Oliver Wendell Holmes

OLIVER WENDELL HOLMES

A Life in War, Law, and Ideas

STEPHEN BUDIANSKY

W. W. NORTON & COMPANY

Independent Publishers Since 1923

NEW YORK * LONDON

For information about permission to reproduce selections from this book, write to
Permissions, W. W. Norton & Company, Inc., 500 Fifth Avenue, New York, NY 10110

For information about special discounts for bulk purchases, please contact
W. W. Norton Special Sales at specialsales@wwnorton.com or 800-233-4830

Maps by Dave Merrill
Manufacturing by LSC Communications, Harrisonburg
Book design by Helene Berinsky
Production manager: Anna Oler

Library of Congress Cataloging-in-Publication Data

Names: Budiansky, Stephen, author.
Title: Oliver Wendell Holmes : a life in war, law, and ideas / Stephen Budiansky.
Description: New York : W. W. Norton & Company, 2019. | Includes bibliographical
    references and index.
Identifiers: LCCN 2018054671 | ISBN 9780393634723 (hardcover)
Subjects: LCSH: Holmes, Oliver Wendell, Jr., 1841-1935 | Judges—United States—
    Biography. | United States. Supreme Court—Officials and employees—Biography.
Classification: LCC KF8745.H6 B83 2019 | DDC 347.73/2634 [B]—dc23
LC record available at https://lccn.loc.gov/2018054671

W. W. Norton & Company, Inc., 500 Fifth Avenue, New York, N.Y. 10110
www.wwnorton.com

W. W. Norton & Company Ltd., 15 Carlisle Street, London W1D 3BS

1 2 3 4 5 6 7 8 9 0

CONTENTS

To have doubted one's own first principles
is the mark of a civilized man.
—OLIVER WENDELL HOLMES JR.

OLIVER WENDELL HOLMES

Justice Oliver Wendell Holmes in Washington, 1914

PROLOGUE

"What a Medley of a Man!"

As he approached his seventy-fifth year in the winter of 1916, Justice Oliver Wendell Holmes of the United States Supreme Court was almost as recognizable a sight to tourists wandering the nation's capital as the Washington Monument or the Smithsonian Institution.

Every afternoon, when the Court was in session, the justice would walk back from the Capitol to his brownstone at 1720 I Street, just west of the White House. Impeccably dressed in the manner of the perfect Edwardian gentleman, he cut a commanding figure as he briskly strode his daily two miles home: his six-foot-three frame held erect like the soldier he had once been, magnificent white moustaches like a cavalry colonel's, always turned out in formal top hat, high wing collar, cutaway coat, and striped trousers purchased from the best shops in London on his frequent visits there.

He reported to friends his facetious relief that he had so far escaped being referred to in any of the newspaper articles about his upcoming birthday as "the venerable jurist"—"which is the sacramental phrase."[1] He was one of those rare men who had actually grown more handsome with age, possessed of a full head of white hair, blue eyes that shone with undiminished intenseness beneath bushy brows, and a beautiful baritone voice that carried the now vanished patrician mid-Atlantic accent that ordinary Americans would become familiar with from Franklin D. Roosevelt's fireside chats.

Dean Acheson recalled the "arresting" impression he made upon

1

him at their first meeting, just after Acheson's arrival in Washington to take up his position as Justice Louis D. Brandeis's legal secretary. "Possessed of a grandeur and beauty rarely met among men," observed Acheson, "his presence entered a room with him as a pervading force."[2]

There were certainly no hints of his slowing down. "I . . . most of the time feel as I did fifty years ago," he told the American diplomat Lewis Einstein, one of his many considerably younger friends, "except that I am much happier." He still bounded up the stairs to his study two at a time and still began each day with a bracing cold bath—a practice he carried on until age eighty-eight, when he finally gave it up in favor of a warm bath at bedtime.[3]

To the young lawyers in Washington for whom he always had time for a "jaw," regaling them with a sparkling stream of talk about philosophy, law, and literature, his wit ever at the ready to skewer the pomposities and self-delusions of men, the years vanished altogether. "It could never to occur to a younger man that he was not talking to one of his own age," said one acquaintance forty years his junior. Charlie Curtis recalled how as a student at Harvard Law School in 1916 he had been invited to tea with Holmes, and at once found himself so deep in a lively conversation that—to his horror as he replayed the scene in his mind on the way home—he was "telling the justice what the law was." Curtis caught himself just as he was about to tap the great man on the knee to emphasize a point.[4]

As oft noted as the justice's mental and physical vigor was his extraordinary embodiment of the sweep of history. As a Union officer in the Civil War he had barely escaped death at Ball's Bluff and Antietam when musket balls tore through his chest and neck, missing heart, spine, and carotid artery by an eighth of an inch. He had spoken to Grant and shaken hands with Meade at the Battle of Spotsylvania, and seen Lincoln dodge enemy fire at Fort Stevens during Jubal Early's raid on Washington. As a boy he knew Ralph Waldo Emerson as a family friend and dimly remembered Herman Melville, a summer neighbor, as "a rather gruff taciturn man."[5] Traveling Europe after the war, he climbed the Alps with Leslie Stephen, better known to later generations as the father of Virginia Woolf; while in law school he became fast friends with Henry James and his brother William, soon to become, respectively, the novelist and philosopher of their generation. To Holmes they were "Harry" and "Bill." On visits to England he met the young Winston Churchill and the old Anthony Trollope; in Washington, Bertrand Russell stopped by more than once to talk philosophy.

A quiz show in the 1960s posed the question, "Which American met, during his lifetime, both John Quincy Adams and Alger Hiss?" The answer of course was Holmes, who had met the sixth president of the United States—another family friend of his Boston boyhood—when he was five years old, and who had employed the future Soviet spy as one of his last law secretaries in 1929.[6]

But it was the Civil War that was his touchstone. "I hate to read about those days," he told friends; he had no interest in reliving the war's "squalid preliminaries," or "the blunders and worse" of its battles.[7] When a cousin sent him the British writer Lord Charnwood's biography of Lincoln he felt obliged to tackle it but halfway through confessed, "I . . . should praise God if I had finished the book or someone stole it."[8]

Yet he was keenly alive to the war's lasting meaning for *him*, the profound way those terrible and ennobling experiences of youth had shaped his life. A drive to Fort Stevens was always part of the program for out-of-town visitors and for each year's new secretary. He marked each anniversary of his brushes with death by solemnly drinking a glass of wine "to the living and the dead," and never failed, when writing a letter or postcard to a friend around those dates, to note the occasion:

1908
the anniversary of Antietam, where <u>1862</u> / 46 years ago (!) I was shot through the neck.[9]

If the war destroyed forever the idealism and optimism of the world of his boyhood, the naïve Boston Unitarian faith in the inevitable triumph of moral virtue, guided only by education and man's innate rationality, it had substituted a profound lesson in the practical courage of everyday life. "The men who have been soaked in a sea of death and

As a young officer in the Civil War, 1862

who somehow have survived, have got something from it which has transfigured their world," he said in a speech to the veterans of his old Army corps the year he arrived in Washington to take his place on the Supreme Court. "They know the passion and irony of life."[10]

He had no illusion of the role that chance had played in determining who survived and who did not. "It almost humiliates me to think of my luck," he remarked years later. But he keenly felt his good fortune not only in emerging with his skin intact, but in having had the chance to learn at an early age that for "most things in this world, half their terrors vanish when you walk up and tackle them." Once "you lay hold of the lion's skin it comes off and the same old donkey is underneath."[11]

Or, as he summarized his philosophy of life and work as he approached his ninetieth year:

My old formula is that a man should be an enthusiast in the front of his head and a sceptic in the back. Do his damndest without believing that the cosmos would collapse if he failed. One should have the same courage for failure that many have for death.[12]

If all else failed one could be "a good soldier," he insisted. He thought it simply bad form to parade one's fears or give way to "prophesying evil or drumming on the void," like his overrefined Boston intellectual friends Henry and Brooks Adams. "To file in and do your damndest remains now as heretofore the only solution, to my mind." It was the only way to real happiness; it was also more likely to do some actual good for the world than more self-conscious striving at altruistic ends.[13]

In Washington he ran his life with military promptitude, beginning with breakfast every day at 9:30. Hiss was awestruck at the standard Holmes morning meal: coffee; a whole orange, which the justice would try to peel in a single continuous piece; a large bowl of porridge with cream; then a poached egg on a slice of toast, first spread with "an absolute mat" of anchovy paste. "It would be enough to take the head off an ordinary person," Hiss said. When several years later he saw Holmes described by one writer as a "morose" and fundamentally unhappy man, he dismissed the idea out of hand: no one could possibly be unhappy, he thought, who could dispatch a breakfast like that each morning with such "gusto."[14]

At precisely 11:25 the justice would prepare to leave for the Court— "a solemn rite," one of his secretaries described it: the justice helped on with shoes and rubbers; mohair housecoat changed for formal suit coat; morocco-leather-bound docket handed to his messenger; a few last-minute words of chaff from his wife, Fanny, on the way out the door ("Straighten up, or you'll be an old man before your time!"); then down the steps, where his driver Charlie Buckley waited at the curb with horse and buggy. Then return from the Court around 5, work until 7, dinner at 7:30, work again until 9; then downstairs to play solitaire and listen while Fanny read aloud. Midnight to bed; lights out at 1.[15]

Each fall he and Fanny scheduled their return from their summer home at Beverly Farms on the North Shore of Boston at the last possible moment before the start of the Court's term on the first Monday in October; they usually took the overnight train to Washington to arrive on the Wednesday morning of the week before. His new secretary, selected each year from the graduating class of Harvard Law School, was instructed to show up on Friday at 11 a.m. More than one anxious young man understandably arrived early, only to discover that the judge meant to be taken literally.

Barton Leach would forever remember his introduction to the justice's well-regulated household. "I got to the house about 10:30, decided I was too early; squirmed for fifteen minutes on a bench in the little park at the corner of Connecticut Avenue and Eye Street where there is a statue of Farragut . . . rang the bell and found that I was still too early and would not be received until precisely eleven." (On a subsequent walk through the neighborhood, Leach recalled, the justice shared his schoolboy glee in pointing out how the statue of the Civil War admiral was "most amusing when viewed from one particular angle," the unfortunate effect of the telescope the admiral is holding at waist level.)[16]

The determination with which Justice Holmes attacked his work disconcerted everyone, not least his more sober or plodding brethren. When, in his mid-fifties, he took up riding a bicycle for the first time, he joked to friends that he proceeded "at a comfortable judicial speed."[17] No one would have used those words to describe the pace at which Holmes "fired off," as he always put it, his Supreme Court opinions. While the Court was sitting, the justices met every Saturday morning to deliberate and vote on the cases they had heard during the week; after the conference the chief justice would decide which justice would write which opinions, sending the assignments by messenger to the justices' homes late Saturday afternoon.

Most waited to begin work on their cases until the Court went into one of the regular two- or three-week recesses that were scheduled throughout the term just for that purpose. But "Holmes was positively uncomfortable until his assignment was completed," noted Chauncey Belknap, his secretary for the 1915–16 term.[18]

This was before the modern practice of judges having law clerks draft their opinions for them: Holmes wrote every word himself, in a flowing if not always easily decipherable hand, using a steel-nibbed pen and ink while standing at an upright mahogany desk that had belonged to his grandfather, a judge on the Massachusetts Supreme Judicial Court before him. He would launch into the work at once, starting on Saturday the moment his assignment arrived, putting in an hour or two before dinner, continuing on Sunday, and invariably delivering the final draft in time for it to be printed and circulated to the other justices by Tuesday. If he had a second case to write, as he often did, that was done by the following Saturday, at which point he frequently importuned the chief justice for still more work, offering to take the load off his slower brethren.[19]

"Why don't you send me a real stinker that will be a real relief to you?" he once asked.[20] When Chief Justice Melville Fuller occasionally delayed getting out the justices' assignments until Monday, Holmes found it unbearable:

> Dear Chief
>   Will you let me know as soon as convenient the cases you assign to me. I worry until I know. Nil actum reputans dum quid superesset agendum.[21]

The Latin quotation was from Lucanus's epic poem about Caesar. It translates to, "He believed nothing done, so long as anything remained undone."

"I would like to write them all if I could," he confided to his friend and North Shore neighbor Ellen Curtis in 1903, shortly after joining the Court. He was not actually joking. He did not write them all, but he did produce 873 signed opinions—still a record, even among the justices who exceeded his twenty-nine years on the bench—along with 30 separate concurrences and 72 dissents.[22] He had felt exactly the same way when he was on the Massachusetts high court, where he wrote nearly a thousand opinions over twenty years.[23]

He brought that same zest for duty to everything. In 1865, at age twenty-one, he began keeping a list of every book he read, noting them down in tiny handwriting in a small leather memorandum book, known to his secretaries as the "Black Book." By the time of his death the list exceeded four thousand, which worked out to more than a book a week for seventy years.[24] The range was extraordinary: law, philosophy, sociology, literature, religion, history, economics, murder mysteries, poetry, science. He read the classics and the latest authors, Montaigne, Virginia Woolf, Dickens, Freud, Saint Augustine, Karl Marx, Shakespeare, Voltaire; he read *Very Good, Jeeves* by P. G. Wodehouse ("which makes me roar"), Hemingway, Spinoza, the Federalist papers, Balzac, James

Joyce. He read Proust in French ("it tells of nothing much, in long sentences of not too easy French, but it seemed to call up all the melancholy of youth"); Homer in Greek; Dante's *Inferno* in Italian, a language he claimed not to know, but said he could manage by drawing on his knowledge of Latin and French. He similarly tackled "The Lusiads," the great epic poem of the sixteenth-century Portuguese national poet Camoens, with the aid of a French translation to help construe the original.[25]

He quipped that a man would get credit in heaven for all the "dull but worthy books" he read; wryly referring to himself as "one who has Boston duty in his bones" (or "this poor Calvinist gone wrong"), he attributed his zealous reading to an inability to shake the gospel of self-improvement absorbed in his youth. In his eighties, he began reading Thucydides in Greek for the first time. To his wondering secretary he explained, "When I appear before *le bon dieu*, he may say to me, 'Holmes, can you recite on Thucydides?' If I have to say, 'No, Sire,' think what a fool I'd feel."[26]

He had a rule that a book once started had to be finished. James Rowe, his last secretary, remembered the then-retired justice literally groaning aloud over one deathly dull political tome Brandeis had pressed on him yet steadfastly refusing to abandon it. The only book any of his secretaries could ever remember him giving up on was D. H. Lawrence's scandalous novel *Lady Chatterley's Lover*. Holmes was then in his ninetieth year, and had begun having his secretary read aloud to him. The increasingly red-faced young man reached page 107 before Holmes finally interrupted, "Sonny, we will not finish this book. Its dullness is not redeemed by its pornography."[27]

If he took duty seriously, he thought the one deadly sin of mankind was to take itself seriously. His deep strain of philosophical skepticism was inseparable from an equally deep sense of humor, usually mordantly focused on the folly of human overimportance. "An angel of average intelligence would smile at what we call our aspirations," he wrote to his young English friend Ethel Scott. He enjoyed giving all of his acquaintances his homespun distillation of the skeptic's creed: "Having made up your mind that you are not God," he admonished them, "don't lie awake nights with cosmic worries."[28]

Or, as he more seriously explained late in his life, "The Army and the other stings of life made it impossible for me, I think, to have a swelled head." He thought skepticism "a saving grace if it takes in enough of oneself"; and, conversely, that self-importance was simply incompatible with self-awareness, maturity, or experience. "When I see a man with a really swelled head," he told his old friend Nina Gray, "I revere his innocence and unsophistication."[29]

The wit that crackled through his talk and letters to friends became part of an enduring legend; inevitably, like Mark Twain, Winston Churchill, and Oscar Wilde, many famous quips, old and new, were attributed to him that he almost certainly never said. (Some had been uttered by his father and namesake, also renowned for his wit, and mis-attributed to the son.)

A few stories in particular stubbornly refuse to die. "A second-class mind, but a first-class temperament," his oft-quoted assessment of Franklin D. Roosevelt, holds an indelible place in the FDR literature even if it has no basis in reality.

"Oh, to be eighty again"—what the ninety-year-old justice was said to have remarked on eyeing a pretty girl in the street—wasn't bad, but wasn't Holmes, either; variations go back at least a century before him.

But many wry observations about aging were indubitably his. "One of my greatest problems," he casually observed to his secretary one day, "is to find available vices for old age." Starting at age seventy he always warned the young man selected to be his secretary for the coming year that the offer was "subject to my right to die or resign."[30]

As for Washington personalities, some of his one-line putdowns have achieved well-deserved immortality. Dean Acheson once asked Holmes what old Justice John Harlan of Kentucky had been like. Holmes: "Harlan's mind was like a vise, the jaws of which did not meet. It only held the larger objects."[31]

And he always spoke with bemused humor about his own position among the high and mighty. "About to sally forth to some hashhouse for vittles" meant going to dinner at the finest hotel in Washington; "the boys" meant the fellow justices of the highest court in the land— as in, "I think I'll lay it on the boys and see if they swallow it," as he remarked to Belknap once upon completing an opinion. He loved telling of the time the berobed justices were filing in stately procession across the corridor of the Capitol to their courtroom in the old Senate chamber when an awed spectator from the heartland punctured the solemnity of the moment by bursting out, "Christ, what dignity!"[32]

His favorite and arresting explanation to his secretaries of how he "fired off" his decisions was that writing a Supreme Court opinion was "just like pissing: you apply a pressure, a very vague pressure, and out it comes." He told his secretary Mark DeWolfe Howe that the thought had first come to him while standing in the lavatory at the Boston Court House, though added that the lawyer next to him, to whom he immediately related his insight, "didn't seem much impressed by the simile."[33]

America was not a country to make a celebrity of a judge, much less an intellectual—which was the only thing Holmes ever wanted to be known for; he scorned ambition of office for its own sake. "I wouldn't do much more than walk across the street to be called Chief Justice instead of Justice," he insisted. Rather, as he jokingly—or not—told Nina Gray in 1910, "I confine my aspirations to being the greatest legal thinker in the world."[34]

Certainly not many members of the public knew of Justice Holmes as the author of the single most important book in the history of American legal scholarship. *The Common Law* appeared in 1881, when Holmes was just forty. It was a work of profound learning, and revolutionary, even shocking, implications. Tracing the development of the law to its most ancient roots, Holmes demonstrated that the common law of England, which America had inherited, had *always* changed and adapted to meet "the felt necessities of the time." As he put it, "The law embodies the story of a nation's development through many centuries, and it cannot be dealt with as if it contained only the axioms and corollaries of a book of mathematics."[35]

It was the genius of the common law, in Holmes's analysis, that judges over the course of time fashioned workable solutions to society's needs even as they decided individual cases—elucidating standards of conduct for the relations between landlord and tenant, buyer and seller, employer and servant, injured and injurer, in an ever-changing and increasingly complex world.

The Common Law was the genesis of "the most influential school of twentieth-century American legal thought and practice," in the words of the legal scholar and U.S. circuit judge Richard A. Posner— the so-called Legal Realist movement, which understands and explains the law through its concrete effects, rather than in moral abstractions such as rights and duties or in formalistic rules, as had largely been the practice before.[36]

A century and a half later the book remains a classic known to every law student. Few lines in the annals of legal prose have been more quoted than Holmes's memorable opening salvo: "The life of the law has not been logic: it has been experience."[37]

Yet if the public did not know or care about Judge Holmes as a pioneering legal scholar, his remarkable way with words, which he first displayed in *The Common Law*, was one steady road to the wider fame that would come. Holmes wrote like no one else, with a style as American and distinctive as Mark Twain or Walt Whitman. To Judge Learned Hand, one of the few in the profession who rivaled him in eloquence of expression, Holmes had a "matchless gift of compression," an ability to reduce an idea to its essence as did a great poet[38]—expressing an elusive, subtle, and complex argument with a single, perfectly turned metaphor, aptly timed colloquialism, or startling juxtaposition that exploded like a jack-in-the-box, releasing its concentrated meaning in what did seem like almost a physical jolt when encountered the first, or the fourteenth, time.

In a day when even the leading newspapers offered little more than a few perfunctory quotes from the justices' published opinions in their far-from-comprehensive coverage of the Supreme Court, Holmes was always one who was quoted. For one thing, he almost completely avoided legal jargon and cant phrases in his judicial writing. But more than that was a freshness of his prose that reflected a clarity of thinking which commanded attention: one of the other qualities Hand praised in Holmes's opinions was "a deadly eye" for "question-begging words" that disguised shallow thinking, which Holmes would then blow to pieces with one of his epigrammatic hand grenades:

The common law is not a brooding omnipresence in the sky.[39]

The construction of a statute does not take a party's property without due process of law simply because it takes him by surprise.[40]

The petitioner may have a constitutional right to talk politics, but he has no constitutional right to be a policeman.[41]

Ordinary street cars must be run with reference to ordinary susceptibilities.[42]

When the common law developed the doctrine of trade-marks and trade names, it was not creating a property in advertisements more absolute than it would have allowed the author of Paradise Lost.[43]

I think it a less evil that some criminals should escape than that the Government should play an ignoble part.[44]

Pretty much all law consists in forbidding men to do some things they want to do.[45]

The Quakers have done their share to make the country what it is . . . I had not supposed hitherto that we regretted our inability to expel them because they believed more than some of us do in the teachings of the Sermon on the Mount.[46]

It is said that this manifesto was more than a theory, that it was an incitement. Every idea is an incitement.[47]

The striking words embodied striking thoughts: to Holmes, the act of writing was above all the act of thinking. Finding the right words was not rhetorical ornamentation: it was very the essence of his work of thinking through a complex legal problem.

By the same token, words and set phrases had a way of tyrannizing and paralyzing thought the moment they became familiar. "The minute a phrase becomes current it becomes an apology for not thinking accurately to the end of the sentence," he warned; it was a danger a judge had to consciously and constantly guard against.

He must not stop at consecrated phrases, which in their day were a revelation, but which in time, from their very felicity, tend to stop the endless necessary process of further analysis and advance. He must throw down his naked thought, unswaddled in pompous commonplaces, to take its chance for life. He must try to realize the paradox that it is not necessary to be heavy in order to have weight.[48]

No one knew how to strip off excess judicial verbal poundage better than Holmes. Even in his day he stood out as unusual for the economy and brevity of his decisions. Nowadays, when judges think nothing of issuing a sixty-page ruling on a procedural motion, he would be in a minority of one. The standard model for judicial opinions today is the law review article—unsurprising, given that nearly all appellate opinions are now ghostwritten by law clerks fresh from law school—its style summarized by one law professor with depressing accuracy as "colorless, prolix, platitudinous, always erring on the side of inclusion, full of lengthy citations and footnotes—and above all dull."[49]

Holmes never worried he might be leaving out an essential point because he viewed everything but the decisive crux of a case as extraneous. "One has to try to strike the jugular and let the rest go," he said. He abhorred—his word—"those long opinions which are treatises," filled with "long winded expositions of the obvious," "padded like a militia brigadier general."[50] His model for a written opinion, he often said, was the ruling that judges traditionally would issue orally from the bench promptly upon completion of an argument. "It should read that way."[51]

His secretary Francis Biddle, who was later attorney general under FDR, struggled like many of Holmes's admirers to describe exactly what was so powerful, even magical, about his legal prose. "The language of the opinions—'the skin of the living thought within' (to use one of his phrases)—had been plucked to the bone, so spare, so concentrated, and yet phrased with such grace," Biddle observed. "His style was close to the nature of his thought, and one could not separate them."[52]

It was another way of saying that Holmes was a great judge at heart because he was a great thinker: his jurisprudence reflected not only a profound study of the law, but more deeply, of the purpose and meaning of the law in life, and indeed of life itself.

What was more remarkable in a way was that his fame, when it came, came on his own terms. "Holmes made himself an embodiment of an ideal," concluded his biographer Sheldon Novick, one "widely shared and deeply felt" among ordinary Americans. That was the ideal of the impartial judge, who stood above the storms and fashions of his times, bringing wisdom, integrity, and the common touch to his job.[53]

HOLMES'S REPUTATION has swung wildly over the years since his death in 1935. His standing among practicing lawyers and judges has always held its own, thanks in no small measure to the bountiful stock of aphorisms about their profession he left behind that lawyers never tire of quoting.

The opinion of the legal professoriate has been another matter. In the 1940s and 1950s Holmes's reputation came under ferocious attack from Catholic legal scholars who saw his rejection of "natural law"—the idea that law derived its authority and substance from moral precepts originating with God—as a dangerous and "alien" philosophy, inviting immorality, chaos, even fascism. (In *The Common Law*, Holmes pointed out that most law had its origins not in morality but in the distinctly unholy spirit of vengeance.) "If totalitarianism ever becomes the form of American government," wrote one Jesuit law professor, "its leaders, no doubt, will canonize as one of the patron saints Mr. Justice Holmes."[54]

Around the same time, liberals were dismayed to discover in the newly published volumes of Holmes's correspondence that he had been willing to uphold the rights of unions, free speech for socialists, and regulation of the economy not from any ideological sympathy for liberal causes but often in spite of a magnificent contempt for them. And in the aftermath of World War II many were left deeply uncomfortable over what remains Holmes's most notorious decision, *Buck* v. *Bell*, his

1927 ruling upholding Virginia's law for the involuntary sterilization of the "feebleminded."

There was the usual kind of historical amnesia at work. Catholic legists and exponents of the natural law philosophy in Europe had no trouble with fascism, just as they had had no trouble earlier with hereditary monarchy: many were notably among Mussolini's most ardent early supporters.[55] And however much the Nazi genocide forever discredited the eugenics movement, it is at least worth remembering that, in 1920s America, eugenics enjoyed the enthusiastic support of many progressive-minded intellectuals, the founders of Planned Parenthood among them.

There is however a nasty and personal tone to some academics' vituperations about Holmes that suggests deeper antipathies. Agnes Meyer, the influential Washington journalist, philanthropist, and social activist (her husband later owned the *Washington Post*), was a neighbor and friend of Holmes's who got to know him well, and she later observed that his superabundance of charm came back to haunt him after his death. While Holmes was "too gifted," in her view, ever to "trade on his personality, as many charming men and women do," it nonetheless "gave him a following of sycophants, who overdid the Holmes cult and hurt rather than helped his place in history."[56]

There is nothing so infuriating as hero worship in others, and Holmes's secretaries and the many young Washington lawyers who flocked around him freely admitted to succumbing to that emotion. Whether it is fair to call them sycophants, there was no denying the single-mindedness with which they tended the image of their hero, both before and after his death. Felix Frankfurter, Harvard lawyer, energetic reformer, New Deal insider, and future Supreme Court justice; and Harold J. Laski—"an astonishing young Jew," in Holmes's words, a polymathic British scholar and wunderkind who met Holmes in 1916 and exchanged hundreds of remarkable letters with him in the following years—were especially active. They arranged for Holmes's speeches to be published and made sure that a special issue of the *Harvard Law Review*, dedicated to his life and work, appeared on each of his significant birthdays; they filled liberal publications like the *New*

Republic with articles, some signed and some not, extolling his opinions upholding social legislation and free speech; they commissioned imposing portraits of the justice to hang at Harvard Law School and the U.S. Supreme Court.

Holmes for his part did little to endear himself to the academic legal community. He notoriously counseled Frankfurter against a career as a law professor, warning that "academic life is but half life," and dismissively observed that "professors as a class . . . dogmatize on unrealities."[57] He almost never cited articles by law professors in his opinions.

And then there is the fact that moralists of all political persuasions are not exactly renowned for their sense of humor, and humorless moralizing is the predominant mode of thought in much of academia today. Many of Holmes's academic critics, however, seem not only incapable of perceiving Holmes's jokes but even of grasping that such a thing as a joke exists. A more enduring fact about academic life is that taking on the great is the most reliable way for those who will never attain greatness themselves to gain attention for themselves.

The result has been a stream of anti-Holmes vituperation that at times borders on the hysterical. He has been called "dark" and "destructive," unprincipled and cynical, obsessed with "morbidity" and "war, power, and struggle."[58] The law professor oddly chosen to take over Mark DeWolfe Howe's unfinished official biography of Holmes after Howe's death in 1967, Grant Gilmore (who in turn died in 1982, having done little more than write a rambling introduction), published a brief and scathing assessment typical of Holmes's latter-day academic detractors:

> Holmes is a strange, enigmatic figure. Put out of your mind the picture of the tolerant aristocrat, the great liberal, the eloquent defender of our liberties, the Yankee from Olympus. All that was a myth, concocted principally by Harold Laski and Felix Frankfurter, about the time of World War I. The real Holmes was savage, harsh, and cruel, a bitter and life-long pessimist who saw in the course of human life nothing but a continuing struggle in which the rich and powerful impose their will on the poor and weak.[59]

Even Holmes's more admiring biographers of the past thirty years—law professors all—seem nonplussed that he uttered things unsayable in the faculty lounge, and see dark shadows in his psyche at every turn: his enthusiasm for work mere calculating "ambition," his lively correspondence an exercise in "self-absorption" or a desperate search for "flattery," his friendships with female acquaintances "womanizing," his reflections on the war a symptom of "survivor guilt," his jokes about old age a masquerade for his deepest fears.[60]

"Biographers," cautions one of the best practitioners of the art, "have a duty to be sympathetic to their subjects. As soon as I begin to discover that a biographer is treating his subject with malice, envy, dislike, or contempt, I begin to suspect the quality both of his motives and of his human understanding."[61]

A sympathetic view of Holmes might begin with those who actually knew him. None of them described a Freudian basket case: they saw a man of unequaled moral courage and philosophical wisdom about life, great human kindness and generosity, and abiding good humor. He left a deep impression on the son of one old friend. Sir Frederick Pollock was an English jurist whose friendship with Holmes spanned sixty years, their warm and wide-ranging correspondence filling hundreds of pages. Once, Pollock's son invited the already famous American judge to visit him at Cambridge University for the weekend. John Pollock was a callow undergraduate; Holmes, then sixty years old, was the chief justice of Massachusetts's highest court. "He stayed in a set of the less good undergraduate rooms in college empty for the moment," recalled the younger Pollock, "took his meals with me, walked with me, met my friends, smoked and talked as only undergraduates can, enjoyed himself, to all appearance, hugely, and left, without, I believe, the Master and Fellows having an idea that they had had a man of note within the gates."[62]

Holmes devoted himself to friendship with the same energy he gave to his work and other pursuits. He wrote literally thousands of letters to friends over his life—there are an estimated ten thousand personal letters among his papers at the Harvard Law School archives, most of them as yet unpublished—that chronicle scores of warm and abiding friendships that he worked hard to keep up across the natural gulfs of time, distance, and age. He wrote of his work and thoughts, the books he was reading, the flowers and birds he saw on his walks; he seldom would permit even a single day to pass without replying whenever a letter from a friend arrived on his desk.

The dozen or so mostly rather younger female friends to whom he wrote affectionately throughout his life laughed off his occasional flirtatious remarks and treasured his openness, his emotional and mental intimacy, and the way he treated them as complete intellectual and spiritual equals. Anna Codman, a neighbor on the North Shore thirty years his junior, whom Holmes called on once a week for an hour's talk during his summers, described their remarkable and enduring relationship in a letter she wrote to Mark Howe in 1942, when he was beginning work on his Holmes biography:

> Our friendship lasted over thirty years. Begun in somewhat a flippant manner it ripened into real affection. . . . I marveled at the extent and variety of his reading; it was a mental excitement for him to discourse about his books. He talked often far above my understanding, but I was an attentive listener and many of his words, that seemed to float upon the surface, have sunk into my deeper comprehension and borne fruit.[63]

On Holmes's ninetieth birthday she wrote to him,

> My very dear friend . . . what I admire most, perhaps because it comes more under my ken, is the beautiful serenity which surrounds you like a halo. Another quality which is so rare, because people often detach themselves from closer associations, is your faculty for intimate friendship, and what you have given me in this way for the last thirty years. I am deeply grateful.[64]

Holmes's longtime friend Nina Gray, wife of his even older friend John Chipman Gray, professor at Harvard Law, carefully preserved the hundreds of letters he wrote her, often penciling a note on them describing their subject and content. On one she wrote: *What a medley of a man!*[65]

No friendship is without nuances of selfish motives, yet Holmes throughout his life had plenty of friends who were no sycophants or flatterers, and who also knew a thing or two about greatness. Dean Acheson late in his life said that no one he had met in his many years of public service touched Holmes, not even George Marshall whom he revered as an exemplar of "transfiguration through duty"; Holmes was "one of the immortals." In 1960 a Harvard undergraduate sent Acheson a paper he had written about the justice, full of the superior wisdom of youth. Acheson replied:

> One of the slipperiest words I know is "great." But I think the "greatest" man I have ever known, that is, the essence of man living, man thinking, man baring himself to the lonely emptiness— or the reverse—of the universe, was Holmes. . . . Don't patronize Holmes. . . . And, perhaps—only perhaps, throw your paper away and start over again.[66]

He was an elitist but never a snob; that too was something the war had done for him. He had no patience with pomposity or putting-on of social airs. When, in 1915, his nephew announced that he was thinking of volunteering for military training "as an example" to others, Holmes was enraged. "I told him if a son of mine talked about doing anything as an example, I would boot him out of my house."[67]

"The army," he explained to Laski, "taught me some great lessons":

> To be prepared for catastrophe—to endure being bored—and to know that however fine a fellow I thought myself in the usual routine there were other situations . . . in which I was inferior to men that I might have looked down upon had not experience taught me to look up.[68]

He never evinced any of the anti-Semitism or anti-Irish prejudices of many of his Boston circle (his own wife included). If he disparaged socialism as "humbug" and "drool" and social and economic equality as utopian nonsense, he was equally disdainful of the idle rich and their empty-headed pursuits: the "culture folks" who amassed works of art without understanding or appreciation; "the brute power of wealth" paraded by the New York plutocrats who decorated their Fifth Avenue mansions with ornate mantelpieces wrested from French chateaus; the society ladies who spent their days playing bridge and "going to a lunch with dresses costing $1000. I own I view such a manifestation with disinterested loathing."[69]

The love he so plainly stirred in those who worked with him and for him for years is a testament that ought at least give pause to academics spouting Freudian theories about his "profound detachment" from his fellow man.[70] The day in 1932 when Chief Justice Charles Evans Hughes called to gently tell him the time had come for him to resign, Holmes took the news stoically; it was Hughes, as he came down the stairs, and Holmes's devoted housekeeper, Mary Donnellan, as she knelt before her ninety-year-old employer, whom his secretary H. Chapman Rose saw with tears "just streaming down" their faces.[71]

After Holmes's death, Arthur Thomas, the last and longest-serving of the three African American messengers who had worked for him (they were employed by the Court but did everything from deliver mail to serve as valets and cooks for the justices), went every year to Arlington Cemetery on the anniversary of his death to lay flowers on his grave, and always placed a small notice in the *Washington Star* newspaper:

HOLMES, MR. JUSTICE OLIVER W.
An upright man, unpretentious gentleman and an impartial judge.
HIS MESSENGER ARTHUR A. THOMAS[72]

Holmes's skepticism likewise deserves more sympathetic understanding than it has been treated with by his more virulently contemptuous academic detractors. Far from a manifestation of cynical immorality or bitter pessimism, Holmes's skeptical view of life was the living soul of a tolerant, democratic, and restrained judicial philosophy.

If he disdained moralizing in the law it was because he knew from bitter experience—this was another lesson of the war—that moralists are the most dangerous of men, oblivious to the nuances of life in their certainty of their own virtue and rightness. "When you know that you know," he said to Frederick Pollock, "persecution comes easy."[73] To Holmes, general principles were the enemy of the hard choices where true moral reckoning took place.

His favorite skeptical maxim could also have served as a statement of the ideal of judicial impartiality, of putting aside one's own prejudiced assumptions and parochial loyalties, which Holmes far more than most actually attained in practice. "To have doubted one's own first principles," he said, "is the mark of a civilized man."[74]

His philosophical skepticism was the force behind every one of his most important and enduring contributions, as scholar and judge, to the law. It was what convinced him to reject certainty in favor of tolerance in his revolutionary transformation of freedom of speech in America; in his demand that judges honestly lay bare their reasoning behind complex issues rather than hiding their prejudices with appeals to abstract rights; in the remarkable triumph of the ideas he set out, starting in *The Common Law,* that the law should be based on external standards of conduct rather than subjective moral judgments. Ideas that are now commonplace in the law, such as the "reasonable man" as a yardstick to determine fault and negligence, and the balancing tests that have supplanted rigid formulas in nearly every branch of the law, owe much to Holmes's pioneering legal scholarship, all grounded in a philosophy of life in which skepticism was his abiding cautionary principle.

As for constitutional interpretation, Holmes would have snorted at the idea that the answers were to be found with nothing more than a dictionary and a literal reading of the words of the text, much less by divining what the Founders might have thought about the matter—as latter-day "textualists" and "originalists" are wont to assert. He would have been equally scornful of the contention that judges face a binary choice of "strict construction" or "judicial activism." As Holmes frequently took pains to point out, most questions of constitutional law come down to claims of competing rights, which the Constitution itself cannot possibly settle; judges who purported to find certainty in the broadly worded precepts of the Constitution, he observed, were more guilty of imposing their personal political prejudices on the law than those who faced up to the duty to draw difficult lines in fashioning workable solutions. He trained his same skeptical eye on the Constitution that he trained on everything, and if that is one of his less successful legacies in our day—when left and right routinely invoke the Constitution as the trump card and final word of every partisan battle—it is more our loss than his failure.

For a constitution, cautioned Holmes, is not a set of "mathematical formulas"; it does not "divide fields of black and white"; it is not "the partisan of a particular set of ethical or economic opinions."[75]

It is rather "a frame of government for men of opposite opinions and for the future."[76]

CHAPTER 1

Dr. Holmes's Boston

It is always difficult to have a famous father, but Dr. Oliver Wendell Holmes was not just famous: he was the living symbol of his time and place—the Boston whose sense of social conscience, learning, and culture his son would carry "in his bones" long after that world of his youth had vanished.

In the words of Van Wyck Brooks, the ironic chronicler of New England's rise and fall as the intellectual and literary mecca of America, Dr. Holmes "stood for Boston in its hour of triumph."[1] He was born in 1809, the same year as Lincoln and Darwin. In 1857, along with Emerson and other prominent Boston writers, he founded the *Atlantic Monthly*—and it was Dr. Holmes who came up with the name for the new journal that would place American letters on the world map, with Boston its capital.[2] He composed hundreds of poems and three novels.

But it was the monthly installments in the *Atlantic* of his light-hearted monologues of the egotistical and talkative polymath known as "The Autocrat of the Breakfast Table" that made his reputation at home and abroad—as well as making the magazine an immediate and resounding success. "In his airy way," wrote Brooks, "he had scattered freely . . . the ideas that had made his town a center of culture."[3]

It was Dr. Holmes, too, who came up with the name "Boston Brahmin," and who was the first to remark that Bostonians looked upon the State House on Beacon Hill as "the hub of the solar system."[4] That was meant as satirical commentary on his neighbors' boundless sense

Dr. Holmes

of self-importance, but the city did his joke one better by adopting "The Hub" as its nickname, which endures to this day.

His choice of the term "Brahmin" was pointed. Today, a Boston Brahmin has come to mean just about any old-money Yankee blueblood, but that was not what Dr. Holmes meant. Like the priestly caste of India, his Brahmins were that distinctive local class of intellectuals and scholars—a "harmless, inoffensive, untitled aristocracy," he called the New England version—that regarded itself as the hereditary guardians of culture and morals for society. Boston's Brahmins had ties to wealth and power, but their authority was their own, one that rested on the deep reverence for learning that had marked the Bay Colony from the time of the Puritans' arrival on its shores.

That Boston in the first half of the nineteenth century was the center of culture and learning for the new republic was the subject of much wry comment, but no real dispute. "Boston folks are full of notions," was what Rhode Islanders said; cartoonists for New York newspapers habitually depicted the city's residents, even babes in the cradle, as squinting, bespectacled bookworms. Bret Harte, whose short stories featuring the rough characters of the California gold rush were the harbinger of a new kind of regional American writing, remarked on his first visit to the city that it was impossible to shoot in any direction on the street without bringing down a writer of two or three volumes. It was likewise said that a lady at a loss for conversation with a Boston man she had just been introduced to need only ask, "How is your book coming on?" to guarantee a copious flow of talk.[5]

An English visitor in 1857 wrote,

Boston is the great metropolis of lecturers, Unitarian preachers, and poets. . . . In walking along Washington Street, and meeting a gentlemanly-looking person with a decent coat and a clean shirt, the traveller may safely put him down as either a lecturer, a Unitarian minister, or a poet; possibly the man may be, Cerberus-like, all three at once. In Boston the onus lies upon every respectable person to prove that he has not written a sonnet, preached a sermon, or delivered a lecture.[6]

"Tomorrow night I appear for the first time before a Boston audience," Mark Twain wrote his sister when a speaking tour took him to the city, "—4,000 critics."[7]

It was easy to make fun of, and Bostonians usually tried to be the first to do so themselves, but no other community in the history of the world had done so much to spread the opportunities and benefits of education. The Massachusetts Constitution of 1780 devoted an entire section to a veritable paean to literature and learning:

Chapter V.
 Section II. The Encouragement of Literature, etc.
 Wisdom, and knowledge, as well as virtue, diffused generally among the body of the people, being necessary for the preservation of their rights and liberties; and as these depend on spreading the opportunities and advantages of education in the various parts of the country, and among the different orders of the people, it shall be the duty of legislators and magistrates, in all future periods of this Commonwealth, to cherish the interests of literature and the sciences, and all seminaries of them; especially the university at Cambridge, public schools, and grammar schools in the towns; to encourage private societies and public institutions, rewards and immunities, for the promotion of agriculture, arts, sciences, commerce, trades, manufactures, and a natural history of the country; to countenance and inculcate the principles of humanity and

general benevolence, public and private charity, industry and frugality, honesty and punctuality in their dealings; sincerity, good
humour, and all social affections, and generous sentiments among
the people.

The "university at Cambridge" was, of course, Harvard, founded
in 1638 as a seminary to train Congregational ministers and since
become the lodestar in Boston's cultural firmament. From its Georgian brick buildings in Harvard Yard radiated a passion for learning
that reached towns and farms across New England; jokes from English
travelers about an overabundance of lecturers aside, the lyceum was a
fixture of towns large and small. There were a thousand throughout
New England, and speakers as famous as Emerson regularly made the
circuit. In 1839 one of the heirs to the Lowell family textile fortune left
half his estate in trust to fund a series of free lectures for the public;
each year as many as ten thousand people would apply for tickets to
the Lowell Institute, to hear Emerson deliver a series of biographical
sketches, the Harvard poet James Russell Lowell discuss literature and
poetry, Yale's Benjamin Silliman explain the latest discoveries in chemistry. Greek antiquities, the geography of Palestine, the steam engine—
it didn't matter; the hall was always full.[8]

Massachusetts was the first in the nation to offer free public school-
ing, in the 1820s; the first to establish normal schools for the training of
teachers, in the 1830s; the first to make school attendance mandatory,
in the 1850s. The rustic Yankee farmer or mechanic who spent his evenings in the lecture hall or working his way through Virgil's *Aeneid* in
Latin was a stock character in nineteenth-century New England, but
he was drawn from life. Charles Eliot Norton, who taught art history
at Harvard, related to Rudyard Kipling the time he had been driving
in the countryside with a fellow professor. While stopped at a farmhouse to water his horse, Norton turned to his colleague and remarked,
"According to Montaigne . . . ," and proceeded to quote a passage. The
stolid Yankee farmer, who had been silently holding a bucket for the
horse, spoke up. "Tweren't Montaigne," he corrected the Harvard professor. "Twere Mon-tes-ki-ew." ("And 'twas," reported Kipling.)[9]

In one of his more serious moments, Dr. Holmes wrote that while Boston may be "full of crooked little streets," it "has opened, and kept open, more turnpikes that lead straight to free thought and free speech and free deeds than any other city of live men or dead men."[10] There was no shortage of tangible proofs which the city could—and to every visitor, did—point to for the truth of that statement. Beginning in the early 1800s ideas and deeds had come together in the founding of an astonishing number of pioneering public institutions that gave tangible substance to the city's lofty ambition to be the "Athens of America."

That bold epithet had been bestowed by a member of one of the city's many literary clubs—there was the Saturday Club, the Thursday Evening Club, the Anthology Society (which would become Boston's famous Athenaeum)—that were "bursting with ideas," in the words of Boston's historian Thomas O'Connor. The clubs were one place where wealth and learning overlapped; merchants and industrialists, doctors and lawyers, clergymen and poets met for dinner and intellectual discussion, and not incidentally to reinvent the world. "Firmly convinced that what they were doing was extremely important," wrote O'Connor, "they wanted everybody in America to know what they had to say about philosophy and religion, about the arts and the sciences, about what life and society should be like in the changing world of America."[11]

Through a combination of private philanthropy and reform-minded governance, Boston's civic and intellectual leaders put those thoughts into action. In 1810 two of the city's physicians—one was Dr. James Jackson, who would be Dr. Holmes's preceptor at Harvard Medical School, and whose niece he would marry—composed a circular letter to the city's leading citizens. Appealing to them as the "treasurers of God's bounty," the doctors sought their support for a hospital that would serve the "whole family of man." A door-to-door fundraising campaign supplemented what God's trustees generously provided, and $100,000 was quickly raised to begin construction of the Massachusetts General Hospital. Fittingly, like the other new public institutions in the Athens of America, it was in the Greek Revival style, solid granite with massive Ionic columns and a domed roof. It was the first of its kind, a beautiful, modern hospital dedicated to alleviate the suffering of the poor. In 1846, the first operation using ether to render a patient unconscious took place there, one of many medical milestones that would take place within its walls. Dr. Holmes coined the word *anesthesia* to describe the revolutionary innovation.[12]

Josiah Quincy, Boston's mayor from 1826 to 1828, instituted a series of high-minded yet thoroughly practical improvements in the health, safety, welfare, and beauty of the city, cleaning up the notoriously foul Town Dock and rerouting sewage outfalls to the more-distant mud flats; ordering the streets cleared of refuse (six thousand tons of it—he knew, because he had it weighed as it was collected); and building one of Boston's most prominent Greek Revival monuments, the Faneuil Hall Market, known to Bostonians then and now as Quincy Market. With its colonnades and copper-clad elliptical dome, it resembled a temple to the gods more than a place to buy codfish and apples. The first sight to greet visitors as they approached the city's waterfront from the sea, it was a dramatic statement of Boston's vision of itself.[13] And then—only in Boston—Quincy capped his six years as mayor by becoming president of Harvard the following year.

In 1854—when Oliver Wendell Holmes Jr. was thirteen years old—the Boston Public Library opened. It was the first free, publicly supported library in the country, and the first to allow its books to be borrowed. When the library moved four years later to a larger building, its seventy thousand volumes were carried in grand procession down the street on New Year's Day, accompanied by city officials, militia companies, brass bands, and Harvard's professors marching in cap and gown.[14]

———

IF BOSTON SEEMED to be fired with a religious zeal to promote learning, literature, and culture, it was because it was.

Religion in New England had always made social morality, and by extension civic duty, its business. "To the New England mind," wrote Henry Adams, "roads, schools, clothes, and a clean face were connected as part of the law of order or divine system. Bad roads meant bad morals." Or, as the historian Richard Hofstadter more seriously put it, deep in the Yankee Protestant tradition was "the idea that every-one was in some very serious sense responsible for everything."[15]

The democratic spirit of the Revolution had brought about a revo-lution in Boston's churches that galvanized anew that sense of every-one being "responsible for everything." The stern Calvinist doctrine that thundered from generations of New England pulpits offered the faithful a powerful and wrathful God, saw sinfulness and corruption as the inherent state of mankind, and capped it with the hopeless fate of predestination, by which men were already assigned to the elect and the damned. Americans who had overthrown a despotic king could not now help bridling at a despotic God. "We cannot bow before a being, however great, who governs tyrannically," declared William Ellery Channing, a Congregational minister and founder of the movement that would come to be called Unitarianism.[16]

The inscription at the base of his monument in the Boston Pub-lic Garden reads, "He breathed into theology a humane spirit." From its beginnings among the liberally minded clergy of Harvard around 1800, Unitarianism within a decade swept into the pulpits of nearly every Congregational church in and around Boston. When a conserva-tive Presbyterian minister, Lyman Beecher, arrived in Boston in 1816, he found that "all the literary men of Massachusetts were Unitarian; all the trustees and professors at Harvard College were Unitarian; all the elite of wealth and fashion crowded Unitarian churches."[17]

Unitarianism's fundamental tenet was that God had given man a rational nature and a moral conscience, and expected him to use them. Salvation was no longer to be found in outward conformity to rigid doctrine or unquestioning obedience to an unknowable God, but lay rather within each man's own conscience. Nowhere did the new belief differ more dramatically from the old than in its emphasis on the innate goodness and perfectibility of man, a complete reversal of the "total depravity" that Calvinism saw as inextricable in man's nature.

To later generations, Unitarianism was usually the punch line of a joke about lukewarm faith. Fanny Holmes once humorously explained to her husband's secretary that they were Unitarian because "in Boston you had to be something, and Unitarian was the least you could be."[18]

Unitarianism derived its name from its rejection of the doctrine of the Trinity; the old joke in Boston was that a Unitarian was a person who "believes in at most one God."

But the generation that grew up with its liberating ideas had all the moral zealotry of its sinners-in-the-hands-of-an-angry-God forebears, now channeled into a faith that made self-improvement, the cultivation of virtue, and social conscience the ultimate expression of God's will. Unitarianism was sometimes summarized as "Calvinism without God," but for that first generation it would have been more accurately described as Puritanism without Calvinism. "The Unitarians, born Unitarians, have a pale, shallow, religion," Emerson commented in his journal; "but the Calvinist born & reared under his vigorous, ascetic, scowling creed, & then ripened into a Unitarian, becomes powerful."[19]

That power expressed itself most manifestly in the irrepressible optimism and enthusiasm for causes that filled the Boston of Dr. Holmes's generation. Libraries, schools, and hospitals were merely the start. "Not a reading man but has a draft of a new Community in his waistcoat pocket," said Emerson in 1840. To every social ill and vice that had beset mankind throughout the ages—poverty, war, criminality, mental illness, drunkenness, prostitution—Boston had a solution. Appealing to the better nature that lay within every human being was the answer. There were societies to promote thrift and savings, societies to rehabilitate "fallen women," societies to uplift the morals of sailors in port, by providing them with reading rooms and religious services. Prisons would become "reformatories" to foster repentance and rehabilitation; the temperance movement would awaken the populace to the undeniable evils of drink; workhouses would inculcate the poor with the moral virtues of frugality, industry, and punctuality, and so eliminate beggary and idleness.[20]

Boston's faith in education ultimately reflected Unitarianism's faith in man's inherent rationality and goodness. If the answers lay within, politics mattered less than self-improvement through learning and self-mastery through the cultivation of conscience; moral advancement would follow inevitably, of its own accord, once men were acquainted with the truth, and achieved the wisdom to embrace it. "How much was then expected from reforms in education," the Unitarian minister Edward Everett Hale ruefully remarked many years later. "There was the real impression that the kingdom of heaven was to be brought in . . . if we only knew enough."[21]

It was, said the philosopher Alfred North Whitehead, the age when "wise men hoped."[22] Those of the next generation, seared by the reality and bloodshed of war, would use less charitable words when they looked back upon the political naïveté and easy moralizing of the intellectual leaders of the faith that had filled the days of their youth. Henry Adams, friend and contemporary of Oliver Wendell Holmes Jr., grandson and great-grandson of presidents, instructor in history at Harvard, described the comfortable beliefs of prewar Boston with none too gentle sarcasm from the perspective of a half century later:

> Viewed from Mount Vernon Street, the problem of life was as simple as it was classic. Politics offered no difficulties, for there the moral law was a sure guide. Social perfection was also sure, because human nature worked for Good. . . . Education was divine, and man needed only a correct knowledge of facts to reach perfection. . . . Difficulties might be ignored; doubts were a waste of thought; nothing exacted solution. Boston had solved the universe.[23]

THE UNITARIAN REVOLUTION arrived in the Cambridge home of Dr. Holmes's youth in a rather different, and more personal, fashion.

The doctor's father, Abiel Holmes, was indubitably a member of the Brahmin caste. He possessed a library of two thousand books. His first wife was the daughter of the Reverend Ezra Stiles, president of Yale College. His own family tree had roots and branches extending to many Boston names of eminence—Quincy, Cabot, Bradstreet, Jackson.

As minister of Cambridge's First Congregational Parish, Abiel Holmes was a mild Calvinist, but a Calvinist nonetheless, in the least hospitable spot in all of Massachusetts for a preacher of the old creed. The family home, facing Cambridge Common, was as close to Harvard

THE HOLMES HOUSE.

The old Holmes house next to Harvard Yard

Yard as any private residence could be. (Its site was just to the west of the present-day Littauer Center, in the North Yard.) In 1828 the liberal majority of the Reverend Holmes's congregation began addressing a litany of increasingly confrontational complaints to their more orthodox pastor, who had apparently decided, after thirty years in the pulpit, suddenly to take a stand against creeping doctrinal innovation. His congregation was particularly incensed that their minister had barred Unitarian-minded preachers of other churches in the area from giving sermons in his church and that he had instituted evening lectures intended to "prosylete the liberal part of the parishioners" to the "harsh, unreasonable & unscriptural creed" of the "Calvinistic exclusive system."[24] The following year he was forced out, taking sixty of his parishioners with him.

Abiel Holmes seems to have been far less strict in the religious instruction of his own children, which hints that he may have had

more doubts than he cared to admit publicly. "I had an old worn-out catechism
as my text-book on the one hand,"
Dr. Holmes recalled, "and a Unitarian atmosphere in the other, surrounding me as soon as I stepped
out of my door." His father made
him do little more than recite the
catechism to his mother, but that
was enough to make him a lifelong
skeptic. "My mind early revolted,"
he said, at being informed that "we
were a set of little fallen wretches,
exposed to the wrath of God by the fact
of that existence which we could not help."
The doctrine of original sin, Dr. Holmes
thought, had "spread its gloom over the

Holmes's grandfather, the
Reverend Abiel Holmes

whole world of Christendom," and "enslaved" the human intellect.[25]

His recollections of the interminable Sundays of his youth, walking to church for his father's second service of the day, the "three
hymns more or less lugubrious, rendered by a village-choir, got into
voice by many preliminary snuffles and other expiratory efforts,
and accompanied by the snort of a huge bass-viol which wallowed
through the tune like a hippopotamus," completed a picture of Calvinist oppression he was eager to escape. The new world of science
offered not only an intellectual, but a spiritual, haven. "Ever since I
paid ten cents for a peep through the telescope on the Common, and
saw the transit of Venus," he wrote, "my whole idea of the creation
has been singularly changed."[26]

Still, Dr. Holmes remained a lifelong churchgoer, attending Unitarian services at the venerable King's Chapel in Boston, a point that
his far more skeptical son occasionally twitted him for. "Of course
my father was by no means orthodox," Holmes told his philosopher
friend Morris Cohen many years later, "but like other even lax Unitarians there were questions that he didn't like to have asked . . . so that

First Congregational Parish in Cambridge

when I wanted to be disagreeable I told him that he straddled, in order to be able to say, whatever might be accepted, well I always have recognized etc. . . ."[27]

But the fact was that Boston religion was too much a part of the air that both Oliver Wendell Holmes senior and junior breathed in their youths ever to dispense with altogether; in their own ways, even as they rebelled, religion always remained the context of their rebellion.

———

THROUGHOUT HIS LIFE, Dr. Holmes could do anything except stick to anything.

Fortunately for him, he had the talent and the circumstances to get away with it. "I, then, Oliver Wendell Holmes, Junior in Harvard University, am a plumeless biped of the height of exactly five feet three inches when standing in a pair of substantial boots," he described himself at age eighteen in a letter to a boyhood friend. "I am rather lazy than otherwise, and certainly do not study as hard as I ought to. I am not dissipated and I am not sedate."[28]

The year after he graduated from Harvard he published in the *Boston Daily Advertiser* a poem decrying the navy's plan to dismantle the *Constitution*, the Boston-built frigate whose famous victories against the British Royal Navy had turned the tide in the War of 1812. "Old Ironsides" exactly caught popular feeling with its indignant exhortation,

> *O, better that her shattered hulk*
> *Should sink beneath the wave*

It gave the young Holmes a name as a poet, and in the ensuing wave of public protest the navy reversed its decision.

He enrolled in Harvard Law School, but neglected his studies when a college periodical "tempted me into print," he confessed. "And there is no form of lead-poisoning which more rapidly and thoroughly pervades the blood and bones and marrow than that which reaches the young author through mental contact with type-metal."[29]

The next year he switched to medicine, reporting his "startling position" to his friend with no further explanation than, "I did not like the one, and I do like the other."[30]

Completing his medical studies, but not the thesis required for graduation, he announced he was going to Paris. His parents, who had vaguely uneasy ideas about what young men wanted to go to Paris for, worried but needn't have. He wrote home with enthusiasm about the "concentrated scientific atmosphere" of the city, the ease with which he had mastered the language ("I understand my French lectures almost as perfectly as English"), the number of interesting cases he was able to attend, and the culture, food, and theater.[31] He saw the sights of London and Rome, then returned home to learn that if he was to receive his medical degree from Harvard that year, he had only three days to submit his thesis—which he did. Later that year he was invited to present the Phi Beta Kappa poem at Harvard's bicentennial, and delivered his poem, an hour and ten minutes long, from memory.[32]

He made a brief if brilliant foray into medical research, publishing two scientific papers that showed a startling clarity and grasp of statistical methods, as well as a poetic deftness with a revelatory turn of phrase that his son would later bring to the law. To the outrage of the medical establishment, Dr. Holmes argued that puerperal, or childbed, fever—a fatal infection that afflicted thousands of women following childbirth—was spread from patient to patient by attending doctors and midwives. This was in 1843, before the germ theory of disease was known, but from an extensive survey of cases he found that the illness was always associated with a handful of practitioners in any given locale, confirming its contagious nature:

> It does appear a singular coincidence, that one man or woman should have ten, twenty, thirty, or seventy cases of this rare disease, following their footsteps with the keenness of a beagle, through the streets and lanes of a crowded city, while the scores that cross the same paths on the same errands know it only by name.[33]

He concluded that a doctor who had had even a single case should consider his next patient at risk of death, and upbraided his colleagues for not washing and changing their clothes after performing autopsies. Given the irrefutable facts, he declared, the deaths of women from such an entirely preventable cause "should be looked upon not as a misfortune but a crime."[34]

He took on homeopathic remedies with equal fearlessness, in a lecture that to this day is one of the most lucid expositions of the fallacies of medical quackery and the placebo effect. He pointed out that while some patients receiving useless treatments might "have been actually benefited through the influence exerted upon their imaginations," that no more justified pseudoscience than would "justifying the counterfeiter and giving circulation to his base coin, on the ground that a spurious dollar had often relieved a poor man's necessities."[35]

Both papers provoked furious counterattacks; both are striking for how far ahead of their time they were. Yet it was typical of Dr. Holmes's more serious attempts at recognition that for many years a later paper by another researcher was credited with the discovery of the contagiousness of puerperal fever, his own groundbreaking contribution of nearly two decades before forgotten.

He could never sit still. In the early years of his marriage he went on the lecture circuit, earning the not inconsiderable sum of $1,200 a year delivering popular talks ("Love of Nature," "The English Poets," "History of Medicine"), even as he bemoaned the dissipation of the mind and spirit that came from delivering the same talk over and over. ("All lecturers, all professors, all schoolmasters, have ruts and grooves in their minds," the Autocrat observed.)[36]

He saw patients, but never made much of an effort to build his practice, admitting that the thing he liked most about practicing medicine was that it required him to keep a horse and chaise, which he enjoyed driving—inexpertly, his acquaintances recalled with a shudder—at high speeds through the streets. He often jokingly threatened to hang a sign at his door announcing, "The smallest fevers thankfully received." As his biographer and nephew John T. Morse Jr. noted, it made people with no fevers laugh but those with fevers think they might prefer to consult someone who took the matter a little more seriously.[37]

He knew that you could be funny or you could be a doctor, but he could not help it, and composed a funny couplet expressing the dilemma:

It's a vastly pleasing prospect, when you're screwing out a laugh,
That your very next year's income is diminished by a half.[38]

After a few years he let his practice dwindle away: his son vividly remembered the day Dr. Holmes went out and sawed the "Dr." off the front of his name on the sign that hung at their front door.[39] He continued to teach anatomy at Harvard Medical School; he was second to none in his dissection skills, and kept his students awake with a string of memorably bizarre comparisons of anatomical structures to everyday objects, while exhorting them to "fearlessness in meeting the unknown," a colleague recalled. But it was never enough to occupy his mind.[40]

He invented a new stereoscopic viewer, but could not be bothered to patent it; he taught himself photography, developing his own plates using the difficult wet process of the day; he amused himself building an electrical apparatus that could make sparks an inch long leap through the air, and dabbled in experiments in chemistry and mineralogy; he knew everything about trees, bookbinding, prizefights, boating, and trotting horses. At one point he decided to take up the violin, to the bewilderment of his friends who had suffered through his "unmusical" attempts at singing. Every day, he shut himself in his study to practice upon his instrument "with surprising industry," Morse recalled, "and a satisfaction out of all proportion to his achievement."[41]

WHAT DR. HOLMES would be famous for was none of these things. His fame was for being a talker, in a city that prized talk. In fact, said Van Wyck Brooks, he was "more than anything else a talker." Dr. Holmes himself regarded talking as "one of the fine arts—the noblest, the most important, and the most difficult." He described his own method of practicing this art as "interviewing himself," and the answers he gave formed a stream of "whimsical discursiveness" that leapt nimbly from topic to topic. A few of his contemporaries complained of his habit of monopolizing conversation—he was never invited to join the town's Friday Club because the other members feared they would never get another word in if he were a regular member—but none faulted his ability to keep his listeners entertained.[42]

Holmes's own famous Saturday Club met once a month at the Parker House hotel, and even with Longfellow, Hawthorne, Emerson, James Russell Lowell, Charles Eliot Norton, and the renowned orator and senator Charles Sumner and the eminent scientists Asa Gray and Louis Agassiz at the table, Dr. Holmes was who they mostly listened to, hours on end, sometimes into the early morning hours. He had a knack, said one, not just of having something witty or insightful to say on just about everything, but of creating the sense that it *was* a conversation no matter how much *he* talked: he played off the thoughts and suggestions of others like a jazz musician improvising a riff.

Talk was a Holmes family trait; they all had it. At age six, the future justice's first teacher sent home a report card: "Talks too much." "Is

The Holmes family: left to right, Edward, Mrs. Holmes, Amelia,
Wendell, Dr. Holmes

it true," the president of Harvard Charles Eliot once asked Justice
Holmes, "that when the Holmes family sat down to breakfast together
they all talked at once without really expecting to be listened to? Your
father once gave me a very amusing picture of that performance." Wendell Jr.'s tactic for dealing with this "free for all" was recounted by his
younger brother, Edward: "Wendell ends every sentence with a 'but' so
as to hold the floor till he can think of something else to say."[43]

The real wit and talker of the family, according to the justice's
own estimate many years later, was Dr. Holmes's younger brother.[44]
John Holmes was not famous at all, except among a close circle of
devoted friends.

He had done his brother's dilettantism one better by abandoning

John Holmes

any pretence of working for a living at all. The ne'er-do-well bachelor was as rugged a New England archetype as the Brahmin, and Holmes's Uncle John played it to the hilt. He had graduated from Harvard and Harvard Law School but after a short and none-too-serious effort to practice law gave it up forever. He then went to sea as a common sailor on a square-rigged sailing ship, returning two months later with a lame leg and no further ambition but to live in the old family home and look after his widowed mother.[45]

With a small income from some rental property in Cambridge he had inherited, he did just that, moving to a smaller house near Cambridge Common after his mother died in 1862. He played whist and conversed with James Lowell and other friends who regularly dropped by to see him (among them the publisher John Bartlett, then at work on his first book of quotations); kept stacks of dimes and quarters on the windowsill to hand out to neighborhood children and other passing strangers; regularly attended Harvard commencement; and composed long whimsical letters in the persona of an old Yankee seafarer from Kennebunk, Goliath Tittle, to his young nephew Ned.[46] To others he wrote letters and spun dialogues involving biblical patriarchs trying to tie their shoelaces, Calvinist preachers reassessing the doctrine of infant damnation after a few mellowing mugs of toddy, and a loquacious dog on a desert island. It was from his Uncle John, Holmes told his fellow justice Charles Hughes many years later, that he learned "not to be afraid of vulgar talk," something he definitely would not have learned from his father.[47]

The more important difference between the two brothers, though, when it came to their wit and talk, was the distinction Lowell pointedly drew: "Wendell markets all his goods, John gives his to his friends."[48]

Dr. Holmes had indeed found a way to make talk pay. Not long after his *Autocrat* stories first showed him just how much the market would pay for his goods, he was regaling his nephew and some of his nephew's college friends after dinner for an hour or so, when he suddenly leapt up from the table, and exclaimed, "Why! I believe I've wasted a hundred dollars worth on you boys tonight!" He was kidding, but not really.[49]

The genius of *The Autocrat* was indeed that it *was* Dr. Holmes's conversation. With no Boswell to record his table talk, "he had Boswellized himself," Brooks wrote.[50] The index of the book was a minor comic masterpiece in itself; a random selection perfectly captures the "whimsical discursiveness" of the doctor's talk:

Abuse, all good attempts get; Authors, hate those who call them droll; Beauties, vulgar, their virtuous indignation on being looked at; Bores, all men are, except when we want them; Canary-bird, swimming movements of; Children, superstitious little wretches and spiritual cowards; Conversation, very serious matter; Dandies, men are born; Feeling that we have been in the same condition before, modes of explaining it; Gil Blas, the archbishop served him right; Heresy, burning for, experts in, would be found in any large city; Huckleberries, hail-storm of; Knuckles, marks of, on broken glass; Log, using old schoolmates as, to mark our rate of sailing; Minds, jerky ones fatiguing; Minister, my old, his remarks on want of attention; Norwich, how not to pronounce; Novel, one, everybody has stuff for; Old Age, how nature cheats us into; Profession, literary men should have a; Rum, the term applied by low people to noble fluids; Seven Wise Men of Boston, their sayings; Shakespeare, old copy, with flakes of piecrust between its leaves; Sin, introduction to; Thoughts, tell worst to minister and best to young people; Toy, author carves a wonderful, at Marseilles; Walking arm against arm, laws of; Youth, American, not perfect type of physical humanity

One typical passage of the *Autocrat* not only demonstrates Dr. Holmes's breathless "tendency to linguacity," as he himself described his relentless style of talk, but also expressed what would become a favorite maxim of his son's:

> All generous minds have a horror of what are commonly called "facts." They are the brute beasts of the intellectual domain. Who does not know fellows that always have an ill-conditioned fact or two which they lead after them into decent company like so many bull-dogs, ready to let them slip at every ingenious suggestion, or convenient generalization, or pleasant fancy? I shall allow no "facts" at this table. What! Because bread is good and wholesome, and necessary and nourishing, shall you thrust a crumb into my windpipe while I am talking? Do not these muscles of mine represent a hundred loaves of bread? and is not my thought the abstract of ten thousand of these crumbs of truth with which you would choke off my speech?
>
> (The above remark must be conditioned and qualified for the vulgar mind. The reader will, of course, understand the precise amount of seasoning which must be added to it before he adopts it as one of the axioms of his life. The speaker disclaims all responsibility for its abuse in incompetent hands.)[51]

Nobody had done this before; like Mark Twain's Mississippi steamboat captains and gold rush desperados, Dr. Holmes's Autocrat was not a character out of a book but a character out of life—and American life at that—and he did it before Twain. "*The Autocrat* is not a picture of New Englandism," observed Morse, "it is an actual piece of New England, a sample cut solidly out of the original body."[52] Each of the Autocrat's papers ended with an original poem, a gimmick Dr. Holmes had used in his popular lectures, and among the Autocrat's are two that remain Dr. Holmes's best and best known, "The Chambered Nautilus," and "The Wonderful One-Hoss-Shay."

And yet, as his sharper literary contemporaries recognized, there was always something flash and superficial about the doctor's performances. "He could always write or speak *to order*," Emerson pointedly noted in his journal, "partly from the abundance of the stream, which can fill indifferently any provided channel." The doctor's irreverence and endless juggling of ideas and words (he loved bad puns, while pretending to deplore them) was always an end itself, never a means to deeper reflection. "He laid trains of thought that later became abuses," admitted Brooks. "In fact, he was a wit and not too wise."[53]

The humor of an earlier time rarely translates well to a later generation, but Dr. Holmes's best-known creation was so closely identified with its author that it barely outlived him at all. "Unsupported by his physical presence," the critic V. L. Parrington wrote just thirty years after his death, "his writings seem far less vital than they did when the echoes of his clever talk were still sounding through them." The doctor's attempts at more lasting literary accomplishment went nowhere. No one took his serious novels seriously, and Parrington's final verdict on Dr. Holmes's place in literature was acute, and deadly. "He was always an amateur," Parrington concluded; "life was too agreeable for him to take the trouble to become an artist."[54]

When the doctor's friend Henry Bowditch heard that Dr. Holmes was proposing to write Emerson's biography, he threw his head back and laughed at the idea that the wit of Back Bay considered himself equal to a subject as profound as the Sage of Concord.[55]

———

TRACING A FATHER'S influence is always a difficult proposition, all the more so in a relationship that combined intellectual competitiveness, family pride, and sarcastic humor in equal measures. In his later years, nothing so irritated Justice Holmes about his father as his incurable dilettantism and contentment with easy popularity.

When the justice was in his seventies, he wrote his friend Clara Stevens,

> I think my father's strong point was a fertile and suggestive intellect.
> I do not care as much as he would have liked me to for his poetry
> and novels—but I think he had the most penetrating mind of all that

lot. After his early medical work, which really was big (the puerperal fever business) I think he contented himself too much with sporadic aperçus—the time for which, as I used to say, when I wanted to be disagreeable, had gone by. If he had had the patience to concentrate all his energy on a single subject, which perhaps is saying if he had been a different man, he would have been less popular, but he might have produced a great work. I often am struck by his insight in things that he lightly touched. But, as I said, it is the last five percent that makes the difference between the great and the clever.[56]

Holmes remarked to several of his secretaries and friends that "distracted into easy talk," his father had "dissipated fine talents on literary trivialities."[57]

Dr. Holmes's irrepressible flippancy was a constant blister in the relations between father and son, whose very similarity in intellect and verbal facility made abrasion inevitable. As a father he had early adopted a frivolous manner of speaking about his offspring—"a second edition of your old acquaintance, o.w.h.," he referred to his son in one letter to a friend—which he never abandoned. When Holmes, at age forty, was appointed to the Massachusetts Supreme Judicial Court, his father wrote a friend with the news, "To *think* of it,—my little boy a Judge, and able to send me to jail if I don't behave myself!"[58]

Sensitive about his own diminutive stature, Dr. Holmes more unpleasantly made his son's appearance a target of his mocking humor. Years later Holmes told Felix Frankfurter that while his father "certainly taught me a great deal and did me a great deal of good," he wondered if he "didn't also do me some harm by drooling over the physical shortcomings of himself and his son and by some other sardonic criticisms." Once, as a young man still living at home, Holmes returned late at night from a club dinner having had too much to drink, and passed out just inside the front door. His father found him there the next morning. "Sonny, my father never let me forget this for weeks," he told his secretary sixty years later. "My mother, being a much wiser woman, never said a word. That hurt me much more than my father did. My father just got my back up."[59]

Holmes took a certain vengeful satisfaction in finding among his father's papers "a letter or two from *his* father to him at school inculcating virtue in the same dull terms that he afterwards passed on to me. If I had a son I wonder if I should yield to the temptation to twaddle in my turn."[60]

He always mordantly referred to his father as "the governor" or "the old man." When both were on the program for Harvard's 250th anniversary in 1886, Holmes to address the Law School Association and his father to deliver a poem, Holmes could not resist the chance to stick the knife in. He began his speech with a not very veiled allusion to his father's having dropped out of the Law School: "Perhaps, without revealing family secrets, I may whisper that next Monday's poet also tasted our masculine diet before seeking more easily digested, if not more nutritious, food elsewhere." In his house in Washington, the two desks that had belonged to his grandfather Judge Jackson went into his library; his father's desk, where he wrote *The Autocrat of the Breakfast-Table*, was relegated to the adjoining office for his secretary's use.[61]

He kept up at least a humorous rivalry with his father's ghost long after Dr. Holmes had departed. Holmes's secretaries, gathering to reminisce about the justice after his death, recorded an anecdote from James Nicely, his secretary in 1923–24.

O.W.H. and Nicely disputed as to the meaning of a word. O.W.H. conceded that Nicely's meaning was permissible but was only a secondary meaning. He told Nicely to look it up in the dictionary. Nicely did and discovered that his meaning was given as the primary meaning and that by way of illustration a quotation from O.W.H. Sr. was given. He showed it to the justice.

O.W.H.: "Well, well, so the poor old Governor was wrong, too."[62]

William James dined at the Holmes house in 1873, when Holmes was thirty-two, and reported to his father afterward, "No love is lost between W. *pere* and W. *fils*." But a more poignant picture of the understanding that Holmes Sr. showed for the complexity of the relationship between fathers and sons was recorded by Alice James, who wrote in her diary of her father coming home from a meeting of the Saturday Club and telling her that Dr. Holmes had asked him if *his* sons did not despise *him*—and "seemed surprised" when the elder James said no. "But after all, it is only natural they should," Dr. Holmes exclaimed, "for they stand upon our shoulders." In a speech in 1870, Dr. Holmes remarked more humorously, if more pointedly, "The young Feejeean carries a cord in his girdle for his father's neck; the young American, a string of propositions or syllogisms in his brain to finish the same relative."[63]

Still, Holmes always defended his father if anyone else criticized him; it was only to himself that he "reserved the right to criticize and praise," said Donald Hiss, who served as the justice's secretary in 1932–33, three years after his brother. Holmes remarked to several friends his lifelong frustration that he had had no ready comeback when a supercilious British writer he was introduced to on an early visit to London, Andrew Lang, drawled to him, "Oh, you're the son of the man who writes those dreadful novels," then abruptly turned on his heels and left the room. He was still fuming a half century later. "How I have regretted that I was not quick enough with rapier or bludgeon to hand him one back before he vanished," he told Laski.[64]

When he came across some manuscripts of his father's long after his death, he had them bound into volumes and placed on a shelf in his library. It gave him "an agreeable sense" of having got the better of "my governor," he told Ethel Scott, "as he never realized that I would take any trouble to do him honor, I not spending my time in adoring him when he was alive. He even suggested to me making a little worm of a nephew his literary executor. . . . [I] intimated that perhaps after all I might be trusted not to wish to belittle his reputation!"[65]

Along with Holmes Sr.'s and Jr.'s shared love of books, learning, and life; great talent for talk; and unique gift for distilling complex ideas into a beautifully wrought metaphor or epigram, Dr. Holmes had a sympathy for the travails of others that his son acquired by heredity or example, too. The doctor's friends always thought part of his reason for giving up medical practice was that he felt the suffering of his patients too acutely. His assistant in his anatomy lectures recalled that

Dr. Holmes could not even bear to see a rabbit euthanized with chloroform, but would rush out of the room until it was done.[66]

Dr. Holmes's preternatural kindness in answering every letter from bores, cranks, and—worst of all—aspiring writers seeking help getting their poems and stories published ("I have always tried to be gentle with the most hopeless cases. My experience, however, has not been encouraging") echoed Justice Holmes's later insistence that his secretary read even the most obvious crank mail. "He was always afraid that some genuine wrong would be left unrighted if he threw them aside," his secretary Arthur E. Sutherland remembered.[67]

Mark Howe recorded in his diary the story Holmes told him in 1934 of an incident during the great Boston fire of 1872, when his father worried about his son's irreplaceable notes for his revisions to Kent's Commentaries, his first major work of legal scholarship, while Holmes worried about some of his father's property that also lay in the path of danger. "Holmes was much pleased by the way in which each thought of the other," Howe noted.[68]

At age eighty-four, Holmes wryly remarked to his secretary Barton Leach, "Well, I suppose that if I live long enough I may yet come to appreciate the governor."[69]

CHAPTER 2

A New England Boyhood

D r. Holmes had moved to a house in the heart of the old Boston of crooked little streets upon his marriage in June 1840. His eldest son and namesake was born there just less than nine months later, on March 8, 1841. Two other children followed: Amelia Jackson Holmes, named after her mother, in 1843, and Edward Jackson in 1846.

Tremont Street in 1860, looking toward the Common from King's Chapel.
Montgomery Place is halfway down on the left

Montgomery Place was a tiny lane of elegant townhouses just off Tremont Street. From the corner, King's Chapel was one block to the right; Boston Common, one block to the left. The Athenaeum library—after its move in 1849 to its new (and present-day) home — was just across the Old Granary Burying Ground, on the opposite side of Tremont Street.

At the other end of Montgomery Place a set of small steps led down to Province Street; from there it was a two-block walk to the Old Corner Book Store, which was also the offices of Boston's famed publishing house Ticknor

The "little steps" at the end of Montgomery Place, in 1934

and Fields—"the lounge resort of all the literary celebrities of Boston and Harvard University," a contemporary guide to the city noted. Dr. Holmes always stopped in "to give and receive the news of the day," and Emerson usually wandered by when he came to town, hoping to find someone to have lunch with.[1]

Montgomery Place is now Bosworth Street, and a modern brick and glass high-rise hotel and condominiums now cover the block where the Holmes house stood at No. 8, but the "little steps" at the end of the street that were a touchstone of Holmes's own earliest boyhood memories—"more venerable to me than the Cenotaph of Romulus," he called them—still lead down to Province Street. Revisiting Boston eight decades later and gazing upon those steps, he wrote his friend Frederick Pollock, "I can get the mystery of the past. . . . By there I was born and they have not changed, and with memory they call up a Boston of two centuries ago."[2]

In its physical contours the Boston of his youth was in many ways unchanged from the early eighteenth century. There were still pumps in the backyards to supply water; light came from whale oil lamps "that it always was a bore to get started," he recalled; and even in the city, outhouses were the norm and "the admirable contribution of Messrs. Gayetty and others to the comfort of the toilet were unknown." That was a reference to the inventor of the first commercially marketed toilet paper; in an amusingly persistent recollection, Holmes added, "I seem to remember not only newspapers, but extra sheets of some work of my father's performing the function."[3]

The city's massive landfill project to convert Back Bay into a neighborhood of boulevards, parks, and stately residences was still two decades in the future; the mixture of stagnant water and untreated sewage that filled the dammed-off "Receiving Basin" came up to Arlington Street, where Holmes remembered fishing with a pin hook as a boy, and the land that is now the Public Garden was "a dreary waste."[4]

Even the Unitarian Boston of Holmes's youth was "still half-Puritan Boston"; the old Puritan strictures against representational art, secular music, public statues, even celebrating Christmas as a holiday, held Boston "half-stifled in its bonds." (The Puritans regarded Christmas Day festivities as superstitious popery; Boston exchanged gifts on New Year's Day.)[5]

Sundays hung over Holmes's youth every bit as oppressively as they had for his father. "Oh—the *ennui* of those Sunday morning church bells, and hymn tunes, and the sound of the citizen's feet on the pavement—not heard on other days. I hardly have recovered from it now," he recalled to Laski in 1918. Sunday was "Dismal Day," Holmes said, and he never did recover from its association with the tapioca pudding that was the invariable dessert at the Holmes house on the Sundays of his boyhood. "Stick-jaw," he called it with loathing, and one guest to lunch at Beverly Farms remembered watching the justice literally throwing a bowl of it out the window when it showed up on the table there.[6]

The woman Dr. Holmes had married, Amelia Lee Jackson, was "well off" as they said in Boston—not quite the same thing as possessing "a fortune," but sufficient to allow the couple to marry without delay (the house on Montgomery Street was a gift to the couple from her father,

Judge Charles Jackson). Dr. Holmes had got to know her through her uncle Dr. James Jackson; another uncle was Patrick Tracy Jackson, a leading Boston merchant and financier. He, along with Francis Cabot Lowell, had founded the new textile manufacturing center on the Merrimack River forty miles northwest of Boston that bore Lowell's name. As one of the Boston Associates, the forty or so families who controlled nearly all of the textile mills of northern New England, Patrick Jackson had subsequently expanded his interests into banking and railroads.[7]

These were men of business and civic power, the financial counterpart to the Brahmin caste of Dr. Holmes's family. Even Judge Jackson was more a businessman than an intellectual: he owed his appointment to the state's high court to the connections he had developed over his years of practice as a commercial lawyer, rather than to any contributions to legal scholarship or public service.[8]

It was from his mother, Holmes said, that he inherited his melancholy streak, such as it was, his father by contrast being "almost too bright and cheerful." He remarked once that his mother had also given him his skeptical temperament—implying perhaps that his father's ready insights into everything did not impress his more practically reared wife as much as it did the admiring members of his literary and intellectual circle.[9]

An inheritance of $2,000 she received in 1849 allowed the family to build a country retreat in Pittsfield at the western end of Massachusetts, and as a boy Holmes spent every summer there, from age eight to fifteen. The land had been in the family going back to Dr. Holmes's great-grandfather Jacob Wendell, who in 1738 bought a thirty-six-square-mile tract from the Province of Massachusetts Bay. The original parcel had included nearly all of the land of present-day Pittsfield, though by Dr. Holmes's time all that remained in the family's possession was a 280-acre tract, located south of town on the road to Lenox, known as Canoe Meadow.[10]

It was a beautiful New England farm, with hills, fields, streams, and meadows, and the Housatonic River meandering through the middle. (There is still a Holmes Road there today, and a Massachusetts Audubon Society wildlife sanctuary called Canoe Meadows.)

The Holmes place in Pittsfield

With his usual energy Dr. Holmes threw himself into country life, ordering seedling trees from English nurseries, putting up fences, chairing the judging committee of a plowing contest at the Berkshire County fair.

But "one thing led to another," the doctor found. The house, which an architect had assured him could be built for the $2,000 Mrs. Holmes had inherited, grew increasingly elaborate, more country estate than summer cottage, sprouting window pediments, roof gables, dentil moldings, corner quoins, gingerbread porch railings, and ended up costing twice as much. Then the doctor decided he needed a barn, and then a horse and wagon; and then, as usual, he gave it all up. It was too expensive, and too far away from Boston to take care of properly.

"I loved the trees, and while our children were little it was a good place for them," Dr. Holmes wrote, "but we had to sell it; and it was better in the end, although I felt lost without it for a great while." He had planted nearly all of the trees with his own hands, and leaving them behind seemed to hurt the most; he "never had the courage" to visit the place again, he sadly told a friend.[11]

But the love for the New England countryside that his son acquired during those idyllic summers in Pittsfield was part of his life ever after. His father reported that Wendell spent most of his days there fishing, swimming, shooting, and drawing. The outdoor life did him good; he was growing tall and slim. His nickname was "Leany Holmes," in notable contrast to his cousin John, who was "Fatty Morse."[12]

Sixty summers later Holmes wrote a friend, "This country has my earliest associations and they largely affect if they don't control our deepest loves and reverences. Among the foundations of my soul are granite rocks and barberry bushes."[13]

━━━━━

LIKE MOST BOYS of his class and time, Holmes was placed in the charge of private schoolmasters for his early education. He took to it from the start, as a member of the Holmes family would have been expected to. After a year at a "dame's school," the equivalent of a kindergarten for boys and girls, run by a schoolmistress—that was where he had earned his report for talking too much—he attended a boys' school that met in the basement of the Park Street Church, a block from the Montgomery Place home.

"Young as he is," reported his schoolmaster three years later, "his habits of application are confirmed, while his proficiency in all the English branches, and his love of study are remarkable for his age." That was for a letter of introduction to the headmaster of the Private Latin School, where Holmes, at age ten, began in the fall of 1851. The headmaster was Epes Sargent Dixwell. In the small world of Boston Brahmins, Dixwell had studied law for a year in the office of Judge Jackson, but had abandoned the profession to accept an offer to become headmaster of the Boston Latin School a few years later.[14]

Dixwell had decided to open his own school in the spring of 1851 when the city adopted an ordinance requiring public school teachers to live within the city limits; Dixwell had a home in Cambridge, at

Holmes's schoolmaster and future
father-in-law, E. S. Dixwell

58 Garden Street, that he had built around 1840 and where his growing family lived comfortably in a quiet neighborhood filled with Harvard professors and other members of the Cambridge intelligentsia, just a few blocks north of Harvard Yard.[15] John Holmes said that so little ever happened in Cambridge that, if two cats crossed the street, all the neighbors rushed to the windows to watch.[16] But Garden Street, with its spacious homes, old trees, and well-tended gardens was in fact a welcome and bucolic haven amid Greater Boston's rapidly increasing growth and commercial bustle of the mid-century, which by 1859 would drive Dr. Holmes to move from his downtown Boston homes twice in a decade in search of quieter neighborhoods.

E. S. Dixwell's wife was the daughter of Nathaniel Bowditch, a self-taught mathematician and astronomer who in 1802 published *The New American Practical Navigator*, which to this day remains the standard reference work in navigation, universally known to sailors as "Bowditch." His eldest daughter was Fanny Bowditch Dixwell—who would marry her father's new pupil twenty-one years later.

Dixwell was a renowned classical scholar. But the main focus of his school—as it had been at Boston Latin—was to prepare students for admission to Harvard, which meant cramming them with Latin, Greek, ancient history, and mathematics, the only subjects covered on the college's entrance examination. A contemporary said that Dixwell ran a "classical grind-mill." It probably says more about his young charge's intellectual curiosity than about the headmaster's instructional methods that Holmes emerged with his love of learning apparently intact. But Dixwell was a kind and generous man, and between the rote lessons he hammered into his pupils' skulls he seems to have at least not closed the door to the intellectual vistas beyond; years later, when Holmes was appointed to the Massachusetts Supreme Judicial Court, the schoolmaster wrote his son-in-law and former pupil of his fond recollections of the days "when you used to wait after school to walk along with me and talk of all topics as I went home. It was a very pleasant relation we then held and is still alive with me."[17]

Years later Holmes recalled to friends the "futile shrinking from new things" that had kept him from learning in his childhood to ride or drive a horse, to ice skate, or dance, but he was not referring to physical timidity; it was rather that he already had a sense of what it took to truly master a subject, and an inkling of the dissatisfactions of half-knowledge.

"Alas I know too much in other directions not to divine how much there is to know," he told Mrs. Gray, explaining why in later years he similarly could never apply himself to learning about the rocks and birds of the North Shore that he loved. He knew he could not give such

The Dixwell house on Garden Street in Cambridge

subjects the attention required to do them justice, and would only be frustrated at dabbling. He felt the same way about games like bridge. "I give up in advance all games that require intelligence," he remarked to Lewis Einstein. "I am sure I never could do them well just as I am almost equally sure I never could have been a good fencer, and at least doubt if I ever could have been a good dancer."[18]

———

HARVARD MIGHT HAVE broadened minds or it might have trained them in useful occupations for a growing nation, but in the 1850s it did neither, and proudly so. For Holmes's Class of 1861, as for previous generations at Harvard, there was no choice of major, few electives, barely any modern science, and a great deal of Latin, Greek, and Rhetoric, all taught by rote recitation.

Henry Adams, who was three years ahead of Holmes, was scathing in his assessment of what passed for education at the Harvard of their day when he looked back a half century later. "It taught little," Adams said, "and that little ill." What was taught in religion, ethics, philosophy, history, literature, art, and science, "stood nearer the year 1 than to the year 1900." But "any other education would have required a serious effort," Adams observed, and "no one took Harvard College seriously. All went there because their friends went there, and the College was their ideal of social self-respect."[19]

Harvard's undergraduates were graded on an elaborate point system (eight points for a perfect recitation in a class, twenty-four for a perfect written exercise) with an equally elaborate system of deductions for disciplinary violations (eight points for being late to compulsory daily morning chapel). For each student, the tally of points per semester ran to the thousands, all meticulously recorded, and just as universally derided. At the end of his freshman year, Holmes received a demerit of thirty-two points for creating a "disturbance" in the Yard following his last examination.[20]

His more serious college rebellions involved ideas.

One of the required subjects for all Harvard freshmen was Religious

Instruction, consisting of a semester each of classes in "Christian Morals" and "Christian Evidences."

The instructor was the Preacher to the University and Plummer Professor of Christian Morals, Frederic Dan Huntington. His instruction consisted mainly of arguments for the truth of the Christian faith and the simple perfection of its moral precepts.[21] During one class, he told his students that it was under any circumstance and in all cases evil and wrong to lie. Holmes, fifteen years old, promptly challenged him. Would it be equally evil and dishonest, he asked, if a white woman being chased by a band of Indians tried to fool her pursuers by concealing herself in a swamp and placing a piece of moss over her head? Was not that equally an attempt to convey an untruth to another person, which is the essence of a lie? When Holmes told the story to Mark Howe seventy years later he could not remember what Huntington's reply had been, but did recall that he had proceeded to explicate to the Plummer Professor of Christian Morals "the fallacious distinction between falsehood in word and action."[22]

In his sophomore year Holmes published an essay, entitled "Books," in the December 1858 issue of *Harvard Magazine*, an undergraduate literary journal. It was Holmes's first published work; it exhorted his classmates to reject the conventional wisdom of organized religion and think for themselves about the urgent questions of life.

A hundred years ago we burnt men's bodies for not agreeing with our religious tenets; we still burn their souls. And now some begin to say, Why is this so? Is it true that such ideas as this come from God? . . . And when these questions are asked around us,—when we, almost the first of young men who have been brought up in an atmosphere of investigation, instead of having every doubt answered, It is written,—when we begin to enter the fight, can we help feeling it is a tragedy? Can we help going to our rooms and crying that we might not think? . . . It will not do for Ruskin to say, Read no books of an agitating tendency; you will have enough by and by to distress you. We *must*, will we or no, have every train of thought brought before us while we are young, and may as well at once prepare for it.[23]

Following his own advice, he began devouring as many books outside the narrowly prescribed college curriculum as he could lay his hands on, particularly philosophy, art, and art history. By his senior year, and now one of the editors of the magazine, he was regularly provoking his more conventionally devout classmates—and the college authorities, as well—with articles questioning Christianity's claim to moral superiority, the adequacy of Harvard's curriculum, and the competence of its professors.

In an essay in the October 1860 *Harvard Magazine*, Holmes argued that even the great religious art of the past, as exemplified by Albert Dürer's engravings, does not ultimately depend on "religious form" or the "stories" and "simple and childlike faith" of the Christianity of those earlier times. He added, "Nowadays we see that duty is not less binding had the Bible never been written, or if we were to perish utterly tomorrow."[24]

That brought an outraged reply from a fellow student who accused Holmes of copying Emerson and of adopting a flippant attitude toward Christian virtue.

But the authorities were more incensed by an article that had appeared in the previous issue attacking the Reverend Huntington— who, to the astonishment of the Harvard community, had announced he was resigning from the college and joining the Episcopal Church. The article, which was written by Wendell Phillips Garrison, son of the abolitionist leader William Lloyd Garrison, offered as a parting shot the opinion that Huntington had "never won the hearts of the students," "was not frank and open," and had pursued a course of "sectarian and religious narrowness."[25]

Harvard's president, Cornelius Felton, was so scandalized that he wrote Dr. Holmes asking him to rein in his disruptive son—and warning that the faculty would certainly shut down the magazine if it continued to print articles "disrespectful in tone and language."[26]

As an undergraduate Holmes was serious, but he was not a prig. If nothing else he was too gregarious and cut too striking a figure to play the part of the brooding intellectual, much less a monkish one. Passing Emerson and his daughter on the street in Cambridge one day during his sophomore year, he ran back to pay his respects; Emerson afterward commented to his daughter, "He was a handsome stately fellow, it was pleasant to see him."[27]

For his whole time at Harvard, Holmes lived in a private rooming house near the Yard, Danforth's, that was filled with other young New England men of his social class; if he avoided there some of the more puerile undergraduate high jinks of window breaking and other pranks that characterized life in the dormitories, he also avoided some of its constraints on conviviality.

His family position in Boston society and his own conversational gifts, social ease, and commanding looks guaranteed his entry into Harvard's most exclusive social clubs and organizations, Porcellian, Hasty Pudding, Alpha Delta Phi, none of which placed their ostensible literary or intellectual ends above their fundamentally social purpose.[28] (Porcellian was the most exclusive. Holmes's father had not been invited to join during his time at Harvard, though was later made an honorary member; Franklin Delano Roosevelt did not make the cut, either, in his day. But among its members would be a number of men who would come to play important parts in Holmes's life, including Theodore Roosevelt, Massachusetts's senator Henry Cabot Lodge, and the writer Owen Wister.)

When Alpha Delta Phi gave a dinner in Holmes's honor in 1912, he recalled how that club more often than not met in his room in Danforth's, "which had the advantage of being outside of the College Yard. . . . In those days the Club used to listen to essays by its members before the business of the bottle began."[29]

And yet, as the literary critic Louis Menand astutely observed, "It is a mistake to discount—even when he was still a student—the severity of his character as an intellectual." This, Menand noted, "is a side of the young Holmes's personality it has proved easy to miss." But there was a "chastity about his intellectual style," which Holmes had modeled directly on Emerson, that revealed an underlying deadly serious-

An etching by Holmes, made while
a student at Harvard

ness.[30] It was chastity not in the sense of moral innocence, but in a kind of austere purity and rigor about the process of thought itself.

In his "Books" essay, Holmes spoke admiringly of Emerson's breadth and depth of reading, his rejection of "the authority of others" that led most people to scorn the teachings of Confucius, or the sacred texts of Buddhism and Zoroastrianism, sight unseen; Emerson insisted on seeing for himself. Emerson consistently warned against subordinating individual integrity of thought to the tyranny of prefabricated ideas. That applied equally to the conventional wisdom of organized religion and the pat moralizing of the new reformers; conformity was the enemy of conscience. ("Each 'Cause,'" Emerson said, however "subtle and ethereal" at first, quickly becomes "a little shop" where the article is "made up into portable and convenient cakes, and retailed in small quantities to suit purchasers.")[31]

In his essay on Dürer, Holmes had not only thought for himself about art and philosophy and religion but had gone into some detail on the technical aspects of engraving. Building on his earlier studies of drawing, he actually executed several etchings of his own during his time at Harvard; a surviving print of a man and a goat, after the seventeenth-century Dutch master Berchem, shows considerable technical mastery.

In the fall of his senior year Holmes published a paper on Plato in the *University Quarterly*, an intercollegiate journal; it won a twenty-dollar prize for the best undergraduate essay of that year. Many years later Holmes recounted to one of his young lawyer friends in Washing-

ton the advice and inspiration that Emerson, "who fired me into reading Plato," had given him on approaching his subject.

> He said, "You must hold him at arm's length. You must say, 'Plato,
> you have pleased the world for two thousand years; let's see if you
> can please me.'" I read Plato and I wrote my first article in the
> short-lived University Quarterly, and I laid it at Mr. Emerson's feet.
> About a year later when I saw him, he said, "I have read your piece.
> When you strike at a king, you must kill him." Weren't those fine
> things for the old fellow? Of course, it made me feel damn bad at
> the time. But I always thought they were a model of what the old
> can do for the young.[32]

The day he ran back to pay his respects to Emerson on the street,
Holmes remembered telling him in a burst of adolescent enthusiasm,
"If I ever do anything, I shall owe a great deal of it to you."[33]

He may or may not have actually said that, but it was clearly what
he felt. Emerson remained one of the few enduring heroes of his life,
long after the Civil War had caused the moral world of Emerson and
Holmes's own youth to crumble. "The only firebrand of my youth that
burns to me as brightly as ever is Emerson," he remarked when he
was almost ninety. Emerson, he said, "had the gift of imparting a fer-
ment. . . . That gift is genius."[34]

————

HOLMES GOT IN more trouble in his senior year.

President Felton informed Dr. Holmes that the faculty had voted to
issue a "public admonition" to his son for "repeated and gross indecorum in the recitation room of Professor Bowen."[35]

As the Alford Professor of Natural Religion, Francis Bowen taught
all Harvard seniors two required courses, "Philosophy" and "Ethics."
They offered an ever-so-slightly more sophisticated version of the arguments that God was a Christian that his students had already endured
in their mandatory freshman courses in religious instruction. The first
semester of his class used Bowen's own book *The Principles of Meta-*

physical and Ethical Science Applied to the Evidences of Religion as its principal text; the second, his even weightier, 546-page tome *The Principles of Political Economy*.[36]

Orthodox in his religious views and conservative in his politics, Bowen was described as "dogmatic and unpleasant in controversy," and "one of the abler men of the nineteenth century . . . who managed, because of his orthodox and conservative bias, to be wrong about almost every important intellectual tendency of the age." He dismissed as self-evidently absurd the new scientific theories that man shared "fraternity, or a common pedigree, with the reptile and the brute," and ridiculed Emerson for believing—in Bowen's words—that a "vague conception of virtue takes the place of religion as a guide of life."[37]

If Bowen was an orthodox Christian, his orthodoxy was still that of a Harvard Unitarian, and much of what he taught his class reflected the optimism and Boston parochialism of the time. "Francis Bowen inferred the benevolence of God from the overwhelming happiness of the human race, and this overwhelming happiness he inferred from the contented situation of his own social class. He apparently could not believe that any sufferings bourgeois Bostonians did not experience were a very important part of human existence," Daniel Howe wrote in his history of Harvard Unitarianism.[38]

In his textbooks, Bowen proved that the laws of laissez-faire economics were ordained by Providence for the benefit of mankind. He asked how many of his readers had suffered "famines, inundations, earthquakes, the assassination of friends, robbery, ravenous beasts, tyranny, the necessity of slaying a fellow creature for sustenance, or the like," suggesting that the answer verified the conclusion that the Earth was in the hands of a benevolent power.[39] Exactly what form Holmes's "gross indecorum" took during the spring semester when Bowen's class was reciting back such passages was not spelled out in the letter to Dr. Holmes, but it is not hard to imagine the later Holmes's reaction to such simpleminded moral reasoning.

And yet, just as Holmes once told Morris Cohen that he had absorbed a sense of Darwin's ideas and "the scientific way of looking at the world" from something that "was in the air" in his college days, so he absorbed more than he later acknowledged of the Unitarian outlook that was most assuredly in the air of the Harvard of 1860. He reread Bowen's political economy book at least once, right after finishing law school, and throughout his life his library contained the works of other leading Unitarian thinkers, notably William Channing's.[40]

Cohen had no difficulty tracing Holmes's powerful sense of duty, work, self-improvement, and recognition of the higher claims of society to "his Calvinistic faith." That was true enough in the way Cohen meant it, though it was really Calvinism as reinterpreted by Unitarianism. Holmes's obsessive practice of maintaining a list of the "worthy books" he had read was something he shared with nearly all of the Boston Unitarian moralists of the first half of the nineteenth century.[41] So was his relentless drive, even as a man of ideas, to take his part in the "the practical struggle of life," and resist the temptation to retreat to his library "to enjoy a certain mild delirium of the mind, regardless of the claims of society," as one early nineteenth-century Boston Unitarian minister cautioned against. (The Reverend Channing admitted that in his early years he had succumbed to that error himself, being a "dreamer" and "castle builder" before duty called him back).[42]

In fact, Holmes's admonishment to Frankfurter in 1913 that the academic life

> is a withdrawal from the fight in order to utter smart things that cost you nothing except the thinking them from a cloister. . . . Business in the world is unhappy, often seems mean, and always challenges your power to idealize the brute fact but it hardens the fibre and I think is likely to make more of a man of one who turns it to success

echoed almost exactly the warning Channing had issued a century earlier to the man of letters: a strong character could only be developed in contact with society, and it was only action that gave ideas meaning. "The revolving of elevating thoughts in our closet does little for us," wrote Channing. "We must bring them home to the mind in the midst of action and difficulty."[43]

One of the things Unitarian moralists like Bowen objected to about Calvinism was that it fostered divisive theological controversies on theoretical points of doctrine. Bowen frequently criticized a reliance on "abstract reasoning" over empirical knowledge, the "abuse of general theories" by "the logician" and "the specularist" without "respect for the limitations suggested by experience," the "habit . . . of dwelling on first principles and abstract truths."[44] That was equally a threat in politics as in religion, he stressed. For the same reason, the Unitarian moralists rejected absolutist notions of rights in law, emphasizing that social harmony and integration were always more important than individual interests.

It is striking how many of Bowen's statements of Unitarian principle on these points—not just in their substance, but even in their precise wording—resemble many of his disrespectful student's later famous aphorisms about logic, rights, law, and the danger of taking "isms on faith."[45]

HOLMES	BOWEN
General principles do not decide concrete cases.[46]	Absolute certainty belongs to the proposition, only when couched in general terms. It can be applied to particular cases only by approximation.[47]
The felt necessities of the time . . . have had a good deal more to do than the syllogism in determining the rules by which men should be governed.[48]	[Laws] are not contrivances of human wisdom, but are necessary products of men's habits and wants.[49]
The provisions of the Constitution . . . are organic, living institutions transplanted from English soil.[50]	The most important provisions . . . constitute the original inheritance of the American people, which they brought over with them from England. . . . Constitutions are not made, but they grow by an inherent law of progress and adaptation to changing circumstances.[51]

[All rights] are limited by . . . principles of policy which are other than those on which the particular right is founded . . . Limits [are] set to property by other public interests.[52]

Property is a social institution and must therefore be subject to those limitations and instructions which increase its tendency to . . . the general welfare.[53]

The most fundamental of the supposed preexisting rights . . . is sacrificed . . . whenever the interest of society . . . is thought to demand it.[54]

If he prefers to live with others, the rights of the society take precedence of his rights as an individual.[55]

A trouble with a system of religious and moral teaching based on challenging the very idea of doctrine and authority was that it sowed the seeds of its own destruction. It was a losing proposition to tell a bright nineteen-year-old that he must cultivate his own sense of reason and conscience, then punish him for "indecorum" and "disrespectfulness" when he did so. Holmes's skepticism about human certainty would be powerfully reinforced in the cataclysmic events that were about to close in on him and his fellow members of the Class of 1861. But the seedbed was prepared. In challenging the received wisdom of Harvard's Professor of Natural Religion, Holmes was applying one of the first lessons of Boston Unitarianism's moral thought.

———

IT WAS THE looming confrontation over slavery that would throw Boston's humane, patient, tolerant, and optimistic worldview into the crisis from which it would never recover.

Slavery divided Boston. Its conscience was on one side, its financial interests the other. The mills that had made the Lawrence and Lowell families their fortunes ran on Southern cotton. Nearly all of Boston's moral leaders opposed slavery, but Unitarianism's abhorrence of social strife, and its optimistic faith in the power of moral suasion and steadily advancing enlightenment, offered the comforting hope to Boston's financial leaders that they could keep their consciences without losing their fortunes, or vice versa. Slavery would end of its own accord when the South recognized its moral error; until then it would only stir "passion" and contention and risk hardening Southern opposition to fan political flames, as the more wild-eyed abolitionist preachers were beginning to do. Channing was typical of Boston's Unitarian leaders in associating the abolitionist movement with the excesses of religious revivalism; they viewed the Boston Brahmin abolitionist orator Wendell Phillips, with his fiery portrayals of the horrors of slavery and the evils of slave owners, as little more than an aristocratic demagogue.[56]

The alternative to continued patient compromise was immediate disunion, and most of Boston's civic and moral leaders, Francis Bowen and Dr. Holmes among them, supported the Compromise of 1850 that held the Union together by acceding to Southern demands on the status of slavery in the new territories and the capture and return of escaped slaves.[57]

The bias in favor of not upsetting the status quo that was inherent in Unitarianism's opposition to political activity was fundamentally conservative, however liberal its underlying moral views. The convenient hypocrisy of that straddle was growing increasingly untenable as the national crisis over slavery intensified following the Compromise of 1850. Emerson, already disenchanted with the cold rationality of Unitarianism, sardonically observed that "Boston or Brattle Street Christianity" consisted of "the best diagonal line that can be drawn between Jesus Christ and Abbott Lawrence."[58]

The provisions of the new fugitive slave law that the South had insisted upon as its price for remaining in the Union brought matters to a head. The Constitution required that any "person held to service or labor in one state" shall be "delivered up on claim of the party to whom such service or labor may be due," but did not specify how it was to be enforced. The Fugitive Slave Act of 1793 permitted owners to cross state lines to recapture escaped slaves and bring them before a local magistrate or federal court to establish their ownership, yet gave slaves no right to habeas corpus, trial by jury, or the opportunity to testify in their own behalf. In response to the obvious abuses this invited, many Northern states enacted personal liberty laws designed to protect, in particular, free blacks whom slave hunters sometimes unscrupulously attempted to kidnap to the South under cover of the law.

The new fugitive slave act went much further, establishing throughout the North a new office of federal commissioners who could order a slave returned on an affidavit from a Southern state, without hearing evidence at all. Commissioners would be paid ten dollars if a certificate of approval was issued, five dollars if it was denied. Anyone aiding a fugitive or interfering with his return was subject to a fine of up to a thousand dollars. Federal marshals and deputies were required to assist in recapturing and returning slaves, with all expenses to be borne by the United States government.

On April 19, 1851—the anniversary of the shots at Lexington and Concord that began the American Revolution, a grim coincidence not lost on Massachusetts—a black man named Thomas Sims who had been seized in Boston with the assistance of a huge force of police and troops arrived back in Georgia. He had stowed away from there on a ship a month earlier in a bold bid for his freedom. In Savannah's public square, Sims was whipped thirty-nine lashes across his bare back.[59]

"I do not think the blood of even Boston merchants could bear it," said the Boston abolitionist leader and Unitarian minister Thomas Wentworth Higginson. A week later, the Massachusetts legislature chose a fiery antislavery candidate, Charles Sumner, to fill the U.S. Senate seat of the retiring Daniel Webster, the moderate Whig who had engineered the Compromise of 1850. It was the first crack in the "State Street power" of Boston's financial captains that had been holding back the abolitionist tide.[60]

Four years later, another overwhelming display of federal power on behalf of the slave owners sent Boston over the edge. Anthony Burns, an escaped slave from Virginia, was arrested in the city on May 24, 1854. This time Higginson organized a group of militant abolitionists in a desperate bid to free the captive. Armed with axes and pistols, a storming party broke down the doors of the courthouse before being driven back by a line of club-wielding policemen.

Higginson, a thirty-year-old Harvard graduate and Unitarian minister who personally led the charge with a battering ram in his hands, changed forever any ideas about Unitarian confidence in the sufficiency of moral suasion. He would go on to command the first black regiment in the Union Army during the Civil War, the First South Carolina Volunteers. For the rest of his life he bore a scar across his chin from the courthouse raid.[61]

In response, President Franklin Pierce ordered Marines, cavalry, and artillery to Boston. "Incur any expense to insure the execution of the law," he telegraphed. A week later Burns was marched down State Street, guarded by a thousand federal troops, to a revenue cutter that Pierce had dispatched to stand by to carry him back to Virginia, and slavery. Fifty thousand Boston citizens lined the streets and rooftops in ominously silent witness, as the city's church bells slowly tolled the death knell. For the first time, Boston's merchant elite joined the protests. Black bunting draped the offices of the financial district; on the side of one building hung a coffin with the word "Liberty" on it. The return of Anthony Burns to slavery cost the United States $100,000, about $3 million in the currency of the early twenty-first century.[62]

"We went to bed one night old fashioned, conservative, Compromise Union Whigs," the textile heir Amos A. Lawrence wrote a friend in the wake of the shattering show of force on behalf of slave power, "& waked up stark mad Abolitionists."[63]

Still, there were many—Dr. Holmes among them—who feared more than ever where militant abolitionism would lead. Speeches on both sides in Boston became more inflammatory, marked by catcalls, brawls, and outright violence. In 1855 Dr. Holmes gave a speech arguing that slavery was a "physical fact," against which it made no more sense to rail than the Allegheny Mountains. He said that the white man "must be the master in effect" of the black races "whatever he is in name," and that having made its pact with the South in the adoption of the Constitution, the North had forfeited any right to criticize its morals:

Shall we of the North feel and act to these Southern men as equals and brothers; shall we treat them always in the spirit of Christian love; or shall we proscribe, excommunicate, anathematize, vituperate and irritate them until mutual hatred shall ripen into open warfare?

For this he was loudly hissed by part of the audience.[64]

His son felt no inclinations to temporize. Holmes would later recall being "deeply moved by the Abolition cause" in his years at Harvard before the war. In his sophomore year "a Negro minstrel show shocked me" with its demeaning representation of blacks.[65] When Wendell Phillips was scheduled to address the Massachusetts Anti-Slavery Society in Tremont Temple on January 24, 1861, Holmes readily volunteered to serve on his bodyguard.

The threat of violence was not theoretical: four days earlier a huge antiabolitionist mob had set upon Phillips as he made his way to the Music Hall to deliver a speech. Phillips, the most radical of the Boston abolitionists, who advocated complete equal rights for all races—and who now carried a gun whenever he left his house—made it to the hall thanks only to a phalanx of one hundred brawny German and Yankee supporters who cleared the way for him through the streets of downtown Boston.[66]

Nor were the issues at stake for the country theoretical anymore: by then half the Southern states had declared their secession from the Union in the wake of Abraham Lincoln's election.

The older brother of Norwood Penrose Hallowell, who was Holmes's close friend, classmate, and housemate at

"Pen" Hallowell

"Little" Abbott

Danforth's, sent Holmes a note confirming the arrangements for the twenty-fourth. The Hallowells were Quakers, whose antislavery furor would lead them to place their Quaker principles aside and take up arms in the coming war. Richard Hallowell told Holmes to come by the family's store to pick up a "William"—that was a jocular term for a billy club—but added, "I do hope you will not receive personal injury tomorrow and trust you will not use a weapon except as a last resort." In the end Holmes's services were not required; after a raucous confrontation between the speakers and a shouting mob in the balcony the afternoon before Phillips's speech, the mayor sent the police to shut the hall and lock the doors.[67]

On April 14 the surrender of Fort Sumter put an end, at least for the moment, to the divisions between Unionists and abolitionists in Boston. Dr. Holmes announced his full-throated support for the war, and for the abolition of slavery. His son had friends at Harvard who had been on both sides; all now enthusiastically volunteered. By the twenty-fifth of the month Holmes had withdrawn from Harvard and enlisted as a private in the Fourth Battalion of the Massachusetts Volunteer Militia.

Joining him were Henry Abbott and Pen Hallowell, the two men who would become his closest comrades in arms, as well as the most enduring symbols to him for what the war had meant.

Abbott, who had been a year ahead of Holmes at Harvard, never had anything but contempt for the cause he fought in—deriding the abolitionists and Lincoln, dismissing Dr. Holmes as "a little fool" for his newfound jingoism. Yet his courage in action, Holmes would recall, was "sublime." His death in the Wilderness apotheosized for Holmes the heroism of doing one's duty heedless of its end, a luminous picture of transcendent greatness that would survive even his darkest disillusionments with the war.[68]

And Hallowell, whose idealism never died—after the war he carried on the heartrending fight for the rights of the freed slaves to his very end—was always to Holmes the embodiment of a youthful ideal that even his later realism could not gainsay. When Hallowell, "my oldest friend," died in 1914, Holmes eulogized him to Lewis Einstein as "a savage abolitionist, a fighting Quaker who blushed at his own militancy, intolerant of criticism or opposition, but the most generously gallant spirit and I don't know but the greatest soul I ever knew. . . . He gave the first adult impulse to my youth."[69]

On April 25, the young men from Harvard arrived at Fort Independence in Boston Harbor to begin training for the fight that, all were confident, would be over by summer's end.

CHAPTER 3

Harvard's Regiment

Of the 578 Harvard men who served in infantry units in the Union Army during the Civil War, 124 died and 86 were seriously wounded, a staggering 36 percent casualty rate. The regiment many of those Harvard graduates would join, the Twentieth Massachusetts, saw more men killed than only four other regiments in the entire Union Army. At Gettysburg, more than half of the "Harvard Regiment," including ten of its thirteen officers, were killed or wounded. By then it had earned another nickname: the Bloody Twentieth.[1]

By the time the war was over, 260 of the men and officers of the Twentieth Massachusetts had died in battle, including its colonel, lieutenant colonel, two majors, its adjutant, and its surgeon; another 149 had succumbed to fatal illnesses; and hundreds more had been seriously wounded or taken prisoner, a casualty list that far exceeded its entire original strength of 750.[2]

In the spring of 1861, however, war still seemed a lark and an adventure, especially to the young Harvard men who had eagerly dropped their books in the surge of excitement following the firing on Fort Sumter. Within days, regular life on campus came to a standstill. "Very little studying going on," noted the college librarian. In all, fifty-one of the eighty-one members of the Class of 1861 would take up arms in the fight. On April 25, many stood in the ranks of the 120 young men—Holmes, Abbott, and Hallowell among them—who boarded the ferry boat *Nelly Baker* for the two-mile voyage across Boston Harbor to Castle Island, where Fort Independence waited to receive them.[3]

The vigorous outdoor life they enjoyed there for the next month had all the release of a sudden holiday. "I'm in bully condition and have got to enjoying the life much," Holmes wrote his mother a few days after his arrival. It was an escape not only from the classical subjects that few of Holmes's fellow Harvard students ever had much real interest in, and from the college's oppressive atmosphere of paternalistic rules and regulations, but also from a sense of aimlessness and uselessness that had burdened many of these young men of privilege.[4]

Henry Abbott, whose Harvard career had consisted of little more than an unbroken string of punishments culminating in two temporary expulsions—his violations included "neglect at mathematics," "indecorum at prayers," "tardiness at recitations," "throwing articles from a window of a college building," and "visiting sundry freshmen at a late hour for the purpose of annoying them"—confessed to his mother that before enlisting, "I felt that I had never done any thing or amounted to any thing in the whole course of my existence. . . . And what is more, that seemed to be the opinion of every body else. I couldn't help concurring with every body else, & so got disgusted with being nothing & doing nothing." Despite being "constitutionally timid," he decided that "nothing could possibly be so good for me" as to "do what so many other young men were doing."[5]

Getting up at dawn, drilling six hours a day, parading in formation every evening at six, learning to handle a musket in regulation fashion, even tending to the mundane duties of camp life gave a flush of competence to men who had never had to do much of anything for themselves. "Yesterday I made a pretty good omelet," Holmes's friend Henry Ropes of the Class of 1862—who would die at Gettysburg—proudly reported to his brother a few months after joining up. William Francis Bartlett, also of the Class of 1862—he would end the war a brigadier general, after losing a leg during the Peninsula Campaign—wrote on his return from Fort Independence, "I value the knowledge acquired in the last month more highly than all the Greek and Latin I have learned in the last year. . . . I look back on the past month as one of the pleasantest and most useful that I remember."[6]

By the time Holmes returned home on May 25 from his month of militia drill, preparations for war had already begun to take a more serious and ominous turn. Immediately after Fort Sumter, Lincoln had issued a call for 75,000 militiamen for ninety days' service. In May the Confederacy authorized the enlistment of 400,000 men, in addition to 100,000 already called up.

Ceremonial state militia units like Massachusetts's Fourth Battalion were going to be a sideshow in this kind of a war, and the northern states were already forming new regiments in anticipation of the expected call for mass mobilization. When Congress returned in July it did just that, authorizing a million men for three years' service. Holmes and anyone else looking to be sent into the fight began seeking commissions in one of the newly organizing volunteer regiments.

Crossing Harvard Yard one day in June, Holmes spotted Colonel Henry Lee Jr., the governor's aide-de-camp, and immediately went up to him to ask for a commission in the Twentieth Regiment. Lee was a cousin of Dr. Holmes's. The colonel's first assessment of the gangly six-foot boy was "pity for your youth and delicacy," as he told Holmes many years later, but agreed to help.[7]

As far as Holmes was concerned, he was done with college life. He was the only one of his class who did not even bother to receive permission from the college authorities before departing.[8] When Harvard announced it would allow the seniors who had gone to Fort Independence to come back so they could graduate, Holmes ignored the offer of clemency. So did his friend Hallowell. On June 10 the faculty voted that "Hallowell and Holmes, Seniors, be informed that they must return to College and pass the usual examination of their class as a condition of receiving their degrees." Once again President Felton found himself writing to Dr. Holmes to plead with him to intercede with his hardheaded son, expressing surprise that he had "not rejoined his class since he was relieved of duty at the Fort." He added, "Not knowing where he is at present, I must rely on you to communicate this notice to him."[9]

Apparently the doctor did. At the Class Day exercises on June 21,

Hallowell was the Class Orator, Holmes the Class Poet. Dr. Holmes remained incensed, however, that the faculty had insisted on deducting from his son's academic score the penalties he had incurred from missing class for a month, which not only disqualified him from a part on the program of the official commencement exercises on July 17 but reduced his class standing from the top twenty to the bottom half. Though his son had never uttered "a word of complaint" or even gave "any thought upon the matter," Dr. Holmes wrote Felton on July 24, for his part he considered it unpatriotic for the college to stick to its rules when the future of the nation hung in the balance:

> He left college suddenly, no doubt, but if he did not stop to kiss his Alma Mater, neither did many other volunteers stop to kiss their mothers and wives and sweethearts. . . .
>
> His case was entirely exceptional. Revolutions do not follow precedents nor furnish them. The enforcement of the scholastic rule in this instance seems to me harsh and unworthy of the occasion. If a great General receives an L.L.D. for military services [General Winfield Scott had been awarded an honorary degree at the commencement exercises], it seems hard that a poor private or Lieutenant should be publicly humiliated,—or his friends through him,—for being too prompt in answering the call of the Commander in Chief.[10]

(President Felton replied, "With the most kindly feeling towards your son, who is to an unusual degree a favorite of mine, I must still think that the course of the Faculty was right."[11]

The younger Holmes's final act of farewell to his Alma Mater was to submit a biographical sketch for the Class Album. "The tendencies of the family and of myself have a strong bent for literature, etc., at present I am trying for a commission in one of the Massachusetts Regiments, however, and hope to go south before very long," he wrote. "If I survive the war I expect to study law as my profession or at least for a starting point."[12]

Dr. Holmes was meanwhile pulling his own strings to help his son secure a commission and obtained from the governor's military secretary a letter of introduction to Colonel W. Raymond Lee, the commander of the Twentieth Regiment, whom the doctor proceeded to visit in person at the regiment's training camp in Readville, southwest of Boston.[13]

On July 23, two days after the Battle of Bull Run dashed any lingering illusions for a ninety-day war, Holmes and Hallowell received their commissions as first lieutenants. Holmes had just borrowed Hobbes's *Leviathan* from the Athenaeum library and was walking home past the State House when an acquaintance told him his commission had just been issued by the governor. He turned around, returned the book, and prepared to leave for war.[14]

THE TWENTIETH REGIMENT of the Massachusetts Volunteer Infantry was riven with unusual tensions from the start.

Governor John Andrew of Massachusetts was a populist and an abolitionist, but he was also an experienced politician who recognized the importance of solidifying the support of Boston's conservative old guard behind the war effort.[15] The officers he chose for the Twentieth read like a page from Boston's social register: Cabot, Crowninshield, Revere, Lowell, Putnam, Palfrey, Whittier, Macy. One half of the regiment's officers literally were Harvard graduates, and in all at least two-thirds were drawn from the city's social elite. None had military experience. But none believed that mattered. They all shared the belief—as did Governor Andrew—that being a gentleman was more important when it came to commanding men in battle.

The enlisted men, by contrast, were working class, and mostly non-Yankee. One half were foreign-born, mostly Irish and German.

Ironically, a number of the Germans, "gentlemen" or not, *did* have real experience on the battlefield, having fought in the Prussian Army—or against it, as an *Achtundvierziger*, a "Forty-eighter"—during the failed democratic uprising in the Revolution of 1848. Ferdinand Dreher, one of the small minority of non-Yankee officers of the regiment, was a thirty-nine-year-old, barrel-chested carriage painter from Baden who had broken out of a German prison after the rebellion and made his way to the United States.[16] He commanded Company C, one of the three predominantly German companies of the regiment, and among his noncommissioned officers were many similarly experienced veterans of the European wars, well versed in modern infantry and artillery tactics. After Ball's Bluff, he would complain bitterly about the "young men, belonging to a certain aristocratick clique" who were lording it over the regiment despite their patent military incompetence. "I would take all the military Science out of [these] gentlemen and put them in a Private, it would not make the best Sergeant we have," he complained to Governor Andrew.[17]

Another German officer of the Twentieth agreed: when it came to the traits that make a good officer, the difference between "those that style themselves gentlemen" and "those that earn their bread by the labor of their hands," he emphasized, is "not perceptible to the unprejudiced observer of men." He too thought that many of the sergeants had more of a grasp of "military science" than the "gentlemen" officers.[18]

The other fault line in the regiment was political. The Germans were passionately opposed to slavery. The working-class Boston Irish, however, made it clear from the start that they were fighting to preserve the Union, and not from the least sympathy for the "nigger-worshippers" and the abolitionist cause. Conspicuous among the troops that had marched Anthony Burns to the wharf was an all-Irish militia artillery unit. Strongly Democratic in their political leanings, Boston's Irish had cast their votes overwhelmingly for Lincoln's rival Stephen Douglas in the 1860 presidential election. The Roman Catholic Church for its part had been conspicuously silent on the issue of slavery, and Boston's weekly Catholic newspaper warned in June 1861 that "not one volunteer in a hundred" from their community had stepped forward in order "to liberate slaves."[19]

Most of the Twentieth's Brahmin officers agreed. Besides Holmes and Hallowell there were only a handful of officers (one was James Russell Lowell's nephew James Jackson Lowell) with any kind of Republican and abolitionist leanings at all. Henry Abbott's father, a state judge, was the leader of the state's Democratic Party and Henry in his letters home regularly derided the radical Republicans, dismissing Governor Andrew as "that miserable old lying, bloated, bragger of the State House" and Charles Sumner as "that miserable old humbug." Bartlett openly sympathized with the South, admitting that in joining the army he "would be fighting rather against my principles, since I have stuck up for the South all along."[20] Following Lincoln's Emancipation Proclamation, the Twentieth would be known as one of the leading Copperhead regiments in the Army of the Potomac, opposing Lincoln and siding with his hapless but charismatic commander General George McClellan in seeking peace with the South.

Many of the antiabolitionist officers were also deeply xenophobic, further inflaming the tensions within the unit. Abbott scorned the foreigners as cowards, dismissing them as "Dutch boors, Maccaronis, & Frogratecs, in short the rag tag & bobtail of all creation, little short beastly fellows with beards & more stupid than it is possible for an American who has never seen them to conceive of."[21]

The Twentieth did not even enjoy the cohesion that most Civil War regiments could count on from the traditional practice of filling each company with men from a single town. By the time the Twentieth began organizing, competition for recruits was making it difficult to find a hundred men from one place ready to enlist together.

The regiment's senior officers did, however, have some important experience, if not specifically military, in commanding men and in understanding the lives of Irish workingmen and others from outside their social class. Colonel Lee had attended West Point, though left before graduating to work as a civil engineer, leading survey crews and becoming a major railroad executive. Major Paul Revere, grandson of his famous namesake of the Revolution, had overseen the rebuilding of a burned-out wharf his family owned in one of the toughest of Boston's Irish waterfront neighborhoods, and his experiences there had drawn him into helping the homeless children of the city's most abject poor. And Captain Bartlett, his Harvard pedigree notwithstanding, had spent much of his time at college hanging around billiard parlors and saloons, where he had learned much about the practical side of life as well.[22]

All of the officers were ordered to help fill the ranks. The Germans—along with the regiment's sole Irish officer—did the best, bringing in hundreds of recruits from their ethnic communities, but Bartlett led all the Harvard men, with twenty-five. Lieutenant Holmes, dispatched to Pittsfield, came back with a respectable eleven volunteers from among the friends and acquaintances of his boyhood summers there.[23]

──────

THIRTY MILES NORTHWEST of Washington, the Potomac River divides for two miles around a low, narrow strip of land known as Harrison's Island. On the Virginia side, the narrower of the two streams flows along the base of a hundred-foot-high bluff that towers over the river for a few hundred yards, cut on each end by a deep ravine where creeks empty into the river.

Ball's Bluff was fated to be the scene of a relatively minor skirmish of the opening months of the war, one that on the scale of carnage Americans were about to become shockingly accustomed to would barely register a year later, with fewer than one hundred killed and three hundred wounded. But in the wake of the devastating defeat at Bull Run three months earlier, the Union's debacle at Ball's Bluff would come as a terrible psychological blow to the country. The setback would also bring painfully to the fore the deep political divisions throughout the North over the purpose and meaning of the war that divided Holmes's own regiment.

To Holmes and his fellow officers, though, Ball's Bluff had a different meaning. It was their first chance to see if they could face fear and death with the courage they knew was expected of them, but which many honestly wondered if they would find within themselves when the moment came. Most performed with extraordinary bravery in the midst of the chaos and bungling leadership for which Ball's Bluff is principally remembered by military historians today. A military disaster, but an individual triumph: Holmes would always look back on his baptism by fire through that intensely personal lens.

The Twentieth had arrived in Washington in the predawn of September 7 and encamped within sight of the unfinished Capitol building, its long-planned expansion halted in mid-construction with the start of the war, leaving a decapitated collar where the soaring new dome was to rise.[24]

Unlike many of the state forces that were being rushed to defend the city, the Massachusetts regiments had arrived well equipped. "Have you arms, uniforms, ammunition, &c." asked McClellan when Colonel Lee reported to him on arrival. "My regiment, Sir, came from Massachusetts," Lee proudly replied. Their competence was another matter. Henry Abbott's brother Edward, who had been in the field for two months already in the Second Massachusetts, stopped by to visit and saw the same jittery nerves and rookie greenness among the Twentieth's officers that his own regiment had been through when they first arrived, "thinking a fight was going to take place every five minutes. They actually believed that they were going to march to meet 30,000 men that very night." The regiment's surgeon, Nathan Hayward, observed, "Our men are clumsy enough at camping, and take three times as long as is necessary to get things to rights."[25]

A few days later, Holmes wrote his mother, "I feel *very* well & in *very* good spirits and I think I am learning as I certainly am trying." Though the camp buzzed with rumors about their destination, the food was plentiful and good; the officers were able to buy milk, eggs, peach and apple pies even if the supply of meat came and went; he reported to his mother that he now weighed 136 pounds.[26]

By the fifteenth the regiment was camped at Edward's Ferry, two miles south of Harrison's Island along the Potomac and the C & O Canal that closely parallels it on the Maryland side.

Across the river they could see Confederate pickets, and from the tops of tree could occasionally spot larger bodies of men and horses moving closer to the small town of Leesburg to the north. Once in a while the pickets would exchange desultory shots, but they also sometimes laid down their arms and met halfway across the river on one of the several shallow fords to chat and exchange newspapers, or called back and forth chaffing remarks: "When are you going to Richmond?" "The day before you go to Washington."[27]

There was certainly no plan or expectation for any serious action along the front where they were deployed. McClellan had designated the 6,500-man division north of Washington, under the command of Brigadier General Charles P. Stone, the "Corps of Observation." Its job

"Head Quarters" 20th Regt Mass Volo.
Camp Benton. Md.

Headquarters of the Twentieth Massachusetts near the Potomac, autumn 1861

was to keep an eye on the Confederate forces across the river and guard against a surprise crossing at any of the fords or ferries.

The unintended battle that began on October 20 has been studied ever since as a model for how not to conduct a military operation. Vague strategic objectives, confused lines of command, ambiguous orders, miscommunications, woefully insufficient reconnaissance, and a disastrous absence of logistical planning would have placed even the most experienced troops in an impossible position. Worst of all was the decision—such as it was—to place seventeen hundred men along the top of an indefensible cliff edge with a sheer drop and an unfordable river to their rear.[28]

At midday on October 20, McClellan telegraphed to Stone that he was sending a division under Brigadier General George A. McCall to march toward Leesburg from its camp in Langley, Virginia; the aim was to assess the size of the Confederate force in the town, and perhaps even induce it to withdraw altogether in the face of this show of force. "Perhaps a slight demonstration on your part would have the effect to move them," McClellan suggested.[29]

McClellan later insisted he had never intended Stone to send any troops across the river at all. But after a small scouting party that night crossed over and spotted what they took to be a small Confederate

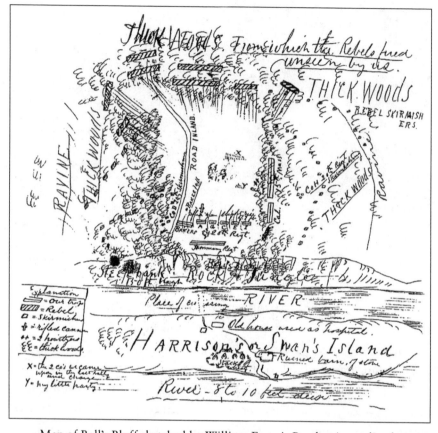

Map of Ball's Bluff sketched by William Francis Bartlett immediately after the battle. Holmes was shot close to where A Company is shown at the far left of the line.

camp of fifteen or twenty tents—they would later turn out to be gaps between trees where the night sky shone through—Stone authorized a raid to destroy the camp and, if the way were open, to continue on to Leesburg. The Twentieth was to wait on Harrison's Island and then cross to the top of the bluff to cover the retreat of the Fifteenth Massachusetts, which was to lead the raid.

Everything went wrong from there. The only boats available to cross the swift-flowing currents of the second channel, from Harrison's Island to the Virginia side, were a small rowboat and two small skiffs, capable of carrying a total of thirty men at a time. Three larger scows, each carrying forty men, were available for the crossing from Maryland to the island, and after some difficulty a rope was stretched across the channel to guide the boats, but that still left a growing bottleneck of men on the island. It was taking an hour or more to move a hundred men all the way across the river. Once there, the only way up the bluff was a steep switchback trail that, as the regiment's official historian later described it, was little more than a "sheep-path," wide enough for only a single man.[30]

Arriving at the top, Captain Bartlett thought "it looked rather dubious." There was a small grassy field of about six acres in front of them, with only a thirty-foot-wide line of trees at the top of the bluff's edge for cover. The field was no more than five hundred yards wide, barely enough room for one regiment to deploy in line of battle. "It was in fact one of the most complete slaughter pens ever devised," Abbott afterward said.[31]

Meanwhile, unbeknownst to Stone, McCall's force was already marching back to Langley, having completed its reconnaissance toward Leesburg earlier that morning. It was not until midday that McClellan had an inkling that Stone had decided to turn his "slight demonstration" into a major reconnaissance-in-force of his own, right into enemy territory. Stone reported confidently, however, that having found no enemy camp after all, the way to Leesburg was open, and that he could take it that day. He ended his message with a line that has entered the annals of military fiasco: "We are a little short of boats."

Stone now ordered several additional regiments to cross the river, and placed them all under the command of Colonel Edward D. Baker, who led a brigade of California troops being sent to join the action. Baker had no military experience. Before the war he had been a senator from Oregon, and he had become a close friend of Lincoln's: the president named his second son after him.

Baker exuded an air of confidence, even as he perceived the precariousness of the situation. Riding up to Colonel Lee he politely introduced himself, saying, "I congratulate you upon the prospect of a battle." But Baker's inexperience told from the start. Rather than using his time to study the terrain of the battlefield and position his troops, he spent two hours on Harrison's Island personally super-

vising the slow ferrying of men across the rising waters of the Potomac. Due to earlier confusion over plans and orders, a cavalry patrol
intended to look for the enemy never went out, and Baker remained
unaware that a force of almost two thousand Confederates was rapidly approaching from Leesburg.

Major Revere recalled his men marching up the hill "happy and
gay, ready for the fight." By three o'clock they were in the fight of their
lives. The Confederate troops, firing from the shelter of the woods on
the far side of the field, quickly had the Union troops surrounded on
three sides. Holmes was in the thick of it on the left end of the front
line. But hemmed in on their tiny front at the bluff's edge, many of the
Union soldiers were unable to return fire without hitting their own
men directly in front of them. Individual companies time and again
rallied to charge the Confederates, but the piecemeal attacks repeatedly failed. The crews manning two howitzers that had been hauled
by brute strength up the path were hit by friendly fire; horses pulling
another gun panicked and plunged back down the cliff.

"Our men were shot on every side of us," Abbott recounted afterward, describing the desperation of the situation. But like Bartlett,
Revere, and the other officers, Abbott found himself able to carry on,
coolly encouraging his men by walking up and down the line, heedless
of the enemy fire. "Why Lit, aren't you hit yet?" Bartlett kept calling
out in a show of devil-may-care humor, using Abbott's army nickname,
short for "Little."[32] Hallowell showed exceptional courage, too, leading
a small group of men stealthily up to the rebel line behind a row of trees
to let loose a volley on their flank.

Two hours into the battle, at about four thirty, Holmes was out
in front of his men of Company A when a nearly spent round struck
him just below the ribcage, knocking the wind out of him and sending
him sprawling to the ground. He started to crawl back, and was being
helped to his feet by his sergeant when Colonel Lee passed by and said,
"That's right Mr. Holmes—Go to the rear." But suddenly feeling "that
I couldn't without more excuse" leave the field, he turned and rushed
forward to where he heard Lee just then cheering the men on to charge.

"I waved my sword and asked if none would follow me when down I went again by the Colonel's side," Holmes recounted in the letter he wrote his mother two days after the battle.[33]

This time the bullet had passed through his chest from left to right. He later found the ball still in his clothes. Bleeding heavily from the mouth, Holmes was carried down the bluff to where the small boats, already heavily laden with wounded men, were making their precarious way across a hundred and fifty yards of water to Harrison's Island.

By now the position had collapsed completely. Around five o'clock Colonel Baker was shot through the head simultaneously by several bullets, dying instantly. Bartlett, Abbott, and Hallowell organized sixty men in a desperate rearguard action, charging from the grove into the open field to buy some time for the men now tumbling in panic down the side of the bluff. Men were shot as they plunged into the river or waited for the boats that were still slowly trying to ferry the wounded. The water's surface, recalled Bartlett, "looked like a pond when it rains, from the withering volleys that the enemy were pouring down from the top of the bank."[34] Howell was one of the last to make it; hanging his watch around his neck and holding his sword aloft, he swam across, then helped man a jury-rigged boat made of fence rails to return with a few more of the wounded.

As Holmes lay half-conscious at the river's edge, he heard another wounded man groan. As he wryly recounted to Mrs. Curtis sixty years later, the thought went through his mind for a moment of "playing Sir Philip Sidney," and saying, "have that other feller put in the boat first"—referring to the legendary story of Sidney handing his canteen to a dying soldier with the words, "Thy necessity is yet greater than mine." Holmes decided instead to "let events take their course."[35]

At a crude field hospital on the island, his first sight was of a severed arm lying on a red blanket in a pool of blood. At last Dr. Hayward approached to inspect his wound.

"How does it look, Doctor, shall I recover? Tell me the truth for I really want to know," Holmes said.[36]

"We-ell, you *may* recover," the doctor cautiously responded. Holmes had supplied himself with a small bottle of laudanum to hasten his end if ever he were suffering intolerable pain, and that first night "I made up my mind to die," he later confessed to his mother.[37] But another surgeon came by and gave him a dose of something to help him sleep, and when he waked he found the bottle of laudanum had been taken away from him. He never again worried about making such preparations for the end.

In his half-dream, half-nightmare state Holmes remembered Pen Hallowell appearing and kissing him, and feeling a terrible anxiety to make sure that someone would write home "& tell 'em I'd done my duty" if he died.

He later was struck forcefully by "how rapidly the mind adjusts itself" to new circumstances, how contingent even the most fundamental truths seemed to be. "I thought for awhile that I was dying, and it seemed the most natural thing in the world—The moment the hope of life returned it seemed as abhorrent to nature as ever that I should die." More matter-of-factly he recalled that "one of the thoughts that made it seem particularly hard to die was the recollection of several fair damsels whom I wasn't quite ready to leave."

Holmes wrote down most of these impressions about two years after the battle; they were on loose sheets placed inside a diary of his war experiences, and at the end of his account of Ball's Bluff he appended a brief explanation of why he had so carefully plumbed the memories of his first wound.

> At first I only intended to show the rapidity of thought & queer suggestions which occur when one is hit, but as I always wanted to have a memorandum of this experience—so novel at that time to all & especially so to me from the novelty of my service and my youth—I have told the whole story from the time I was hit until apprehension had left me.

Most striking was the vivid sequence of philosophical reflections about life itself that passed through his mind in that falling-down log hut on Harrison's Island, as men lay groaning and dying around him:

Of course when I thought I was dying the reflection that the majority vote of the civilized world declared that with my opinions I was
en route for Hell came up with painful distinctness—Perhaps the
first impulse was tremulous—but then I said—by Jove, I die like a
soldier anyhow—I was shot in the breast doing my duty up to the
hub—afraid? No, I am proud—then I thought I couldn't be guilty
of a deathbed recantation—father and I had talked of that and were
agreed that it generally meant nothing but a cowardly giving way to
fear—Besides, thought I, can I recant if I want to, has the approach
of death changed my beliefs much? & to this I answered—No—
Then came in my Philosophy—I am to take a leap in the dark—but
now as ever I believe that whatever shall happen is best.

Later, he vaguely recalled being carried across the island in a blanket, lying on the bank comatose, "swearing terrifically," finally being
placed aboard a canal boat; then, being driven in "one of the two
wheeled ambulances which were then in vogue as one form of torture,"
with a balky horse and a man who didn't know how to drive, with Captain Dreher as his companion. For the first time he saw the extent of
Dreher's ghastly head wound. "Two black cavities seemed all that there
was left for eyes—his whiskers & beard matted with blood which still
poured black, from his mouth—and a most horrible stench."

After a week at the camp's field hospital near Poolesville and then at
a hotel in Washington, Holmes arrived on October 31 in Philadelphia
to stay with his Quaker abolitionist friends the Hallowells and continue
his recuperation. A few days later a local doctor, William Hunt, sent
Holmes's father a report on the patient. The wound was improving, he
found, though still separated by only "a very thin partition" from the
vital organs. "Now Sir you can judge from this description what a narrow escape your son has had from immediate death."[38]

Although Dr. Hunt advised that there was no need to come to Philadelphia, Dr. Holmes rushed there at once. Holmes was deeply embarrassed and irritated by his father's overly emotional greeting on his
arrival, and, as he recounted to his secretary Chauncey Belknap in
1915, "I showed my young soldier's contempt for his lack of restraint."[39]

But Dr. Holmes was in his element, bustling about with arrangements. After a stopover in New York, Dr. Holmes reserved six seats on the train to Boston and had a bed placed on them so the wounded soldier could make the rest of the trip in more comfort. They left at eight in the morning on Saturday, November 9, arriving in Boston at a quarter to five that afternoon. A carriage Dr. Holmes had ordered was waiting at the station to take them home.[40]

Dr. Holmes had recently moved to 21 Charles Street, a house overlooking the Charles River. Mrs. Holmes kept a guest book recording all the "Visitors to the Wounded Lieutenant" who came to the house. There were 133 during the month of November.[41] Charles Sumner came twice; Anthony Trollope, on a visit to the United States, stopped in; most often there was a virtual pack of pretty young girls surrounding the wounded lieutenant's bedside. Fanny Dixwell called twice, bringing flowers on one occasion.

Dr. Holmes, having quickly recovered his sarcastic equanimity, described the scene to his friend the historian and diplomat John Lothrop Motley. "Wendell is a great pet in his character of young hero with wounds in the heart, and receives visits *en grand seigneur.* I envy my white Othello, with a semicircle of young Desdemonas about him listening to the often told story which they will have over again."[42]

By the end of the month he was up and walking. He paid a call to Harvard's curator of engravings, Louis Theis, who "opened his arms and embraced and kissed me and produced a bottle of wine and cigars," and then "let me have some ripping A. Dürer woodcuts and his St. Jerome in a room and other things," which became the start of Holmes's own small but well-chosen collection of prints. And from the Athenaeum library he checked out a raft of books, on political theory, philosophy, and military history, which he read as he finished his amazingly brief recuperation.[43]

═══════

IN THE AFTERMATH of Ball's Bluff, the enmities within the regiment that had been temporarily set aside reemerged with venomous spite. Besides the two hundred Union troops killed and wounded in the battle, more than seven hundred of the seventeen hundred men who had crossed the river were taken prisoner, Colonel Lee among them. The Twentieth had sustained a staggering 281 casualties, including four of its ablest German officers. In their absence, the political differences within the regiment quickly resurfaced in rivalries and maneuverings for promotion that threatened to tear the unit apart.

In early December, Governor Andrew received an explosive letter from one of the regiment's officers—Andrew subsequently cut out the signature to protect the writer's identity, but called him "a reliable source." The writer complained that "the Complection of the regiment was different before the battle. Then we had Schmitt, Dreher, Babo, Putnam, Wesselhoeft, Lowell, Holmes,—Anti-Slavery heroes all, Abolitionists most. None of our Anti-Slavery officers, save one, returned unhurt from Ball's Bluff."[44]

More damagingly, the writer reported an incident in camp that added a sensational new charge to already smoldering rumors that General Stone was not just a bungling commander, but was actively aiding the enemy. In the first week of December two black men had come into the camp to sell cakes and pies to the soldiers. Lieutenant George Macy, a member of a wealthy family from Nantucket, promptly ordered the men arrested, and, according to the report Andrew received, sought out the Maryland slave owner whose property they were and returned the fugitives to him, under an armed guard.

Pen Hallowell was livid. "By what authority do you make New England soldiers do such work?" he angrily asked Macy.

"In pursuance of my orders from Gen. Stone," Macy replied.

Hallowell said, "I didn't think that any New England gentleman would do such dirty work."

In February, following a congressional hearing into his conduct at the Battle of Ball's Bluff, Stone was arrested and held for six months, without formal charges, on suspicion of treason. Macy had meanwhile successfully promoted himself for the vacant captaincy of Dreher's Company B, nearly setting off a revolt among the German troops. For months Macy kept up a campaign of petty harassment of the German officers and men, ordering them to perform menial personal tasks for him and imposing collective punishment when they refused. Macy also refused to speak to Hallowell, deeming his honor as a gentleman insulted by their exchange of words.[45]

But Holmes's friend Abbott, though he despised abolitionists as fiercely as any of the gentlemanly clique of the Twentieth, had a very different reaction. It went to the heart of what to both men would come to be the overwhelming meaning of the war for them. "I was a coward before I went & now I ain't," Abbott told his sister. His first experience in battle had led him to rank courage above everything else. In a letter to his father after Ball's Bluff, Abbott praised Hallowell's bravery, and later strongly defended his claims to promotion.[46]

Abbott's friendship with Holmes was cemented by their shared sense that they had stood up to the ultimate test of war. Abbott would tell his father later in the war that though "one can't help despising" Dr. Holmes—"a miserable little mannekin, dried up morally & physically, & there is certainly nothing more aggravating than to have such a little fool make orations & talk about traitors & the 'man who quarrels with the pilot when the ship is in danger' &c, &c"—the son was a different man entirely. "He is a devlish fine fellow & a devlish brave officer":[47]

> Oliver Junior, though you have an instinctive dislike to his specu-lative nature, is infinitely more manly than the little conceited doc-tor. . . . A man here in the hardships & dangers of the field can easily detect what is base in a man's character, & it is particularly trying to Holmes, who is a student rather than a man of action.
>
> But since I have seen him intimately, he has always been most cool, cheerful, & self sacrificing. . . . He is considered in the army a remarkably brave & well instructed officer, who has stuck to his work, though wounded often enough to discourage any but an honorable gentleman.[48]

On March 25, 1862, Holmes rejoined his regiment in Washing-ton. Lieutenant Colonel Francis W. Palfrey—to whom Governor Andrew had sent a sharp rebuke over his part in the fugitive slave incident—was acting commander. "Don't like the looks of things under Palf. wish Lee was here," Holmes wrote home the same evening he arrived.[49]

Two days later, the regiment boarded ships for Fortress Monroe at the mouth of the James River. During the first week of April they trudged forward toward the Confederate defenses near Yorktown, the site of the last battle of the Revolutionary War. McClellan's grand plan was to flank General Robert E. Lee's army, which blocked the most direct route from Washington to Richmond, and move up the peninsula formed by the James and York Rivers to reach the Confederate capital from the southeast. It was a huge logistical feat: the Twentieth was part of a force of 100,000 men, 300 artillery pieces, and 25,000 horses carried on 400 ships.[50]

It was also the first but not last demonstration of McClellan's limitless capacity for self-delusion and blaming others for his failures. Always convinced that the enemy outnumbered him, he always demanded more reinforcements before moving against the enemy. Lincoln had been dubious about the entire plan, telling McClellan he would "find the same enemy, and the same, or equal intrenchments" whichever route he took. As McClellan settled into a prolonged siege of the Confederate trench works at Yorktown, Lincoln kept urging him to strike before the enemy could shift his army and block his entire plan. "*You must act*," Lincoln wired finally, which prompted McClellan to write in disgust to his wife that if the president wanted an immediate attack "he had better come & do it himself," and complained of "the rebels on one side, & the abolitionists & other scoundrels on the other."

When Confederate general Joseph E. Johnston inspected the defenses at Yorktown in late April he was appalled by their inadequacy. "No one but McClellan could have hesitated to attack," he informed Robert E. Lee. After McClellan spent a month emplacing his heavy siege guns, the Confederates evacuated their trenches overnight and slipped back to a well-prepared line around Richmond.[51]

Nothing happened fast. Roads churned to mud under the heavy artillery and horses, bridges swayed and flooded under pouring rain, and all of the men of the Twentieth suffered under filthy conditions. "It's a campaign now & no mistake—No tents, no trunks—no nothing," Holmes wrote home. The dysentery that would be a constant companion to life in the army added to the misery. "While on picket my bowels played the Devil with me owing to cold & wet and want of sleep," he reported. By June nearly all of the officers of the Twentieth discovered they had body lice ("caught perhaps from the men, perhaps from the dirty places we have been forced to live in or enter") and symptoms of scurvy were starting to appear as a result of their inadequate rations, often little more than hard bread and coffee day after day.[52]

The three-month long Peninsula Campaign was a more sobering introduction to the uglier realities of war for Holmes and his fellow officers than the brief skirmish at Ball's Bluff had been. At the Battle of Fair Oaks on May 31 and June 1, Holmes had had to pull out his revolver and threaten some of his own men—"Swore I'd shoot the first who ran or fired against orders." Toward the end of the fight some of the rebel troops panicked and threw down their guns; the Twentieth continued to fire on them until Hallowell ordered them to stop. "Remember Ball's Bluff!" a man shouted. "I told him that was just what I did remember," the Quaker officer replied.[53]

During the Seven Days Battle fought on the outskirts of Richmond at the end of June, Holmes remembered "looking at the sun and saying God why can't it go down faster so that we can rest."[54] At the start of the Battle of Glendale on June 30, as the Twentieth stood ready to advance, the officers standing at the head of their companies, Holmes looked down the line and saw his cousin James J. Lowell. "We caught each other's eye and saluted," Holmes recounted in his famous address on Memorial Day twenty-two years later. "When next I looked, he was gone." Shot in the abdomen, Lowell fell mortally wounded.[55]

By then the Army of the Potomac was in retreat, McClellan having abandoned the operation, blaming the politicians for his failure. Some of the officers of the Twentieth who had shown their bravery at Ball's Bluff began to crack under the strain. Holmes himself later acknowledged, "I was a devilish sight more scared in later engagements than I was in the first when one was keyed up to meet the unknown."[56]

But he at least managed to keep his fears to himself. All the way down the peninsula, the captain of Company A, Henry Tremlett, kept predicting that "we *must* surrender or be cut to pieces within 36 hours." Years later Holmes recounted to one of his young Washington friends this encounter with defeatism, remarking that if he had been older he would have known that "the proper thing to do was to throw something in the fellow's face" and challenge him to a duel on the spot. "It is best after all never to admit in public the things which in your heart you all too tremulously feel may happen."[57]

By the start of September the regiment was back in Washington where it had started five months earlier, and about to face an even greater ordeal.

———

"I REMEMBER JUST BEFORE the battle of Antietam," Holmes wrote to his young Chinese friend John Wu in 1923,

> thinking and perhaps saying to a brother officer that it would be easy after a comfortable breakfast to come down the steps of one's house pulling on one's gloves and smoking a cigar to get on to a horse and charge a battery up Beacon Street, while the ladies wave handkerchiefs from a balcony. But the reality was to pass a night on the ground in the rain with your bowels out of order and then after no particular breakfast to wade a stream and attack the enemy. That is life.[58]

The Battle of Antietam remains the bloodiest single day in the history of the United States Army, its casualties on that hot September day in the Maryland countryside twice those it would experience even in the D-Day landings against Nazi-occupied France.[59] The morning of September 17, 1862, found Holmes's regiment encamped on the east side of Antietam Creek a few miles outside the town of Sharpsburg, Maryland. By seven thirty they were on the move, part of a huge second wave of two divisions being sent to reinforce the Union attack that had begun at dawn and which had ground to a halt under a massive Confederate counterattack. Crossing the large cornfield that had been the scene of intense fighting an hour before, the men of the Twentieth tried to avoid stepping on the wounded men who lay amid the dead and the litter of war—dismounted cannon, broken caissons, abandoned guns and knapsacks.

Although later in the war infantry assault formations employed looser tactics, with individual soldiers using available cover to advance, most battles of the first years of the war were fought with soldiers in closely spaced lines, marching ahead in lockstep. That was partly to keep men moving forward unquestioningly amid the chaos and din of battle but it also reflected tactics suited to the older era of smoothbore muskets, which had an effective range of at best eighty yards and whose inaccuracy could only be compensated for with concentrated fire. The horrific casualties suffered by attacking forces throughout the Civil War was largely a result of the collision of traditional tactics with the vastly increased firepower of newer weapons: rifled muskets that could be accurately aimed to five hundred yards and lethal to a thousand yards, and cannon that could sweep the field with curtains of canister shot.[60]

To make matters worse for the men of General Edwin V. Sumner's Second Corps, under which the Twentieth Regiment was now assigned, Sumner was a former cavalry officer whose ideas of how to space his lines reflected tactics more suitable for men on horseback. The Twentieth was on the far left of the second of three lines that advanced across the cornfield; the men of the five regiments of the second line, stretching across a front some four hundred yards wide, practically touched shoulders, while scarcely thirty yards separated them from the lines in front and behind, making it all but impossible for the reserve ranks to fire.[61]

Entering the grove known afterward as the West Woods, they halted on a slight rise at the far edge of the tree line. A cart path, well concealed by limestone ledges and woods, ran along the base of the hill just to the south, connecting the A. Poffenberger farm and the Dunker Church on the Hagerstown Pike.

A few minutes later, the entire Second Corps was hit by a murderous flank attack from five brigades of Confederate troops that had moved up stealthily along the path. The Twentieth was by this point bunched

The Battle of Antietam, September 17, 1862

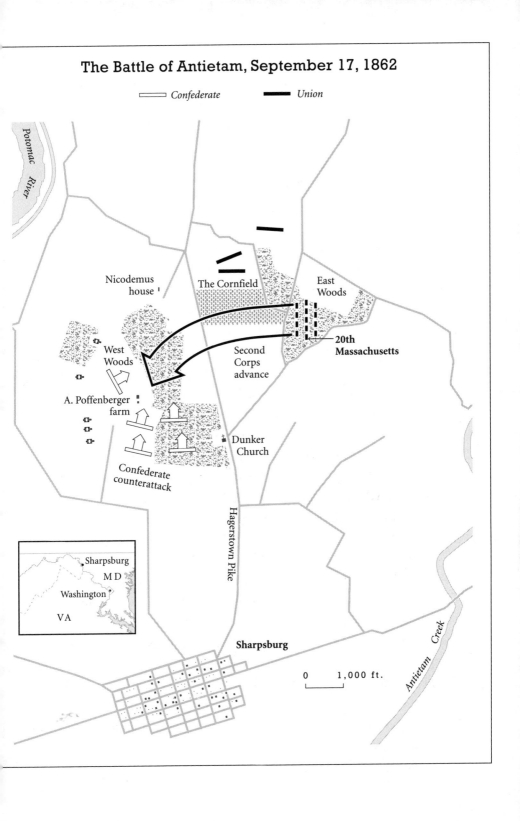

Confederate   Union

Potomac River

Nicodemus
house

The Cornfield

East
Woods

West
Woods

20th
Massachusetts

Second
Corps
advance

A. Poffenberger
farm

Dunker
Church

Confederate
counterattack

Hagerstown Pike

Sharpsburg

MD

Washington

VA

Sharpsburg

Antietam Creek

0   1,000 ft.

up so close to the Massachusetts Fifteenth just in front that "we could have touched them with our bayonets," Holmes recounted, and "could do nothing" but retreat with alacrity when Sumner gave the order.[62]

The Second Corps took twenty-two hundred casualties in twenty minutes, nearly half its numbers. Holmes was running to the north with the rest of the regiment—he was probably about a hundred yards to the northeast of where the Fifteenth Regiment's majestic "fallen lion" monument now stands—when a bullet tore through his neck. He managed to walk the rest of the way to the small field hospital in the Nicodemus farmhouse, a few hundred yards to the north of the woods. Hallowell was already there, lying on the floor with a shattered arm.

One of Holmes's first thoughts was another ironic flash about romantic notions of war: he recalled how after Ball's Bluff an article in *Harper's Weekly* had made much of Lieutenant Holmes's being struck "in the breast, not in the back; no, not in the back. In the breast is Massachusetts wounded, if she is struck. Forward she falls, if she fall dead." "Chuckling to myself," Holmes wondered what the papers would make of him this time, "hit in the back, and bolting as fast as I can."[63]

The Nicodemus house for a while lay between the two lines and its windows were shattered by shellfire that, in Hallowell's description, "ploughed up the wounded in the yard." But the house itself was miraculously unhit. Late that afternoon ambulances carried the wounded off to the Union field hospital at Keedysville, a few miles to the east.[64]

William G. Le Duc, a staff officer, wired Dr. Holmes with the news; he later told the doctor how he had found his son lying unattended at the hospital, and had importuned a surgeon to tend to his wound. But the surgeon "shook his head," and "said his duty was to try to save those who had a chance of recovery." Le Duc asked if there was anything he could do for the wounded man. "Wash off the blood, plug up the wound with lint, and give him this pill of opium, and have him keep quiet," the surgeon impatiently replied. But the patient, Le Duc reported, was full of black-humor wisecracks. "I'm glad it's not a case for amputation, for I don't think you'd be equal to it, Le Duc," Holmes said, and joked that being shot in the neck—which was army slang for being drunk—was "disgraceful for a temperance man."[65]

Three days later Holmes was making his way up a street in the outskirts of Hagerstown "in a pretty groggy fashion," with a bandage around his neck, when a little boy ran out from a house and inquired "if the ladies" who had sent him could do anything to help. Holmes asked for water, and was invited in to rest for a few minutes.

"I spied around and observed a grand piano and one of my father's books," he recalled, telling the story fifty years later, "and decided it looked like a pretty good thing." When a box of "excellent cigars" was brought out, "I decided it was an adventure worth seeing through," and accepted the family's invitation to stay. The head of the house was a widow, Frances Kennedy, whom Holmes would thank on his return to Boston for her "womanly kindness and motherly tenderness." There was also an attractive young cousin visiting from Philadelphia who, over the following week, would be his constant companion and "would discourse on the universe or play the piano, to my choice."[66]

Hoping to avoid another embarrassing reunion with his father, Holmes delayed sending word home of his whereabouts. "Finally, they told me I really must communicate with my family." His arm temporarily incapacitated by the nerve damage to his neck, he dictated the letter, beginning with a line in Latin explaining that his "beautiful amanuensis" was writing for him. (It turned out she could understand Latin, and "she cautioned him that he was becoming a little too personal concerning herself in mood and tenses.") Holmes sharply informed his father that he planned to start for home in a day or two "& I may remark I neither wish to meet any affectionate parent half way nor any shiny demonstrations when I reach the desired haven."[67]

Holmes never forgave his father not only for once again making a spectacle of himself, but for subsequently writing up a sentimental account of his "Hunt for the Captain" in a long article for the *Atlantic Monthly* that appeared just a month later. The climactic scene of Dr. Holmes's tale was encountering his son at last on the train at Harrisburg, Pennsylvania, and their heroically stoic greeting:

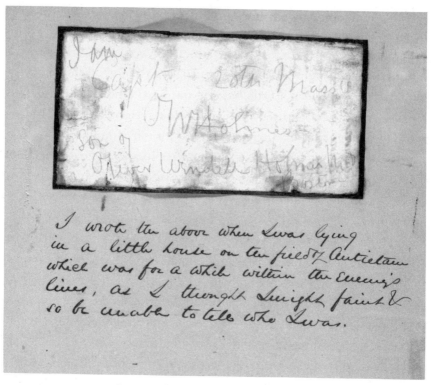

From Holmes's Civil War scrapbook

"How are you, Boy?"

"How are you, Dad?"

"Such are the proprieties of life, as they are observed among us Anglo-Saxons of the nineteenth century," Dr. Holmes explained.[68]

His son told at least two different versions of how their meeting had actually unfolded. He apparently told a writer for the *New Republic* to whom he agreed to speak off the record for a rare profile of him in 1926 that his real reply had been, "Boy, *nothing*." But the account he gave his secretary Chauncey Belknap a few years earlier rang truer: that his father, remembering the withering response he had received on the previous occasion, had been chastened into an artificial show of restraint, which his son ironically echoed. "This was play-acting," Holmes explained to his secretary, "and we both knew it."[69]

The war had physically distanced him from his sometimes over-bearing father, but it had done something more: it had given him the moral claim, earned in the hard experience of battle, to directly confront his father in a way he had never quite done before. And yet, as he had lain on the floor of the Nicodemus house, worried that he might lose consciousness and no one would know who he was if he fell prisoner, he had scrawled a penciled note: "I am Capt. O. W. Holmes 20th Mass. Son of Oliver Wendell Holmes M.D. Boston." Like the bloodstained handkerchief he had dropped on Harrison's Island and that was returned to him by a relic collector a few months after Ball's Bluff, he carefully preserved it for the rest of his life.[70]

CHAPTER 4

The Wilderness

Antietam was a tactical draw, but just enough of a strategic victory for the North to halt British and French thoughts of extending official diplomatic recognition to the Confederacy, and to provide Lincoln the favorable moment he had been waiting for to issue the Emancipation Proclamation. McClellan's failure to pursue Robert E. Lee's forces as they withdrew back to Virginia, and his increasingly open alignment with the Democratic Party in opposing the proclamation and Lincoln's war policies, convinced the president to relieve him of his command on November 7.

Another casualty of the battle was the Twentieth Regiment's commander, Colonel Lee. After being taken prisoner at Ball's Bluff, Lee, Major Revere, and five other Union officers were selected as hostages to be executed in retaliation if death sentences against the crew of a captured Confederate privateer were carried out. For four months all seven Northern men were confined to a seventeen-by-eleven-foot cell in Henrico County Jail. Through the two tiny barred windows of the cell they could see local slaves led to a lashing post in the yard and whipped for various misdemeanors. The first was a young woman, who screamed until she lost consciousness. Revere at first thought the scene had been staged as "a contrived indignity" to the Northern prisoners, but it turned out that every Saturday was "whipping day."[1]

Lee was exchanged before the Peninsula Campaign and seemed to recover, but after the slaughter of his men in the West Woods he fell to

Dunker Church at the edge of the Antietam battlefield

pieces, unable to "do any thing," Abbott reported. Two days after the battle he mounted his horse and rode off without a word to anyone. Macy found him later that day in a barn in Keedysville, blind drunk, his clothes covered in his own excrement.[2]

Two months later Lee resigned his commission. A farewell letter Holmes composed on behalf of the regiment's officers offered a tribute to what their colonel had shown them in his nobler days. "Your example taught us more perfectly than we could learn elsewhere to strive not only to acquire the discipline of soldiers but the high feelings and self-sacrifice of chivalrous gentlemen."[3]

Devoted to McClellan and scornful of Lincoln, most of the officers of the Twentieth were profoundly demoralized by the turn of events. "The president's proclamation is of course received with universal disgust," Abbott wrote his aunt that winter, "particularly the part which enjoins officers to see that it is carried out. You may be sure that we shan't see to any thing of the kind, having decidedly too much reverence for the constitution."[4] Holmes recalled talking during the war with a fellow Massachusetts officer, Charles Russell Lowell, about who from the war would be remembered as a great man; "he mentioned Lincoln, but I think we both smiled." Holmes's own assessment of Lincoln changed only many years later. "Until I reached middle age I believed that I was watching the growth of a myth about Lincoln," he told Lewis Einstein in 1924. "In the war time like other Bostonians I believed him a second rate politician. But later I saw and read things that convinced me that I was wrong."[5]

In the middle of November, Abbott, who also had been at home in Boston on sick leave, joined Holmes to head south to return to the regiment. They were on the road together for a week, crossing at times through "debatable land" where they were cautioned Confederate guerrillas were on the loose.[6]

It was a small adventure, and they enjoyed each other's company. "Have been more or less blue of course but Abbott has made the journey easier & pleasanter," Holmes wrote home on November 16. Looking back on their trip a year later, Abbott wrote his friend, "That was after all a devlish pleasant journey to look back on. I have felt a sort of brotherhood ever since."[7]

Holmes found Washington a "modern Gomorrah," with its dram shops and brothels, and "vulgar, selfish & base" political types. From Washington they headed fifty miles west to Warrenton, Virginia, where the headquarters of the Army of the Potomac had moved, only to "find the Corps is the Lord knows where. . . . Hunting up a Regt isn't what it's cracked up to be and everyone seems to hold that you are a nuisance for not having stayed at home."[8]

They finally learned that the regiment had been ordered the day before to Falmouth, Virginia, just across the Rappahannock River from the still Confederate-held city of Fredericksburg. That meant reversing direction and heading fifty miles to the southeast. A train would take them about a dozen miles east to Catlett's Station, but the rest of the way would be on foot.

They walked over twenty miles one day, finding a decent house to stop at overnight, "with a motherly old gal who advised us to go home & get stronger." The Virginia woman was courteous to her guests but swore that "the South will stick it out to the end." They finally found their regiment on the nineteenth.[9]

Reading of the physical hardships soldiers were enduring in the trenches in World War I, Holmes once remarked to Einstein regarding his own experiences in the Civil War, "I know I expected dysentery to begin every time I went back."[10] The disease killed more men than enemy bullets over the course of the Civil War.

This time was the worst. It was bitterly cold in Falmouth, and on December 11, the day the Twentieth was sent forward into the streets of Fredericksburg in yet another of the most horrific slaughters of the entire war, Holmes lay in the hospital tent too weak even to stand as he suffered the agonies of bloody diarrhea. A man who had just died from the illness was being carried out as Holmes was brought in, and another lay groaning near death next to him. He could hear the battle raging and knew that for the first time his regiment was going into a fight without him, "a feeling worse than the anxiety of danger." But he was too honest with himself not to admit the mixed emotions of the moment. "I cried, and yet knew that my hide was safe."[11]

The Twentieth had been sent to cross the river and clear the town of rebel snipers who were still firing from the rubble of buildings leveled by a massive cannonade. Union engineers had been working since before dawn to lay pontoon bridges, but all day the sharpshooters prevented them from completing the uppermost of the three crossings. In midafternoon, taking matters into their own hands, the men of the Twentieth filled the pontoon boats, the Nantucket whaling men of Macy's Company I manning the oars, and rowed across the Rappahannock under murderous fire, then stormed into the tight street grid of the town that rose sharply from the river's edge. In the desperate house-to-house fighting that followed, the companies of the Twentieth engaged in the fiercest part of the battle once again suffered half their number killed and wounded in a few hours.[12]

Holmes left an indelible tribute to Abbott's courage that day in an extended passage in his most-well-known public speech, his Memorial Day Address delivered in Keene, New Hampshire, in 1884.

> There is one who on this day is always present to my mind. He entered the army at nineteen, a second lieutenant. . . . His few surviving companions will never forget the awful spectacle of his advance alone with his company in the streets of Fredericksburg. In less than sixty seconds he would become the focus of a hidden and annihilating fire from a semicircle of houses. His first platoon had vanished under it in an instant, ten men falling dead by his side. He had quietly turned back to where the other half of his company was waiting, had given the order, "Second platoon, forward!" and was again moving on, in obedience to superior command, to certain and useless death, when the order he was obeying was countermanded. The end was distant only a few seconds; but if you had seen him with his indifferent carriage, and sword swinging from his finger like a cane, you never would have suspected that he was doing more than conducting a company drill of the camp parade ground. He was little more than a boy, but the grizzled corps commanders knew him and admired him; and for us, who not only admired, but loved, his death seemed to end a portion of our life also.[13]

In the fighting that day was also Captain Dreher, who had incredibly survived his wounds at Ball's Bluff to return to the regiment and even to serve briefly—to the disgust of Abbott and the other "gentlemanly" officers—as its temporary colonel following Lee's incapacitation.

Dreher was by his own description "a half cripple" by then, his jaw permanently smashed, his hearing gone on one side, the shock to his nervous system leaving him prone to bouts of angry and incomprehensible outbursts. Deeply bitter over the machinations that had removed him from command, he had nonetheless insisted on leading his company in the street battle on December 11. He was hit in both legs. Gangrene set in, and his right leg was amputated, but too late to save him. He died four months later.[14]

Two days after clearing the town, the regiment was again at the lead in a wave of assaults launched against the indomitable position Confederate general James Longstreet had occupied atop Marye's Heights overlooking the town to the rear. The brigade-sized Union attacks—fought uphill, over stone walls and a canal, across a field on which Confederate artillery on the heights above poured canister shot—were "as courageous and hopeless as anything in the war," wrote the historian James McPherson. The Confederate lines held, and the Union forces suffered thirteen thousand casualties. "It can hardly be in human nature for men to show more valor, or generals to manifest less judgment," a newspaper correspondent reported. Forty-eight members of the Twentieth Regiment were killed or mortally wounded, its greatest loss of any battle in the war.[15]

"If there is a worse place than Hell, I am in it," Lincoln said when he heard the news of the disaster at Fredericksburg. A few weeks later General Ambrose Burnside, who had commanded the failed Union attack, rode out to review the troops at Falmouth. The men of the Twentieth remained sullenly silent as the divisional commander called out, "Now, three cheers for General Burnside!" Henry Ropes wrote to his brother describing the humiliating scene, reporting that when the general passed another corps, calls of "Butcher!" greeted him from the ranks.[16]

Abbott sent a despondent letter home. "All the evening the regiments were groaning Abe Lincoln & cheering Jeff Davis," he wrote, then wrote again a few days later imploring his father to burn his last letter, for fear it would be considered treasonable. "The state of the army is terrible," he nonetheless confessed. But then he added, "Thank God we can trust our regiment perfectly!"[17]

Little Abbott's end would come a year and a half later, in the Battle of the Wilderness; by that time he seems to have acquired the same kind of suicidal contempt for the war that would mark the bitter heroism of Britain's First World War generation. The greater the folly of the generals, the less his belief in the cause he was fighting for, the more Abbott flaunted his indifference to his own safety.

Holmes never reached that suicidal edge himself. Nor did he ever nurse hatred for the enemy. But after Fredericksburg he made it clear that he did hate war. He also grew disdainful of the high-minded talk of people at home who did not grasp that any good the war might still accomplish was being threatened by the evil it had itself become. Many years later, mentioning his oft-repeated formula that rights are merely "those things a given crowd will fight for," he remarked that he still "would fight for some things" to make the kind of world he wanted.[18]

But he was growing increasingly annoyed with his father's jingoistic armchair generalship and his inability to see that the other side was just as convinced that theirs was a cause worth dying for. This was one argument where he felt he undeniably had the upper hand, and the chance of evening the score for all the times he had dutifully submitted to his father's pontifications and domineering manner was too much to resist. With mounting irritation, he told his father that he was no longer going to be lectured to on matters that he knew far more about than his father possibly could. Although the letter from Dr. Holmes that prompted one particularly exasperated reply has not survived, its tone was apparent from the letter Holmes fired back on December 20. Referring to some articles by John Motley on the conduct of the war that his father had enclosed, Holmes wrote just a week after the shattering events of Fredericksburg,

I never I believe have shown, as you seemed to hint, any wavering in my belief in the right of our cause—it is my disbelief in our success by arms in wh. I differ from you & him—I think in that matter I have better chances of judging than you . . . I see no farther progress—I don't think either of you realize the unity or the determination of the South. I think you are hopeful because (excuse me) you are ignorant. But if it is true that we represent civilization wh. is in its nature, as well as slavery, diffuse & aggressive, and if civ[n] & progress are the better things why they will conquer in the long run, we may be sure, and will stand a better chance in their proper province—peace—than in war, the brother of slavery—brother, it is slavery's parent, child and sustainer at once. . . . I am, to be sure, heartily tired and half worn out body and mind by this life, but I believe I am as ready as ever to do my duty—But it is maddening to see men put in over us & motions forced by popular clamor . . .[19]

In expressing his continued readiness to do his duty, Holmes held fast to the one ideal that had survived contact with the enemy. As he told Mark Howe many years later, there was a feeling of "real horror" while it was going on, but "you simply do it because you have to." In a war where romantic chivalry, high-minded zeal for a great cause, and even heroism in the conventional sense of the word had lost its meaning in an orgy of almost random death, duty was one thing he could cling to. "I hate to hear old soldiers telling what heroes they were," Holmes said at a gathering of veterans of the Twentieth Regiment thirty-five years later. "We did just what any other American, what the last generation would have done, what the next generation would do if put in our place." Even winning was no longer the purpose; the only meaning left to the war was to do one's job.[20]

In January 1863, after a few weeks of sick leave spent as usual with the Hallowells in Philadelphia, where his parents visited him, he was appointed provost marshal overseeing the occupation of Falmouth.[21]

In late March, referring to a further tense exchange of views he had apparently had with his father, Holmes wrote home, "My Dear Old Dad I had my blowoff in one of my last and now let bygones be bygones—if *you* will." Reflecting his newfound determination to treat the war as a bad job to make the best of, he expressed pride in the Twentieth's disdain for attention-getting and in the cool and unflashy professionalism with which it went about its work. The commander of the brigade the Twentieth had been attached to at Fredericksburg, he noted, had told him approvingly, "The 20th have no poetry in a fight." Holmes ended the letter saying he was a bit melancholy but it was "just a passing cloud." And then he got in one small last dig at his father's attempts to instill him with high-minded thoughts. "It's very well to recommend theoretical porings over Bible & Homer," he said. "One's time is better spent with Regulations & the like."[22]

On the morning of May 3, the Twentieth was sent back across the bridges to Fredericksburg, retracing its assault on Marye's Heights where the Confederates remained dug in. Waiting to cross the canal at the base of the hill, the Union forces came under heavy artillery fire from the heights. Holmes's company was exactly in range. The men

A battle-hardened Holmes, in April 1863

hit the ground as shells of case shot burst overhead. Shrapnel from the second incoming round tore Holmes's knapsack supporter to shreds. The third sent an iron ball through his shoe and into his heel.[23]

His ironic thought this time about receiving an inglorious wound was realizing, a minute later, that "it could have been worse": not just his lower legs but his posterior had been exposed above the rock he had tried to take cover behind.[24]

But "to show how much he hated the war" by that point, he "was praying that his foot might be cut off so that he wouldn't have to go back." Holmes's comrade Charles Whittier sent a jocular letter teasing him about his big feet having given the enemy such a large target and kidding that "I do believe that it was an arranged thing." But he also reported that "Dr. Hayward said 'Holmes seemed to be rather sorry that he wasn't going to lose his foot.'" Instead, Haywood chloroformed him and extracted a piece of shattered bone, and told him he would probably be able to keep his foot after all.[25]

THOUGH NOT CRIPPLING, and hardly as dramatic as his first two wounds, the injury to his heel was slow to heal; it would keep him at home for eight months. Back in Boston this time, he took a small cynical satisfaction in describing the war as "an organized bore"—"to the scandal of the young women of the day," he later recalled, "who thought that Captain Holmes was wanting in patriotism."[26]

His father did not make life easier with his nonstop levity. The surgeon treating the wound had used a plug from a slice of carrot to keep it open, which prompted Dr. Holmes one day to pinch his son's heel and ask him what vegetable he had turned it into.

No response.

"Why a Pa's nip!" Dr. Holmes gleefully declared.[27]

The wounded soldier also found himself cringing in advance whenever a visitor entered the room, anticipating the inevitable remark: "Ah, Achilles!" ("I early acquired . . . conviction of the mechanical action of the human mind," he later recalled, "by seeing the self-congratulatory smile with which man after man would say 'Achilles' to me when I was wounded in the heel. Each thought he was being and manifesting a personality.")[28]

But for all the minor irritations of his convalescence, Dr. Holmes reported in a letter to Dr. Hunt, his son seemed "in excellent spirits, not at all nervous, as when he was last wounded." Holmes had received a letter from Hallowell offering to recommend him for a commission as major in one of the first black regiments being formed in the U.S. Army, the Fifty-fourth Massachusetts. To Abbott's satisfaction, Holmes, for whatever reasons, declined the opportunity. Abbott remained disgusted with Hallowell's decision to join the new regiment, as its lieutenant colonel: he wrote Holmes that Hallowell "has written me a letter that I should have expected from any abolitionist except him. . . . I thought at first that he must have been joking . . . but since I have made up my mind that he was drunk, as the letter is dated from the Parker House."[29]

Owing to his seniority, Holmes remained in line for promotion within the Twentieth, but the situation was complicated by senior officers who had been sidelined with injuries and whose places had been temporarily filled by acting commanders. Although Holmes was commissioned a lieutenant colonel by Governor Andrew later that summer, he could not be mustered into the Twentieth at that rank as long as the current officer of the same rank in the regiment remained on the rolls. After Revere was killed and Macy wounded at Gettysburg, Abbott became the acting commander of the regiment, a position he would hold until his death a year later, yet still unable to advance beyond the rank of major.

Holmes offered to step aside so that Abbott could receive the lieutenant-colonelcy, but Abbott refused to hear of it, telling his father, "Holmes is one of the best friends I have. & I assure you I should a thousand times rather see him in the place his rank entitles him to have, than to have him offer it me, for of course I should only return it to him."[30]

His injury kept him from Gettysburg, where the Twentieth was again in the maelstrom, positioned front and center on the line atop Missionary Ridge that received the full force of Pickett's Charge on July 3. But this time it was the Union army that had the high ground and the murderous artillery commanding the long, uphill field the enemy had to traverse. "The moment I saw them," Abbott told his father afterward, "I knew we should give them Fredericksburg. So did every body. We let the regiment in front of us get within 100 feet of us, & then bowled them over like nine pins."[31]

Even so, the Twentieth's losses were again horrific. Three of its thirteen officers were killed and seven wounded; of its 231 enlisted men, more than half, 117, became casualties.[32]

One of the dead was Henry Ropes, one of Abbott's dearest friends. He was the brother of John Ropes, who after the war founded the Boston law firm of Ropes and Gray with John Chipman Gray, who was to become Holmes's lifelong friend. Henry was hit by a prematurely exploding shell fired by a Union artillery gun behind him as he sat on a hillside the morning of the battle, quietly reading Dickens. "His men actually wept when they showed me his body," wrote Abbott, "even under the tremendous cannonade, a time when most soldiers see their comrades dying around them with indifference." He quoted the words of another officer, who said, "Henry had the real flame of patriotism & not the newspaper stuff."[33]

The coffin arrived in Boston on July 7. John Ropes wrote Holmes asking if he would serve as a pallbearer, describing in gruesome detail the glimpse he had had of his brother's mutilated body.

My dear Wendell,

The body arrived this morning. It is, I am grieved to say, not in a state to be seen. It would not do to open the coffin. All that can be seen through the glass-plate is the breast, which is bare, and in which is a fearful wound in the region of the heart, which must have caused instant death. I think I can discern a fragment of shell imbedded in the breast. It is a sad & shocking sight. Nothing of the face can be seen but the chin, round which is a handkerchief.

If you would take any satisfaction in seeing what can be seen of poor Henry's mortal remains, you can do so by coming at 10 a.m. at the house of Lewis Jones, undertaker, rear of St. Paul's Church.[34]

Two weeks after Gettysburg, on July 18, Pen Hallowell's brother Ned, who had accepted the position of major in the Fifty-fourth that Holmes had turned down, was badly wounded in the colored regiment's famous assault on Fort Wagner, South Carolina. The regiment's colonel, Robert Gould Shaw, was killed; infuriated by the sight of black men under arms, the Confederate defenders gave no quarter. After the battle a Confederate officer rebuffed a request for Shaw's body to be returned, replying, "We have buried him with his niggers."[35]

"What an awful month July has been for us. I mean you & me," Ned Hallowell wrote Holmes in August from Philadelphia, where he was recuperating from his wounds. "I feel at least one year older since I left Boston. Do you ever see John Ropes? How completely broken he must be."[36]

Anticipating his promotion to field rank, Holmes began taking riding lessons that summer. Abbott wrote to express his pleasure that Holmes had declined another approach from Pen Hallowell, who was now the colonel of a second colored regiment, the Fifty-fifth Massachusetts, formed to absorb the flood of black volunteers. "I haven't time to tell you how much I am delighted at your decision to stick to the old mother," Abbott told him. "I believe you have done not only what is agreeable to yourself & us, but what is thoroughly right and proper, instead of absurdly wasting yourself before the shrine of the great nigger." The Twentieth, by contrast, Abbott told his father after Gettysburg, was now a solidly "Copperhead regiment. . . . Not an abolitionist in it, with the exception of one officer."[37]

Abbott also assured Holmes that he should not think of resigning out of concern that he was taking another deserving officer's place during his extended recuperation, and not to feel pressure to return before his wound was fully healed. "If any impudent stay-at-home wide-awake asks you when you are coming back," Abbott told him, "punch his head."[38]

Charles Whittier now wrote Holmes with another possibility: Whittier was now on the staff of General John Sedgwick's Sixth Corps, and he assured Holmes it would be an easy matter to obtain a detail for him to the headquarters of one of the corps's divisional commanders, General Horatio C. Wright. Back in March, Whittier had told him that Sedgwick had been impressed by Holmes when he had stopped by to visit his friend at headquarters, saying afterward, "Tell Capt. Holmes he must come over again soon I want to hear him talk."[39]

Being able to ride was a necessary skill for a staff officer, and Whittier, when he wrote in August, said, "I am glad that you are about

"Farley," headquarters of the Sixth Corps near Brandy Station, March 1864

to parade your equestrianism."[40] In early January 1864 Holmes once again headed south, and for the war.

⸻

YEARS LATER, HOLMES often remarked to New England friends that though the fall colors of Virginia could never quite rival the blazing red brilliance of the sugar maples of home, springtime in the South was incomparable.[41] Spring of 1864 found him in one of the most beautiful spots of the Virginia Piedmont, along the Hazel River about eight miles from the town of Culpeper and a few miles up the old Winchester Turnpike from Brandy Station, a tiny stop on the Orange & Alexandria Railroad. Holmes would forever after express an abiding love for the glories of the Virginia countryside awakening from winter: the "misty blurs" of browns and grays that filled the woods as the first trees budded in March; then carpets of bloodroot and crocuses and windflowers, and the blooming red and pink dogwoods; finally the immense white flowers of the magnolias bursting forth with the first fireflies and the smell of honeysuckle that filled the evenings of late spring, along with a deafening chorus of frogs from hidden ponds that would suddenly fall silent as one approached.[42]

Farley, the headquarters of the Sixth Corps, was an elegant plantation manor house, perched in a shallow bowl on a hillside that rose gently over the surrounding countryside, with a sweeping panoramic view of the Blue Ridge to the west. Throughout the quiet months when both sides had waited for the muddy roads to become hard enough to send hundreds of thousands of men on the march, the Sixth Corps had rested in its winter camps spread across the rich farmland and apple orchards that covered the area northeast of Culpeper, its pickets guarding the fords and pontoon bridges across the Hazel River.

As an officer on a division general's staff, Holmes would no longer be leading infantrymen directly into the face of enemy fire, but the position was anything but cushy or a safe billet in the rear. Junior staff officers had the responsibility to scout out roads ahead of troop movements; to deliver messages and orders, which not infrequently risked

Crossing the pontoon bridges at Germanna Ford

running into enemy cavalry patrols; and to reorganize the front lines in the midst of battle. In fact, he was about to enter the most intense and nightmarish episode of the entire war for him, nine weeks of nonstop moving, fighting, and killing that would find him often falling asleep in the saddle from sheer fatigue, escaping death by inches, and witnessing carnage on a close-up scale that eclipsed even his own previous experiences on the front lines at Ball's Bluff, Antietam, and Fredericksburg.

On May 3, Holmes bought a mare from another officer for $150 and next morning "at 4 a.m., nominally, we started on the Spring Campaign," Holmes noted in his diary.[43]

Three years into the war the Union army had reduced moving men across obstacles to a science. The country that the Army of the Potomac was about to enter in its relentless pursuit of Lee's army was traversed by swamps, deeply cut rivers, and tangled woods. But where McClellan had spent days arduously constructing bridges in his slow movement up the Peninsula, Ulysses S. Grant's army of two years later had river crossings down to a choreographed sequence that could throw a span across a deep waterway in a couple of hours.

By 5:30 a.m. the day the army began to move, a train of wagons carrying canvas and wooden pontoon boats had already arrived at the first crossing, Germanna Ford on the Rapidan River. The boats were quickly anchored parallel to the stream as other wagons brought up long wooden stringers that were placed over the boats from shore to shore, and then wooden cross boards to fill in the bridge decking. The Sixth Corps crossed at midday, part of an unbroken stream of troops pouring over the two temporary spans.[44]

As they headed south, the Union troops sensed there was something different this time, that this at last might be the decisive campaign that would end the war. The new spirit came from the top: in Grant, Lincoln had finally found the commander he had been vainly seeking for three years, one who understood that the only way to win was to force Lee into a fight and to keep doing so without letup. "Lee's Army will be your objective point," Grant instructed his army commanders. "Wherever Lee goes, there will you also go." On the second day of the campaign, a twenty-four-year-old cub reporter from the *New York Tribune* volunteered to ride back to Washington with the first news accounts of the clashes with the enemy. When Grant heard he was going, he stopped him and said, "If you see the president, tell him for me that, whatever happens, there will be no turning back." When Lincoln received the message, his deeply lined face broke into a huge grin, and he kissed the man's cheeks.[45]

The Wilderness took its name from the nearly impenetrable tangle of second-growth thickets, deadfall, and brush that had filled in woods cut down for years to supply fuel for local iron- and gold-smelting furnaces and to corduroy the surface of the plank roads that intersected from the north and west at a tiny inn known as the Wilderness Tavern. Visibility was rarely more than a few hundred feet. "As a battleground," remarked one Union officer, it "was simply infernal."[46]

By daybreak on May 5 the Sixth Corps was advancing down the Germanna Plank Road just north of the crossroads. "At one point . . . were very accurately shelled from the left," Holmes recorded, "one struck within a yard of quite a number of us who were sitting on horseback & bounced under the horses—Others threw fragments round constantly

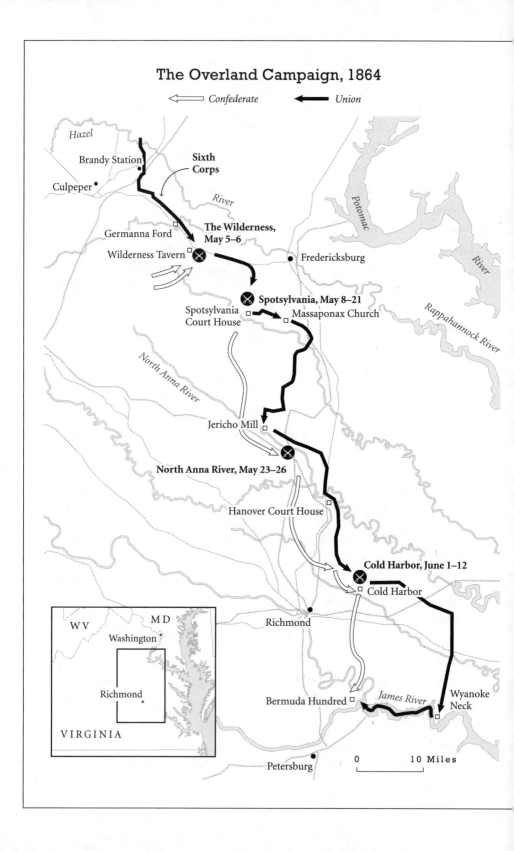

The Overland Campaign, 1864

⇐ *Confederate*   ⬅ *Union*

Hazel

Brandy Station

Culpeper

Sixth Corps

River

Germanna Ford

The Wilderness, May 5–6

Wilderness Tavern

Fredericksburg

Potomac

River

Rappahannock River

Spotsylvania, May 8–21

Spotsylvania Court House

Massaponax Church

North Anna River

Jericho Mill

North Anna River, May 23–26

Hanover Court House

Cold Harbor, June 1–12

Cold Harbor

Richmond

WV

MD

Washington

Richmond

VIRGINIA

Bermuda Hundred

James River

Wyanoke Neck

Petersburg

0   10 Miles

for a few minutes & as a Regt. was filing by to the right a shell or roundshot striking in it covered many of the staff with brains."[47]

In a pitched battle the following day Grant managed to put seventy thousand men into action to the west of the plank road. Sedgwick's corps held the right end of the line, and as the fighting died down at day's end the men were cooking their evening meal when four brigades of Longstreet's men came crashing down on their unguarded flank. They had made their way along the unfinished roadbed of a railroad unmarked on any map, but which the local Virginians knew well. Two of Sedgwick's brigades panicked and ran. "There was a stampede of these Brig-s. back to plank road," Holmes wrote in his diary. "Up all night in the saddle—establishing new line."[48]

Years later, Holmes recalled "one who taught me a lesson when our right was turned in the Wilderness." Henry R. Dalton was assistant adjutant of the corps, and later a North Shore neighbor of Holmes's. "He had the coldest head on the spot and reasoned as serenely among a lot of half crazy men as if he were discussing it now," Holmes wrote Clara Stevens after returning from Dalton's funeral in September 1914. "He had no complex views of the cosmos, but I learned to take off my hat to many a simple minded man like him."[49]

In the fiercest of the fighting earlier in the day, the Twentieth had been ordered to mount a desperate charge to shore up the Union position in the face of a powerful counterattack by Longstreet. A third of the regiment fell in the first hail of Confederate bullets. Abbott, leading the charge, ordered his men to lie down and continue firing; he alone remained standing, walking the line as enemy bullets literally rippled the edge of his clothing. This was so madly courageous that it crossed over the line to suicidal. A minute later he was struck in the abdomen, and died a few hours later. Holmes learned the news the next day.[50]

"My brigade lost in him its best soldier," Abbott's brigade commander said in his official report. Holmes never mentioned Abbott by name again in anything he wrote. But it was Abbott whom Holmes undoubtedly had in mind in his speech "The Soldier's Faith" that he delivered thirty-one years later on Memorial Day of 1895 to the Harvard graduating class. He spoke of the pure and simple faith of the soldier that impels him "to throw away his life in obedience to a blindly accepted duty, in a cause which he little understands, in a plan of campaign of which he has no notion, under tactics of which he does not see the use." Abbott's madly heroic death affirmed for Holmes the idea that had been fermenting in his mind ever since he had come to hate the war and doubt the ideals that had fired him: that a man can still achieve something great and beautiful even without a cause, without belief, without even a worry for what he was accomplishing, just by giving his utmost to the job at hand, with magnificent indifference to fate.[51]

In every previous battle, the exhausted armies withdrew to lick their wounds and slowly regroup. But now Grant did not hesitate to press on, at once. When a panicked brigade commander insisted that Lee had outwitted them, Grant snapped back, "Oh, I am heartily tired of hearing about what Lee is going to do. Some of you seem to think he is suddenly going to turn a double somersault, and land in our rear and both of our flanks at the same time. Go back to your command, and try to think what we are going to do ourselves, instead of what Lee is going to do."[52]

What Grant did was send his whole army marching south, aiming to flank Lee and again force him into an open fight. The weary Union troops pulled back to the east toward the Wilderness crossroads, anticipating the usual defeated withdrawal. But when they turned south instead of north at the turning, cheers went up as they realized that this time they were going to stay on and finish the job.[53]

What followed truly began to take on a nightmarish quality for Holmes as days of no sleep and endless galloping back and forth blurred into one. Over the nine weeks of Grant's Overland Campaign the Sixth Corps marched over two hundred miles, but Holmes must have easily covered twice that distance on horseback.

Throughout the night of May 7 the entire Army of the Potomac filed south, traveling in huge parallel columns to maximize the speed of the movement. A little after noon the next day, a few miles after passing the Piney Branch Church northeast of Spotsylvania, Holmes saw "woods afire & bodies of Reb[s] & our men just killed & scorching." Holmes

Confederate entrenchments near the "Bloody Angle"

was ordered to gallop ahead and notify Sedgwick of orders to hurry the Corps forward. He searched in vain for the general at the Army of the Potomac Headquarters "& got snubbed by Gen. Meade" but finally located him, returning to the front "so tired I could hardly sit up."[54]

On May 9 he was on horseback next to Sedgwick; a minute after he left him Sedgwick was chaffing a man for ducking at the shots from a rebel sharpshooter concealed in the woods—"Why man they couldn't hit an elephant here at this distance," the general scolded him—when a bullet struck Sedgwick in the head, killing him instantly. He was the highest-ranking Union officer to die in the war. "Today is the 7th day we have fought," Holmes wrote his mother two days later, "averaging a loss I guess of 3000 (three thousand) a day at least."[55]

Both sides by this point in the war had learned to immediately start digging trenches and felling trees to throw up ramparts whenever they stopped. The worst of the fighting in the Battle of Spotsylvania took place on May 12 at the notorious "Bloody Angle," where the Confederate trench lines came together at a vulnerable right angle at the edge of a long sloping field. In the midst of the fight Holmes was sent to place a New Jersey regiment into the line. In "The Soldier's Faith" he recalled the horror of the scenes he witnessed. Those in his audience would understand what he was speaking of, he said,

> if you had ridden by night at a walk toward the blue line of fire at the dead angle of Spotsylvania, where for twenty-four hours the soldiers were fighting on the two sides of an earthwork, and in the morning the dead and dying lay piled in a row six deep, and as you rode you have heard the bullets splashing in the mud and earth about you . . . [56]

Trees at the edge of the field had been reduced to slivers from the bullets. In one space twelve by fifteen feet between two lines of trenches at the angle lay 150 bodies, Holmes noted in his diary.[57]

On May 16 he wrote to tell his parents that he had seen enough of war.

> Before you get this you will know how immense the butchers bill has been—And the labor has been incessant—I have not been & am not likely to be in the mood for writing details. I have kept brief notes in my diary wh. I hope you may see some day— Enough that these nearly two weeks have contained all of fatigue & horror that war can furnish—The advantage has been on our side but nothing decisive has occurred & the enemy is in front of us strongly intrenched—I doubt if the decisive battle is to be fought between here & Richmond—nearly every Regimental off[icer] I knew or cared for is dead or wounded—
>
> I have made up my mind to stay on the staff if possible till the end of the campaign & then if I am alive, I shall resign—I have felt for sometime that I didn't any longer believe in this being a duty & so I mean to leave at the end of the campaign as I said if I'm not killed before. . . .
>
> The duties & thoughts of the field are of such a nature that one cannot at the same time keep home, parents and such thoughts as they suggest in his mind at the same time as a reality—Can

hardly indeed remember their existence—and this too just after the intense yearning which immediately precedes a campaign. Still your letters are the one pleasure & you know my love.

Your Aff. Son

O W H Jr[58]

Again Grant pressed on, pulling his entire army out of the line and turning south. Again Holmes found himself in the saddle around the clock, riding past the Massaponax Church in the dead of night as the Sixth Corps swung far to the east to flank Lee's army, now joining the race southward.[59] They were now in rough and uglier country, the beauty of the Piedmont far behind, their view hemmed in by dark woods surrounding swampy bottomlands, the winding lanes cut by innumerable creeks.

Holmes reached Jericho Mill on the North Anna River late at night on the twenty-third. He recorded in his diary the next day, "A nasty hot dusty day devoted to what was called rest but wasn't. . . . Ev'g severe lightning & thunder just as we changed our H.Q. across the ford." After a brisk but fierce battle they were again on the move, this time to Hanover Court House thirty miles to the southeast. "A stunning night's rest—The loveliest morning we have had," he finally recorded on May 29.[60]

Late the following afternoon General Wright handed his junior staff officer an urgent dispatch for General David Russell, whose division was ahead leading a large Union probe toward Confederate lines, "& told me not to spare my horse." The Sixth Corps had its headquarters west of Hanover Court House, near the town of Studley, at the Jones house, a former home of Patrick Henry. About a mile north of the plantation, where the farm lane turned onto a road, a scout came tearing back to warn him he had just been shot at. Holmes decided he must go on, pushed his horse into a gallop, and ran directly into a line of twenty horsemen, who called on him to surrender.

At first thinking it was a mistake and that they were friends, he started to pull up—but then saw the gray uniforms, and instead spurred his horse right for them. Holmes started to draw his saber, but the thought then crossed his mind that as cavalrymen the Confederates were probably much better swordsmen than he. He pulled his pistol instead. One rider came alongside and was unslinging his carbine when Holmes clapped his pistol to his breast and pulled the trigger, but the gun misfired. Ducking down on the side of his horse he "did a Comanche" and galloped through the line unscathed.[61]

The bracing episode—"my narrowest escape," he called it—helped to reassure Holmes he was not giving in to simple fear in deciding to leave the army at the end of the current campaign, which in the normal course of events would end by winter. "Fortunately I have a jewel in the head of this campaign in the shape of my adventure," he boasted to his mother.[62]

The next day he wrote another long explanation to his parents, apparently in response to a sermonizing reproval his father had sent in reply to his first letter:

recᵈ y'r letters of 21ˢᵗ 22ᵈ the latter fr. dad, stupid—I wish you'd take the trouble to read my letters before answering—I am sure I cannot have conveyed the idea, rightfully, that I intended resigning before the campaign was over . . . I must say I dislike such a misunderstanding, so discreditable to my feeling of soldierly honor, when I don't believe there was a necessity for it—I shall stay on the staff and wish you'd notify the Governor to commission new field officers to the 20th I waive promotion—I am convinced from my late experience that if I can stand the wear & tear (body & mind) of regimental duty that it is a greater strain on both than I am called to endure—If I am satisfied I don't really see that anyone else has a call to be otherwise—I talked with Hayward the mentor of the Regt & told him my views on the matter—I am not the same man (may not have quite the same ideas) & certainly am not so elastic as I was and I *will not acknowledge the same claims upon me under those circumstances* that existed formerly. . . . We are going to have another of those killing night marches as soon as we can start out of a country worse than the wilderness if possible.[63]

On the back of the envelope he wrote, "Write as often as poss. It is still kill—kill—all the time—"[64]

━━━━━━

HOLMES YEARS LATER admitted having doubts about whether he was quite as justified as he felt at the time about leaving the army.

"It is required of a man that he should share the passion and action of his time at peril of being judged not to have lived," he declared in his Memorial Day Address. No one could say he had not done that. But he was honest enough with himself to recognize that behind his strident insistence that he had fulfilled his duty was a desperate yearning to live and have his chance at life. At the start of the brief Spanish-American War in 1898, he wrote Lady Pollock that he thought old men should fight instead of the young. "If you are killed as a young one you feel that you haven't had your chance," he wrote. "The real anguish is never to have your opportunity," he remarked to Frederick Pollock in a similar vein. "I used to think of that a good deal during the war." When Felix Frankfurter mentioned his own plans to join the Army if America entered the First World War, Holmes replied that he hoped he would not suffer too much of a disruption to his legal career, but added, "I agree, on the other hand, that now I should allow less than I did in my own case 50 years ago to the consideration of the special faculties that one may attribute to oneself as a ground for not taking the chances of war."[65]

On June 3, Grant ordered a frontal assault on the Confederate earthworks at Cold Harbor, an attack that cost the Union forces seven thousand casualties in two hours. "I regret this assault more than any one I have ever ordered," he said afterward.[66] In a harbinger of the grinding trench warfare of the First World War, the two sides remained locked in a ten-day stalemate at Cold Harbor, in the brutal heat.

A few days later Holmes wrote his mother a more measured letter about his intentions. He allowed himself another small boast about his

Burial party at Cold Harbor

run-in with the cavalry patrol—his fellow officers "intimated that they thought it rather a gallant thing," he said—then continued,

> The campaign has been most terrible yet believe me I was not demoralized when I announced my intention to leave the service. . . . I started in this thing a boy I am now a man and I have been coming to the conclusion for the last six months that my duty has changed—
>
> I can do a disagreeable thing or face a great danger coolly enough when I *know* it is a duty—but a doubt demoralizes me as it does any nervous man—and now I honestly think the duty of fighting has ceased for me—ceased because I have laboriously and with much suffering of mind and body *earned* the right which I denied Willy Everett [a fellow Harvard student who had left to spend the war in England] to decide for myself how I can best do my duty to myself to the country and, if you choose, to God— . . .
>
> I hope that this will meet your approbation—you are so sure to be right—at all events I have tried to decide conscientiously & I have decided.[67]

At Cold Harbor he again deliberately exposed himself to danger, perhaps to test himself one more time, going out "on the front line of works drawing them & dodging bullets. . . . Sharpshooters put a bullet wherever you show a head." He wrote a girl he knew in Pittsfield—she later married his old captain, William Bartlett—"how often in these weary nights and days when the sun seemed to have stopped a second time to prolong the fighting, have I thought of those peaceful and most happy days at Pittsfield."[68]

Grant's final move of the Overland Campaign was a prodigy of logistics. Traversing the route the Army of the Potomac had followed three years earlier, the entire army of 100,000 men, with 50,000 horses and mules and 5,000 wagons, cut across the Peninsula to Wyanoke Neck, where engineers in seven hours constructed a 2,100-foot bridge on 101 pontoons spanning the deep water of the James River. The Sixth Corps's headquarters and two divisions boarded boats that carried them to Bermuda Hundred, a neck where the river abruptly narrows a few miles southwest of Richmond. "These last few days have been very bad," Holmes wrote his parents June 24. "This morn'g I spent on the picket line it was being pushed forward—hot & nasty as Orcus. . . . Father'd better not talk to me about opinions at home. . . . I tell you many a man has gone crazy since this campaign begun from the terrible pressure on mind & body. . . . I hope to pull through but don't know yet."[69]

Three weeks later the Sixth Corps was rushed north to Washington to defend the northern capital from Jubal Early's raiders, taking it out of Grant's campaign against Lee's army. Holmes's last taste of enemy gunfire came at Fort Stevens, where he saw Lincoln standing precariously conspicuous in his stovepipe hat atop the ramparts, watching the action.[70]

On July 23, his three-year enlistment expired, he received a mock farewell order from a Massachusetts comrade:

Dear Holmes
. . . I now send the "ultimatum" of the US Govt. in yr case. The final discharge.

Take it, young man, and as you become again a citizen of Massachusetts, remember us kindly, and omit to enquire why the Army of the Potomac dont move.

I see you in spirit (too deeply in spirit I fear) at Parkers and I would I could see you there in body also.

Hail and Farewell

Francis A Walker.

ADC

2nd Corps[71]

By then he was home, with his life and his chance to do something with it intact.

CHAPTER 5

"Society of Jobbists"

In the letters and diaries of the soldiers of Holmes's generation who survived the Civil War, one very seldom finds expression of the belief that their lives had been spared for a purpose. Death had been too promiscuous and capricious for the survivors to see their fate as anything but the chance fortune of a kind of mad lottery. But Holmes spoke to the heart of what many of his fellow veterans felt when he said that the war had set them apart. No words about the meaning of the Civil War to the men who fought and survived it have been more quoted than the passages in Holmes's two Memorial Day speeches in which he spoke of how the war had forever changed them, instilling them with the courage—and the drive—to live life to its fullest.

"You know your own weakness and are modest," he told his fellow veterans; "but you know that man has in him that unspeakable somewhat which makes him capable of miracle, able to lift himself by the might of his own soul, unaided. . . . We have shared the incommunicable experience of war; we have felt, we still feel, the passion of life to its top."[1]

And probably his most famous words of all, which he spoke on Memorial Day in 1884:

Through our great good fortune, in our youth our hearts were touched with fire.[2]

The boys who had become men, in Holmes's words to his mother, had done a lot of growing up in a few short years. "When I was twenty-one," Holmes could not help boasting to the twenty-one-year-old son of a Boston lawyer friend who once called to visit, "I had taken my degree, received a commission, and had been wounded in battle." If it made them serious before their time it also made them unusually confident for their age. He frequently told friends that the great lesson of the war for him had been that it taught him early on to face with courage and calmness the inevitable hardships of life—the setbacks, the moments of tedium and boredom, the self-doubt that everyone experiences at times. Fanny Holmes more bluntly once told Felix Frankfurter's wife that if it were not for the Civil War, "Wendell would have been a coxcomb."[3]

Holmes, being the kind of thinking man he was, was able to wrap the horrors of war quickly in a kind of intellectual scar tissue. Holmes often recalled how Dr. Hayward, the Twentieth's surgeon, had divided the world into internal men and external men—or, as Holmes himself later humorously termed them, ideasts and thingsters. Holmes was an ideast, an internal man, and he looked upon his searing experiences of the war much as he looked upon the physical scars left by his three physical wounds: they were trophies of what had tried to kill him but could not.[4] "I am converting misfortune into a source of satisfaction," he told Laski in 1917, fifty-five years after Antietam, when he began experiencing a pain in the left side of his face that brought back the neuralgia he experienced right after the bullet had passed through his neck. The doctor had told him that sooner or later some such nerve trouble was to be expected to recur from his old wound. "So I at least can pretend to myself that my discomforts came from that source—and inwardly swagger," Holmes boasted.[5]

If he steadfastly refused to read any of the thousands of books that most of his fellow veterans devoured to relive the great adventure of their lives, he also by all appearances managed to avoid reliving its nightmares. He never suffered from any of the traumas that later generations would call shell shock or post-traumatic stress disorder. Throughout his life he got seven or eight uninterrupted hours of sleep most nights. He had promptly put the war in a glass case, and like the note he had written on the floor of the Nicodemus farmhouse he kept it there the rest of his life, to display on his own terms.[6]

His limitless capacity for work was undoubtedly an emotional escape but it was also a need that he shared with many who had been through the intense experiences of war: civilian life just did not seem that exciting by comparison, without the constant stimulation of new challenges. "If I should pursue simpler amusement for a week I should feel as if I had eaten too many chocolates," he once told Lewis Einstein. His emotional self-control and intellectual detachment struck some as cold, but to Holmes they reflected the paramount emotional and intellectual lesson of his war experience. To the Wendell Holmes who returned to Boston in the summer of 1864, the war, in other words, had become both a metaphor and a lesson for life. "Repose is not the destiny of man," he observed. Life is a struggle, and it is the struggle that gives it meaning. The only thing to do was to give one's all, and leave the consequences to fate.[7]

———

MANY HISTORIANS ASSESSING how the Civil War changed American society have quoted Louis Menand's trenchant observation about what the war did to Oliver Wendell Holmes: it did not merely make him lose his beliefs, Menand wrote, "It made him lose his belief in beliefs." Walt Whitman, for one, agreed. Looking "at our times and land searchingly . . . like a physician diagnosing some deep disease," he wrote in an 1871 essay in which he bemoaned America's loss of moral identity in the wake of war and industrialization, "genuine belief seems to have left us."[8]

The truth for Holmes was more complicated. After the war he destroyed a number of his diary pages and letters to his parents. In a letter to his mother on July 4, 1862, he mentions that he is sending a page from his diary "to show my feelings" after the Battle of Fair Oaks, two weeks earlier. On the envelope he afterward wrote, "letter referred to within destroyed—rather pompous."[9]

It was not clear whether he was embarrassed by some high-minded thoughts about the abolitionist cause, or whether it was some naive gush of romantic chivalry that he found "pompous" after having experienced the full brutality of war. He did speak later of how distant seemed the fiery enthusiasms for abolition that had filled his youth: relating to Laski in 1926 how he had been one of the "little band intended to see Wendell Phillips through if there was a row after the meeting of the Anti-Slavery Society," he observed, "How coolly one looks on that question now."[10] Unlike his friend Pen Hallowell, he was largely unmoved by the plight of the freed slaves after the war. He sealed off his idealism for the cause he had fought for, just as he had sealed off the experience of the war itself.

But he never lost his belief in man's capacity *for* ideals, nor his personal conviction that ideals mattered. "Of all humbugs the greatest is the humbug of indifference and superiority," he wrote his friend Lady Castletown in 1897. "Our destiny is to care, to idealize, to live towards passionately desired ends." He always dismissed the nihilistic attitude "it is all futile," which he termed "the dogmatism that often is disguised under scepticism. The sceptic has no standard to warrant such universal judgments. If a man has counted in the actual striving of his fellows he cannot pronounce it vain."[11]

What the war did make him question was the morally superior certainty that often went hand in hand with belief: he grew to distrust, and to detest, zealotry and causes of all kinds. "The abolitionists had a stock phrase that a man was either a knave or a fool who did not act as they (the abolitionists) *knew* to be right," Holmes wrote Pollock in 1929. "So Calvin thought of the Catholics and the Catholics of Calvin. So I don't doubt do the more convinced prohibitionists think of their opponents today. . . . It is as well that some of us don't know that we know anything." Every cause, Holmes said, was at heart a kind of despotism—an attempt to force one's own views on others. "I don't care to boss my neighbors and to require them to want something different from what they do," he told Laski, "even when, as frequently, I think their wishes more or less suicidal."[12]

The worst thing about the Boston moralists before the war was not only their superior assumption that they were right, but their disdain for troubling themselves with the practical consequences of that certainty. The war had shown what those consequences were: he had seen, Holmes said, the "the power that prejudice gives a man" to hate, and fight, and kill. And if he would come to insist as a cornerstone of his legal philosophy that law is fundamentally a statement of society's willingness to use force—"every law means I will kill sooner than not have my way," as he put it—it was because he did not want the men who threw ideas around ever again to escape responsibility for where those ideas led. It was the same reason he lost the enthusiastic belief he once had in the cause of women's suffrage: political decisions had better "come from those who do the killing."[13]

More than once he cautioned his friends about "the irresponsibility of running the universe on paper," as Frankfurter summarized Holmes's counsel. Or, as Holmes explained it to John Wu, "The test of an ideal or rather of an idealist, is the power to hold it and get one's inner inspiration from it under difficulties. When one is comfortable and well off, it is easy to talk high talk."[14]

A corollary was that nothing in life comes without a price, and it was best to know in advance what the bill was going to be. "Remember, my friend, that every good costs something," he cautioned Einstein. "Don't forget that to have anything means to go without something else. Even to be a person, to be *this* means to be *not that*."[15]

But the war had done more than that: it had been a cataclysmic reproach to the very idea that there was even such a thing as a common interest of society, much less one that would be embraced by all as a self-evident good on nothing more than a few lectures, sermons, and pamphlets by Boston intellectuals.

The manifest failure of Boston's Unitarian optimism had itself engendered "a certain tough-mindedness" that Holmes's entire generation shared, Daniel Howe observed: "The very fact of war went far to destroy the hopefulness which had characterized so much of antebellum Unitarian thinking and gave the Boston Brahmin mind a more somber cast. No longer was it possible to put so much faith as before in voluntary moral suasion as a means of effecting progress." Even Dr. Holmes acknowledged as much; in his postwar novel *Elsie Venner* he drily observed, "'The beauty of virtue' got to be an old story at last. 'The moral dignity of human nature' ceased to excite a thrill of satisfaction, after some hundred repetitions."[16]

It was not just slavery that had revealed the divisions in society; the war had forced on Boston the unsettling truth that it was just one town, Einstein remembered Holmes telling him, and that discovery had upended the entire comfortable and secure world that Holmes had grown up in. "He told me," said Einstein, "that after the Civil War the world never seemed right again."[17]

That had as much to do with what the war had done to Boston as what it had done to Holmes. America, as seen from Boston, "had once been as vague as Australia," wrote Van Wyck Brooks. But as news came from battlefields as far west as New Mexico and as far south as New Orleans, "In every house & shop, an American map has been unrolled, & daily studied," Emerson wrote in his journal. "We will not again disparage America. . . . The war is a new glass through which to see things."[18]

The war accelerated a shift in political and economic power away from New England that underscored the parochialism of its views and values. Grant, elected president in 1868, represented the rising power of the West, along with a new kind of politics that had little time for the refined moral and intellectual sensibilities or social airs of Boston's prewar leaders. Grant hated Charles Sumner for his English tailored clothes, despised Dr. Holmes's diplomat friend John Motley "because he parted his hair in the middle." New England's statesmen, wrote Brooks, "were unhorsed at once and, it seemed, forever." That same year the Cunard line moved its main port of entry from Boston to New York, confirming Boston's eclipse as the railroad hub and trade and financial center of the nation. Fortunes made on the new western frontier in mining, railroads, and commerce overshadowed New England's old wealth, built on the declining textile and shipping industries.[19]

Even Boston was not Boston anymore. Members of the city's burgeoning Irish population had fought with incredible bravery in the war, giving them a claim on the city's conscience that could not be ignored. Boston's Irish had come from the poorest of the poor, looked down on in the years before the war as at best objects of pity and charity and at worst an alien pestilence to be contained. From 1846 to 1849, during the worst of the potato famine, 125,000 Irish had arrived in Boston, most from the destitute western counties, most settling in Boston only because they were too poor to travel anywhere else upon disembarking from the immigrant ships at their first port of call. The part played by the heavily Irish Columbian Artillery company in the return to slavery of Anthony Burns in 1853 had added to the anti-Irish wave that propelled the nativist Know-Nothing party to power in the state the following year, and to a deepening conviction that the Irish shared none of America's true values as seen from Beacon Hill.[20]

But when, in the weeks immediately following Fort Sumter, the commander of the disbanded Columbian Artillery stepped forward to raise a new Irish regiment to join the fight against the Confederacy, all the old moral certainties became less certain. "This is my country as much as the man who was born on the soil," Peter Welsh wrote to his wife from Virginia, where he was serving with the Boston Irish regiment, the Ninth Massachusetts Infantry. The forty-four men of the Fighting Ninth killed or mortally wounded in the Wilderness exceeded even the losses of the Twentieth. Boston could not help noticing. When the Ninth's commander Thomas Cass was killed in the Peninsula Campaign, the city erected a monument to his memory in the Public Garden. And in 1861 Harvard awarded an honorary Doctor of Divinity degree to Boston's Catholic bishop, John B. Fitzpatrick, a recognition unthinkable a few years earlier.[21]

After the war, as the Back Bay project and new industries including electric, telephone, and gas utilities created new and better-paying opportunities than the pick-and-shovel jobs the Irish had been lucky up until then to get, the Irish began moving rapidly out of the crowded waterfront tenements to new neighborhoods in the expanding city; though it would be another generation or more before the "lace-curtain" Irish (or the still later "two-toilet" Irish) made their first inroads into the city's more affluent suburbs, their rising prosperity brought political power and a new brand of rough-and-tumble politics that turned Boston's guardians of civic virtue on their heads. To the Irish, whose

Old World mores based on family ties "placed strong personal loyalties above allegiance to abstract codes of law or morals," as Richard Hofstadter noted, politics had nothing to do with the pursuit of public virtue, the greater good, or the disinterested progress of the community, and everything to do with personal obligations and deal making. Boston's moral spokesmen now suddenly seemed "less the natural leaders of a unified commonwealth," Daniel Howe observed, "than one interest group within a pluralistic society."[22]

Likewise the Unitarian movement, which had long resisted the idea of forming an association because they viewed their ideas as self-evident Christian moral truths that would transcend sectarian divisions, in 1865 abandoned their dream of universality and set up a regular denomination, in competition with every other squabbling church faction.[23]

What had seemed universal certainty in prewar Boston now seemed to depend entirely on where one was sitting.

"WHEN I CAME BACK from the war my head was full of thoughts about philosophy," Holmes told Frankfurter in 1932, but "I was kicked into the law by my Governor." Francis Biddle, not always the most reliable relater of Holmes anecdotes, told in his brief 1942 biography of the justice how Holmes had gone to visit Emerson in Concord not long after his return from the war. He had spent the evening talking over whether he should try to emulate Emerson's own life's work, and in the end decided that philosophy was too far removed from the roar and battle of life ever to satisfy him.[24]

But of course Holmes himself had earlier declared his intention to go to law school, when he wrote his Class Album sketch upon graduating from Harvard just before he left for the war, and whatever "kicking" Holmes Sr. did may have been more to get his son back on his already announced track. Holmes told Frankfurter he had even in "a vague way" thought about medical school, which was such an unlikely idea on all counts that that may have been what really provoked his father to tell his son to get serious and stop woolgathering. Holmes offered a slightly facetious amendment to his initial description of his father kicking him into the law which acknowledged that in fact his father had merely pointed out an obvious truth: he "put on the screws to have me go to the Law School—I mean he exerted the coercion of the authority of his judgment."[25]

Harvard Law School was then a two-year program, and Holmes applied himself to the work with an intensity not dampened by the intellectual incoherence of the subject as it was then presented to students. "It required blind faith—faith that could not yet find the formula of justification for itself," he recounted decades later.

> There were few of the charts and lights for which one longed when I began. One found oneself plunged in a thick fog of details—in a black and frozen night, in which there were no flowers, no spring, no easy joys. . . . One heard Burke saying that law sharpens the mind by narrowing it. One heard in Thackeray of a lawyer bending all the powers of a great mind to a mean profession. One saw that artists and poets shrank from it as from an alien world. One doubted oneself how it could be worthy of the interest of an intelligent mind.[26]

"Truth sifts so slowly from the dust of the law," he wrote to H. H. Brownell, a poet of the Civil War who had himself begun in the law, at the end of his first year of studies. But, he added, "I think my first year at law satisfies me. Certainly it far exceeds my expectations both as gymnastics and for its intrinsic interest." He liked to drop in on John C. Ropes and talk over the technical points he was mastering, sipping a gin toddy and smoking a cigar. Ropes later remarked to William James that "he had never known of anyone in the law who studied anything like as hard as Wendell."[27]

From the start he took heart in the belief that mastery of a subject, and thorough professional expertise, was the only way to accomplish anything significant in life. A year and a half after receiving his degree, and still thoroughly immersed in a now self-directed program of voluminous readings in the law, he wrote William James of his "ever increasing conviction that law as well as any other series of facts in this world may be approached in the interests of science and may be studied, yes and practised, with the preservation of one's ideals. I should even say that they grew robust under the regimen."

But that meant one could not pick and choose what was pleasant; to pursue a profession required total commitment of a kind that was the exact opposite of his father's enjoyable dilettantism:

> Since I wrote in December I have worked at nothing but the law. Philosophy has hibernated in torpid slumber, and I have lain "sluttishly soaking and gurgling in the devil's pickle," as Carlyle says. It has been necessary,—if a man chooses a profession he cannot forever content himself in picking out the plums with fastidious dilettantism and give the rest of the loaf to the poor, but must eat his way manfully through crust and crumb—soft, unpleasant inner parts which, within one, swell, causing discomfort in the bowels.[28]

Holmes was hardly alone in feeling that the generalism of his father's generation was an anachronism in the postwar world. "Holmes's rejection of the intellectual style of prewar Boston," Menand observed, "mirrored a generational shift. To many of the men who had been through the war, the values of professionalism and expertise were attractive; they implied impersonality, respect for institutions as efficient organizers of enterprise, and a modern and scientific attitude—the opposites of the individualism, humanitarianism, and moralism that characterized Northern intellectual life before the war."[29]

His personal experience on the battlefield, where moral ardor and gentlemanly attainment had proved no match for technical competence in military science, was repeated in the larger lessons of the war's organization and management. At the start of the war a number of Boston women had rushed to form aid societies for the soldiers at the front: they rolled bandages and knitted socks and mittens and launched a variety of well-meaning but largely uncoordinated efforts to improve hospital care. It was all very much in the style of prewar Boston's philanthropic support for social causes of all kinds. But these amateur efforts were quickly supplanted by far more professional organizations, notably the U.S. Sanitary Commission, run by businessmen who deliberately played down any sentiment of philanthropy or good deeds and instead emphasized their practical dollars-and-sense approach to problem solving: they employed professional fund raisers, hired and paid a staff of experienced managers, and quickly showed what could be done with modern business practices. They sent stocks of medicine to the field, bought and equipped wagon trains and steamships to evacuate the wounded, and gathered statistics on diseases and sanitary conditions to see where improvements were needed.[30]

But more broadly, the failure of Boston's amateurism and idealism to yield much of *anything* of use in "the workaday world" had been brought into sharp relief by the war; the Boston moralists now looked not only "precious, snobbish, overrefined, softly sentimental," but simply incompetent as well. "The gap between their promise and their achievement in science, the arts, evangelism, pedagogy, and politics," wrote Daniel Howe, was "too obvious to be ignored."[31]

The new spirit of the age was nowhere more evident than at Harvard. "Our new President, Eliot, has turned the whole University over like a flapjack," Dr. Holmes reported to his friend Motley. Charles Eliot was not only not a clergyman, he was a chemist, and he proceeded in quick order to throw the classics overboard, introduce electives and majors, and revitalize the teaching of science and modern languages. "He loved skill," Brooks observed, and it would be no coincidence that just a few years later he would hire the twenty-nine-year-old Oliver Wendell Holmes Jr. as University Lecturer on Constitutional Law.[32]

Holmes would later in life jocularly formulate his idea about the paramount virtue of professionalism in what he called "my imaginary society of jobbists." As he described his conceit to Wu, its members "were free to be egotists or altruists on the usual Saturday half holiday provided they were neither while on their job. Their job is their contribution to the general welfare and when a man is on that, he will do it better the less he thinks either of himself or of his neighbors, and the more he puts all his energy into the problem he has to solve."[33]

As he more seriously explained it, this "little army of specialists" was the new democratic elite, one based not on privilege or vague attainments of culture, but on hard technical competence that spoke for itself:

> They carry no banners, they beat no drums; but where they are, men learn that bustle and push are not the equals of quiet genius and serene mastery. . . . They set the example themselves; for they furnish in the intellectual world a perfect type of the union of democracy with discipline. They bow to no one who seeks to impose his authority by foreign aid; they hold that science like courage is never beyond the necessity of proof, but must always be ready to prove itself against all challengers. But to one who has shown himself a master, they pay the proud reverence of men who know what valiant combat means, and who reserve the right of combat against their leader even, if he should seem to waver in the service of Truth, their only queen.[34]

It was an idea he frequently repeated in speeches and in letters to friends throughout his life. In life, as in war, it was best not to worry about the larger meaning of it all, but just get on with the job.

———

After receiving his law degree in the spring of 1866 Holmes set off on a tour of Europe. It was his first trip abroad. He loved London instantly for the women and the conversation, and every time he returned over the next half century he felt the same surge of intellectual and romantic excitement.

"I always feel twice the man I was, after a visit to London," he once told an English friend, Lady Burghclere. Having to think on one's feet and bandy wits with "people who being in the center of the world have seen all kinds of superlatives" was a bracing experience:

> Nothing is put up with but *real* personality. It must be the stiletto not a bogus masonic sword or stuffed club. You can't stick your hand into your waistcoat and stand on a pedestal and be august. . . . You have to pay your way in London. No one takes

you on faith—and I love it. You must be gay, tender, hardhearted when something misses fire, give your best, and all with lightness.[35]

"The pace is tremendous," he wrote Nina Gray in the middle of one of his later visits. "A lady said to me 'You Americans disconcert one by waiting for us to finish our sentences.'" He found the English women an agreeable change from the bluestocking daughters of Cambridge and Boston intellectuals that had formed his chief circle of female acquaintances at home. "Women let their eyes wander while they talk to you, very freely—wear lower necked dresses than at home," he wrote in his diary after one of his first dinners in London society. As he observed to Lady Pollock, "You may say what you like about American women—and I won't be unpatriotic—but English women are brought up, it seems to me, to realize that it is an object to be charming, that man is a dangerous animal—or ought to be—and that a sexless bonhomie is not the ideal relation."[36]

Holmes arrived in May with a sheaf of letters of introduction to London society from prominent Bostonians including Charles Sumner, and a dutiful list of sights to see ("Pharaoh at British Museum"; "Johnson's House") and shops to patronize. More important, his entrée was eased by Henry Adams's father, who was the American ambassador. Henry was there as well, as his father's secretary, and the Adamses took their visiting countryman under their wing. He dined and lunched with them regularly—"sat on Mrs A's right as Lt. Col." he noted in his diary on the first occasion—and enjoyed a mild flirtation with Henry's sister Mary ("each time prettier & more charming than the last").[37] He also met there Clover Hooper ("a perfect Voltaire in petticoats," Henry James would later describe her).[38] She was visiting from Boston, and in a few years would become Henry Adams's wife.

With the Adamses, Holmes was taken to dinners and receptions where he met and conversed with leading Liberal politicians, including the Duke of Argyll, and then the Grand Old Man himself, Prime Minister William Gladstone. Handsome, brilliant, and a wounded veteran to boot, Holmes was an instant success. "Had quite a long talk with the great Panjandrum G. himself whereat people stared—G in consid[n]

Holmes, in September 1865

of my wounds made me sit & I was a great gun," he wrote after an evening at the prime minister's house.

Invitations poured in: from John Stuart Mill to meet him at the House of Commons and accompany him to a dinner and discussion at the Political Economy Club; to Oxford, where he dined in Hall and saw a cricket match; and to observe the many courts of law in London. He heard a case before the Court of Arches, England's ecclesiastical court—"the wife of a parson was telling how another parson solicited her favors"—and was invited by Lord Cranworth, the Lord Chancellor and Speaker of the House of Lords, to dinner and then the next day to attend the Court of Chancery. When the Chancellor saw him enter the chamber he motioned to him to come up and sit next to him on the bench: "People looked at me & grinned."

He saw the Magna Carta and the mummy at the British Museum, left his card for the Dean of Westminster Abbey, heard Dickens give a reading, and visited the famous art galleries. And on June 12 Leslie Stephen invited him to a dinner with the members of the Alpine Club.

Stephen was from a prominent English family of Christian social reformers and abolitionists, and had met both Holmes and his famous father on a visit to Boston in July 1863. "He is a very jolly, chirpy man," Stephen reported of Holmes Sr. at that time, "whose principal fault is that when he has once got started in talking," no one "could get a word in."[39] In 1865 Stephen had renounced his religious beliefs, resigned as a minister of the Church of England, and begun a career as critic and man of letters; as editor of the *Cornhill Magazine* he would publish works by Trollope, George Eliot, Arthur Conan Doyle, and Henry James, among others, and would later launch the monumental *Dictionary of National Biography.*

He was also a serious Alpinist, one of the wave of English mountaineering enthusiasts who from 1855 to 1865 conquered sixty Swiss peaks for the first time. In 1861 Stephen had made the first ascent of the Schreckhorn, a 13,379-foot peak in the Bernese Alps. He had since become president of the Alpine Club. In 1866, at age thirty-four, he was described as "tall and lean as a young Lincoln," and "one of the fastest climbers of his time."[40]

At the London dinner, Holmes saw some of the surviving members of the party that had "tumbled down the Matterhorn" the year before: three English climbers and a guide in the first party to reach its summit had been killed in the descent. It had thrown the entire sport into a crisis, with public accusations that climbers were reckless egotists; it was Stephen's job to try to restore the image of the club. When he invited Holmes to join him on a climb in the Alps the next month, Holmes readily agreed.

A week later he was crossing to Paris, where he had arranged to meet Stephen on July 2. He saw and talked with Lincoln's former secretary, John Hay, at the American legation; bought shirt studs and ate lobster mayonnaise and turbot that "was the best I ever tasted"; went to a foot doctor and submitted to the "ignominy" of having painful corns removed; and ogled the pretty French art students at the Louvre copying the famous pictures: "Wanted to talk to 'em but darant."

Carrying only a carpet bag, umbrella, and satchel he boarded the overnight train for Basel with Stephen, and his first glimpse of the Bernese Alps the next morning left him awestruck at the challenge he had rashly agreed to undertake. "This is not the place for squirts," he wrote in his diary.

They climbed the Balmhorn a few days later, inching up on ropes and on a precipice with sheer drops on either side, "like going along the edge of an oyster shell." The next day they made the summit of the Tschingel Glacier in five hours, a blazing pace, Holmes cursing all the way with all the swear words in "use among the army of the

Potomac," as Stephen later cheerfully reminded him; Stephen periodically calling down to his straggling neophyte companion, "Can you come up, Yank?"[41]

Holmes made it to the top horribly sunburned, his stomach violently deranged. "I had eaten nothing and after several vain attempts signalized the top by departing with the little I had summarily." Then another even higher peak a few days later, Mönch, with guides to cut steps in the ice and fourteen hours in the snow. "There is nothing to say about that most horrible grind," he wrote afterward. "It almost recalled an army march."

He watched as a party of English climbers who hoped to be the second to ascend the Matterhorn set out, their local guides kneeling in front of the church as they departed to be crossed with holy water. The next day they returned, the guides having "funked."

He returned to Paris July 26. At the Louvre, the "same girls copying—I was stared at I was so burned." At his hotel he found invitations awaiting him to spend August at the country homes of Sir John Kennaway, a Conservative politician, and the Duke of Argyll.

His final weeks in Britain were a throwback to what seemed a feudal world: shooting parties for grouse and roe deer; flirting with the daughters of peers; reciting "The Old Sergeant" to the admiration of the ladies in the drawing room after dinner; driving through the lanes of Devon with Miss Kennaway, as men touched their caps and women curtsied; Sir John assembling the servants each morning for prayers, at which he "read & expounded the Bible in patriarchal fashion." Then days of festivities to mark the coming of age of the duke's son at Inveraray Castle, with Highland games; a party for the tenantry in an outbuilding erected for the occasion, where Holmes danced with the daughter of the duke's man of business, a Miss Jessie Robertson, who snubbed him, then wrote a letter apologizing for her rudeness, to which he replied "soothing her"; and a county ball at which he misbehaved himself but was rescued by a Scottish peer "and no one was wiser." Then more fishing and shooting, and flirting with several aristocratic Miss Campbells, who warned him they had sided with the South in the American Civil War.

Then back across the Atlantic in berth 183 of the Cunard steamship S.S. *China*, which docked in Boston on September 11, after a quick ten days' passage.

Holmes called his subsequent election as "an unworthy member of the English Alpine Club" one of a number of undeserved honors he had "squeaked into" by chance. He never climbed again. But his weeks in the Alps ranked among the most moving of his life. "The great emotions that I have known from external events was due to the Swiss Mountains, a storm at sea, battle, and a total eclipse of the sun," he related to a friend a half century later.[42]

To his intimate friend Lady Castletown he offered the same list, but added one more item: "Women." But he also told her that "the romance of the mountains is in my soul forever" from that "brief but vivid experience of the Bernese Oberland." He never forgot, he said, "the silence of the snow or the passion of the return to life when one first hears running water on the descent."[43]

———————

WHILE HE WAS in London, he had received a small warning from his mother that his friend William James was taking advantage of his absence to moon about his old schoolmaster's daughter Fanny Dixwell:

> Fanny is living quietly in Cambridge with the exception of visits from Bill James, who appears to go there at any time from 9 o'clock in the morning. I told her to let me know how the flirtation got on—she says he is a person who likes to know his friends well. I had a little fun with her, about him, & told her I should write to you about it.[44]

"She said you told her you shouldn't write," his mother added. Prompted by the hint Holmes immediately sent Fanny a note, enclosed in a letter to his mother, which Mrs. Holmes promised to relay at once.

Fanny was not at all a beauty, but she had the attractions of youth and a lively wit, which gained her more than a few admirers. Holmes's sister reported that one particularly persistent caller that summer,

Fanny Bowditch Dixwell,
c. 1870

whom they nicknamed "Taurus," was "besieging their house now, inquiring for her—He comes once a week, but rarely gets in."[45]

William James wrote his brother Wilky that spring describing his own infatuation. "I have made the acquaintance of the eldest Miss Dixwell of Cambridge lately. She is about as fine as they make 'em. That villain Wendell Holmes has been keeping her all to himself out at Cambridge for the last 8 years; but I hope I may enjoy her acquaintance now. She is *A1*, if any one ever was."[46]

Holmes had met William James for the first time when he was at home in Boston recovering from his wound at Antietam. Their fathers were acquainted already. Henry James Sr., a philosophical enthusiast and writer of self-financed works of distinctly less than fully baked diktats on Utopianism, Swedenborgianism, and the Realm of Divine Love, had known Emerson since 1842; in 1863 he was invited to join Dr. Holmes's famous Saturday Club.[47]

When Holmes and William James met again after the war they became fast friends. James, a year younger than Holmes, was studying medicine at Harvard. His brother Henry, after a misbegotten year at Harvard Law School, had already decided he would try to make a living writing.

The James children had suffered from a bizarre upbringing. Henry James Sr. disbelieved in all organized education just as he disbelieved in all organized religion, and had moved the family to Geneva, London, Paris, Boulogne, Paris again, Boulogne again, Newport, Geneva yet again, Bonn, Newport, and finally Cambridge in pursuit of educational opportunities for his children. William had studied science, painting, science, painting again, before finally settling on chemistry and medicine.[48]

William and Henry were understandably more than a little awed by Holmes's self-confident sense of direction. "The only fellow here I care anything about is Holmes," William James wrote an acquaintance in 1866, "who is on the whole a first-rate article, and one which improves by wear. He is perhaps too exclusively intellectual, but sees things so easily and clearly and talks so admirably it's a treat to be with him."[49]

William, who was already plunged into the explorations of psychology and philosophy that would be his life's work, met Holmes once a week for philosophical chats and nearly always came away feeling inferior, even as he was drawn to him.[50] "You have a far more logical and orderly mode of thinking than I," he wrote Holmes a couple of years later, "and whenever we have been together I have somehow been conscious of a reaction against the ascendancy of this over my ruder processes—a reaction caused by some subtle deviltry of egotism and jealousy . . . as if you threatened to overrun my territory and injure my own proprietorship."[51]

He blamed his own "meanness" for those feelings, and while he was away in Germany for a year he admitted to Holmes, "I . . . cursed myself that I didn't make more of you when I was by you, but . . . threw evening after evening away which I might have spent in your bosom, sitting in your whitely-lit-up room, drinking in your profound wisdom, your golden jibes, your costly imagery, listening to your shuddering laughter, baptizing myself afresh, in short, in your friendship."[52]

William was also intimidated by Holmes's war record and ease with women, neither of which he shared. The two younger James sons had been in the war; Wilky was Shaw's adjutant and seriously wounded in the assault on Fort Wagner. But their father had apparently discouraged his two older sons from enlisting, wanting to save them for the great work he thought he saw in them, and Henry, at age eighteen at the start of the war, had suffered what he called a "horrid even if an obscure hurt" while helping man a fire pump that gave him a more legitimate excuse.[53]

But William and Henry were both tormented over their timidity in having sat out the war. Visiting Wilky at the army camp at Readeville, Massachusetts, Henry "gaped" at the display of military manhood,

Minny Temple

sardonically observing of himself, "By the blessing of heaven I could in default of other adventures still gape." Later, in the "bronzed, matured faces" of the returning veterans—and even more in their "bronzed, matured characters," possessing a "stored resource of overwhelming reference"—he caught a glimpse of a world he would forever be a stranger to.[54]

If William was mooning hopelessly around Fanny Dixwell, he mooned hopelessly about a series of other girls as well: he vaguely pursued Clover Hooper, and then her sister, both of whom had other plans. And all of the men of their circle were smitten with the Jameses' cousin Mary Temple, known as Minny. She was slender, dark-haired, lively and outspoken, possessed of a keen sense of the "play of life in others," "ever the heroine of the scene," Henry James later wrote, and she was dying of tuberculosis.[55]

An early short story of Henry James's, "Poor Richard," re-created a trip he, Holmes, and John Chipman Gray made in August 1867 to North Conway in the White Mountains of New Hampshire where the Temples were also vacationing, and the title character's hopeless feelings of inferiority as a rival of the two young soldiers for the heroine's affections.[56]

"Every one was supposed I believe to be more or less in love with her," Henry wrote his brother after her death. In fact, neither Holmes nor Gray was, from the available evidence of her letters, but both James brothers may well have been, in their usual ineffectual way.[57] The Jameses' mother in any case expressed relief in early 1867 when Holmes seemed to be out of the running, telling their sister Alice that

Minny had become "quite disenchanted, and evidently looks at Holmes with very different eyes from what she did; that is she sees him as others do, talks of his thinness and ugliness and pinchedness, as well as of his beautiful eyes—and seems to see his egotism."[58]

Years later, when some of Minny Temple's letters were published in Henry James's *Notes of a Son and Brother*, Holmes wrote to John Gray's wife, Nina,

> I knew Minnie Temple with the rest—quite well I think I may say. Oh yes she had charm—the psychological insight of the Jameses with aristocratic feelings from the Temple side made a strange mixture. Her death affected me more than almost any that I have had to lament. She had her judgment of all of us.

"Few spirits have been more free than hers," William James agreed, and said that her death in 1870, at age twenty-four, left a mark on them all. "We felt it together as the end of our youth."[59]

Henry James's feeling of inadequacy next to Holmes was so palpable it overshadowed everything in their relationship. Their friendship had begun with the exuberance of youthful confidence; Henry's first letter inviting him to North Conway begged him to come as a relief to Henry's spiritual isolation: "It's tolerably cool; there are woods; there are women. Put two and two together. The woods are not vast; neither are the women; but they will perhaps hold you a week or so. . . . If you disappoint me, you kill me—or rather, I kill you."[60]

But Henry's jealousy was never far from the surface. When Holmes was away in London in August 1866 "on his 1st flushed and charming visit to England," Henry wrote in his diary, he had stopped in at the house on Charles Street "and saw his mother in the cool dim matted drawingroom of that house (passed, *never*, since, without the *sense*), and got the news, of all his London, his general English, success and felicity, and *vibrated* so with the wonder and romance and curiosity and dim weak tender (oh, tender!) envy of it." He traced his own impulse to settle in England ten years later to that moment of envy.[61]

Over the next few years Henry alternated between professions of friendship and pique toward Holmes, sometimes in the same breath; he wrote his brother more than once threatening simultaneously never to speak to Holmes again, and to write to him at once:

> I get no news at all of O.W.H. jr.—Tell him—I hate him most damnably; I never knew till the past few months how much; but that I yet think I shall write to him.

> Do tell me something about Wendell Holmes. One would think he was dead. Give him my compliments and tell him I'm sadly afraid that one of these days I shall have to write to him.[62]

Holmes's relationship with William was more nuanced. They, too, would drift apart over the years, but their intense shared interest in questions of fundamental philosophical truth was one of the last great formative experiences of his youth. Early in their friendship Holmes wrote him,

> Ah! dear Bill, do me justice. My expressions of esteem are not hollow nor hyperbolical. . . . In spite of my many friends I am almost alone in my thoughts and feelings. And whether I ever see you much or not, I think I can never fail to derive a secret comfort and companionship from the thought of you. I believe I shall always respect and love you whether we see much or little of each other.[63]

Overwhelmed by the problem of free will in a world apparently meaningless, "void," and "evil," in 1869 William James plunged into deep depression. He exhibited a raft of psychosomatic ills—insomnia, backaches, gastrointestinal disturbances, exhaustion, panic attacks so severe he could not walk alone in the dark—and began thinking of suicide. "The difficulty: 'to act without hope' must be solved," he wrote in his diary.[64] Throughout his life he attempted to reconcile his skepticism with the possibility that man's beliefs still mattered in a world without God. He posited a "duty to believe," then "the will to believe," and later "the right to believe."[65]

Around the time he began to pull out of his depression, James, along with Holmes and a few other like-minded radical thinkers, began meeting regularly to argue over their skeptical ideas. "[Holmes], my brother, and various other long-headed youths have combined to form a metaphysical club, where they wrangle grimly and stick to the question," Henry James told Charles Eliot Norton. "It gives me a headache merely to know of it." Naming it "a metaphysical club" was more than half-sarcastic: it was if anything an antimetaphysical club.[66]

Holmes later paid tribute to the lasting influence that one member of the group, Chauncey Wright, had in shaping his basic philosophical views. Wright was a mathematician whose day job was calculating astronomical data for nautical almanacs, but he mostly devoted his time, when not drinking and brooding, to inventing card tricks, juggling and making mechanical toys, writing impenetrably dull book reviews—and tirelessly arguing philosophy. President Eliot tried to help this troubled but obviously brilliant young man by letting him teach a class at Harvard on mathematical physics. One student enrolled.[67]

Holmes in 1929 described Wright to his old friend Pollock as "a nearly forgotten philosopher of real merit" who "taught me when young that I must not say *necessary* about the universe, that we don't know whether anything is necessary or not." Wright himself summarized his argument thus: "No *real* fate or necessity is indeed manifested anywhere in the universe—only a phenomenal regularity."[68]

Holmes would distill those ideas in his oft-repeated aphorism that "I mean by truth simply what I can't help accepting"—adding, "My can't helps are not necessarily cosmic can't helps." But more than that, Holmes thought true skepticism meant recognizing that the universe cares nothing about our existence, and that man ought to return the favor, and get on with life. The question that drove his friend William James to the edge of suicide he considered a waste of time. The universe was predictable enough from a statistical point of view that one could operate on the basis of likelihood even in a world where no certainty existed. He liked to say he considered himself not a necessitarian but a "bettabilitarian." Being able to make a reasonable bet on the outcome was good enough.[69]

He also thought there was something absurd in arguing the limits to knowability from a philosophical position that itself was presented as the final word, as he thought James always tried to. "I heartily agree with much," he wrote James after reading his book *Pragmatism* in 1907—"but I am more sceptical than you are. You would say that I am too hard or tough minded. I think none of the philosophers sufficiently humble."

> Philosophy generally seems to me to sin through arrogance. It is like the old knight-errants who proposed to knock your head off if you didn't admit that their girl was not only a nice girl but the most beautiful and best of all possible girls. I can't help preferring champagne to ditch water,—I doubt if the universe does.[70]

Or as he explained in another letter to his old philosophical sparring partner, "I think the demands made of the universe are too nearly the Christian demands without the scheme of salvation. . . . This you will recognize as my ever recurring view ever since we have known each other."[71] Holmes said he thought railing against the universe was like damning the weather or firing a gun at the sky; the only change it produced on the relation between man and the cosmos was the kick of the gun on the man who fired it. "It seems to me that the only promising activity is to make *my* universe coherent and livable, not to babble about *the* universe," he wrote James in 1907.[72]

On the way down from one of their climbs in the Alps, Holmes and his lapsed-minister friend Leslie Stephen had talked "comfortably of metaphysics." Holmes later sent Stephen a criticism of one of his articles, noting his "bitterness." Stephen admitted "it is quite true that I generally am too savage," but "having wasted a large part of my life in the damnable fetters of the Thirty-nine Articles," had reason to be.[73] Stephen, like William James, having been brought up with God, was like the agnostic who an English writer of the next generation would describe as furious at God for not existing.

Holmes's agnosticism was milder because it encompassed even itself: it was possible to live a moral and useful life without even worrying about the question. It was part of why he always managed to get along with devout believers like his friend John Wu, who converted to Catholicism, or the Irish priest Canon Patrick Sheehan, whom he met near Lady Castletown's home in County Cork and warmly corresponded with for years. Wu admiringly said of Holmes after his death that he was always "*skeptically* skeptical," never "dogmatically skeptical."[74]

Holmes's skeptically philosophizing friend Chauncey Wright died in 1875, age forty-five, of a stroke brought on by his dissolute life; Henry James was at his bedside.[75] Wright was one of the few influences Holmes ever openly acknowledged in his intellectual development, and Wright's clarifying insights completed what the war had more practically taught him, that certainty not only leads to dangerous consequences, but is not even necessary to life.

Before Holmes had even begun to think of developing a comprehensive philosophy of law, he had worked out a philosophy of life.

CHAPTER 6

The Common Law

In later years Holmes often recalled the uncertainties and doubts that are a young man's lot. Remarking on his own nephew in 1897, he observed, "Just now he is in the great fog bank that lies around 25 and thinking poorly of himself." Reading Proust in his eighties, Holmes was struck by its evocations of that still-familiar existential loneliness of youth. "Other melancholy and lonely lads," he told Ethel Scott, "had had the same futile yearnings."[1]

But he also often mentioned the more acute feelings of isolation that he had experienced from his determination to blaze his own trail through the law from the start. "One cannot cut a new path as I have tried to do without isolation," he told Lady Castletown in 1896. "I have felt horribly alone." And he confessed to John Wu, "I had many black years."[2]

Original work by its very nature means cutting oneself loose from the usual sources of encouragement and reassurance to one beginning a career—and it also means constantly having to overcome doubts about failure. His dream of making his mark as a legal thinker meant he was seeking to blaze a trail through a wood he was not sure even existed.

In the midst of the intense scholarly research that would culminate a few years later in his public lectures and book on the common law that would make his reputation, Holmes wrote his old mentor Emerson, "I have learned, after a laborious and somewhat painful period of probation that the law opens a way to philosophy as well as anything else, if pursued far enough, and I hope to prove it before I die." A decade later, in a lecture to Harvard undergraduates on "The Profession of the Law," he was able to declare, "I say no longer with any doubt—that a man may live greatly in the law as well as elsewhere; that there as well as elsewhere his thought may find its unity in an infinite perspective; that there as well as elsewhere he may wreak himself upon life, may drink the bitter cup of heroism, may wear his heart out after the unattainable."[3]

He told a number of people that he had felt he *had* to accomplish something by age forty.[4] One night, working late at the law library at the Suffolk County Court House, he invited a younger lawyer he often saw there, George Upham—he was a distant cousin by marriage—to join him for a walk across Boston Common on their way home when the library closed. Upham recalled their talk sixty years later, in 1936, a year after the justice's death:

> He told me he had a theory that anyone could accomplish anything he wished, if he only wished it hard enough, continuously, morning, noon, and night, and perhaps subconsciously while sleeping. . . .
>
> I asked what he wished to do. He replied he was trying to write a book on the common law which he hoped would supplant Blackstone and Kent's Commentaries. Pressing him to tell me of further ambitions he said he wished to become chief justice of the supreme court of Massachusetts, and eventually, impossible as it might seem, a justice of the Supreme Court of the United States.[5]

It sounds too pat a story, remembered only after all its prophecies had come true. But Holmes repeated that same general advice, at least, to others. He counseled John Wu, a half century later, that to achieve anything of importance "takes time, the capacity to want something fiercely and want it all the time, and sticking to the rugged course." And none of his friends doubted he was destined for great things. In 1869, noting his preternatural dedication to his legal studies, William James prophesied, "This must lead to Chief Justice, U.S. Supreme Court."[6]

Even before his admission to the bar in March 1867, Holmes had taken on a major new task in legal scholarship, contributing regular book reviews to a new journal that Ropes and Gray had just founded. The *American Law Review*, though aimed at practitioners, was unusual in publishing theoretical essays on the law and covering legal developments in England as well as America. Within a few years, Holmes had become one of its coeditors as it rose to become the preeminent legal publication in America. At the same time, he was beginning the practice of law himself, while still finding time to wrangle philosophy late into the night. "In comes Bill James and we had the Cosmos hot and heavy till half past eleven," he recorded in his diary on February 14, 1867.[7]

Admission to the bar in Massachusetts in 1867 involved being examined in person by two current members of the bar named by a judge. "Made a devilish poor show I thought," Holmes wrote after his second interview. But he did well enough to pass, and recorded the great milestone in his life on March 5: "My first day as a lawyer . . . The rush of clients postponed on account of weather."[8]

While preparing for his examination Holmes had begun working for one of Boston's leading law firms, Chandler, Shattuck and Thayer. The firm specialized in litigation for major commercial clients, notably railroads, banks, and mercantile houses. Holmes would remain with them for the next three years, arguing his first cases. He would later say, "I owe to Mr. Shattuck more than I ever have owed any one else in the world, outside my immediate family."[9]

In his own way as a practitioner, George Otis Shattuck, who was just twelve years older than Holmes, impressed on his new associate the absolute need, as Holmes wrote in his diary, "to immerse myself in

George Otis Shattuck

law completely—wh[ich] Shattuck says, a man must at some period of his career if he would be a first rate lawyer, though of being that I despair."[10]

Shattuck, in his prime, was "the ablest advocate I ever knew," Holmes recalled many years later. He had both the law and a deep understanding of human nature at his fingertips. Holmes would write upon Shattuck's death at age sixty-eight in 1897 that "young men in college or at the beginning of their professional life are very apt to encounter some able man a few years older than themselves who is so near to their questions and difficulties and yet so much in advance that he counts for a great deal in the shaping of their views or even of their lives. Mr. Shattuck played that part for me."[11]

> He taught me unrepeatable lessons. He did me unnumbered kindnesses. To live while still young in daily contact with his sweeping, all-compelling force, his might of temperament, his swiftness (rarely found with such might), his insight, tact, and subtlety, was to receive an imprint never to be effaced. My education would have been but a thin and poor thing had I missed that great experience. . . .
>
> His work may not always have had the neatness of smaller minds, but it brought out deeply hidden truths by some invisible radiance that searched things to their bones.
>
> He seemed to like to take great burdens upon himself,—not merely when there was a corresponding reward, but when his feelings were touched, as well. He was a model in his bearing with clients. How often have I seen men come to him borne down by troubles which they found too great to support, and depart with light step, having left their weight upon stronger shoulders. But while his calm manner made such things seem trifles, he took them a good deal on his nerves. I saw the ends of his fingers twitch as he quietly listened and advised. He never shunned anxiety, and anxiety is what kills.

Shattuck's skill in cross-examination was a model of force and tact. He never asked a question he did not already know the answer to,

Holmes noted—and from his later experience as a trial judge, he had seen all too many lawyers "hurt their case" with ill-prepared cross-examinations—and his closing arguments to the jury "carried everything before them like a victorious cavalry charge."[12]

Holmes's eulogy of his old mentor, delivered from the bench of the Supreme Judicial Court thirty years after beginning his own career, was a mirror of the human qualities Holmes would prize throughout his life in the law. Shattuck had tested his abilities on the firing line, where real consequences were at stake. "Many of those who are remembered have spared themselves this supreme trial, and have fostered a faculty at the expense of their total life," Holmes said. "It is one thing to utter a happy phrase from a protected cloister; another to think under fire—to think for action upon which great interests depend."[13]

Working for Shattuck, and later with him as a partner of the firm Shattuck, Holmes and Monroe that Shattuck would establish in 1873, Holmes regularly appeared before the Massachusetts Supreme Judicial Court and the U.S. District Court, arguing maritime, insurance, and tax cases for Boston's downtown business interests. He argued one case all the way to the U.S. Supreme Court, a complex admiralty matter involving the liability of partners for an unpaid prize claim on a vessel captured during the Civil War. In that single appearance before the highest court of the land, he won a victory against the government's attempt to recover the money—if relying on a highly technical argument to do so.[14]

Shattuck was both a close friend and a partner in their years at the bar together. Holmes was a frequent visitor to his senior partner's summer home in Mattapoisett on Buzzard's Bay, just west of Cape Cod, and a few years later Holmes bought a place nearby himself. An enthusiastic sailor, Shattuck often took Holmes on his yacht on expeditions across the bay to the closer islands, or even to Nantucket or Provincetown at the very tip of Cape Cod. He was enough of an old Yankee farmer in his roots—he grew up on a farm in West Andover that had been in the family since 1725—that he always loved to ride and drive and to try to "subdue the stubborn soil of his rough acres" by the sea. "I think he had a sympathy with the great, quiet forces which he saw at work, and a sympathy with the animals of his farm," Holmes said.[15]

In the midst of everything else going on in his life then, Holmes got married. He wrote his old savior Mrs. Kennedy in Hagerstown on March 11, 1872, with the news. "I am engaged to Miss F. B. Dixwell who has been for many years my most intimate friend and who will now I hope soon be my wife." Three months later, he recorded in his reading-list notebook, among the books on Early Roman Law, Principles of General Jurisprudence, and a French translation of Kant, *Eléments metaphysiques de la Doctrine du Droit*, that he was reading, two noteworthy events:

June 17 *Married sole editor of Law Rev.* July no. *et seq.*[16]

Their friends thought it a perfect match. Dr. Holmes said of Fanny that he and Mrs. Holmes "both knew her well and love her much" and that it had been plain for some time that the couple "were entirely devoted to one another." A young friend and neighbor of the Holmes family thought that in marrying Fanny, Wendell had shown far more character and substance than she had given him credit for. "O.W.H. has gone up in my opinion most amazingly," Rose Hooper wrote a friend on hearing of the engagement. "I have always liked him very much but never quite believed in his disinterestedness even in his affections—and I feel quite ashamed now I think I have not appreciated him better. I think she is just the wife for him & I can quite conceive of their being happy 'ever after.' "[17]

Because of his work and Fanny's ill health—she was struck with a serious case of rheumatic fever just a month after their marriage, and was bedridden for months—they had to postpone their wedding trip for two years.[18] But in May 1874 they set off on a grand tour of England and the Continent. Fanny kept a diary of the trip, filled with humorously caustic observations of the dress and manners of English society: she described their aristocratic host at one evening party as "a twinkling hippopotamus" and recounted a dean of the church, "very disagreeable in black stockings, long coats, black sash and rib-

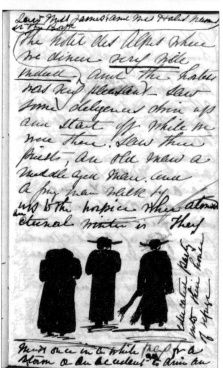

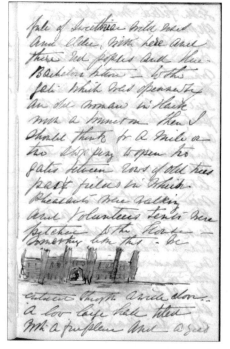

Pages from Fanny's diary of their trip to Europe, 1874

bon round his neck," producing a precious witticism about "St. Peter's daughter—and he, you know, was not a married man," causing three matrons "with immense bosoms and larger stomachs both adorned with gold and precious stones" to flip their fans quickly over their faces, while the dean did the same with his hand "to conceal his face from his own joke."[19]

And then there was "Wendell off on the rampage" at intervals to call on some of the "charmers" he had met on his previous trip to London. Fanny did not seem to take any of these rivals very seriously. "Wendell to see his charmer and return the book," she drily recorded. "Brought the book back with him."

They dined with the leading lights of the London literary and legal worlds; at one dinner Fanny sat between Anthony Trollope and Tom Hughes, the author of *Tom Brown's School Days*. It was on this trip that Holmes formed a number of lifelong friendships within the fraternity of English legal scholars. At a dinner at the Alpine Club with Leslie Stephen, he met Frederick Pollock for the first time. Pollock was four years younger than Holmes and in the midst of his first major legal work, a textbook on contract law that together with a second textbook on torts would modernize legal education in England. "There was no stage of acquaintance ripening into friendship," Pollock recalled of their meeting; "we understood one another and were friends without more ado."[20]

They also saw James Bryce, a leading Liberal politician and legal scholar whom Holmes would see again many times over the coming years, notably in Washington when Bryce was named Britain's ambassador in 1907; and had breakfast with Sir Henry Maine, the chair of historical and comparative jurisprudence at Oxford and the author of a renowned work of historical legal scholarship, *Ancient Law*, that sought to explain the evolution of law in society.

They spent three weeks touring Paris, Switzerland, and Italy, returning to Boston in early September.

Holmes had continued to live with his parents ever since his return from the war, and on his marriage Fanny joined him in the new house that Dr. Holmes had bought in 1870 at 296 Beacon Street, part of the

296 Beacon Street

new neighborhood created by the Back Bay landfill project. The project had been both public-spirited civic improvement and a calculated bid to keep the wealthy in the city, whose tax base and political institutions the old guard feared were being threatened by the surging population of the "foreign class," in the words of the state commission that reported on the plan. The centerpiece of the design was a broad tree-lined avenue modeled on Paris's Champs-Élysées, with parallel avenues of stately Victorian brownstones. The state carefully regulated the sale of the new land to keep prices up; 40 percent of the new space was set aside for parks, squares, gardens, and other "public purposes"; and the legislature stipulated that half the net proceeds would be dedicated to educational and cultural purposes, divided between the public school budget and the state's universities and museums. In the end the project yielded a profit of $3.5 million after all expenses were paid.[21]

Following their return from abroad the couple finally moved into their own place, a flat at 10 Beacon Street back in the heart of Old Boston. It was right next to the Athenaeum and a short walk from the library at the courthouse where Holmes spent many of his evenings, while Fanny occupied herself with her fine embroidery work that won prizes in art shows, and the admiration of Oscar Wilde when he once visited.[22] "All young couples should begin housekeeping in a tenement, economize on the necessities of life, and indulge in the luxuries," Holmes once advised a young acquaintance, just before her marriage. A half century later he fondly remembered how they would get the cheap seats to events at the Athenaeum's museum "and sneer at the snobs" and "was devilish glad to get pine boxes for my books"; he told Laski it was a great moment when, for their summer place in Mattapoisett, "we decided to invest in a wheelbarrow for manure." [23]

Thirty years into his own marriage he wrote another young friend who was about to be married, "Marriage, of course, is one of the most serious steps in life." But it "makes the world more beautiful," he said, and "a man as well as a woman finds life enlarged and glorified by marriage. The adjustment of personality is easy to people who think nobly."[24]

———

HOLMES'S FRIENDS WERE at times amused by, and occasionally put off by, the single-minded determination with which he devoted himself to his chosen field in his early years.

In the first years of his marriage Holmes continued to see William and Henry James regularly at a club of young men who, like his father's Saturday Club, met for dinner once a month at the Parker House. (The members also included his cousin John T. Morse Jr., his legal colleagues

John Ropes and John Chipman Gray, and the coeditor of the *American Law Review*, Arthur Sedgwick.)[25] "He grows more and more concentrated upon his law," William James noted in 1872. "His mind resembles a stiff spring, which has to be abducted violently from it, and which every instant it is left to itself flies tight back." The picture of a tightly wrapped intellect held together by sheer force of will suggested to James another vivid image on another occasion: "Wendell amuses me by being composed of at least two and a half different people rolled into one, and the way he keeps them together in one tight skin, without quarreling any more than they do, is remarkable."[26]

In the midst of his depression James had found himself more violently irritated by Holmes's intense focus on his work, and once bitterly accused him of "a cold-blooded, conscious egotism" that "poisoned" all of his "noble qualities." But that probably said more about James's own wretched feelings of self-loathing and envy of his more accomplished friends during that slough of doubt than anything about Holmes; he lashed out at his other best friend, Thomas H. Ward, in almost identical words at the same time.[27]

James offered a more measured picture of the way Holmes set himself to the task he had embraced in life in an affectionate description he sent his brother of a visit he made to Holmes and Fanny at their weekend place in Mattapoisett a few years later. The property was thirty-seven acres right on the water, with an old double house, half of which was occupied by the farmer who looked after it for them; it had an ancient fireplace "into which one could put half a tree," Holmes remembered, and he recalled it always as "a center of romantic delight."[28] James was amused at the picture of a rustic Wendell Holmes:

> I spent three very pleasant days with the Holmes's at Mattapoisett.
> I fell quite in love with she; and he exemplified in the most ridiculous way Michelet's *"mariage de l'homme et de la terre."* I told him he looked like Millet's peasant figures as he stooped over his little plants in his flannel shirt and trousers. He is a powerful battery, formed like a planing machine to gouge a deep self-beneficial groove through life; and his virtues and faults were thrown into

singular relief by the lonesomeness of the shore, which as it makes every object, rock or shrub, stand out so vividly, seemed also to put him and his wife under a sort of lens for you.[29]

Michelet was a French intellectual and historian, and the passage James alluded to was one where he had gone on for pages, as only a French intellectual can, expressing the oneness with nature he had experienced in a mud bath at a spa—and James's point was that Holmes's homely surroundings at the shore had similarly worked only to accentuate, to anyone who knew him, the impossibility of forgetting for a moment the intellectual drive and ambition that animated his whole being.

In the first years of his career and marriage Holmes had taken on still another ambitious assignment of legal scholarship, in addition to editing the *American Law Review*, lecturing on constitutional law at Harvard, and beginning his own legal practice. In 1869 James B. Thayer, the junior partner at Chandler, Shattuck and Thayer, had been approached to prepare a revised edition of *Commentaries on American Law*. The American counterpart to William Blackstone's famous *Commentaries on the Laws of England*, it had been first published in 1826 by Chancellor James Kent of the New York State courts, and had since become the standard reference work of American case law. Like Blackstone, Kent presented a compendium of the major appellate decisions that practicing lawyers needed to be able to cite as precedents. To stay current, however, any such work needed regular updating with recent important judicial opinions.

Kent's grandson owned the copyright and agreed that Thayer would receive $3,000 to serve as editor of the new, twelfth edition. At the very start, Thayer proposed bringing in his young associate to help. "Mr. Holmes who will have the laboring oar is getting together the material & getting it into shape."[30]

It took the oarsman about two weeks to move to the helm. The *Commentaries* had suffered from an accumulation of notes in previous editions that had done little more than dump recent cases "in sprawling heaps at the bottom of each page," as Mark Howe aptly put it. Holmes told Thayer he thought they should insist on the right to completely jettison these additional notes and substitute their own—and, more dramatically, to write the new notes not merely to supplement the text with recent developments, but to present a thorough review of the law on matters of "present fighting" interest to the bar.[31]

Holmes ended up doing even more than that. Kent's original work was more legal botanizing than analysis: it itemized rules in a long list of specific categories with little larger rhyme or reason or effort to synthesize and contrast how similar concepts were applied across different sorts of cases. "His arrangement is chaotic—he has no general ideas, except wrong ones—and his treatment of special topics is often confused to the last degree," Holmes observed about halfway through the task.[32]

Holmes not only began overhauling the notes, but simultaneously writing a series of essays for the *American Law Review* that dealt with many of the larger points in considerably greater depth, and his new notes for Kent referred readers to these longer articles for those in search of a fuller discussion.

In a voluminous note to Kent's simplistic rule that "the common law very reasonably" does not hold a seller accountable for the quality of his merchandise, Holmes analyzed more than fifty relevant cases in English and American courts on implied warranties, and offered a crisp categorization of the circumstances under which goods may in fact be returned to a seller for a refund: if they do not reasonably answer the purpose for which they were sold; if they differ in kind from particular bargained-for specifications; or if they fall short of the normal standards of a "merchantable" item in the trade. (Six decades later a leading authority in commercial law cited Holmes's note as—still—the clearest analysis ever written on the subject, supplanting the "fuddled groping" that preceded his explanations.)[33]

He similarly clarified a welter of chaotic cases on property easements by comparing easements to other sorts of limited rights on another's property, such as licenses and leases. He pointed out the common thread in tort law that imposes vicarious liability under certain circumstances even in the complete absence of moral fault, such as on a nonnegligent owner of a ferocious animal that escapes and causes injury, or on an employer for a servant's negligence.[34]

The work quickly became something close to an obsession for him. "I have as you know given up all my time to Kent's Commentaries and during the past year especially have hardly touched any other business," Holmes wrote to Thayer in July 1872; he said he thought it more important to take the time to do the job thoroughly than meet the original deadline of two years, even though "it has been at considerable pecuniary sacrifice that I have done as I have."[35]

As he approached the completion at last in late 1873, he was gripped by the agonizing first author's fear of losing his manuscript. Mrs. James, in a letter to her son Henry at the time, described Holmes's haggard appearance:

Wendell Holmes dined with us a few days ago. His whole life, soul and body, is utterly absorbed in his *last* work upon his Kent. He carries about his manuscript in his green bag and never loses sight of it for a moment. He started to go to Will's room to wash his hands, but came back for his bag, and when we went to dinner, Will said, "Don't you want to take your bag with you?" He said, "Yes, I always do so at home." His pallid face, and this fearful grip upon his work, makes him a melancholy sight.[36]

While living at 296 Beacon Street, Holmes had had the family and servants practice monthly fire drills: the first mission was to rescue the green bag, which he would place just inside the front door before going to bed each night.[37]

Whatever their physical and psychological toll, Holmes's labors gave him an extraordinary familiarity with the leading cases across the entire breadth of the law, from property to admiralty. Years later, Chief Justice Charles Evans Hughes emphasized to Mark Howe that the reason Holmes was able to turn out his decisions so quickly as a judge was a direct consequence of this early and total immersion in the law from his work on Kent, which "had given him an unusual and complete mastery of common law decisions and history. The effect of this in his habit as [a] judge was that, where others would be compelled to devote an enormous amount of time to the rediscovery of law, Holmes needed to make no re-examination—the law was at his finger tips."[38]

The original agreement with Kent's grandson was that Thayer and Holmes would be recognized as coeditors in the preface to the twelfth edition, but not on the title page. Having done all the work, Holmes—without consulting either the copyright holder or the signer of the contract—decided to place his name alone on the title page, as editor.

The week before Christmas 1873, an express package from the publisher, Little, Brown, arrived at Kent's New York address; inside were finished copies of the book. It was the first news he had that the book was even done. Kent wrote Thayer immediately to say he was "much provoked" and rather candidly confessed that in making the original deal, "I wanted your *name*" in "first place." Holmes probably described Thayer's actual role with complete accuracy in the preface, in which he thanked Thayer for reading and commenting on his drafts, and left it at that. When Thayer declined to contest the top billing, Kent told him, "*You* are a saint. I am an ordinary mortal."[39]

Kent enclosed in this letter to Thayer a rather cold note to Holmes that, while thanking him for his "labor, learning, and research," informed him that "by a mistake on your part, I have been obliged to change or rather to request that two words, in your preface, shall be dropped. I sent the marked copy to Little & Brown." Kent was irked by a line in the preface where Holmes seemed to slight the work of his father, William Kent, who had edited a previous edition, and by the fact that "they have left out grandpa's original preface and introduction, a most stupid blunder. They are not 'Kent's Com.' without that."[40]

But four days later, after receiving an apparently mollifying explanation from Holmes himself, Kent wrote to apologize for his initial "annoyance," and assured Holmes he never suspected him of deliberately wanting "to wound my feelings." He had made such a point of wanting to know when the book was coming out that to receive the finished copy by express "without a word of warning . . . was too much for one day." But Kent now conceded that it was best to leave the preface "as it is," and enthusiastically praised Holmes's work:

Each time I take up the book, I am impressed with the care & labor you have expended on it, & more & more pleased with the "spirit of law" you have thrown into the notes.

Should lecture business or pleasure bring you to New York, I am sure you will let me know, & permit me to turn our pleasant acquaintance if possible into something stronger.

With my sincere regards

I am my dear sir

Yours very truly

James Kent[41]

Thayer, however, remained rankled. A decade later, when Holmes abruptly left Harvard Law School to assume his first judgeship, Thayer vented his irritation in a note in his personal memorandum book that revived all his earlier resentments about being shown up by his more able, if less tactful, junior: "My experience with him in editing Kent, which I had been willing to forget, comes all back again and assures me that this conduct is characteristic—that he is, with all his attractive qualities and his solid merits, wanting sadly in the noblest region of human character—selfish, vain, thoughtless of others."[42]

But, with some justice, Holmes always insisted that he had never been ambitious in the conventional or craven sense, for money, fame, office, or power. When Henry James, one of the last times he saw him, made some arch comments about his brother's and Holmes's accomplishments in life, Holmes sent a slightly irritated account to Mrs. Gray afterward:

He says "poor Wendell" and "poor William" have chosen success— hum . . . it is not always disgraceful to succeed. I never knew anyone to elect against it for the sake of avoiding it—but I think I may say that since I chose the law, or rather was kicked into it by my father, I never have sacrificed an internal demand for an external end, and when the occasion seemed to require it have chosen what seemed to bar success.[43]

Success to Holmes above all meant accomplishing something original and of intellectual merit. By the time he finished his work on Kent in 1874, he still had seven years left to achieve that goal, before his self-imposed deadline of age forty.

=====

"Deciding to give Lowell Lectures on the Common Law, a matter which the weight of a hair decided, changed the whole course of my life," Holmes recalled when he had been on the Supreme Court for a decade.[44]

He had been working on some of the key themes ever since his research for Kent had left him dissatisfied with "what sounded so arbitrary" in Blackstone and other leading authorities.[45] In a series of articles for the *American Law Review* in the late 1870s Holmes began to work out the basic ideas. The task was immense, but it was where his heart lay, he told his English legal colleague James Bryce in the summer of 1879:

> I wish that the necessity of making a living didn't preclude any choice on my part—for I hate business and dislike practice apart from arguing cases. . . . As it is I console myself by studying towards a vanishing point which is the center of perspective in my landscape . . . but that has to be done at night for the most part and is very wearing. My articles though fragmentary in form and accidental in order are part of what lies as a whole in my mind—my scheme being to analyze what seem to me the fundamental notions & principles of our substantive law, putting them in an order which itself is a part of or results from the fundamental conceptions.[46]

His aim was nothing less than to try to make sense of the entire body of common law. An invitation in 1880 to deliver a series of twelve public lectures to the Lowell Institute that winter spurred him to complete the job in earnest.

The common law in America traces its origins to the Middle Ages in England, particularly the century following the Norman invasion in 1066. The Normans brought with them a body of customary law that, under Henry II, was extended across England by judges of the King's Bench who traveled on circuit to hold court: the new law was "common" in the sense that it was presumed to apply throughout the realm, superseding or at least supplementing a hodgepodge of local customs.

Its key feature was that, unlike the Roman civil law that was becoming the foundation of the legal systems on the Continent at the same period, the English common law was not a written code of rules but rather rested upon a set of procedures and actions for redress of wrongs. The common law left it to judges, through their decisions in individual cases, to declare what the law *was*, and as early as the twelfth century the emerging class of legal professionals in England began preparing and circulating written digests of cases that judges and barristers could consult to see how courts had ruled in previous cases that raised similar questions to a matter at hand. The system was flexible and conservative at once: reliance on precedent helped to create uniformity in the administration of justice and avoid abrupt change, while also allowing cumulative growth and movement in new directions to deal with new situations over time.

Holmes's famous dictum that the "common law is not a brooding omnipresence in the sky" was an allusion to the quasi-mystical reverence for the common law as a kind of Platonic ideal that, however, had come to be the accepted view by the nineteenth century. The approach taken by Blackstone and Kent reinforced the idea that judges merely "discovered" what was already existing in the law; they reached their decision in any particular case by deducing logical conclusions that flowed ineluctably from the law's fundamental postulates.[47] Legal scholars such as Holmes's law school colleague Christopher Columbus Langdell—who pioneered the case study method of teaching the law, having students learn its principles by examining specific cases rather than memorizing rules and formulas—saw their role primarily as elucidating that ideal preexisting order in the received corpus of the law.

Langdell thought his approach "scientific." But if so, it was, as Louis Menand observed, a distinctly pre-Darwinian kind of science. In an unsigned review of Langdell's casebook in the *American Law Review*, Holmes rather more contemptuously described Langdell as "the greatest living legal theologian," more concerned with reaffirming the law's elegant consistency than questioning its reasoning.[48]

Holmes set out to study the history of the law for the same reason Darwin studied fossils: to elucidate the actual purpose and functions underlying its accumulated appendages and outer forms. The first hundred pages of his "Black Book" were filled with his notes for the project, written in precise script often as tiny as a sixty-fourth of an inch high, covering an enormous range of sources, going back to ancient Rome and the Germanic tribes.

His research spanned the gamut of the law: liability, crime, contracts, property, wills, bailments. His important discoveries emerged in three key themes that he emphasized throughout his lectures. All were strikingly original, as well as a radical assault on legal tradition.

First was that the law changed—but did so in a way that tended to hide the fact, by continually inventing new explanations for old rules that survive long after their original justifications have been forgotten.

Second was that common law judges did not just make law, they made policy: acknowledged or not, they fashioned solutions that addressed actual problems and needs of society.

And last, and in a way most shocking to conventional sensibilities, the law as it actually was applied had little concern with moral culpability: in all branches of the law, there had been an evolution away from trying to determine whether a man had acted with evil intent, substituting rules based on external standards of conduct that reflected social needs and norms of behavior.

Holmes's exposition of how old forms and rules in the law were put to new uses bore more than a passing similarity to biological evolution. Although Holmes did not read Darwin until 1907, Darwin's *Origin of Species* had been published while Holmes was in college, and its ideas,

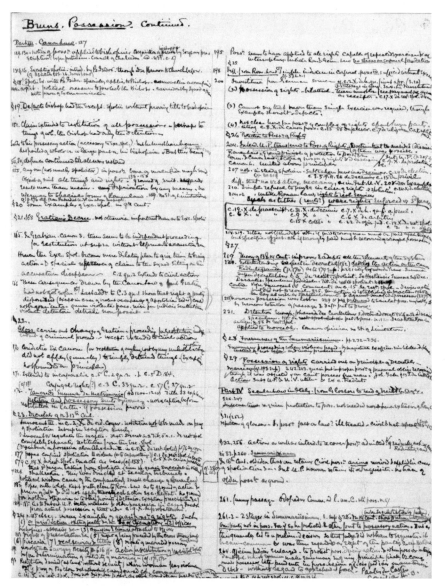

A page of notes for *The Common Law*

as he told Morris Cohen, were "in the air." He would later say that that no writer of English "has done so much to affect our whole way of thinking about the universe" as Charles Darwin.[49]

The law, Holmes observed, above all adapted to its surrounding environment, just as Darwin saw biological species did. Property law of the twelfth century, for example, was almost entirely concerned with land tenure and inheritance. But English law courts in the ensuing centuries evolved an entire body of commercial law to cope with the emerging money economy, fashioning new rules for contracts, partnerships, buying and selling, payment of debt, stocks, insurance, and all the other appurtenances of modern business life.

As Holmes explained in the famous lines with which he began his first lecture, the law has always kept pace with the "felt necessities of the time"; more than that, it mirrors the prevailing zeitgeist as a whole, reflecting "prevalent moral and political theories, intuitions of public policy, avowed or unconscious, even the prejudices which judges share with their fellow-men."[50]

The effect of applying new reasoning to old precedents, however, was often to hide this reality of the law as a living, evolving organism. The entire process was unseen, even unconscious to judges themselves as they worked its gradual evolution over time:

> The substance of the law at any given time pretty nearly corresponds, so far as it goes, with what is then understood to be convenient, but its form and machinery, and the degree to which it is able to work out desired results, depend very much upon its past. . . . It is forever adopting new principles from life at one end, and it always retains old ones from history at the other, which have not yet been absorbed or sloughed off.[51]

That meant, for one thing, that any search for coherence and logical consistency in the law was bound to be futile. Exposing the forces that shaped the law over time would not only clarify its true purpose, but also open the way to a rational reevaluation of rules that heretofore had been taken on faith:

> When we find that in large and important branches of the law the various grounds of policy on which the various rules have been justified are later inventions to account for what are in fact survivals from more primitive times, we have a right to reconsider the popular reasons, and . . . to decide anew whether those reasons are satisfactory. They may be notwithstanding the manner of their

appearance. If truth were not often suggested by error, if old implements could not be adjusted to new uses, human progress would be slow. But scrutiny and revision are justified.[52]

A prime example Holmes gave was the rule in admiralty law that a ship involved in a collision can be seized and detained, and later sold to pay for the damages if at fault. That, Holmes noted, is justified by good sense: a foreign owner is usually beyond the reach of the court, thus "the ship is the only security available" to insure that an injured party is compensated.

But that was *not* where the rule had come from, he found in delving into its history: its origin, in fact, lay in an ancient legal formula that held even inanimate objects as legitimate targets of retribution. In Edward I's time, if a man fell from a tree and was killed, the tree itself was forfeited to the dead man's kin, or chopped to pieces as a token of vengeance. Everywhere else in the law the notion had sensibly died away, as recompense took the place of vengeance. "No one would think of claiming a right to seize the horse and wagon" of a livery stable whose customer had run over a man in the street, Holmes noted. The survival of the old formula in admiralty law was apparent in the formality, still followed to this day, of naming not the ship's owner or crew as the defendant but the ship itself, for an offense "committed by the vessel." Yet the real justification for retaining this archaic formula was an entirely new one, adopted for sound reasons of current policy needs.[53]

A point Holmes recurred to was that many of the new rules that had evolved reflected efforts by courts to work out a balance between competing interests in society and establish standards of conduct so as to avoid conflict. That meant the law was as much about setting policy as doing justice in individual cases: "In substance the growth of the law is legislative," he insisted.[54] To American legal theorists, that was an especially heretical idea. They had been adamant that judges were not "legislators": that was a power reserved to the democratic will of the people, expressed through their elected representatives.

Holmes's most telling counterexample came from tort law, the body of law that provides redress for injuries. The traditional legal authorities had deduced in liability law a morass of confusing "duties" owed to others: landowners to trespassers, innkeepers to customers, railroads to passengers, owners of straying cattle to neighbors. Holmes's key insight was that a better way to get at the underlying purpose of the law was to begin by asking under what circumstances the law actually held a man to account.

In all cases, Holmes found, the law adjusted fault not to the gravity of the injury done or the intent to injure another person, but to other considerations that reflected a balancing of competing social needs. It is important not to encourage people to act recklessly; it is also important not to make it impossible to carry on normal and useful business by assigning fault every time someone is hurt. Examined in this light, Holmes concluded that in "a pretty sensible way," the law weighed the probabilities of harm under different situations based on actual experience, and held people to account when they failed to act as a prudent member of society would be expected to. The law, in other words, set standards based on accepted social norms and real-world knowledge of what activities are particularly dangerous and what safeguards are reasonable to demand.[55]

For actions that are inherently dangerous—pulling the trigger on a pistol in a crowded street without checking first to see if it is loaded, constructing a reservoir that can flood neighboring land if it gives way—the law tends to apply a standard of absolute or strict liability: a man proceeds at his own peril, and is fully responsible for any injury that results, foreseen or not, intended or not. Actions that serve an important social end, by contrast, are sometimes shielded from liability even when they are almost certain to cause direct and undeniable harm at times. The law of slander even traditionally protected an employer who unintentionally makes false and damaging statements in providing a reference for a servant. That was a striking exception to the usual rule that innocent intentions are no excuse when it comes to harming another person's reputation. But in this instance, Holmes noted, "the law considered the damage to the plaintiff of less importance than the benefit of free speaking."[56]

Most tort cases, though, fall in a middle ground, where liability is tied to negligence. But even there, Holmes emphasized, "negligence" is not a statement of moral failing ("guilty neglect"), but rather a proxy for a generally agreed rule of conduct: in practice, it means a failure to take the normal precautions or care that is generally expected in the usual course of life.

That was a pattern he called attention to throughout the law: although the law "abounds in moral phraseology," with terms like wrong, malice, fraud, intent, obligation, and duty, those words had lost their original moral meaning as they were actually applied by the courts. Malice, for example, did not in practice mean evil intent, but rather reckless disregard for certain agreed standards of behavior. The law, Holmes concluded, "is continually transmuting those moral standards into external or objective ones, from which the actual guilt of the party concerned is wholly eliminated."[57]

Holmes's great clarifying contribution to liability law and negligence was the concept of the "reasonable man." Holmes did not invent the term, but his writings and many subsequent decisions on the Massachusetts high court were greatly influential in securing its place in both American and English common law. The standard instruction to juries in injury cases is a direct legacy of these ideas: juries are told to consider how the defendant's actions compare to what a reasonable person would have done in similar circumstances—and not what the defendant intended, or what his personal motivations were.

As Holmes explained it, the "reasonable man" by its very nature embodied a community standard that ignored individual variations in blameworthiness or culpability in determining when a person should be held accountable for an injury that arises from his actions. "When men live in society, a certain average of conduct, a sacrifice of individual peculiarities going beyond a certain point, is necessary to the general welfare," Holmes stated in his third lecture, devoted to trespass and negligence. A man, after all, might be born awkward or accident-prone, and "no doubt his congenital defects will be allowed for in the courts of Heaven," Holmes noted, "but his slips are no less troublesome to his neighbors than if they sprang from guilty neglect. His neighbors

Huntington Hall

accordingly require him, at his proper peril, to come up to their standard, and the courts which they establish decline to take his personal
equation into account."[58]

It was another way of saying that assigning risk is always going to
be a judgment call, but that practical experience was the best guide
to making that judgment. And the less it was couched in the moral
language of individual guilt and more in the express acknowledgment
that it was about necessary social norms, the more consistent and pur-
poseful the result was likely to be. "Experience is the test by which it
is decided whether the degree of danger attending given conduct under
certain known circumstances is sufficient to throw the risk upon the
party pursuing it," Holmes concluded.[59]

He began the lecture series the night of November 23, 1880. The
site was Huntington Hall at MIT, a large semicircular lecture room
that the Lowell Institute had chosen just the year before as its new
venue—relocating from a slightly seedy chapel in downtown Boston just a half block from Holmes's boyhood home on Montgomery

Place, but now hemmed in by music halls and hotels that the institute's trustees thought cast a "commercial" air inappropriate to the intellectual tone they were hoping to maintain. The *Boston Daily Advertiser* reported that the hall for Holmes's first talk was nearly full, and in contrast to the usual audience for the Lowell Institute lectures, it was made up mostly of young men. But Dr. Holmes was also there; as was Horace Gray, the chief justice of Massachusetts and half-brother of Holmes's good friend John Chipman Gray; and also the president of the Massachusetts Senate, and other important state officials and lawyers. "Mr. Holmes proved a ready, interesting lecturer, speaking well without being confined to his notes," the paper reported.[60]

He continued for six weeks, Tuesdays and Fridays, concluding the series on December 31. Still feeling "superstitious enough" to want his magnum opus published before he turned forty, Holmes hurried to get the text ready for the printer. For the rest of his life he kept in his desk drawer a champagne cork on which he had inscribed: *First copy of book, March 3, 1881.* He had opened the bottle of champagne at Mattapoisett to celebrate. It was five days before his fortieth birthday.[61]

The reviews were largely favorable; a few criticized it for obscurity, but Pollock wrote a glowing notice in *The Saturday Review*, praising its originality and holding it up as proof that English lawyers were "being outrun by their American brethren in the scientific and historical criticism of English legal institutions and ideas."[62]

Holmes later conceded some of the criticism, but defended the book's faults as the price of originality. "Obscurity has been my trouble," he admitted to Mrs. Curtis in 1908. But, he added, "Obscurity sometimes means, with me as with others, that one still is out on the fighting line of thought. It is only when the battle is over that one can arrange one's forces. When a thought has become commonplace to you, you can state it clearly. For that I take no shame."[63]

Responding to a later legal critic who savaged the book a third of a century after its publication for, as Holmes put it, having had the temerity to point out that "judges make law," as well as for a series of small alleged errors, he wrote to Laski:

I think the material thing to be that I gathered the flax, made the thread, spun the cloth, and cut the garment—and started all the inquiries that since have gone over many matters therein. Every original book has the seeds of its own death in it . . . but it remains the original.[64]

Shortly after he finished the book Holmes faced a brief panic of mortality. Looking at his exhausted and gaunt appearance, some of his friends were worried he had so worn himself out from his labors that he would not live another five years, and for a few days Holmes feared the same. Noticing blood in his mouth one day while brushing his teeth, he was convinced it "meant the end," and that like his lost friend Minny Temple he was fated to die of tuberculosis before his time.[65]

He happened to come across a reference to Casanova's memoirs, and went to the Athenaeum library to try to find them; the librarian had to retrieve the ten volumes from the strongbox, where the notorious work, recounting the sexual exploits of an eighteenth-century Italian libertine, was kept safe from casual eyes. "That was just what I wanted then," Holmes later recounted to Ethel Scott. "I don't like dirty books or care for indecent ones, but there sometimes goes with the freedom that they imply, a temperament—a smack—a gusto . . . that puts life into one."[66]

As he told the story to another young English woman friend, Lady Askwith, "I took that book and it put a wiggle into me and then the doctor said that at that age the tooth brush often made the gums bleed and people think that something had happened—and that was the end of that."[67]

CHAPTER 7

Holmes J.

In the fall of 1881, still basking in the triumph of his Lowell Institute lectures and the publication of *The Common Law*, Holmes was asked by President Eliot if he would consider joining the faculty of Harvard Law School full time. The salary would be $4,500, considerably more than the $300 per course he had been receiving as a part-time lecturer.[1]

An endowment first had to be raised for the chair, but James B. Thayer, now a professor at the law school, offered to take charge of the effort, assuring Holmes and Eliot it would not be difficult. He had the more than able assistance of an enthusiastic and very-well-connected recent graduate of the school. Louis D. Brandeis had met Holmes two years earlier, when he returned to Boston from St. Louis to become legal secretary to Massachusetts's chief justice, Horace B. Gray. The two men had celebrated Brandeis's admission to the Massachusetts bar that year together, drinking champagne and beer late into the night. Since then, Brandeis had launched a successful career in commercial law in partnership with Samuel Warren, who had earlier worked with Holmes at Shattuck, Holmes & Monroe, and had also begun teaching classes part-time at the law school, where he had gotten to know both Holmes and Thayer as academic colleagues.[2]

Brandeis assured Thayer that he could raise the $100,000 needed to endow the chair from some of his fellow alumni: he knew, he said,

JUDGE HOLMES.

THE SURGEON-POET'S SON PLACED ON THE SUPREME BENCH.

HIS APPOINTMENT AS SUCCESSOR OF JUDGE
LORD—SKETCH OF THE LEGAL AND MILI-
TARY CAREER OF MR. HOLMES—THE SU-
PREME BENCH, AS REORGANIZED BY GOV-
ERNOR LONG.

Oliver Wendell Holmes, jr., was appointed yesterday afternoon by the governor and council to
the place on the supreme judicial bench made

Boston Daily Advertiser,
December 9, 1882

"a number of young fellows as likely to help and perhaps as likely to give it all." A few days later, Brandeis was crossing Boston Common when he ran into William Weld Jr. Brandeis had been his tutor a few years earlier when Weld was a law student at Harvard, and struggling to complete his last year of studies. Weld had left the school without graduating. But in the meanwhile he had inherited $3 million under his grandfather's will. Brandeis and Thayer clinched the deal with their well-heeled former student the next day.[3]

On February 11, 1882, the Harvard Corporation confirmed Holmes's appointment as the Weld Professor of Jurisprudence. Eliot wrote to Holmes, "So begins happily a relation which, I trust, will prove lasting, fruitful and fortunate."[4]

He was mistaken on all three counts. Holmes had barely begun his teaching duties, delivering his first classes on torts, agency, mortgages, and jurisprudence in the fall of 1882, when he was hit by "a stroke of lightning which changed the whole course of my life," as he later described it.[5]

On Friday, December 8, while having lunch with his law school colleague James Barr Ames, his old mentor and partner George Shattuck suddenly appeared. He had just come from the governor, John Davis Long, a Republican who was to be succeeded in four weeks by the Democratic victor in the fall election, Benjamin Butler.

Shattuck reported that the governor was prepared to offer Holmes the seat on the state's Supreme Judicial Court vacated that day by the resignation of Justice Otis P. Lord. But he had to give his answer by three o'clock. Shattuck had rushed to Cambridge, stopping only to pick up Fanny Holmes, who was now waiting outside in the carriage. It was one-thirty: there was not a moment to lose. Shattuck bundled Holmes into the carriage and they tore back to Boston.[6]

Upon seeing the governor, Holmes accepted on the spot. He explained his decision to his friend and British legal colleague James Bryce a few weeks later.

> My motives so far as I could disentangle them in half an hour which is all the time I had to decide the momentous question—were in a word that I thought the chance to gain an all round experience of the law not to be neglected and especially that I did not think one could without moral loss decline any share in the practical struggle of life which naturally offered itself and for which he believed himself fitted. I had already realized at Cambridge that the field for generalization inside the body of the law was small. . . . I was however as happy as a man could desire but I felt that if I declined the struggle offered me I should never be so happy again—I should feel that I had chosen the less manly course.[7]

Holmes never looked back with an ounce of regret at leaving the law school. He admitted that his brief stint in the ivory tower had done little more than leave him feeling trapped. "My wife thinks I unconsciously began to grow sober with an inarticulate sense of limitation in the few months of my stay at Cambridge," he told Frankfurter many years later.[8]

Thayer, however, was incensed that Holmes would abandon his job so soon, and in the middle of the academic year, and took it as a personal betrayal. Thayer poured out his bile in a long memorandum to himself. He acknowledged that Holmes had every right to take the judgeship, and that Governor Long had in fact insisted on an immediate answer, but faulted Holmes for having "made no struggle for more time" so that he could properly inform President Eliot before the appointment was publicly announced. That sounded petty, and it was: Thayer had spent days poking into the matter, hoping to dig up something discreditable to Holmes.[9]

But, as Eliot informed Thayer when he saw him about it, Holmes in his original letter of acceptance to Harvard had explicitly reserved the right to resign at any time if he had a chance for judicial appointment. "If a judgeship should be offered me I should not wish to feel bound in honor not to consider it," he had written, and Eliot had agreed, "You remain free to accept a better position or more congenial employment elsewhere." The treasurer of the university also backed Holmes: "As he expressly reserved the right to accept a judgeship, we cannot complain," he wrote to Weld. That failed to satisfy Thayer, however, who cattily wrote in his memorandum book: "Holmes, of course, is entitled to the excuse which this may furnish!" and continued to insist that Holmes had behaved in "an unhandsome, and indecent" manner. "He lost his head perhaps?"[10]

Holmes felt enough of a pang of conscience himself that on taking his oath of office he enlisted an outside legal consultant to review the entire matter and tell him if he was under any legal or moral obligation to repay part of his salary to Harvard. The lawyer, Francis E. Parker, concluded he was not: he had earned his pay the previous spring not only "in consideration of service to be rendered," but as compensation for the income he had given up by leaving his lucrative legal practice. And however disappointed the law school might be in losing Holmes, Harvard was still "the gainer," having raised $90,000 on "the attraction of Mr. Holmes's name."[11]

If anyone might have felt embarrassed by Holmes's abrupt departure it was Brandeis, given his personal role in soliciting Weld's gift. But on reading of Holmes's appointment to the Supreme Judicial Court in the newspaper, Brandeis immediately sent a brief, gentlemanly, and graceful note that bore none of Thayer's rancor. "As one of the bar I rejoice," he told Holmes. "As part of the Law School I mourn. As your friend I congratulate you."[12]

———

A FEW MONTHS into his new job, Holmes wrote to his friend Pollock, "Well, I like my work far more than I dreamed beforehand. The experience is most varied—very different from that one gets at the bar—and I am satisfied most valuable for an all round view of the law. . . . One sees too a good deal of human nature, and I find that I am interested all the time."[13]

Part of the pleasure, too, he reported, came from the feeling of being on the firing line and getting out of the artificial tranquility of the cloister, where "the professor, the man of letters, gives up one-half of life that his protected talent may grow and flower in peace." Having to "make up your mind at your peril upon a living question,

Portrait of Holmes by Clover Adams, 1884

for purposes of action" was by contrast bracing and filled him with a sense of life.[14]

The workload was, however, overwhelming. His friend Oakes Ames, congratulating him on his appointment, recalled how he had once described the qualifications of the ideal judge: "In the first place he should be a corpulent man," Holmes had joked. Holmes himself was anything but: Owen Wister remembered him in those days "as lean as a race horse." The reality for a judge on the Massachusetts high court was that he needed to have the stamina of a trained athlete. "We are very hard worked and some of the older Judges affirm that no one can do all the work without breaking down," Holmes wrote Pollock shortly after joining the court. He later said that the work—literally—"has killed some men who took it too hard."[15]

But, he added in his letter to Pollock, "I have not yet made up my mind—at all events it is more interesting than if we had less to do."

Besides hearing appeals sitting *en banc* in sessions of the full court at locations around the state, the individual justices of the court each had a heavy caseload of trials to preside over: all divorces, all murders (in which two of the justices sat together), many cases involving contracts and other business disputes, all suits relating to wills and trusts, and the entire body of disputes that came under the heading of equity. Common law courts were limited to awarding monetary damages, but in equity proceedings a court could order other kinds of remedies, including injunctions or revising the actions of public bodies and corporate boards. Following the traditional English practice, some states maintained entirely separate courts of equity—the equivalent of the English Court of Chancery—but even states like Massachusetts that had a single court system held separate sessions in law and equity during Holmes's time.

A heavy travel schedule added to the stress of the work. Writing once from Worcester, in the middle of the state, Holmes called the days in early September when the judges went on circuit to hear appeals and sit in trials "one of the hardest weeks of the year"; at the end of each day he went back to his hotel room after dinner too worn out to do anything but "play a game of solitaire on my bed, read a little Hegel and turn in early."[16]

The printed schedule of assignments of the Massachusetts Supreme Judicial Court ran to fourteen printed pages each year, with a series of tables laying out where each of the seven justices was to be each week of the year. In September and October, five of the justices, sitting as the full court, heard appeals at various locations around the state, while rotating duty sitting as single justices at trials of common law actions in each of the counties they visited. The full court then returned to Boston for appellate sessions in November, December, January, and March. There were single-justice equity sittings every Tuesday and Friday for two-month sessions throughout the year in Boston, and on the first Mondays of December, February, June, and August in Springfield, at the far western end of the state. Divorces were heard in May and October by the justice assigned to the Boston equity session during those months, as well by other justices during their travels to the other counties. Finally, in April and May, came the "spring circuit," with five of the justices each visiting a different county for one or more days to hold law trials.[17]

Holmes's record as a trial judge during his twenty years on the Massachusetts high court has tended to be overlooked, but it was an enormously important influence in shaping his understanding of human nature and the way law actually bears upon life. In his first sitting in the equity session in Boston, in November and December 1883, there were seventy-nine cases on his docket; on the spring circuit in Boston two years later he conducted twenty-two jury trials.[18]

Over the course of his time on the Massachusetts court he presided over hundreds of trials, and the experience gave him an acquaintance with a side of life that someone of his background and class would seldom otherwise encounter. To Holmes's courtroom came an endless parade of cases of scheming lovers, shady stock deals, fraudulent wills, gory accidents, overpromising real estate agents, hysterical streetcar passengers, overflowing sewage ponds, collapsing warehouses, reeking sausage factories, drunken barroom shootings, and the goings-on of assorted gamblers, con men, cranks, women of no visible means of support, and colorfully named fraternal orders. There were also many that involved the increasingly complex world of modern business: insurance, trademarks, intellectual property, futures contracts, bankruptcy, industrial pollution, economic competition and regulation, and the many new conflicts that arose from the rapid growth of cities, railroads, and markets.[19]

Years later, when they were colleagues on the United States Supreme Court, Brandeis would express wonder at Holmes's apparent grasp of real-world problems. "It's perfectly amazing," Brandeis told Frankfurter in 1924, "that a man who has had no practical experience to speak of . . . should be so frequently right as to matters that have significance only in their application."[20]

Yet much of Holmes's understanding of the practical considerations that arise where concept meets application undoubtedly came directly from his two decades of listening to and ruling on the drama and complexity of real life as a trial judge. Writing appellate opinions, a justice never came face to face with witnesses or the parties to a case, and it was all too easy to retreat into theoretical abstractions about the law and forget the human consequences. But in his role as a trial justice, Holmes was on the sharp edge of the law, seeing and hearing firsthand all of the tangled dramas of the courtroom, sizing up the honesty of often conflicting witnesses, rendering decisions that had immediate and dramatic consequences—the breakup of families, financial ruin, even death—to the people standing right before him. It was also a chance for him to demonstrate the breadth of his mastery of the law.

ONE OF THE CASES he tried his very first year on the bench made headlines almost immediately, and it was a chance to put into action his ideas about external standards. On Sunday, November 18, 1883, railroads across the United States adopted a new uniform system of "standard time" to replace the separate time standards each railroad line had previously used. Most cities and towns, meanwhile, continued the time-honored practice of resetting clocks to noon each day at the sun's zenith, resulting in a different time in every locality. Boston became the first municipality to order its public clocks to be changed to standard time when the new railroad time went into effect on the eighteenth.

Two days later a debtor who had been ordered to appear before the Commissioner of Insolvency at nine o'clock arrived at 9:49 a.m. Eastern Standard Time, which would normally be considered within the appointed hour. But by Boston's old meridian time it was already 10:04 a.m., and the commissioner found the man, Horace B. Clapp, in default and ordered his immediate arrest. Clapp then filed suit in Holmes's equity court for an order prohibiting the arrest warrant from being carried out.

The commissioner argued that his order to Clapp to appear was issued before the new time took effect, that nobody said the courts were bound to use standard time, and that "everyone knows how to correct to Boston mean time." But Holmes ruled that the only essential

THE NEW TIME STANDARD LEGAL.

BOSTON, Dec. 4.—Judge Holmes, of the Supreme Court, to-day, in the case of Clapp against Jenkins. directed a writ of prohibition to issue against the defendant to prevent him from further proceedings against the plaintiff under the poor debtor law. Clapp was cited to appear before Jenkins, Commissioner of Insolvency, Nov. 19, between 9 and 10 A. M. On the morning of Nov. 19 Clapp appeared at the office of Jenkins at 9:45, according to the new time. The magistrate refused to recognize the new time standard, and as it was 10:01 by the old time Jenkins defaulted the debtor. Judge Holmes decided that Clapp had a right to be governed by the new standard, which. by its universal adoption, became the usage of the community the day. it went into effect.

New York Times, December 5, 1883

point was whether "the new time had been adopted by usage," which might take a long time or might establish itself in as little as twenty-four hours. Holmes said he had little doubt the usage *had* changed, but wished to satisfy himself on the point before making a final order; a week and a half later he found for Clapp and issued the writ of prohibition. The case made the *New York Times* and other papers across the country, the *Times* story in particular calling attention to Holmes's use of a community standard in reaching his decision.[21]

That first autumn on the bench he was plunged at once into the full panoply of human and legal dramas that fill a court of law. He dismissed a suit to halt construction of a canal across a plaintiff's land, ordered that an agent hired to sell five hundred shares of stock in the American Hoop Dressing Company be paid his commission, allowed a private stable to be constructed on a lot in Back Bay, and issued an injunction against the seller of a milk delivery route from continuing to sell milk himself in violation of his agreement.[22] He found for a Jewish family who had been harassed by their landlady into abandoning their lease when she aroused the neighborhood with "racial and religious bias," and ordered their advance rent repaid. He allowed the Boston Standard Cab Association to regain its lease of an office in Post Office Square after a member of the association tried to claim the space for himself.[23]

The divorce, inheritance, and murder cases he presided over, however, offered the real window on human nature at its rawest. That fall of 1883 he heard his first divorce cases, sitting in Pittsfield—where the local newspaper reported the arrival on the bench of the new justice, referring to him as "a son of the poet O. W. Holmes, and looking much younger than his 42 years."[24]

Divorce in Massachusetts was possible at the time only on the grounds of desertion, cruelty, adultery, or "gross and confirmed habits of intoxication," and the testimony in divorce cases accordingly tended toward the salacious. More than once Holmes allowed the wife in a divorce case to offer her testimony in a low voice, or told the reporters in the courtroom that "if out of respect for delicacy" they would move out of earshot, "I should think it very proper." ("I should not have felt right in requiring it," he said, but the reporters complied.)[25]

In other instances he intervened to protect a wife from legal consequences she did not want or anticipate. In a case in Pittsfield, he dismissed the husband's claim that his wife had deserted him after she testified that she did not want a divorce, and that the only reason she would not share his bed was that he refused "to wash himself and change his filthy and soiled and bad smelling clothing" and could not get near him "without making herself sick."[26]

In a high-profile divorce case his first year on the bench involving a prominent Back Bay couple—he was described in a newspaper account as "the president of a large manufacturing company," she "a buxom, comely woman of 30 or thereabouts, stylish, accomplished, and a general society favorite"—the wife did want a divorce, but the only grounds available were her own adultery. Despite a lengthy deposition from a "lady detective" who had followed the woman and her lover from their rendezvous at the Christian Science Church on Park Street, to the Boston Common, onto a streetcar to Upham Corner, and then into the woods where they had lain behind a stone wall—where the detective "saw them in the act of adultery"—Holmes somewhat implausibly ordered the case dismissed for lack of proof. He explained in a memorandum, which he ordered "not to be filed among papers in the court,"

> With regard to the charge of adultery . . . in no event could I find it sustained without insisting that Mrs. Seaver should be represented by counsel and an opportunity given to put in such evidence and make such cross examination as should be thought necessary. Mrs. Seaver does not appear to understand that so far as the case before me is concerned the divorce which she says she wants can only be decreed on the ground that the disgrace she says she does not deserve and wishes to avoid, is proved . . . or that if it were granted she might not be allowed the custody of her child.[27]

He broke legal ground in several of his divorce cases. In a landmark case on visitation rights, he took lengthy testimony from both parents, as well as relatives, the family physician, and the child's nurse, to work out a detailed arrangement for the father to see his daughter once a week at his expense at a hotel in Boston.[28]

In another case, he ruled that a husband, in arranging to have a telegram sent to him so he could pretend to go out of town on a business trip, did not "connive" in his wife's adultery when he returned that night with a witness and surprised her in bed with their lodger. The wife appealed, arguing that a husband had a common law duty to guard his wife from unchastity. But the full court upheld Holmes's decision, agreeing that "by modern law and usage the right of a husband to control the conduct of his wife has largely, if not wholly, disappeared . . . if she commits adultery against his wishes, and without his procurement, he ought to be permitted to obtain evidence of it."[29]

On the U.S. Supreme Court, Holmes once snapped in conference to a fellow justice who had praised their arriving at a "just" decision, "Hell is paved with *just* decisions": he explained to Mrs. Curtis at the time, "I am in the habit of saying to my brethren I hate justice— meaning thereby that when I hear a man appealing to that I expect to find it an apology for not playing the game according to the rules— dodging some settled principle without articulate discrimination."[30] Yet as a trial justice in Massachusetts he seemed willing, at least at times, to stretch a point to avoid a manifest injustice.

In two cases involving beneficiaries of a fraternal order's fund for widows and orphans, he showed an understanding of the problems of daily life in ordering an equitable result despite the strict letter of the law. In both cases the lodge members had named as their beneficiary a nondependent—obviously a longtime, unmarried girlfriend—which fell afoul of the organizations' charters and Massachusetts insurance law. To make matters worse, one of the men had submitted a sworn affidavit to his order's supreme lodge falsely declaring that the woman *was* his dependent. But Holmes found a way around even that, noting that the local lodge had seemed to be aware of the subterfuge, and ruling, "I must assume that this affidavit was not true, but there is no evidence other than its untruth that it was fraudulent"—and ordered the death benefits to be paid to the members' chosen beneficiaries.[31]

In one of the last trials he conducted on the Massachusetts court, he set a new precedent on the witnessing of a will that loosened the traditional, draconian standard. Holmes ruled that if it was even physically possible that the witnesses *could* have been within the line of sight of the signer of the will, it deserved the benefit of the doubt.

> The only question tried before me was whether the codicil was signed by two of the witnesses in the presence of the testatrix. She lay in bed in one room, two of the witnesses signed in another on the other side of an entry, and the codicil immediately thereafter was shown to the testatrix. The doors were open. The distance from door post to door post diagonally along the line of vision was about nine and one half feet. The table at which the witnesses sat was just inside the door of their room, and the distance from the table to the bed of course was a few feet greater. The evidence as to the exact positions of the table and of the bed was conflicting and somewhat uncertain. I was satisfied, however, that the doors were open, and that the bed was in such a position that the testatrix, by rising slightly, her legs remaining in the same place, could have seen into the other room and could have seen the witnesses as they signed. Whether she could have raised herself so as to see is more doubtful. I did not find that she could have done so. I ruled that these facts did not exclude a finding that the codicil was witnessed in the presence of the testatrix, and I found as matter of fact and also ruled as matter of law that the witnesses signed in her presence.[32]

In a number of other will cases he likewise consistently placed the manifest interests and intentions of the deceased ahead of whatever was said on paper. There was the case of a huge bequest left by a ninety-five-year-old widow to her remarkably named sons Verrazano, Odanathus, and Longinus, under a will that Verrazano had obviously drafted himself, leaving almost everything to him alone, which Holmes invalidated; and an almost-as-large estate of one Ann White Vose, to be distributed to two dozen different charitable institutions and more than fifty individuals under a voluminous codicil containing thirty-six sections "which seems to have been drawn without the help of a lawyer, and which raises difficulties of the kind to be expected under such circumstances," Holmes drily wrote in his findings. He spent fourteen pages untangling its contradictory and imprecise instructions, answering nineteen specific questions the bewildered executors had asked the court ("To whom shall the Vose clock, mentioned in section fifth of said memorandum or codicil of June 10, 1895, be given by the executor?"), and ruling that the testatrix had probably not really meant to exclude from the $2,500 bequests, designated for each of her first cousins not otherwise "remembered by a legacy," the two cousins who had been singled out to receive, respectively, a hat-stand and a chromolithograph print.[33]

IN TWO LENGTHY courtroom trials, Holmes had the opportunity to make the acquaintance of a pair of exceptionally talented con artists who almost certainly would never have crossed the normal path of life of a Boston Brahmin.

Deshon v. *Wood* involved an affable wheeler-dealer named John F. Wood who put on air of prosperity to court a divorcée even as he was plunging into bankruptcy. On the witness stand he continued to breezily insist that his financial affairs were in perfect order, brushing off evidence presented in cross-examination of his increasingly desperate pleas for advance payment of rents he tried to collect—"do try and save me," read one—as merely the "usual form" "common in mercantile usage."[34]

The crux of the case was his promise to give his wife-to-be $20,000 in bonds in the Exeter Wood Pulp Company, a sawmill he owned in Maine. He had shown her the property, placed the bonds in her hands, and promised he would transfer ownership when they were wed. In fact, he was deeply in debt, leaving behind him a trail of dubious transactions—pledging stock from one venture to borrow for another and serving as vice-president of an insolvent manufacturer of emery wheels that had nonetheless paid out a 35 percent dividend to its officers after the factory burned down, and a $60,000 insurance payment collected. Shortly after his marriage he was declared insolvent and his assets placed in the hands of a receiver.[35]

Like Wood's other property, the sawmill had also burned down in the meanwhile, yielding a $6,000 insurance payment, which remained one of his few tangible assets. The receiver was now suing to recover the bonds, alleging that the transfer to Mrs. Wood was little more than a sham to hide his assets from his creditors.[36]

Holmes agreed, ruling that the statute of frauds required prenuptial agreements to be made in writing to be valid against a third party. It was a fine point of law, ultimately turning on whether the bonds were transferred as a gift or through a contract, and the full court narrowly divided 4–3 in upholding his decision.[37]

The most bizarre slice of human experience Holmes probably witnessed in his courtroom was the case of a fifty-year-old unmarried woman, who, to the astonishment of her family, suddenly changed her will, naming as her sole beneficiary a thirty-eight-year-old man whom she had recently met—whom she then also legally adopted as her son. She had been a believer in spiritualism and, when her aunt died and left her the house they had shared, had refused to allow any of her aunt's belongings to be touched. But after meeting the younger man, she sold all of the aunt's prized possessions, moved out of the house, grew suspicious and hostile to her family, and changed her legal adviser.

When she died, her sisters sued to have the will invalidated, telling a sordid tale of her having been kept in isolation by the adopted son in her last days, confined to a room in her house as she was dying of cancer, and denied visits of friends or even medical attention.

The case presented a paradoxical legal problem: if the will was invalid, the son would *still* inherit her estate as her sole heir, which meant that the sisters had no legal standing to challenge the will in the first place. There was little basis in law to challenge an adoption unless a fraud had been perpetrated on the probate court, and even then it seemed as if the sisters would *first* have to have the will invalidated, to gain standing to be a party to any action there. Holmes denied a motion to present the case to a jury on the question of the will alone, and the full court again agreed with his judgment.[38]

Shortly after Holmes joined the court in 1883, its trial caseload was lightened by dividing jurisdiction over equity cases with the Superior Court; in 1887 divorce cases were transferred to the lower court as well; and in 1891 the legislature ended the high court's role in murder trials.[39] Holmes presided at the trials of four particularly lurid murders before the change was made: there was the ex-policeman who shot his estranged and pregnant wife, who had left him because of his extreme drunkenness; the murder of a man on an egg-buying trip, killed for the thirty dollars in his pocket; the elderly couple who did in their eighty-eight-year-old lodger with an axe; and the drunken doctor who shot a cab driver in a dispute over change from the fare. The trials lasted only a few days, all but the last ending in a death sentence (the doctor was convicted of manslaughter).[40]

Two years after joining the court, in a speech to the Suffolk Bar Association, Holmes asked in what other profession but the law "does one plunge so deep in the stream of life,—so share its passions, its battles, its despair, its triumphs, both as witness and actor?"[41] In seeking to live life on the firing line, he had realized his ambition in presiding over the daily drama of the courtroom.

———

Paying tribute to a departed judicial colleague, William Crowninshield Endicott, toward the end of his own term on the Massachusetts Supreme Judicial Court, Holmes praised the qualities that Endicott had embodied, a perfect balancing of intellect and heart:

> He sat without a thought of self, without even the unconscious pride or aloofness which seemed, nay, was, his right, serenely absorbed in the problems of the matter in hand, impersonal yet human, the living image of justice, weighing as if the elements in the balance were dead matter, but discerning and collecting those elements by the help of a noble and tender heart.[42]

It was clearly a reflection of his own model of the ideal trial justice, and Holmes relished the challenge of issuing judgments on the fly, sizing up a witness's credibility, and being absorbed in a living drama of the moment even while maintaining a rigorous intellectual independence. Hiller B. Zobel, who served on the Superior Court in Massachusetts a century after Holmes's time, and who made a thorough study of Holmes's trial records, wrote that he was an "exemplar" of a highly efficient and active trial justice, with a command of both the law and his courtroom. "He issued difficult, complicated legal rulings from the bench," Zobel noted, "explained evidentiary decisions as he made them," and "charged juries clearly," never using boilerplate instructions but carefully explaining how they were to weigh the evidence before them.[43]

Holmes also liked to run a tight ship when it came to courtroom decorum. Once, on circuit in Worcester, a young lawyer—it was Webster Thayer, who would later be notorious as the judge who presided over the Sacco-Vanzetti murder trial in 1921—was "lounging" in the courtroom with his feet up on the bar toward the bench. After a while Holmes beckoned to the court officer. "Tell that feller I'm tired of looking at his ass," he said. The message was relayed in more decorous language, and Thayer took his feet down.[44]

The one thing he did not like about the job was the tediousness of lawyers. "Dear me, hardly anyone knows how to argue a case," he confided to Mrs. Gray. "You can twig in one minute what a man will take from 5 to 15 minutes to utter with due rhetorical emphasis." Waiting for lawyers to catch up with his understanding of their case, he often busied himself writing letters to friends. "I now am listening to an argument which is to determine who shall be Mayor of Worcester—an impertinent distraction when one is writing to a lady," he wrote to Mrs. Curtis on another occasion. He later acknowledged to Dean Acheson that his letter writing on the bench gave him "an undeserved reputation for attention and industry," as courtroom observers understandably assumed he was taking meticulous notes of the case he was hearing.[45]

He wrote to Lady Castletown one day from the courtroom that the lawyer arguing an insurance case before him at the moment made him think of the interminable Wagner opera he had been to the night before ("If anyone has to go down stairs each step takes a quarter of an hour, and a kiss is as long as a Puritan sermon"). Another time he wrote her from the bench,

> Just now I am holding court ... and am suffering from a take down in the hint that the younger men—or I daresay the bar generally, think I talk too much on the bench and don't give 'em chance enough to develop their ideas. I will be a monument hereafter but I think it uncivilized to have to listen to speechifying instead of telling at once where my trouble is when I am the man they want to convince.[46]

The few complete transcripts of his trials that exist show Holmes frequently trying to move the case along, cutting off repetitive questioning or taking over the examination of witnesses himself to try to get to the point more quickly. "Is it worthwhile pressing that any further, Mr. Richardson? Of course I understand the thing," he impatiently interrupted one lawyer while questioning a witness. "Cannot you abridge these long preliminaries a little?" he asked another who was too enamored of the sound of his own voice.[47]

The bar nonetheless thought well of him. "I like to try a case before Judge Holmes," one prominent lawyer, a retired federal judge, told a committee of the legislature that was considering ending the Supreme Judicial Court's trial jurisdiction altogether. "He is open-minded, magnanimous and lets you know what is the matter."[48]

His experiences in the trial court may not have made him sympathetic to long-winded counsel, but it did give him a perspective of the trial judge's role that he carried with him as an appellate judge, both in Massachusetts and later on the U.S. Supreme Court. In a number of his appellate decisions he stressed that it is not enough for an appeals court judge to say that he would have reached a different conclusion on the original evidence: many questions had to be left to the discretion of the trial judge for the system to work at all, and it would only sow chaos and uncertainty to second-guess the man on the spot absent a clear finding of legal error.

"Petitioners have had their day in court," he ruled in denying a further hearing on a case he had already dealt with while sitting as a single justice. He held that the award of costs was in a trial judge's discretion and not reviewable; that having an inept lawyer who failed to appear in court, and did not notice the default judgment entered in the case, was no excuse for missing a one-year deadline for a rehearing; that in the absence of "manifest injustice" a court would not intervene merely to revise an unfavorable tax assessment; and that a will accepted by the probate court, and then affirmed on appeal, cannot subsequently be challenged, even with new evidence.[49]

Holmes's own record on appeal was respectable: about four-fifths of his rulings at trial were upheld by the full court, one-fifth were overturned. As a member of the full court he participated in reviewing his own decisions, and in a few instances he actually wrote the affirming opinion himself. Twice, he wrote the full court's decision *overruling* his own previous judgment at trial, apparently after being convinced by his brethren that he had failed to properly apply a relevant precedent, which showed a certain manful willingness to face up to mistakes.[50]

A MORE DIRECT chance to see his theoretical ideas about the law put into action came in dozens of important cases Holmes tried that raised new questions of law amid the strains of a growing and urbanizing society.

From 1860 to 1880 the population of Boston doubled, half of the increase coming from immigration and a rising birthrate and half from the absorption of outlying neighborhoods. By 1880, 80 percent of Massachusetts residents lived in urban places, a huge change from the village and rural landscape of just a few decades earlier. The demand for city services and new public utilities supplying gas, electricity, and telephones created new kinds of work and a vastly expanded role of municipal government, constructing and operating schools, transit networks, water and sewage, police and fire departments.[51]

By the 1880s Boston's horse-drawn streetcars covered 560 miles of track (and employed eight thousand draft horses); by the end of the

decade Boston would be among the first cities to begin running electric
streetcars, and in the 1890s would be the first to complete the change-
over from horsepower to electricity on its street railways and would
begin work on the nation's first subway. Electric streetcars tripled the
distance commuters could easily travel from home to work, further
stimulating the suburbanization of outlying towns.[52]

New England still led the country in textile manufacturing, and 80
percent of the region's entire textile industry was located within sixty
miles of Boston, but the Civil War had struck a blow to the region's
traditional industries that they would never recover from. The legion
of skilled mechanics who had built and maintained the mills' custom-
made equipment were no longer needed as mass production standard-
ized the machinery, and the new high-speed ring-spinning machines
being installed in Lowell could be tended by largely unskilled women
and children, in place of trained adult males.[53]

Boston remained a center of innovation, with machine shops, metal
fabricating, and instrumentation and electrical companies, but the very
nature of work was changing as the relation between employer and
employed became more impersonal, and factory owners sought to regulate the hours and behavior of their workforce. And even as the Irish
were beginning to be an accepted part of the city's fabric, a new flood
of immigrants, mainly Italians and Jews from Russia, Poland, and
Lithuania, were arriving and by the mid-1880s had overtaken the Irish
among the city's newest immigrants.[54]

All of these forces created challenges to a legal system that was still
rooted in forms and rules that had evolved in a society of farmers and
small tradesmen. The question was whether the law was still flexible
enough to adapt to "the felt necessities" of a time that was changing
more swiftly than ever.

At least in Holmes's hands, it generally was. Throughout the 1880s
and 1890s he tried a number of cases that directly took on the collisions
of the new industrial and financial age with the law's traditional ideas
about property, competition, and morals. Disputes over the siting of
bridges and railroad crossings, purchase of land for schools, assessment
of taxes for road improvements, the decisions of school boards and cor-

porations, and the responsibility of employers for the safety of unskilled and often non-English-speaking workers created a raft of cases.

Typical of the new problems was the complaint of the owner of a millpond on the Concord River in Lowell that Holmes heard in his equity session in 1884. Since 1841 the city had been directing water from two street sewers into the pond. For the first thirty years the water had mainly consisted of surface runoff and sand, and the owner had used the reservoir for both manufacturing and drinking. But with the introduction of public water in 1873 and the installation of indoor water closets in houses on the streets, a constant flow of "house sewage of a noxious character" had been filling the pond, giving off foul gases and forming a layer of ooze and sludge two and a half feet deep at the bottom.

The owner sought an injunction against the city to stop the flow and remove the accumulated deposits. Holmes rejected the city's claim that it had acquired a right by longtime use, noting that the owner could not have anticipated back in 1841 the changes that urbanization and indoor plumbing would bring, and ordered the city to halt the discharges and pay for at least a portion of the cleanup.[55]

Other cases confronted questions about economic relations in an age of corporations, distant communications, and financial markets that spanned the nation. Holmes consistently ruled that both the common law and statutes passed by the legislature had to be interpreted in terms of their actual effects in the real world, and not by resort to traditional formulas or dictionary definitions.

Traditionally, for example, the common law generally declined to recognize contracts in restraint of trade, such as agreements forbidding the seller of a business to open a new, competing business for a set period of time. At most, the courts would enforce such noncompete agreements only if they were restricted to the immediate locality, to protect the so-called goodwill in a business a buyer had purchased.

But when one of the owners of three electrical supply companies that had agreed to merge violated the terms of his noncompete agreement by establishing a new electrical business in Boston, Holmes issued an injunction against him after finding that "the business of the plaintiffs is of a nature that may extend over the whole country." In upholding his decision, the full court noted that "provisions which are reasonably necessary for the protection of the good will of many kinds of business are very different now from those required in the days of Queen Elizabeth," when the common law first took notice of the problem. The ease with which someone could change professions or businesses in the modern era, and the ability of manufacturers from all over the world to compete for markets everywhere, had changed the old rationale that such agreements could harm competition or leave a community with only a single seller of a necessary good or service.[56]

Holmes was more willing than the full court, however, to recognize the reality of new financial markets in the case of a Boston brokerage house that had speculated heavily in pork and other commodities on the Chicago Board of Trade. The brokerage had entered into more than $500,000 in futures contracts over a period of thirty days, losing $23,042.84 when the investments failed to pay off. The Chicago Board sued to collect the debt, and on an auditor's report Holmes found for the board, declining to rule on a motion for the brokers that because their clients had no warehouses, no intention of receiving the goods, and had agreed merely to settle the difference between the contracts and market price when they came due, the transactions were unenforceable "wagers."[57]

But when the case reached the full court, it ran directly into the traditional-minded views of the law of Chief Justice Walbridge Abner Field. Holmes did not write a dissent to Field's decision for the court overturning his finding at trial, but did take the extraordinary step of carrying on his argument with Field in a memorial remembrance of his predecessor on his death in 1899. Holmes said that Field conceived of the law not as "an empirical product of history," but as "embodying absolute right" and "general principle." In a clear allusion to the brokerage case, Holmes went on to observe, "If a contract struck him as aiming at a gambling result, he would not enforce it, however much his refusal might encounter the daily practice of a whole board of brokers. He had his view of policy, and he did not doubt that the law agreed with him." Holmes had many warm things to say about Field in his tribute, but just could not let it go when a matter that so touched his fundamental thinking about the law was concerned.[58]

INTERPRETING A STATUTE enacted by the legislature poses its own special set of problems for a judge, but here too Holmes tried to ask how the law actually functioned in society when applying it to specific cases in his courtroom. In 1883 the Massachusetts legislature passed a law intended to insure that laborers brought into the state to build the Cape Cod Canal would not become paupers requiring public support. The canal company was required at the outset to place $200,000 in a fund to pay "all claims for labor performed or furnished in the construction" of the canal. The venture failed, and among those left unpaid were its president, chief engineer, and clerks, who then brought a claim against the fund for their salaries.[59]

Holding that white-collar work was not "labor" within the meaning of the statute, Holmes ruled that they were not eligible for a payout—and he pointedly rejected the voluminous efforts of their attorneys to show how the words "labor" and "construction" were defined in other laws. "A word is not a crystal, transparent and unchanged," Holmes would later write in a U.S. Supreme Court decision that turned on the definition of the word income: "it is the skin of a living thought and may vary greatly in color and content according to the circumstances and the time in which it is used." Or, as he wrote in another case that involved interpreting the intent of the legislature, "It is not an adequate discharge of duty for courts to say: We see what you are driving at, but you have not said it, and therefore we shall go on as before."[60]

There were foreshadows, too, of key threads of his future jurisprudential philosophy on the Supreme Court in several trials in which he confronted questions about the limits of government power. One in particular, *Bent* v. *Emery*, strikingly anticipated his long-running battle on the Supreme Court against the absolutist view of the conservative majority which regularly overturned economic regulation as an infringement of "property" or "liberty," while resorting to a euphemism Holmes always loathed—"police power"—to excuse the inevitable exceptions. He would always consider that a mealymouthed excuse for facing facts, and an evasion of the duty to weigh the real competing interests at stake. And it gave him an opportunity to reiterate his grown-up philosophy that everything ultimately comes down not to simplistic absolutes, but to matters of degree:

> We assume that one of the uses of the convenient phrase, police power, is to justify those small diminutions of property rights, which, although within the letter of constitutional protection, are necessarily incident to the free play of the machinery of government. It may be that the extent to which such diminutions are lawful without compensation is larger when the harm is inflicted only incident to some general requirement of public welfare. But whether the last mentioned element enters into the problem or not, the question is one of degree.[61]

He similarly ruled that it was within the authority of the town council of Taunton to spend $200 on band concerts under a statute authorizing small appropriations to celebrate holidays "and for other public purposes." Although public concerts "look rather more obviously to increasing the picturesqueness and interest of life than to the satisfaction of rudimentary wants," Holmes wrote in his decision, "we know of no simple and merely logical test by which the limit can be fixed. It must be determined by practical considerations. The question is one of degree."[62] That would be his watchword on the bench for a half century to come.

CHAPTER 8

Labor, Capital, and Dames

Soon after Holmes's appointment to the Massachusetts high court, he and Fanny began looking for a house, but after one attempt to involve her husband in the process, Fanny announced that he had better leave it all to her.

"The next thing I heard was an enquiry if I would dine that night at No. 9 Chestnut Street," Holmes recalled. "After I gave my august consent to this house," Fanny went to work "altering and getting it into shape, determining what should be my library and even the color of the shelves against the will of the architect and coming out clearly right." They moved in at the end of 1883.[1] The house still stands on a historic block of brick townhouses one block north of the Common, in the shadow of the State House.

Throughout their marriage Holmes knew better than to second-guess her when it came to running the household. He handled the checkbook and bills, but left just about everything else to Fanny. "If my wife should consult me as to the household I should be an imbecile," he once told Lewis Einstein. "My function there is that of God, a terrific idol to be appealed to on condition that it remains dumb."[2]

Fanny was such an intensely private person that she left few hints of her views of their marriage and life together. Holmes's friends who managed to catch glimpses of her depth all liked and admired her, but her shyness and deliberate isolation remained the most visible feature of her character. That has led some of Holmes's biographers, with little solid evidence, to portray her as an odd, even unstable figure. Recalling their long life together shortly after her death in 1929, Holmes acknowledged to Einstein, "I like solitude with intermissions, but she was almost a recluse. . . . She shocked Gifford Pinchot once by saying, 'I have no friends'; and it was true that there was no one except me with whom she was very intimate." Fanny wrote very few letters; "nothing short of a charge of dynamite . . . will get even a line out of her," Holmes once explained to Ethel Scott, who had worried something was amiss between her and Fanny when she did not reply to her letters.[3]

Fanny was also distant from her family, and never comfortable in Boston society—though as one family friend recalled, "Boston society was not a cordial one" then. One relation remembered her literally hating her sister Mary, as well as the snobbery and smugness of the Wigglesworth family that she had married into.[4]

There was much speculation, too, that she was bitterly unhappy over her husband's flirtations with other women. "There is something so grim as to be out of nature in that poor woman's life and character," Alice James wrote in her diary in 1889. "What is there but ugliness in any relation between two beings which doesn't work to soften their hearts and open their minds to their kind?"[5]

Yet those who were able to see the pair in unguarded moments sensed something very different about their relationship. Several of Holmes's secretaries in Washington who got to be favorites of Fanny's wrote affectionately of her strength of character and her sharp wit that was every match for her husband's. Tommy Corcoran said later that "in many ways, she was stronger than her husband and she guided him through his times of crisis with the courage that accepts and faces the problems of life." Einstein also remarked on her imperturbability, saying that she "would keep cool in the crater of Vesuvius"; and after her death he told Holmes, "I recall on one or two occasions the real warmth of her heart which she did her best to hide, and there was true generosity in her sympathy for those who needed it."[6]

John E. Lockwood, who was Holmes's secretary the year Fanny died, also noted "the artistry" with which she always kept her husband "on his toes." Every April 1 she played some silly practical joke on him, accompanied by a crude stick figure drawing announcing "April-lie Foollie," or the like. One year he arrived at his desk to find the ink bottle knocked over and a huge ink blot almost completely covering a just-completed opinion. On closer inspection the "blot" turned out to be a cut-out piece of black paper.[7]

Corcoran sent Felix Frankfurter a verbatim account of a typical bit of Holmes-Fanny repartee he witnessed. Fanny had interrupted her husband and Lockwood while they were working through a long list of petitions asking the Court to accept a case for review.

Holmes (to Lockwood): "Remove this impediment to the business of the nation."

Fanny: "Justice Holmes!"

Holmes: "Madam?"

Fanny: "Sir, I have been reading this morning of a woman who divorced an unimaginative husband—and kept him around the house for a handyman. I hereby give you notice that if I am ever again treated in this manner, I shall divorce you in like manner—and keep you around the house to pay the bills!"[8]

She addressed him, at least in front of others, as "Holmes" or "Holmes J." He often called her "woman." But their longtime servants remembered their being very affectionate and happy with one another when no one else was around to watch. His pet name for her was "Dickie" or "Dickie bird." Charlie Buckley, Holmes's driver for nearly all the years he was in Washington, told Alger Hiss that when they would get into the back seat and pull the lap rug over them, they would kick each other in the shins like "flirting adolescents."[9]

Agnes Meyer recalled an indelible scene of their marriage she witnessed one day near her home in Washington. She had always felt that Fanny had both a "brilliant" and "subtle" mind to which Holmes owed much, as few others were aware. But she also felt that she had glimpsed in their marriage a "relationship between man and wife . . . of the rarest beauty." That day on Connecticut Avenue she saw the couple, then in their eighties, strolling ahead of her. So absorbed were they in each other that, at one point, "they stopped, oblivious of the passersby, and conversed with the intensity of a young couple under the spell of first love."[10]

After Fanny's death, Holmes told several friends that "for sixty years she made life poetry for me," a phrase that some took as a poetic metaphor itself, but which he meant a little more literally than perhaps they realized. He recalled times she had noticed and tended to the small beauties of life that might have passed him by but for her. Once, remembering their lean early days at their apartment at 10 Beacon Street, he recalled to her how she had brightened their life: "You even made roses bloom on a broomstick."[11]

And one day in 1910, when they were driving between Beverly and Gloucester, she made them stop at a farmhouse where a small sign, in the style of a beautifully illuminated manuscript, announced "Robert W. Hyde, Limner." In a letter to his friend Ethel Scott he wrote at the time, Holmes described Fanny's beautiful and serendipitous discovery:

Looking into the two little windows on the two sides of the door you see engrossed on pieces of parchment medieval looking inscriptions, so that the impression is of the scriptorium of a monk. Fanny was so struck by the general look that we went in, and found a little room lighted also from one side like Albert Durer's St. Jerome; and in it a very good looking young man, who had made this his occupation. . . .

Anything more remote from the fashionable world of these shores would be hard to imagine. We bought one or two and F. asked him to do the beginning of the prologue to the Canterbury Tales through "Then longen folk to gon on pilgrimages" as a sort of spring song for this house—or Washington. F. has taught me how many poems and pictures are to be seen all about one, if one looks.

He added, "I am afraid I should have passed the place every day without even noticing it."[12]

———

THE ONE SOURCE of sadness Fanny did mention to a few others was not having children. The wife of Holmes's nephew and sole surviving heir told Mark Howe in the 1950s "that she had destroyed a number of exceedingly personal papers of Fanny Dixwell Holmes—including poems—which reflected her profound regret that she had had no children." Katharine Bundy, the wife of one of Holmes's secretaries, became closer to Fanny than most of their Washington acquaintances, and she said their not having children "was great grief to both of them."[13]

Holmes himself dropped a few hints, however, that he was just as happy to have avoided fatherhood. Whenever forced to admire a baby, he trotted out a wisecrack about endorsing infant damnation;[14] and when he was in his fifties he wrote a wry account of the miseries of dealing with a visiting adolescent cousin, which suggested he did not feel he had missed much in not having had a daughter of his own. It was probably his young cousin Dorothy Upham, who would later live with them in Washington after her parents died, to whom he was referring in an account to Mrs. Gray of a week she spent at Beverly Farms in the summer of 1895:

> It is a spike in one's celestial crown to try to please a young woman of 13 whose dislikes seem to be her only articulate consciousness— who never speaks—and lets everything drop flat. There is a theory that she adores me—but if she does not hate me by the end of this week I shall think myself lucky.[15]

Learned Hand recalled Holmes saying late in his life that "this is not the kind of world I want to bring anyone else into," which sounded like a bit of formulaic justification.[16] But around the same time that he made that remark to Hand, he wrote to Einstein a more nuanced expression of his feelings about the subject, referring at the outset to a dinnertime conversation he had had with an English judge during his and Fanny's first trip to England in 1874, just after their marriage:

> Once at dinner in England old Sir Fitzroy Kelly on hearing that we had no children said le bon temps viendra. But I am so far abnormal that I am glad I have none. It might be said that to have them is part of the manifest destiny of man, as of other creatures, and that he should accept it as he accepts his destiny to strive; but the latter

he can't help and part of his destiny is to choose. I might say some sad things but I won't. Whatever I may think of life, the last years of mine have been happy and are so now. Of course, if I should break down before dying it would be awkward, as there is no one to look after me as a child would. But I daresay my nephew and my friends would cook up something.[17]

There was a suggestion in this that he had chosen deliberately not to have children, but, again, others who knew Fanny vehemently rejected that suggestion.[18]

There was also a rumor that Holmes was impotent, which his cousin John Morse rather nastily spread, but the medical evidence is at best highly speculative. Holmes did suffer from prostate problems in his late fifties; in a passage that Mark Howe cut from his edited edition of Holmes's correspondence with Pollock, Holmes wrote of having to halt his foray into bicycle riding because of a flare-up of the condition: "Although I have an ideal saddle arranged so as not to bear on the prostate, rather a bumpy ride the other day seemed to make some disturbance in that region and I prudently knocked off to avoid the risk of trouble." Twenty years later he had emergency surgery to remove his prostate. The symptoms were consistent with what today would be recognized as benign prostatic hyperplasia, or an enlarged prostate. But whether these troubles ever seriously impinged on his sex life at any point is impossible to say.[19]

Almost no correspondence between Holmes and Fanny survives, nor is there anything in Holmes's papers that gives a hint of the nature of his and Fanny's sexual relationship (despite one extravagant over-reading attempted by Sheldon Novick).[20] It was not an age when people opened the most private aspects of their lives to others, and the true reasons for their childlessness remained theirs, and theirs alone.

————

FANNY HOLMES WAS certainly aware from the start that putting up with her husband's flirtations came with the territory of being the wife of Oliver Wendell Holmes Jr.

He often commented that he much preferred the company of women to men. In his sophomore year at Harvard he wrote to a girl he had met, Lucy Hale, "Now almost all my best friends are ladies and I admire and love ladies' society and like to be on intimate terms with as many as I can." He earnestly explained to her that he did not want to be on the same footing as "these flatterers" and "fellows who don't care what harm they do a girl if they only have their fun." He wanted to talk to her about the things *she* really cared about, he said.[21]

"I hate men's dinners," he told Mrs. Curtis a number of years later. "My male friendships, at least, make a queer company—they have included a fair share of cranks." Even to the one woman who would touch his affections more deeply than any other, Lady Castletown, he explained that what he valued above all in the company of women was "the unspecialized interest which women bring to conversation and the greater personal warmth which is present however unconscious, in the most Platonic relations with them."[22]

The intensity and number of his friendships with women, however, certainly raised eyebrows around Boston. "I never meet you when I am with a woman but you begin to grin. Why is this?" he facetiously asked John Morse one time in 1887. Owen Wister remembered how "certain ladies in those Boston days" would tell him with great concern that certain other Boston ladies "were spoiling Wendell Holmes." During his years on the Massachusetts bench Holmes nearly always went to see Mrs. Gray at her home on Beacon Street for a long talk every Tuesday afternoon.[23] He also became exceptionally close to a number of the young wives on the North Shore on whom he similarly paid regular calls in the summers: there was a story that one young husband threatened to divorce his wife if Judge Holmes came by one more evening to read her poetry and amuse her with his witty conversation.[24]

Mrs. Gray was eleven years younger than Holmes, but the age difference with most of his female friends was considerably greater: most were in their twenties or early thirties when he first met them in his fifties or sixties. They were also, nearly without exception, notably attractive and prominent in Boston or New York society, as well as intellectually and artistically accomplished. Nina Gray, from a wealthy Boston family, the Lymans, published poetry. (It was said of her husband, John Chipman Gray, who carried on his very lucrative practice as a property lawyer while teaching at Harvard, that "he made a million and married a million.")[25]

Bas-relief of Nina Gray by Augustus Saint-Gaudens

Anna Codman, who lived almost directly opposite the Holmes summer place at Beverly Farms, was the daughter of a professor of chemistry at MIT and the author of one novel, and later the translator of the journal of a German U-boat commander published during the First World War—"a civilized woman," Holmes described her to Mrs. Gray. Ellen Curtis, whose husband raced yachts with the Lowells and Saltonstalls at Marblehead and led hunting expeditions to British East Africa when he was not practicing law or serving as Boston police commissioner, could also "hold her own" intellectually.[26]

Clara Sherwood Rollins was another young and socially prominent novelist whom Holmes drew quite close to. She was in her twenties and separated from her husband when Holmes met her in the 1890s; her subsequent marriage in 1899 to Joseph S. Stevens—Harvard graduate, star polo player, member of Teddy Roosevelt's Rough Riders in the charge up San Juan Hill—made her one of the wealthier women in America, with a mansion on Madison Avenue and homes in Newport, Rhode Island; Aiken, South Carolina; and Colorado Springs, Colorado.[27] The New York society pages regularly noted her appearances at Long Island horse shows, Newport tennis tournaments, and teas with Mrs. Cornelius Vanderbilt and visiting European royalty, always carefully describing the clothes she wore, and reported on her exploits as one of the few female polo players of the time.

Portrait of Ellen Curtis by
John Singer Sargent

Mark Howe interviewed in the 1940s and 1950s everyone he could find who knew Fanny and Holmes at the time and asked them point-blank if Holmes had affairs with these young women. Not one believed he did. "Charlie Curtis says that both his mother & J. T. Morse asserted with complete confidence that OWH was never unfaithful to his wife—& emphasized that they should know," Howe noted in a memorandum. Clara Stevens's son likewise was "thoroughly convinced that OWH had nothing that might be called an 'affair' with his mother or other women—but that he turned to them for their youth, their beauty, their intelligence and their admiration."[28]

"My own suspicion is that he talked a good game," said James Rowe, Holmes's last secretary. Tommy Corcoran, Francis Biddle, and Isabella Wigglesworth (who was married to Fanny's nephew) all recalled Holmes telling them in later years some variation on the words, "I've always loved the dames, but I've never stepped over the edge." And several shrewder feminine observers of Holmes in his later years, including Katharine Bundy and a North Shore neighbor, Katherine P. Loring, thought that in playing the part of "a very dangerous flirt," Holmes was just showing off more than anything else. "He was a very handsome man and he knew it," said Katharine Bundy. "He adored adulation."[29]

A psychoanalyst might read into this urgent need for attention and reassurance of his desirability from much younger women compensation for something unfulfilled in his own life. There was no doubt something highly unusual in the lengths he sometimes went to in his letters—hinting at stronger feelings he dare not express, longing for the next time they might meet, expressing jealousy of other men (though not their husbands, many of whom were his good friends as well). This was more than mere flirtation. Yet it was not the way lovers in a passionate sexual relationship talked. It was only very late in life that he ever addressed Nina Gray, "Dear Nina" or "My dear friend" in his letters; it was always "Dear Mrs. Gray,"

Clara Sherwood Rollins Stevens

just as it was "Dear Mrs. Codman" and "Dear Mrs. Curtis."

What these women got from their friendship with Holmes was the respect and attention of a brilliant and warm man, who above all took them seriously. His correspondence with Nina Gray, Clara Stevens, Ellen Curtis, and a dozen other women was indeed extraordinary, all the more so for the time. He wrote Nina Gray 330 letters from 1888 to her death in 1932. His letters to women are the most intimate record of his life during this period. But they are literature as well as biography: he discoursed with wit, zest, and ability on ideas, religion, literature, personalities, the nature of human creativity, his work on the court, the follies of mankind, thinkers ancient and modern, and questions in the law that interested him, often all in one letter. "A letter is not a composition but a talk, a breathing out of the casual contents of one's mind," he once said. "I think that it may be intelligent or strange or any other damned thing that gives the writer's thought or want of it."[30]

Mark Howe observed that if you cut out a few lines at the beginning and end of his letters to women, where he offered courtly formulas of his devotion, what remained was generally indistinguishable from those to Harold Laski, Lewis Einstein, Frederick Pollock, and his other male legal and philosophical colleagues.[31] But that was not entirely true: he opened up to women far more, revealing his hopes and apprehensions and occasionally much more personal reflections.

Holmes destroyed most of their letters to him, but judging by some of his replies they apparently now and then asked him to tone down his more eager efforts to elicit expressions of affection. But they all plainly cherished his way of treating them as intellectual and human equals.

He was never condescending. "You don't need to dazzle me with a list of brilliant women. . . . I have had too many deep and truly reverent friendships to require a reminder," he wrote Margaret Bevan, the fifteen-year-old daughter of English friends with whom he corresponded for several years when he was on the U.S. Supreme Court. "Don't ever feel that writing is a duty," he told her. "You took it up for your own satisfaction. Chuck it when you don't feel like doing it longer or at the moment." But whenever she did write, he instantly responded with a thoughtful, touching, four-page letter that treated her completely as an adult.[32]

She asked him about his views on equality between men and women. He replied,

As between men and women it never occurs to me to make the kind of contrast you suppose. One meets a human being—one is curious as to this new personality—one wants to know its feelings and views and to lay one's own cards on the table and submit them to the acceptance or rejection of the other. It is human being, not man or woman. Not of course that one's feelings are not profoundly modified by the difference of sex. A woman hardly would wish them not to be, I should think. Indeed you speak of the inspiration our sex gets from you—and it is quite true. Gallantry is probably consistent with absolute intellectual respect. I think I can swear that I take thoughts and opinions simply as such without regard to where they come from and do my best to weigh them. . . .

While no woman ever had a right to feel that I didn't take her intellectual ideas just as I should take a man's, I don't see much good in an attempt to weigh the sexes against each other. . . . It is enough for me that I have seen plenty of women whose genius, or intellects, or characters impressed me—sometimes with awe and humility, sometimes with the joy of companionship—just as I have seen multitudes of men whose company I did not desire except on the footing of simple gregariousness.

Lest in something I have said I seem to swagger, let me add my favorite quotation from I forget whom, but quoted by Schopenhauer in his big book: "In the vulgar herd there is one more than each of us suspects." I never forget that.[33]

Clara Stevens based a minor character in her 1897 novel *Threads of Life* on him, and her Mr. Herbert Fiske is an unmistakable sketch of his real-life counterpart's conversational flair, sympathy, and love of female company in those years in Boston in the 1890s:

A smile, a rare one for a man, made his stern face beautiful for a moment as he took her hand. . . . The world—the great world—was in the marrow of his bones, but he was intensely human with all his worldliness.

He called cynicism the smallpox of the nineteenth century, and believed that only those vaccinated with humanity escaped the disfiguring disease. He had been vaccinated. Perhaps the hardships of war had taught him that sympathy for pain of all sorts so uncommon in men. A man who had been wounded for the love of his country can guess at the joys of maternity. He has turned a leaf in the book of life that is uncut by most men.

Once he laughingly said of himself, "I am like La Fontaine, 'Un vain bruit et l'amour ont occupées mes ans.'" But the noise was not vain, and he had only loved one woman with his whole soul. . . .

He liked an audience. A listener was always inspiring to him. His ideas were like champagne—eager to be free—effervescing as readily in the pewter mug as in the crystal goblet. A responsive mind was a keen delight to him, but if his companion were unable to assist in the conversational game, he enjoyed playing return-ball with his own thought. . . .

Talk was like a clearing house to his brain. He found out where he stood, what he had received, and what ideas he had on hand. Still, he was a good listener, and eager to draw out the best from his companion. . . .

The *ewig weibliche*—particularly when well dressed—attracted him. There are men who by instinct can single out at a glance the most attractive woman in a room full of feminine prettiness. Herbert Fiske was such a man.[34]

Stevens remained forever touched by Holmes's sympathy and intelligent understanding when she was going through her divorce, remarriage, and separation from her five-year-old son. A few of her letters to Holmes survive, and they speak plainly of the love "deeper than passion" that she alluded to in a poem she wrote for him.

> *Say my love is deep*
> *Deeper than passion. Love of soul and mind*
> *Transcends all love—yet—were I at his side!*[35]

From Paris, where she had gone with her husband in part to escape the publicity and disapproval of Boston society following her remarriage, she wrote,

No account of joy, no combination of new and enchanting experiences can stop the ache that comes from the tearing away of old friendships and associations. Of course the pain of longing for my little boy is a separate physical thing which I reckoned with before I married Jo. And though there have been days when it was worse than I imagined it could ever be, still there has never been a pang of regret. It was best. It had to be. But here my whole life is breathed in as it were through my husband. . . .

If you come to England this summer I *must* see you. Please don't stop caring for me dear. I miss you more and more, there never was any one like you. No one ever was to me what you were. If I could only see you from time to time for one of the old soul reviving talks![36]

His young English friend Ethel James similarly wrote him, on the eve of her marriage in 1896 to the barrister Leslie Scott, to thank him for what he had done for her when they had met at an English country house on his recent trip. "I shall always entertain a very vivid recollection of you & of your kindness at Abinger. . . . You did me a very great deal of good—much more than you can have any idea of. I felt it as you talked & I wished so much I had known you before. So you will understand that I am not likely to forget you."[37]

Fanny kept her feelings about all of these flirtations and friendships to herself, and friends and relatives had varying impressions of how much she was affected by her husband's carryings-on. Several thought she was very hurt, even if she mostly hid it. Austin H. Clark, a prominent zoologist who married one of Holmes's young cousins, told Mark Howe that Fanny was "greatly troubled," extremely jealous, suspicious even of Holmes's young cousin Dorothy Upham when she lived with them. But others said they never saw any signs of jealousy on Fanny's part, and took her occasional arch comments about her husband's "charmers" as proof she had rightly sized up all of these young beauties as no real threat to her or her marriage.[38]

Only one letter of Fanny's hints at her feelings; it was an

With Ethel Scott, in Ireland

undated letter to her husband written while she was staying at Beverly
Farms at the end of the summer while he was working in Boston and
joining her at the shore for the weekends. She concluded with a tart
reminder that just because they were apart during the week, he should
not think he was free to gallivant about as if he were a single man. "I
don't suppose you intend to go to New York after Miss Bradley's friend,
she herself being well out of the way. If the fancy has come into your
mind banish it. You have a wife once a week."[39]

Outwardly, she put on an air of stoicism. Many of her acquaintances
noted how Fanny made no effort to improve her appearance. "In her later
years she really did look like a little monkey," observed one friend, her
hair pulled back from her forehead as tightly as possible. Charlie Curtis
thought her "studied effort to be plain and to wear unbecoming clothes"
was a shrewd way to "defy the notion that she was jealous of his philander-
ings, an effort to show that she didn't care—though of course she did."[40]

Fanny was sensitive enough about her looks, however, to refuse ever
to be photographed, though remained self-mocking enough that when
her husband kept asking her to have her portrait taken so he could
have a picture of her, she finally presented him with a postcard of an
ancient Buddha.[41]

And every once in a while, with studied deadpan humor, she would
stick a monkey wrench in her husband's attempts to impress pretty
young things. Once, Holmes was pouring out a stream of beautiful
philosophical talk to an attractive young woman in the drawing room
at Beverly Farms (she was the wife of a young Boston lawyer friend,
Richard W. Hale). Just as Holmes paused for his conclusion, Fanny
interjected—"like a needle against a balloon," Hale would always
remember—"George! You do talk pretty!"

Holmes, to his credit, delighted in telling the story on himself. "That
woman!" he would say, "she took me just as I was well satisfied that I
had plumbed the universe and—look what she did to me!"[42]

———————

In 1888 they traveled across the country to California as George
Shattuck's guests in a private railcar. He was a director of the Atchi-

son, Topeka & Santa Fe and, as the *Boston Daily Advertiser* noted on their departure from Boston on May 5, "The judge has been looking overworked of late and as if just such an ideal mode of travel and new sights were needful." In Chicago they were introduced to Melville Fuller, who had been just nominated by Grover Cleveland as chief justice of the United States, then traveled on to San Francisco and Oregon, where they were taken on a steamboat that shot the rapids to Portland. Holmes gave the local newspaper a diplomatic quote, saying they had never seen anything in Europe to equal the grandeur of the scenery.[43]

"Home again. 9000 miles in one car!—everything an immense success," Holmes wrote his friend Owen Wister a month later. They spent two months at Niagara Falls later in the summer, Holmes using his time to read the Bible through, which inspired him to observe that the constant roar of the falls was "like living on familiar terms with the prophet Isaiah."[44]

The following spring, in May 1889, Holmes left on his own for a trip to England. His widowed sister, Amelia Jackson Sargent, had just died that April, at age forty-five, following a few weeks' illness. She had been living with and looking after Dr. Holmes since the death of their mother the previous year, and Holmes and Fanny decided they now had little choice but to take Amelia's place in Dr. Holmes's house, and move back once again to 296 Beacon Street.

Fanny moved in at once, and Dr. Holmes was grateful for her company, describing her to a friend as "a very helpful, hopeful, powerful as well as brilliant woman," who kept the household running smoothly and even cheerfully amid his sorrow. But Fanny told her husband she thought it might ease the friction between father and son in the new arrangement "and make the first summer easier" if he were absent. She had sworn never again to go abroad after her first experience at sea on their 1874 trip, but they did go once more together, spending a leisurely three months in Europe in the summer of 1882 touring England, Switzerland, Germany, and Holland. But after that she never again accompanied him abroad. Knowing how much he enjoyed going to England, however, she always afterward took the burden on herself to insist that he go whenever he wanted to, and to come up with reasons that would alleviate him of the guilt of leaving her behind.[45]

On the boat going over was William James, to attend a psychological research conference in Paris later in the summer. Holmes "making himself delightful to all hands," William archly reported. Alice James, who was living in London at the time, added her own catty observation in her diary shortly after Holmes's arrival: "They say he has entirely broken loose and is flirting as desperately as ever."[46]

Desperately flirting or not, he met a number of charming young women who became lifelong correspondents. Ethel Grenfell, known as "Ettie," was the twenty-one-year-old niece of Henry Cowper, a Liberal MP whom Holmes had met on his first trip to England in 1866. She visited the Holmeses in Boston in September 1888 and had recently married a member of Parliament twelve years her senior; as Lady Desborough she would be well known as a confidante of prime ministers and as a prominent society hostess in the political and intellectual circles that included Winston Churchill, Oscar Wilde, and H. G. Wells—and known too for her numerous love affairs. On Holmes's return home that summer, he and Ettie began a warm and vivacious correspondence. She wrote him a few years after his visit,

> My very dear friend . . . what *perfect* letters you do write. I should like to read one every morning like the "Times"—quite apart from the dear kind personal part which I love, there is no one in this world or ever has been who fills every page he writes with such vivid suggestion, farce, & spontaneity. You fire one afresh with every letter, half with longing to be farther along the road you have travelled, half with a proud joy thinking, "I too in my life have loved the great things passionately, as such fragments of them it was given me to apprehend."[47]

He also met Margot Tennant—later Lady Asquith, famous as author, wit, and wife of a prime minister—who became a faithful correspondent; and was introduced, by Henry James, to Lucy Clifford, a novelist and the widow of a brilliant mathematician and philosopher,

William K. Clifford. ("Mrs. Clifford happened to confide to me yesterday how madly she loves you," James wrote him afterward. "So poor woman *now*! Damn your greatness, my dear Wendell.")[48]

And at the magnificent country estate of the Earl of Pembroke, Wilton House in Salisbury, he made the acquaintance of a thirty-six-year-old Anglo-Irish noblewoman, Clare, Lady Castletown. Three years later, when he sent her a copy of his book of speeches that he had just had printed, she wrote back,

> I feel quite flattered at your remembering my existence after all this time! I suppose you have been back in England again since that time at Wilton but I have been laid up almost ever since (with a spine that I damaged out hunting) so we haven't had a chance of meeting. I hope however that if you come over this year you will write & let us know & come & stay with us.[49]

ANNA CODMAN, with her novelist's eye, once observed to Mark Howe that Holmes "is known for his superlative mentality, but the greater the man the more interesting are his minor reflexes." Holmes, she said, had "tender little weaknesses that he toyed with like a chaplet, and that were as much part of him as the power of his mind and the kindness of his heart."[50]

A letter Holmes wrote Nina Gray in the summer of 1891 was perfectly typical of the lively mind and small reflexes that he revealed in his correspondence with women, as well as capturing a vivid portrait of him halfway through his career on the Massachusetts high court.

> Dear Mrs. Gray:
> . . . Your letter pulls the trigger, and here goes. The day or day before I received it Brooks Adams had been giving me pleasure by speaking ill of [the journalist and editor Edwin] Godkin, who now seems to be a feature in your landscape. He is one of the properties of culture but as I have always avoided associating with the cultured class I don't know much of him, beyond

supposing that he has not done quite all he expected to, of which I am glad.

The main change since I last wrote has been in the advent of my dear little Brooks. We go into water together and talk sadly of life and man's futile destiny & then I go home and read Locke on the Understanding. I have written a few sentences for future use touching my departed brother Wm. Allen which I own I think A.1. and which sing in my head—it would serve me right if the programme were changed and I should not be deputed to answer the resolutions of the bar in September.

I think my health is improving slowly. Sometimes I suspect that I am not so impervious to internal strain as I have supposed and that my various maladies mean that I have overtaxed my nerves with work etc.—but I know not. If I could make up my mind to go away I think that it would be a good plan for me to move either in your direction or toward the serener skies of the South Shore. . . .

I suppose it to be possible that an exquisite and learned spirit should take true delight in Aristophanes—but I have supposed that most of those who did either were simple pedants or dilated with the wrong emotion as Ruskin did in a passage where he cited and misunderstood according to the late Sophocles whom I consulted. In fact there's a deal of truth in [William Dean] Howells' remark that the classics are dead. Only like Aristophanes it is caviar to the general.

Strange—Here at Bev. Farms we are surrounded by good and gifted beings, yet I see them not nor wish to. I can impart to them neither my aspirations nor my sardonic dislikes—philistine respectables—bourgeois or canaille fashionables. But this also is but the philistine dogmatism of temperament. There is nothing so dogmatic as tastes—and nothing therefore which lays a deeper foundation for the ironic view of man and his destiny. I have a headache this morning or perhaps I should think better of my neighbors. I can't abide sugar in my coffee—ten years ago I couldn't abide coffee without sugar. Is all our idealizing equally arbitrary? I could amplify on this theme but I will not. . . .

My Brooks has come and gone. We have *buffeted the bilious* interchanged further *mediances*—so now I am cheerful and happy. Sturgis Bigelow had been trying to persuade him that it was possible to imagine thinking without a body whereat Brooks was justly irate and contemptuous. Also we came to the conclusion that the reason why we didn't care for people was because they hadn't genius enough. Also we sized up your sex—ever a diverting theme—and generally played round like young bulls in old china shops. I am fond of Brooks.

My remarks above as to the people here are not exhaustive. There are some good people in Beverly—I believe the Eliot Cabots to be such. I do not think I should hate them, but then they are not on hand when I want 'em and when they are on hand I don't want 'em.

I am dying, Egypt, dying (very gradually)—every man of 50 is—and as I have to take in my skyscrapers and other fancy sails—or less figuratively, limit my interests in various ways, I pitch into my neighbors and try to make out that they are to blame for my not sharing all their sports and joys.

Goodbye dear Madam I kiss your fair hands and am sincerely yours,

O. W. Holmes[51]

―――――

THAT YEAR OF 1891 brought the first of several cases where Holmes would break sharply with his fellow justices over the issue of workplace and economic regulation and the rights of labor. In the 1880s the country was swept by a wave of strikes, reaching a peak in the early 1890s. In 1891, hundreds of thousands of workers in the textile, leather, metal-working, construction, and railroad trades engaged in two thousand strikes in an effort to force employers to accept the right of unions to bargain for wages and working conditions.[52]

Most workers labored sixty hours a week, but layoffs were common: factories regularly shut down for months at a time, leaving employees to fend for themselves when demand for products dropped or the rivers that powered the mills froze over in winter. Even during good years as many as a third of all employed workers in Massachusetts were out of a job for an average of three or four months of the year. As confrontations between labor and management intensified, the issue was less wages than control of working conditions, hours, and safety. Between 1888 and 1891 one cotton mill in Lowell recorded seventy-one serious accidents, including two deaths, most occurring because workers were expected to clean, maintain, and remove jams from machinery without first stopping the equipment.[53]

In 1891 the Massachusetts legislature passed a law forbidding employers in woolen mills from withholding the wages of workers for imperfections in their weavings. On December 2, the Massachusetts high court declared the law unconstitutional, finding it a violation of the right of property guaranteed by the state constitution, as well as the U.S. Constitution's prohibition on any state passing a "law impairing the obligation of contracts."

Holmes was the lone dissenter. It was only his third dissenting opinion in his nearly ten years on the bench. As a rule, he said, he disliked the practice; he thought it better to "shut up" than file a lone dissent, and in his entire twenty years on the Massachusetts bench he would issue only a dozen written dissents in all: as he wrote in one of those opinions, "when I have been unable to bring my brethren to share my convictions my almost invariable practice is to defer to them in silence."[54] But the majority's opinion in *Commonwealth* v. *Perry* he did *not* feel he could let pass in silence. "I have the misfortune to disagree with my brethren," he began, but "considering the importance of the question" felt "bound to make public a brief statement."

> I do not see that [the statute] interferes with the right of acquiring, possessing, and protecting property any more than the laws against usury or gaming. In truth, I do not think that that clause of the Bill of Rights has any application. . . .

If . . . speaking as a political economist, I should agree in condemning the law, still I should not be willing or think myself authorized to overturn legislation on that ground, unless I thought that an honest difference of opinion was impossible, or pretty nearly so. . . .

I suppose that this act was passed because the operatives, or some of them, thought that they were often cheated out of a part of their wages under a false pretense that the work done by them was imperfect, and persuaded the Legislature that their view was true. If their view was true, I cannot doubt that the Legislature had the right to deprive the employers of an honest tool which they were using for a dishonest purpose.[55]

Holmes often made clear that "as a political economist," he *did* consider such legislation pointless, even counterproductive, in improving the lot of the masses. No "tinkering with the institution of property" was going to change the fundamental fact that "the crowd now has substantially all there is." He once told Laski, "I never read a socialist yet from Karl Marx down, and I have read a number, that I didn't think talked drool." Nor did he look upon as a Utopia a world "cut up into five-acre lots and having no man upon it who was not well fed and well housed," if the price was to give up all that was great and romantic in the world.[56]

But his objection to the court's decision in *Perry* was not just a difference over a technical point of law; he was deeply bothered by politics masquerading as objective legal analysis.

"When socialism first began to be talked about, the comfortable classes of the community were a good deal frightened," Holmes observed a few years later. "I suspect that fear has influenced judicial action both here and in England. . . . Something similar has led people who no longer hope to control legislatures to look to the courts as expounders of Constitutions." But in upholding "economic doctrine which prevailed about fifty years ago," judges were "taking sides upon debatable and often burning questions." It was Holmes's skeptical temperament to the core: he never mistook his own views for eternal truth. Precisely his

belief that "certainty is illusion," he said, made him reluctant to insist
that "one rule rather than another has the sanction of the universe. . . .
I have noticed the opposite tendency in minds that regarded our corpus
juris as an image, however faint, of the eternal law."[57]

He had in fact gone out of the way to understand political views he
disagreed with, calling on one Boston labor leader "at his very humble
shrine." He described their meeting to Pollock:

> "Sir," I said, "I am Judge H. of the Supreme Judicial Court. I have
> no ulterior motives and no particular questions to ask or observa-
> tions to make, but I thought in the recently published interviews
> you talked more like a man of sense than the rest, and as a Judge
> and as a good citizen I like to understand all phases of economic
> opinion. What would you like if you could have it?" So we have
> discoursed several times with some little profit.[58]

Holmes was likewise the lone dissenter the year after *Perry* was
decided when the Massachusetts House of Representatives asked the
court for an advisory opinion on the constitutionality of a proposed
law allowing cities and towns to operate coal and wood yards. "The
majority say they can't—I say they can and so this morning I appear
in the newspapers as a blooming communist," Holmes wrote to Mrs.
Gray. He added to his friend Bryce with irritation, "I suppose some
people thought I was posing as friend of the proletariat."[59]

The following year, 1893, he dissented yet again, this time joining
Justice Marcus Perrin Knowlton in declining to overturn a law requiring railroads in the state to accept tickets from other lines on an equivalent per-mile basis. As in the other cases, the majority found the law
an unconstitutional violation of property rights.[60]

His larger point was that "the present has the right to govern itself
so far as it can." In only one case in his twenty years on the Massachusetts bench did he hold a statute unconstitutional.[61] Before a judge took
such a step, he wrote in a dissenting opinion in which he argued that a
statute permitting a referendum would be constitutional, "We should
remember that [a constitution] is a frame of government for men of

opposite opinions and for the future, and therefore not hastily import into it our own views, or unexpressed limitations derived merely from the practice of the past." He saw no grounds for courts to declare that the state's constitution allowed the government to provide education, but not wood, to its citizens; or to take land for railroads and public markets, but not to write rules governing their operation. The question to ask was not whether the constitution specifically authorized a certain power, he said, but only whether it prohibited it.[62]

THE DEATHS OF his mother, sister, and brother within a few years of one another cast a shadow on his otherwise busy and energetic life at the time. "My spirit is somewhat collapsed and flat for the moment," he told Owen Wister. His brother, Edward Jackson Holmes Sr., had died in 1884, at age thirty-seven, leaving a wife and an eleven-year-old son. Edward had been ill ever since contracting malaria in Washington, where he had gone just after law school to work as Senator Charles Sumner's secretary and clerk of the Foreign Relations Committee. After that he had dabbled in archaeology, traveling to Italy for his health and to research antiquities. He died in his sleep, having just finished correcting the proofs for a report of the examining committee he chaired to recommend improvements to the Boston Public Library.[63]

There were other melancholy reminders of the disappearing world of Holmes's youth. Walking through Montgomery Place one day in 1885, his father had seen workmen tearing out the insides of their old house, preparatory to its demolition. "We Americans live in tents," Dr. Holmes had joked in relaying the news. The house in Cambridge the doctor had grown up in had been sold to Harvard after the death of his mother in 1870, and it too had recently been demolished. A "case of justifiable domicide" Dr. Holmes acknowledged in his usual facetious way, but there was unmistakable sadness in his finding that "not a vestige is left to show where our old Cambridge house stood."[64]

In 1888 a neighbor at Mattapoisett started a fire that swept across a dry stubble field and burned down Holmes's summer house on Buzzard's Bay. After that, Holmes and Fanny began joining Dr. Holmes

Beverly Farms

in the summers at the place he rented each year at Beverly Farms, on the North Shore. Dr. Holmes had been amused by the pretentiousness of his neighbors who had stationery printed announcing their address as "Manchester-by-the-Sea," and began heading his letters "Beverly-by-the-Depot"—this was in the days he had first summered there, and rented a cottage near the train station.[65]

But the house he now had each summer was a few hundred yards from the water, a large and rambling Victorian clad simply in clapboards and shingles, with eight bedrooms and a wide wraparound porch. Set on a secluded three-acre hillside lot of lawn and pines and dramatic granite outcroppings, it was swept with salt air breezes, and a glimpse of the sailboats and ocean could be seen from the second-floor windows. It would become Holmes's own summer residence for the rest of his life.

In October 1894 Dr. Holmes died at his home on Beacon Street, at age eighty-five. The British humor magazine *Punch* published a eulogy in verse with the lines,

From that Boston breakfast table,
Wit and wisdom, fun and fable,
Radiated
Through all English-speaking places.
When were Science and the Graces
So well mated?[66]

"My father's death although of course a very great event in my life seems to me to have come at a fortunate moment," Holmes wrote to James Bryce. "I was fearing many things for him and he painlessly avoided them—having had all that he could expect from life. . . . I expect that we shall keep on living at 296 Beacon St. for though I don't wholly like the house, my parents built it and died in it and my brother and sister were buried from it."[67]

The deaths of his father and sister made Holmes, for the first time in his life, an independently wealthy man. His salary as a justice of the Massachusetts court in 1894 was $6,500 plus a $500 travel allowance. His sister had no children, and she left him in her will a $130,000 trust that almost doubled that income. (She had inherited a substantial fortune from her husband, Turner Sargent, a member of the famous family of artists.) She also left him her house at 59 Beacon Street, which, along with some commercial property on State Street that he inherited from his father, brought in $4,000 a year in rental income. The sale a few years later of Cambridge properties Holmes inherited with his cousins from his Uncle John netted him $33,000 cash.[68]

And when Fanny's father died a few years later, he left an estate of over $300,000. All told, by the late 1890s their income was some $20,000 a year, at a time when the average household in Massachusetts earned less than $700.[69]

All his life Holmes kept his Yankee attitudes toward money. "I am not stingy—but I am canny. I like to be a little richer at the end of the year," he told Lady Castletown. In particular, he never lost the old-money abhorrence of dipping into capital. He once chided Tommy Corcoran when his secretary returned from the drugstore with a roll of

Life Savers. Corcoran offered the justice one. He took it, then sharply demanded, "Sonny, do you know what you've done?"

"I bought a package of Life Savers," Corcoran replied.

"Do you know how much you paid for it?"

"I paid five cents."

"Do you know how much you really paid? You paid out the interest on one dollar for a year." Corcoran was similarly amused by Holmes's Yankee frugality in recording his annual list of books read on the scattered blank pages he had left unused when making his original notes for *The Common Law* in his by then half-century-old Black Book.[70]

That said, Holmes never stinted on his household or indulging his interests after he came into money. "When in doubt do it is a general rule of life, and when in doubt buy it," he told Mrs. Gray. He and Fanny always had a cook, maids, a gardener, and other servants. He spent hundreds of dollars a year ordering whatever books he wanted, while Fanny loved to shop at an importer of oriental wares on Summer Street, picking up exotic screens, tables, baskets, and other items that struck her fancy. They were able to take over the $1,000 rent for the Beverly Farms house each summer, and always went first class and stayed in the best hotels wherever they traveled. "I couldn't live as I do on my salary," he remarked years later, when his income as a U.S. Supreme Court justice was $20,000, the equivalent of about $300,000 today.[71]

He had done nothing to seek wealth, but his inheritances guaranteed that financial concerns would not be a factor in any of his career decisions to come.

CHAPTER 9

Ideals and Doubts

In his first ten years as a judge there were few hints of the eloquence in his judicial writing that the later Justice Holmes would be renowned for. In part, he was learning himself. As he later confessed, he did not always spend enough time organizing his thoughts before leaping in. "In Massachusetts they pitched into me for writing obscure opinions. I used to say I took for granted that a man understood his business, and I didn't need to put in the platitude—but then I decided there was another thing, to have each thought follow in sequence and avoid sticking a thing in when you think of it. I said to myself, I have been guilty of this, and I have had it in mind since."[1]

But there was also the constraint of having to accommodate himself to his colleagues, which at times put a crimp in his aspirations to philosophic eloquence or originality. He noted more than once having to trim his sails to meet the objections of his fellow justices, who were uneasy whenever he tried to elaborate more general ideas about the law. "I think this is the ground of a great number of cases," he told Pollock about an 1891 decision that had turned on whether a person could be held liable for the actions of an intervening party, "but I only gave a hint of my general view which is all I can do now."[2]

The case was of a husband who had sued two of his wife's friends who had advised her to leave him. Holmes thought it belonged to a special class of cases where intent did matter, an important exception to his general ideas about external standards. But, as he subsequently related to Pollock, "It was thought advisable to cut down the discussion in which I aired some of my views." He confined himself in his opinion to the matter at hand, ruling that for a person to be answerable for his advice having been followed, it was necessary to prove that it had been given dishonestly or malevolently.[3] He would end up having to save most of his larger ideas on the subject for an article he published three years later in the *Harvard Law Review*, "Privilege, Malice, and Intent," that presented his theory of malicious intent being the key consideration in finding fault in otherwise privileged actions.

The court's tradition of collegiality and unanimity sometimes led to opinions being narrowly drawn to steer clear of controversy when the judges had differed on the reasoning behind the conclusion, which left even less scope for Holmes to elaborate on basic ideas about the law. "As there is considerable difference of opinion among the members of the court, we shall not discuss this case further than to say that, in the opinion of a majority, . . . the plaintiff was guilty of gross or wilful negligence," Holmes wrote in one such case. In a number of his opinions for the court Holmes even wrote a decision he himself disagreed with: "Had the decision rested with me alone I probably should have ruled the other way," he stated in one opinion before presenting the majority's conclusion.[4]

Behind the scenes things were not always collegial. "We are in a long consultation in which every man's hand is more or less against everyone else," Holmes wrote Lady Castletown during a break in the middle of one lengthy day of deliberations. "I walk into my neighbors and intimate in more or less polite language that they are talking what Brooks Adams delicately terms hogwash—and when they go for me (but my turn hasn't come yet, as my cases are later) I am ready to maintain that every word is better than any part of the 10 Commandments."[5]

He later candidly described Chief Justice Field's maddening habit of wanting to explore every possible question and remove every possible doubt before reaching a decision:

His mind was a very peculiar one. In the earlier days of my listening to him in consultation he seemed to me to think aloud, perhaps too much so. . . . It was hard for him to neglect the possibilities of a side alley, however likely it might be to turn out a *cul-de-sac*. He wanted to know where it led before he passed it by. If we had eternity ahead this would be right and even necessary. But as life has but a short number of working hours, we have to choose at our peril; we have to act on the presumptions afforded by our present knowledge as to what paths are most likely to lead to desired goals. . . . One has to try to strike the jugular and let the rest go.[6]

Still, Holmes made a point of maintaining cordial relations with all of his colleagues, and he spoke admiringly of Field's kindness and "heroic temper," the "greatest thing" about him: "I used to notice, even in little matters, that he always looked his own conduct in the face and did not equivocate, apologize, or disguise."[7]

The two also shared a gift of repartee that created a camaraderie between them. "I used to delight in giving him opportunities to exercise it at my expense, for his answers were sure to be amusing and they never stung," Holmes recalled. He related one such instance to Mrs. Gray: "Field told my father in law the other day that I was a born pagan and repeated a mot which seems to have pleased him as much as it did me when he got it off originally. An ass had been spouting godliness at us and in the consultation room I let off my disgust at his cant— whereupon the C.J., 'Holmes hates virtue so much that he can't stand even the pretence of it.' "[8]

Field also ragged Holmes about his notorious handwriting, saying once, "Holmes, you are indictable as a fraud at common law because your handwriting looks legible but it isn't!" Holmes always had a comeback to that. "It is not enough to be able to write," he would primly observe. "One must learn to read also."[9]

———

BY THE 1890s Holmes was finding his judicial voice, and also finding more opportunities to bring his ideas about the law to expression in his decisions.

The flashes of Holmesian epigrammatic insight and wit began to appear with regularity in his written opinions. "A horse car cannot be handled like a rapier." "The plaintiff has no copyright on the dictionary." "A man cannot justify a libel by proving that he has contracted to libel." "When a man makes such a representation, he knows that others will understand his words according to their usual and proper meaning, and not by the accident of what he happens to have in his head." "General maxims are oftener an excuse for the want of accurate analysis than a help in determining the extent of a duty or the construction of a statute."[10]

In one of his rare dissenting opinions, he took issue with the full court's refusal to enforce a contract made by a married man who promised his estranged wife he would create a trust for her if she returned to him. Noting that prenuptial agreements were enforceable, he archly disposed of the majority's reasoning: "No one doubts that marriage is a sufficient consideration for a promise to pay money. I do not quite understand why it should be more illegal to make such a promise for the resumption than for the assumption of conjugal relations."[11]

The notion of the external standard and the reasonable man as the test of legal culpability which he had developed in *The Common Law* he slowly but steadily began weaving into his appellate decisions as well. One early case that reached the full court on appeal gave him the chance to extend the same test to the criminal law. "If my opinion goes through it will do much to confirm some theories of my book," he told Pollock with satisfaction.[12]

Commonwealth v. *Pierce* was an appeal of the manslaughter conviction of a doctor who had kept a patient wrapped for three days in flannels soaked with kerosene. Her skin was severely burned and blistered, and she died a week later. The doctor's attorney cited an old Massachusetts case in which the court held that "there is no law which prohibits any man from prescribing for a sick person with his consent, if he honestly intends to cure him by his prescription."

But in his opinion upholding the conviction, Holmes made a pointed parallel to the law of negligence in civil actions, where

> it is very clear that what we have called the external standard
> would be applied, and that, if a man's conduct is such as would be

reckless in a man of ordinary prudence, it is reckless in him. . . . The law deliberately leaves his idiosyncrasies out of account, and peremptorily assumes that he has as much capacity to judge and to foresee consequences as a man of ordinary prudence would have in the same situation. . . .

The recklessness of the criminal no less than that of the civil law must be tested by what we have called an external standard. . . . We cannot recognize a privilege to do acts manifestly endangering human life, on the ground of good intentions alone.[13]

Or, as he put it in an attempted murder case a few years later, "the aim of the law is not to punish sins, but to prevent certain external results."[14]

He consistently sought to apply the external standard to other cases that came to the full court on appeal. He ruled that a man was bound at his peril as "one of the first principles of social intercourse" to know what words commonly mean and how they will be understood in a business contract; that a streetcar passenger cannot expect a conductor to make special allowances for her nervous disposition when carrying out the necessary and legal act of ejecting a drunk from the car; and that the circumstances "of a large part of the community may be taken into account" in deciding whether an impoverished mother exercised due care in leaving her children briefly unattended on the front steps of her house.[15]

In that last case a four-year-old boy was killed at a grade crossing when a freight car—which had come detached and was rolling on its own some distance behind the train—struck the boy as he stood on the tracks waving "good-by" to the train that had just passed. The railroad maintained that, owing to the mother's negligence, there was no case for the jury to consider, and the trial judge had agreed.

But Holmes in his opinion found that the case should have gone to the jury, explaining, "The poor cannot always keep their children in the house or always see that they are attended when out of doors. In this case the evidence warranted a finding that the mother reasonably might expect her children to obey her, and that leaving them where she did for the short time that she left them there, occupied as they were, was not negligence.

For the most part, however, Holmes in his opinions in tort cases took every chance to narrow the scope for juries to determine negligence. He once sardonically observed to Lady Pollock that the only real purpose of a jury "is to let a little popular prejudice into the administration of law—(in violation of their oath)." In his view, it was for the courts to define standards of conduct for guilt or negligence under the law. As he asserted in one opinion, "It is not necessary to go on forever taking the opinion of the jury in each new case that comes up."[16]

═══════════

In late 1895 or early 1896 Fanny became seriously ill again with rheumatic fever. She lost much of her hair, adding to her plain appearance, and her recovery was painfully slow. He had been looking forward to traveling to England that summer of 1896, but now hesitated. He wrote to Mrs. Gray,

> I almost hate to go when it comes to the point because my wife has had the rheumatic fever and although much better still seems weak. But I reflect that it will rub off one's rust to get among a new lot of people with different modes of thought, although when I try to state to myself any specific benefit to be expected, I fail. . . . Perhaps it is well for a recluse to realize the charms of the world the flesh and the devil—a moral advantage which London offers in its plentitude.[17]

He finally decided to go, and made a reservation at Mackellar's Hotel on Dover Street. It was one of the most expensive in London, but he had stayed there before, and "the advantage of this place," as he later remarked to Lady Pollock, was that he could get a bedroom and parlor on the ground floor and "a lady could come into the parlor so conveniently. When one has to climb, it seems more questionable."[18]

His calendar in London was jammed with his usual lunches and dinners. A week after arriving, he left his card for Lady Castletown at her London residence at 101 Eaton Place. That same day he received a reply from her. "Dear Mr. Holmes I remember you well & am so sorry to have missed you this afternoon—but do come to luncheon one of these days? per-haps W-dy.? We *may* be away on Monday & Thursday—Yours sin-cerely, Clare Castletown."[19]

He had lunch with her several times, took her to an exhibition of pictures, and then received an invi-tation to her Irish estate, Doneraile Court, for mid-August when all of fashionable London retreated to the countryside.[20]

She was twelve years Holmes's junior, the descendant of an old Anglo-Irish family, the St. Legers,

Clare, Lady Castletown

who were a legendary name in the horse world; the St. Leger Stakes horserace was founded by a distant ancestor and the first steeplechase race was run from Doneraile in 1752. She was a classic aristocratic beauty, who had married at age twenty into an equally wealthy and venerable Anglo-Irish clan. Her husband, Bernard Edward Barnaby FitzPatrick, the 2nd Baron Castletown of Upper Ossory, had inherited a huge estate of his own, consisting of 22,000 acres in Queen's County, with his principal residence at Granston Manor at Abbeyleix, and they divided their time between their two Irish estates, their London town-house, and frequent foreign travels.

Lord Castletown had all the air of the none-too-bright British aris-tocrat. He had been elected to Parliament in 1880, then served in the House of Lords after acceding to his hereditary title three years later. But as one contemporary observed, "No one except Lord C. himself can, I think, say what his political principles are: I should make even that reservation with reservations." At various points in his political life he was listed as Conservative, Liberal, Liberal Conservative, and Liberal Unionist. His memoir, *Ego*, published in 1923, is devoted mainly to accounts of his travels to distant locales and the various large animals he shot there.[21]

The Castletowns' marriage was friendly, but with little evidence of deep passion. Lord Castletown scarcely mentions his wife in his memoir. In her private letters to him she calls him "my old big bear" or "old man," and mostly writes about arrangements for shooting parties, entertaining guests, and the usual problems of the landed nobility in dealing with servants and managing the estate. They had no children of their own, though he had had a mistress who had borne his child; she was now ensconced in Paris and the recipient of a regular and secret annuity from him.[22]

During Holmes's two months in London, Henry James had sent him a blizzard of gushing letters about visiting him at his cottage in Rye, two hours away, then repeatedly canceling the arrangements with elaborate explanations of his complicated schedule and other guests; they finally saw each other at the very end of Holmes's stay in the metropolis: "H. James to tea—stayed & saw me off for Ireland," Holmes wrote in his diary on August 16.[23]

Holmes had jotted down in his diary Clare Castletown's instructions for getting to Doneraile: the night train at 8:25 from Euston Station to Holyhead, then the boat to Kingstown on Dublin Bay, then on the next morning by the train to Maryborough to Buttevant. At the station he was met that afternoon for the drive to Doneraile through the tiny bowered lanes and improbably green fields of the Irish countryside. The entrance to Doneraile Court was through a triumphal arched gate at the end of the village, then along a curving drive over a stone bridge that crossed the river Awbeg, sited to give a dramatic view of the house on a low rise ahead.

Clare's maternal grandfather had been a foreign officer in the British government and collected seeds for Kew Gardens wherever he traveled, sending some to his daughter at Doneraile at the same time, and the grounds were an exemplar of the English landscape style and filled with specimens of beautiful exotic trees.

Doneraile Court

The house dated to the late seventeenth century, built in the grand Georgian style, with curving window bays on each end, soaring ceilings filled with ornate plasterwork, an Ionic-columned entrance hall, and a three-story-high floating elliptical staircase that rose to a dome at the top. An early St. Leger had had the river rerouted so a shimmering waterfall formed the distant focal point looking out the front windows. A sunken ha-ha fence left an uninterrupted vista of the fields beyond and the grazing cattle and roe deer.[24]

There were only a few other guests staying at Doneraile, and Lord Castletown was off to Norway, elk hunting. Holmes later twitted Clare for having had one fellow "who was invited for fear the Yankee experiment should prove tedious." But, he triumphantly recalled, "it was not I who was sent to shoot rabbits." He stayed five days, and left hopelessly in love.[25]

"It is the stopping so sudden that hurts," he wrote her the evening he left, as he ate his solitary dinner at his hotel in Queenstown, the port near Cork where he was to embark on the *Etruria* the next morning. He had Room S, the "best on the ship," he noted in his diary, but that was little consolation. He filled the six days' passage chatting to an Irish priest and to an ex-Confederate officer, Gordon McCabe, who ran an Episcopal boys' school in Richmond and who amused him with stories of the war and insults to the Yankees. ("I'm afraid—no I'm not—I think we are friends for life," he told Clare three months later, after receiving what he humorously described as "a regular love letter" from McCabe.) He was roped into giving an after-dinner speech at a charity concert one night, but his mind was not on it. A young, newly married couple he knew, who he ran into, found him pacing the deck one evening trying to come up with his speech. "Morton," Holmes told the young husband, "the perfect after-dinner speech should contain an introduction, an anecdote, and a cosmic observation. I have the first and the last, but cannot get the second." But he wrote Clare that at least it was a distraction from his misery: "If I try to think of something to say I shall not have to think of you."[26]

He landed in New York on Saturday, August 29, and took the train to Boston. Fanny, and his nephew and newly engaged fiancée, were expecting him at Beverly Farms at seven-thirty that evening—"all was prepared to receive me," he knew—but worn out, and his head full of his "curly headed early Norman angel," as he called Clare, he simply went to 296 Beacon Street, and to bed.[27]

He woke the next morning to find Fanny there: she had hired a carriage and driver and pair of horses and had posted through the night the forty miles to meet him, arriving at one-thirty in the morning, not waking him. It was a sign of his guilt and confusion that he told the whole story to Clare in his first long letter to her on arriving home. "Imagine my joy—but also my shame to have her make the effort rather than myself," he wrote her.[28]

He wrote to Clare every few days, calling her "My dear Lady" or "Beloved Hibernia," always asking her to write more often, reminding her of the time they had sat in the conservatory at Doneraile together, of how intimately their minds had met so quickly, begging for a reassuring word that he was not being a fool in feeling more for her than perhaps she did for him, given her "whims." One night at dinner he ordered an Irish whiskey to remind him of her, and was disappointed that the waiter brought him a Scotch; he asked for her picture and had it framed and hung it in "a place of honor" in his library.[29]

When Holmes's letters to Lady Castletown were discovered among Mark Howe's collection of Holmes materials in the 1980s by a former congressman and amateur historian, John S. Monagan, and excerpts from them published, they naturally caused a sensation over the secret "affair" of Mr. Justice Holmes.[30]

But while there was no denying his feelings for Clare went far beyond those for his other young women friends, to read them after

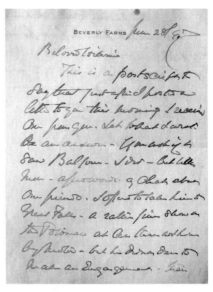

To "Beloved Hibernia," June 28, 1897

reading his letters to Ellen Curtis and Clara Stevens and Ethel Scott and Anna Codman and a half dozen others makes the difference seem more of degree than of kind. He wanted her love and attention and to feel she was opening her mind and soul to him, but he did not write to her as a real lover any more than he did to any of the others; he wrote of "kissing her hand" but never anything more, and bridled when she apparently teased him with a bit of sexual banter, complaining of her "blague," of her playing the usual game of the "war between man and woman and each to get as much as they can," of trivializing his desire for "the infinite" with her suggestion he cared only for "the finite"—"a nasty dig," he riposted. "You do me wrong." Even as he begged her not to spurn his "romantic feeling"—which it would "cut me to the heart to have you repudiate," he told her—at the very start he also made a point of telling her, "My life is in my wife and my work."[31]

There is good reason to think that Clare never took any of it as seriously as Holmes did, even as a romantic excursion. For one thing, she already had a lover, a fellow foxhunter and equestrian named Percy La Touche. His letters to her crackled with the rude possessiveness that only a man in a sexual relationship usually dares to use. Holmes was jealous when he heard about La Touche ("has he happily demised?" he inquired a few months later), but La Touche told Clare he really wanted to kill her Yankee admirer. "I don't know how much you will do or how far you will go and I am not happy," La Touche wrote her. He called her "a snake" in one letter, and roughly told her, "I have played for the highest stake for which ever man gambled." Holmes wrote of kissing her hand; La Touche rapturized about her breasts.[32]

In any case, Clare took her flirtation with Holmes lightly enough that she teased her husband with it, writing him about her mock-heartbreak a week after Holmes's departure at the end of August:

> The conservatory is really *very* nice now, with its fountain & comfy seats & sweet smells—& I am sure you will like it—though I am afraid you wont read to me erotic poetry—& make love to me generally as the surroundings decidedly demand!! My Yankee suited it exactly—& I mourn his departure more & more & dont see how anything is ever going to comfort me.[33]

There was no physical connotation to "make love": that was a Victorian way of saying whispering sweet nothings. The next line of Clare's letter to her husband was to ask whether he was getting his newspapers. Mostly she wrote about the troubles she had had those last few weeks of August organizing the village bazaar. "I am still disconsolate about my Yankee," she teased him a week later.[34]

Only a very few letters from Clare to Holmes survive; in one she expressed her unhappiness that he had presumed to begin his last letter to her "Dear Clare," and asked him not to do it again. "I *do* like to be given my name by you but not in that bold sort of way!" She asked him to "go back to the old 'Hibernia' or to no name at all."[35]

━━━━━━━━

FOR ALL HIS anxiety over her feelings for him, his love for her invigorated him with a renewed zest for everything in life that fall of 1896 upon his return home. An invitation to deliver an address to Boston University's law school was a chance again to make a major statement

about his ideas of the law, and he poured himself into the task with an
intellectual vigor unequaled since *The Common Law.*

As he organized his thoughts, one recent case was very much on
his mind. Sitting as single justice in the Boston equity session in the
spring of 1895, Holmes had heard a request by the owner of a furniture factory for an injunction against a group of striking upholstery
workers. The owner, Frederick Vegelahn, had refused a demand for
higher wages and fired the group's leader, George Guntner. In response,
the workers called for a boycott of the business by other tradesmen
and began picketing the factory, pressuring replacement workers not to
cross their lines.

Holmes issued an injunction against physical intimidation by the
strikers, but refused Vegelahn's request to halt the picketing altogether:
as long as they refrained from violence or threat of bodily harm, they
were free to use persuasion or social pressure to achieve their aims.[36]

Vegelahn appealed, and on October 26, 1896, the full court reversed
Holmes's decision, issuing a sweeping injunction barring picketing and
persuasion of any kind that interfered with the employer's "right to
engage all persons who are willing to work for him, at such prices as
may be mutually agreed upon."[37]

This time Holmes wrote a lengthy dissent, laying out his strongest
case yet that whenever judges considered questions like this, "The true
grounds of decision are considerations of policy and of social advantage, and it is vain to suppose that solutions can be attained merely by
logic and the general propositions of law which nobody disputes. Propositions as to public policy rarely are unanimously accepted, and still
more rarely, if ever, are capable of unanswerable proof."[38]

It was a theme he had begun to develop in his 1894 article "Privilege, Malice, and Intent," and which would form the impassioned core
of his dissent in *Vegelahn* and his upcoming lecture at Boston University. There were many instances, Holmes noted, in which the law
carved out a privilege for intentional infliction of damage "because it
regards it as justified" on policy grounds. The classic illustration was
economic competition. "It has been the law for centuries that a man
may set up a business in a country town too small to support more than

one, although he expects and intends thereby to ruin some one already there, and succeeds in his intent," he wrote in his dissent in *Vegelahn*. "The reason, of course, is that the doctrine generally has been accepted that free competition is worth more to society than it costs, and that on this ground the infliction of the damage is privileged."[39]

But that, like almost all instances of privilege in the law, reflected a policy choice, a fact judges could disguise only by resorting to circular reasoning. "Questions of policy are legislative questions, and judges are shy of reasoning from such grounds," Holmes observed in "Privilege, Malice, and Intent." "Therefore, decisions for or against the privilege, which really can stand only upon such grounds, often are presented as hollow deductions from empty general propositions . . . or else are put as if they themselves embodied a postulate of the law and admitted of no further deduction, as when it is said that, although there is temporal damage, there is no wrong; whereas, the very thing to be found out is whether there is a wrong or not."[40]

Moreover, the conflict between labor and management was every bit as much economic competition as the competition between rival businesses, and it was hard to see why one should be privileged and not the other, he wrote in his dissent in *Vegelahn*:

> I have seen the suggestion made that the conflict between employ-ers and employed is not competition. But I venture to assume that none of my brethren would rely on that suggestion. If the policy on which our law is founded is too narrowly expressed in the term free competition, we may substitute free struggle for life. Certainly the policy is not limited to struggles between persons of the same class competing for the same end. . . .
>
> One of the eternal conflicts out of which life is made up is that between the effort of every man to get the most he can for his ser-vices, and that of society, disguised under the name of capital, to get his services for the least possible return. Combination on the one side is patent and powerful. Combination on the other is the necessary and desirable counterpart, if the battle is to be carried on in a fair and equal way.[41]

Previously Holmes had suggested that the law generally absorbed through gradual and unconscious evolution the necessities of the times. But now he was advancing a much bolder idea: that judges had a duty to make thinking about social need an *explicit* part of their decisions. Avoiding the policy questions did not make judges impartial: it only disguised their prejudices.

In his talk to the students at Boston University on January 8, 1897, he laid out the entire argument. Entitled "The Path of the Law," the lecture reflected the culmination of his thinking about the purpose of law in society and the role of judges.

There is a concealed, half conscious battle on the question of legislative policy, and if any one thinks that it can be settled deductively, or once for all, I only can say that I think he is theoretically wrong. . . .

I think that the judges themselves have failed adequately to recognize their duty of weighing considerations of social advantage. The duty is inevitable, and the result of the often proclaimed judicial aversion to deal with such considerations is simply to leave the very ground and foundation of judgments inarticulate, and often unconscious.[42]

He made two other points that were equally intended to rattle the complacency of his listeners. The first was what would become his subsequently oft-repeated insistence that general propositions do not decide concrete cases. Later, sitting on the U.S. Supreme Court, Holmes would like to needle his fellow justices in conference by saying, "I will admit any general proposition you like and decide the case either way." But the law, as he observed in "The Path of the Law," is fundamentally empirical, not theoretical: "The logical method and form flatter that longing for certainty and for repose which is in every human mind. But certainty generally is illusion, and repose is not the destiny of man."[43]

Even in a narrow sense, the process of formulating general rules in the law was really only as valuable as the data the generalization was based upon. "College boys and girls read clever or brilliant generalizations and then think they are on a level with the man who made them," he observed to one correspondent. "Whereas the worth of a generalization is only as a shorthand statement of particulars—and one's knowledge of the generalization is measured by one's knowledge of the particulars, largely if not wholly." Or, as he often liked to put it, "I always say that the chief end of man is to form general propositions—adding that no general proposition is worth a damn."[44]

In "The Path of the Law," Holmes offered his so-called prediction theory of the law, which boiled down this legal empiricism to a simple test: the law, he proposed, is really nothing more than a prophecy of how courts will rule. It was easy to take that as cynicism. The humorist Ambrose Bierce, in his famously cynical *Devil's Dictionary*, might actually have had Holmes in mind when he defined *lawful* as, "Compatible with the will of a judge having jurisdiction." But Holmes's point was that the law *is* what it *does*; it is not a theoretical collection of axioms or moral principles, but a practical statement of where public force will be brought to bear, and that could only be derived from an examination of it in action.[45]

And the best way to understand *that*, he said—this was his other deliberately provocative point—was to regard the law as would a "bad man" who cares nothing about morals, but only wants to know what he can get away with. "A man may have as bad a heart as he chooses, if his conduct is within the rules," Holmes had pointed out in *The Common Law*. And likewise, a legal right is nothing more or less than a description of how far the aid of public force will be given a man in support of a claim he may assert—"and this right is the same whether his claim is founded in righteousness or iniquity."[46]

He elaborated on the idea in "The Path of the Law." Holmes underscored that in putting forward his hypothetical "bad man," he was *not* suggesting that the law does not reflect and embody the moral growth of civilization. But it was a good way to get to "a business-like understanding of the matter," free from sentiment and self-righteous pieties:

A man who cares nothing for an ethical rule which is believed and practised by his neighbors is likely nevertheless to care a good deal to avoid being made to pay money, and will want to keep out of jail if he can.

I take it for granted that no hearer of mine will misinterpret what I have to say as the language of cynicism. The law is the witness and external deposit of our moral life. Its history is the history of the moral development of the race. The practice of it, in spite of popular jests, tends to make good citizens and good men. When I emphasize the difference between law and morals I do so with reference to a single end, that of learning and understanding the law.[47]

Three days after the lecture he wrote Clare,

On Friday I fired off my long projected discourse—on the law— with unexpected success. I had so much to say that I read it in order to get it inside an hour—and to read instead of speaking is bad for the hearers—the room was crowded the air not too good—and I was preceded by more than an hour of prayer and discourse on the finance of the institution (a relatively new Law School) and summaries of the little glories achieved by graduates until I saw the listeners eyes begin to roll with poisoned slumber—and I started sadly enough—but to my great satisfaction I had them all wide awake pretty soon and kept them so.[48]

He did more than keep an audience full of law students awake. With "The Path of the Law," observed the legal historian Morton J. Horwitz, "Holmes pushed American legal thought into the twentieth century." It was in retrospect a defining moment when belief in the law as independent from politics and separate from social reality—the idea that the law was "discovered," not made—was dealt the stunning blow from which it never recovered, and the Legal Realist movement born. His talk, published later that year in the *Harvard Law Review*, came just a year before William James's first essay on pragmatism, in which James proposed that the only test of an idea is its "practical consequences." As Horwitz noted, Holmes was in that sense part of a deeper change in the American consciousness that renounced "theological and doctrinal modes of thought" that had dominated the nineteenth century.[49]

Holmes's decisions putting these ideas into action would be among his most lasting legacies as a judge on the Massachusetts high court. Making plain the clashing policy considerations that lay beneath a claim of wrong became a recurring theme in his judicial opinions in the late 1890s. "As in many cases, perhaps it might be said in all, two principles or social desiderata present themselves, each of which it would be desirable to carry out but for the other," he wrote in a case in which a flapping sheet on a freight car that was being unloaded frightened a passing horse. "It is desirable that as far as possible people should be able to drive in the streets without their horses being frightened. It also is desirable that the owners of land should be free to make profitable and otherwise innocent use of it. . . . A line has to be drawn to separate the domains of the irreconcilable desires. Such a line cannot be drawn in general terms."[50]

When the American Waltham Watch Company sued a competitor for placing the word "Waltham" on its watches, Holmes wrote a decision that became classic in the law of trademarks and unfair competition: "In cases of this sort, as in so many others, what ultimately is to be worked out is a point of line between conflicting claims, each of which has meritorious grounds and would be extended further were it not for the other. It is desirable that the plaintiff should not lose custom by reason of the public mistaking another manufacturer for it. It is desirable that the defendant should be free to manufacture watches at Waltham, and to tell the world that it does so." Emphasizing again that it is not possible to weigh such competing claims "by abstractions or general propositions," Holmes found for the plaintiffs on evidence that the name Waltham had come to be associated in the public mind with its particular watches.[51]

"Between 1910 to 1920 in virtually all fields of law a balancing test overthrew the earlier system of legal reasoning based on logical deduction from general premises," Horwitz observed, "marking the demise of the late-nineteenth-century system of legal formalism." More than any other figure, Holmes provided "the intellectual ammunition" for this revolution in legal thought.[52]

―――――

WHEN HOLMES'S DISSENT in *Vegelahn* v. *Guntner* was published in the fall of 1896, he told a Boston lawyer friend, Arthur D. Hill, "I have just handed down an opinion which has shut off the possibility of judicial promotion." When the issue of strikes and boycotts came up again a few years later in a case that turned on efforts by a union to enforce a closed shop, Holmes was again the lone dissenter; in *Plant* v. *Woods* he repeated his conclusion that it is "lawful for a body of workmen to try by combination to get more than they now are getting"—even as he took pains this time to add that he thought it "pure phantasy" that strikes would do much to achieve that end.[53]

He confided to Clare that while it would be nice to sit on the U.S. Supreme Court and know "that my word was always the last," politics and chance counted for so much in such appointments that "a man w[oul]d be a donkey who allowed himself to bother about such things." He was also aware that his personality, as much as his perceived political sympathy for unions and strikers, were against him: "Many I dare say, because I have a light way, and like to talk to women, find it harder to suppose me a serious person than if I looked august, wore black, and thought only about business and going to church," he wrote to Clare.[54]

On Memorial Day that spring of 1897 he got out his old Civil War uniform to be present at the unveiling on the Boston Common of the bronze memorial to Colonel Shaw and the Fifty-fourth Regiment created by the sculptor Augustus Saint-Gaudens. "It stirred old memories, I can tell you," he told Clare. He proudly reported that "unlike most of the fighters," he was still able to button his uniform around his waist. But when he got his sword out he found the belt had crumbled away and the sword rusted—"more than thirty years nearly 35 years since I laid it by as a relic because it was covered with blood from my last wound." William James was one of the speakers, but Holmes thought

Dedication of the Shaw Memorial on Boston Common, 1897

"the chap that just obliterated all his predecessors in the speaking was a black man." It was Booker T. Washington.[55]

That summer, he and Fanny went by horse and carriage to Windsor, Vermont, for the wedding of his nephew, Edward Jackson Holmes Jr. He afterward wrote Mrs. Gray a long lyrical description of what he called "one of the most enchanting times we ever had in our lives":

> We had a Yankee driver who has driven us for years—with horses from his stable so that we were not bothered with that responsibility—and personally to me delightful Yankee equality with great tact. . . .
>
> There was room also for a lunch basket out of which Mrs. Holmes (who bossed the whole show with a forethought which never went wrong) produced at psychologic moments all manner of comforting things—from pate de foie gras to chewing gum! The latter not a bad thing by the way in the hot and dusty part of a drive, low as it sounds. We saw all manner of beautiful scenery, including a show of laurel such as I never dreamed of, though I knew it of old in Pittsfield. The hotels and inns were always com-

fortable and sometimes excellent—we dodged the heat by traveling early and late and dined and snoozed and read about polar
regions and played solitaire during the midday hours. We slipped in
between showers so that we never got wet, we talked with Yankee
landlords and exchanged experiences with old soldiers whom we
found scattered about in the hills after having seen the world and a
good deal of this continent.

We took our hand in the wedding and came back by a different
route seeing something of the enchanting part of the Connecticut
valley with its enriching hints of Indian warfare here and there.

Oh it was adorable.[56]

It was a glorious break from the relentless pace of his life, but he
could never find satisfaction very long without having his time filled
by some activity. He reported his satisfaction in making progress with
his bicycling and had ordered his own bike, happily bragging that he
had survived being shot over the handlebars a number of times: "It is
no slight thing for an old gentleman to learn that he can tumble off
and not break. I was as pleased as a boy at the discovery. It is curious
what glee such a physical outlet gives one," he wrote to Mrs. Gray.
He rode about five miles each afternoon in the summers, reveling also
in the "great democratic bond" the recreation fostered. "I find myself
consulting with laboring men who also are learning on most brotherly
terms—and another is my teacher guide philos. & friend."[57]

In the winter of 1898 he began thinking of traveling to London the
coming summer to see Clare again. Tormented by Clare's alternating
hints of deeper feeling for him with her "light hardhearted" tone of "blag-
ging" that left him "deeply uncomfortable"; fidgeting over his own state
of health; guilty about leaving Fanny on her own, he changed his mind
a half dozen times. "I keep saying to myself Oh if I *should* see her this
summer—my wife rather eggs me on to go. It is pure generosity on her
part because she thinks I shall enjoy it etc.," he wrote to Clare in January.[58]

In March, after hearing from her that she might not be in London
for the summer, he sent her a fevered reply,

My dear lady I am dreadfully cast down by your letter telling me that everything is less certain. If it is not certain that I shall see you it is not certain that I shall even try to come to England ... if you are not there what is to hinder my seeing you somewhere in England or in Ireland. Please answer at once if you have the least scrap of doubting our meeting somewhere, if I come over—because the solid earth fairly reeled under me as I read your letter on the bench this morning.[59]

The looming possibility of America's going to war with Spain, and not being sure if he would be excused from the judges' final conference in June, added to his uncertainty. "England this summer seems more doubtful and everything is shaky except my affection," he wrote on April 1.[60]

On April 15 he reserved a stateroom on the Cunard line's *Umbria*. On June 6 he wrote her, "I am dreadfully shaky about going over this year." The next day he wrote again, reversing course: "Today it looks more as if I should come. The vicissitudes I go through with regard to the chances of seeing you next summer are really very wearing." Two days later he wrote *again*, "I am nigh insane with the question of coming to England. I had made up my mind that I ought to put it off and my wife now urges me to and threatens horrid results to me if I do not. I fear I shall be a selfish pig if I do, and I don't know. . . . Life seems short and its chances few."[61]

Two weeks later he canceled his stateroom reservation, then immediately changed his mind and bought his ticket. "Mrs. Holmes made up her mind that I needed the change, and I deferred, if I did not come round, to her way of thinking," he weakly explained to Mrs. Gray. He wired Lady Castletown in London, "Just settled sail Umbria June twenty five." He signed it "Justice."[62]

In London he went for drives in hansom cabs with Mrs. Clifford and dined with Lord Castletown at his club, the Travellers, meeting him for the first time. Making his final arrangements to see Clare alone in Ireland had him again in a nervous dither. "To go to Ireland is a complete diplomatic lesson, in the correspondence for a stateroom—and for a sleeping berth—and the search on the train for your name in the window &c. . . ." he told his friend Lady Burghclere.[63]

As before at Doneraile he and Clare spent their days together in the conservatory or strolling in the garden and the lime walk, while the few other guests busied themselves with country pursuits.[64]

There was a new intensity in his letters to her afterward. "I am here in the kind of collapse that comes after nervous tension," he wrote to her on his arrival back at Beverly Farms in September. He had developed a painful condition during his stay, which he first thought was eczema, then gout, but which finally turned out to be shingles. It kept him up at nights; "an ignominious but painful disease . . . and my shoulder still aches and the small of my back does the like," he told Pollock three months later.[65]

He poured out his heart to Clare in letter after letter. "Oh my dear what joy it is to feel the inner chambers of one's soul open for the other to walk in and out at will. It was just beginning with you. Do not cut it off because of a little salt water." And just a few days later, "Do assure me that the pain of separation does not outweigh the joy of confidence and belief in the abiding."[66]

When she responded to one of his letters in early May of 1899 by telling him, "It is *impossible* to really keep in touch," he indignantly replied, "It is possible to be unchanged after 20 years—I care for you just as much as when we were together and with every year new little roots grow out and bind you tighter. You don't mean anything to the contrary of that I am pretty sure. For you are a faithful wretch. But I hate any suggestion of less nearness. Write and say that you are not taking back anything that you said when I was there."[67]

But the fact was that Holmes could never be more than a pleasant idea to her; her husband and Percy La Touche were real, and at hand. And whatever the complications of her marriage, its bonds ran deep. Her marriage in fact had been very much on her mind when she tried to brush Holmes away with her remark about the impossibility of their keeping in touch. April 23 was her twenty-fifth wedding anniversary, and that day she had written her husband a touching note of the genuine ties that held them together; she told him she had worn all day the engagement ring he had given her,

> and we have sentimentalised a lot about it all, I & the dogs—& they have sympathised thoroughly in my sorrow at your being away . . . bless you & thank you for all your loving kindness & forbearance during these many years which have not blunted our affection for each other much I think? & I know that I care for & love you more now than I did at the beginning when I hadn't yet learnt what a good true brave man you were.[68]

When Holmes then did not hear from her for several weeks, he finally wrote Lord Castletown. He answered on June 18. She and Percy La Touche had both taken falls from their horses while out riding in early May; Clare had been seriously hurt, bedridden for weeks with an injury that threatened the use of one eye. She was slowly recovering. "My wife . . . is much charmed by your letters," Lord Castletown assured him, "& hopes soon to be able to write herself."[69]

Later that year Lord Castletown left for South Africa to join the British campaign in the Boer War, and Clare followed when she was again able to travel; they remained abroad for nearly two years. Holmes would see Clare again in Ireland in 1901, 1903, 1907, and 1913, and briefly in London in 1909 when he traveled to Oxford to receive an honorary degree. None of Holmes's letters to her from 1900 to 1911 survive. But there is a hint of the inevitable cooling that time and distance wrought in a letter he dashed off to Mrs. Gray at the end of his 1901 visit that sounded very much like a man quickly seeking another woman's company as consolation for the one who had just disappointed him. He was then sixty, Clare forty-eight. He saw her every few days during his five weeks in London, then stayed at Doneraile from August 9 to 23. "I have had the most complete time of all my times," he wrote Nina on his return to Beverly Farms. "But nothing impressed me so much as a kind of resentment which I felt in the end at continuing the pursuits of pleasure. . . . I am gladder than ever before to be an American, and I am happy to be back or shall be as soon as I see you."[70]

━━━━━━

IN LATE JULY 1899 Holmes learned from a newspaper reporter that the governor had just nominated him to succeed Chief Justice Field, who had died on the fifteenth of the month.[71] It was news to him, but no real surprise. Field had been ailing for months and in his absence Holmes had been acting chief and was the obvious person to assume the position.

As chief justice he was relieved of circuit duty, but if anything he drove himself harder than ever. "I am mad with work and high pressure and the consequence is that I fairly need discourse with you," he wrote to Mrs. Curtis. "We are smashing through the docket and everything is going with a whiz."[72]

He loved "bossing the show," he said. One small change he ordered was for the justices to resume wearing robes, a practice they had abandoned in 1792 when the Massachusetts chief justice, incensed over the appointment of a judge he considered uncouth and unqualified, refused to wear his robe so all the others would be forced to follow suit, and thus deprive the new appointee of the trappings of dignity he felt he did not deserve. In response to a petition by the bar, Holmes decided the time had come to bring judicial attire back. (The first day, the judges were struggling to tie their robes properly when the minister who was to read the prayer for the opening session of the court entered the room. "Ah, an expert!" Holmes welcomed him, and the clergyman proceeded to show the bewildered justices how it was done.)[73]

In February 1902, Associate Justice Horace Gray of the U.S. Supreme Court, who had been ailing for some months, suffered a stroke. Though he did not immediately resign his seat, the news set off a wave of behind the scenes political maneuvering over his replacement. Custom dictated the seat would be filled by another man from New England, most likely from Massachusetts, as was Gray. "I am as out of politics as it is possible to be—so much so that if I were willing instead of profoundly unwilling to pull wires for myself in case Gray resigns I hardly should know what to do," Holmes wrote to Mrs. Stevens.[74]

That was not entirely true. One of Massachusetts's senators was Holmes's old friend Henry Cabot Lodge, whom he had known since Lodge was a boy, and who was a close adviser to President Theodore Roosevelt. Lodge was already lobbying hard for Holmes's appointment. But the rule of "senatorial courtesy" dictated that judicial appointments have the support of both senators of the state the candidate was from, and Massachusetts's other senator was George Frisbie Hoar, a much older man who was definitely not well disposed to Holmes. Hoar thought his lawyer nephew was the perfect candidate for the job—and that in any case Judge Holmes was *not*. "His accomplishments are literary and social," Hoar sniffed to Lodge, "not judicial. In his opinions he runs to subtleties and refinements, and no decision of his makes a great landmark in jurisprudence."[75]

Through the summer Hoar kept up a barrage of anti-Holmes barbs. "I always talk with lawyers, when I meet them about the State, about the Court," he wrote Lodge again two weeks later. "I never heard anybody speak of Judge Holmes as an able judge. He is universally regarded as a man of pleasant personal address . . . but without strength, and without grasp of general principles." "The whole thing is an awful blunder," he insisted.[76]

Boston's conservative business community—the men who had regarded Holmes as "dangerous" for his labor decisions—stuck in some quiet knives of their own. Eben S. Draper, a leading textile manufacturer, wrote Lodge to warn that the bar considered Holmes "erratic, and that he is not a safe man for such an important position." But Roosevelt liked what he had seen about Holmes: he was a romantic who shared his view that "life is a great adventure"; his "Soldier's Faith" speech spoke TR's language; and, as Lodge was quick to assure the president, he was a loyal Republican.[77]

Roosevelt also considered Holmes's labor decisions a strong point in his favor: "The ablest lawyers and greatest judges are men whose past has naturally brought them into close relationship with the wealthiest and most powerful clients," the president wrote Lodge, "and I am glad when I can find a judge who has been able to preserve his aloofness of mind so as to keep his broad humanity of feeling and his sympathy for the class from which he has not drawn his clients."[78]

But he did want reassurance on one point. The Court had recently ruled 5–4 to uphold a tariff on sugar and tobacco imported from Puerto Rico and the Philippines, American possessions. Justice Gray had been one of the slender majority. Protective tariffs were a bedrock Republican principle, and other similar cases were likely to come up again. "Now I should like to know that Judge Holmes was in entire sympathy with our views . . . before I would feel justified in appointing him," Roosevelt told Lodge.[79]

Roosevelt arranged for Holmes to meet him secretly at his Long Island summer home, Sagamore Hill, on July 25. When Holmes arrived he found the president was out for the day on his yacht—so "dodged the reporters," who "were not on the lookout"—and was left on his own to entertain the Roosevelt children at dinner with stories of his Civil War adventures. ("Gathered afterwards that I gave satisfaction.") A telegram then arrived that the president was fogged in and would not be back until the next day. The next morning he saw Roosevelt at nine. "I had a little talk with him in which he said just the right things and impressed me far more than I had expected and then I bolted so as not to be seen."[80] The appointment was announced August 11.

The Senate was in recess until December, and Roosevelt had at first wanted to give Holmes a recess appointment so he could take his seat immediately. But knowing of Hoar's opposition, Holmes was uneasy about giving up his place in Massachusetts without the assurance of the Senate's confirmation, and asked Roosevelt to just submit his name to the Senate and wait for December. The president said he would consult Lodge about the recess appointment, but reassured him he had nothing to fear:

My dear Judge:
    I have your letter of the 17th. Pettigrew said that South Caro-
lina was too small for an independent republic and too large for
a lunatic asylum. The Senate is not too large for a lunatic asylum,

and if there is any opposition whatsoever to your confirmation, I shall certainly feel that it fulfills all the conditions of one. Seriously, I do not for one moment believe that a single vote will be cast against your confirmation. I have never known a nomination to be better received.[81]

Meanwhile, Holmes's Massachusetts colleague Marcus Knowlton, desperately eager for the chief justice position and knowing that the current governor would appoint him but the next one might not, started to ominously warn Holmes that he *must* resign immediately, no matter what: to do otherwise would be a grave insult to the Senate. Holmes was amused by the transparency of Knowlton's motives, but asked Roosevelt what to do; Roosevelt wrote two days later to report that Lodge had agreed there was no necessity for a recess appointment, and "meanwhile, I strongly feel that you should continue as Chief Justice of Massachusetts."[82]

On December 4, 1902, he was unanimously confirmed, and was on his way to a new life in Washington, on the eve of his sixty-second birthday.

CHAPTER 10

"So Great and So Different"

It was a realization of ambition but it was also the closing of a chapter. As Holmes had prepared for the move to Washington that fall, he sank into a melancholy that surprised him for a while. "The principal and rather absurd thing is the depth of gloom in which I was plunged for a time on what so far has been a triumph," he told Clara Stevens. To John Gray he confided that "the sense that this is the last quarter of the race" weighed on his spirits.[1]

Paying his farewells and cleaning out the house reminded him also how deeply rooted he was to the town of his birth. He wrote to Clara Stevens later that fall,

> Lord what a job it is to empty a single desk. I burned some papers the other day that had been a shrinking dread for 25 years—more. Some of my earliest law experiments and I just simply feared and loathed looking at them . . . destroyed the whole boodle—pouf— one feels better—and yet part of one's past disappears—one's roots grow in the dead accumulations. And when you have purged your home of everything that is not vital now you feel like a cut flower.

He added: "How many years have we known each other. How long is it since I paid you a visit I never made to Emerson."[2]

He was also painfully sensitive about what the newspapers were saying about the appointment. Though he was bitterly stung by a few columns that called him "more brilliant than sound," or, as the *New York Evening Post* had archly commented, "more of a 'literary feller' than one often finds on the bench," the praise if anything annoyed him more. "They make my nomination a popular success but they have the flabbiness of American ignorance," he complained to Pollock. "It makes one sick when he has broken his heart in trying to make every word living and real to see a lot of duffers, generally I think not even lawyers, talking with the sanctity of print in a way that discloses to the knowing eye that literally they don't know anything about it."[3]

Most of the positive comment focused on his siding with labor in the *Vegelahn* case—yet without "the slightest discrimination or notion, favorable or unfavorable, of what my work had amounted to," Holmes recalled to Einstein twenty-five years later, when it obviously still rankled.[4]

It was a deeper nerve this all had touched, because for all of his philosophical belief in work as an end in itself, he had been thinking a lot about what he had actually accomplished, and had his doubts. Two years before, at a dinner given him by the Bar Association of Boston the night before his fifty-ninth birthday, in March 1900, he had grown wistful looking back on how quickly the years had gone by and wondering "what is there to show" for "this half lifetime" he had spent on the bench:

> I look into my book in which I keep a docket of the decisions of the full court which fall to me to write, and find about a thousand cases. A thousand cases, many of them upon trifling or transitory matters, to represent nearly half a lifetime! A thousand cases, when one would have liked to study to the bottom and to say his say on every question which the law ever has presented, and then to go on and invent new problems which should be the test of doctrine, and then to generalize it all and write it in continuous, logical, philosophic exposition, setting forth the whole corpus with its roots in history and its justifications of expedience real or supposed!
>
> Alas, gentlemen, that is life. . . . We cannot live our dreams. We are lucky enough if we can give a sample of our best, and if in our hearts we can feel that it has been nobly done.[5]

Now, with the end of his career on the Supreme Judicial Court definitely in sight, he had a feeling of facing "a day of judgment on how I have done my work so far," he told John Gray. "Of course for purposes of action and courage one goes ahead on his own will, whatever may be said. But for purposes of joy one needs recognition—intelligent and to the point. One is always so near to despair that it does not take much to bring in the black humor."[6]

But as the time finally approached, courage began to win out. "Those who run hardest probably have the least satisfaction with themselves, but they find, I am sure, that they know most of the joy of life when at top speed," he proclaimed in a speech that fall in Chicago, where he had been invited to join in the dedication of the Northwestern University Law School. And at the banquet the Middlesex Bar Association gave him on the eve of his Senate confirmation in December, he concluded his remarks of thanks with a rhetorical flourish full of images of battle, of making ready to storm the enemy earthworks, climaxing with the call, "Bugler, blow the charge!"[7]

Holmes's colleagues sometimes thought he talked about the Civil War just a bit too often, and one young Boston lawyer who was at the banquet, Dixon Weston, sent his cousin—Chief Justice Melville W. Fuller—an account of Holmes's speech, with the amused warning, "There is about to be a charge upon your Court."[8]

It turned out to be a more serious prediction than either realized.

═══════════

HOLMES HAD BEEN to Washington just once since the end of the Civil War, when he had argued his case before the Supreme Court in 1878. He reminisced to his Boston colleagues at their farewell banquet, "The capital, with its asphalt pavements, is not quite unknown to me. But my notion of Washington still is the notion of the Washington of war times, where mule teams sank to their knees in mud, where at every other door one saw signs bearing the words 'Embalming the Dead,' with an occasional alleviation in the form of 'Sample room in the rear.'"[9]

Washington had filled out the monumental framework of streets, squares, and broad diagonally crossing avenues of Pierre L'Enfant's original plan, but it was still "a small, gangling southern city," as Dean Acheson recalled it in those early years of the century. Washington's population at the turn of the century was 278,000, almost exactly half that of Boston's. Its streets were uncrowded with traffic, and the broad sidewalks of Connecticut Avenue leading from the White House to the fashionable residential district toward Dupont Circle were twice their present-day width, shaded by a double row of sycamore trees. Throughout the city flowering magnolias abounded.[10]

Where the Mall now stands was a chain of public parks, laid out in the naturalistic style. The largest and most picturesque was the forest-like grounds of the Smithsonian Institution between Seventh and Twelfth Streets, a glade of winding footpaths and drives that followed gentle hills under the shade of magnificent chestnuts, in the days before the blight eliminated that stately epitome of American parklands and woodlands. Potomac Park, formed from a massive landfill of the swampy banks of the river where the Lincoln Memorial stands today, was just starting to be landscaped under a beautification plan approved by Congress. Along Rock Creek, which stretched from the African American shanties and industrial areas of Georgetown into wilder parts to the north and west, the National Zoological Park had opened just a few years earlier—its grounds designed by the preeminent landscape architect Frederick Law Olmsted—and miles of quiet bridle trails penetrated the untamed woods of the adjacent park, which were filled each spring with carpets of wildflowers.

The whole city seemed bright and fresh, recalled Francis Biddle, a marked contrast to the dirty streets of his native Philadelphia. The pace of life was distinctly slow, southern, and "feminine in its charm." The Shoreham Hotel, at Fifteenth and H streets, was a "period piece of southern hostelry," Acheson fondly remembered, with a "serene dining room decorated in white with mirrors and chandeliers," where Washington's power brokers took their leisurely luncheon every day.[11]

The day Holmes arrived in Washington he was met at the train station by "an elderly colored man," as Holmes later related his arrival, who informed him that he had been his predecessor Mr. Justice Gray's messenger, and would now perform the same service for him.[12]

The Court's messengers were a venerable institution, as well as a vivid reminder of the capital's irredeemable Southern ways. All of the messengers were African American men who held the job for life; some had inherited their position from a father or uncle before them. The messengers did not just handle the justices' mail and deliver sensitive documents, such as proofs of draft opinions, but performed any menial services the justice required—chauffeur, valet, cook, barber, waiter—or for that matter did not require. They were actually still often referred to as "body-servants," and for justices unused to such a quaintly feudal Southern institution, it came as something of a shock. "My body-servant is the most annoying thing I have experienced," a justice from Ohio remarked in the 1880s. "The fellow is the first man I see in the morning and the last man I see at night. He forces his way into my bedroom in the morning and orders me down to breakfast, taking my order himself to the cook. I cannot get rid of him in any way. He haunts me all the time. I try to think of places to send him, but he is back again as quick as lightning. That fellow will be the death of me. I have this satisfaction, however; the other justices are tortured in the same way."[13]

Despite the servile nature of the duties, the positions offered pay and security far beyond what most African American workers at the time could expect; the salary was about $1,000 a year, six times what an African American laborer made then. And in a world full of daily indignity for men of color, the position was one of stature and respect. When Holmes attended the funeral of his first messenger, John Craig, a few years later, the pastor of the Metropolitan A.M.E. Church, after pronouncing the eulogy, invited "The gentlemen of the Supreme Court" to rise and be recognized. As the justice was about to get to his feet, he saw that all the men standing were Craig's fellow messengers.[14]

The Court in those days met in the old Senate chamber of the Capitol; it would not be until 1935 that it finally moved into a building of its own. The chamber was austere but dignified, a semicircular half-domed room forty-five feet wide with a mahogany screen and a colonnade of marble Ionic columns forming the straight wall behind the judges' elevated bench and a line of marble pilasters along the curving wall with busts of the former chief justices between. The floor was carpeted in soft brown and the benches for the public cushioned in red velvet.

The dignity was sometimes of the genteel shabby kind, as upkeep did not always have a high priority; only when the carpet was reduced to threads was it finally replaced, and then in exactly the same brown hue as the original. The dim lighting provided by three tiny windows above the screen made one reporter think of a parlor more than a courtroom, while the "imperfect" heating and ventilation left parts of the room cold and other parts hot and the "air in any part has only remote relationship to the fresh breeze which you may have been enjoying if you have walked up Capitol Hill," the reporter observed. "I wonder that the Judges have endured it as long as they have."[15]

Still, it was a vast improvement over the previous home of the Court, which was in the Capitol basement in a room that reminded one reporter of a "potato hole," lacking even a robing room for the justices, which offered the daily spectacle of the justices filing in and taking their robes in turn from a peg along the wall, and donning their judicial dress in full view of the lawyers and public. With their courtroom in the old Senate chamber the judges had a robing room across the hall, which allowed for a more dignified entrance through a roped-off passageway between the assembled spectators in the corridor.[16]

The disadvantages of the Court's location in the Capitol had a number of consequences that had become so routine as to go unnoticed until circumstances forced attention on them. Notably, there was no space for offices for the justices, all of whom accordingly worked from home. The Court provided each a $2,000 allowance for furniture and a set of law books—which, however, were often so dilapidated and incomplete as to be useless.[17]

The Court convened at noon each day that it was in session, with a break from two to two-thirty, then resumed until four-thirty. The judges had no real facilities for eating lunch, which was delivered to the courtroom by their messengers every day and quickly consumed during the half-hour recess. That in itself was a major innovation reluctantly introduced by Chief Justice Fuller—who "hated to change anything," Holmes said—just before Holmes's time: previously the Court

The old Supreme Court chamber

met without break from noon to four, and the judges took turns, two at a time, ducking behind the screen to the rear of the chief justice's chair to eat their hasty meal, "clashing their knives and forks" as the lawyers' arguments went on out front. Holmes had his meal carried to the Court from his home or a restaurant in an old Civil War–era painted ammunition tin, which he used as his lunchbox for his entire time on the Court.[18]

The Court's library and its conference room, where the justices met each Saturday morning for their deliberations, were even more inconvenient, small, cluttered, ill-ventilated rooms in the Capitol basement. During long conferences, Justice Charles Evans Hughes remembered, "the room became overheated and the air foul . . . not conducive to good humor." He added, "I suppose that no high court in the country had fewer conveniences."[19]

Nonetheless the old courtroom was loved by many. "Isn't a beauty," Holmes told Mark Howe in 1933. "I wouldn't want to sit anywhere else," he said, and expressed no regret he would never have the chance to occupy the new Supreme Court building. Frankfurter later said he thought it was "almost a desecration of tradition" for the Court to forsake its familiar room for the new "marble palace" a block away. There was also a worry that the Court had lost some of its connection with the life of the nation when the justices were no longer seen walking the corridors of the Capitol, brushing elbows with the hordes of visiting tourists each spring, as did the senators and congressmen.[20]

The plainness of the old courtroom, with its low bench and close proximity of judges and counsel, Dean Acheson thought, "combined dignity with true republican simplicity." An observer at the time described the questioning of counsel by the justices in that intimate setting as "more like a confidential conversation" than the inquisitorial ordeal it sometimes seemed to terrified lawyers appearing before the high court for the first time.[21]

TAKING NO CHANCES—and getting in a small humorous dig at his impatient successor Knowlton—Holmes waited until literally the last minute to give up his old job. As he strode forward through the Supreme Court chambers to take the oath of office on Monday, December 8, 1902, he handed the Court's reporter, Charles Butler, a telegram addressed to the governor of Massachusetts, and asked him if he would have the marshal of the Court forward it: noting that he could not very well be a justice of two courts at the same time, it officially informed the governor of his resignation as chief justice of Massachusetts.[22]

Two weeks later he wrote Mrs. Curtis in tearing high spirits, the gloom of the fall entirely vanished in the rush of new duties:

> I wish I could have a talk with you—this experience here has been so much more impressive than I dreamed. . . . My past work is a finished volume—the new is a beginning of life over again. I have not looked upon a woman save in the way of kindness. All my interest and energy have been taken up in this mighty panorama of cases from every part of our great empire involving great interests,

raising questions I never have heard of, argued by the strongest men the country can show or submitted for peremptory action on big records which you have to get the point of in half an hour.

I am glad to find that some of my brethren despaired when they first came here. I did for 48 hours—and I had a rheumatism and a horrid cold to emphasize the point, as I sat in a barren room of a hotel. But I am now in a temporary house—looking out on Lafayette Square—the White House just across the road—wonderfully convenient and sufficiently comfortable.

I have begun to get the hang of the work. I think I can do my share all right. I am better in health—and I begin to be cheerful. I wrote my first decision this last week and yesterday at 11 sent it to the printer. When I got home the proofs were waiting. I shall have nine copies of the corrected thing tomorrow and give them to the other gents to pick at. For the first time in my life I have had flashes of a sense of responsibility. You know that I always have said one should not have. One should think about the question—to feel responsibility is steam out of the boiler—egotism in disguise—but things here are so solemn and tremendous that the thought will break in at times.[23]

"You were right in predicting that the vague awe would wear off," he told her a few weeks later. "I don't see that the cases need such a very long time to write them in, as is imposed. I have touched off mine pretty quick—to the amusement of my brethren. I think they like me and my work—but everything is so diplomatic here that I wouldn't swear to anything. Anyhow I still am happy and glad that I tackled the great adventure."[24]

He was unsure at first how his practice of writing short opinions would go over. Many of the justices felt compelled to address all the points that had been raised by the attorneys in their briefs so that they would feel their arguments had been taken seriously. Holmes insisted it was necessary only to deal with the decisive crux of the case. "I don't believe in the long opinions which have been almost the rule here," he told Mrs. Gray a few weeks into the job. "I think that to state the case shortly and the ground of decision as concisely and delicately as you can is the real way. That is the English fashion and I think it civilized. Therefore I try each week when we are sitting to turn off my case, and to announce it the following Monday. I think it pleases the chief who as an executive officer likes to get work done."[25]

When the nine printed copies of the corrected proofs of an opinion were circulated, the justices indicated their approval or disapproval on their copy and sent it back to the author. The "returns," as they were called, often contained little more than a brief handwritten comment— "I concur" or "Fine" if the justice agreed, "I dissent" if they did not— though sometimes they made lengthier comments, raised questions, or suggested specific changes or marked edits directly on the proofs.

By the end of the first week of January, Holmes had already circulated three opinions and was pleased with the warm response he had received from the brethren. "As clear as a bell. Concur. E. D. W.," Justice Edward D. White wrote on his return of Holmes's first opinion. Justice Henry Billings Brown offered some praise that Holmes found particularly reassuring, given his untraditional belief in writing short and to the point: "I hope your opinion may call the attention of our brethren, including myself, to the value of brevity, in respect to which I think we are all sinners. H.B.B."[26]

Holmes's own returns to the other justices brimmed with his usual uninhibited high spirits, and were apt to include oddball slang, cornball pseudo-French, snatches of poetry, and self-deprecating wisecracks: "A sockdolager." "Yes—twice if I can get in two votes." "Wee Mussoo—I float in a fairy bark to the bight and serenely anchor there with you." "I am in it with both feet." "Yes, with humility. I now see what you have been about when I was giving parties their constitutional right to jaw while I slept." "Ye crags & Peaks, I'm with you once again." And once: "I dissent. 'Loan' is not a verb."[27]

His speed and brevity did cause problems when an unusually large number of petitions for rehearing were filed his first year, the lawyers in the cases refusing to believe the justices could possibly have given due consideration if a decision came back in just two or three weeks. "Such humbugs prevail!" Holmes fumed to Pollock. "If a man keeps a case six months it is supposed to be decided on 'great consideration.' It seems to me that intensity is the only thing. A day's impact is better than a month of dead pull."[28]

His satisfaction with his initial plunge made him only want to work faster. "I am in full blast here," he told Clara Stevens in January, 1903, and began peppering the chief justice with notes asking for additional cases to be assigned to him:

Dear Chief Justice

    I am on my last case barring the one you told me not to write until further notice . . .

    If you will give some of yours I will be grateful.

    P.S. I shall finish the last tomorrow.

Dear Chief Justice

    . . . If there are 2 more weeks—I can write almost any old thing that anyone will give me. A case doesn't generally take more than two days if it does that.[29]

He was so eager to take on additional assignments that once he offered to help out a fellow justice who was struggling with the opinion for the Court in a case Holmes had dissented to. Holmes ended up drafting the entire decision for him, one of the only times a justice wrote both majority and dissenting opinions in the same case.[30]

Fuller, who labored over his own writing, was plainly pleased to have such a zealous new colleague. Appointed chief justice by Grover Cleveland in 1888, Fuller had come to the Court with less experience in public life than anyone ever to occupy the position. He had never been a judge or held federal office. But he was a successful lawyer from Chicago, and a staunch Democrat, and Cleveland was looking for a candidate from Illinois for the usual reasons of geographic balance, and his first choice—Judge John Schofield of the Illinois Supreme Court—had declined the nomination because he did not want to raise his nine children in Washington. Newspapers called Fuller the most obscure man ever named to the position. His appointment, wrote a Harvard Law

School classmate, "was a genuine surprise to himself, to the profession and to the country at large."[31]

Fuller was so small a man that he had to have his chair elevated and a hassock placed under his feet to keep his legs from swinging in the air. "Oh, but there were giants on the Court in those days," Fuller had said, no doubt half in jest. But in fact a number of the senior associate justices were towering men, which accentuated their comical contrast in physical stature.[32]

No one thought Fuller's strength was in writing opinions, or even in setting a direction for the Court, though he had consistently joined the Court's majority in its increasingly reactionary and pro-business interpretation of the Constitution during his twenty-two years as chief justice. In 1895 the Court had ruled the income tax unconstitutional, and had so narrowly restricted Congress's power over interstate commerce as to invalidate virtually any efforts to regulate business or economic activity through federal legislation: only measures focused exclusively on the movement of goods across state lines could meet their new test of constitutionality. In 1897 the Fuller Court had likewise held most *state* laws regulating business unconstitutional, as a violation of the Fourteenth Amendment's guarantee that no state shall "deprive any person of life, liberty, or property without due process of law." And in *Plessy* v. *Ferguson*, the Court upheld state-imposed racial segregation, establishing the notorious "separate but equal" rule that would be the law of the land for more than half a century.

The most forceful and certainly the most colorful figure on the Court was John Marshall Harlan, whom Holmes described as not only the last of the tobacco-spitting judges but a "savage," though capable of tender-hearted gestures: on Holmes's birthday he placed a little bunch of violets at Holmes's place on the bench. Harlan had been appointed in 1877, the longest serving of any of the justices by more than a decade at the time Holmes joined the Court. A contemporary observer described his "grey eagle of a face, surmounted by a massive dome of a head." He had a booming voice, and "his was not the temper of a negotiator," said Attorney General George W. Wickersham, who argued many a case before him.[33]

The Fuller Court

As Holmes too would be known in his later years, Harlan was called "the great dissenter." A Kentuckian who had been a pro-slavery Unionist during the war, and who had opposed even Lincoln's reelection in 1864, Harlan had filed a powerful and impassioned dissent in *Plessy*, arguing that segregation was by its very nature a "badge of slavery" and a "brand of servitude and degradation" that the Thirteenth Amendment had put an end to, along with slavery itself. "The law regards man as man," he declared, "and takes no account of his surroundings or of his color when his civil rights as guaranteed by the supreme law of the land are involved. . . . The thin disguise of 'equal' accommodations . . . will not mislead any one, nor atone for the wrong this day done."

Announcing his dissent in the income tax case, Harlan had become so furious that he grew red in the face and banged on the bench, glowering at the chief justice. *The Nation* called it "the most violent political tirade ever heard in a court of last resort."[34]

"His is a simple nature, but a forcible intellect and a personality that it would be hard to replace—under superficial shortcomings a great engine—and a noble courage," Holmes wrote to Mrs. Curtis shortly after joining the Court. The two never got along, but Holmes would humorously deflect Harlan's assaults when discussions in conference grew heated by calling him "my lionhearted friend."[35]

Although Holmes at sixty-two was well past the average age for appointment to the Court, there were only two justices younger than him at that point. One, with whom he hit it off immediately, was Edward Douglass White, a Louisianan who had fought as a private in the Confederate army for two years, before being taken prisoner at the surrender of Port Hudson following Grant's capture of Vicksburg in 1863. White's father had been a governor of Louisiana and he himself had been a U.S. senator before being appointed to the Court in 1894.

White lived in a massive stone Victorian townhouse at 1721 Rhode Island Avenue, five blocks north of Holmes's rented house in Lafayette Square, and the two justices soon fell to walking home together each day. "A fertile mind and charming man," Holmes described him to Mrs. Gray. "White and I are getting to be pals, as we walk together. He is stout and goes slow and I get half frozen and if I peep he says it was on my account and soon we lapse back as before."[36]

The intellectual wattage of the rest of the Court was distinctly dimmer. Dean Acheson once asked Holmes what Justice Rufus W. Peckham, another key figure of the Fuller Court, had been like, intellectually. "Intellectually?" Holmes replied, in great puzzlement. "I never thought of him in that connection." Holmes later summarized Peckham's judicial temperament: "I used to say his major premise was God damn it, meaning thereby that emotional predilections somewhat governed him on social themes."[37]

Peckham had been the leading force on the Court in reading laissez-faire economics into the Constitution via the doctrine that the Fourteenth Amendment embodied the absolute protection of "liberty of contract"—which Peckham had extolled in one opinion as a right of man "endowed by his Creator."[38]

The other justices were so unremarkable that the authors of a comprehensive set of biographies of Supreme Court justices strained to pierce "the shroud of anonymity" that enfolded their lives and careers. The retirement of Justice George Shiras Jr. in 1903, they wrote, "attracted little notice, and his death even less, for Shiras appeared to have been an undistinguished justice."[39]

For all of his shortcomings as a jurist himself, Fuller was an able administrator of the Court, and well liked by his fellow justices. Along with White, the chief quickly became Holmes's closest friend among the brethren. Some saw opportunism in Holmes's cultivation of Fuller, but there was genuine regard and a simple warmth of feeling in Holmes's affection for his senior colleague, for all of their differences. Opposites in political affiliation, religious belief, and intellectual style, they nonetheless enjoyed a friendship, Fuller's biographer wrote, that was "one of the most notable in the history of the Court."[40]

When Fuller's wife died in 1904, Holmes visited him every Sunday morning to keep him company on what would otherwise be a lonely time of the week. "Poor gallant little man—he is hard hit by the death of his wife," Holmes told Mrs. Curtis, "and I think likes to have me come. . . . So I make it a rule to do it."[41]

Holmes always spoke with genuine admiration of Fuller's ability to get the business of the Court done "easily, swiftly, with the least possible friction, with imperturbable good-humor, and with a humor that relieved any tension with a laugh." It was Fuller who inaugurated the custom—still followed to this day—of all the justices shaking hands with one another every morning, as a way to defuse the tensions that arose from their inevitable disagreements.[42]

For Fuller's part, he was grateful for Holmes's reliability and readiness to tackle any assignment. Just before the Court's February recess, Fuller told his wife that, thanks to "The Nimble Holmes," they were likely to dispose of fifty cases at their next meeting—more than ever before.[43]

HOLMES'S VERY FIRST OPINION, one of two he delivered the first Monday of January 1903, was a shot across the bow.

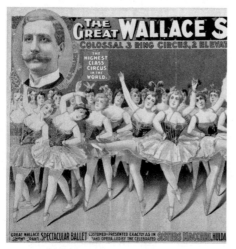

One of the circus posters in the copyright case *Bleistein v. Donaldson Lithographing* (1903)

Otis v. *Parker* had been brought as a challenge to a provision in California's constitution that banned buying stock on margin. It gave Holmes the chance to enunciate several of his favorite themes, as well as directly take on the Supreme Court's growing use of the Fourteenth Amendment to invalidate state laws. In writing the majority opinion for the Court he carried all of the justices with him but Peckham and David J. Brewer in asserting that there were limits to how far the Court might substitute its own judgment for that of legislators. "General propositions do not carry us far," he began.

> While the courts must exercise a judgment of their own, it by no means is true that every law is void which may seem to the judges who pass upon it excessive, unsuited to its ostensible end, or based upon conceptions of morality with which they disagree. Considerable latitude must be allowed for differences of view, as well as for possible peculiar conditions which this Court can know but imperfectly, if at all. Otherwise, a constitution, instead of embodying only relatively fundamental rules of right, as generally understood by all English-speaking communities, would become the partisan of a particular set of ethical or economical opinions, which by no means are held *semper ubique et ab omnibus.*
>
> Even if the provision before us should seem to us not to have been justified by the circumstances locally existing in California at the time when it was passed, it is shown by its adoption to have expressed a deep-seated conviction on the part of the people concerned as to what that policy required. Such a deep-seated conviction is entitled to great respect.

He took equal satisfaction in an opinion he delivered the first Monday of the following month, finding that a chromo-lithographed circus poster was entitled to the protection of the copyright laws. "It would be a dangerous undertaking for persons trained only to the law to constitute themselves final judges of the worth of pictorial illustrations," he wrote in his opinion, noting that "the taste of any public is not to be treated with contempt."[44]

Chicago Record-Herald,
February 3, 1903

He wrote Mrs. Curtis, "Last Monday I fired off a decision upholding the cause of low art and deciding that a poster for a circus representing decolletées and fat legged ballet girls could be copy-righted. Harlan, that stout old Kentuckian, not exactly an aesthete, dissented for high art. . . . The Chicago Record-Herald has a cartoon of me in my gown pointing with a stick at one of the numerous sketches of high kickers on the wall, with the legend, 'The Supreme Court says they are all right.' "[45]

———————

THE SOCIAL RULES of Washington in the early 1900s had aspects of a Renaissance court, transported to the Old South. The prominent members of Washington society who owed their standing to something other than position in government were mostly descendants of old Maryland and Virginia families, who had decidedly antebellum views of caste, as well as mostly unreconstructed views of the Confederacy. "The cave dwellers," Belknap and his young group of friends called them. Mrs. Ralph Cross Johnson, a wealthy widow who would be Holmes's neighbor and friend, living right across the street at 1735 I Street, never ceased thinking it amusing to call him "a damned Yankee." A highlight of the Washington social season was the Ladies' Southern Relief Society ball at the Willard Hotel, which raised funds for destitute Confederate veterans. The United States Marine Band provided the music and one thousand "Dixie Belles" and their consorts, the *Washington Post* reported, attended the annual event.[46]

"The types that strike me here with the most freshness are the snob and the Gracious Lady," Holmes told Mrs. Gray. "The snob needs no comment. The Gracious Lady is generally large . . . imperfectly educated—more or less rich—and plays at demi-princess who inhabits or ought to inhabit a demi-palace with some good and many poor things in it." He added to Richard Hale, "You couldn't get into a drawing room without tripping over a dozen of them."[47]

The ex-Confederate from Virginia he had met on the *Etruria* back in 1896, W. Gordon McCabe—who had indeed become "a friend for life," as he had predicted to Lady Castletown—offered a good specimen of the antebellum, if not antediluvian, attitudes he encountered in moving to Washington, so marked a contrast from democratic New England. "They all have a sort of stiff-lipped solemnity of adhesion to an ideal—their rather rudimentary notion of a gentleman," Holmes said of the Southerners he had met. He enjoyed talking to McCabe about books and listening to his stories, and occasionally gently challenged his romantic talk of the "graciousness" and "civilization" of "the Old South," but other times his patience was sorely tried. McCabe would start going on about this and that person from Richmond or Charleston, invariably referring to them as "gently born." Holmes would finally explode. "Did every even numbered house in Charleston and Richmond have a Van Dyke and every odd one a Rembrandt? Gently born! What a bawdy expression! Down in the South don't they have any whores and muzzle loaders?"—a muzzle loader being Civil War slang for a backward or crude person, the opposite of a rapid-firing breech loader.[48]

Official Washington maintained a strict protocol of who would invite whom to dinner when and on what day of the week the ranking ladies were to be "at home" to receive the homage of the other wives and any other callers. Monday was for the Supreme Court; Tuesday, members of Congress; Wednesday, the Cabinet; and so on through Saturday, for the diplomatic corps. Cards would be left—two of the husband's, one of the wife's, with their corners turned down—and ceremonial tea consumed.[49]

Holmes and his wife found themselves dining out nearly every night, but also were invited by the Roosevelts for informal family suppers and accompanied them to the theater several times. "They seem to like us there," he said.[50] The formal occasions, however, could be burdened to the point of deadliness by the rules of precedence that dictated who would sit where and in what order the guests would be received or take their leave—"a ridiculous bore insisted on in a rather snobbish way by some of them here," Holmes said. "If anybody is not put in his or her precise place he or she sulks."[51]

He got the full experience of Washington—and Southern—social mores at the annual official reception for the justices, which took place just a month after they arrived. He sent Mrs. Curtis a bemused account:

> I don't believe much more in my own canons of taste than I do in those of others—only they are mine and govern me. There was a reception at the White House, for the judges this week—and it is said that Southerners bolted because there was a negro present. I noticed that one of my colleagues gave offence to our Empress, Mrs. Chief Justice, by making his bow before she and her man did. He left for some reason at once and he is a Southerner. He is a pal of mine—but to me he played the naif. It seems as if everybody smiled and lied. I don't do that sort of thing—but am as my wife says, a child of nature. . . .
>
> You might say that this place does not make you feel proud of your country and yet I believe there is a vast amount of ability and public spirit here.[52]

He told other friends, "To see a common soul mistaking itself for uncommon because its body sits on the right of the hostess or walks first out of the room! I see several, or one poor little snob in particular, always trying to get ahead of his place & it makes me grin." "As I said to John Hay, if a man can write better opinions than I he may go out ahead of me and if he can't I don't care whether he does or not."[53]

His own stature in Washington, however, he found was still under his father's shadow. At one afternoon tea, the wife of a western congressman began telling him that his was a household name to her, and assuring him how much she had always enjoyed *Elsie Venner* and all of his other "splendid books." Holmes tried to explain that that was his father, not him; at which the woman even more insistently expostulated that he was being "entirely too modest" and should not hide his literary light under a bushel. Holmes wordlessly resumed drinking his punch. The *Washington Post* caught wind of the story and ran a brief account under the headline JUSTICE HOLMES SIGHED.[54]

—————

To THE AMAZEMENT of acquaintances who had known her reclusiveness in Boston, Fanny took to the part expected of the wife of a prominent official with aplomb and even apparent ease, going out to dinners and "rushing about madly returning calls on people she doesn't know." She kept a visiting book dutifully logging the hundreds of calls made and received throughout the season, and began pasting newspaper articles of Washington news and events in a scrapbook to keep up with the talk of the town.[55]

"Little as she cares for society she takes it like a little man and you would think to see her that she liked it thoroughly," Holmes reported to Mrs. Curtis in mid-January, adding a few weeks later,

> She has been a great success although she won't believe it. Mrs. Lodge said she wrote to Boston the other day that my wife was It. But she gets more pleasure from solitude than from society and I think that some day when we have paid back some of our social debts (the people keep an exact account here—another thing I don't admire) we shall drop out—or quiet down a good deal. But at present we are on the top of the wave.[56]

Agnes Meyer, who was much taken by Fanny when she got to know her a few years later, thought few people in Washington realized how much her husband owed to this "brilliant woman who was content to play second fiddle to the maestro." On at least one occasion Holmes privately gave her credit for a witty thrust he worked into one of his Supreme Court opinions. Holmes held that the performance of a piece of music in a restaurant without paying a royalty to the publisher was an infringement of copyright, as the restaurant profited even if it did not directly charge for the performance. "The object is a repast in surroundings that to people having limited powers of conversation, or disliking the rival noise, give a luxurious pleasure not to be had from eating a silent meal," he wrote in the line he told Mrs. Curtis that Fanny had come up with.[57]

Meyer thought Fanny's "plain appearance, restraint, and modesty" made it easy to overlook her subtle mind, and likewise her "conversation was so playful and artful that its incisiveness escaped any but the most careful listeners." One whom it did not escape was President Roosevelt: her mordant wit made her an instant hit with him. At their first dinner at the White House, she remarked to the President that "Washington is full of famous men and the women they married when they were young," which made TR roar.[58] And she completely flummoxed the Russian ambassador, notorious for repeating salacious stories to ladies. When he tried one on her, she showed not the slightest surprise or disapproval, merely countering with an even more risqué one of her own. The ambassador reportedly never told a dirty joke to an American woman again.[59]

One of her other quick comebacks became a famous story in the Holmes household. When one "gracious" Southern gentlewoman she was introduced to began prattling on about how she had met a Mrs. Holmes in Boston years earlier, "But, my dear, quite an old woman. I scarcely think she would be living now," Fanny—who quite remembered their earlier meeting—deadpanned, "That must have been the Judge's first wife."[60]

Deputed to assist at Mrs. Holmes's weekly Monday "at homes," Belknap was amused by the stream of sardonic sotto voce comments she would make to him about her guests. "Most of these occasions were as tepid as the tea," Acheson remembered, observing that "Washington social talk, like that of all single interest societies, is repetitious and dull." Mrs. Holmes would try to get rid of the boring wives of congressmen as quickly as possible. "She would sometimes whisper to me, 'Give that pouter pigeon over there this little glass of Cherry Bounce and see if it will bounce her out,'" Belknap recalled. She also, unlike her husband, did not worry about letting the Southern Gracious Ladies know what she thought of their Confederate nostalgia: at one White House dinner for the justices, she apparently snubbed or insulted the widow of the Confederate hero General "Stonewall" Jackson, which caused the president's military aide, Archie Butt, a young Georgian full of Southern pride, to refuse to shake her hand afterward whenever they met.[61]

In some ways, Belknap and many others thought, Fanny was a shrewder judge of Washington society and character than her husband. Fanny once related to Belknap the time their friend Arthur D. Hill, a lawyer from Boston, was invited to dine at the White House, and stayed with them. When Hill returned from his dinner, Fanny, who was thoroughly familiar with TR's political charm offensives, asked him if he had had a wonderful time, and then said, "Let me tell you what happened. The President put you on his right hand. He talked to you more than anybody else during the evening. He talked about what you might do for him in politics in Boston, in Massachusetts, and then from time to time he would verge off into a discussion of the ancient Irish sagas or something equally erudite."

Hill looked at her in amazement and blurted out, "Mrs. Holmes, were you behind the door?"[62]

The gossip of the town could, however, be sharp-tongued, and as Holmes told Mrs. Gray, "One realizes here the possibility of having enemies, which one rather thought a romantic fiction in Boston. But here rivalries—envies—ambitions—grow fierce. I believe Hoar regards my appointment as a chronic grievance—and I think he doesn't lie awake nights loving me, but I may be wrong." Everything in Washington, he found, was politics and political advantage: "One learns in Washington—or ought to, I never shall, to suspect ulterior motives, and to ask 'why did he say that.'" As he told Clara Stevens a few years later, "Most Washington friendships one must stand ready to unhook at short notice and other changes with politics or hair."[63]

If he had not lost his eye for pretty young women, he found Washington not as conducive to flirtation as London, or even Boston. He facetiously complained to his female correspondents that his rank required him always to be seated at dinners next to "dowagers," but conceded that perhaps that was just as well "in this center of gossip." At one White House dinner where Holmes, as usual, was stuck between two older women, Roosevelt looked on with amusement, then remarked to Fanny, "Look at him—the sex instinct is strong enough in him to make him talk to Mrs.——. I wish I could do that. Do you suppose it is real or is he putting it on!"[64]

But with Fanny now accompanying him on social occasions for the first time, "I have all the companionship I need," Holmes said. When he did have the opportunity to work his charm on younger women he now mostly made it into an obvious bit of play acting, bringing his wife into the scene to rebut any implications that might set Washington tongues wagging.[65]

He sent Mrs. Codman a tongue-in-cheek account of one such foray: "I went to the reception and vainly urged my wife to introduce me to a being in pink of possibly bad form but certainly good shape—to repeat a little joke I made. I told my wife I wished to drop gracefully on one knee raise the lady's hand to my lips and devote to her the shattered remnant of a romantic existence. But it was no go." A few weeks later, at the wedding of the daughter of a fellow justice attended by all official Washington from the president on down, he "somehow" found himself talking to the same "very pretty girl" of good shape, and played the farce to its conclusion:

We gave each other notice of hostile intentions and that we were out for scalps & she told me that I might play in her backyard if I didn't play with other girls—and jabbered French to me tutoying me at once. But I fear the tragedy ends there—as I don't have time to play in backyards, and for other reasons too numerous to mention.[66]

"My whole time passes in writing opinions and adoring you," he playfully told Mrs. Codman. One of the few exceptions to his avoiding new relations with pretty young women in Washington was the serious friendship he struck up with the Baroness Moncheur, the American wife of the Belgian ambassador. She was twenty-seven; her husband, a widower with three young daughters, was twenty years older. They had met a few years earlier when her father was the American ambassador to Mexico, where Baron Moncheur was also posted. Their Washington home was one block from the house Holmes and Fanny bought the year after their arrival. Hers was one of Holmes's last new friendships in the mold of his deep romantic and intellectual attachments to younger women, and they exchanged numerous letters about their lives and thoughts. A few years later from Turkey she wrote him,

> My dear friend—You needn't worry about your advancing years nor the distance between us nor anything else that I can think of while your letters bring me the exquisite thrill that so far has always accompanied them. Seriously & thoughtfully I always feel that my separation from you is one of the great deprivations of my life & I haven't talked as you & I talk since I told you goodbye.

"Don't let the joy of our intimacy fade out," he told her. "I don't expect to make new friends now."[67]

———

IN FEBRUARY 1903, during that first winter in Washington, was also when he met Lewis Einstein for the first time. Einstein had just joined the State Department, and at age twenty-six was already the author of an erudite work on the Italian Renaissance in England. He would subsequently write a book that proved to be an accurate prophecy of the First World War, as well as a biography of Theodore Roosevelt and a vivid account of his time in Constantinople during the disastrous Dardanelles campaign and the Turkish genocide of the Armenians.

Einstein had previously met Lady Castletown in England, where he also met his soon-to-be wife, a twice-divorced Anglo-Greek beauty named Helen Ralli who was fourteen years older than him. Lady Castletown asked him to call on her friend Justice Holmes in Washington, and Einstein later recalled the rented house in Lafayette Square, hung with fox-hunting prints, which struck him as particularly incongruous. The two men stayed up well past midnight talking about art and philosophy.[68]

Posted shortly afterward to Paris on his first diplomatic assignment, Einstein sent a letter to Holmes—"I don't recall how or why"—and Holmes immediately replied. That began a correspondence that continued for thirty years, with Holmes sending his young friend more than two hundred letters, filled with his thoughts and reflections that are some of his finest.[69]

When the spring came, Holmes and Fanny went for a drive in a horse-drawn cab to Cabin John's Bridge in Maryland, and for the first time since he was carried down the C & O Canal after the Battle of Ball's Bluff he saw the canal again, and the bluffs of the Potomac, which he found beautiful and enchanting.[70]

He also made a visit to the haunting sculpture Henry Adams had commissioned from Saint-Gaudens that stood over the otherwise unmarked grave in Rock Creek Park of his wife, Clover, who had committed suicide in 1891. The bronze depicted an androgynous hooded and cloaked figure. Magazine writers had named the sculpture "Grief" or "Despair," but Holmes wrote to Mrs. Gray, "I should not call it despair any more than hope. It is simply the end and silence. The universe escapes epithets. It is enough if you find it beautiful and awful."[71]

As the end of the term approached, he wrote to Mrs. Curtis, "At bottom I am profoundly happy, because the task I have undertaken is so great and so different. I would not give it up for anything." He had written twenty-nine decisions, beating or tying everyone but the chief, despite having started three months into the term. "Having the last word and knowing that there isn't any incompetent idiot who can reverse you or do anything but swallow what you say" was a pleasure; but more than that, for the first time in his life he felt "up against a greatness that comes from outside," and "feeling a vast world vibrate to one's determinations."[72]

"The importance of the things we have to deal with makes me shudder from time to time but I don't lie awake over them, and try to think of them merely as problems to be handled in just the same way whether they involve $25 or the welfare of a state or a people," he told Mrs. Gray that May. "I think you would worry sometimes if you had the job."[73]

But, he said, "I do just love my job."[74]

CHAPTER 11

Due Process

That summer of 1903 Holmes was off to England again, by himself again. This time he stayed at the Hotel Curzon in the fashionable Mayfair district, but other than that his London holidays were now a routine. "I am once more an habitué of London," he wrote Mrs. Gray. He had lunch and dinner every day with one of his friends— Lady Castletown, the Pollocks, the Scotts, Mrs. Clifford, Ethel Grenfell, Lady Burghclere; he went to the theater—Sarah Bernhardt in *Plus que Reine*—and to the opera; and he indulged in a veritable shopping spree at London's tailors, bootmakers, haberdashers, and hatters, buying shirts, coats, formal trousers, vests, cravats, gloves, merino socks, a silk umbrella, and an opera hat.[1]

As usual, he spent August in Ireland, but this time the Castletowns were entertaining a raft of guests at Granston and Doneraile for the whole time. "I suppose I must earn my living by trying to make myself agreeable to casual guests," he complained in a letter from Granston Manor in mid-August, and found himself reluctantly dragged along with the Castletowns' horsey set to the Dublin Horse Show and the Cork Races. Near the end of his stay at Doneraile he wrote Mrs. Gray, "Houseful of people with a garden party in prospect—how I hate such disturbances of a quiet life!" The evenings were occupied with bridge, which left Holmes to read a book or talk to "a chance lady"; during the day the others did "sporting things" that equally left him to his own devices. "I prefer the role of Samson in the lap of Delilah so far as permitted," he ruefully said, suggesting it was not permitted as far as he had hoped. "It is not without a tragical side to come to places and think how more than possible it is that it is for the last time," he told Mrs. Gray, but he would in fact have two more visits there before time and circumstances put an end to his travels abroad.[2]

It was during this time at Doneraile that he met Canon Patrick Sheehan, who had admired his father's books and asked Lord Castletown to introduce him to his distinguished American visitor. Sheehan was a local literary celebrity in his own right, the author of several Irish-themed novels and Catholic devotional works. From whatever odd mixing of human chemistry, the two men took an instant liking to one another.

Holmes's agnosticism was of the tolerant kind, but he never had much intellectual patience with the dogmatism and superiority of religious faith. "I think man has taken himself too seriously, to which he has been helped very much by the clergy," he once said, and often complained that "the humility of the Christian is based on the arrogant assumption that he has been let in on the ground floor by God."[3] He loathed empty shows of public piety—the politician who called for "prayers for peace" provoked him to remark, "Prayers are like nettlerash—anything from heat to champagne may bring them out."[4]

But just as he never lost his admiration for Emerson, or Pen Hallowell, or the other idealists who had fired his youth, he was moved by traditions and beliefs that men were willing to give their lives to, even if he did not share them himself. He once told Einstein of spending a few days in a small settlement in the middle of Illinois, where he and the young Cabot Lodge had gone grouse hunting just after the Civil War. "I realized that Cotton Mather would not have seemed out of place there. The Minister impressed me more than any other clergyman ever did. I said to him, 'I should not think life would be happy with your beliefs.' He answered, 'It is not.' And his face had deep lines."[5]

On his return home from Doneraile, Holmes sent the Irish priest a copy of his speeches, and Sheehan sent the American jurist a copy of his mystically poetical memoir *Under the Cedars and Stars.* Holmes found himself absorbed at once, reading the canon's book to the exclusion of all the others he had planned to get to, deeply moved by "the song of the words" and the "love and exaltation" it expressed.[6]

Holmes wrote to Sheehan a few days after he had begun the book. "I am as far as possible from being on your side—but I still hope you will have room for a little pleasure when I say that your book moves me more intimately by old world feeling than anything that I have

Canon Patrick Sheehan

read for a great while and that if you did not regard me as an enemy I think it might be that we should recognize each other as friends."[7]

But Sheehan felt a kindred spirit in Holmes's tolerant skepticism, moral courage, and philosophical resignation—which, he pointed out to his agnostic friend, mirrored the Catholic teachings of charity and vocation. Sheehan later told Holmes of the excitement he felt whenever a letter arrived with his familiar handwriting on the envelope. Several years after their first meeting, when Sheehan was in the hospital in Cork—a sudden collapse "brought me to the gates of death," he said—he wrote to Holmes, "Your friendship is one of the sheet-anchors of life."[8]

"Odd as it seems that a Saint and a Catholic should take up with a heathen like me," Holmes told friends, he found Sheehan "a gentle poetic cultivated lonely soul." He said to another Irish friend, the historian Alice Stopford Green, "I love him. He has a lovely soul. He is almost always savagely Catholic in his books and yet finds a place for me in his affection. I wonder if ever priests are not quite so cocksure as they say."[9]

══════

Before leaving for England, he had agreed to buy the house at 1720 I Street—which was customarily written in those days as "Eye Street," to avoid confusion with 1st Street—which would be his permanent Washington home. "I long for the time when I shall be in a house of my own," he wrote to Mrs. Gray. "I expect to feel more at home there than I ever did in Beacon St. That was my father's house—not mine!" As before, when they had bought their house on Chestnut Street in Boston, he left the project entirely to Fanny, "only requiring that I be asked no questions."[10]

As soon as they returned to Washington just before the start of the Court's term on the first Monday in October, Fanny hired an architect to oversee a complete remodeling of the house, and she also busily went to work shopping for furniture and draperies at the Woodward & Lothrop department store, ordering lighting fixtures and wallpaper, signing contracts for new plumbing equipment, and arranging for servants for their new home. Holmes reported a few months later that his wife was working "like a strenuous Bostonian—which is quite a different thing from the work of the normal Washingtonian. Here they promise whatever you like and take their ease." Against "every kind of obstacle," Fanny was able to overcome "the detailed incompetency and general slackness of most people in this town," and they were looking forward to settling in at last by the end of December.[11]

The remodeling, which included completely redoing two rooms on the second floor into a study and library for Holmes to work in, came to $13,357.44, to which the architects added their 10 percent fee; the total was equal to about $400,000 today. Fanny spent thousands of dollars more on everything from curtain rings to lampshades to bird cages to movers' bills: among the crate-loads of household goods shipped from Boston were Holmes's four tons of books, waiting to be unpacked and placed on the shelves of the new bookcases built into the library, secretary's study, and drawing room. Holmes said he would be happy once again to be surrounded by his familiar books, to able to find his handkerchiefs, and to take his underclothes from a drawer instead of the trunks they had been living out of for a year.[12]

Facing the plunge back into his work on the Court that fall, Holmes thought that his time in London had been good mental preparation. "There are many Londons, but mine is the enemy of the *banal*—makes you fire snap-shots, talk short, be casual, and take your chances of missing when you say your best thing. It helps one to write better decisions when he gets back—no padding in mine, if I can help it," he wrote to Mrs. Gray. "I have not yet got very *grave* with the prospective cares of my work, but there are many little things to think of and do before I go, and once more give the newspapers a chance to declare me either a person of second rate reputation or a brilliant jurist, according to their liking of some decision in which I take part."[13]

The newspapers were one thing, but it was inescapable that the Supreme Court's judgments would be viewed through the lens of politics, much more so than Holmes had experienced as a judge on the Massachusetts Supreme Judicial Court. Felix Frankfurter would always tell the story of the time John Chipman Gray, one of the foremost authorities on the law of property, was asked to teach a course at Harvard on constitutional law. After one semester, horrified, he swore never to do it again. Constitutional law, Gray despairingly said, "was not law at all, but politics."[14]

That was true in the sense that constitutional questions inevitably had political consequences. But as Holmes's Harvard Law colleague James Thayer had pointed out in several much-noticed essays on constitutional law published a few years before Holmes went to Washington, the Supreme Court in the last two decades of the nineteenth century had chosen to insert itself into legislative questions in a way that sharply departed from past practice, and which had greatly raised the political stakes of its rulings.

For its first hundred years, the Supreme Court had exercised great caution in declaring legislative acts invalid, generally holding that a statute had to be in violation of the Constitution "beyond all reasonable doubt" before a court would overturn the "will of the people." This was not just a matter of deference to the legislature, Thayer said, but a recognition that no constitution was ever meant to dictate a prescription for every situation that might arise. For judges to invalidate statutes based on a "pedantic and academic treatment" of the text, while disregarding the legislative purpose behind an act, was to ignore the reality that any constitution is going to be subject to differing interpretations. Courts do have a duty to stop legislatures from manifest abuses of power—passing a law giving its current members seats for life, for example—but short of that, Thayer argued, "Whatever choice is rational is constitutional."[15]

But beginning around 1886, the Supreme Court began striking down scores of laws that it deemed to be "unreasonable." In the two decades before Holmes joined the Court, it had invalidated some seventy state laws and a dozen acts of Congress, most on the grounds that the legislation violated the Fourteenth Amendment's Due Process Clause, or went beyond a very narrow reading of Congress's enumerated powers under the Constitution.

A conservative majority led by Justice Peckham held that state laws setting rates on railroads, requiring inspection of meat or stockyards, allowing an owner the chance to redeem his foreclosed property, regulating the purchase of insurance, or licensing salesmen all deprived persons of "liberty" or "property" without due process of law, in violation of the Fourteenth Amendment. As Peckham read the Due Process Clause, the Constitution permitted practically no government interference with private property or the economy except what was absolutely necessary to protect public health or safety.

Many state high courts had taken a similar tack, striking down laws regulating businesses or protecting the rights of workers. While on New York's high court before he joined the United States Supreme Court in 1895, Peckham had denounced a law setting the rates grain elevators could charge as "vicious in its nature, communistic in its tendency" and a violation of "the most sacred right of property and the individual liberty of contract." Whatever economic abuses might exist in society, he wrote in his opinion in *People* v. *Budd*, would automatically be corrected "by the general laws of trade, supply and demand," not by "paternal government."[16]

The movement to read laissez-faire economics into the Due Process Clause had not come about by chance. It was the direct result of a calculated legal strategy aimed at undermining the progressive Reconstruction state governments in the former Confederate states, and simultaneously vitiating protections for the newly freed slaves in the three constitutional amendments adopted in the aftermath of the Civil War. John Archibald Campbell, a Louisianan and former U.S. Supreme Court justice who had resigned his position to join the Confederate government, had filed a series of lawsuits beginning in 1868 seeking to limit the power of the state government to establish public schools, impose taxes, or enact other progressive legislation.

He was also incensed by the sight of "Africans in place all about us," serving as jurors, post office clerks, and legislators. When the racially integrated Republican state legislature passed a law to improve sanitation in New Orleans by creating a central slaughterhouse and requiring the city's butchers to operate from this single public market, Campbell saw an opportunity, and filed suit on behalf of the butchers alleging a violation of the Fourteenth Amendment's right of liberty.[17]

It was a creative legal maneuver, since it aimed to turn an amendment adopted with the purpose of guaranteeing the equal civil rights of the emancipated slaves into a tool of conservative retrenchment. Although in 1873 the Supreme Court upheld the Louisiana statute in a 5–4 decision, it was a victory in disguise for Campbell.[18]

For one thing, the majority opinion almost completely gutted one of the Fourteenth Amendment's other key protections of the rights of the freedmen. The authors of the amendment had clearly understood it to make the individual rights guaranteed by the Constitution binding on the states and directly enforceable by federal legislation. The key provision for this was the Privileges or Immunities Clause, which declared that "no state shall make or enforce any law that shall abridge the privileges or immunities of citizens of the United States." The amendment further declared that all American citizens were citizens both of the state they reside in and of the United States, and gave Congress the power to enforce its terms with appropriate legislation.

Those provisions, like the rest of the Fourteenth Amendment, had been aimed squarely at the "Black Codes" that the first, all-white, Southern state legislatures reconstituted immediately after the Civil War had adopted. Their avowed intention was to keep the freedmen in as close a condition to slavery as possible, forbidding them to own or rent farmland, enter any trade except agricultural labor without a special license, assemble in groups, keep firearms, or live with whites, and requiring them to enter into annual labor contracts or face summary arrest.

But in the *Slaughter-House Cases* the Court majority held that the only "privileges or immunities" of a citizen of the United States were such uniquely federal responsibilities as the right to obtain a passport: free speech, freedom of assembly, the right to counsel, and the other provisions of the Bill of Rights were not included. Ten years later, in the *Civil Rights Cases*, the Court further drained much of the Fourteenth Amendment of its original purpose when it struck down a federal civil rights law prohibiting racial discrimination in public accommodations. The Court held 8–1 that even though the Fourteenth Amendment explicitly empowered Congress to enforce its provisions, the amendment's guarantee of equal rights applied only to action by states, not private parties; thus Congress had no power to restrict the "individual invasion of individual rights" by innkeepers, railroads, or theaters.

As in *Plessy*, Harlan was the lone dissenter, writing bitterly that by narrowing the Fourteenth Amendment's scope to state action, the Court had reduced its soaring promises of equality for all to "splendid baubles, thrown out to delude those who deserved fair and generous treatment at the hands of the nation."[19]

The minority opinion in *Slaughter-House* was Campbell's other secret victory. Within a decade, the dissenters' reasoning had been adopted by many state courts, and a few years later by the United States Supreme Court as well. Their key "discovery" was that the Due Process Clause did not merely guarantee what would come to be somewhat tautologically referred to as "procedural due process": namely, the right to a fair trial before the state exacted a penalty entailing loss of life, liberty, or property. It also, the Court said, embodied protections of "substantive due process" for other, unspecified rights—chiefly the economic "right" to pursue any lawful occupation or business without interference by the government.

Notably, an 1885 decision by the New York high court invalidated a law prohibiting cigar factories in tenement buildings, finding that limitations on a person's choice or place of work were "infringements upon the fundamental rights of liberty, which are under constitutional protection."[20] The U.S. Supreme Court elevated the *Slaughter-House* dissent to the law of the land in 1897 in *Allgeyer* v. *Louisiana*, with Peckham writing the decision that a Louisiana law prohibiting the purchase of insurance from an out-of-state company violated the "right to contract."

As the legal historian Bernard Schwartz wrote, "*Allgeyer* did more than enshrine liberty of contract in the constitutional pantheon. It made due process dominant as the doctrine virtually immunizing economic activity from regulation deemed contrary to the laissez-faire philosophy of the day."[21] And so it would be when Holmes faced the first major case of his third full year on the Court.

═══════

IN 1895, the New York State legislature passed a law regulating sanitation and working conditions in bakeries. At the turn of the century about 90 percent of commercial bakeries in New York were located in the basements of tenement buildings. These were about the worst possible places to work, much less prepare food. Floors and walls were usually nothing more than packed dirt, leaking sewer pipes fouled the air, ventilation was nonexistent, lighting minimal. Profit margins were low in the baking industry, so owners often employed child labor to keep down costs. The work was long and hard, often going late into the night and beginning in the predawn to be ready for customers on their way to work.

The New York statute, modeled on a British law, barred workers from sleeping in the bake room, set minimum sanitary standards, and limited work to ten hours a day and sixty hours per week. An upstate

New York basement bakery at the turn of the twentieth century

bakery owner, Joseph Lochner, who had been fined for exceeding the ten-hour limit for his employees, decided to fight the law. He lost his initial appeals in state and federal court, but was determined to go all the way to the U.S. Supreme Court.

On February 23, 1905, the justices heard oral arguments in the case. Eight weeks later Justice Peckham delivered the Court's 5–4 decision striking down the law. It was a pure expression of the kind of reasoning from abstract propositions that Holmes had always scorned, going back to *The Common Law*. The Court had previously upheld a Utah law limiting workers in underground mines to eight hours a day, accepting that as a legitimate exercise of the state's "police powers" to protect public health and safety, though warning that "the police power cannot be put forward as an excuse for oppressive and unjust legislation."[22] In *Lochner* v. *New York*, Peckham held that no such justification applied to bakers: "Clean and wholesome bread does not depend upon whether the baker works but ten hours per day"; the law was rather "an illegal interference with the rights of individuals, both employers and employees, to make contracts regarding labor upon such terms as they may think best." Were the Court to uphold the New York law, Peckham ominously warned, "no trade, no occupation, no mode of earning one's living could escape this all-pervading power."

Both Harlan and Holmes wrote dissents. Harlan's is forgotten; Holmes's is one of the most famous judicial opinions of all time, known to and studied by every law student to this day.

Holmes's views about judicial deference to the legislature closely followed Thayer's reasoning. He once offered Laski his own version of Thayer's "beyond reasonable doubt" test, opining that a court should never invalidate a statute "unless it makes us puke."[23] But Holmes went beyond Thayer's ideas in two important respects. One was that his view was based not merely on acceding to the will of the people, but was rooted fundamentally in his skepticism, and even his ironic philosophical approach to life itself.

As Richard Posner observed of Holmes, "He was a wit, and wit implies a sense of incongruity, including the incongruity between one's pretensions and one's achievements. If you do not take yourself very seriously you are unlikely to fool yourself into thinking that you have all the answers. A judge who, like Holmes, does not think he has all the answers is less likely to challenge the decisions of the other branches of government than a know-it-all judge."[24] In his willingness to uphold legislation even when he disagreed with it, Holmes was not just saying that he thought it his duty to accept the dominant opinion of society; he was also saying that his—or anyone's—opinions might be wrong, and that the only way to find out was to allow the states and Congress room to experiment.

The other factor behind Holmes's belief in judicial restraint was his realism—his insistence that a judge had a duty to examine the actual operation of a law in the real world rather than retreat to legalistic formulas. As Holmes had argued about the common law, assertions of basic principle do not get one very far: almost all legal decisions come down to weighing competing and equally valid claims of rights and interests, and drawing a line between them. That was even more so when it came to the broad, vaguely worded precepts of the Constitution. A judge who retreated to "the Constitution made me do it" to reach his conclusion, without considering the purpose behind legislation or the balancing of social interests at stake, was *more* likely to impose his own unarticulated prejudices than one who took the trouble to understand and assess the "felt necessities of the time," as he had said in *The Common Law*. Or, as he told Alice Stopford Green a few years later, "I took occasion at luncheon to define constitutional law to my brethren as the prejudices of nine old pedagogues read into an instrument that did not contain them, which I hope gave pain."[25]

Holmes's dissent in *Lochner* was extraordinarily brief, barely six hundred words long; it was completely free from legal jargon; it was, in Posner's words, a "rhetorical masterpiece" that violated every rule of a "good" judicial opinion to become "merely the greatest judicial opinion of the last hundred years."[26]

> I regret sincerely that I am unable to agree with the judgment in this case and that I think it my duty to express my dissent.
>
> This case is decided upon an economic theory which a large part of the country does not entertain. If it were a question whether I agreed with that theory, I should desire to study it further and long before making up my mind. But I do not conceive that to be my duty, because I strongly believe that my agreement or disagreement has nothing to do with the right of a majority to embody their opinions in law. It is settled by various decisions of this court that state constitutions and state laws may regulate life in many ways which we, as legislators, might think as injudicious, or, if you like, as tyrannical, as this, and which, equally with this, interfere with the liberty to contract. Sunday laws and usury laws are ancient examples. A more modern one is the prohibition of lotteries. The liberty of the citizen to do as he likes so long as he does not interfere with the liberty of others to do the same, which has been a shibboleth for some well known writers, is interfered with by school laws, by the Post Office, by every state or municipal institution which takes his money for purposes thought desirable, whether he likes it or not. The Fourteenth Amendment does not enact Mr. Herbert Spencer's Social Statics. The other day, we sustained the Massachusetts vaccination law. United States and state statutes and decisions cutting down the liberty to contract by way of combination are familiar to this court. Two years ago, we upheld the prohibition of sales of stock

on margins or for future delivery in the constitution of California. The decision sustaining an eight hour law for miners is still recent. Some of these laws embody convictions or prejudices which judges are likely to share. Some may not. But a constitution is not intended to embody a particular economic theory, whether of paternalism and the organic relation of the citizen to the State or of *laissez faire*.

It is made for people of fundamentally differing views, and the accident of our finding certain opinions natural and familiar or novel and even shocking ought not to conclude our judgment upon the question whether statutes embodying them conflict with the Constitution of the United States.

General propositions do not decide concrete cases. The decision will depend on a judgment or intuition more subtle than any articulate major premise. But I think that the proposition just stated, if it is accepted, will carry us far toward the end. Every opinion tends to become a law. I think that the word liberty in the Fourteenth Amendment is perverted when it is held to prevent the natural outcome of a dominant opinion, unless it can be said that a rational and fair man necessarily would admit that the statute proposed would infringe fundamental principles as they have been understood by the traditions of our people and our law. It does not need research to show that no such sweeping condemnation can be passed upon the statute before us. A reasonable man might think it a proper measure on the score of health. Men whom I certainly could not pronounce unreasonable would uphold it as a first instalment of a general regulation of the hours of work. Whether in the latter aspect it would be open to the charge of inequality I think it unnecessary to discuss.[27]

Herbert Spencer's *Social Statics* was the bible of laissez-faire economics, and Holmes mentioned to several correspondents how satisfied he was to get in that dig at his fellow justices.

———

WHEN HE WAS able to write the opinion for the Court in other cases that ran up against the same question of liberty of contract, but where the majority was willing to grant that the circumstances fell within one of the "police powers" exceptions to its normal hostility to social legislation, Holmes never missed the chance to try to slip in the more general arguments he had made in *Lochner*, and fire off another broadside against the Court's use, or rather misuse as he saw it, of the Fourteenth Amendment to void state legislation.

Upholding a Texas law that fined railroads for allowing noxious weeds to grow in their rights of way, Holmes, writing for the Court, rejected the claim that this violated the Fourteenth Amendment's guarantee of equal protection of the laws, and worked in at the end of the very brief opinion an admonition: "Great constitutional provisions must be administered with caution. Some play must be allowed for the joints of the machine, and it must be remembered that legislatures are ultimate guardians of the liberties and welfare of the people in quite as great a degree as the courts."[28]

The last point was also one of Thayer's central premises in counseling judicial restraint: even when it was unavoidable for judges to hold laws unconstitutional, he had emphasized, it was nonetheless an evil—because "the people thus lose the political experience, and the moral education and stimulus that come from fighting the question out in the ordinary way, and correcting their own errors. . . . Under no system can the power of courts go far to save people from ruin."[29]

Just two weeks before *Lochner*, the Court rejected by 6–2 a challenge to a Kentucky law that assessed property owners for the paving of adjacent roadways. A railroad had objected to paying the assessment, arguing that it gained no benefit from the paving of roads next to its rights of way. Holmes again seized the chance; in his opinion for the Court he admonished that "it is important for this Court to avoid extraction from the very general language of the Fourteenth Amendment a system of delusive exactness" to invalidate government powers which were widely accepted at the time the amendment was adopted.[30]

In a similar case involving assessments for opening of alleys in the District of Columbia, Holmes wrote, "Constitutional rights, like others, are matters of degree." Most ordinances restricting the height of buildings would be held as valid under the police power, he noted, though if it were set at five feet it would require compensation under eminent domain. "I took pleasure," he told his friend John Wu, "in pointing out that a man's constitutional rights . . . might be a matter of feet and inches."[31]

But more often he found himself, as in *Lochner*, filing a dissenting opinion by himself, or occasionally joined by one other justice. In a case challenging Kentucky's tax on out-of-state property owned by a company incorporated within the state, the Court agreed that it was a violation of the Due Process Clause. Holmes was left to write in bafflement, joined by only Chief Justice Fuller, "The result reached by the court probably is a desirable one, but I hardly understand how it can be deduced from the Fourteenth Amendment."[32]

———

THE CASES THAT really stirred up a political hornet's nest, more than those involving the Fourteenth Amendment and state legislation, were a series of challenges to federal labor and antitrust laws by businesses hoping to halt the progressive movement in its tracks. The Supreme Court's implacable hostility to unions and readiness to invalidate laws that touched private business gave them hope that they might be able to achieve in the courts of law what they been unable to in the court of public opinion. And here Holmes found himself facing a barrage of political attacks for his dissenting opinions unlike anything he had ever before experienced.

During his first two years in office, Roosevelt had vowed to take on the big railroad, oil, and other "trusts" as a central part of his public image as a progressive reformer. At the start of the election year of 1904, a major antitrust case reached the Supreme Court. Previous cases brought under the 1890 Sherman Antitrust Act had taken aim at price-fixing arrangements between competitors in the same market. But *Northern Securities* v. *U.S.* was the first time the government sought to break up a monopoly in the interests of competition.

The Northern Securities Company had been created by J. P. Morgan and the railroad tycoon James J. Hill to consolidate the Great Northern and Northern Pacific railroads. A state law had barred the merger, but Northern Securities was designed to get around that by serving as

Awaiting a verdict in the trust cases:
New York Times, April 23, 1911

a "holding company" to take control of the two companies' stock, a legal maneuver that effectively accomplished the same end, doing away with the competition on the parallel lines the two companies operated from the Midwest to the West Coast.

On March 14, 1904, a deeply divided Court announced its decision. By 5–4, the Court upheld the federal government's action to dissolve the company. Holmes delivered one of the two dissenting opinions. He was painfully aware of the political attention the case had drawn, noting at the start of his dissent, "Great cases, like hard cases, make bad law. For great cases are called great not by reason of their real importance in shaping the law of the future, but because of some accident of immediate overwhelming interest which appeals to the feelings and distorts the judgment."

It was far from Holmes's clearest or most-well-written opinion, either. But it reflected, fundamentally, his view that while a conspiracy by two competitors to keep a third company from entering the same market might be an illegal restraint of trade, bigness in and of itself was no crime. Economies of scale and the greater efficiencies of concentrated control were an irresistible force driving mergers and combinations. As he remarked later to many of his friends, he thought the Sherman Act "an imbecile statute," which "aims at making everyone fight but forbidding anyone to be victorious."[33] He thought people who say "damn Rockefeller" were ignoring the fact that Rockefeller and his fellow monopolists had merely recognized ineluctable economic forces better than others. They might as well say "damn God, or the order of the universe." He told President Taft a few years later, "If they could make a case for putting Rockefeller in prison I should do my part, but if they left it to me I should put up a bronze statue of him."[34]

Holmes's dissent in *Northern Securities* did not sit well with the White House. A story that first appeared in print thirty years later had it that on learning of Holmes's failure to back up the administration, the president scornfully declared that he "could carve out of a banana a Justice with more backbone than that." That may or may not have actually happened. There were also newspaper stories at the time that a furious Roosevelt had summoned Holmes for a personal dressing-down, which definitely did not happen.[35]

But Holmes "heard rumors of wrath" at the White House—no doubt from Henry Adams, who wrote an acquaintance at the time, "Poor Wendell Holmes is the immediate victim. . . . Theodore went wild about it, and openly denounced Holmes in the most forcible terms of his sputtering vocabulary."[36] Holmes himself had been anguished beforehand over how the president would take his dissent. "The case was not without its painful side as it involved going against one's natural crowd," he told his lawyer, John Palfrey. "If however his seeming personal regard for us was based on the idea that he had a tool," he wrote Mrs. Curtis a few days after the decision was announced, "the sooner it is ended the better—we shall see."[37]

Roosevelt made a point of maintaining an outward show of cordial relations, however, inviting Justice and Mrs. Holmes just a few weeks later with the Lodges to an intimate dinner and musical recital at the White House. He and the president continued to have "charming" talks, and Holmes was somewhat amused at himself by the way he always fell under Roosevelt's charismatic spell whenever they were together, as much as he now saw through it. "Of course I went off with the glamour that he always leaves," he wrote Baroness Moncheur after one such session at the White House.[38]

Years later Holmes told Pollock,

It broke up our incipient friendship, however, as he looked on my dissent to the *Northern Securities* case as a political departure (or, I suspect, more truly, couldn't forgive anyone who stood in his way).

We talked freely later but it never was the same after that, and if
he had not been restrained by his friends, I am told that he would
have made a fool of himself and would have excluded me from the
White House.[39]

Roosevelt was too good a politician to break openly with anyone
who might still be an ally, but long after his initial anger died away
he continued to regard Holmes's decisions in *Northern Securities* and
other "political" cases as a betrayal, if not of him personally than of the
Republican Party. As he told Henry Cabot Lodge in 1906,

Nothing has been so strongly borne in on me concerning lawyers
on the bench as that the *nominal* politics of a man has nothing to
do with his actions on the bench. . . . Holmes should have been an
ideal man on the bench. As a matter of fact he has been a bitter
disappointment, not because of any one decision but because of his
general attitude.[40]

Roosevelt was somewhat mollified when Holmes wrote the opinion
for the Court in a 1905 case upholding another of the administration's
major antitrust suits, this one targeting the "Beef Trust." Six large meat
packers controlled 45 percent of the nation's entire beef market, and
accounted for 98 percent of the beef purchased at eight principal cattle
markets in the Midwest and West. Unlike *Northern Securities, Swift &
Co. v. U.S.* involved a clear case of anticompetitive collusion: the buyers
agreed not to bid against one another, blacklisted competitors who did
not go along, and occasionally bid up prices for a few days so the market reports would draw large shipments from out- of-state sellers, only
to bring the prices back down again.[41]

"For once thank the Lord we were unanimous," Holmes wrote Mrs.
Green when the decision was announced. It "excited a good deal of
talk—and I appear in caricatures as a toreador or as lassoing a mad
bull." The opinion was in Holmes's view "only a rather mechanical
development of a necessary result but some of the lads liked it—I dare
say because I was not on the other side."[42]

The case did break ground in one key area, and would in retrospect be seen as a landmark ruling halting the Court's trend of ever-narrowing readings of the Constitution's Commerce Clause: Holmes held that even though the sales at stockyards took place within one state, they were part of a "current of commerce" among the states that came within Congress's power to regulate.

Approaching the end of his administration in 1908, Roosevelt also made very public show of appreciation toward Holmes in a speech on conservation to the state governors at their meeting in Washington. Roosevelt concluded his remarks by quoting from Holmes's ringing opinion in a recent case that had upheld a New Jersey law barring the out-of-state sale of water from its lakes and rivers. "The state, as quasi-sovereign and representative of the interests of the public, has a standing in court to protect the atmosphere, the water, and the forests within its territory. . . . There are benefits from a great river that might escape a lawyer's view."[43]

Another recent opinion of his had offered an equally emphatic support for the government's power to protect natural resources, a cause that TR had made as much a part of his presidency as his crusade against the trusts. Holmes's decision had affirmed an injunction sought by the state of Georgia against copper plants in Tennessee that were poisoning its forests with sulfur emissions. There was a question whether a state had standing to bring a suit for damage to property in private hands, but Holmes ruled that "the state has an interest independent of and behind the titles of its citizens, in all the earth and air within its domain. It has the last word as to whether its mountains shall be stripped of their forests and its inhabitants shall breathe pure air."[44]

Holmes was in the audience for Roosevelt's speech to the governors, and that night was invited to a private dinner at the White House. "Had a very nice talk with the President (in which incidentally we said one last word about the old No. Securities Case & that matter is finished)," he reported to Mrs. Gray. But he added: "We like each other by temperament though I cannot again take his friendship seriously."[45]

What irked Holmes more than anything was the failure of the president—and the newspapers and the interest groups—to see that politics had nothing to do with his judicial opinions, however great their political consequences. "I think he hardly realizes what I repeated to him last night that a question before a judge is a problem—with which personal matters and preferences have nothing to do," he said of Roosevelt, as the president prepared to leave office.[46] Holmes had the same annoyance when he dissented strongly in a labor case that year, *Adair* v. *U.S.*, in which the Court struck down a federal law that as part of an effort to ensure labor peace had prohibited railroads from enforcing "yellow-dog" contracts, which made it a condition of employment that workers pledge not to join a union.

The majority, applying the same reasoning it had used in holding that the Fourteenth Amendment barred the states from infringing on "liberty of contract," ruled that the due process protections of the Fifth Amendment similarly constrained Congress. Holmes protested that the act "simply prohibits the more powerful party to extract certain undertakings, or to threaten dismissal or unjustly discriminate." He reiterated his view that "the word liberty in the amendments has been stretched to its extreme by the decisions" of the Court.

But he was equally irked at a dinner for labor leaders he attended at the White House later that year where he listened to a series of speeches attacking the courts for their antilabor decisions. "As we were leaving I told the man who was most savage on the judiciary—a plasterer I believe, that he didn't appreciate us—that the workingman didn't think anything was good except what was on their side—that my job was simply to see that the parties were held to the rule of the game and that when I was on my job I didn't care a damn for him or the President or Morgan and Rockefeller." He complained to Clara Stevens, "I suppose the capitalists think me dangerous and the labor people think me an eccentric slave of capital—so I hope I am all right. Nobody wants a dispassionate man."[47]

Nonetheless, he invited a young lawyer he had sat next to at the dinner, a union man "who had fought his own way up," to come and see him, and the next morning they had a lively half hour's talk at 1720 Eye Street. Holmes was genuinely sorry when he could not stay for luncheon. "I wish I could have talked more than I had the chance to with the labormen," he said.[48]

<hr />

AT THE END of each term of the Court, Holmes felt like "a mere law machine," he quipped. "Put the problem in the hopper and it would grind you out a result pretty quick—but not much good for general conversation."[49]

He always looked forward to his rejuvenating trips to London to shake off the effects of seven months of single-minded focus on the law. He continued to insist that it was Fanny who urged him to go for a rest and change of scene. But one of Fanny's few surviving letters—it was written just after Holmes boarded the *Saxonia* in New York on June 11 to sail to England in the summer of 1907—revealed the more torn feelings that both experienced about these jaunts of his.

Fanny had come to New York to see him off. Whether to hide her own sorrow or from the crush of the crowd, she had turned away abruptly at their parting on the deck, and had caught a look of hurt and anguish on her husband's face when she glanced back again. On her return to Beverly Farms she wrote,

> My dearest—dearest—Dearest
>
> Please Please you did not think that I did not care. I was in a maze and I shall be in it till Heavenly September comes. I wanted to throw myself away when you went out of sight—Why could my wings not have sprouted and carried me into your state room for five minutes. I am so glad those men had their way and took the snap shot for when I got down here your poor face all filled with loss and grief as I saw it last made me almost faint. But the Blessed Herald had another last look for me when I opened it and saw you again I almost shouted He did know I was his old loving wife his other half left here to love and long for him.

It is cold and apple blossom here pretty enough for those who like it. Everything that the servants can do to make me comfortable they are doing. Even Katie made some good biscuits for my tea. Dorothy staid with me till after luncheon and saw me on the express to Mount Desert. She went to Salem.

But Fanny without her husband finds the joyless house very mournful tonight.

Dont ever think I am rough or cold or anything but your—

Adoring wife

11 June 1907

How did you dare to weep when I could not reach you to comfort you Dont dont again Please please dont[50]

In England, Holmes visited his friends the Scotts in the country—"from whom I receive I really believe the most generous, absolute and disinterested love I ever received from anyone except my wife. It fortifies one's soul even while it makes one tremble lest he should not deserve it"—and "ran over to Paris for two days," where a "fair friend" took to him to lunch at Versailles, and where he was amused at the mix of "Western School Marms" and "painted ladies" he encountered in the foyer of the Marigny Theater.[51]

When Baroness Moncheur expressed some mild disapproval of his gadding about and accepting invitations in London to dinners and weekends, he bristled defensively. "What the deuce should I do if I didn't?" he shot back. "Improve my mind in the British Museum and National Gallery I suppose?"[52]

He ended with a visit to the Castletowns in Ireland for the last two weeks of August. "My usual routine, this time more intent on old friends than on new acquaintances," he wrote Mrs. Gray.

But I have talked with all sorts, from princesses to haberdashers, and tried to get their touch of human nature that alone pays one for the trouble of talking. A dinner at which one only gets one's victuals is a failure. . . . I whizzed about in motors a little, but I don't like them except when there is some special reason for getting over the ground in a hurry. The Scripture says that the horse is a vain thing for safety, but the motor is a shade or two worse.[53]

Still, he said, he did not think he would do England again alone. "It is getting too hard and anxious to leave my wife."[54]

CHAPTER 12

1720 Eye Street

True to his word, Holmes had not only refrained from offering any opinions about Fanny's remodeling and furnishing of their new house in Washington; he had not even set foot in the house until a few weeks before they moved in. But when he was at last given a tour he pronounced "every room from kitchen to trunk room" perfect, and "charming." Everything, he said, was much more spacious than their Boston house. "I really have got a home," he told Mrs. Gray.[1]

The library on the second floor was two large adjoining rooms, each fitted with white-painted bookshelves covering all four walls from floor to ceiling, enough to hold most of his twelve thousand books. The south room, at the back of the house, was Holmes's study, and its two tall windows faced the sunlight and looked out on "a trim little yard with borders and grass in the middle."[2]

In the yard were magnolias and double-flowering apples and a paulownia tree with delicate perfume-scented purple flowers and a wisteria that climbed the adjoining wall, all of which provided a succession of flowers through the spring. Holmes marveled to friends that roses "grow here if you simply stick them into the earth." Within a few years there were profusions of climbing roses on the fence beneath his window "and some more pretentious ones in the border," he wrote Clare.[3]

An alley running across the back protected the lot from "the danger the sunlight will be cut off by a big apartment house—such as spoil half the houses here." It had the feel of living in a "large country town," Holmes said. "One sees and hears crows (which I adore) and wild birds light and sing sometimes even in my backyard." In the distance, almost directly south over the intervening roofs, the Washington Monument was framed in the two library windows. "I love that monument for the eternal wonder of changing light upon it—at times an aerial dream—at times a plain stone fact—but never the same," he said.[4]

1720 Eye Street, with Holmes's 1926 Packard out front

The library was the undoubted life center of 1720 Eye Street. The justice wrote his decisions there, usually working at his grandfather's stand-up mahogany desk that directly faced the right-hand window, his head ringed in a halo of smoke from one of the large cigars he ordered by the hundred—Puerto Ricans for himself, more-expensive Havanas for his friends—from the old Boston grocers S. S. Pierce.[5] His grandfather's other desk, where he sat when he was not writing, was a seven-drawer Federal-style cherry piece with beautiful simple lines, the top of which Holmes always kept carefully covered with a sheet of blotting paper. It had its left end against the wall between the two windows, so the chair was directly in line with the other window of the study, to Holmes's left.

The library was where he received his important visitors, and when he and Fanny had dinner parties the men would gather there afterward to smoke and talk. A pair of crossed swords that had been his great-grandfather David Holmes's in the French and Indian War hung over the fireplace on the west wall, and framed photographs of Clare

In the study, with his secretary H. Chapman Rose

Castletown, Mrs. Curtis, Margot Tennant, and other friends hung about the room.

There were some comfortable chairs, but mostly there was a kind of rugged simplicity. "He did not favor any of the modern paraphernalia of an office," recalled his secretary Augustin Derby, and Holmes never budged from the nineteenth century in that regard: "How I loathe conveniences," was one of his cherished sayings. His secretary sat in the adjoining north room; a pair of glass doors looked out into the hall at one end of the room; the sliding doors at the other end that divided the two studies were always open, so the secretary could see the justice at work and respond to any call without the need of a buzzer or any other gadget. A telephone had only recently been installed when he arrived for the 1906 term, Derby learned, but it was placed in his room; Holmes disliked using the phone himself, claiming he found it difficult to hear. A typewriter a subsequent secretary attempted to smuggle in to answer the justice's correspondence was discovered after a few days and promptly ejected.[6]

The rest of the second floor had the Holmeses' bedroom and bathroom. On the third floor, Fanny had arranged a suite of rooms for Holmes's young cousin Dorothy Upham. When they moved in in December 1903 she was in her senior year at Smith.[7] Ever since her mother died in 1897, the Holmeses had played an increasing part in her life, inviting her to visit during school holidays and looking after the trust fund she had inherited from Holmes's sister. Her father, Oliver Wendell Holmes Upham, who was Dr. Holmes's nephew, had apparently been in declining health or competency for a number of years. Amelia Jackson Sargent in her will had provided a trust for O.W.H. Upham's wife and children, but left nothing to him directly. In 1901 Holmes and his other cousin, William P. Upham, had set up a trust to provide him an income out of the estate of John Holmes—who had likewise apparently not thought O.W.H. Upham fit to handle an outright bequest, as the others received.[8]

After her graduation in 1904 and her father's death the following year, Dorothy came to stay at 1720 Eye Street. "Dorothy is a cousin whom I call my niece and commonly is called as, who lives with us. She was left alone and we saw no other way," Holmes explained to Clara Stevens. The Holmeses took Dorothy with them to several White House receptions during the Roosevelt administration, and Mrs. Holmes hosted some lunches for her and other young women; but though Dorothy told Mark Howe years later that she "loved OWH who was always sweet and kind," it had to be a somewhat stifling existence for a young woman right out of college. The justice, she recalled, was always correcting her pronunciation of words, and Mrs. Holmes had strict rules that Dorothy was not to receive male visitors without a chaperone. The one time Fanny came in on her sitting chaperoneless in the drawing room with a young man, she had ordered him out of the house immediately. The next morning when Dorothy came down to breakfast, she found Holmes alone, having been sent by Fanny to deliver a stern lecture. She remained with the Holmeses until her marriage in March 1909 to Thomas Wayland Vaughan, a noted oceanographer

Dorothy Upham Vaughan

and geologist, who later became director of the Scripps Institution of Oceanography.[9]

The more public rooms of the house reflected the bygone age of servants and formal entertaining and manners that, within a generation, would seem from another world entirely. On the first floor was a small formal reception room where visitors would wait while they were announced, a larger front drawing room where Fanny spent much of her time and where guests were entertained, and a substantial dining room at the back with a table that could seat two dozen. In a half basement were the domestic offices: kitchen and pantry, the "help's sitting room," and the "colored man's room." In the attic were bedrooms for the other servants.[10]

As Holmes's secretary Arthur Sutherland later recalled, the house "would have given an interior decorator severe pain." It was furnished in a complete hodge-podge of styles: New England heirlooms passed down from the Holmeses and Jacksons—Chippendale and Hepplewhite chairs, a Sheraton and a Duncan Phyfe table, fine family silver—side by side with all sorts of geegaws Fanny had picked up at The Pagoda ("importer of oriental oddities") and other local shops, including lampshades covered with artificial butterflies, bronze Chinese dogs and Buddhas, carved figurines, and a varying collection of a half-dozen tame birds and the occasional cat to complete the household. But as Sutherland noticed, Holmes and Fanny liked things just "as they were; were completely poised in their own tastes, and the suggestion that they should have complied with somebody else's idea of how to live would only have amused them."[11]

Until they drew back from their official entertaining around the time

"Would have given an interior decorator severe pain": the reception room at
1720 Eye Street, looking into the front parlor

of the First World War, they filled the house with a number of large dinner parties; Fanny drew up seating charts and the guests included the
Lodges, the Baron and Baroness Moncheur, the Russian ambassador,
the secretary of state, and Holmes's fellow justices.[12]

Holmes did not believe in economy when it came to ordering the
best food or having help to run the household. There was always a full-
time staff consisting of cook, waitress, one or more maids, Holmes's
Court messenger, and another African American man, Earle H. Jones,
whom Holmes employed for years as an "inside man" (which he found

in Washington was rather grandly known as a "butler") to help with the housework, run errands, and look after the house during the summer.

His driver Charles Buckley, who drove the justice everywhere in a horse and carriage until 1925, when a large Packard sedan finally took their place, also worked full time, but Holmes employed him as an independent contractor—his secretaries always believed he did so to limit his liability in case of an accident, having observed that Buckley was never entirely comfortable with the transition from coachman to chauffeur. (One time Buckley narrowly missed hitting a truck. Holmes turned to his secretary who was riding with him, and exclaimed, "My Lord, sonny! What a blow to jurisprudence if he'd killed both of us!")[13]

Holmes easily spent twice his salary each month just keeping the household running in the style he enjoyed. Each month he cashed a check for $300 to pay his servants; he paid Buckley $87.50 (later increased to $100.00) twice a month; there were regular bills of $800 a month or more for the food consumed by the Holmeses, their guests, and their servants. With all their other household bills—flowers, laundry, coal, ice, electricity, gas, phone, repairs, maintenance—their expenses ran well over $2,000 a month, at a time when the average *annual* household income in America was less than half that.[14]

Until Prohibition began in 1920—and even after, because Holmes had put in a large stock of champagne, and the law did not forbid private consumption, only the manufacture, importation, and sale of liquor—he always enjoyed "the fizzly water," as he called it. All of the provisions for their ample meals came from the fancy shops patronized by fashionable Washington—Magruder's grocery, right across Connecticut Avenue; Rauscher's caterers at Connecticut and L Street, which regularly supplied ice cream, cakes, rolls, and brioche to the house; the Marlborough Market, for meats, poultry, fish, game, hothouse fruits; and the Chevy Chase Dairy, which delivered a daily stream of cream, milk, butter, and eggs. And there were the indispensable orders to S. S. Pierce not only for Holmes's regular boxes of cigars but other luxury items he and Fanny missed from the famous Boston purveyor, including marmalade, anchovy paste, and candies.

As Holmes once remarked thoughtfully to Alger Hiss as they were enjoying one of the usual very good lunches at 1720 Eye Street, "If they put all the cattle and sheep that I've eaten in my life in boxcars, it would be an awfully long train." After Holmes's death, his last secretary, James Rowe, and the household staff that stayed on to look after the house had gone on ordering food as usual until John Palfrey, as executor of Holmes's estate, came down from Boston and ordered Rowe to start getting their groceries from the local supermarket. The food bill dropped to a third of what it had been.[15]

HOLMES WAS AN exception among the justices in employing a secretary. In 1886 Congress had provided each of the justices an allowance of $2,000 a year for a "stenographic assistant." Holmes's predecessor Justice Horace Gray decided to use the money instead to hire a young lawyer who could provide him assistance with legal research. He had his brother John Chipman Gray select a top graduating student from Harvard Law School each year, and, as he conceived the position, it was as much an apprenticeship as assistant. Gray liked to "do his thinking aloud," recalled one of his clerks, and would debate his cases with his young charges; as preparation he would often ask them to write their own draft opinion. The drafts invariably ended up in the trashcan, but the experience was heady and invaluable. One of Gray's former clerks remembered his amazement at how the justice "would patiently and courteously listen to the crudest deliverances of youth fresh from the Law School."[16]

None of the other justices followed Gray's example, and except for Holmes and Brandeis (and White, who paid for a legal secretary out of his own pocket) none would employ a legal assistant until Congress in 1919 appropriated funds to provide the justices with both a "stenographic clerk" and a more highly paid "law clerk," at $3,600 a year.[17]

Holmes was not sure he would know what to do with a secretary. He certainly had no use for a stenographer, since he wrote his decisions himself in longhand, and he knew the law so thoroughly he had no need to have precedents looked up to figure out how to decide a case. There were many more letters needing attention than he had to deal with in the past "that a secretary might answer, if I had one," he admitted to Mrs. Codman shortly after arriving in Washington. "But I have not the habit and tremble on the brink. I don't quite see what a secretary could do for me in the legal way, as my mode of writing is to get into a kind of frenzy when I should not want anyone bothering round and then the thing is done."[18]

The first year he ended up hiring a local man who had applied to him for the position, Charles K. Poe; Holmes said he had taken him on "because he wanted to study law and had no other chance." But when Poe left at the end of the 1905–6 term, he decided to revive Justice Gray's practice of selecting a Harvard Law graduate, and he wrote Nina Gray to ask if her husband might look out for a secretary for him, as he had for his half brother:

> I presume that we should want the same kind of man—presentable, clever, not unwilling or unable to make out my checks for me at the beginning of the month, etc. and up in the latest fashions of the law school law. I think it is rather a good thing to have the place regarded as a sort of yearly prize in the law school—if I do not misappreciate.[19]

They all quickly discovered what his first secretary from Harvard, Augustin Derby, observed when he took up his duties: Holmes really did not need a secretary. What the justice wanted was a young companion to accompany him on his walks, represent him and be "a contribution to society" around Washington, and handle confidential personal matters like keeping his checkbook, making out his tax returns, and periodically going to his safe deposit box at Riggs National Bank, a block from the White House, and cutting off the coupons of his maturing bonds.[20]

The legal duties were at best a formality. "Don't bother about preparations for coming here," Holmes assured one of those selected for the job, telling him not even to worry about reading the reports of the recent opinions of the Court: "I don't regard it as necessary as a qualification." The first task he always assigned his new secretary, when he arrived as instructed at precisely 11 a.m. on the Friday before the Court began its term the first Monday of October, was to unpack and sort out the large "cube" of books and pamphlets that had accumulated over the summer.[21]

During the year Holmes sometimes had his secretary read briefs, motion papers, and petitions and prepare summaries of them, but even that was more an exercise than real work: "Perhaps he thought that he had given legal assistance; but the Justice read all the briefs and papers himself," Derby noted. "He never asked me to find the law. He knew the law." The only substantive contribution the secretaries were asked to make to Holmes's opinions was to find citations that backed up his points, preferably from his own previous decisions. "Please embellish this with citations from my favorite author," Holmes would say as he handed over his completed opinion to his secretary.[22]

He would sometimes read a finished opinion aloud to the secretary, "not soliciting our comment," Chauncey Belknap said, "but rather, it seemed, to let his ear test the cadence of the sentence." Belknap wrote in his diary a month and a half into his year with Holmes that even though the justice freely discussed his decisions "as if I were on an equal plane of learning and powers," he could not ever imagine screwing up his courage to offer his own views. "Even if there were doubts in my mind, I should have to get myself into the state of mind of a court overruling a jury before venturing to differ."[23]

Harvey Bundy did once cautiously venture to make a suggestion. "I think, Sir, that the opinion is splendid, except for the last paragraph which seems to me not to be quite clear," he said.

"What the hell do you mean—not clear? Give it to me." Holmes reread the offending phrase. "Well, if you don't understand it I suppose there will be some other damn fool who won't, so I'd better change it."[24]

Holmes once explained that he liked to have a new secretary each year so he could continue to draw on his fund of favorite stories without being accused of repeating himself. "The Judge liked to walk with his secretary and expound his philosophical ideas to a ready audience— if you will, a quite willingly captive audience," Bundy recalled. Their usual walk in the afternoons when he returned from the Court at about five o'clock was a three-quarters-of-an-hour loop around the immediate neighborhood—up to Connecticut and Seventeenth Street, or around the White House—though sometimes they would make it to Rock Creek Park. On days the Court was not sitting, he would often take his secretary along for a drive in the morning to one of his favorite spots: Fort Stevens, the Soldiers' Home, the unknown soldier monument at Arlington Cemetery, the zoo.[25]

In fact, there was "more walking than law," Barton Leach remembered. The topics of Holmes's talk on these occasions was as free-ranging as his letters; there was nothing that did not interest him, Donald Hiss noted, "except athletics."[26] The Civil War, literature, the personalities of his fellow justices, people and life in general were all likely to be covered over the course of the year.

Holmes called his secretaries "Sonny" when he was pleased with them; he would say, "Don't be an idiot, boy," when he was not. Donald Hiss vividly recalled Holmes's efforts to drill his philosophy of life into him. "Sonny," he suddenly asked him one day, "if you were at war and had your rifle raised and brought into your sights an enemy figure and God tapped you on the shoulder and said, 'If you let that man live, he'll be a great doctor some day,' what would you do?" Hiss replied it was a difficult question and he did not have a ready answer. "Don't be an idiot, boy," Holmes shot back. "He's the enemy and you'd shoot him of course. You're not God, you are merely a soldier fighting a war."[27]

Francis Biddle thought Holmes enjoyed "the sense of resistance that youth sometimes gives to age," but there were limits. Donald Hiss once began challenging Holmes to explain what he meant when he said that J. Pierpont Morgan was "an intellectual giant." After enduring several minutes of Hiss's persistent questioning, Holmes turned to him and said, "Sonny, I am not an anvil on which you can beat out your impressions of life," at which Hiss dissolved into laughter and abandoned his interrogation.[28]

But what Holmes clearly liked most was simply the contact with the young, the feeling he was not losing touch with "the latest fashions" of the law, as he had put it, and the connections his secretary provided to the younger set in Washington. At the start of the year, Holmes told

Belknap that one of his duties, at least as important as any legal work, was to make sure that "all of the liveliest gals in town turned up" for his weekly Monday afternoon reception. "As there was not one of them who didn't regard an hour with the Holmeses as about the best fun there was to be had in Washington, this part of the job gave me no trouble," Belknap noted. Some of the young ladies would sit on the floor, literally at the justice's feet, listening to his talk.[29]

Holmes's one rule for his secretary was that the man chosen for the position had to be single. As he told Frankfurter, who took over the job of selecting Holmes's secretaries after Gray's death, "It is true that the work is not very much but if baby has the megrims, papa won't have the freedom of mind and spirit that I like to find."[30]

But the four who violated the rule—Harvey Bundy, W. Barton Leach, Arthur E. Sutherland Jr., and Alger Hiss—were all promptly forgiven. Bundy was engaged, though not yet married, when he arrived in Washington and Holmes was "quite upset" to learn the fact. But at some point during the year Fanny said to Bundy, "Why don't you two get married," and they did. Derby later heard the story of one of the miscreant secretaries: the justice gave him a thorough dressing down for his outrageous behavior, then said, "Here is three hundred dollars, young man," and handed him a check.[31]

When Hiss got married halfway through his year, Frankfurter was worried enough that he sent Brandeis an urgent telegram asking him to go over to 1720 Eye Street at once and try to smooth out the situation. Hiss confessed to Frankfurter that he had only learned from a law school friend, about ten hours before the wedding, of the justice's rule. But when Brandeis arrived on the scene he found Holmes "in the best of form, rollicking, playful in spirit & entirely without worry of any kind. I concluded he needed no assurance about Hiss." Holmes had shown no annoyance, giving Hiss his blessing the evening of the ceremony and his "welcome into the brotherhood" the next morning, and invited the newlyweds to lunch a few days later.[32]

But still Holmes did not drop the general rule against his secretaries being married or engaged, and reiterated to Frankfurter that it would be best to make sure the man chosen for the job understood: he wanted "a free man" who could be a part of Washington society and bring back the latest quips, as well as the "liveliest gals."[33]

The job was so undemanding and the role expected of them such an abrupt change from the intense three years they had just spent at Harvard Law School that it was a bit bewildering. "The discouraging feature of the job is that they are both so nice to me that I wonder at times whether I am secretary, guest, or prodigal son," John Lockwood wrote to Frankfurter a month into it. "I have a suspicion that I shall never have another boss whom it will be so difficult to convince that I should be allowed to help him—nor one whom I shall be so anxious to help." Belknap remembered Mrs. Holmes informing him at the start of his year—"with mischief in her eye"—"that I would usually find her right downstairs, and if the Justice did not behave himself or did not treat me properly I must be sure to let her know immediately."[34]

A month later Belknap wrote in his diary, "I am the master of a magnificent leisure." During his year, Leach found himself filling most of his hours while the Court was sitting playing golf or reading. Bundy spent so much time at the Chevy Chase Club improving his tennis game that he won the club championship his year.[35]

For a bachelor in that vanished world of Washington society in the first decades of the twentieth century, there was no lack of dinners, outings, dances, and debutante parties, which added to the sense Holmes's secretaries had of the slight unreality of their year with the justice. Washington was "terribly short of men," and society hostesses were ever in need of extra male guests to fill out their tables, Bundy recalled; there was always "a blizzard of invitations" to grand houses and embassies for dinners, with "six butlers and three kinds of wine." Francis Biddle idled away his spare time with all-day riding parties on Sundays in Rock Creek Park, lunches at the Metropolitan Club with cosmopolitan acquaintances he had made among the young staff members of the British and Russian embassies, and lavish picnics put on by a wealthy retired Army colonel and his wife who liked young people, featuring "a fabulous lunch from picnic baskets unpacked by solemn men servants, and all the champagne we could drink."[36]

All sorts of celebrities streamed in and out of the colonel's house, and Biddle was able to score one coup that greatly pleased the justice when one Sunday afternoon he met Maggie Teyte there. She was a twenty-three-year-old soprano who was making a sensation in the opera world, and she asked Biddle if he would take her to Court the next day, when the justices announced their opinions. In the solemn hush of the courtroom she suddenly leaned over and whispered in Biddle's ear that she felt an uncontrollable urge to sing—perhaps the Jewel Song from *Faust*—and would that be all right? She came to tea that afternoon and related the story, causing Holmes to shout with laughter when she explained that the only thing that stopped her was the look of complete horror on his secretary's face.[37]

Although the job may not have been much of a legal apprenticeship, one after another of his secretaries called their year with Holmes the greatest of their lives. Long before he became a household name, Holmes was a figure of renown to the law students at Harvard—"I believe the casebooks we studied at the Harvard Law School contained more opinions by Holmes than by any other judge, living or dead," said Belknap—which gave the feeling of "being admitted to a charmed circle" for the young graduates selected for the job.[38]

But what really made the year magical in their memories was what Biddle called Holmes's "spontaneous unforced sympathy" for the young—and what Alger Hiss described as the aura of Holmes's "moral and physical courage, fierce independence of spirit" and example of duty and personal honor.[39] "The intellectual excitement of being with him was just extraordinary," Hiss recalled a full half century later. "It was probably the greatest intellectual, emotional experience any of us had." John Lockwood wrote at the end of his year of having had his "budding tastes" educated by the "contagious" affection Holmes had for nature and art—"a tulip tree, a statue, or a group of etchings . . . I feel certain that my eyes see more, that I think in broader channels than I did." And Horace Chapman Rose sent Holmes a parting tribute in a burst of ingenuous enthusiasm, "You gave me insight into a way of life more perfect than any that I shall know again."[40]

Nearly all of Holmes's young protégés went on to exceptional careers. Of his thirty secretaries, eleven became founders or partners of prestigious law firms, including his two Jewish secretaries, Lloyd H. Landau and Robert M. Benjamin, in an era when institutionalized anti-Semitism in the legal profession generally closed the door to that possibility; four became law professors at Harvard, W. Barton Leach, Mark DeWolfe Howe, Arthur E. Sutherland Jr., and Augustin Derby, and one, Stanley Morrison, at Stanford; nine held prominent positions in politics and government, including Francis B. Biddle (attorney general), Harvey H. Bundy (assistant secretary of state), James Henry Rowe Jr. (assistant attorney general), H. Chapman Rose (undersecretary of the treasury), Laurence Curtis II (congressman from Massachusetts), Erland F. Fish (president of the Massachusetts Senate), Day Kimball (Supreme Court of Bermuda), and Thomas G. Corcoran (intimate adviser to FDR and drafter of key legislation of the New Deal, including the Federal Housing Act of 1933, the Securities Exchange Act of 1934, and the Fair Labor Standards Act of 1938); and four rose to the top ranks of business and industry, including Irving S. Olds (president of U.S. Steel) and George L. Harrison (president and chairman of the board of RCA).[41]

Leach, who had a less happy year than most and who was willing to make some fairly caustic comments in later years about Holmes's judicial performance, nonetheless concluded the remarks he was asked to deliver when Holmes's portrait was unveiled at Harvard Law School by observing, "But let there be no doubt about this: Whatever cliché may have been uttered about great men and their valets, Holmes, J. is a hero to his secretaries."[42]

———

HOLMES'S "BOYS" WERE NOT adopted sons or surrogates for the children he never had, as some of the more romantic portrayals of his life have implied, but they helped fill a void of companionship that he felt acutely as he approached his seventieth year, and the passing years took their inevitable toll on the lives and happiness of his older friends.

"This year has been full of disaster and death," he wrote Baroness Moncheur a week before Christmas 1910. That April he had heard from Mrs. Green that his friends the Scotts were having difficulties in their marriage. Leslie as a rising barrister and politician was absorbed in his career, while Ethel "has been overworked and overwrought ever since I have known her," Holmes wrote back. "I wish that I could help the situation, but I have nothing except an anxious affection for both. . . . They both think nobly about life and yet one feels a kind of despair."[43]

On the Fourth of July, 1910, Chief Justice Fuller died at his summer home in Sorrento, Maine. Holmes spent four nights on trains traveling to Maine for the funeral, back to Boston, to Chicago for the burial, then again home. "The services at Sorrento moved me through and through," he wrote to one of Fuller's old friends the day after arriving back at Beverly Farms on July 11. "It was a beautiful day, and there was no false note. The coffin, spread with a coverlet of flowers, was put on a buckboard to go from the house to the church; the birds were singing; the clergyman, a fine fellow whom I dare say you know, read extremely well; a little choir of four young men sang touchingly. . . . It is rare indeed for me to find everything so conspire with the natural feeling of the moment."[44]

He confided to Baroness Moncheur that "the Chief died at just the right moment, for during this last term he had begun to show his age in his administrative work, I thought, and I was doubting whether I ought not to speak to his family, as they relied upon me." But, he added, "He loved me and I shall miss him as long as I sit on the Bench." Holmes did not read the newspapers as a rule—"superficial, silly things," he called them—but could not help reading the articles about him or the Court from time to time, and he was cast down to see how much more attention the papers gave to the Johnson-Jeffries heavyweight championship fight that same day than "to a great man dead."[45]

In August, William James died, and Holmes attended the funeral in Cambridge, where he caught a glimpse of Henry James looking "distinguished but far from well." It was another closing of a door to the past, even if, as he told Baroness Moncheur, "our relations had ceased, practically," separated not just by distance and time but by mutual irritations that the very closeness of their onetime friendship and intellectual kinship exacerbated over the years.[46] James, ever resentful of Holmes's freedom from the moral earnestness he could never abandon himself, complained in his later years of Holmes's "childish" exuberance in action for action's sake; Holmes, equally annoyed at what he called the "amusing humbug" of James's efforts to reconcile a mechanistic universe with free will, sniped that James was always trying to "sneak in the miraculous at the back door." In their later years they had mostly seemed to talk past one other, still agreeing at heart but unable to admit it.[47]

And then, just before his return to Washington at the end of September, the old first sergeant of his regiment, Gustav Magnitzky, a Prussian Pole "who enlisted on principle shortly after his arrival in this country," and later was the bookkeeper and general manager of Holmes's law firm in Boston, died. "There were few men for whom I had so sincere an affection," he told Ethel Scott.[48]

"The familiar faces are nearly all gone now," he said; driving around Beverly Farms, he found the houses "now inhabited by strangers and ghosts." But, he remarked of his feelings toward death, "As one grows older one gets like the eels accustomed to being skinned. Indeed the war accustomed me to it when I was young."[49]

<hr/>

FULLER'S DEATH set off the usual political scramble over his replacement. Public speculation strongly favored Justice Charles Evans Hughes for the job. Hughes, who had just been appointed to the Court as an associate justice by President Taft, and not yet even taken his seat, had been all but promised the chief justiceship as a reward for giving up a possible challenge to Taft for the 1912 Republican nomination. But now, abruptly faced with the decision, Taft backpedaled, and after months of "prayerful consideration" and much political consultation, in December 1910 announced his choice of Justice White instead.[50]

The political calculus was complex. Though Hughes had been a progressive-minded governor of New York, he had run afoul of TR over a matter of patronage, which neutralized any favors Taft might hope to score with the Roosevelt wing of the Republican Party by elevating him to chief justice. Roosevelt let Taft know he preferred White, as did more conservative Republicans; as a Democrat, White would also automatically command the support of the opposing party in the Senate. When Taft's choice of a Democrat was announced, the Republican Speaker of the House, Joe Cannon, grumbled that "if Taft were pope he'd want to appoint some Protestants to the College of Cardinals," but it was a shrewd political move: the Senate approved the nomination in a unanimous voice vote the same day it was sent up.[51]

"I suppose Hughes was bitterly disappointed at not getting the place as everyone expected that he would—including, I guess, the President up to the evening before the choice was announced," Holmes wrote to Mrs. Green. "White is a bigger man and I am glad it fell to him. Hughes has taken it admirably. Poor old Harlan who was the senior and who was skipped is heart broken, I am afraid." Taft was, too, in his own way. "There is nothing I would have loved more than being chief justice of the United States," he told his attorney general the day White was confirmed. "I cannot help seeing the irony in the fact that I, who desired the office so much, should now be signing the commission of another man."[52]

Holmes disavowed any ambition in the position, or disappointment that he was not selected; he told Mrs. Gray, who had apparently written a word of consolation when he was passed over,

My ambitions as you know are internal. An appointment as Chief Justice would do nothing towards satisfying them and I never thought of it for an instant as a possibility for myself. . . . Naturally one's feeling of attainment goes up and down—as my father used to say self estimates are a stock of fancy goods—sold at auction they don't bring much. I was feeling down when I felt the touch of your soothing hand.[53]

But it all left him "gloomy," he admitted to Lewis Einstein, and musing about the nature of accomplishment and recognition. "One has a despairing sense that popularity or popular appreciation is to be had only by the sacrifice of ideals."[54] He had been briefly buoyed when Oxford awarded him an honorary degree the summer of the previous year; he made a "flying visit" to England that June, but did not feel he could be away long from Fanny, who had had a long "pulldown" after an operation in May 1908 that kept her hospitalized for several weeks.[55]

During the Oxford ceremony, "while the learned Doctor of Laws who presented me was making a Latin speech as to my merits," he recounted, an undergraduate "sung out from the gallery, 'Can you translate it, Sir?' which made me grin." He was given the opportunity to buy his scarlet doctor of law's robes, which he briefly considered for the pleasure of horrifying his brethren by appearing in them in the justices' robing room, but decided that "my evil impulse wasn't worth 8 guineas."[56]

"Out of the blue" in October 1910 he also was awarded an honorary degree from the University of Berlin, an "encouragement" that "really pleased me," he told Einstein. But those recognitions had been balanced by the bittersweet pang he felt when White remarked to him that "he didn't know any man in the country who had so little reputation in proportion to what he had done—I was half pleased, if half sad."[57]

"It all makes me speculate as to what I shall do—keep on or retire— when my 10 years are out if I am still alive and all right on Dec. 8, 1912," which was when he would be eligible to retire on his full salary, he told Baroness Moncheur when he wrote her at Christmastime 1910 at the end of that year of "disaster and death." A. V. Dicey, a British jurist he had known since 1870, remarked when he saw him at his degree ceremony at Oxford that "he would rather have people say why the devil does he than why the devil doesn't he." But for now, Holmes was still finding he could do his work with ease—even if that some-times seemed an omen in itself: "A pen writes best when it is nearly worn out," he ironically observed.[58]

The final disaster of the year was the news from Ireland. Clare Castletown had had a painful operation on her eye that summer, and Holmes received a letter from her in December "which beside speak-ing with discouragement about ever getting back the sight of one eye, almost casually said that they were reduced to great poverty." Holmes cautiously asked Canon Sheehan if he knew the details, and the full story slowly emerged. Lord Castletown had sold out all of his pur-chased land, plunged wildly in foreign investments, and lost everything. Receivers were sent to take charge of the estates at Granston and Doneraile, and Canon Sheehan wrote of hearing the crack of guns all day as the deer herd was shot out and the carcasses sent to the market in London to try to raise what small amount they would bring.[59]

The following year, Lord Castletown broke down completely under the strain and was committed to an insane asylum, from where he sent piteous letters to Clare begging to be allowed to return home ("I am *perfectly well* & as *sane* as any man in Ireland . . . I give you my word of honor you will have no trouble with me . . . I can do you no harm as I am quite well"). He did come home after several months.[60]

Holmes, in the first of his letters to Clare that exists after a decade's gap, wrote her in the midst of the crisis in the spring of 1912 that he was "extremely glad" she had apparently decided against leaving her husband:

> I can't but believe it wiser, on selfish grounds, and I also have the notion, for which I have no documentation or definite evidence, that at other moments he has been pretty loyal to you. And altogether magnanimity is your most judicious as well as most beautiful role. It is easy for me to talk, away off here, I know, but I tell you what I believe.[61]

His tone was much altered from the passionate outbursts in the wake of their 1898 meeting; he now wrote her just as another old friend. A week later he sent her the news that "many who were known and loved here" had gone down with the *Titanic*, including Archie Butt, the president's aide.[62]

In the summer of 1913 he made his final trip to England and Ireland. He was again worried about leaving Fanny, and was "very unwilling" to travel without her. A few days before he was to go, he fell hard on his knee at the bottom of the stairs, which left him black and blue ("I beat Turner for colors from there to the sole of my foot"). But as usual in the end he went.[63]

The Castletowns had been allowed to retain a life estate in their houses, and he saw them again at Doneraile, and visited Canon Sheehan every day, who "said he was dying but I hoped otherwise," he wrote to Mrs. Gray. But shortly after his return to Washington he read of the canon's death on October 5. As a parting gift Sheehan had asked him to pick out a book from his library, and Holmes took a folio of the seventeenth-century Jesuit Francisco Suarez's work on the philosophy of law, *De Legibus*.[64]

"A beautiful spirit," he said to Mrs. Green of his departed friend. "I am afraid I should not have talked quite so freely to him!"[65]

THE DEATHS OF his old friends gave Holmes even more pleasure in the young. "I . . . perhaps should be lonely but for the young men that seem to like to come in and see me from time to time. I always have one on hand in the form of my secretary, who has to sit and hear my views (if you can *hear* a *view*) on law and economics, not to speak of excursions into the cosmos at large," he told Ethel Scott. Aside from his secretary there was suddenly a new group of young, lively, brilliant, and enthusiastic friends in Washington whose company he found invigorating and encouraging.[66]

The most brilliant and enthusiastic was the twenty-eight-year-old Felix Frankfurter, who had burst into Holmes's life bearing a letter of introduction from John Chipman Gray. Frankfurter was the son of Austrian Jewish immigrants; he had arrived in New York at age eleven not knowing a word of English, but had flourished in New York's public schools, in part thanks to the tough Irish teacher at P.S. 25 who threatened the other German-speaking students in her class with her fists if she caught them talking German to the new pupil. After graduating from City College, he applied to Harvard Law School with more than a little trepidation, fearing he could not afford it and would not be welcome there. But he found the law school the most "democratic" institution he would ever experience, later saying that he had a "quasi-religious" feeling for the way intrinsic value and ethical considerations permeated everything about the place. He quickly soared to the top of his class, and was selected as an editor of the law review.[67]

When he graduated in 1906 he was brushed off in interview after interview with New York law firms, until one finally offered him a job—the first Jew they had ever hired—though one of the partners suggested he change his last name to something less "odd." Then a phone call changed his life. Manhattan's U.S. attorney Henry Stimson, a blue-blood patrician who had given up a $20,000 a year position with a Wall Street law firm (equal to $600,000 today) to help advance the progressive agenda of the Roosevelt administration, had asked the deans of the top law schools for recommendations of their best recent graduates. Frankfurter was at the top of the list, and Stimson hired him as a junior assistant. Over the next several years Frankfurter played a lead role in the government's prosecution of the sugar trust, winning several key convictions in court.[68]

When Stimson was named Taft's secretary of war in June 1911, he brought Frankfurter to Washington with him as law officer for the department's Bureau of Insular Affairs, overseeing U.S. territories acquired in the Spanish-American War.

Frankfurter was five foot six, with a babyish face, and by his own telling had come off to his Harvard roommate as "a mamma's boy" when he arrived with a trunk of clothes that he admitted his mother had packed for him. But he had an unselfconscious love of ideas and people and talk and an optimistic spirit that, Holmes later said, "walked deep into my heart." If the uncanny ability that Holmes also detected in Frankfurter "of wiggling in wherever he wants to" was self-promoting, it was also perfectly genuine. "Felix has two hundred best friends," his future wife once remarked. She also said, "Do you know what it's like to be married to a man who is never tired?"[69]

Holmes invited him to lunch, and Frankfurter wrote enthusiastically to Gray immediately afterward, "I came away with the keen relief of having been on Olympus and finding that one's God did not have clay feet. There is a brilliance and range in the justice's conversation. . . . But over and above his keen penetration, his contempt for mere words and formula, and his freshness of outlook, give lasting zest and momentum to one's groping and toiling."[70]

Frankfurter soon became a regular visitor. Holmes later remarked to Frankfurter how struck he was by the "exquisite moral susceptibil-

"House of Truth," c. 1913: standing left to right, Denison,
Valentine, Frankfurter; seated, Christie

ity" that, he said, seemed to be "the gift of many Jews." But more than
that, Frankfurter cheered him up. "He . . . has the encouraging tone
that seems to be a point of conscience with the Jews," he told Baroness
Moncheur. "At all events Felix always is comforting."[71]

Frankfurter lived with several other young men near Dupont Circle.
The group quickly became the nucleus of a lively social circle, as well
as a hotbed of progressive opposition inside the Taft administration.
The small, three-story townhouse at 1727 Nineteenth Street where
they lived (which still stands) had been rented by Robert G. Valentine, Taft's commissioner of Indian affairs; when his wife had to return
to Boston to obtain medical care for their infant daughter, the forty-

year-old Valentine invited several younger friends who shared his liberal views to move into the house and help pay the rent and keep him company. Frankfurter was the first, moving in in May 1912, and two other young attorneys soon followed: Winfred T. Denison, an assistant attorney general who had worked with Frankfurter and Stimson in the sugar trust cases, and Loring Christie, who had graduated from Harvard Law three years after Frankfurter and come to Washington to work in Denison's office.[72]

The last to join the household was Lord Eustace Percy, a British diplomat and the seventh son of the Duke of Northumberland. Frankfurter described him as "much more of a dreamer and a mystic than the son of a great landowner," but he shared the group's interest in public affairs and social progress. On the floor of the living room the young men once spent four days working out an eight-page plan of reform, which they modestly titled, "A Tentative Social Program."[73]

The justice and Mrs. Holmes became regular visitors to the house, with its conversation-filled dinner parties and five-hour-long Sunday lunches. "How or why I can't recapture," Frankfurter said later, "but almost everybody who was interesting in Washington sooner or later passed through that house." Herbert Hoover; the British ambassador James Bryce, Holmes's old legal friend; Attorney General James McReynolds; Louis Brandeis, on his many trips to Washington to argue public-interest cases, all dined there, along with artists, newspapermen, writers, and a raft of pretty girls. One night Holmes looked on with fascination as the sculptor Gutzon Borglum sketched on the tablecloth his conception of a memorial to Robert E. Lee and other Confederate heroes that he had a vision of carving out of the solid stone face of a mountainside in Georgia—the plan he would later realize as the monument to presidents on Mount Rushmore.[74]

The house acquired a self-mocking name, "The House of Truth," which Percy recalled "some humorist conferred upon us" in token of their earnest discussions.[75] Holmes took his young friends' "asms for isms" and "upward and onward" talk with amused tolerance. He was particularly unmoved by the universal enthusiasm in the house for Teddy Roosevelt's Bull Moose campaign of 1912. TR had galvanized progressive reformers by seeking a comeback as a third-party candidate after losing his challenge to Taft for the Republican nomination that year. But as Holmes observed to Einstein, "The Bull Moose manifestos struck me as exhibiting a strenuous vagueness that produced atmospheric disturbance without transmitting a message."[76]

Still, Holmes said, "I can talk with those young chaps more easily than with most of the older men who have lost their enthusiasm." A notable example of the latter was his old Boston friend Henry Adams, who lived just north of Lafayette Square, and whom Holmes used to stop in and see on his way home from Court. But he had finally given it up as too much work. "At times he poses as an old cardinal and wears on your nerves by telling you that everything is dust and ashes," Holmes told Baroness Moncheur.[77]

And Holmes always liked telling how Walter Howe, one of the young admirers of TR to whom he had been expressing his doubts, "stuck me under the fifth rib" with his riposte, "You would found legislation on regrets rather than on hopes"—which Holmes said he thought a good comeuppance to his perennial skepticism. It was a pleasure, he said, to see "more faith and enthusiasm" among "the young chaps" than he himself could always muster.[78]

———

HOLMES DROVE HIMSELF so hard during the Court term that when the work ended each June it took him several weeks before he could feel he had "settled down to vacation." As much as he looked forward to getting away to Beverly Farms each summer, the arrangements for the trip were a torment; he would fidget over sending off the trunks, dread missing the train. "I am a bad case of train fever and am more worried by things of this sort than by a great constitutional case," he admitted. "The kind of thing that women have to deal with all the time, the simultaneous pressure of many little things to be attended to, drives me mad." They would get to the station hours ahead of time, just to be safe. Once he had his secretary hunt up the stationmaster to let them board a full hour before the scheduled departure time. "Sonny," he announced with satisfaction as he settled into his private room, "this is the way to catch a train!"[79]

The servants usually went a week ahead of time to take care of the final preparations of opening the house, but that meant additional worries and disruptions to his comfortable routine that also frayed his nerves. His old attendant from the court in Boston, James Doherty, would meet the "girls" at Boston's South Station, see that their luggage was forwarded, and get them in a taxi to North Station for the train to Beverly.[80]

But once the turmoil of the trip was behind him Holmes was able to indulge himself in a summer of "busy idleness." In 1908 he had agreed to purchase the Beverly Farms property, paying $17,000 for a two-thirds interest and buying the other one-third later. The Holmeses added a small rose garden ("bossed by this great expert") on a steep slope behind the house; Holmes later bought an additional piece of land at the bottom of the hill to preserve the row of trees and masses of rhododendrons that grew there, and to block a rumored private road that might have run right along his fence.[81]

But overall little changed in their reclusive existence there. "To keep off strangers," the phone, 14 Beverly Farms, was listed under Fanny's name. He played solitaire, slept, and went for long drives with Fanny along "beautiful seashores and pretty inland farms" every day the weather was fine. "I am very quiet and duties have ceased, if I only could get rid of the feeling that there must be something that I ought to be doing," he wrote to Ethel Scott during a typical summer there. They occasionally had close friends to stay for a few days, like the Pollocks or Ethel Scott when they visited America, but other than that saw very few people, and had less and less to do with the fashionable world of summer residents around them in Beverly Farms and Manchester.[82]

Most of all he looked forward to reading. He tried to devote some time to "books that bear on the foundations of the law in one way or another"—economics, sociology, science, and "even law." But toward the end of the vacation he would give up, and pursue "lighter themes." Only Holmes could call Plato's *Republic* or Homer's *Odyssey* in the

A portion of Holmes's 1911 reading list, including Plato's *Symposium* in Greek, the letters of Flaubert to George Sand in French, Alfred North Whitehead's *Introduction to Mathematics,* and *The Industrial History of the United States,* by the social activist and economist Katharine Coman

original Greek light reading, but to "sport with ideas" was always his greatest pleasure.[83]

So during his summers at Beverly he finished Dante, reading *Purgatorio* and *Paradiso* ("the last I think on the whole is my favorite of the three, and I suppose it is the least read. People prefer stories of bad boys to those of good ones"); worked his way through the *Oxford Book of French Verse* ("poetry or prose, the Mussoos mean business when they make love to a lady"); ordered Descartes, Aristotle, and Berkeley from the Everyman's Library ("they are bores invariably, but they leave a residuum"); dipped into Epictetus, which he had never before read ("an astonishing book") and Montaigne, which he had, but which struck him in a new light when he picked it up in the right mood on one vacation ("What a reasonable bird he was! I don't know whether one would have liked him in the flesh"); tackled Spinoza's *Ethics*, which pleased him ("his dream of the Universe, which he prefers to call God, and I call X is more nearly mine than that of any of the older writers that I know") and Henry James's *The Ambassadors*, which did not ("a narrow world of taste and refined moral vacillations. . . . My general attitude is relatively coarse: let the man take the girl or leave her. I don't care a damn which"); and forced himself, on his English friends' enthusiastic praises, to give Jane Austen another try, though he admitted— writing the two words in very tiny print in a letter to Pollock—that he found her "a bore."[84]

Tolstoy and Dickens held his interest better when it came to fiction, as did "frisky French" novels and the spy thrillers of John Buchan: he devoured *Mr. Standfast* almost in one day, lying on the couch from breakfast to midday dinner.[85]

Usually by the end of the summer he succeeded in feeling "richly idle," though he half-jokingly told Clara Stevens that even his regular games of solitaire had a way of feeling like a duty he did not dare to neglect.[86]

Then the return to Washington was another frenzy of packing and travel arrangements; the servants were usually given their annual vacation then, so the Holmeses were again on their own for a couple of weeks when they arrived back at 1720 Eye Street.

One September they broke their journey with a visit to New York, but Holmes did not care much for the feel of the city:

> I don't like hurry as an ideal. . . . I don't like money as so exclusive a criterion. My wife said the churches used to reach nearest to heaven but now business looks down on the steeples. But Grants

Tomb brought the tears into my eyes. . . . Central Park and the Met Art Museum are noble. . . . I went to some not too high shows. . . . But I am glad to be out of it and still solvent. I remembered what Cohen is said to have remarked on his receiving his hotel bill. "I've got more than that."[87]

On returning to Washington every fall one of his first acts was to copy into the Black Book the list of books he had read over the summer, which he had jotted down in the back of his checkbook while he was away. He also made a solemn ritual of placing on the shelf of his library the printed set of his opinions from the previous term. He would drop off the pages with a bookbinder in Boston each year on his way north, to be bound into a handsome leather volume, stamped on the spine in gold letters MR. JUSTICE HOLMES' OPINIONS U.S. SUPREME COURT. "I never feel that the last term's work is finished until I have solemnly deposited my little vol. of decisions in the shelf by the side of the others," he told Leslie Scott. "Also I don't feel as if books had been read until they are entered on my permanent list."[88]

He added: "And this is a man supposed to be entitled to the respect of his fellows!"

CHAPTER 13

Holmes Dissenting

The elevation of White to chief justice was one of a half dozen appointments that Taft made in just over two years from 1909 to 1912 that completely remade the Court.

Taft had repeatedly bemoaned the aging Court and what he feared was its declining vigor and reputation. "The condition of the Supreme Court is pitiable, and yet those old fools hold on with a tenacity that is most discouraging," he wrote in 1909 to a good friend—Horace H. Lurton, a federal circuit judge whom he would name to the high court when the first vacancy during his term opened up. "Really the Chief Justice is almost senile; Harlan does no work; Brewer is so deaf that he cannot hear and has got beyond the point of the commonest accuracy in writing his opinions; Brewer and Harlan sleep almost through all the arguments. I don't know what can be done."[1]

On the eve of his successor Woodrow Wilson's inauguration on March 4, 1913, Taft called in the newspaper reporters to his office for some farewell observations on the successes and failures of his administration. He told them that the thing he was proudest of was having appointed six of the nine current justices. "And I have said to them, 'Damn you, if any of you die, I'll disown you.'"[2]

The appointments did little to alter the Court's ideological balance, which retained its conservative, if vacillating cast. The Court would continue as before to strike down most progressive labor and economic

Chief Justice White

laws, with only the occasional not very clearly reasoned exception. But there was no doubt that Taft's selections injected new life and prestige into the Court. Joseph H. Choate, a leading member of the bar, declared at a dinner given in Taft's honor by the American Bar Association: "Mr. Taft has rehabilitated the Supreme Court of the United States."[3]

Of Holmes's colleagues when he joined the Court, only White and Justice Joseph McKenna remained. As second in seniority among the associate justices, Holmes now sat at the center of the bench on the chief justice's immediate left; McKenna was on the right.

Holmes mostly liked the new brethren, even if he was mostly unimpressed by them. The most able, he thought, were Hughes and Willis Van Devanter, a Wyoming man appointed to fill White's seat. Van Devanter was an expert on Western land law, and Holmes found his careful edits on the returns of his opinions incisive and nearly always accepted them. But when it came to writing his own opinions Van Devanter suffered from what one of his closest friends called "pen paralysis." Hughes later observed that if his careful and well-grounded statements in conference could have been taken down stenographically they would have made excellent opinions with little editing, but Van Devanter just could not get himself to begin writing and was always behind in his assignments.[4]

Taft's final two appointments were Joseph R. Lamar, a former justice of the Georgia Supreme Court, chosen mainly because Taft was seeking a Southerner for geographical balance, and Mahlon Pitney, who had been chancellor of Delaware's court of equity. Lamar was an amiable man who, like White, looked like a justice from central casting, tall, with a deep, resonant voice and a domelike head; a reliably cautious economic conservative, he embraced liberty of contract and upheld economic regulation only when it could be justified on the grounds of public health, safety, or morals.[5] Pitney aggravated Holmes at first with his long-windedness, though after Pitney's death in 1924 Holmes told Frankfurter, "I learned to appreciate more and more his faithful, serious devotion to his job, his great industry and . . . his intellectual honesty. It is hard to get a man as good as he was, whatever reserves one may make in superlatives."[6]

Holmes gave Baroness Moncheur his "*very private*" assessment of the new Court:

> Lurton thinks like a lawyer, though I suspect his economics are superstitions. Hughes has taken hold of work with industry and acuteness. I doubt if he has great analytic power—time will show. . . . Van Devanter knows a great deal about certain departments of the work and is pleasant. Lamar has not written yet, but seems a very nice fellow and intelligent. . . . I think the new Chief worries over his work—he thinks like a legislator of consequences, all the time—and sees the ruin of the republic in a wrong decision—which makes it harder for him, but is valuable for the Court.[7]

Holmes constantly complained in private, though, of his colleagues' tedium in conferences. They "bore me with their not unavailed opportunities for repeating the arguments that already bored me once," he told Mrs. Green. Holmes prided himself on not losing his calm even when the discussions got heated. But he could not always resist a veiled swipe. "I stop from a scalping expedition in which I am trying to remove the place where the hair ought to grow from the head of one of my brethren," he wrote to Mrs. Gray during a break in one conference. "As of old my brethren pitch into me for being obscure and when I go nasty I say that I write for educated men—of course, as if referring to some others than my interlocutor."[8]

Most of all he chafed at having to submit his written opinions to "the censors who prune my exuberance," and forced him to substitute "some pap that would not hurt an infant's stomach." Again, Holmes would always "good naturedly agree" to the changes imposed on him, Hughes observed, but he never stopped being privately irked.[9]

The most severe of his "censors" were McKenna and William R. Day.[10] Though Holmes said he was "very fond" of Day, who had joined the Court just after him, he once remarked that Day's "opinions set like plaster of Paris; there is no budging them." A small-town corporation lawyer from Ohio, firmly rooted in nineteenth-century laissez-faire individualism and a narrow view of the federal government's powers, Day had been unexpectedly catapulted onto the national stage when McKinley had made him his secretary of state during the Spanish-American War. Dean Acheson thought Day looked more like one of the Seven Dwarfs than one of the nine justices: a "small, frail man whom a breath of air would carry off," with a balding head too big for his body and protuberant ears.[11]

McKenna—another small man, "bearded, birdlike," who Acheson remembered always appearing in rubbers, white scarf, and overcoat no matter the time of year or the weather—had intended to become a priest before switching to law, and Holmes also had kind things to say about him as a person, calling him "a truly kind soul" and possessing "a sweet nature."[12]

But time and again, to keep their votes in an opinion he was given to write, Holmes was forced to remove the arguments he thought most germane and the turns of phrase that most pleased him. "The boys keep a pretty sharp watch on me," he wryly remarked. "When I get some phrase that strikes me as vivid the other lads are apt to think it had better come out. So I tell them that I prepare a plum pudding and then one pulls out one plum and another another until I have to offer to the public a mass of sodden dough as my work."[13]

To Frankfurter he offered a more striking metaphor to describe the process his prose was subjected to. After he was forced to cut a line from his opinion in *Western Union* v. *Speight*, in which he had reiterated one of his favorite dicta that it was not "evading" a law to walk right up to the line the law allows, he told his young friend, "As origi-

Justice McKenna

nally written, it had a tiny pair of testicles but the scruples of my brethren have caused their removal and it sings in a very soft voice now."[14]

HIS EXUBERANT STYLE more than once caused some of fellow justices
who had voted with Holmes in conference to withhold their support
once they read his draft opinion.

In one not terribly important case Holmes had been assigned, his
first draft caused one or more of the justices to switch their vote, losing the majority. He then circulated a second draft, ruling the opposite
way, but *again* losing the majority. He finally sent to the Court printer
a one-paragraph memorandum for circulation bearing the title THIRD
ATTEMPT TO GET A MAJORITY. He proposed to simply dismiss the case in
an unsigned "per curium" opinion, based on a narrow technical precedent that Justice Brewer had called to his attention. The Court agreed.[15]

But he was never happy about the compromises he had to make
on more substantial cases. One that rankled him ever after was a very
high-profile decision he delivered at the end of the 1913–14 term. The
Pipe Line Cases arose from a law that required owners of pipelines to
transport the oil of any shipper. The legislation was aimed directly at
Standard Oil, which owned most of the pipelines in the country and

which forced owners to sell their product to the company before they would allow it to enter one of their pipelines. Because transportation by pipeline was much cheaper than by rail, Standard Oil could keep the prices it forced the sellers to accept artificially low.

The case for the government was argued by Solicitor General John W. Davis on October 15, 1913. Weeks, then months went by with no word from the Court on its decision.

On the very last day of the term, June 22, 1914, Holmes delivered his opinion for seven of the other justices, with Chief Justice White writing a separate concurring opinion. Holmes had been given the case just the week before, after one or more of the other justices had tried and failed to produce an acceptable decision, and White finally turned to Holmes, as the Court's nimble draftsman, to come up with something that would allow them to get the case off their backs. The very morning the decision was announced Holmes was still making revisions in an effort to satisfy the majority. "I replied to everyone that I would strike out everything between title and conclusion" if that was what it took "to enable me to get the case off per contract," he said with exasperation.[16]

In his original draft, Holmes had forthrightly asserted that Congress has the power to discourage monopolies by declaring oil pipelines to be common carriers, thus requiring them to offer their services to all comers at the same rate. He received only a single concurring return, this time from Day.

In response, he ended up cutting out several entire sections that constituted the substance of his argument, weakly concluding that there was no need to rely on any disputed powers of Congress to *make* pipelines common carriers, because they already *were* common carriers in everything but name.

It was a classic example of begging the question—assuming the very conclusion that the case had been brought to establish—and Holmes was privately disgusted with the outcome, vowing never to do it again. "I put my name to something that does not satisfy or represent my views," he wrote his retired colleague Justice William H. Moody a few months later. "I never was so disturbed but I thought it my duty to let it go as the majority was content and the case had hung along in other hands for months."[17] Holmes added a handwritten annotation on the printed copy of the final opinion in his bound volumes: "I regard this as inadequate reasoning, but was compelled to strike out what I thought the real argument, and assented to prevent the case going over the Term."[18]

Some of the brethren's "pruning" reflected prim disapproval of Holmes's rhetorical style: his colloquial language, literary allusions, epigrams, and invocations of common knowledge that they worried sounded undignified or unjudicial—though they were the very qualities that made his opinions so memorable, readable, and to the point. And even some of his allies on the Court worried at times that Holmes's brevity and linguistic flair had a way of shading into glibness: that he sometimes was ignoring not just irrelevant arguments but genuine difficulties in disposing of cases so handily. "The old man leaves out all the troublesome facts and ignores all the tough points that worried the lower courts," his later colleague Justice Harlan Fiske Stone once complained to his law secretary. "I wish I could make my cases sound as easy as Holmes makes his."[19]

As in Boston, his style also gave his enemies outside of the Court a handle, echoes of the dismissive comments that he was more of a "literary feller" than a serious jurist. When a lecturer at Northeastern University Law School, John M. Zane, a few years later published an ad hominem attack on Holmes dripping with academic condescension and charging Holmes with "legal heresy"—Holmes's sins included his *Lochner* dissent, his rejection of natural law, and his "indefensible" and "atrocious" theory that "courts can and do make law"—he first damned Holmes with faint praise as "a man of letters" and "a master of epigrammatic expression" before going on to dismissively assert that "epigrams, unfortunately, are either half-truths or not truths at all."[20]

But the more substantive objections his fellow justices on the White Court raised to his opinions went to the heart of the Court's muddled due process jurisprudence, and what Hughes called their inclination to "squirm at some of Holmes's generalities, fearful of their implications."[21]

Holmes never ceased trying to strike a decisive blow against the inconsistencies the Court had worked itself into in that area, boldly stating his fundamental views on the flexibility that the Constitution was intended to give future generations. "We must be cautious about pressing the broad words of the Fourteenth Amendment to a drily logical extreme," he wrote in the majority opinion in *Noble State Bank* v. *Haskell*, upholding a state deposit insurance law. "Many laws which it would be vain to ask the court to overthrow could be shown, easily enough, to transgress a scholastic interpretation of one or another of the great guaranties in the Bill of Rights." But even that was watered down from what he had originally written—which had criticized judges who "get pedagogical and read into Constitutions prohibitions of whatever doesn't suit their social or economic prejudices," he told Mrs. Gray—leaving him to complain again about the "sodden mass" he was left with.[22]

In the 1913–14 term he had similarly used his majority opinion overturning a contempt conviction against the labor leader Samuel Gompers to point out,

> The provisions of the Constitution are not mathematical formulas having their essence in their form; they are organic, living institutions transplanted from English soil. Their significance is vital, not formal; it is to be gathered not simply by taking the words and a dictionary, but by considering their origin and the line of their growth.[23]

He scorned what he saw as the mealymouthed evasions and slippery logic his fellow justices resorted to to avoid committing themselves. White, although he and Holmes shared "points of keen mutual understanding," had an opaque style and "his mode of expression rarely strikes me as felicitous or as at all doing justice to his great ability." White was indeed the master of the slippery-slope argument: Acheson described how "he would start with a reasonably fair statement of a litigant's position, followed by restatements progressively more disadvantageous to the side about to lose—each preceded by 'or to put it another way,' or 'in other words'—until the position was palpably absurd."[24]

Holmes told Acheson that he thought White's slipperiest dialectical feat as chief justice was devising "the rule of reason" as the test of whether a company's actions violated the Sherman Antitrust Act. "The moment I saw that in the circulated draft I knew he had us," Holmes said. "How could you be against that without being for a rule of unreason?" It had been a way to appease the Court's conservatives while still upholding the government's action to break up Standard Oil, with the vague promise to limit the scope of future government antitrust actions. As Holmes remarked to Acheson—with a twinkle in his eye—"The thought did occur to me that the rule might not prove to be self-elucidating." That kind of rhetorical evasion, Holmes thought, was nothing but "a cloud of cuttle-fish ink," intended to obscure a judge's unwillingness to take a clear stand.[25]

When Holmes thought of retiring from the Court, it was the loneliness and feeling of intellectual isolation among his brethren that were uppermost in his mind. None of the other justices even seemed to share his larger intellectual interests in the law, much less his views on particular cases. The companionship he had struck up with White never ripened into the friendship he once thought likely; though there "never was any alienation or coldness," their intellectual worlds were just too far apart. "You can't expect as one does with men of the great world a reciprocity of interest," Holmes told Mrs. Green. "The things and points of view that most occupy me he cares little for . . . and his view of life and of the law naturally does not hit me."[26]

The spring of 1914 had brought other melancholy feelings of loneliness and of the fading past. "I grow, again gradually, more inwardly solitary," he wrote Clara Stevens. In April his oldest friend Pen Hallowell had died—"classmate—companion in the Regiment, first inspirer of a man's ideals," Holmes said of him. Hallowell's death brought back a flood of memories, as did the publication that spring of Henry James's autobiographical *Notes of a Son and Brother*, which was full of recollections of James's father and Minny Temple during the time they all "were very intimate," he told Stevens.[27]

In his own way, the visit of Gordon McCabe just a week after Hallowell's death did too, since all he ever talked about was the Civil War. "McCabe is here, and in pretty good form—Roaring insults to Yankees, telling funny stories—one or two actually new to me—eternally dwelling on the war—and pretty deaf—but withal such a gallant highminded little man, that one must love him as well as honor," Holmes wrote to Mrs. Gray. "You have to take the southerners on their own footing and make ironic allowances."[28]

———

WHEN HE WAS appointed chief justice, White vowed that he was "going to stop this dissenting business." The practice of judges' writing separate dissenting opinions in decisions they disagreed with had a long and contentious history. By the turn of the twentieth century many legal commentators in America had come to denounce the practice altogether, arguing that it only sowed confusion and undermined respect for the judgments of a court of last resort. "Dissenting opinions may be as pleasant to the minority judge as it is for a boy to make faces at a bigger boy across the street, whom he can't whip," wrote one critic, "but what good does that do?"[29]

It was hardly a new phenomenon, however. For a thousand years, the King's Bench had followed the custom of each judge delivering his opinion in turn at the conclusion of a case, without prior consultation among themselves, and that model was adopted by the early multijudge tribunals in America. Thomas Jefferson, for one, viewed such "seriatim" opinions as more open and democratic, and was outraged when the United States Supreme Court under Chief Justice John Marshall began issuing "opinions of the court"—which Jefferson charged were "huddled up in conclave" only through the silent acquiescence of the more "lazy or timid" judges. Justice Henry Billings Brown, who overlapped with Holmes's early years on the Court, expressed the view of many who defended written dissents and disagreed with the contention of justices like White that it undermined confidence in the majority's decision. "If the authority of the Court is weakened by a dissent," Brown said, "it is probably because it ought to be weakened."[30]

Still, dissenting opinions remained the rare exception in Holmes's time, especially when compared to present-day practice, when it is not unusual for the Court's decisions to be accompanied by multiple dissenting and concurring statements; in recent years the Court has even on occasion issued nine separate opinions in a single case, one from each justice. The White Court decided 95 percent of its cases without any dissenting opinions, a rate that would fall to less than 50 percent a century later; the number of cases with separate concurrences increased over the same period from about 1 percent to more than 40 percent.[31]

Despite his reputation as a dissenter, Holmes actually did so less often than many of his fellow justices; overall, he joined the full Court's opinion more than 96 percent of the time, and according to an analysis of available notes of deliberations in conference, he was also one of the justices most likely, in the interest of collegiality and unanimity, to go along with an opinion he had initially opposed.[32]

Holmes regarded that as both a matter of principle and of effective tactics. He often said it was pointless to keep dissenting in case after case only to raise the same objection; in such situations he would usually silently acquiesce once he had had his initial "whack" at the issue. As he noted in one of his dissents, "There are obvious limits of propriety to the persistent expressions of opinions that do not command the agreement of the Court."[33]

And Brandeis observed that there was a fundamental difference between "ordinary" cases such as business disputes—where it actually did not matter very much which way the Court decided "so long as it is settled," and where "there is a good deal to be said for not having dissents"—and constitutional cases, which raised important matters for the future where "nothing is ever settled."[34]

Holmes was insistent that good manners as well as respect for the Court's authority required that even in a dissent, however, it was important to avoid direct criticism of the majority's opinion or reasoning. Holmes disliked even the traditional formulation, "Mr. Justice Holmes, dissenting" in the Court's printed opinions, he told Laski: "We are giving our views on a question of law, not fighting with another cock." Insisting once that Brandeis remove one offending sentence before agreeing to join a dissenting opinion he had circulated, Holmes wrote, "I think it better never to criticize the reasoning in opinions of the Court and its members. I feel very strongly about this. Of course it is OK to hit them by indirection as hard as you can."[35]

McKenna, however, violated that rule constantly. His rivalry with Holmes soon began to grow into something resembling an obsession. From 1910 until his retirement in 1925, one-third of McKenna's 117 dissents and separate concurrences were to opinions by Holmes, and their tone became increasingly personal and intemperate. He accused Holmes of weakening the Constitution, attempted ironically to quote Holmes's previous opinions against him, and once dismissively asserted, "The question in the cases is without complexity and the means of its solution ready at hand."[36]

Holmes replied with at most an oblique thrust. In a famous concurring opinion he filed to McKenna's opinion for the Court in another case in the 1913–14 term, *LeRoy Fibre* v. *Chicago, Milwaukee & St. Paul Railway,* he took issue with the absoluteness of McKenna's finding that a property owner who stacked flax straw near a railroad right of way could not be considered contributorily negligent when a spark from a locomotive ignited the stack. While agreeing with the outcome in the particular case, Holmes said the decision in other situations remained a matter of degree: if combustible material were placed so close to the tracks that the danger of fire could be foreseen by a reasonably prudent person, the railroad indeed might avoid liability. Then, in an undeniable dig at McKenna, he concluded:

> I do not think we need trouble ourselves with the thought that my view depends upon differences of degree. The whole law does so as soon as it is civilized . . . and between the variations according to distance that I suppose to exist, and the simple universality of the rules in the Twelve Tables, or the *Leges Barbarorum*, there lies the culture of two thousand years.

Jealous of Holmes's speed and facility in turning out his assigned cases, McKenna not only tried to beat him in the race to get the work done, but even attempted to emulate his epigrammatic dash, with a result that ranged from incoherent to ludicrous. Taking on Holmes in a stylistic duel was hardly a winning strategy for someone of McKenna's distinctly limited writing ability.[37]

Yet the two men remained on friendly terms. Theirs was a rivalry—if an odd one on McKenna's part—not a feud, the legal historian Alexander Bickel observed. One June, heading north on the train, Holmes ran into McKenna, and found him "very pleasant, as usual." Declining to join a Holmes dissent, McKenna once wrote on his return to Holmes, "But I like this. It gratifies my Irish heart to see heads hit even if one of them is my own."[38]

HOLMES ADMITTED THAT despite his reluctance to make a habit of it, he found it a relief to write the occasional dissent: he could say exactly what he thought without having to trim his views to "suit the squeams" of the brethren. "A dissent once in a while offers you a chance to go as you please and let out a little poison," he explained to Baroness Moncheur.[39]

But the more serious purpose of a dissent, as he well knew, was the hope it might speak to the future where its views had failed to carry the present. Justice Hughes had made this point in one of the most succinct defenses of the practice:

> A dissent in a court of last resort is an appeal to the brooding spirit of the law, to the intelligence of a future day, when a later decision may possibly correct the error into which the dissenting judge believes the court to have been betrayed. Nor is this appeal always in vain.[40]

That was true of no one in the history of the Court more than Holmes, whose dissents not only feature prominently among the classic opinions in the annals of the United States Supreme Court, but which, time and again, became the majority view a decade or more later. Beginning with *Lochner*, his appeals to the intelligence of a future day were astonishingly successful.

The 1914–15 term saw the beginning of a nearly unbroken series of Holmes dissents over the next fifteen years that would be his most lasting legacy to American constitutional law. The first came in another of his strikes against the use of the Fourteenth Amendment to invalidate state laws protecting the rights of labor. Writing for the majority in *Coppage* v. *Kansas*, Pitney held unconstitutional a Kansas law that, like the federal law struck down in *Adair*, outlawed yellow-dog contracts. Holmes's dissent was but a single paragraph, but it distilled the counterargument to its essence.

> In present conditions, a workman not unnaturally may believe that only by belonging to a union can he secure a contract that shall be fair to him. If that belief, whether right or wrong, may be held by a reasonable man, it seems to me that it may be enforced by law in order to establish the equality of position between the parties in which liberty of contract begins. Whether in the long run it is wise for the workingmen to enact legislation of this sort is not my concern, but I am strongly of opinion that there is nothing in the Constitution of the United States to prevent it, and that *Adair* v. *United States* and *Lochner* v. *New York* should be overruled.

He concluded with a citation to his two dissents on the Massachusetts Supreme Judicial Court that had taken exception to injunctions against striking workers, *Vegelahn* v. *Guntner* and *Plant* v. *Woods*. "I still entertain the opinions expressed by me in Massachusetts," he stated.

His second major dissent of that year was a plunge into previously uncharted constitutional territory, and it revealed the intensity of his feeling of outrage when the rules of the law were flouted. In the early morning hours of April 27, 1913, the bruised and bloodied body of a thirteen-year-old factory worker, Mary Phagan, was found by the night watchman in the cellar of the National Pencil Factory in Atlanta. Two days later the factory's manager, Leo Frank, a rising member of the small Jewish community of the Southern city, was arrested and charged with her murder.

The evidence was scant, nearly all of it based on the inconsistent testimony of Frank's chief accuser, an African American employee who was almost certainly the real killer. But the murder received sensational and lurid coverage that suggested Frank had also raped the girl, and for months Georgia newspapers treated the crime as the lead story.

Four months later Frank was sentenced to hang; his appeal to the Georgia Supreme Court affirmed his conviction; and on November 21, 1914, his counsel applied to Justice Lamar, who was designated to hear appeals to the U.S. Supreme Court from the circuit that included Georgia. Lamar denied it. The Court's rules of procedure allowed other justices to then be applied to, and the appeal came to Holmes next.[41]

The right of appeal to the U.S. Supreme Court from the judgment of a state supreme court at that time was basically in the hands of the state court; if it did not certify a writ of error, there was no federal jurisdiction to take the case, and the Georgia court had found no errors at trial, effectively shutting off the effort to have Frank's appeal moved to the federal courts.

Holmes agreed with Lamar's ruling on procedural grounds, but immediately zeroed in on what all of the procedural niceties were overlooking: the trial had been conducted amid outright intimidation of the judge, jury, defendant, and counsel. "I very seriously doubt if the petitioner has had due process of law," Holmes wrote in a brief memorandum of his decision, "because of the trial taking place in the presence of a hostile demonstration and seemingly dangerous crowd, thought by the presiding judge to be ready for violence unless a verdict of guilty was rendered."[42]

Holmes had not intended his memorandum to be published; it was meant "only as a suggestion to my brethren if any of them could see a way to giving relief." But it received enormous attention in the press, and Holmes found himself getting both "letters from sensitive females crying for mercy" and praise from the *New York Times* and other Northern and liberal publications for pointing out the manifest injustice of Frank's trial. "Justice Holmes deserves the highest commendation for this human departure from the dry legal formula," the *Times* wrote.[43]

It also pointed to another avenue for appeal: that Frank could seek a writ of habeas corpus in the federal courts, raising the claim that he was illegally confined by the state of Georgia because he had effectively had no trial at all as guaranteed by the Due Process Clause of the Fourteenth Amendment. If a federal court issued the writ, then a federal district judge could proceed with a hearing and order his release or a new trial if he found a violation of Frank's rights under the U.S. Constitution.

For four months the habeas corpus appeal wound its way through the federal courts. On April 19, 1915, the Supreme Court issued the final decision. By a 7–2 vote, with Holmes and Hughes dissenting, the Court denied the writ.

Holmes's dissenting opinion was extraordinarily unusual for him. It recounted in dramatic narrative detail the circumstances of the case, something he almost never did in writing opinions. His fundamental point was that the record of the trial was irrelevant when the trial itself was "a farce," as he later termed it.[44] And he pointedly alluded to his own experience as a trial justice in understanding the reality of how juries behave under duress.

"The trial began on July 28, 1913, at Atlanta, and was carried on in a court packed with spectators and surrounded by a crowd outside, all strongly hostile to the petitioner," Holmes wrote.

> On Saturday, August 23, this hostility was sufficient to lead the judge to confer in the presence of the jury with the chief of police of Atlanta and the colonel of the Fifth Georgia Regiment, stationed in that city, both of whom were known to the jury. On the same day, the evidence seemingly having been closed, the public press, apprehending danger, united in a request to the court that the proceedings should not continue on that evening. Thereupon, the court adjourned until Monday morning. On that morning, when the solicitor general entered the court, he was greeted with applause, stamping of feet and clapping of hands, and the judge, before beginning his charge, had a private conversation with the petitioner's counsel in which he expressed the opinion that there would be "probable danger of violence" if there should be an acquittal or a disagreement, and that it would be safer for not only

the petitioner but his counsel to be absent from court when the verdict was brought in. . . . When the verdict was rendered, and before more than one of the jurymen had been polled, there was such a roar of applause that the polling could not go on until order was restored. . . .

Whatever disagreement there may be as to the scope of the phrase "due process of law," there can be no doubt that it embraces the fundamental conception of a fair trial, with opportunity to be heard. Mob law does not become due process of law by securing the assent of a terrorized jury. We are not speaking of mere disorder, or mere irregularities in procedure, but of a case where the processes of justice are actually subverted. In such a case, the Federal court has jurisdiction to issue the writ. . . .

This is not a matter for polite presumptions; we must look facts in the face. Any judge who has sat with juries knows that, in spite of forms, they are extremely likely to be impregnated by the environing atmosphere. And when we find the judgment of the expert on the spot—of the judge whose business it was to preserve not only form, but substance—to have been that if one juryman yielded to the reasonable doubt that he himself later expressed in court as the result of most anxious deliberation, neither prisoner nor counsel would be safe from the rage of the crowd, we think the presumption overwhelming that the jury responded to the passions of the mob. . . . It is our duty . . . to declare lynch law as little valid when practised by a regularly drawn jury as when administered by one elected by a mob intent on death.[45]

The case affected Holmes far more than usual for him. He mentioned to Einstein "a dissent as to which I feel a good deal," and alluded to the case in a half dozen other letters at the time. His old friend John Chipman Gray had died just two months earlier, at the end of February, which had been a strain and a shadow over his life, he told his friends, and may have added to the acuteness with which he felt the matter.[46]

Holmes had written to Gray as soon as he heard the news of his terminal illness that his wife, Nina, had sent him in confidence; enclosing it with a covering note to Nina—"Of course, I write to him as I should at anytime. If it isn't suitable to his condition just chuck it into the fire"—his letter was full of warm reminiscences of their pleasant times together. The news of the death of his oldest friend a week later came as no surprise but inspired some poetic reflections on the passing of the years that he sent his young friend Baroness Moncheur:

> A very well mannered old party, time. He doesn't speak loud, or come bulging in on you as some ingenuous young secretaries will, but he comes up as soft footed as a cat . . . and by a by he lays a soft paw on your sleeve, so gently. And then slowly, like the dog in Faust's study, he begins to swell, and grow more like a tiger. And the door is locked and one must await his doings.[47]

At the end of the term death struck in a more violent form. On June 22 his sixty-year-old messenger George Marston was badly burned trying to put out a blaze in his home that began when the curtains caught fire, and he died two days later in Freedmen's Hospital in the District. Holmes stayed for the funeral, delaying their departure to the north. "His death was a good deal of a shock, and I was attached to him as he had been with us in one capacity or another almost from my first going to Washington," he told the baroness.[48]

The Frank case remained in the headlines throughout the summer. Although Holmes took his usual tough-minded satisfaction in shocking one woman who "began to talk to me about his innocence"—by telling her that he "never had read the evidence and didn't care whether he was innocent or guilty"—he was oddly moved to receive a long letter from Frank. It was written from the State Prison Farm in Milledgeville, Georgia, just a few weeks after the governor, "at peril of his own life" as Holmes correctly noted, commuted Frank's death sentence to life imprisonment the day before his scheduled execution on June 22.[49]

Frank wrote that now that all of his appeals were exhausted, he felt free at last to thank the justice for having "diagnosed the situation with rare insight and sagacity," and for recognizing that "my trial could not have approximated justice." He concluded, "My life is preserved, and

I live on in the confident trust, in God and man, that the day is not far distant when Truth and Reason will hold sway."[50]

A month later, a lynch mob, openly organized by the leading citizens of Phagan's home town of Marietta—calling themselves the "Knights of Mary Phagan," they included a former governor of Georgia, the town's former mayor, and the current sheriff of the county—abducted Frank from prison and hanged him on an oak tree in broad daylight. Picture postcards of the lynching were sold throughout the South.

Despite Holmes's insistence that he had no opinion or concern about Frank's guilt or innocence, Frankfurter recalled years later Holmes saying to him that a man who could write to him so sensitively "couldn't have raped and murdered a girl."[51]

THE COURT MAJORITY's willingness to read the word "liberty" to encompass the right of a railroad to fire an employee who joined a union, but not protect a man convicted of murder under the threat of mob violence, was another stark reminder to Holmes of his isolation on the Court. Hughes was his one reliable ally. "There have been and will be other cases in which Hughes and I stand back to back," Holmes remarked right after their *Frank* dissent. Hughes was a man of "character and courage" and had been "good wise and consoling company" in several other important cases as well.[52] But at the end of the 1915–16 term Hughes resigned to accept the Republican nomination for president to run against Wilson in the fall.

Outside of the Court, Holmes's young friends remained a source of companionship as well as encouragement to keep fighting for his views. There was a new group living at the House of Truth as Frankfurter and the original residents moved out, but the dinners and conversation remained as lively and engaging as ever. Introduced by Frankfurter to the other young lawyers who had taken his place at the house, a series of Holmes secretaries lived there during their years with the justice, beginning with George Harrison in 1913, followed by Bundy in 1914, and Belknap in 1915.[53]

On Holmes's seventy-fifth birthday, in March 1916, Fanny organized a surprise party, sneaking the whole group of young people into 1720 Eye Street after Holmes had gone upstairs following a quiet dinner with a few friends. Suddenly the whole house came alive with the sound of birds. Coming down to investigate, he found the drawing room filled with "all the gang," tootling away on bird calls, which Fanny had purchased from a street vendor she had noticed on F Street. Just as he began to "think in dismay" that he had nothing to offer his guests, the doors to the other room opened and there was a supper laid out, with a bowl of "very judicious punch." They stayed up laughing and talking past midnight. Describing it all afterward to Baroness Moncheur, he wrote, "These younger men (lawyers from the Departments, etc.) and women (some of them making their own living and good looking and intelligent) are very good to the old fellow and help to keep him young."[54]

Among the other regular visitors to the House of Truth now were two "able chaps," Walter Lippmann and Herbert Croly, who had impressed Holmes with the precociously masterful books they had written on American politics. Proposing a new approach that rejected both "the chronic partisans and the social revolutionists," they had appropriated the label "liberal" from its nineteenth-century connotation of laissez-faire to describe their ideas. Liberalism, Lippmann explained, was not a political ideology but an intellectual transition from the old party politics; it emphasized protection of civil liberties and pluralism in society along with meaningful social legislation to democratize the new industrial economy. "These same fellows," Holmes reported to Ethel Scott, "have just started a weekly paper The New Republic that I am hoping well for, not without anxiety."[55]

While as usual unmoved by their enthusiasm that "universal bliss would ensue if the world would only get a move on and obey when the New Republic says Hocus—Pocus—Presto—Chango," as he put it, he was flattered by the articles in the magazine praising his decisions, notably his dissents in *Coppage* ("the opinion of a judge who deals with things, not words, and who realizes that a document which is to rule a great people must in its very nature allow for a wide and growing field for experimentation") and *Frank* ("the delivered opinion of the most distinguished intellectual and moral membership of the United States Supreme Court").[56]

And on his seventy-fifth birthday Lippmann had written a beautiful tribute in the magazine explaining "why young men feel themselves very close" to Justice Holmes. "He wears wisdom like a gorgeous plume," Lippmann wrote, "and likes to stick the sanctities between the ribs."[57]

Just when it looked as if his intellectual isolation on the Court had hit bottom that summer, Holmes was joined by the man who would be his closest friend on the Court for his remaining fifteen years on the bench, and his most potent ally in his efforts to make a lasting mark with his ideas of the Constitution, and of the purpose of law in society.

———

THE NOMINATION OF Louis D. Brandeis to the Supreme Court by Woodrow Wilson in January 1916 was the first ever to be subjected to the scrutiny of a Senate committee hearing. Brandeis had made his share of enemies, and all were now out to get their revenge by testifying against the nomination. Adding to the campaign against him was a scarcely veiled undercurrent of anti-Semitism, stirred up to block the first Jew ever named to the high court.

In Boston, Brandeis had made a million dollars by age fifty, and another million over the next decade, as an extremely successful corporate lawyer, representing leading business interests of the city. He had then turned his considerable energies to working for the great public causes that fired him. The press dubbed him the "People's Attorney" as he took on the abuses of large insurance companies and railroad conglomerates. He once explained that just as some wealthy men bought diamonds or yachts, his "luxury" was to invest his surplus income in solving a problem "for the people" without compensation.[58]

He had experienced little overt anti-Semitism in his early years in Boston, and was so inner-directed that he had scarcely seemed to notice the few snubs that were directed his way. But when he took on the New Haven Railroad in 1912 as an "unregulated monopoly," the company fired back by subsidizing a rabidly anti-Semitic publication that

Brandeis, in 1914

accused him of doing the bidding of a secret cabal of international Jewish bankers. Brandeis had also earned the resentment of the Boston bar and Beacon Street by upholding the very moral standards that were once the birthright of Brahmin society, but now were giving way to the rough-and-tumble of free-market capitalism. Brandeis insisted that companies owed a duty not just to shareholders but to the community, and refused to trade favors in the usual professional courtesies with opposing counsel, insisting that he owed his duty to his client alone.[59]

The nomination hearings began with a barrage of hostile witnesses who accused Brandeis of "dishonorable" conduct for working against the interests he had once represented as an attorney. Taft wrote to a newspaperman he knew,

> It is one of the deepest wounds that I have ever had as an American and a lover of the Constitution and a believer in progressive conservatism, that such a man as Brandeis could be put in the Court. . . . He is a muckraker, an emotionalist for his own purposes, a socialist, prompted by jealousy, a hypocrite, a man who has certain high ideals in his imagination, but who is utterly unscrupulous . . . a man of infinite cunning.

President Abbott Lawrence Lowell of Harvard circulated a petition opposing the nomination that bore the signatures of many leading Brahmin names, and letters in opposition poured into the Senate from Wall Street firms.[60]

Holmes privately worried that the controversy would hurt the Court no matter what the outcome, but he wrote to Mrs. Stevens during the nomination fight, "All that I can say is that I have known him ever since Sam Warren got him to come to Boston—and that he always has left me when he has called feeling encouraged about the world and that I have met a good man."[61] On June 1, 1916, the Senate finally approved Brandeis's nomination on a 47–22 vote, with all but three Republicans opposed.

Holmes sent a one-word telegram to his old friend: WELCOME.[62]

———

IN EVERYTHING BUT intellect, Brandeis could have been the anti-Holmes. A moral idealist where Holmes was a skeptic, an ascetic where Holmes was a bon vivant, Brandeis above all worshipped facts—and Holmes loathed them. One of Brandeis's favorite sayings was a line from a sonnet by Goethe: *In der Beschränkung zeigt sich erst der Meister*, in working within limitations the master reveals himself. He exhaustively prepared his cases and was a devastating cross-examiner, sticking to the point relentlessly with a preternatural calm that was far more disconcerting than attorneys who bellowed at or badgered witnesses.[63]

In 1908, in the landmark case *Muller* v. *Oregon*, in which he successfully defended Oregon's law limiting working hours for women to ten hours per day, Brandeis had filed a brief that ran 113 pages, only two of them dealing with the law; the rest was a compendium of social science research, statistics, medical evidence, reports on the effects of similar legislation in other countries. Known immediately as a "Brandeis brief," it forever changed the way cases were argued before the Court.[64] As a justice, Brandeis would send his secretaries to hunt up data from obscure sources and expect them to stay up all night writing up their findings, then work with him through endless revisions of his footnote-studded opinions, as different a life from that of a Holmes secretary as could be imagined.[65]

Brandeis's secretaries called him "Isaiah," and never detected any but the faintest glimmers of a sense of humor in him. ("You liked him like you like the Washington Monument," the journalist Marquis Childs observed.) Brandeis lived in the Stoneleigh Court apartment building on Connecticut Avenue, around the corner from Holmes's

The Stoneleigh Court apartments

house, and was notorious for the austere simplicity of his life there, and the meager meals he provided his guests. One of his secretaries recalled slices of roast beef carved so thin "you could see through" them. It became standard knowledge that anyone invited to the Brandeis home for dinner had better eat a full meal ahead of time.[66]

Yet the friendship that Holmes and Brandeis instantly formed was above all a kind of electric recognition of intellectual kindred spirits. Holmes found Brandeis's intelligence a welcome relief to the isolation he had felt among his distinctly less brilliant brethren, and his new colleague's unwavering faith that ideas vitally mattered in the law as they did in life buoyed him in his doubting moments. Brandeis, who would call Holmes's companionship "the crown of his life," wrote to Laski a few years after joining the Court, "I am impressed even more with the great work Judge Holmes has done and by the beauty of his character. He deserves the Great Gift of Eternal Youth with which he has been endowed."[67]

It was now Holmes and Brandeis who walked home together from the Court each day; sometimes they would each insist on walking the other to his door, and crossed and recrossed the street until one gave way. Brandeis called on Holmes almost every day when the Court was not in session, and in Holmes's later years, his housekeeper remembered, his eyes would light up and he would exclaim, "My dear friend" whenever Brandeis came to visit.[68]

Brandeis's Jewishness was never an issue to Holmes, who not only was almost totally free of conventional prejudices but had been finding that "quite without my being aware" of it, "most of the men I have taken a shine to within the last few years have been Jews," as he wrote Clare Castletown in the summer of 1916. "They are all men of extraordinary gifts and a kind of high goodness."[69]

More than one of Holmes's old Boston acquaintances, and even his wife, Fanny, were not so tolerant. There was an old story that Holmes's Dutch ancestors, the Wendells, were originally Jews, and when Fanny would make some disapproving observation about his Jewish friends, Holmes would counter that he'd "rather have the brilliance of the Jews" through those supposed forebears of his than the "god-damned Anglo-Saxon wing."[70]

Some who tried to explain the Brandeis-Holmes friendship suggested that they had both felt themselves to be "outsiders" in Boston society. But there was much more to it than that. If not by blood than by deeply rooted values, there were more than a few areas of intellectual and moral kinship between the Brahmins and the Jews, which Holmes's lack of bigotry allowed him to see: a love of learning, a sense of social duty, and a reverence for the life of ideas, all of which Holmes and Brandeis fully shared. When Mrs. Gray made an arch comment about hoping he would "stay thoroughly Anglo-Saxon," Holmes retorted, "I take the innuendo to be that I am under the influence of the Heb's. I am comfortably confident that I am under no influence except that of thoughts and insights. Sometimes my brother B. seems to me to see deeper than some of the others—and we often agree."[71]

The vicious anti-Semitism of one of Wilson's other new appointees to the Court, James R. McReynolds, troubled Holmes much more than it did Brandeis. As Wilson's attorney general McReynolds had prosecuted several antitrust actions, but upon joining the Court in 1914 he

Holmes and Brandeis

had revealed himself not the progressive Wilson had supposed but an archreactionary, as well as a man of towering bigotries. Taft called McReynolds "fuller of prejudice than any man I have known."[72] The few times a woman or African American lawyer appeared before the Court in the 1920s and 1930s, the Kentucky-born McReynolds ostentatiously rotated his chair and sat with his back to the courtroom.[73]

There was a widely repeated, though inaccurate, tale that in 1924 McReynolds had refused to pose for the traditional Court photograph because it would have required him to sit next to Brandeis. But other stories of his anti-Semitism were completely true. McReynolds would immediately get up and leave the room whenever Brandeis spoke during conferences. When the Court was invited to Philadelphia to attend the dedication of the State House where the United States Supreme Court first sat, McReynolds sent a note to the chief justice declining to accompany them: "As you know, I am not always to be found when there is a Hebrew abroad. Therefore my 'inability' to attend must not surprise you!"[74] He once wrote on a return to Holmes, in a case in which Holmes and Brandeis were dissenting, "Did you ever think that for four thousand years the Lord tried to

Justice McReynolds

make something out of Hebrews, then gave it up as impossible and turned them out to prey on mankind in general—like fleas on the dog for example."[75]

McReynolds was also the most personally unpleasant man ever to sit on the Court, Taft later said, "selfish beyond everything," taking "delight in making others uncomfortable," unbelievably rude and domineering. Brandeis ignored his crude hostility, viewing him more as a curious natural phenomenon—a *Naturmensch*, he called him, a primitive man, a child of nature: "He has very tender affections & correspondingly hates."[76]

But Holmes was appalled by McReynolds's behavior and did what he could to ease the strains. Frankfurter came in for the McReynolds treatment when he appeared before the Court in January 1917 to defend an Oregon law limiting the workday for all workers to ten hours. McReynolds kept hectoring him, interrupting his arguments, finally demanding in a sneering tone, "Ten hours! Ten hours! Ten! Why not *four*?"

Child mill workers in North Carolina

Frankfurter walked over to stand before McReynolds at the end of the bench. "Your honor," he said, "if by chance I may make such a hypothesis, if your physician should find that you're eating too much meat, it isn't necessary for him to urge you to become a vegetarian."

"Good for you! Good for you!" Holmes boomed.[77]

Holmes did once wryly remark of Brandeis that for all of their real friendship and intellectual companionship, "I am not sure that he wouldn't burn me at a slow fire if it were in the interest of some very possibly disinterested aim."[78] But their alliance on the Court was cemented in several powerful dissenting opinions that directly challenged the old guard and reflected their shared philosophy of the law as an evolving response to the needs of society.

Near the end of the 1917–18 term, Brandeis joined Holmes's dissent in *Hammer* v. *Dagenhart*, in which the Court struck down an act of Congress banning from interstate commerce the products of cotton mills employing child labor. Noting that the Court had upheld laws prohibiting the interstate movement of lottery tickets and liquor, Holmes asked why the Court thought Congress's exercise of the Commerce Clause was "permissible as against strong drink but not as against the product of ruined lives."

A week later Brandeis joined a second Holmes dissent, *Toledo Newspaper v. U.S.*, the case of a newspaper that a federal district judge had held in contempt and slapped with a substantial fine for publishing an unflattering political cartoon about him. "I confess that I cannot find in all this or in the evidence in the case anything that would have affected a mind of reasonable fortitude," Holmes archly commented in his written opinion, and suggested that contempt under the relevant statute was limited to actions that directly impeded the enforcement of a court order or disrupted courtroom proceedings.

"My last two cases in Court were marked by two dissents that I imagine the majority thought ill timed and regrettable as I thought the decisions," Holmes wrote to Pollock.[79]

———

THE WAR IN Europe cast a solemn mood over Washington that spring. The war had brought back to him all of his old memories and feelings about the transformative experience of battle. To his English friend Lady Askwith, whose son lost an arm in the early fighting, he wrote,

> I truly believe that young men who live through a war in which they have taken part will find themselves different thenceforth—I feel it—I see it in the eyes of the few surviving men who served in my Regiment. So, although I would have averted the war if I could have, I believe that all the suffering and waste are not without their reward. I hope with all my heart that your boys may win the reward and at not too great a cost.[80]

"I have lived through so many wars, including that which overshadowed the beginning of my adult life that I do not feel that even this one is the end of all things," he told Baroness Moncheur. "But my heart aches underneath."[81]

From the start of the war, Holmes's heart was entirely with

England, and he had been chagrined to receive from a German law professor he knew a long letter praising his speech "The Soldier's Faith" as if it supported the German cause. Worse, he learned from friends in England, the professor, Otto von Gierke, had made the letter public even before Holmes received it and excerpts had been published in newspapers.[82]

It was not the first time that speech had caused him grief: he repeatedly had complained to friends that it "was not intended, as it stupidly was taken by many, to advise young men to wade in gore," but on the contrary to express "the eternal idealism of man"—even if his paradoxical praise of the man who dies in a cause in which he does not believe almost invited such a misunderstanding.[83]

The sentimentality being expressed by both supporters and opponents of the war, however, rekindled all his smoldering toughmindedness. His secretary the year America entered the war, Shelton Hale, was a socialist and pacifist, and announced to Holmes that war was irrational. "I find myself very fond of him," Holmes remarked, but Hale's observation brought "blood in my eye," and he had riposted that "war is the ultimate rationality": when two nations disagreed, the only logical recourse was to try to impose their will through force.[84]

Holmes said he felt like the English officer he read of who said "he didn't hate the Germans, the people at home did that, he only wanted to kill them. I think that is the usual feeling of men at the front in any war." He related to Einstein his reply to "a nervous dame" who had reproached him for his "detached attitude" toward the war: "I said that I saw no good in unproductive emotion that merely detracts from one's working force; that I hoped I would go out and be shot in an hour for the cause, but that I wouldn't lie awake for it if I could help it, and I could." Or, as he had earlier remarked to Einstein, "If men die so shall I. It is not a sufficient reason for not using one's time."[85]

But he confessed that during one night in that spring of 1918 when "the news seemed black from the front," he had lain awake with dyspepsia, despite his boast. A few days later he drove out to the park "and saw the bloodroot with its dazzling white stars . . . but the ache was under it all, and the spring seems only to embody the inexorable."[86]

As he and Fanny prepared to head north at the end of the term, he had his usual feeling "as if the bottom had dropped out when work stops." But he expected that after his usual bout of "train fever," and a fortnight's "emptiness and collapse," he would be ready to alternate between a book and slumber at his summer retreat.[87]

CHAPTER 14

Free Speech

Holmes and Fanny had decided to spend a few nights in New York on their way up, and on the morning of Wednesday, June 19, 1918, they boarded the train from New York to Boston. By chance, on the same train, heading to his summer home in Cornish, New Hampshire, was Judge Learned Hand of the federal district court in New York. Hand not only knew and respected Holmes, thirty-one years his senior, but looked upon him as "the epitome of what a judge should be," "the example of all that I most cherish." As a member of the editorial board of the *New Republic*, Hand had written a number of the magazine's unsigned editorials praising Holmes's dissenting opinions.[1] At some point during the train ride Holmes ran into his fellow jurist, and sat down for a talk that would hold a place in the annals of the right of freedom of speech in America.

Hand's intellectual and philosophical touchstones were strikingly akin to Holmes's. From a strict Calvinist upbringing in Albany, New York, he had gone to Harvard where he majored in philosophy, graduated summa cum laude, and under the teaching of William James and George Santayana emerged a confirmed skeptic.[2] He had then gone on to Harvard Law School and a distinguished career as lawyer and judge. Although he would never sit on the U.S. Supreme Court—owing mainly to having incurred Taft's enduring enmity by supporting Roosevelt's Bull Moose campaign of 1912—Hand would become one of the coun-

try's most influential judges, with a
name as famous to students of the
law today as Marshall, Holmes,
and Brandeis.

But unlike Holmes, he was beset
with anxieties and self-doubts, and
never could redirect the Calvinist
guilt instilled in him by his mother
into Holmes's exuberant joie de
vivre. His unusual first name added
to his self-consciousness: Learned
was his mother's family name, and
though he worried it made him
sound like a "sissy," he thought it
was better than his full given name,
which was Billings Learned Hand;
it was certainly better than his fam-

Learned Hand

ily's name for him, which was "Bunny." His friends called him "B."[3]

The "constant anxiety complex" he carried with him from his
upbringing made it impossible ever to have a "happy, contented disposition," he acknowledged, and his self-deriding inclination to identify
himself with the cartoon character Caspar Milquetoast was deepened
by the unhappiness in his marriage. His wife, a Bryn Mawr graduate
whom he had met when he was twenty-nine having had little experience with women previously, was a determinedly independent woman
who had announced from the start that she had no intention "to be the
door-mat of a man of genius." She had taken to spending longer and
longer intervals at Cornish in the company of another man, a professor
of French at nearby Dartmouth College, for which Hand only blamed
himself even as he begged her to stay with him at least a bit more often.
"I don't know if I can take this," he admitted to a friend when she
began talking about buying a permanent home there, but he was heading to see her for a brief vacation together that day in June when he
encountered Holmes on the train.[4]

Despite his inner torments, Hand had a mastery of his work that was very much like Holmes's: an exhaustive understanding of the law and precedents, an ability to penetrate to the core of the matter at hand, and a skill at expressing his reasoning in luminously clear prose—along with a fervent conviction that skepticism dictated judicial restraint and a willingness to question one's own prejudices. And what was on his mind that day was a case in which he had taken a bold, deeply reasoned, and distinctly unpopular stand defending the rights of freedom of speech against government censorship.

The case arose under the 1917 Espionage Act, passed by Congress shortly after America's entry into the First World War. Among its other provisions, the act made it a crime punishable by imprisonment to "wilfully obstruct the recruiting or enlistment service of the United States." The act also gave the postmaster general the authority to bar the mailings of publications violating its provisions.

An article in *The Masses*, a "monthly revolutionary journal" with a circulation of twenty thousand, immediately fell afoul of the postal authorities by praising conscientious objectors and antiwar agitators who had been convicted of obstructing the draft. When the publishers were informed that their next issue would be excluded from the mails, they promptly went to court seeking an injunction to stop the order from being carried out. On July 24, 1917, just six weeks after enactment of the law, Hand granted the injunction, in a broad decision that sharply limited the government's power to ban criticisms of its policies.

The traditional common law of criminal and seditious libel held that speech that has a "bad tendency"—that is likely to lead to a breach of the peace or defiance of government authority—can be punished, and that was the theory on which Postmaster General Albert Burleson had applied the Espionage Act to publications like *The Masses*. But Hand countered that suppressing hostile criticism was "so contrary to the use and wont of our people" that no such subjective assumptions about tendencies could be read into the act. He proposed a strict and objective legal standard to assess whether speech could be punished: a speaker, he said, should not be responsible for others who were moved to illegal action by his words unless the words in and of themselves directly advocated forcible resistance to the law.

Although Hand did not base his decision on the First Amendment, it was deeply rooted in his thinking about the importance of free speech in a democracy and the dangers of allowing the government to ban speech based on what it might possibly lead to. "To assimilate agitation, legitimate as such, with direct incitement to violent resistance, is to disregard the tolerance of all methods of political agitation which in normal times is a safeguard of free government," he wrote in his decision. "The distinction is not a scholastic subterfuge, but a hard-bought acquisition in the fight for freedom."[5]

But few others on the federal bench or the legal profession shared his views. As he later noted with disappointment to Zechariah Chafee Jr., a young Harvard Law professor who was one of his few stalwart allies on free speech, his decision "seemed to meet with practically no professional approval whatever." Hand's order was overturned by the Circuit Court of Appeals three months later, his direct-incitement test decisively rejected. Permanently barred from the mails, *The Masses* never published again.[6]

Hand's cousin, a federal judge who served with him on the Southern District of New York, needled him that he was just displaying his "natural perversity." But Hand wrote back, "I never was better satisfied with any piece of work I did in my life." The importance of tolerance for opposing views, not just as a bedrock foundation of democracy but as a reflection of fundamental skepticism about certainty, continued to gnaw at him; and when he had what he described to Holmes as "my good fortune in meeting you on the train," he tried to lay his case out to his eminent senior.[7]

He did not get far. They talked most of the way to Boston, but although Hand's argument was very much in tune with Holmes's own oft-repeated rejection of the claim of anyone to possess absolute truth, Holmes had little enthusiasm for the idea that human beings possessed any rights simply by virtue of being human. Holmes always liked to provoke friends who he thought were being sentimentally idealistic by saying, "all society rests on the deaths of men," and frequently asserted that a "right" was nothing more than "those things a given crowd will fight for—which vary from religion to the price of a glass of beer."[8] He had flummoxed Hand into silence by facetiously rebuffing his talk of free speech as a right by countering that Hand wanted to strike at *his* "sacred right to kill the other fellow" if he disagreed with him.

But after stewing for a few days, Hand decided to try again, and wrote to Holmes to rejoin the fight:

> I gave up rather more easily than I now feel disposed to about Tolerance on Wednesday. Here I take my stand. Opinions are at best provisional hypotheses, incompletely tested. The more they are tested, after the tests are well scrutinized, the more assurance we may assume, but they are never absolutes. So we must be tolerant of opposite opinions or varying opinions by the very fact of our incredulity of our own. . . .
>
> You say that I strike at the sacred right to kill the other fellow. . . . Not at all, kill him for the love of Christ and in the name of God, but always realize he may be the saint and you the devil . . . and what you may die for, some smart chap like Laski may write a book and prove is all nonsense.[9]

Holmes replied cordially, "Rarely does a letter hit me so exactly where I live as yours, and unless you are spoiling for a fight I agree with it throughout," and closed by saying, "I enjoyed our meeting as much as you possibly could have and should have tried to prolong it to Boston but that I feared my wife would worry."[10]

But in fact he did not, at least not yet, buy Hand's argument that freedom of speech had a greater claim than any other rights; "free speech stands no differently than freedom of vaccination," he wrote to Hand. It would only be after some steady effort by Hand and other legal thinkers, and some more visceral personal encounters with the evils of intolerance for unpopular views, that Holmes would make the cause his own, and in so doing change forever the way the courts, and Americans, thought about free speech.

———————

THAT SUMMER HAROLD Laski and his wife rented a cottage on the water at Rockport at the tip of Cape Ann, about fifteen miles from Beverly Farms. He had met Holmes two summers before when Frankfurter brought him to lunch, and their friendship had blossomed in a blizzard of correspondence; by the end of the year they had exchanged forty letters, and continued to do so at a scarcely undiminished rate over the following two decades. In Laski, Holmes had found his equal as a correspondent: Laski replied as quickly as Holmes, and filled his letters with a dazzling array of allusions to literature, political philosophy, church history, and earnest assurances of his affection and friendship.

He laid it on thick enough at the start that it put Holmes a bit on guard: when their correspondence was published in the 1950s Learned Hand said he was "glad to see that O.W.H. kept his fond disciple at a greater distance than I had feared; and was vaguely aware of the net that was being thrown for him." A few months after their initial meeting, Holmes wrote to Laski, "The sinister thought has arisen in my mind whether you young fellows were ironically trying how much the old man could stand in the way of flattering things." But he quickly added, "I hardly need say that I believe in and reciprocate the affection that I get from men like you and Frankfurter too sincerely to have any doubt."[11]

Laski was just twenty-one and

Laski, his wife, and daughter, in 1918

teaching at McGill University when Frankfurter had met him in the spring of 1915, and was so impressed he immediately arranged introductions that led to his becoming a regular writer for the *New Republic* and, the following year, an instructor in medieval history at Harvard.[12]

He was short, Jewish, leftist, and never let the truth get in the way of a good story, of which he had a seemingly inexhaustible supply. As an undergraduate at Oxford, fired with the cause of women's suffrage, he had briefly flirted with radical extremism, planting a gasoline bomb in the men's room of a railway station in a village in Surrey. The device detonated but failed to fully explode, doing minimal damage. Laski decamped to Paris for a few days, earning back the money he had borrowed for his getaway by giving tours of the city to visiting Americans, until the police lost interest in the "Oxted Station Outrage" and he quietly slipped back to Oxford. After that he confined his political agitation to words alone.[13]

When the Holmes-Laski letters were published they also confirmed to the world what all of his friends knew: that Laski was full of charm, brilliance, and fabulations. His stories were always fascinating, involving famous people or astounding coincidences: finding a set of astonishingly rare books inside a locked seventeenth-century desk that he picked up for three pounds at an antique shop; beating the American champion at tennis; being arrested in Manchester, England, when he was mistaken for a notorious wanted jewel thief; meeting the British prime minister Lloyd George, who at the end of a two-hour-long intimate dinner asked, "You don't like me, Laski?"[14]

A later colleague at the London School of Economics, Edward Shils, described Laski's "unsteady relations with the truth whenever he told about some experiences of his own."

> His very recounting of any experience that he said he had was immediately discounted. No one ever said: "Harold told me . . ." with the expectation that the retelling of the story told by Laski would be taken at its face value. It was known that, despite his *soi-disant* Marxist egalitarianism, one of Laski's greatest pleasures was to be in the company of the great and the mighty and that his

very greatest pleasure was to say that he had been in their company. . . . His irrepressible need to elaborate and to fabricate came to be accepted by everyone who had any dealings with him. . . .

The creation of these tales was not regarded as a vice; Laski was never called a liar. It was regarded rather as a foible.[15]

Charlie Curtis, who was a student at Harvard Law School at the time Laski arrived in Cambridge, recalled that "it was not until the morning after an evening with Laski that I used to wonder whether my belief had not been keeping pace with my enjoyment." The English social reformer Beatrice Webb, who also heard many of Laski's accounts of intimate talks with prime ministers and other famous people, observed in her diary, "He is never malicious or mischievous, but the tales he tells, if they are not all true, are vivid anticipations of what might have happened."[16]

Holmes was not completely taken in by all of Laski's stories, either. "I hope some day in a flush of conscience you will confess to faking a little—pour épater les bourgeois," he once wrote to him. Another time Holmes caught him out boasting in a newspaper interview of his private conversations with President Wilson. "I did not know that you ever were in contact with him," Holmes wrote. "When and what was it?" Laski replied that the reporter must have mixed him up with someone else.[17]

Yet if it was not always easy to separate truth from fiction in his stories that was at least in part because extraordinary things really *did* happen to him, and he really did know the great and mighty wherever he went. One of his more astounding real-world experiences was to have been selected as a juror in the libel action brought by Sir Michael O'Dwyer against an Indian jurist who had accused him in print of instigating the 1919 Amritsar massacre, in which British troops fired on and killed hundreds of peaceful protesters: Laski was the lone holdout against a verdict for the plaintiff.[18]

Leonard Woolf, one of the British intellectuals active in advising the Labour Party, recalled Laski's astonishing performance—"one of the most brilliant intellectual pyrotechnical displays I have ever listened to"—when Gandhi met with a group of Labour people in London a few years later to discuss future action toward Indian independence. After each of the participants had said his piece, Gandhi asked Laski if he would summarize the discussion.

> Harold then stood up in front of the fireplace and gave the most lucid, faultless summary of the complicated, diverse expositions of ten or fifteen people to which he had been listening in the previous hour and a half. He spoke for about 20 minutes; he gave a perfect sketch of the pattern into which the various statements and opinions logically composed themselves; he never hesitated for a word or a thought, and, as far as I could see, he never missed a point. There was a kind of beauty in his exposition, a flawless certainty and simplicity which one feels in some works of art. Harold's mind, when properly used, was a wonderful intellectual instrument.[19]

As Shils concluded about his colleague, "Despite the mists of ambiguity and embroidering, there was much that was real in both his fame and his learning. . . . His capacity to arouse affection and to show affection was the most visible and least fabricated thing about him."[20]

The affection between Holmes and Laski was certainly genuine, on both sides. Holmes described his new young friend to Pollock as "one of the very most learned men I ever saw of any age," as well as "an extraordinarily agreeable chap." If any of his young friends ever filled the role of surrogate son, Laski came the closest. Holmes called him "dear lad" or "my son" and Laski—whose own father had broken off all connections when he defied his parents by marrying, at age eighteen, a non-Jewish woman eight years his senior—was more than happy to play the part.[21]

"Here we are at last—and I hope before long to see you," Holmes wrote to Laski in Rockport a few days after arriving at Beverly Farms for the summer of 1918. A few days later he wrote to confirm their first planned meeting, "I am dying to talk with you." They saw each other for a number of long talks; when Holmes got tied up for several days straightening out his bank statement ("my Heavenly Father never meant me to do sums"), he wrote, "Just a word to say how I miss you." At the end of August Laski invited the Holmeses to have dinner with him and his wife at their cottage, and afterward wrote to say how much it moved him "that you both have broken bread with us."[22]

Laski was juggling an incredible number of projects. In addition to teaching and writing for the *New Republic*, he was contributing scholarly articles to the *Harvard Law Review* on everything from the liability of charitable corporations to the effect of orders-in-council on Magna Carta, while also running its book review section, helping to fill in while many of the students had enlisted for the war—the only time in the history of the *Review* that one of its editors was not registered at the Law School.[23]

Laski at that time threaded a careful line between liberalism and communism, but one of the key ideas that animated him at Harvard was enthusiasm for what he called "pluralism"—the idea that government was just one of a number of institutions that contributed to the public good, and that the freedom of people to organize competing associations such as labor unions, churches, and civic associations was essential to progress and democracy. His belief in freedom of speech flowed directly from that. A divergence of views over even the most basic questions allowed new ideas to develop and be tested; but diversity was also an inevitable consequence of liberty itself: in a society where people did not slavishly owe obedience to the state and to conformity, differences of opinion were natural, and should be welcomed.[24]

Holmes had shown Laski his correspondence with Hand, and that summer, as he cultivated his deepening friendship with Holmes, Laski used the opening Hand had given him to keep working on Holmes on the issue, employing a combination of argument and flattery. Holmes responded to Laski's sallies by sticking to his insistence that tolerance is only a product of indifference to the outcome: on matters where we care enough, Holmes insisted, "we should deal with the act of speech as we deal with any other overt act that we don't like." But he added, "To be continued on Friday."[25]

Holmes's self-avowed sense that he had to spend at least part of his summer reading "for improvement" gave Laski another opportunity:

he sent Holmes a list of titles calculated to advance the case for civil liberty—Lord Acton's *The History of Freedom*, Thorsten Veblen's *The Nature of Peace*—and in early August sent him a weighty French legal tome, the second volume of *Science et technique en droit privé positif*.[26]

That was probably a mistake. The work was devoted to the very proposition about the law that Holmes had always most scorned, the idea that there was a "natural law" that underpinned all of human law, in particular man's endowment with certain fundamental rights—as the Declaration of Independence had so notably declared.

In "a kind of a rage," as Holmes later described his mood, he sat down and wrote a short essay distilling his rejection of these views. He showed it to Laski that night he and Fanny came to dinner. Laski flatteringly declared it second only to "The Soldier's Faith" among the "things of yours that, at first sight, have moved me so much," and claimed it for the *Harvard Law Review*.[27]

"The jurists who believe in natural law seem to me to be in that naïve state of mind that accepts what has been familiar and accepted by them and their neighbors as something that must be accepted by all men everywhere," Holmes wrote in his article. "The most fundamental of the supposed preëxisting rights—the right to life—is sacrificed without a scruple not only in war, but whenever the interest of society, that is, of the predominant power in the community, is thought to demand it."[28]

And yet there was a small crack in his argument when he acknowledged at the start the point that would grow to become his clarion call in defense of freedom of speech—if not as a right, then as a necessity. "Certitude is not the test of certainty," he wrote. "We have been cocksure of many things that were not so."[29]

It was exactly the point Hand had tried to make to him on the train, and then reiterated in what Holmes described to Laski as Hand's "mighty good letter" afterward: that our very skepticism about our own certainty ought to counsel tolerance in repressing the beliefs of others.

And then, Holmes wrote to Einstein toward the end of the summer, he had said "To hell with improvement!" and spent the rest of his vacation reading three books of Homer's *Odyssey* ("with more pleasure than formerly"), *Hamlet* ("a bill filler . . . they all talk Shakespeare"), and *Experiences of an Irish R.M.*, the humorous tales of a hapless English resident magistrate constantly outwitted by the locals in his attempts to enforce the law in the Irish countryside.[30]

THAT FALL OF 1918 the flu pandemic that would claim three times as many lives as the entire four years of fighting in the war now at last approaching its end broke out in an army camp near Boston, and spread quickly down the East Coast. In Washington, public buildings were shut, and the Supreme Court delayed the opening of its term so that lawyers from around the country would not have to travel to "a crowded and infected spot," Holmes wrote to Pollock.[31]

Although the *Masses* case had ended with the ruling of the court of appeals that threw out Hand's injunction, several other challenges to the Espionage Act's restrictions on speech were on the Supreme Court's docket for the October 1918 term. One of the very first cases to come up when the Court began hearing arguments again in November was *Baltzer v. U.S.*, an appeal of the convictions of twenty-seven South Dakota farmers who had made the mistake of protesting to the governor what they saw as an unfair draft quota assigned to their community.

The farmers, all socialists of German descent who opposed the war, complained that their county had been singled out in retaliation for their political views and ethnic heritage. In fact, the quotas had been arrived at by deducting the number of men who had already enlisted from each county; and their area, which also contained a large number of Mennonites who opposed military service on religious grounds, had relatively few volunteers, so received a correspondingly high quota. After sending a petition to the governor against what they saw as an injustice, all had been promptly arrested, tried in federal court, and sentenced to one to five years in prison for obstructing the draft.

Several other pending Espionage Act cases garnered considerably more attention. In *Schenck v. U.S.* the government had gone after Socialist Party officials who had much more openly denounced the war and the draft, mailing leaflets to draftees urging them to resist conscription. In *Frohwerk v. U.S.* the editors of a German-language newspaper in Missouri had been convicted for printing articles that, among other things, denounced sending American soldiers to France as "outright murder" and asserted that Germany was conducting a defensive war against the aggressions of England.

The most prominent of the cases was an appeal of the conviction of Eugene V. Debs, the Socialist Party's leader and standard bearer. Debs had unsuccessfully run for president on the Socialist Party ticket four times, never garnering more than 6 percent of the vote, but he was no joke, to either his supporters or his enemies. A fiery orator and veteran union organizer, he had never wavered in his denunciation of the war as a fight between the capitalist powers in which the working class had no stake. In a speech in Canton, Ohio, on June 16, 1918, he thundered that the ruling classes "have always taught you that it is your patriotic duty to go to war and to have yourselves slaughtered at a command, but in all of the history of the world you, the people, never had a voice in declaring war."

Debs, the master orator, made his own closing argument at his trial, speaking for two hours without notes, denying nothing but likening himself to past American heroes who dared to challenge the "respectable majority of their day." This time his oratory fell on deaf ears, and he was convicted of inciting disloyalty to the military and obstructing the draft.[32]

Eager to have a definitive ruling, the attorney general sought an expedited review of all of the cases, which the Supreme Court granted. *Baltzer* was first on the docket. In early December, McKenna circulated his draft opinion for the majority, affirming the convictions of the farmers.

Holmes's decisions up until then in cases involving freedom of speech had not been particularly sympathetic to the idea that speech deserved any special protection from government control. In Massachusetts, he had upheld statutes that banned public speaking and preaching on the Boston Common and that barred police officers from engaging in political activity.[33] He had rejected the argument that in accurately reporting

Eugene V. Debs speaking in Canton, Ohio, 1918

accusations of corrupt dealings by public officials or unethical conduct by a lawyer, newspapers were shielded from libel suits by those named in their stories.[34]

The federal courts for their part had had little to say on the First Amendment. Having ruled in 1833 that the Bill of Rights does not apply to the states, the Supreme Court had heard few cases touching on freedom of speech. One that did reach the Supreme Court, in 1907, was *Patterson* v. *Colorado*. In his unanimous opinion for the Court, Holmes followed the same line of reasoning he had applied in his Massachusetts cases, relying largely on a key 1825 decision by his eminent predecessor on the Massachusetts Supreme Judicial Court, Chief Justice Isaac Parker.[35]

Parker, in a carefully argued analysis of whether the constitutional protections of freedom of the press adopted by the states and the federal government at the nation's founding merely embodied the existing English common law, or were meant to establish a new, more expansive right, Parker came down squarely on the side of the first proposition. The common law rule, which Blackstone had set forth in his influential commentaries, was that the government could not impose a *prior* restraint on speech—such as requiring publishers to submit a work for approval in advance—but that anyone who did publish could still be held to account for his words after the fact.

Moreover, Parker wrote, the constitutional provisions protected "the *liberty* of the press, not its *licentiousness.* . . . The liberty of the press was to be unrestrained, but he who used it was to be responsible in case of its abuse." It could even be an "abuse" to publish true statements, if they threatened a breach of the peace or reckless damage to reputation. If "a minister of the gospel should be guilty of gross immoralities," Parker noted, a member of his parish could properly bring a complaint to the church authorities without risking a libel action. But a "promiscuous promulgation of the same facts" through publication would be "the strongest evidence of malice," fully punishable by the law.[36]

In *Patterson*, Holmes wrote that a fine levied against a Denver newspaper for criticizing a decision of the state's supreme court did not raise a First Amendment issue, since the Bill of Rights did not apply to the states. But he did not stop there. In almost the exact language of Blackstone and Parker, Holmes went on to assert that even if the amendment did apply, it had been adopted only "to prevent all such *previous restraints* upon publications as had been practiced by other governments, and . . . not to prevent subsequent punishment of such as may be deemed contrary to the public welfare." Two years later, upholding a libel judgment against a Chicago newspaper, Holmes had quoted the words of one of England's leading authorities on the common law, the eighteenth-century jurist Lord Mansfield: "Whenever a man publishes, he publishes at his peril."[37]

Baltzer was by far the most aggressive of the government's Espionage Act prosecutions, since it targeted exactly the situation Parker had suggested as an example of protected speech. The farmers had not published or publicly circulated their petition: no one had even seen it but the governor and a few of his aides. Among the First Amendment's explicit guarantees was the right of the people "to petition the Government for a redress of grievances." All of the justices had indicated

SUPREME COURT OF THE UNITED STATES.

No. 320.—OCTOBER TERM, 1918.

Emanuel Baltzer, Gottfried Baltzer, Frit- rich Leneschmidt, *et al.*, Plaintiffs in Error, *vs.* The United States of America.	In Error to the District Court of the United States for the District of South Dakota.

[   ]

Mr. Justice HOLMES dissenting.

The only evidence against the plaintiffs in error is that the petition set forth in the indictment was signed and sent by them to the Governor of the State, and to two other officials probably supposed to have power. The signing and sending of it is taken to amount to wilfully obstructing the recruiting and enlistment service of the United States. Uniting to sign and send it is supposed to amount to a conspiracy to do the same thing and also to a conspiracy to prevent the Governor by intimidation from discharging his duties as an officer of the United States in determining the quota of men to be furnished for the draft by the local board. I can see none of these things in the document. It assumes that the draft is to take place and complains that volunteers have been counted with the result that counties have been exempted. It demands that the Governor should stand for a referendum on the draft and advocates the notion that no more expense should be incurred for the war than could be paid for in cash and that war debts should be repudiated. It demands an answer and action or resignation on penalty of defeat at the polls of himself and 'your little nation J. P. Morgan.' The later phrase was explained by the writer to mean J. P. Morgan's class, as I think it obviously does without explanation. The class is supposed to stand behind the Governor and to be destined to defeat with him if he does not do as he is asked.

It seems to me that this petition to an official by ignorant persons who suppose him to possess power of revision and change that he does not, and demand of him as the price of votes, of course

It was not circulated publicly.

Holmes's undelivered dissent in *Baltzer*

that they were willing to uphold the power of the government to prevent action that harmed the military in wartime, but if the convictions in *Baltzer* were affirmed, that would imply a far greater restriction of fundamental rights of citizens. Brandeis was troubled enough by the precedent that would be set that he went to see Holmes and suggested he write a dissent.[38]

What ensued was a remarkable instance of back-door politicking in the Court. Holmes quickly fired off a dissenting opinion that, while dismissing the petition of the farmers as a "foolish exercise of a right"—and not retreating from his position that "freedom of speech is not abridged unconstitutionally in those cases of subsequent punishment with which this court has had to deal from time to time"—showed that his blood had been stirred, and that Laski's and Hand's appeals had not been wholly in vain.

"We have enjoyed so much freedom for so long that perhaps we are in danger of forgetting that the bill of rights which cost so much blood to establish is still worth fighting for," Holmes wrote in his dissent. He saw nothing wrong with punishing real efforts to aid the enemy or obstruct the law. "But the emergency would have to be very great before I could be persuaded that an appeal for political action through legal channels, addressed to those supposed to have power to take such action was an act that the Constitution did not protect as well after as before."[39]

"I gladly join you," Brandeis replied immediately. Somewhat surprisingly, Chief Justice White did too: "Please state me as joining EDW." Pitney did not, writing on his return to Holmes:

I submit, with great respect, that this reads as if it proceeded from the heart rather than the head—Pitney
  P.S.—a good fault perhaps, but still a fault[40]

Less than a week later, on December 16, 1918, the government abruptly withdrew the case, admitting that the convictions had been in error. The justices' deliberations were strictly confidential, yet the solicitor general wrote an internal memorandum indicating that he had received warning that the government might lose its case in the Supreme Court. What seems likely is that someone tipped him off, and the most likely culprit is Brandeis. Whether the solicitor general simply feared that a powerful dissent by Holmes, joined by the chief justice, would be an embarrassment, or whether Brandeis succeeded in leaving the impression that Holmes's dissent might actually garner a majority, the Justice Department concluded it would be wiser to drop the case altogether.[41]

Holmes had no similar doubts about the guilt of Debs and the others, however. In February 1919, White assigned three remaining Espionage Act cases to Holmes to write, and in early March he announced the decisions for a unanimous Court, upholding all of the convictions. But he told several friends he thought it was foolish for the cases to have been brought at all. He wrote to Baroness Moncheur,

> I had a disagreeable task in writing a decision against Debs, the agitator, for obstructing recruiting by a speech found by the jury to have been made with that intent. There was no doubt in my mind about the law but I wondered that the Government should have pressed the case to hearing—as it enables knaves, fools and the ignorant to say that he really was condemned as a dangerous agitator.[42]

Yet even in upholding the government's position, Holmes had in fact taken another measured step back from the views he had expressed in *Patterson* and in the Massachusetts cases. He had clearly been wrestling with the question Hand had raised in *Masses* about where to draw the line between protected and dangerous speech: he wrote Hand in late February that he had finally read his opinion and that while he would not necessarily have arrived at the same result, "I thought that few judges indeed could have put their view with such force or in such admirable form."[43]

In his opinion in *Schenck*, the case of the Socialist Party leaflets, he proposed a test of his own. He had been thinking by way of analogy to the law of attempted crimes. In two important cases he had decided in Massachusetts, Holmes had addressed the all-important question of intent. Like everything, it came down to a matter of degree. But "as the aim of the law is not to punish sins, but is to prevent certain external results, the act done must come pretty near to accomplishing that result before the law will notice it," he had ruled in affirming an attempted murder conviction in a case where a rat poison ("Rough on Rats") had been placed in the intended victim's moustache cup. He made the same point in overturning a conviction for attempted arson in the case of a man who bought combustible materials with the intention of burning down a building, but changed his mind and turned around when he was still a quarter of a mile away.[44]

In *Schenck* he suggested the test of whether speech advocating illegal conduct was punishable was, similarly, whether it came close enough to the act that it posed "a clear and present danger." As with everything else, that depended on the circumstances: in wartime there was more justification for limiting speech since the danger was proportionately greater. He illustrated the point with an analogy whose subsequent fame may have added more confusion than clarity: "The most stringent protection of free speech would not protect a man in falsely shouting fire in a theatre and causing a panic."[45]

Laski and Hand were unhappy with the decisions, but continued to cajole Holmes in the hope of bringing him around. "I read your three opinions with great care," Laski wrote the justice; "and though I say it with deep regret they are very convincing." Hand, trying one last time to get Holmes to see his point about looking at the words themselves rather than subjectively trying to gauge their implications, began his letter to Holmes, "I haven't a doubt that Debs was guilty under any rule conceivably applicable," which he almost surely did not believe. But Hand worried that a test that still relied on motive and intent was far too sweeping, and he said that the Espionage Act had "certainly terrorized some of the press whose voices were much needed." He admitted defeat, however, on the direct-incitement test he had proposed in his *Masses* decision: "I bid a long farewell to my little toy ship which set out quite bravely in the shortest voyage ever made."[46]

The *New Republic* departed from its usual praise of Holmes with an article by a University of Chicago law professor, Ernst Freund, that took sharp issue with the reasoning in his decisions. "To be permitted to agitate at your own peril, subject to a jury's guessing at motive, tendency and possible effect," Freund wrote, "makes the right of free speech a precarious gift." Holmes went so far as to draft a somewhat stung reply to the magazine's editors, but thought better of it and did not send it, but did show it to Laski—who responded with tactful silence.[47]

In part, that was because Laski was orchestrating some of the critical commentary himself. Few academic lawyers had much interest in the First Amendment at that time, but Chafee had been inspired to delve into free speech when he came across Hand's *Masses* decision while searching for examples of injunctions for a course he was teaching on torts and equity. The scion of a wealthy Rhode Island family, Chafee was a specialist in business law, but Hand's decision piqued his interest. Laski then urged him to start writing on the subject for the *New Republic*.[48]

Chafee's views on free speech reflected his patrician and old–New England feelings of the responsibilities of wealth: his sympathies, he said, were with his class, but to persecute those less well off for their differing views offended his sense of honor. "[I] want my side to fight fair," he insisted.[49]

Following the Espionage Act decisions, Chafee followed up with a lengthier article for the *Harvard Law Review* that also took issue with some of Holmes's reasoning. Notably, the "fire in a theater" analogy, he observed, was shooting fish in a barrel: it was such an easy case that it offered little useful guidance to juries, which would still have far too much leeway to apply subjective notions about what constituted actual danger. "How about the man who gets up in a theater between the acts and informs the audience honestly but perhaps mistakenly that the fire exits are too few or locked?" he asked.[50]

But Chafee sought to make the best of it, and thought that "clear and present danger" was a starting point that could achieve a much broader protection of free speech, despite its shortcomings. As Hand later told Chafee, "You have, I dare say, done well to take what has fallen from Heaven and insist that it is manna."[51] The events of the next few months would show that they were not mistaken in their hopes of continuing to move Holmes to a more encompassing view of the one right, they argued, that all other rights in a free society flowed from.

═══════

WALKING IN ROCK Creek Park at the end of March, a few weeks after his decisions in *Debs* and *Schenck* were announced that spring of

1919, Holmes saw his first bloodroot flower of the season. "In spite of continuing anxieties I can enjoy nature now," he wrote Baroness Moncheur. "I found myself doing so one day and said to myself How is this? And then I answered myself—why the Armistice."[52]

If he thought that, like the anxieties of the war, his recent controversial cases were behind him, the relief was short-lived. Holmes privately hoped the president would pardon Debs, and the "other poor devils with whom I have more sympathy." But his opinions upholding their convictions brought the Court, and Holmes personally, in for a flood of hate mail and public attacks. "Just now I am receiving some singularly ignorant protests against a decision that I wrote sustaining a conviction of Debs, a labor agitator, for obstructing the recruiting service," he wrote to Einstein. "They make me want to write a letter to ease my mind and shoot off my mouth; but of course I keep a judicial silence."[53]

In the early morning hours of April 30, 1919, a postal clerk in Manhattan named Charles Caplan was reading the newspaper on the subway on his way home from his late shift when his eye fell on an article about a bomb that had exploded at the home of ex-senator Thomas W. Hardwick on Peachtree Street in Atlanta. The bomb was in a parcel that had been sent through the mail; when Hardwick's maid opened it, it blew off both her hands and seriously injured the senator's wife. Enough of the packaging had survived, however, to provide a description of the parcel's appearance—and Caplan realized with a start that it was identical to sixteen packages that were sitting at that moment in the parcel-post storage room in Harlem, where they had been held for insufficient postage. He got off the train at the next stop and immediately returned to the post office and notified his supervisor.

By the end of the day, the bomb squad had dismantled all of the devices and confirmed that they were the same as the Atlanta bomb, filled with liquid dynamite and wrapped in a box labeled "Novelties" and stamped with the name of the Gimbel Brothers department store. Among the intended recipients were John D. Rockefeller, J. P. Morgan, Attorney General A. Mitchell Palmer, Postmaster General Albert

Burleson, and Justice Oliver Wendell Holmes.[54]

Holmes, the old soldier, brushed it off. "I haven't thought much about it," he told Einstein, who had written with concern upon reading the news. "As I said to my wife, if I worried over all the bullets that have missed me I should have a job." Holmes likewise belittled the alarmed talk in the popular press of "the Red danger in the U.S." If it was his decision in *Debs* "that led them to want to blow me up," Holmes dismissively observed, that only showed "that they were fools who didn't understand the situation."[55]

Much of the country did not take so detached a view of the "Red threat." Attorney General Palmer launched a sweeping probe of radical organizations

36 WERE MARKED AS VICTIMS BY BOMB CONSPIRERS

Infernal Machines, All Mailed Here, Sent Broadcast on Different Dates.

FIND 16 AT POST OFFICE

Authorities Declare Them the Most Deadly Contrivances in Their Experience.

NOTED MEN PICKED OUT

Burleson, Rockefeller, Landis, Justice Holmes, and Palmer Among Intended Recipients.

New York Times,
May 1, 1919

that would lead to a series of raids later in the year: as many as ten thousand alleged Communist Party members were rounded up and hundreds deported after summary hearings before a Justice Department official, without any access to legal representation.

Frankfurter and Chafee joined a number of prominent lawyers who spoke out against the Justice Department's "illegal acts" in carrying out arrests and searches without warrants and in denying the most basic due process rights to those detained in the Palmer Raids. In response, a young attorney named J. Edgar Hoover at the newly created Bureau of Investigations opened files on hundreds of "subversives" and "radicals" who were aiding communists and "inciting" unrest. Among them were Harold Laski ("an English-Polish Jew, said to be extremely radically inclined"), Zechariah Chafee ("Attorney for Radical Organizations"), and Felix Frankfurter ("a parlor Bolshevist").[56]

Frankfurter, who had spurned Holmes's advice about the limitations of the academic life to accept a position at Harvard Law School in 1914, had already come in for hostile criticism there for his political views. Holmes caught hints that both Laski and Frankfurter were now in serious trouble at Harvard. In April 1919 he wrote Laski, "Every once in a while, faintly and vaguely as to you, a little more distinctly as to Frankfurter, I hear that you are dangerous men. I even heard it said that he was a bad one—(Do *not* repeat this.) What does it mean? They used to say in Boston that I was dangerous."[57]

In fact both were being subjected to a vicious and anti-Semitic campaign by conservative faculty members and influential alumni who wanted them fired. The same "narrow tribe of Beacon Hill and State Street," as Frankfurter called them, that had opposed Brandeis's nomination were now threatening to withhold their support from Harvard's fundraising campaign as long as Frankfurter remained on the faculty. When the dean of the law school, Roscoe Pound, refused to fire Frankfurter, the group began pressuring President Lowell to fire *him*.[58]

Laski, who was already the subject of angry complaints from parents that he was indoctrinating their children with socialist propaganda, came in for much more public attack that spring when he supported striking mill workers in Lawrence. A conservative professor of physics at Harvard, Edwin H. Hall, began writing letters to newspapers calling Laski a "bolshevist" and a "poisonous influence"; though fortunately, Hall concluded, Laski—like "a rattlesnake"—gives warning of his dangerous intentions with his noisy speeches.[59]

Holmes was president of the Harvard Law School Alumni Association and Laski, while playing down the threat to himself, suggested that Holmes might say a word in support of Pound to head off the attack on him and Frankfurter. Holmes's position with the association was a purely honorary one—he mockingly referred to himself as King Log—but in May he wrote a carefully worded letter to the association suggesting they pass a resolution commending Pound for all he had done for the school. He also sent a note to Lowell saying that Pound and Frankfurter were worth far more to the school than any addition to the endowment could be. Lowell responded with a reassuring reply; while not mentioning Frankfurter, he said of Pound, "What you say about his value to the law school I agree with entirely." For the moment at least, Laski's and Frankfurter's positions were safe.[60]

Approaching the end of the Court term, Holmes was again looking forward to a summer of reading philosophy. But, he told Laski, "Talking with Brandeis yesterday (a big chap) he drove a harpoon into my midriff by saying that it would be for the good of my soul to devote my next leisure to the study of some domain of fact—suggesting the textile industry." Holmes diligently ordered a stack of reports and tried to tackle them. "I hope it is good for my soul," he wrote Mrs. Gray as he plodded through a study of women and child wage earners in the United States in 1912. "It certainly is food for the body as it encourages slumber." (The following summer, Holmes happily reported, Brandeis gave up on him: "In consideration of my age and moral infirmities he absolved me from facts for the vacation.")[61]

As Holmes was slumbering over his government reports at Beverly Farms that summer of 1919, Laski's troubles suddenly grew much worse. On September 9, the Boston police went on strike, and several nights of chaos ensued until the state guard restored order, after firing into a mob in South Boston. Police Commissioner Charles Curtis—the husband of Holmes's friend Ellen Curtis—refused to give in to the strikers' demand to form a union, and ordered all thirteen hundred officers dismissed. Laski threw himself into the maelstrom. Addressing a huge rally of the wives and mothers of the fired officers, Laski denounced Curtis's handling of the strike: "We are told the police are deserters. The deserter is Commissioner Curtis, who was guilty at every point of misunderstanding his duties." This time the letters to Lowell demanding his dismissal from Harvard became a torrent.[62]

Holmes was only vaguely aware of just how serious the situation had become for Laski; he wrote him on October 26, "I infer that you have had trouble, I hope not serious, because of your criticism of Curtis." But he drew a direct connection from Laski's and Frankfurter's run-ins with intolerance to the questions of freedom of speech that were very much on his mind—owing to a case that was about to complete his transformation as the Court's foremost champion of the First Amendment. "I fear we have less freedom of speech here than they have in England," he wrote to Laski in that same letter. "Little as I believe in it as a theory I hope I would die for it."[63]

JUST FIVE DAYS before, the Court had heard argument in *Abrams* v. *U.S.* Seven anarchists, all Russian Jews, had been arrested for distributing leaflets in English and Yiddish denouncing America's intervention in Russia in aid of the forces battling the Bolshevist government. In one of their pamphlets they called on American arms factory workers to refuse to assist in the crushing of "the Russian worker." On that basis, five of the defendants were convicted of violating the Espionage Act and given sentences of up to twenty years in prison.

This time, Holmes and Brandeis announced in conference that they planned to dissent. A few days before the Court's decision was delivered on November 10, 1919, Holmes's colleagues McKenna, Pitney, and Van Devanter appeared at the doorstep of 1720 Eye Street. With Mrs. Holmes joining them in the study, they urged him politely but in no uncertain terms not to go through with his planned dissent: given Holmes's great reputation and military record, they told him, it would do great harm that he perhaps was unaware of. They suggested that—under Brandeis's influence—he was taking a "quixotic" view of the case. Fanny indicated she agreed with them. Everything was cordial, but Holmes made clear his mind was made up.[64]

Mollie Steimer, who was deported from the U. S. in 1921 because of her radicalism, has just been exiled from Russia, and for a similar "crime." (*Keystone*)

אלי שטיימער, וועלכע איז ארויסגעשיקט געווארען פון די אמעריקא אלס רעװאלוציער נרעגע אין איצט ארויסגעשיקט געווארען סאוועטרוסלאנד פאר'ן זעלבען "חטא".

Four of the defendants in the *Abrams* case

Holmes would always insist that his dissent in *Abrams* was completely consistent with his earlier opinions in *Schenck* and *Debs*; it was merely a matter of where to draw the line.[65] But no one hearing the ringing words he read out in Court that day would have agreed. Holmes set forth a completely new rationale for the protection of speech that went beyond his "clear and present danger" test, and which embraced fully Hand's pragmatic rationale: that only when competing ideas are heard can they be tested.

He began by making a point of showing up the absurdity of the danger the government alleged by quoting in full the text of the offending leaflets. And then in words that no one but Holmes could have written, he went on,

> In this case, sentences of twenty years' imprisonment have been imposed for the publishing of two leaflets that I believe the defendants had as much right to publish as the Government has to publish the Constitution of the United States now vainly invoked by them. Even if I am technically wrong, and enough can be squeezed from these poor and puny anonymities to turn the color of legal litmus paper, I will add, even if what I think the necessary intent were shown, the most nominal punishment seems to me all that possibly could be inflicted, unless the defendants are to be made to suffer not for what the indictment alleges, but for the creed that they avow—a creed that I believe to be the creed of ignorance and immaturity when honestly held, as I see no reason to doubt that it was held here, but which, although made the subject of examination at the trial, no one has a right even to consider in dealing with the charges before the Court.
>
> Persecution for the expression of opinions seems to me perfectly logical. If you have no doubt of your premises or your power, and want a certain result with all your heart, you naturally express your wishes in law, and sweep away all opposition. . . . But when men have realized that time has upset many fighting faiths, they may come to believe even more than they believe the very foundations of their own conduct that the ultimate good desired is better

reached by free trade in ideas—that the best test of truth is the power of the thought to get itself accepted in the competition of the market, and that truth is the only ground upon which their wishes safely can be carried out. That, at any rate, is the theory of our Constitution. It is an experiment, as all life is an experiment. Every year, if not every day, we have to wager our salvation upon some prophecy based upon imperfect knowledge. While that experiment is part of our system, I think that we should be eternally vigilant against attempts to check the expression of opinions that we loathe and believe to be fraught with death, unless they so imminently threaten immediate interference with the lawful and pressing purposes of the law that an immediate check is required to save the country. I wholly disagree with the argument of the Government that the First Amendment left the common law as to seditious libel in force. History seems to me against the notion. I had conceived that the United States, through many years, had shown its repentance for the Sedition Act of 1798, by repaying fines that it imposed. Only the emergency that makes it immediately dangerous to leave the correction of evil counsels to time warrants making any exception to the sweeping command, "Congress shall make no law . . . abridging the freedom of speech." Of course, I am speaking only of expressions of opinion and exhortations, which were all that were uttered here, but I regret that I cannot put into more impressive words my belief that, in their conviction upon this indictment, the defendants were deprived of their rights under the Constitution of the United States.

Holmes almost never quoted the text of the Constitution in his opinions; he had never before spoken of individuals' rights under the Constitution; he had never before so clearly rejected Blackstone's and Parker's view that the First Amendment merely put in writing the existing English common law on prior restraints. In introducing the notion of the free trade in ideas, he laid the foundation of the single most powerful and enduring rationale for the protection of free speech, one that would be cited repeatedly in future Supreme Court decisions.

Something had aroused him to the core, and that something was not only the reasoned persuasion of Hand and Chafee, but the vivid example of what intolerance had done to Frankfurter, Laski, and his other friends in the red-baiting attacks they had endured.

Holmes rarely admitted he ever changed his mind, but when Chafee asked him a few years later how he had developed the clear-and-present-danger test and come to accept that the First Amendment embraced more than the common law prohibition against prior restraints, he acknowledged that *Abrams* and the other Espionage Act cases had forced him to rethink the assumptions he had expressed in *Patterson*. The law of attempt that he had devoted much thought to in Massachusetts had been one source of ideas. But also, "the later cases (and probably you—I do not remember exactly) had taught me that in the earlier Patterson case . . . I had taken Blackstone and Parker of Mass. as well founded, wrongly. I simply was ignorant."[66]

Laski, Lippmann, Pound, Croly, Frankfurter, Hand, and other friends all sent their praise of his "glorious opinion"; conservative lawyers were almost beside themselves, denouncing what Holmes had written as "a positive menace to society." Holmes's old friend John Wigmore of the Northwestern University Law School, who had invited Holmes back in 1902 to dedicate the school and had often praised Holmes's decisions, wrote a sneering diatribe in the *Illinois Law Review*. Mocking the words of his dissent, Wigmore attacked Holmes for his "obtuse indifference to the vital issues at stake," accusing him of protecting not freedom of speech, but "Freedom of Thuggery."[67]

At Harvard, both Laski and Chafee continued to come in for attacks from conservatives for their stands for free speech, too. Both were hauled before committees to examine their political views and scholarly bona fides. (Chafee was accused of "deliberate falsehoods" in his articles, but by a vote of six to five the committee declined to recommend his dismissal.) Laski laughed off his inquisition, but a month later, in January 1920, he was the victim of one of the ugliest incidents

TRUE MARTYRDOM

"I do not want to be a fly,
I want to be a worm."

Gilman's "A Conservation."

**Reference Books for Mr. Laski's
Political Theories**

1. "Pluto's Republic" or "What in hell?"
2. Laski's "Authority in the Matrimonial State." $3.50 at Coop.
3. "Political Theories of Dunning," How to dodge creditors creditably. (Out of print.)
4. "The World and I—which is the more important?" $3.50 at Coop.
5. "History of Shoe-shining", by Lord Howlong. Three copies. Dunster Book Shop. Every man expecting to pass must have one.
6. "From Gortion to Grotius," by Figits. In Latin with French, German, Greek, and Hebrew notes to facilitate reading.
7. Laski's "The greatest political thinker I have known. An Autobiography." $3.50 at Coop.

Caricature and parodies of Laski from the *Harvard Lampoon*, January 16, 1920

in Harvard's history. The entire issue of the *Harvard Lampoon*, the undergraduate humor magazine, was devoted to a personal, humiliating, and in places crudely anti-Semitic character attack on him. Sixteen pages of poems, parodies, drawings, and caricatures mocked his physique, his Jewishness ("Oi Gewalt! I was delicate"), his politics ("from the firstski to the Laski he's a Red!"), even his hat. Parodied as "Professor Moses Smartelickoff," he was portrayed as an egotistical deadbeat, a coward and shirker, and a lecherous ogler of the Radcliffe girls. The magazine concluded with the wish that "the next Soviet Ark that sailed" might "transport this pseudo-instructor from the United States and from Cambridge."[68]

When Holmes heard about it he was disgusted, he told Frankfurter, "that so serious a scholar and thinker as he should be subject to the trampling of swine." He was particularly incensed that the *Boston Evening Transcript* had joined the attack on Laski with a "dirty" editorial congratulating the students for showing that Laski's radical utterances did not reflect the feelings of the august university. Laski tried to make light even of this, writing to Lowell to ask that the *Lampoon*'s editors not be disciplined. Brandeis sent an encouraging word: "I trust you and Frida are not too much concerned about the Lampoon episode. It is really a great compliment, and has done good service to the cause of freedom." But it was the last straw. In March, Laski wrote Holmes that he had accepted a position at the London School of Economics. "You will know what I mean when I say that my love for you and Felix is the one thing that holds me back."[69]

Holmes replied instantly, "Your decision sounds right to me."

But oh, my dear lad, I shall miss you sadly. There is no other man I should miss so much. Your intellectual companionship, your suggestiveness, your encouragement and affection have enriched life to me very greatly and it will be hard not to look forward to seeing you in bodily presence. However, I shall get your letters and that will be much.[70]

CHAPTER 15

Taft's Court

Returning home one January afternoon following the justices' weekly Saturday conference, Holmes was giving Brandeis his familiar speech about how no rearrangement of property could address the real sources of social discontent, that cutting off "the luxuries of the few"—even from the "rotten second generation that has no idea of responsibility"—would make no appreciable difference in the material lot of "the crowd," that the passion for economic equality was merely "idealizing envy."[1]

Brandeis replied from his deepest wells of moral indignation. Growing "really eloquent on the evils of the present organization of society," as Holmes described it all to Laski afterward, Brandeis dismissed Holmes's thinking as "superficial." He told him his observations did not even touch the real evil, which had nothing to do with luxuries or necessities, but power. "He was fierce and fine," Holmes said, describing men he knew who did not dare say what they thought because of the economic control other men held over them. Brandeis told Holmes that in his sheltered existence he knew *nothing* about the realities of life that people involved in the affairs of the world had seen firsthand.[2]

"He bullies me a little on that from time to time," Holmes said. But he took it all in good part, and never stopped telling friends what a "great comfort" Brandeis was to him on the Court. And for all his pri-

vate comments about taking satisfaction in upholding "imbecile" statutes—"If my fellow citizens want to go to Hell I will help them. It's my
job," he once remarked to Laski—his written opinions in labor cases, as
in Massachusetts, consistently showed sympathy for and understanding of the inherently unequal power between employer and employee.[3]

At the very end of the 1918–19 term the Court had upheld, by 5–4,
Arizona's worker's compensation law. McReynolds in his dissent hys-
terically warned that to impose financial liability upon an employer for
accidents that occurred without fault on his part was "revolutionary
and leads straight towards destruction of our well-tried and successful
system of government."[4]

Holmes had been assigned the majority opinion, but lost Day's vote
when he made the point that there were many instances in the common
law where conduct was punished without moral fault, including the
criminal law and the master-servant rule—one of those generalities of
his that made his fellow justices nervous for their future implications.
Pitney ended up rescuing the majority, while Holmes's opinion became
a separate concurrence.[5]

But the more important lines in Holmes's opinion were those pointing out that social insurance schemes like worker's compensation really
were nothing more than a way to have society pay for what it gets: "It
is reasonable that the public should pay the whole cost of producing
what it wants, and a part of that cost is the pain and mutilation incident to production. By throwing that loss upon the employer in the first
instance, we throw it upon the public in the long run, and that is just."[6]

His attitude toward private philanthropy was marked by the same
mix of coldly rational disdain in the abstract, and human sensitivity
in the specific. He made only the most perfunctory annual charitable
contributions, to the Community Chest, the state firemen's association,
and like organizations. Only after being "importuned" by his secretary
Tommy Corcoran did Holmes come up with a $100 donation to the
Harvard Law School fund. During the First World War he had put all
the money he could spare into Liberty bonds; but that was "duty," he
said, not philanthropy.[7]

He was especially scornful of the kinds of causes and cultural institutions whose support had so filled old Boston with its sense of virtue. He had read Malthus for the first time in 1914 and was thoroughly convinced by his argument that in a world of finite resources, all utopian schemes ran smack up against the inexorable consequences of unbridled population growth. "Being a devout Malthusian I believe that all social improvements . . . are exhausted by propagating up to the dead line," he said.[8] By the same token, social investment came only at the cost of investment in other useful economic activity. In an unpublished passage in a letter to Laski, he related,

> And oh how I did rile my ex-sister in law [Mrs. Walter Scott Fitz, the remarried widow of his brother Edward], by saying that great gifts to public purposes (like Carnegie libraries) were prima facie wrong—and tried to make her see that always there is detriment by wh. the benefit must be paid for—so that one must question very seriously before doing such things. She is rich but thinks no farther than that she is giving from *her* superfluity—and said "I shant tell you the nice things I've been doing for the Art Museum." I answered "Dont" and bid her adieu.[9]

And yet he was always ready to give away hundreds of dollars to help friends or acquaintances. His secretary Augustin Derby related how the cabman who drove Holmes every day to the Court in his early years in Washington, before he had engaged Charlie Buckley as his regular driver, once came to see the justice and explained that his horse had died, and asked if he could borrow $150 to buy a new horse. With great indignation, Holmes sternly replied, "I am not in the business of money lending." Then, with an abrupt change of expression, "I will give you $150." He helped subsidize the sabbatical of the young philosopher Morris Cohen, whose ideas had impressed him, and told Frankfurter that if a plan materialized for his Chinese friend John Wu to come to Harvard Law School as a visiting lecturer he would provide $500, "but that is *strictly between ourselves* and not to be hinted to him or anyone else."[10]

With the failure of the Bull Moose campaign, many of Holmes's progressive friends including Frankfurter and Brandeis had moved to the Democratic Party, but Holmes never lost his lifetime Republican allegiances. He had never been very impressed by the Democrat Wilson, and after returning from one garden party at the Wilson White House, he wrote Einstein, "I think the average democratic politician is even a more odious type than the inferior of republican stripe."[11]

Four days before his eightieth birthday in March 1921, he sat through the inauguration of the new Republican president, Warren Harding, and reported himself equally unimpressed. The inauguration was the "only public show" the Court was expected to attend, and as Holmes always gruffly observed, "Inaugurations are great on killing off old men, as we have to sit out doors in raw weather." This one came off "in less time and ennui than usual," but the new president, Holmes reported to his irritation, "used 'sensed' as a verb or participle three times," as well as some other words "that made me shudder." "I fear that he is a pumpkin not a cantaloupe," he told Mrs. Gray.[12]

For his eightieth birthday Fanny had arranged another surprise, gathering nearly all of his former secretaries and sneaking them into the dining room through the back entrance of the house via the kitchen. It was a Sunday night, two days before his birthday, and he suspected nothing even when Fanny explained it would be more convenient for the servants if they reversed their usual Sunday practice and lunched out and dined at home, and then persuaded him to dress formally before going downstairs in tribute to his last Sunday "in the 79's." When the folding doors to the dining room were opened, "There were 16 or 18 strapping chaps standing around the table," he told Mrs. Curtis in describing the scene afterward. "Of course I was flabbergasted." Fanny told him that he had "yelled with joy when they began to pour our champagne of which we had a case or two left."[13]

Two years before he had sent Einstein a bit of doggerel he had composed on his walk while contemplating his approaching birthday,

I will sit in the seats of the mighty
If I can, until I am eighty (pronounce ity)
And what I'll do then
In the following ten
I leave to the Lord God Almighty.[14]

But now he gaily announced to all his friends that he had "a new ideal—to try to live to 90, and hereafter seek further fame only as a survivor, impressive to look at in civic processions." He had been especially buoyed by the publication of his collected writings on the law that Laski had arranged—and that Frankfurter, Lippmann, Croly, and others of his circle of young admirers made sure received multiple praiseful notices. Morris Cohen, writing in the *New Republic*, called it "an extraordinary book of thoroughly matured human wisdom"; and a second piece in the magazine, by Lord Haldane, the former Lord Chancellor of England, Holmes said nearly overwhelmed him for saying, "Ideas, when great enough, have a penetrative power which extends beyond the boundaries of nations and across oceans."[15]

Learned Hand many years later expressed regret that he and the others had "indulged themselves so much in flattery" of Holmes, and thought it had not always brought out his best side. "As I look back on it, we all did exploit him by playing on his vanity." And yet Hand took pains to emphasize that it was not so much egotism, as a kind of unsuspecting innocence and guilelessness on Holmes's part, that made him so susceptible to praise. Hand described it as an "almost childlike simplicity" "that remains the most endearing of his moral qualities." It never would have crossed Holmes's mind to manipulate others in that way, so it never occurred to him he was being used by those whose words, he once said, made him feel "I have achieved what I longed to do."[16]

Meanwhile they all reassured him he should not think of resigning. What gave Holmes pause—besides the inevitable apprehensions of undetected senility ("one is told that old men can't trust their judgment," he admitted)—was the extraordinary isolation that came with the job. "It is a great place, Judge," Chief Justice White had said on welcoming John Hessin Clarke, who took Hughes's place on the Court in 1916. "But we live in a cave."[17]

Still, unless "the loneliness becomes too intolerable," as he once put it, he intended to keep on as long as he could handle his share of the cases—which he continued to "fire off" as rapidly as ever.[18]

WILLIAM HOWARD TAFT hated being president of the United States; but he worshiped the life of the law. "I love judges, and I love courts," he once said. "They are my ideals, that typify on earth what we shall meet hereafter in heaven under a just God." When he appointed White chief justice he had secured something close to a promise from White that he would merely be "holding the place" until Taft could be named to the position by a future Republican president. With Harding's election, the time seemed to have arrived to call in that obligation. White spared him the embarrassment of pressing the matter by dying two months after Harding's inauguration.[19]

Joining the Court for its fall term of 1921, Taft threw himself into the job he had always coveted. Holmes had disliked Taft's unconcealed ambition for the office and had remarked that he "never saw anything that struck me as more than first rate second rate" about him, but he quickly was won over by the new chief's zeal for administrative efficiency and his unbounded reserves of good humor. Unlike White, Taft took firm control of the conferences, keeping discussions to the point and cutting off repetitious arguments. One of his first aims was to eliminate the enormous backlog of cases clogging the docket: 343 cases had been carried over from the 1920–21 term, and the average time for a case to be heard was eighteen months. Within a few years the backlog was gone and the time from the filing of an appeal to oral argument was reduced to six months.[20]

Taft's larger ambition was a more sweeping overhaul of the entire federal court system, giving the chief justice administrative authority over federal district judges and reforming the outmoded appeals process that was overwhelming the Supreme Court. The centerpiece of his

The Taft Court

proposal was to eliminate most of the automatic right of appeal by writ of error, and to give the Supreme Court the power to decide for itself what cases it would accept.

The legal mechanism for this was the writ of certiorari, which traditionally had been used by a higher court to order the records of a lower tribunal brought up to correct a manifest error. But with the passage in 1925 of Taft's "Judges' Bill," after four years of hard lobbying of Congress by the new chief, applications to the Court for certiorari became the almost exclusive avenue of appeal. Routine appeals of cases already decided by a lower appellate court were eliminated in a stroke. As Taft saw it, the Court would now be able to limit its work to cases where the issues between the parties were of "sufficient importance," owing to the constitutional or national questions they raised, to justify a hearing by the highest court in the land.[21]

While substantially reducing the number of decisions the Court had to render, it added a new burden, however, of reviewing hundreds of applications for certiorari each year—only a small fraction of which were approved. ("A certiorari granted is a certiorarity," Holmes wisecracked. But reading the applications now filled the summer as well as the entire term: "They infest the whole year and make it like a house full of moths," he complained to Nina Gray.)[22]

Taft's other great passion was for "teamwork," and like White he wanted to greatly reduce the number of dissents—"a form of egotism" he called them, that "only weaken the prestige of the Court."[23] He never achieved that aim: the percentage of cases decided with dissenting opinions in each of his years as chief justice years varied between 8 and 21 percent, considerably more than the 4 percent average of the White Court, if still far below the record of his successors.[24] But the sheer ebullience that Taft brought to the job did much to ease friction among the brethren. "The truth is, that in my present life I don't remember that I ever was President," Taft said, and Holmes reported with pleasure that Taft's infectious good humor and ability to keep "things moving pleasantly" with "a smile or a laugh" was a vast improvement. "We get on very pleasantly with the present Chief Justice, who is not a worryer, or if he is doesn't show it," Holmes wrote to Ethel Scott halfway through Taft's first year.[25]

Taft made a point of showing his appreciation for the work of others, tried to assign cases to each of the justices that played to their strengths and particular interests, and often went to great lengths to modify his own draft opinions to meet objections from his fellow justices. Nowhere was his tact more evident than in the gracious way he put aside his past differences with Brandeis. Upon joining the Court, Taft had sent Brandeis a long letter expressing his hope they would work together, and exerted his personal charm to show there were no hard feelings, always offering Brandeis and Holmes a ride home in his car from the Court's conferences. Brandeis, like Holmes, welcomed Taft's administrative abilities and found him "a cultivated man," easy to talk to.[26]

McReynolds and McKenna, however, remained as obdurate as ever, and their fractious behavior and often sheer incompetence left Taft privately in despair. Aside from his outrageous rudeness, McReynolds was the laziest member of the Court, "always trying to escape work," Taft complained; on more than one occasion McReynolds airily announced in the middle of the fall term that he would not be attending Court for several days because "an imperious voice has called me out of town," to go duck hunting on Maryland's Eastern Shore.[27]

McKenna was not only continuing his pointless rivalry with Holmes, but was "the worst and most embarrassing member" of the Court, turning in opinions that missed key points, in one instance actually presenting in conference a draft opinion that decided the case the opposite way from which the judges, McKenna included, had unanimously voted. "He is jealous of Holmes," Taft confided to his brother in April 1922, and tried to complete his opinions as quickly as Holmes, but "does not get the record straight. . . . He and Holmes had a controversy the other day in conference, in which Holmes kept his temper, and McKenna lost his. I wrote a note to felicitate Holmes on the manner in which he bore himself. So you see we are not without our troubles."[28]

In a case Holmes had decided for a 5–4 majority just before Taft joined the Court, McKenna had written one of his most intemperate dissents yet to a Holmes opinion. Holmes made light of the matter to Baroness Moncheur, telling her that his decision "provoked a cry of despair over the downfall of the Constitution from McKenna, but I guess the old document will survive as it has survived many similar predictions in the past." But he told Frankfurter that he thought it was "bad form" for McKenna to go after the majority decision rather than simply express his own views of the law.[29] The case, *Block* v. *Hirsh*, had been brought in challenge to the District of Columbia's rent-control law, enacted by Congress as a wartime necessity. McKenna had written a virtual diatribe in dissent to Holmes's opinion affirming the law, sarcastically suggesting it was "safer" and "saner" to "regard the Constitution as paramount" rather than "weaken it by refined dialectics."

No amount of administrative skill or tactful leadership was going to bridge the fundamental ideological divisions in the Court, however, and Taft came in with an unwavering antilabor stance that solidified the conservative majority and Holmes's and Brandeis's distance from it. "The only class which is distinctly arrayed against this court . . . is organized labor," Taft wrote his brother during his first year on the Court. "That faction we have to hit every little while, because they are continually violating the law and depending on threats and violence to accomplish their purpose."[30]

In one of his first decisions in the fall of 1921, *Truax v. Corrigan*, he did just that. Arizona had passed a statute forbidding courts to issue injunctions against peaceful picketing by strikers. Taft's "rather spongy" majority opinion, as Holmes called it, relied on the usual argument that the law violated the Fourteenth Amendment's protection of property. One absurdity of the majority opinion was that the supreme courts of many of the states had reached the same position as Arizona's statute as a matter of common law—meaning that by Taft's reasoning it was constitutional for a state supreme court to disallow the issuance of injunctions against picketers, but unconstitutional if a state legislature did the same, a point that Brandeis made in his dissent.

Holmes's separate dissent was in a way more pointed, because it went to the heart of the idea that a right of property was involved at all. "By calling a business 'property' you make it seem like land," he wrote. But a business "is a course of conduct and like other conduct is subject to substantial modification according to time and circumstances."

Taft would later grumble about Brandeis's and Holmes's "claques in the law school contingent," and grow increasingly exasperated by their frequent dissents, which he said only gave ammunition to political attacks on the Court from progressives like Senator Robert La Follette who wanted to limit its power to overturn legislation—but which he also knew sucked the force out of his opinions. Holmes, Taft complained, is "a very poor constitutional lawyer . . . he lacks the experience of affairs in government that would keep him straight on constitutional questions."[31]

But he always conceded that whatever their differences, "association with Justice Holmes is a delight," as he told Learned Hand in 1923. "In many ways he is the life of the court."[32] Not least were Holmes's lively interjections in oral argument, which became the stuff of legend among attorneys who appeared before the Court. All kept lists of their favorite Holmes anecdotes. A famous one involved Harding's solicitor general, James M. Beck, a grand orator in the old style who liked to end his arguments with lengthy quotations from Shakespeare, ostentatiously recited from memory. Once Beck was delivering a particularly long quotation, which seemed to be aimed pointedly at the chief justice's view of the case. Holmes leaned over to Taft and whispered—quite audibly—"I hope to God Mrs. Beck likes Shakespeare." And more than once, Holmes came to the rescue of a young attorney who was about to walk into a trap one of his colleagues had laid. "I wouldn't answer that question if I were you," Holmes would genially interject.[33]

Taft acknowledged that whatever "unsound" views Holmes might have on the Constitution, "it is a great comfort to have such a well of pure common law undefiled immediately next [to] one, so that one can drink and be sure one is getting the pure article."[34]

─────────

HOLMES COMPLAINED OF asthma and a cough the following spring of 1922 and though he prided himself that he had never missed a single meeting of the Court up until then, was absent from one Saturday conference by what Taft termed "the positive injunction of his doctor." Holmes observed with humorous dismay to Mrs. Gray, "How I fear I am a venerable man. I called on a young woman the other day and when I left she came down stairs and helped me on with my overcoat." He still took his daily walks with his secretary, who that year was Laurence Curtis II, "a dear rather simple minded true Bostonian," as Holmes described him: "I have a one legged secretary who got smashed up by a fall in an aeroplane when training for the war, and we walk together at a judicial pace, which suits me better than it used to."[35]

For the summer Laski was pushing him to read "something about some industry in Chicago," but he had responded, "Webbs, Industries and generally upward and onward as be damned," and said he meant to "take advantage of my age" and get hold of an unexpurgated edition of Pepys's *Diaries*. But on June 20, 1922, he was hit by "a thunder clap" that upended his peaceful summer plans.[36] He wrote Justice

Clarke from Corey Hill Hospital in Brookline, Massachusetts, a week later with the news:

> I was taken quite by surprise—about 2 days after a doctor and a catheter I found myself here—with a pipe promptly attached to my bladder and awaiting the psychologic moment for them to take my prostate from me. The preliminaries are striking—no sleep—spasmodic yearnings to piss &c &c. But I read books and receive flowers from the dames and am doing as well as could be expected.
>
> I think I shall be philosophical whatever the results. I can write but a line as I am on my back but I send you my love and gratitude.
>
> Yours OWH[37]

The standard procedure at the time was to make an incision a few inches below the navel directly into the bladder and insert a drain tube to relieve the immediate obstruction to urination caused by the enlarged prostate—and then wait as much as several weeks, with the aim of reducing urea levels in the blood that often rose as a result of urinary retention, and which made an operation riskier by elevating blood pressure and putting a strain on the kidneys. The prostate would then be removed in a second operation through the same incision.[38]

Holmes waited three weeks, having to lie on his back most of the time. He wrote to Ellen Curtis that he felt it "providential" he had seen her just before his hospitalization: "You are glad aren't you that we did meet before this broke loose upon me? . . . I am at a low ebb in all but hope." On July 12 he wrote her again, using a pencil because he could not sit up, "Dear Friend Today is the day—they begin on me before long. . . . You have been a good friend. OWH."[39]

He was in the hospital another month before the doctors would let him return to Beverly Farms, but all had gone well. "I think I am a kind of prize patient," he jauntily reported to Mrs. Curtis in August. "I do so hope to turn up in Washington as if nothing had happened—épater les bourgeois."[40]

Anna Codman and her son came to see him in the hospital, and she wrote him afterward,

> The tears were very near my eyes more than once, at witnessing your courageous cheerfulness. Young Russell was also gravely impressed and I am glad he has also a chance of feeling such an affectionate admiration for one of my dearest friends. You have the great gift of drawing young people round you and making them feel at their ease, and they absorb unconsciously deeper thoughts, new to them. . . .
>
> Always affectionately yours,
>
> A. K. Codman[41]

Back at Beverly Farms, Holmes's idea of recuperation was to read *all* of Shakespeare's plays (in the hospital it had been "nothing higher than Kipling" and detective stories) and by the end of August he reported to Mrs. Gray, "I drive for an hour in the morning—walk inches—lie down—read Shakespeare and sleep—a little solitaire—complete irresponsibility—no mental improvement. That's me."[42]

An elevator was being put in at 1720 Eye Street, and while the work was going on the library and front parlor were in a state of temporary chaos; on arriving back in Washington he was pushed from the train to a taxi in a wheelchair ("I blushed but submitted") and he and Fanny went straight to the Powhatan Hotel, where they stayed for two weeks while the work at the house was completed. It increased his troubles, Holmes said, though they had wonderful rooms, "looking over the whole earth."[43]

As always his work proved the best medicine. He immediately wrote the opinion in a case argued the first day of the term, relating to Mrs. Gray that "the guardians of the public taste made me strike out one phrase that I thought happy. I knew they would when I put it in." But, he went on, "As I say to the boys when I smilingly consent to strike out something from an opinion that I knew would turn their stomach, our effort is to please."[44]

The case involved a Pennsylvania statute that reflected a long-standing local custom allowing a property owner to rebuild a wall shared with an adjacent building; in rejecting a Fourteenth Amendment claim against the law, Holmes had originally made a wisecrack about his much disliked phrase "police power," observing that the action here "does not commit even the petty larceny of the police power." He dutifully changed it in the final version to, "does not need to invoke the police power."[45]

Though he still felt weak in the legs, he was able to sit at a table "and do a days work." He said to Mrs. Curtis, "I feel as if it were a close shave."[46]

BRANDEIS HAPPILY REPORTED a few months later, "We met Holmes J. walking alone on K St. yesterday PM. Blooming and buoyant, having practically written the last opinion in his hands."[47]

He and Holmes continued to wage their fight against the narrow view of the Court's majority of what social, economic, and labor laws were allowable under the Fourteenth Amendment. During Taft's nine years as chief justice, the Court struck down almost one hundred state laws, most on the grounds that they interfered with private business activity in violation of "liberty of contract" or right to property under the Due Process Clause. In dozens of these cases Holmes and Brandeis dissented, later often joined by Justice Harlan F. Stone, who replaced McKenna on the Court in 1925.

Taft began to talk about the "enemies of the Constitution," complaining that Brandeis was out to "break down the prestige of the Court" and that Holmes was "so completely under the control of Brother Brandeis that it gives to Brandeis two votes instead of one." Moreover, Taft complained, Holmes seemed to care only about his dissents, turning in perfunctory and "not very helpful" opinions in cases in which he was assigned to write the majority opinion.[48]

The position Holmes and Brandeis took in their dissents was hardly radical: if a legislature had a reasonable basis for enacting a law regulating business, it was not for the courts to say otherwise. The Court's conservative majority, however, continued to hold that except when justified as an exercise of "police powers" in the interests of health, safety, or public morals, or in a very narrow circumstance when a business was "affected by the public interest"—such as the grain elevators in Chicago that stood "in the very gateway of commerce"—all such meddling with private enterprise was unconstitutional.[49]

On that reasoning the Taft Court threw out a Pennsylvania law banning the use of recycled wool in mattresses, a Tennessee law regulating the price of gasoline and a Minnesota law the price of milk, a Wisconsin law subjecting gifts made within six years of death to the state's inheritance tax, a California law requiring the licensing of car services that transported passengers between fixed points, a Pennsylvania law requiring the owners of drug stores to be pharmacists, and a New York law outlawing the scalping of theater tickets. Holmes dissented in all.[50]

In the New York ticket case, *Tyson & Brother* v. *Banton*, Holmes dropped any effort to salvage the majority's theories of "police powers" or a business "dedicated to a public use" in making his case for the validity of state laws regulating a business. Those terms, he wrote in his dissent, are merely used "to apologize for the general power of the legislature to make some part of the community uncomfortable by change."

> I do not believe in such apologies. I think the proper course is to recognize that a state legislature can do whatever it sees fit to do unless it is restrained by some express prohibition in the Constitution of the United States or of the State, and that Courts should be careful not to extend such prohibitions beyond their obvious meaning by reading into them conceptions of public policy that the particular Court may happen to entertain. . . . The notion that a business is clothed with a public interest and has been devoted to the public use is little more than a fiction intended to beautify what is disagreeable to the sufferers.

A notable exception to Holmes's stand against the Court's striking down state laws in the name of property rights came in the fall of 1922, in a case that Taft persuaded him to write while he was still recovering from his operation. Brandeis was the sole dissenter; he told Frankfurter afterward that he thought Taft had caught Holmes at a vulnerable moment, and "played him to go whole hog." *Pennsylvania Coal Co. v. Mahon*, which has never been overturned, held that a state law banning mining of coal within the limits of a city unconstitutionally deprived coal companies of the mineral rights they had retained when selling the land for development. The law was intended to protect buildings from collapse as a result of subsidence from mining, but Holmes held that this time the government had gone too far in infringing on expressly reserved property rights.[51]

But otherwise the battle lines remained deeply drawn as ever. What Justice Clarke called the "Fourteenth Amendment nonsense" so frustrated him that he abruptly resigned that fall. Clarke, a Wilson appointee and the one other voice on the Court to resist the reactionary direction of the majority, was a lifelong bachelor and a confirmed hypochondriac, and there were other things preying on his mind; he was given to bouts of melancholia, and McReynolds's constant insults and torments added to his miseries. But it was the overall sense of futility that most of all led him to give up. Two years later, happily back home in Ohio, he wrote to his former colleague Van Devanter, "The most trying part of it all was the conferences, so futile for the most part and so little like what I had imagined, and what the country imagines they must be."[52]

Holmes dealt with the ongoing impasse over the Fourteenth Amendment with his usual humorous stoicism: Frankfurter related how Holmes once told him that whenever his fellow justices started going on about "liberty of contract," he would pass the time by "thinking of all the beautiful women he had known."[53]

Brandeis on numerous occasions used his dissents to present an exhaustive factual background that he hoped would point out the rationale for the laws that the Court majority was so cavalierly overturning as "unreasonable, arbitrary or capricious." When the Court struck down a Nebraska law setting standard weights for loaves of bread sold at retail, Brandeis "wrote a good dissent," Holmes slightly facetiously told Pollock, "showing profound study of the art of bread making." Even Laski once suggested to Holmes, "If you could hint to Brandeis that judicial opinions aren't to be written in the form of a brief it would be a great relief to the world."[54]

Although Holmes said that "the way in which that cuss is loaded with facts on all manner of subjects leaves me gawping," Holmes himself, as always, relied on rhetorical strikes at the jugular rather than massed assaults of facts.[55] When the Court refused in *Adkins* v. *Children's Hospital* in the spring of 1923 to uphold a law Congress had passed setting a minimum wage for women workers in the District of Columbia, even Taft balked; while not joining Holmes's dissent, he wrote a separate opinion stating that he had assumed the Court had quietly overturned *Lochner* in its intervening decisions upholding Oregon's laws regulating working hours. That the Court was now resuscitating the majority opinion in *Lochner* was seen by most progressives as a huge step backward.

Holmes, though, claimed to be unfazed. "The minimum wage case didn't bother me at all personally as I like to shoot off my mouth without having to secure some one else's agreement," he wrote to Mrs. Gray.[56] But he took direct aim at the idea of liberty of contract in his dissent in *Adkins*, which would join *Lochner* as one of his most famous and prophetic stands against one of the Court's most notoriously misguided decisions. "Contract is not specially mentioned in the text that we have to construe," wrote Holmes. "It is merely an example of doing what you want to do, embodied in the word liberty. But pretty much all law consists in forbidding men to do some things that they want to do, and contract is no more exempt from law than other acts."

For the next fourteen years, until *Adkins* was overturned, four of the justices who had joined the majority opinion—McReynolds, Van Devanter, and two of Harding's new appointees, Pierce Butler and George Sutherland—would form a solid conservative bloc, striking down not only all similar state laws, but much of the early program of the New Deal. Frankfurter dubbed them the "Four Horsemen," as in the biblical riders of the apocalypse.

———————

AMONG TEDDY ROOSEVELT'S sources of "bitter disappointment" with Holmes, besides the *Northern Securities* case, were his decisions "on the negro question."[57] Holmes had in fact shown decidedly little sympathy for the plight of African Americans in the Jim Crow South in a number of cases that reached the Court early in his tenure.

Like nearly all members of his class and time, his only direct contact with African Americans in segregated Washington was as servants, in his case chiefly his Court messenger and household butler. Although Holmes never evinced any racist sentiments himself, and never uttered a word suggesting he agreed with the "scientific" thinking about race of the day that viewed blacks as biologically inferior, he clearly looked upon segregation and the South's maintenance of white supremacy as expressions of "the dominant force of the community," which he always insisted the law inescapably reflected, and which it was vain for courts to oppose.[58] His lack of concern with racial justice in the abstract was no different in one sense from his equal indifference toward other claims of abstract rights. But his complex feelings about the war and the determined walling-off of the fervent abolitionism of his youth had left him with a noticeable blind spot on racial matters, which led him directly to write several of the worst decisions of his career. Only later, when his impassioned defense of due process in criminal trials began to open his eyes to the systematic and brutal nature of racial discrimination in the South, did he begin to question his own thinking about race and to acknowledge the widespread injustices experienced by African Americans in daily life.

In his very first months on the Court—in what was arguably one of his most poorly reasoned opinions—Holmes delivered the decision in *Giles* v. *Harris*, declining to order Alabama to register five thousand black voters in Montgomery. Like every other Southern state at the turn of the twentieth century, Alabama had adopted a new constitution specifically designed to throw black voters off the rolls. Alabama relied mainly on a so-called grandfather clause that imposed permanent literacy and property tests, but allowed lifetime voter registration for a brief initial period for those who qualified under a set of carefully drawn exceptions that only whites were likely to meet—such as having fought on either side "in the war between the states" or being the descendant of a veteran of any of America's wars.

The leaders of Alabama's constitutional convention openly declared that the "paramount purpose" was to "lay deep and strong and permanent in the fundamental law of the State the foundation of white supremacy forever in Alabama," and the result was exactly as intended: after the new constitution went into effect, only 3,000 blacks out of an eligible population of 180,000 in the state were left on the voter rolls.[59]

In an argument that bordered on sophistry, Holmes in his decision asserted that if Alabama's voter registration was corrupt, as the petitioners alleged, then "how can we make the court a party to the unlawful scheme by accepting it and adding another voter to its fraudulent lists?" But probably more reflective of his thinking was his conclusion: "Relief from a great political wrong, if done, as alleged, by the people of a state and the state itself, must be given by them or by the legislative and political department of the government of the United States," Holmes insisted—not the courts.

In other cases challenging Jim Crow rule, Holmes had consistently sided with the Court's majority in maintaining the separate but equal rule of *Plessy* v. *Ferguson*. He even declined to associate himself with the Court's finding that an Oklahoma law allowing railroads not to offer dining or sleeping cars for black passengers on segregated trains violated the Equal Protection Clause. He likewise voted to affirm a Kentucky law that made intermixing of the races a crime, even at private institutions— which was aimed at eliminating the one integrated college in the state, Berea College, founded by idealistic abolitionists after the Civil War.[60]

And in a dissent that was full of ironies—"legalistic in the worst sense of legalism," as Max Lerner, a liberal but clear-eyed admirer of Holmes called it, and ignoring the "simple facts of human experience" that Holmes himself had always maintained judges need to consider in applying the law—he argued for the constitutionality of Alabama's peonage laws, under which thousands of African Americans were arrested for trivial offenses, mostly farm laborers accused of breaking their labor contracts, and forced to pay off their fines as convict labor leased out to private employers.[61]

He had even been planning at first to dissent from the Court's ultimately unanimous 1916 opinion in *Buchanan* v. *Warley* holding as an unconstitutional denial of due process a city ordinance in Louisville,

Kentucky, that forbade any "colored person to move into and occupy as a residence" a house in a predominantly white neighborhood.

The case had its peculiarities. A law cannot be challenged in the abstract as unconstitutional: the Constitution explicitly limits the Supreme Court's jurisdiction to "actual controversies," meaning there has to be a party who can show he was injured and has a plausible legal claim against another. An African American buyer whose offer to purchase a house was simply not accepted by a white seller had no direct standing to challenge the law.

The NAACP's attorneys had been trying to devise a case that *would* create an "actual controversy" at law, and with the help of a cooperative white real-estate agent they finally did so: the agent entered into a contract of sale with a black purchaser, but it included a provision that if any local law prevented the buyer from occupying the property, he would not be required to complete the purchase. The black buyer, citing the Louisville law, accordingly refused to fulfill the contract, and the white seller sued him, arguing that because the Louisville law was constitutionally invalid, the buyer *was* required to meet his contractual obligation.

It was a clever solution, but it troubled Holmes greatly precisely because it was the product of collusion between the parties, the kind of abuse of the legal process that never failed to raise his hackles. Learned Hand often told the story of how one time, visiting Holmes in Washington, he had jokingly called back to him as they parted after sharing a ride to the Capitol, "Well, Sir, goodbye, do justice!"

Holmes spun sharply around. "Come here young feller, come here."

"Oh, I know, I know," Hand replied, aware of what was coming. As he reached him, Holmes said, "That is not my job. My job is to play the game according to the rules."[62]

In his unpublished dissent in *Buchanan*, Holmes made the point that the case did *not* look like playing by the rules. "The contract sounds so very like a wager upon the constitutionality of the ordinance that I cannot but feel a doubt whether the suit should be entertained without some evidence that this is not a manufactured case," he wrote.[63]

Holmes left no clue of why he abandoned his dissent; it was likely one of the many instances in which he ultimately chose to "shut up" rather than to appear as the lone holdout to another unanimous decision. In any event, the Court's decision was the first time it had applied the Due Process Clause in limiting racial segregation, and the first time it had spoken unanimously in a civil rights case involving racial discrimination.

But it was Holmes's very sensitivity to questions of genuine due process, whatever his relative indifference to the lives of African Americans in the segregated South, that began to chip away at his judicial attitudes toward racial discrimination in the cases that came before the Taft Court. The Frank case had touched him at an emotional level that was unusual for him, and he had been equally indignant at the outrage to justice in another early case to come before the Supreme Court in which a lynch mob had made a mockery of legal proceedings. That case had led to the only criminal trial in the history of the Supreme Court, when the sheriff in Chattanooga, Tennessee, was brought up for contempt for allowing a lynch mob to take from his jail a black man sentenced to death for raping a white woman.

It was a typical horrific case of Southern summary justice for a black man accused, on however flimsy evidence, of an "outrage" against Southern womanhood. Under repeated threats that the defendant, Ed Johnson, would be lynched if his trial or execution were delayed, his court-appointed lawyers declined to seek a new trial or appeal. But Chattanooga's leading black attorney stepped in and filed a habeas corpus petition in federal court, and Justice Harlan, and then the full U.S. Supreme Court, granted a stay to allow his appeal to be heard. After receiving a telegram from the Court informing him of the stay—it specifically noted that Johnson was now in the custody of the federal courts—the sheriff, Joseph Shipp, dismissed the jail's guards, and a mob that night raided the jail and seized Johnson. They strung him up from a bridge, then riddled his body with bullets when he did not die quickly enough. A note was pinned to his chest: "To Justice Harlan. Come get your nigger now."[64]

Shipp gave a newspaper interview the next morning. "The Supreme Court of the United States was responsible for this lynching," he defiantly declared. "The people . . . were willing to let the law take its course until it became known that the case would probably not be disposed of for four or five years by the Supreme Court of the United States. The people would not submit to this and I do not wonder at it."[65]

Holmes wrote the Court's opinion unequivocally asserting the Supreme Court's jurisdiction to enforce its decrees and ordering a contempt trial of Shipp and others who were a party to the lynching. The trial was held in Chattanooga by a special master appointed by the Court, and the record sent to the Court for a final verdict. After two hours of oral arguments from both sides and several days of deliberation, the Supreme Court found the men all guilty of contempt. Holmes was especially adamant that the integrity of the Court was at stake and that such a brazen defiance of its orders could not be allowed to pass unpunished. Holmes urged a stiff sentence: "I don't see how we can treat it as less than a grave offense," he wrote the chief justice. "I am inclined to say one year's imprisonment." Fuller gave the men ninety days. When Shipp arrived back in Chattanooga after serving his brief sentence, he was greeted at the station by a cheering crowd of ten thousand, and a band that struck up "Dixie" and "Home, Sweet Home" as he stepped onto the platform.[66]

———————

IN THE WINTER of the Court's 1922–23 term, the Shipp and Frank cases formed the background to one of the most important habeas corpus decisions of the Court to that date, and again the decision was by Holmes. *Moore* v. *Dempsey* presented one of the worst instances yet of a Southern mob-dominated trial to reach the federal courts. On the night of September 30, 1919, several hundred African American tenant farmers were meeting in a church near Elaine, Arkansas, to discuss joining together against the extortions routinely practiced on them by their white landlords. An armed white mob, responding to wild rumors that the black farmers were "planning an insurrection" and intending to "kill all the white people," surrounded the church and opened fire. One white man was killed, and over the next several days white gangs hunted down and killed African Americans in the area with impunity.

The defendants in *Moore* v. *Dempsey* (1923)

With the assistance of federal troops sent to restore order, 120 blacks—and no whites—were arrested. The twelve black men charged with murder for the death of the white man at the church were convicted and sentenced to death in trials lasting less than an hour, in which their court-appointed lawyers called no witnesses and offered no challenges, and the juries returned verdicts in five to ten minutes.[67]

The facts as alleged, Holmes wrote in his decision for the Court's 6–2 majority, "make the trial absolutely void . . . no juryman could have voted for an acquittal and continued to live in Phillips County, and if any prisoner by any chance had been acquitted by a jury, he could not have escaped the mob."

Holmes acknowledged that "it certainly is true that mere mistakes of law in the course of a trial are not to be corrected" through a federal habeas corpus proceeding. "But if the case is that the whole proceeding is a mask—that counsel, jury and judge were swept to the fatal end by an irresistible wave of public passion, and that the State Courts failed to correct the wrong," he wrote, then no assertion that criminal cases are matters to be left to the states "can prevent this Court from securing to the petitioners their constitutional rights."

The majority in *Frank* had allowed that a district court has the authority to consider habeas corpus appeals, but Holmes's opinion in *Moore* took a huge step forward in guaranteeing those rights of criminal defendants in actual practice: he ruled that if the facts as presented to a federal court would, if true, be sufficient to substantiate a claim that a defendant had been denied a fair trial in violation of his constitutional rights to due process, then a federal district judge had an obligation to hold a hearing to determine whether they are indeed true.

The decision provoked a furious dissent from McReynolds, in which, besides misstating the facts of the case (and sarcastically observing that "the fact that petitioners are poor and ignorant and black naturally arouses sympathy"), he ominously warned that "If every man convicted of crime in a state court may thereafter resort to the federal court . . . another way has been added to a list already unfortunately long to prevent prompt punishment. The delays incident to enforcement of our criminal laws have become a national scandal."[68]

Moore marked the first time the Court had intervened in a state court's criminal conviction on due process grounds, but it was not just a victory for abstract constitutional rights: for the first time it also saved the lives of the defendants in a mob-dominated trial. The state agreed to reduce the death sentences to twelve years imprisonment in exchange for dropping the federal habeas proceedings, and in January 1925 the governor furloughed the remaining six men who were still being held, the other six who had been sentenced to death having been earlier released by the state supreme court.[69]

The ruling helped restore progressives' faith in the Court when it was at a low ebb, and the *New Republic* and other liberal publications hailed the decision and Holmes, just months after they had excoriated him for his decision in *Pennsylvania Coal* v. *Mahon*.[70]

"Life certainly is one damned thing after another," Holmes wrote to Einstein that winter.[71]

CHAPTER 16

"My Last Examination"

Writing to an associate following Holmes's return to the Court after his prostate surgery, Taft was barely able to conceal his hope that the recovery would prove only temporary. "An operation at that age has in a great many instances that I have known proved to be merely a suspension of the trouble," he observed. Taft kept wishing that both Holmes and McKenna would retire, but as the months went by he was forced to admit that Holmes, at least, seemed as vigorous as ever—"thirsting for more cases," and always eager to help out by taking on work from the other justices. Taft good-naturedly told Holmes "he would probably live to bury us all," which turned out to be prophetic as far as Taft was concerned.[1]

The newspapers regularly reported Holmes's imminent retirement, which he suspected "must mean that somebody hopes to achieve the result by repeated suggestion." Holmes always responded by quoting to his friends what Chief Justice Fuller had said under similar circumstances: "I am not to be paragraphed out of office."[2]

The rumors that he would resign on his eighty-fourth birthday in 1925 did however "add to the bores who beset me," as his increasing public recognition brought a tide of letters from cranks and others. Among them, he wrote with amused irritation to Einstein, are the "elaborately genealogical to show relationship. . . . When I can I chuck them into the basket. I genuinely regret not being able to say: 'Sir or Madam, I don't care a damn about your descent. I don't believe we are

Holmes on his 85th birthday

cousins and I hope not.' . . . Brandeis says that it is a pity that the Post Office is so cheap." He similarly ignored the requests he was now regularly deluged with for what "they call an autographed photograph." (The "animals who ask this," he observed to Laski, "often add to their offense by 'thanking you in advance.' ")[3]

His eighty-fifth birthday brought another surge of attention; along with the now-customary tributes from the profession there was his picture on the cover of *Time* magazine and a wave of newspaper stories and newsreel features. *Time*'s cover called him "more venerable than his father"—which he no doubt found doubly annoying, both for the comparison to his father and for employing the dreaded word "venerable"—but the accompanying article quoted a prediction that Holmes and Marshall would be seen as "the greatest two men that ever sat in the Supreme Court." Lippmann, Frankfurter, and Hand all wrote unsigned pieces in newspapers and journals singing his unstinted praise. "The true disciples of Holmes are the first-rate men now in law school or just recently graduated. Between him and them there is a sym-

"As venerable as his father":
Time, March 15, 1926

pathy of spirit and a community of method which the pedants and legalists do not understand and look upon with some apprehension," Lippmann wrote in the *New York World*, of which he was the editorial page editor. "He is a thinker who has made thinking, even about law, beautiful."[4]

He took popular fame for what it was. "This public business is like getting rich," he observed to Mrs. Gray. "After you reach a certain point you can't well help getting richer. And after a certain number of influential superlatives the papers go down like a row of bricks." It was only the praise of "competent people," he insisted, that mattered to him.[5]

He steadfastly declined to give interviews, but had spoken off the record to Elizabeth Sergeant, a writer who was doing a series of profiles of contemporary Americans for the *New Republic*. She had shown up at his door a few months earlier bearing a letter of introduction from Frankfurter; she was forty-five, born in Massachusetts, educated at Bryn Mawr, and was an experienced journalist and war correspondent. Holmes was charmed and talked almost nonstop for an hour and a half. Only at the end did she mention she was hoping to write a piece about him; Holmes replied that of course she must not take her call on him as an interview, and that he "couldn't cooperate" with her planned article. But Frankfurter accurately appraised the situation: "You certainly have bagged the Justice," he wrote her.[6]

When her article appeared at the end of 1926 Holmes wrote to Frankfurter, "Miss Sergeant's piece was a wonder of care in collecting facts and so kind that it made me blush." He also wrote to her directly, to correct a few anecdotes, but mostly to implore her to remove one reference to Fanny before republishing the piece in a planned book. It was completely innocuous—Sergeant had quoted the passage from William James's published letters in which James had spoken of Fanny as "A1," back when he was Holmes's rival for her attentions in Cambridge after the Civil War—but Holmes explained that "my wife is so averse to being mentioned in public" that he hoped she would understand: "My wife is not showing up sensitive for this occasion. Ever since we have been in Washington she has taken great pains to keep all mention of her out of the papers."[7]

Sergeant apparently also broached the idea of writing his biography, because Holmes wrote her, "As to the dream of a biography I hope that no one will write one while I live. I could not ask for kinder hands than yours, but I should be sorry to see it done by anybody."[8]

Fanny, unmollified, dismissed Sergeant as a "slimy cat." But she made sport with Tommy Corcoran, Holmes's secretary that year, over one line in the piece which had referred to the justice's secretary as "a new jewel of the Harvard Law School every year." Now when Corcoran arrived each morning, Mrs. Holmes would stop him on the stairs and demand, "Whose little jewel are you?" "I am Justice Holmes's little jewel," Corcoran would reply. "Pass, friend!"[9]

At eighty-five Holmes had begun to outlive even his young friends. Clara Stevens had died suddenly of pernicious anemia two summers before, at age fifty-five. And in March 1927 Lady Castletown died at Doneraile, after a long decline following a fall on the stairs and a concussion she had suffered the year before. Her cousin Ethel St. Leger sent Holmes a long and very personal account of her illness and final peaceful death. "Perhaps you will not mention I have written to you to Castletown," she cautioned. A lengthy and slightly cracked letter followed from Lord Castletown himself a week later, blaming a curse on the house for his wife's death and sadly concluding, "Now all is gone and I have no object in life."[10]

But Holmes told his friends he enjoyed life as much as ever; his last few decades, in fact, had been the happiest he had ever known. "We are private soldiers and do not know the plan of campaign or even whether there is one, but I think the evidence plain that we should fight and not worry," he wrote Baroness Moncheur that spring. He and Fanny never went out anymore, which suited him fine: "I say no to everything except to an invitation to a White House Reception to which I say yes and don't go." He sent Mrs. Gray his old formula for happiness, which he said "consists in the neglect of opportunities. I have neglected many—from D. Webster in Faneuil Hall, when I was a boy, to Wagner at Bayreuth—and no doubt other later ones—and am without regret. (You remember the old lady, French, presumably, who said she had remorse but no regrets.)"[11]

That year he got around to reading *Experience and Nature* by John Dewey, an American philosopher a generation younger than the members of the Metaphysical Club, but who had been deeply influenced by the ideas of Holmes's old circle. Dewey had developed William James's and Charles Sanders Peirce's ideas about pragmatism into a more encompassing political and philosophical theory. "I approached it with distrust although it referred to me as one of our greatest American philosophers, which gave me unusual pleasure, but I give you my word was not my reason for reading the book, or thinking well of it," Holmes told Mrs. Curtis. "It is very badly written . . . and yet I thought it the profoundest and most comprehensive view of the world we know that I ever had read."[12]

Tommy Corcoran reported that Holmes had intrepidly climbed over a half dozen fences in Rock Creek Park on one of their excursions that spring in search of the first bloodroot flower. On an outing to Great Falls a few months later, Fanny had to admonish him like a little boy not to get near the edges of the cliffs overlooking the Potomac. And there were echoes of the same undiminished enthusiasm for conversational free-for-alls that had filled the Holmes dinner table at Montgomery Place in his boyhood, in his amused account of his first meeting with Mrs. Curtis on arriving at Beverly Farms: "I have had a struggle for life with my Curtis (each of us liking to talk—so that it becomes a question of getting the floor and keeping it till out of breath)."[13]

"Life still is vivid to me," he wrote his friend Mrs. Clifford in London.

But I wonder as I look with delight on the symphonies of green about me here—or watch the thunder of the sea upon the Glouces-ter rocks, whether I am saying good bye. I dont worry. I am only a little sadder in my pleasure. I have had my whack—and I have no desire to be immortal. After saying which last one adds in one's mind, but I should like four years more like the present—to turn 90 and die in harness doing one's full share. 3 years and 9 months would get one past the line.[14]

"I used to dream of a final calm under old trees, possibly, no—impossibly, in England or the East," he once told Einstein. But, he had concluded, "one must grow one's trees in one's soul." And meantime, he said as he approached the end of the Court's term in the spring of 1927, "I enjoy my work as much as ever, and have had an interesting lot of cases to write."[15]

———

THE CASE THAT filled the headlines the summer of 1927 was not one that had reached the Supreme Court, but it had swept up Frankfurter and his liberal friends in yet another storm of public controversy. Two Italian anarchists, Nicola Sacco and Bartolomeo Vanzetti, had been arrested in the armed robbery in South Braintree, Massachusetts, of a factory payroll in which the company's paymaster and a guard were shot and killed. The case was a liberal cause célèbre that continued for nearly a century afterward. Although subsequent evidence seems to show that Sacco and Vanzetti did take part in the robbery, their trial was marred by prosecutorial misconduct and biased comments by the judge, Webster Thayer, who was quoted making a raft of prejudiced remarks to acquaintances during the trial, such as, "Did you see what I did to those anarchistic bastards the other day? I guess that will hold them for a while."[16]

Frankfurter had been intensely active in defending immigrant radi-cals against deportation during the Palmer Raids and was importuned to look into the Sacco-Vanzetti case; when he did he was particularly outraged that prosecutors had concealed possibly exculpatory evidence.

Throwing himself into the cause, he meticulously went over the record and wrote a twenty-three-page article that was published in the March 1927 issue of the *Atlantic Monthly*, and subsequently in a short book, exposing what he set forth as a manifest failure of the justice system.

For his efforts, Frankfurter once again found himself under attack from Boston Brahmin society and the conservative legal establishment. Holmes told Laski he had heard from Brandeis that the book "has kicked up a commotion" and "Beacon Street is divided."[17] The usual old-Boston crowd was writing to President Lowell and Dean Pound threatening to withhold their support of Harvard as long as Frankfurter remained there. In response to Frankfurter's *Atlantic* article, John Wigmore, Holmes's erstwhile friend and more recent detractor, attacked Frankfurter in a front-page article in the newspaper of the Brahmin establishment, the *Boston Evening Transcript*, accusing him of committing a "libel on Massachusetts justice." Wigmore began telling colleagues in Chicago that Frankfurter was "the most dangerous person in the U.S."

And Frankfurter's old nemesis Justice McReynolds sent the *Atlantic*'s editor a complaint full of anti-Semitic sneers about Frankfurter's "exotic" and "crooked" mind. "Perhaps I may venture to add," McReynolds concluded his letter, "that to me it is a really annoying thing to find such a man teaching American boys at Harvard."

Sacco and Vanzetti's final appeals having been denied, and an advisory committee named by the governor at the last minute recommending against clemency, their execution in the state's electric chair was scheduled for midnight on August 10. In a last desperate bid, Holmes's old friend Arthur D. Hill, who had taken over as lead counsel for the defense, drove out to the justice's house that afternoon seeking a stay to allow them time to ask for a review of the case in federal court.

All Holmes had read of the case was Frankfurter's book; in March he had cautiously complimented him for his efforts, writing, "Naturally I don't want to express any opinions at present beyond saying that I appreciate the self sacrifice and devotion to justice that led you to write the book."[18] But Frankfurter could not bear to accompany Hill and the three other lawyers on their journey to Beverly Farms.

Holmes listened to them for two and a half hours, then wrote a one-paragraph order declining the request for a stay. The line between this case and *Moore* and the other cases where the Court had intervened was clear-cut. Prejudice on the part of a judge was insufficient to deprive the state court of jurisdiction; this was not a case of a lynch mob that had made the entire proceedings an empty form.

A large group of reporters waited outside for the result. That night the police wanted to station an officer at the house, and Thomas Barbour, Holmes's cousin by marriage, offered to spend the night on his porch as protection. Holmes declined both. But after the house of one of the jurors was blown up and threats mounted following Sacco and Vanzetti's delayed execution on August 22, Holmes reluctantly agreed on Fanny's insistence to have a guard posted at night. Corcoran let slip a mention of the guard in a letter to Frankfurter, who had not known of the threats to Holmes, and was stricken with the news.[19]

Almost no attention was paid to a habeas corpus petition Holmes had granted to another lawyer who had made the drive to Beverly on July 14, just a month earlier. Nathan Bard and Bunyan Fleming, two black men in Madisonville, Kentucky, had been convicted of raping a sixteen-year-old white girl and sentenced to hang. With soldiers armed with a machine gun protecting the courthouse, an all-white jury had convicted Fleming after deliberating for ten minutes; it took them eight minutes the next day to convict Bard. Holmes approved the petition on

Holmes's handwritten order staying the executions of
Bard and Fleming, July 14, 1927

the spot to allow the attorneys time to file an application for certiorari to the Supreme Court as soon as the Court's term resumed in October. But on November 21, 1927, the full Court declined to hear the case, and four days later, in the last public hanging in America, Bard and Fleming, protesting their innocence to the last, were put to death before eight thousand spectators who crowded the Hopkins County jail and surrounding rooftops to watch the spectacle.[20]

The liberal and socialist press continued to whip up outrage over Sacco and Vanzetti, attacking Holmes—and Brandeis, who had also turned down a last-minute petition from their lawyers. But as Holmes noted when he had denied a third request from Hill, "thousand-fold worse cases" of injustice against blacks in the South went unremarked upon by those fired with the cause of protecting the rights of political radicals.[21]

"This world," he lamented to Einstein, "cares more for red than for black."[22]

ANOTHER CASE THAT received less attention at the time was the one that would cast the longest shadow over his reputation. To Holmes, the question raised in *Buck v. Bell* had not been a difficult one. In 1924 Virginia had enacted a law based on a model statute drafted by eugenics proponents. It authorized the sexual sterilization of inmates at state institutions who were afflicted with "idiocy, imbecility, feeble-mindedness" or "hereditary forms of insanity." To answer a possible challenge to the law on due process grounds, an appeals process was provided to allow an inmate or an appointed guardian to contest

Carrie Buck and her mother, at the Virginia State Colony for Epileptics and Feebleminded

a sterilization order in court. The superintendent of the Virginia State Colony for Epileptics and Feebleminded quickly arranged a test case intended to establish the law's validity.

Carrie Buck was an eighteen-year-old who had been committed by her family to the State Colony. After unsuccessfully challenging her sterilization order in Virginia courts, her lawyer filed the appeal that reached the U.S. Supreme Court on April 22, 1927. Compared to drafting men for war or even ordering compulsory vaccinations, Holmes thought, sterilizing those incapable of taking care of themselves or their children was a small imposition on individual rights in the interests of society. In his decision for a nearly unanimous Court, delivered just ten days after hearing argument in the case, Holmes wrote:

> We have seen more than once that the public welfare may call upon the best citizens for their lives. It would be strange if it could not call upon those who already sap the strength of the State for these lesser sacrifices, often not felt to be such by those concerned, in order to prevent our being swamped with incompetence. It is better for all the world if, instead of waiting to execute degenerate offspring for crime or to let them starve for their imbecility, society can prevent those who are manifestly unfit from continuing their kind. The principle that sustains compulsory vaccination is broad enough to cover cutting the Fallopian tubes. Three generations of imbeciles are enough.

What Holmes and the Court did *not* know was that the lawyer representing Buck was a close friend of the doctor who ran the institution, was himself a longtime supporter of eugenics, and was a former member of the board that had ordered her sterilization. At trial he failed to bring out any evidence to challenge the pat medical testimony that both Buck and her mother were "feebleminded," and that Buck's seven-month-old daughter was likewise "not quite normal." In fact, Buck had been a good student in school, her mother was literate, and Buck had been institutionalized after being sexually abused by the nephew of her foster family, who wanted to send her away to conceal the pregnancy—none of which appeared in the record that reached the Supreme Court.[23]

Had Holmes been aware of the collusive nature of the appeal he might very well have taken a different view of the matter. Moreover, Taft had clearly egged Holmes on in assigning him the opinion, and even in suggesting the last brutal sentence for which it would always be remembered. The day after hearing oral argument, Taft sent Holmes the assignment, along with some strong advice:

> Saturday April 23, 1927
>
> Dear Justice Holmes,
>
> I have assigned to you the Virginia sterilization case. Some of the brethren are troubled about the case, especially Butler. May I suggest that you make a little full the care Virginia has taken in guarding against undue or hasty action, the proven absence of danger to the patient, and other circumstances tending to lessen the shock that many feel over such a remedy? The strength of the facts in three generations of course is the strongest argument for the necessity for such state action and its reasonableness.
>
> As ever yours
>
> Wm. H. Taft[24]

Holmes closely followed Taft's suggestions, setting out at length the appeals process provided for in the law—unaware that in Buck's case it had been largely a sham. "This is very good and comprehensive," Taft wrote on his return.[25] Pierce Butler, the Court's lone Catholic, remained troubled enough to register a lone dissent, though without writing an opinion.

Holmes was unusually proud of his opinion in *Buck*, and particularly pleased that for once he had resisted at least some of the suggestions of his brethren to tone down his language. "I purposely used short and rather brutal words for an antithesis, polysyllables that made them mad," he told Laski. "But a man must be allowed his own style. At times I have gone too far in yielding my own views as to the reason for the decision."[26]

Holmes's love for honing memorable and punchy phrases more than once left an exaggerated impression of tough-mindedness: as a writer he understood the power of "brutal words," and he took satisfaction in rattling commonplace thinking with a startling juxtaposition or a lunge for the rhetorical jugular that cut through sentimentality and euphemistic evasion.

But there was also no doubt that his opinion in *Buck* reflected his basic worldview. As he wrote in "Natural Law," society, acting through the law, sacrificed men without scruple whenever the community's interests demanded it. Nor did he see anything particularly sacred about human reproduction in the abstract. In a case that reached the Massachusetts high court, he had ruled that an unborn child is not a person, dismissing a suit brought against a town for a defect in a public highway that caused a woman to fall and suffer a miscarriage. With Malthus much in mind, he had once remarked to Ethel Scott, "Most of the great things have been done with thin populations, and as I am not a Catholic I take no joy in increased numbers of ordinary ugly people."[27]

Likewise, his decisions in tort cases implicitly, and sometimes explicitly, embraced the view that a certain amount of maiming and death was just the price to be paid for the smooth functioning of society. In his appellate opinions in Massachusetts, he had consistently worked to elevate strict standards of due care into rules of law that made it difficult for injured parties to recover in accidents that occurred in the course of what he considered the normal rough-and-tumble of everyday life. As he noted in one of these Massachusetts decisions, "all accidents could be prevented by not building." But, since "it is desirable that buildings and fences should be put up," the law does not throw all the risk on the builder for the injuries that from time to time are bound to occur. He reversed the judgment in the case of a recent immigrant who was injured when she fell into an open coal chute on the street, holding that the practical necessities of coal deliveries in a city made it impossible to require property owners to take special precautions against accidents of that kind. And he overturned the jury's award of damages to a girl whose fingers were cut off in the coffee grinder in a grocery store.[28]

As he explained to Lady Castletown at the time, "When a child of 6 puts her hand into a coffee-grinder in a shop and gets her finger taken off and we say she cant recover because she was hurt in consequence of unlawful intermeddling, we are saying in effect that it is more desirable that property should be respected even from a harmless touch than that one too young to look out for herself should have her finger kept on—not necessarily an absurd proposition but one which wouldn't be so popular if stated that way!"[29]

On the U.S. Supreme Court, in *United Zinc* v. *Britt* (1922), he had similarly overturned a judgment against a property owner for the deaths of two young boys who had gone swimming in a pool of clear-looking but sulfuric acid–tainted water left in the abandoned cellar of a torn-down chemical plant. His zeal to write into the law his draconian views about risk led him to render one of his other most notoriously bad decisions on the Supreme Court just a few months after *Buck* v. *Bell*. In *Baltimore & Ohio R.R.* v. *Goodman* (1927), Holmes held that a railroad was not at fault in a fatal grade-crossing accident where the view of the tracks was obstructed to an approaching driver. Showing if nothing else that he had never learned to drive himself, Holmes ruled as a matter of law that it was a driver's duty to stop, get out of his car, and look down the tracks to see if a train was coming.

The standard which Holmes enunciated in *Goodman* was overturned just seven years later, in an opinion by his successor on the Court, Justice Benjamin Cardozo—who, sounding more like Holmes than Holmes on this occasion, emphasized that the law had to take into account practical realities: "Standards of prudent conduct are declared at times by courts, but they are taken over from the facts of life. To get out of a vehicle and reconnoitre is an uncommon precaution, as everyday experience informs us. Besides being uncommon, it is very likely to be futile, and sometimes even dangerous."[30]

Brandeis thought the Court had had no business taking these cases in the first place and that Holmes had pressed his colleagues to do so mainly because he was "incorrigible when there is an opportunity of curbing the power and province of a jury." But there was no escaping the impression that Holmes had also relished the opportunity to point out the brutal trade-offs that he believed were inherent in law, and life.[31] While in so many areas of the law Holmes would prove decades ahead of his time, his Darwinian attitudes toward injury cases seemed at times almost a throwback to the nineteenth century—holding firm to a conception of tort law that was rapidly being swept aside by the very kind of nuanced balancing tests and apportionment of responsibility between the parties that he otherwise so zealously advanced.

Holmes was always slightly puzzled why his liberal friends never seemed as enthusiastic about his opinion in *Buck* as he was. But he continued to receive their enthusiastic praise in the *New Republic* and the *Harvard Law Review* for other of his opinions in the later years of the Taft Court in which he was unquestionably taking an ever-bolder stand for civil liberties and racial justice, whatever his disparaging comments about human rights in the abstract.

Just a few months before his decision in *Buck* in 1927, he delivered the Court's decision in *Nixon* v. *Herndon*, which held that a Texas law barring blacks from voting in the state's Democratic primary elections was an unconstitutional violation of the Fourteenth Amendment. It was a forceful and direct opinion, declaring in no uncertain terms that the amendment, "while it applies to all, was passed, as we know, with a special intent to protect the blacks from discrimination against them." He dismissed the defendants' claim that the matter was "political" and therefore beyond the jurisdiction of the courts as "little more than a play upon words." He concluded: "It is too clear for extended argument that color cannot be made the basis" of a state's denial of a right to vote. Even McReynolds joined the Court's unanimous opinion.

But, as always, Holmes more often found himself in dissent, joined most often only by Brandeis. The following term Holmes particularly infuriated Taft with his dissent in *Olmstead* v. *U.S.* (1928), an appeal by a bootlegger in Washington State named Roy Olmstead, whose telephones federal agents had tapped. There was no doubt they had the right man. Olmstead was notorious as "the King of the Bootleggers," and the hundreds of pages of transcribed phone conversations documented a vast business enterprise, in which operators took orders from morning till night, and hundreds of cases of liquor smuggled in on motorboats from Canada were delivered each day throughout the Seattle area by Olmstead's fleet of trucks.[32]

A Washington State law made wiretapping a crime. But Taft's opinion for the Court which affirmed Olmstead's conviction brushed that aside: the common law rule had always been that evidence—however obtained—was admissible in a court of law, as long as it was pertinent. Taft also rejected Olmstead's claim that intercepting his conversations violated the Fourth Amendment's protection against unreasonable searches and seizures. Taft said that because agents never actually entered the defendants' homes or offices, and attached their taps to telephone wires at poles on the street or in a common basement area of an apartment building, "There was no searching. There was no seizure."

Holmes's dissent was a classic expression of his view that the law is always a balance between competing and incompatible ends. He suggested there was no need even to consider the question of rights under the Fourth Amendment: a more fundamental principle was at work. Delivered at the very end of the term, in June 1928, Holmes's opinion spoke to his most basic beliefs about the law and the role of the courts:

> There is no body of precedents by which we are bound, and which confines us to logical deduction from established rules. Therefore we must consider the two objects of desire, both of which we cannot have, and make up our minds which to choose. It is desirable that criminals should be detected, and, to that end, that all available evidence should be used. It also is desirable that the Government should not itself foster and pay for other crime, when they are the means by which the evidence is to be obtained. . . . We have to choose, and, for my part, I think it a less evil that some criminals should escape than that the Government should play an ignoble part.
>
> For those who agree with me, no distinction can be taken between the Government as prosecutor and the Government as judge. If the existing code does not permit district attorneys to have a hand in such dirty business, it does not permit the judge to allow such iniquities to succeed.

Taft furiously wrote to his brother that Holmes had written "the nastiest opinion," and added, "If they think we are going to be frightened in our effort to stand by the law and give the public a chance to punish criminals, they are mistaken, even though we are condemned for lack of high ideals." In the past, Taft had called Holmes "a noisy dissenter," but now he began to rage that if the rest of the Court had followed Holmes and Brandeis, "I don't think we would have had much of a Constitution to deal with."[33]

But Arthur Sutherland, Holmes's secretary that year, said he never forgot the magnificent disdain with which Holmes spoke the words "dirty business" as he read out his dissent in Court that day, his careful voice still resonant and filling the room in his eighty-seventh year.[34]

———————

ONE OTHER DEEP and persistent divide between Holmes and the old guard of the Court that came to the fore that term went back to one of his earliest and most basic ideas about the law, which he had first set forth in *The Common Law*.

The law, as Holmes never tired of pointing out, is at its foundation "a statement of the circumstances in which the public force will be brought to bear upon men through the courts."[35] As such, it has meaning only as "the articulate voice of some sovereign or quasi-sovereign that can be identified," he insisted in his dissent in *Southern Pacific v. Jensen*, the 1917 case in which he pronounced his famous dictum, "The common law is not a brooding omnipresence in the sky."

In that case, he had taken exception to the Court's ruling that New York State's workmen's compensation law could not apply to seamen. The majority held that the state law was preempted by the customary rules of admiralty law that dictated compensation for injuries to sailors. But, as Holmes underscored in a subsequent 1922 case in which he was able to command a narrow 5–3 majority on a question that pitted the rules of admiralty law against the government's immunity from claims, the law is not an abstract body of principles that a court can draw upon at will, but only what a sovereign power agrees to enforce. "However ancient may be the traditions of maritime law, however diverse the sources from which it has been drawn, it derives its whole and only power in this country from its having been accepted and adopted by the United States," Holmes wrote. "There is no mystic over law to which even the United States must bow."[36]

One implication of this basic conception of the law that particularly incensed his bête noire John M. Zane was Holmes's explanation for why the government cannot be sued without its consent. In 1907, dismissing a suit against the Territory of Hawaii over a disputed land sale, Holmes wrote, "A sovereign is exempt from suit not because of any formal conception or obsolete theory, but on the logical and practical ground that there can be no legal right as against the authority that makes the law on which the right depends."[37]

That decision had been the centerpiece of Zane's charge of "legal heresy": writing at the end of the First World War, Zane had accused Holmes not only having "completely misled his associates" with one of his "careless and debonair utterances" about the law, but of giving support to the "atrocious German theory" of "uncontrollable power in the state."[38]

Holmes as usual was amused at academic lawyers pronouncing with great certainty what "the law" was. But he was considerably irritated by Zane's fundamental misunderstanding of his point.[39] Far from granting the state "uncontrollable power," his insistence that the law had to be anchored in an ability to enforce it was a check on usurpation of power by the courts. And in a case that was decided in the spring of 1928, Holmes made another indelible mark in a dissenting opinion that lived on after his death as a milestone of constitutional jurisprudence.

The idea that there was a single body of common law for the courts to correctly "discover" was behind the federal courts' long-standing practice of developing their own "general" common law, which they applied in cases where the parties were citizens of different states, a circumstance that fell under the jurisdiction of the federal courts. When the federal courts sometimes differed from a state supreme court in their view of the common law, however, the anomalous result was that a different rule might apply within a state depending on whether the case that raised the question had been brought by a resident or a nonresident.

The case where Holmes most sharply challenged this idea was a particularly egregious instance in which the federal courts' jurisdiction had been exploited to get around a state's reading of the common law. A Kentucky railroad company had entered into a contract with a taxi company in Bowling Green granting exclusive rights to pick up passengers at its depot. Knowing that Kentucky courts held such contracts to be invalid, but federal courts did not, the taxi company first dissolved itself and reincorporated in Tennessee, so that it could seek an order in federal court blocking a rival taxi firm from challenging the arrangement.

In his dissent in *Black & White Taxicab Co.* v. *Black & Yellow Taxicab Co.*, Holmes argued that in cases that were purely a question of the common law of the states, the federal courts had no more business substituting their abstract determination of what "the law is" than did a law professor:

> Books written about any branch of the common law treat it as a unit, cite cases from this Court, from the circuit courts of appeal, from the state courts, from England and the Colonies of England indiscriminately, and criticize them as right or wrong according to the writer's notions of a single theory. It is very hard to resist the impression that there is one august corpus, to understand which clearly is the only task of any court concerned. If there were such a transcendental body of law outside of any particular state but obligatory within it unless and until changed by statute, the courts of the United States might be right in using their independent judgment as to what it was. But there is no such body of law. . . . The common law, so far as it is enforced in a state, whether called common law or not, is not the common law generally, but the law of that state existing by the authority of that state without regard to what it may have been in England or anywhere else. . . .
>
> In my opinion, the authority, and only authority, is the state, and if that be so, the voice adopted by the state as its own should utter the last word.

This "fallacy" of regarding the common law as a transcendent body, Holmes concluded, "has resulted in an unconstitutional assumption of powers by the courts of the United States which no lapse of time or respectable array of opinion should make us hesitate to correct." Again, Holmes was joined only by Brandeis and Stone.

But just ten years later, in the landmark case *Erie* v. *Tompkins*, the Court reversed itself. Brandeis, writing for the Court in one of its most significant decisions of the modern era on the division of powers between the federal government and the states, quoted at length Holmes's dissent in *Black & White Taxicab* in declaring the federal common law void and explicitly overruling a hundred years of precedent. As with his dissents in *Lochner*, *Frank*, and *Abrams*, Holmes's eloquence and clear-thinking would find their most important audience in a future Court that had disenthralled itself from the obduracy of his contemporaries.

———

IN OCTOBER 1928 Holmes surpassed Chief Justice Roger B. Taney as the oldest-ever sitting Supreme Court justice. He finally began to have his secretaries help with some actual legal work, preparing one-page summaries for him of each of the hundreds of applications for certiorari that flooded into the Court each year, but even then he would always leaf through the record to check his secretary's digest for accuracy. And he still was carrying off his unwavering practice of delivering to the court printer on Tuesday the opinion he had been assigned the previous Saturday.[40]

Brandeis thought he literally seemed to be the youngest member of the Court. "The old man is still the keenest one of the lot," Justice Stone agreed. Returning from conference one Saturday, Stone related to his secretary a specimen of Holmes's still razor-sharp legal mind at work. During a long wrangle in which some of the justices were arguing what seemed to Stone an untenable position, Holmes had settled back in his chair and drifted off for his afternoon nap. But as the discussion wore on, Holmes suddenly opened his eyes, and "launched into a summary of the issues so lucid and persuasive" that it was quickly followed by a unanimous vote. "He punctured their arguments like a bubble," Stone marveled.[41]

But on Sunday, April 21, 1929, Brandeis wrote to Frankfurter in dismay about his colleague. "Mrs. Holmes turned seriously ill Tuesday, I judge. O.W.H. was absent from Court that day—has attended since. But yesterday at Conference he seemed crushed, and fully twenty years older than he has been for months—actually the old man." Fanny had fallen three times since the previous autumn; the fourth time, which happened the night before Holmes's absence from Court, she broke her hip. No one was nearby to help, and Holmes had had to lift her into bed by himself. A doctor could not be summoned until morning; when he arrived, he put her hip in a plaster cast, but the outlook was clearly grim.[42]

Holmes wrote to Nina Gray a few days later, "Please do not mention it to anyone—though you may possibly hear it from others. Fanny is very ill and I cannot write at present. You know how she hates to have people talk or know of her private affairs and therefore I say no more than is necessary. I try to keep occupied with work." Brandeis told Frankfurter on the twenty-eighth, "O.W.H. is making a grand fight. But it is a very hard one."[43]

She died on the evening of April 30, and Taft, all of his basic human feeling overcoming whatever professional differences he had ever felt with Holmes, at once hurried to the house and announced he would take charge of all the arrangements. "One thing I do know how to do is run a Unitarian funeral," he said. Holmes had quietly picked out a gravesite at Arlington Cemetery a few years before, and she was buried in the plot next to his.[44]

Holmes told friends he was reconciled to her death. He wrote Ethel Scott, "If my wife had lived it would have been only for pain—and therefore to die in her sleep as she did was the best that could happen—but it leaves little except a little more work for me. I have kept and been kept busy, but expect to go to Beverly Farms as usual June 5–6. I thank you for your cable which was like your faithful self."[45]

His colleagues on the Court were extraordinarily sensitive to his feelings. The day after Fanny's funeral, Brandeis, knowing that the only thing that would help him through was his work, suggested to Holmes that he write a dissenting opinion in an important First Amendment case. "He took the bait—telephoned me himself Wednesday asking me to come to see him & read me his piece—which is fine," Brandeis told Frankfurter. Brandeis arranged with Taft to keep giving Holmes regular assignments, and not to spare him out of misplaced kindness: "I asked the C.J. to give him some opinions to write, one each week. Instead he gave O.W.H. 3, with a promise on the donee's part not to write more than one a week. He is in fine form again, working as of old," Brandeis reported on May 11.[46]

The First Amendment case was an appeal of the government's denial of citizenship to Rosika Schwimmer, a Jewish Hungarian refugee. As a pacifist, she had refused to swear the required oath that she would take up arms to defend the United States. Writing for the Court, Justice Butler dismissed the fact that she had agreed to swear allegiance to the United States and had met all of the other requirements for citizenship—and that, as a fifty-year-old woman, she was ineligible to serve in the Army anyway: "The fact that she is an uncompromising pacifist, with no sense of nationalism, but only a cosmic sense of belonging to the human family, justifies belief that she may be opposed to the use of military force as contemplated by our Constitution and laws," Butler concluded.

Since his *Abrams* dissent Holmes had dissented in several other free speech cases, using each opportunity to restate his views in ever more forceful language. "The United States may give up the post office when it sees fit, but while it carries it on the use of the mails is almost as much a part of free speech as the right to use our tongues," he asserted in a 1922 case, *Milwaukee Social Democratic Publishing* v. *Burleson*, in which he objected to what he termed the "practically despotic power" claimed by the postmaster general to bar from the mails subversive literature. In a second case that same year, he asserted the same principle protects commercial speech from prior restraint. "I cannot understand by what authority Congress undertakes to authorize anyone to determine in advance . . . that certain words shall not be uttered," he wrote in his dissent in *Leach* v. *Carlile*, in which the majority upheld the postmaster general's authority to issue a "fraud order" against the use of the mails by a patent-medicine business. "If the execution of this law does not abridge freedom of speech, I do not quite see what could be said to do so." In 1925, in *Gitlow* v. *New York*, he dissented to the Court's decision upholding the conviction for "criminal anarchy" of a communist pamphleteer, offering the memorable admonition, "Every idea is an incitement." ("The usual notion is that you are free to say what you like if you don't shock *me*," he wrote to Ein-

Rosika Schwimmer, in 1927

stein, explaining his dissent in the case. "Of course the value of the constitutional right is only when you do shock people.")[47]

In *U.S.* v. *Schwimmer* (1929), Holmes added yet another indelible phrase to the lexicon of free speech. Holmes was joined only by Brandeis and Stone in again affirming that freedom of speech and freedom of conscience were the rights upon which all other rights depended in a free society. "If there is any principle of the Constitution that more imperatively calls for attachment than any other," Holmes declared, "it is the principle of free thought—not free thought for those who agree with us, but freedom for the thought that we hate."[48]

Holmes's secretary John Lockwood wrote to Frankfurter, "The Schwimmer dissent is truly a magnificent document. I rejoice at such tangible evidence that the divine fire burns as brightly as ever." Frankfurter added his congratulations: "It was like real, prewar champagne to read your *Schwimmer* opinion and not because Mrs. Schwimmer matters at all to me. . . . It is a glorious piece of writing. We so need the antiseptic play of your humor and wisdom."[49]

Holmes, though in almost every way the very opposite of a pacifist, wrote in his dissent that Schwimmer was obviously "a woman of superior character and intelligence," and after the case was over she wrote to Holmes, fearing it might be a breach of etiquette but saying she had to thank him for his "magnificent expression of true Americanism," which "helped me to take the blow of the refusal without loss of faith in the inherent idealism of your nation." Holmes replied with a kind word of reassurance and thereafter they exchanged a few further cordial messages. Possibly because of Holmes's dissent, Schwimmer was allowed to remain in the United States for the rest of her life as a resident alien.[50]

The case received enormous attention, with the *New Republic* reprinting Holmes's dissent in its entirety. E. B. White wrote in the *New Yorker*, "One profession that is more noble today than that of soldier is Dissenting Justice of the Supreme Court."[51]

═══════

During Fanny's illness Brandeis had written to Frankfurter, "When the time comes, Lockwood should be told to insist on staying with O.W.H. substantially all summer. He is needed as no Secretary ever has been, & is evidently much beloved by O.W.H." Lockwood readily agreed, but found he had to "beg for permission" from Holmes before he would accede to the arrangement.[52]

Lockwood ended up joining him at Beverly Farms from mid-July to the end of that summer of 1929. He would later recall the deep admiration he felt in seeing how Holmes courageously adjusted to his new circumstances: "Here, in the most deeply personal event to occur in his life since the Civil War, I guess, one could see all of his experience coordinated and distilled by him and relied upon."[53]

At Beverly Farms, Holmes continued his old routine. He invited several "discreet dames" to lunch—Mrs. Codman, Mrs. Curtis, Mrs. Gray—telling "one who professed hesitation on solitude with a gent" that at his age "she might as well hesitate about visiting Bunker Hill Monument." When Alger Hiss began as his new secretary in the fall, he managed to convince Holmes to let him take over Fanny's old role of reading aloud to him, and they generally spent an hour in the late afternoon each day with a book. Holmes still was diligently tackling the "Day of Judgment" books he said he needed to have read to get a good mark on his "final examination," but on the recommendations of Laski and others he had discovered Wodehouse and murder mysteries and other light reading, and would usually greet Hiss on his return from the Court, "What should it be this time? Shall we improve our minds, or shall we have a little murder?"[54]

His subsequent secretaries all continued the practice, and between their suggestions and the *New Republic*'s book reviews Holmes tried a few modern writers, who for the most part left him unimpressed with their daring breaking of taboos. He summarized to Frankfurter a novel by the English

With Alger Hiss, in the summer of 1930 at Beverly Farms

playwright and author Charles Morgan, "An able writer but the metaphysics of screwing your neighbor's wife don't interest me"; and once interrupted Mark Howe in the midst of another contemporary work that had been getting much attention—*Three Cities* by Sholem Asch—to ask, in rather more direct language, "Am I to understand that the young man fucked his mother-in-law?" As he drily observed to Laski, "The new generation has discovered the act by which it came into being and is happy in the discovery."[55]

Toward the end of 1929, Taft began noticeably deteriorating mentally and physically. The good humor that had kept the conferences genial and efficient dissolved into dark forebodings. "I must stay on the court in order to prevent the Bolsheviki from getting control," he wrote to his brother in mid-November. By the New Year he was too ill to come to work.[56]

With the Beverly Farms crossing guard, whom Holmes always stopped to talk with on his daily walk

In his absence, Holmes, as the senior justice, took over as acting chief for the first two months of 1930. The duties seemed to revive him almost in inverse proportion to Taft's decline. "He is presiding with great firmness, alertness, and joy," Brandeis happily reported to Frankfurter. "A marked rejuvenescence has been effected; and he is definitely without worry in those unaccustomed duties incident to his new office. It is several years since we have had so good a C.J." Stone said he thought Holmes had run the best conference he had attended since joining the Court, and although Brandeis begged Holmes not to overburden himself by also writing opinions, he assigned two to himself right away, and the next month took on one of the gnarly patent cases he hated. "I felt bound to take it," he told Mrs. Gray, since no one else wanted to write it, though "went home scared to death."[57]

But Hiss did note that by the end of February, Holmes seemed worn down. He had seemed particularly "haunted" at the sight of Taft's vacant expression in an AP news photograph and by the rapidity of the chief justice's ensuing mental collapse. On top of everything, there was a deluge of "fan mail" and greetings for his upcoming birthday to be answered that was taking Holmes two hours every morning. Hiss finally persuaded the justice to allow him to write the replies to three categories of well-wishers: those who Holmes had never heard of; those he knew slightly but only in an official capacity; and those he knew so well he was sure they would not want to trouble him with a personal reply.[58]

On February 3, 1930, Taft sent in his resignation; a month later he was dead. To replace him, President Herbert Hoover appointed

Holmes's old friend and colleague Hughes. "We all loved Taft and grieved at his bodily collapse," Holmes told Nina Gray, "but Hughes is an old and valued friend of mine and I surmise and hope a little nearer to my way of thinking than his predecessor."[59]

That spring Holmes wrote what would be his final dissenting opinion, *Baldwin* v. *Missouri* (1930), and it fittingly summarized his entire case against the Court's misuse of the Due Process Clause to invalidate economic and social legislation, in this instance a state inheritance tax applied to bonds held by an out-of-state owner:

> I have not yet adequately expressed the more than anxiety that I feel at the ever increasing scope given to the Fourteenth Amendment in cutting down what I believe to be the constitutional rights of the states. As the decisions now stand, I see hardly any limit but the sky to the invalidating of those rights if they happen to strike a majority of this Court as for any reason undesirable. I cannot believe that the Amendment was intended to give us *carte blanche* to embody our economic or moral beliefs in its prohibitions. . . . Of course, the words "due process of law," if taken in their literal meaning, have no application to this case, and, while it is too late to deny that they have been given a much more extended and artificial signification, still we ought to remember the great caution shown by the Constitution in limiting the power of the states, and should be slow to construe the clause in the Fourteenth Amendment as committing to the Court, with no guide but the Court's own discretion, the validity of whatever laws the states may pass.

He also made a sly dig at the majority opinion, written by McReynolds, which Holmes pointed out had ignored a number of precedents— including one Holmes had written for the Court in 1903—that argued for deciding the case the other way. "I suppose that these cases and many others now join *Blackstone* v. *Miller* on the *Index Expurgatorius*—but we need an authoritative list," Holmes wrote, alluding to the Inquisition's list of banned works.

McReynolds, when he read out his decision in Court, added a few extremely nasty words not in his formal written opinion. "The result here ought to be clear," he sneered, "to an unclouded mind." The joke, as usual, was on McReynolds: eleven years later the Supreme Court overruled *Baldwin*, citing Holmes's dissent in rejecting McReynolds's opinion as wrongly decided.[60]

"I want to get all that I can out of the old hulk before coming to anchor," Holmes wrote to Ethel Scott. The following year, for his ninetieth birthday, his friends arranged a national radio broadcast over the Columbia Broadcasting System to honor him, with tributes from Chief Justice Hughes, the president of the American Bar Association, and the dean of the Yale Law School. A microphone was set up in his library to carry a few closing words from Holmes himself. He had told Mrs. Curtis that the one thing that "made me not positively refuse to take any part in the radio talk" was that he had a cosmic observation readily at hand: it was a line from a volume of medieval Latin poetry he and Hiss had read the previous summer that had moved him with its defiance of death. He thought he could end his talk with the line, but still needed to come up with a few more words.[61]

But when he sat down to write, as usual the words came in a smooth flow, written in his unhesitating longhand with only a few emendations and cross-outs. There is a recording that survives of his talk, his fine, dignified patrician voice only slightly wavering at the start before falling into his orator's practiced cadence:

> In this symposium my part is only to sit in silence. To express one's feelings as the end draws near is too intimate a task.
>
> But I mention one thought that comes to me as a listener-in. The riders in a race do not stop short when they reach the goal. There is a little finishing canter before coming to a standstill. There is time to hear the kind voice of friends and to say to one's self: The work is done.
>
> But just as one says that, the answer comes: The race is over, but the work never is done while the power to work remains.

The canter that brings you to a standstill need not be only coming to rest. It cannot be while you still live. For to live is to function. That is all there is in living.

And so I end with a line from a Latin poet who uttered the message more than fifteen hundred years ago:

Death—death plucks my ear and says, "Live—I am coming."[62]

He received a tide of congratulatory messages from friends and strangers, schoolchildren and fellow nonagenarians, plus a few patronizing letters from Christians quoting Bible verses and instructing him that "No Latin poet's words will save you—only the blood of Jesus Christ can cleanse all from sin," and suggesting that he would not have such a "hopeless tone" if he were saved.[63]

Other tributes came in; he sat to have his portrait painted and a bust sculpted, and received a hefty gold medal from the ABA which he wrote of wryly to Mrs. Curtis. "This morning the Bar Assoc. Medal arrived—very heavy—a profile of Marshall on one side—and a lady in the buff to her waist on the other pretending to distract you from her person by futile scales & sword. I must go and lock her up."[64]

He wrote his last important opinion for the Court that spring of 1931, deciding a dispute between New Jersey and New York over the use of water from the Delaware River, and he used the opportunity to point out that there were principles of equity that rise above common law rules of property, and that there were interests of a nation that go beyond the words in any document. "A river is more than an amenity," he declared, "it is a treasure."[65]

He had once similarly reminded his fellow justices, and the nation, that the Constitution was not just a body of words or even of laws, but was an act in itself, and that it took a bloody Civil War among other tests to make America a nation: The Founders, Holmes wrote, "called into life a being the development of which could not have been foreseen completely by the most gifted of its begetters. It was enough for them to realize or to hope that they had created an organism; it has taken a century and has cost their successors much sweat and blood to prove that they created a nation. The case before us must be considered in the light of our whole experience, and not merely in that of what was said a hundred years ago."[66]

———

IN THE SUMMER of 1931 he suffered what he called a "pull down" that he could not shake off. He confided to Mrs. Curtis that fall, "Sometimes I think the old hulk is slowly going to pieces." His maid Mary Donnellan had taken over running the household after Fanny's death and she "watches me tigerishly," Holmes said, chastising him when he smoked too many cigars or tired himself out, and "quotes the doctor and is ominous if I don't ease up."[67]

Although his wits remained acute, he simply was no longer able to keep up with the work of the Court. It was obvious to his colleagues that the time had come for him to resign, and Holmes seemed to recognize it too, at least in private: at Thanksgiving he confessed to Nina Gray, "Writing like life comes harder to me as time goes on."[68]

After conferring with Brandeis, Hughes came to see Holmes at noontime on Sunday, January 10, 1932, and gently told him the time indeed had come. Perhaps relieved to have the decision taken out of his hands, Holmes took it without the slightest hint of resentment or opposition, simply asked his secretary Chapman Rose to look up the relevant statute, and wrote out his resignation on the spot—dated two days later, the twelfth, so he could deliver his final opinion the following day. The tears pouring down Hughes's impressive bearded face struck Rose as a remarkable sight, but Holmes, "though his heart was breaking," Mary Donnellan later said, "wouldn't let anyone know it." Brandeis by arrangement showed up at 12:45 to keep Holmes company for the rest of the day. "He was as calm and gallant as ever," Brandeis told Frankfurter.[69]

Knowing how much it would help Holmes in his retirement to continue having the companionship of a young secretary from the Law School, Rose and Frankfurter between them plotted out a plan of campaign to overcome his objections that the position would now have little to offer a prospective lawyer. For Rose's successor they proposed Donald Hiss, knowing how much Holmes had liked his brother Alger, and Holmes gave way "without struggle."[70]

"I am enjoying idleness more than I dared to expect," he wrote to Nina Gray the spring following his retirement. But in another letter he added, "With blank feeling that achievement is over."[71] Laski, who had been as faithful a correspondent as ever since returning to England in 1920, had come to visit on Holmes's ninetieth birthday and did so again in 1933. Learned Hand was a regular visitor, taking the train down from New York every few weeks and staying for an hour entertaining Holmes with dirty jokes. Brandeis, Hughes, and even McReynolds came to see him frequently, too, though Holmes said he had little interest in the Court's work anymore: he wanted to feel like a rock in a riverbed, he said, with the water flowing over it. One exception was the evident satisfaction he evinced when Mark Howe told him the Court had finally rejected the idea of "a business affected with a public interest," upholding a New York law regulating milk prices and effectively embracing Holmes's dissent six years earlier in the ticket-scalping case *Tyson & Bro. v. Banton*.[72]

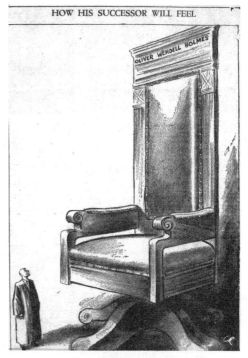

Editorial cartoon commenting on Holmes's retirement

On his ninety-second birthday, four days after FDR's inauguration, Frankfurter arranged for the president to make a surprise visit to 1720 Eye Street. Frankfurter and Corcoran had come to lunch, and Holmes's niece and nephew had produced a bottle of champagne, which they quickly reassured him—no doubt with less than the complete truth— had come from the French Embassy, not a bootlegger.[73] Donald Hiss kept a nervous lookout through the rest of the afternoon for the president's arrival while Holmes napped in his bedroom.

In Rock Creek Park in the spring

When the car pulled up, Hiss hurried to wake him, saying, "Mr. Justice, I think the President of the United States is outside." Coming immediately to life, Holmes barked back, "Don't be an idiot, boy. He wouldn't call on me." Hiss said, "I'm pretty sure it is." He helped Holmes change from his old alpaca coat to a swallowtail jacket, just as the doorbell rang.[74]

The President and Mrs. Roosevelt and Frankfurter joined Holmes in his study, and they had an animated conversation, FDR asking about his great-grandfather's swords over the fireplace, and the talk ranging over history and other topics; and as the president was leaving, he asked if there was anything he could do for him. Roosevelt had just ordered the banks closed as an emergency measure to halt the panicked withdrawals that the Depression had triggered, and Holmes replied, No, nothing, except perhaps he could make an exception and let Supreme Court justices withdraw some cash from their accounts—or "don't make it all Supreme Court justices, just retired justices," he suggested— so they could pay their servants. FDR laughed, and asked if he had any final advice.

Holmes said, "No, Mr. President. The time I was in retreat, the Army was in retreat in disaster, the thing to do was to stop the retreat, blow your trumpet, have them give the order to charge. And that's exactly what you are doing. That is an admirable thing to do and the only thing you could have done."

HOLMES ONCE REMARKED to Barton Leach, "Why should people be afraid to die?"

> I'm not. I'll know the old fellow when he comes around and he'll know me because I've seen him before. I've seen the army doctors pass me by with a shake of the head as they looked over the wounded. . . . The first time was in that hideous log hut on the island in the river at Balls Bluff where our wounded were carried during the battle. . . . The second time was at Antietam when they brought me in with a hole through my neck. And the third time was a couple of years ago when I was operated upon in Boston. The old fellow will look like an old friend when he finally does come around to take me.[75]

In the winter of 1935 Holmes contracted bronchial pneumonia, and died on March 6. He was buried two days later at Arlington Cemetery, on what would have been his ninety-fourth birthday. A long line of cars followed the horse-drawn caisson carrying his coffin, and the president

Holmes's funeral procession at Arlington Cemetery

came to pay his respects at the graveside as a chill wind blew and sleet and rain pelted down from a dark and overcast sky. But Mary Donnellan said, "Soldiers don't mind the rain."[76]

A few summers before, when Felix Frankfurter and his wife, Marion, had visited him at Beverly Farms, Holmes had begun to read his favorite Civil War poem, "The Old Sergeant," but choked up partway through, his eyes full of tears.[77]

They were tears of nostalgia, tears for the futile but beautiful heroism of war, tears for the sadness but wisdom that the experience of battle had filled his entire life with.

When his Washington lawyer, John S. Flannery, opened Holmes's private safe deposit box, he found in it a small paper parcel.[78] Wrapped inside were two musket balls, and on the paper was a note in Holmes's hand:

These were taken from my body in the Civil War

"Men Who Never Heard of Him Will Be Moving to the Measure of His Thought"

In his will Holmes left his nephew, Edward Jackson Holmes Jr., $100,000; his cousin Dorothy Upham Vaughan $25,000; his devoted housekeeper Mary Donnellan and longtime maid Annie Gough $10,000 each; and most of his other servants, including his Court messenger Arthur Thomas, his driver Charles Buckley, and his old Boston clerk James Doherty, $1,000 each. After some other small bequests, and gifts of $25,000 apiece to the Harvard Law School and the Boston Museum of Fine Arts, he instructed that his entire residuary estate, including the house at 1720 Eye Street, be given to the United States Government. The bequest amounted to $263,000, about $5 million today, the largest unrestricted gift the United States had ever received at the time.[1]

President Roosevelt immediately sent a message to Congress urging that this "striking gift" and "noble bequest" be dedicated to "some purpose worthy of the great man who gave it," and a committee was named to develop a proposal that would honor Holmes's legacy to the law.[2]

All of Holmes's secretaries knew that this was not what he had in mind at all, but they equally knew that his intention that the money should simply go into the general Treasury—just as if he had paid it in a tax—would be incomprehensible to those who did not know him. John Flannery, who drew up the will on Holmes's instructions, explained to

Mark Howe that there was a sturdy logic to Holmes's directions. He had passed on to his nephew, his father's sole grandchild, the equivalent of what he had inherited from his father; he had returned to Fanny's family substantially what he had received under her will when she died; and as the residue represented the accumulated investments from what he had saved out of his government salary, it was fitting that it be returned to the public, just as he had returned all his other capital to its source.[3]

The secretaries were asked to submit their views on a fitting use of the fund, and in their discussions among themselves Laurence Curtis tried to summarize Holmes's true intentions, while acknowledging it was probably a lost cause:

> This bequest to the government was a brave and hard gesture, too hard for most people to understand or appreciate. As a young man he had given his blood to his country, and at his death he wanted to give his property to his country. . . . In other words, I think he would have preferred to have his money just go into the common pot, as in his younger days he was prepared to have his life go into the common cause.[4]

James Rowe spoke to several members of Congress and tried to make the case, but Curtis's apprehensions proved exactly correct: "They are completely unable to understand that reasoning behind it," Rowe reported back to the others.[5]

In 1940, the committee appointed by Congress proposed using the Holmes bequest to commission a history of the Supreme Court and to create a garden in Holmes's memory on land the government planned to acquire just east of the Court's new building. Nothing happened for fifteen years, while the funds sat in a non-interest-bearing account. By then the plan to acquire the property next to the Court had been abandoned, foreclosing the idea of the memorial garden. Finally taking the matter in hand, Congress in 1955 voted an appropriation of $158,000 to make up for the lost interest and authorized a committee of scholars under the Librarian of Congress to oversee production of a multivolume "Oliver Wendell Holmes Devise" history of the Supreme Court.[6]

Another fifteen years passed, without any of the volumes appearing. In 1977, the new Librarian of Congress, Daniel Boorstin, publicly declared the situation "deplorable" and a "scandal," and ordered the authors of the still-uncompleted volumes to turn over whatever they had written, in whatever form. One of the authors, a law professor at the University of Chicago, had literally nothing to show for his twenty years on the project, and under threat of government legal action was forced to return the $12,000 advance he had received, plus accumulated interest. The new editor that Boorstin brought in to revive the project acknowledged it had probably been a mistake from the start to assign the work to leading constitutional scholars: It was, he told the *New York Times*, "like getting seven of the smartest lawyers together and asking them to write a novel."[7]

Eighty years after Holmes's bequest, the volume covering the Taft Court, arguably the most important of Holmes's own years on the Court, still had not been issued.

Frankfurter's attempts to arrange for an authorized biography of Holmes that would help permanently enshrine his legacy fared little better. Holmes had never been enthusiastic about having his life written. "Part of the greatness of a great life I think consists in leaving it unadvertised," he once told Lewis Einstein's stepdaughter, just as on more than one occasion he took pride in noting that his regiment in the Civil War had never tried to sing its own praises: "The Twentieth never wrote about itself to the newspapers." When John Wu urged him to write his autobiography, Holmes replied, "A man's spiritual history is best told in what he does in his chosen line."[8]

More than that, he felt that personal details were genuinely unimportant, of nobody's business and of interest only to those who took their own "puny personality" far too seriously.[9] In 1932 he had told Einstein that against any possible future biography, "I have done my best to destroy illuminating documents." He frequently beseeched Nina Gray, Clare Castletown, Clara Stevens, Frankfurter, Laski, and other of his correspondents to burn his letters—a request they all thankfully ignored, though Laski was the most evasive in sidestepping Holmes's entreaties.[10] In December 1921 Holmes had written Laski, "I want to feel sure that what I write to you with openness of heart and spirit is safe from publication after my death. What I want to have made public I make public but it would take all spontancity from me if I thought that the world would have a chance to see my shortcomings from an inside view. *Please reassure* me as to this."[11]

Laski replied vowing his "solemn word that no letter of yours that I have shall be published." But he pleaded not to be held to destroying them, as "there's too deep a delight for me in re-reading them, and I cherish their possession as a monument to the greatest friendship I can ever hope to have." In 1949, Laski gave all of the original letters to Mark Howe, and they were published in 1953.[12]

But Holmes did make good on his own determination to destroy a good many "illuminating documents" in his possession. Alger Hiss recalled the solemn ritual of burning in the fireplace of the study, under Holmes's watchful eye, the manuscripts and proofs of his completed opinions. Hiss thought that this was not from any "narcissistic wish" to shape an image of himself to history, but rather reflected his deep sense of privacy—"he eschewed sentimentality and vulgarity"—and because he saw himself most of all as a writer, who had worked hard to hone his craft, and "what he wanted to say was in his printed work."[13]

But Holmes did unbend a few years before his death, naming Frankfurter to write a book about him after his death and giving his executor, John G. Palfrey, full authority to do whatever he thought best with his papers. Frankfurter replied, "I'm bowed with zest and humility." But Holmes also suggested that while "Felix seems to me the man for the law part," if there were another part "dealing with the old Yankee" that might best be written "by some other Yankee."[14]

After his own appointment to the Supreme Court in 1939, Frankfurter abandoned the idea of writing the entire biography himself and enlisted Mark DeWolfe Howe to take over the project. Howe was not only Holmes's former secretary but so thoroughly a part of Brahmin Boston that his father, Mark Anthony DeWolfe Howe, had written a biography of Holmes's father.

It was an impossible situation. Frankfurter saw it as his mission to safeguard Holmes's memory, and he bombarded Howe with suggestions, his own reminiscences, and constant inquiries about Howe's progress. Holmes's papers meanwhile had been sent to Harvard and set aside for Howe's exclusive use, with no access permitted to other writers or scholars. But Howe's heart was never in writing the book. He organized and transcribed thousands of pages of letters and documents with a scholarly attention to detail that was equal parts dedication and procrastination. Telling Frankfurter that it would be better first to publish some of Holmes's own words, he spent the better part of a decade editing for the press the Holmes-Pollock letters, Holmes's Civil War diaries, and the Holmes-Laski letters, continually putting off a start on the actual biography.[15]

In January 1954 Charlie Curtis wrote Learned Hand,

> The only thing I am quite sure of about Holmes is that Mark Howe holes up this week, on the 5th floor of the Boston Athenaeum, to write his damn biography, which Mark ought to have lived down years ago. I had supper with him Sunday & I think he dreads it. He should. Perhaps he kept putting it off hoping Felix would die, but whether, if so, he didn't want to be watched or whether then he wouldn't have to write it, I don't know.[16]

At the time of his death in 1967 at age sixty, Howe had completed only two slim volumes, covering Holmes's life up to 1882. Frankfurter had died in 1965, and after another abortive effort to have the "official" biography completed, the Law School finally opened Holmes's papers to researchers in 1985. In the end, Frankfurter's effort to so zealously protect his mentor's reputation did much more harm than good, delaying by more than half a century the publication of the first comprehensive biographies of Justice Holmes.

Frankfurter's efforts to portray Holmes as a liberal icon was a false note from the start that also complicated his reputation. It was certainly the case that progressives found much to admire in Holmes, both personally and for his unwavering moral courage in challenging the prevailing legal doctrines that had stifled social reform. But sharper commentators smelled a rat in the assiduous championing of Holmes as a liberal, and the disparity between the image retailed by Frankfurter and the *New Republic*, and the reality that Holmes had certainly never disguised but which was swept aside in the popular imagination, became an easy target for those out to chip away at his reputation later on.

H. L. Mencken, in a remarkably perceptive 1930 article, pointed out that many of Holmes's decisions were difficult to reconcile with "any plausible conception" of liberalism:

> My suspicion is that the hopeful Liberals, frantically eager to find at least one judge who was not violently and implacably against them, seized upon certain of Mr. Justice Holmes's opinions without examining the rest. . . . Finding him, now and then, defending eloquently a new and uplifting law which his colleagues proposed to strike off the books, they concluded that he was a sworn advocate of the rights of man. But all the while, if I do not misread his plain words, he was actually no more than an advocate of the rights of law-makers. There, indeed, is the clue to his whole jurisprudence.

"He is a jurist of great industry, immense learning and the highest integrity," concluded Mencken, "but . . . to call him a Liberal is to make the word meaningless."[17]

However disenchanted latter-day liberals were to find that Holmes was not in fact one of them at heart, his unwavering fight for the principles of respect for the rule of law, judicial restraint, and the interests of the community did infinitely more to secure their vision of a more humane, just, and decent society than any more-partisan striving could have done. The very power of his dissenting opinions that argued for upholding legislation regulating workers' wages and hours, banning child labor, restricting labor injunctions and yellow-dog contracts, and protecting consumers was that they grew *not* from a political concern with the outcome, but from his deep study of the law and its purpose in society. Nor did he write in vain: every one of those dissenting opinions was subsequently embraced by Court's majority, in many instances just a few years after his retirement from the Court.

In 1937, overruling the majority opinion in the 1923 minimum wage case *Adkins v. Children's Hospital,* in which Holmes's dissent had so forcefully refuted the notion of "liberty of contract," the Court specifically cited his dissent as having set forth the better case.[18] In 1938, the same year it issued its decision in *Erie* upholding Holmes's position rejecting the federal courts' usurpation of the common law of the states, the Court laid to rest the half-century abuse of the Due Process Clause by the Court's conservative bloc, establishing the now-definitive rule that "regulatory legislation affecting ordinary commercial transactions is not to be pronounced unconstitutional" unless it is totally without "a rational basis"—a polite rephrasing of Holmes's "puke test."[19]

Again in 1937 and 1938, the Court effectively reversed *Truax v. Corrigan,* holding state and federal laws barring labor injunctions to be constitutional; and in a series of cases over the next few years that upheld the New Deal's 1935 National Labor Relations Act, which barred employers from discriminating against union workers, the Court likewise declared *Adair* and *Coppage* to be dead letters.[20]

And in 1941, citing Holmes's "powerful and now classic dissent" in the 1918 child labor case *Hammer v. Dagenhart,* the Court unambiguously affirmed Congress's power under the Commerce Clause to regulate the national economy.[21]

In at least a dozen less high-profile cases, Holmes's dissents proved equally prophetic, with the Court later reversing itself and adopting Holmes's views on questions of taxation, presidential appointments, and the powers of the states.[22]

Holmes's palpable outrage over the affront to the rule of law in Southern mob-dominated trials that stirred him in *Frank* and *Moore* to demand that federal courts assert jurisdiction was not in vain, either. In 1932, in the famous case of the Scottsboro Boys, the Supreme Court for the first time reversed a state death-penalty conviction and extended the protections of the Fourteenth Amendment for a fair trial to include the right to counsel and to a jury free from racial bias.[23]

Holmes certainly saw nothing particularly liberal, much less activist, in his scornful repudiation of the originalist notion that the Constitution had set in stone forever the worldview and assumptions of its eighteenth-century authors. Holmes is often associated with the idea of the "living Constitution"; but that was not really how he saw it at all. It was not the Constitution that was the living organism, in his view: it was the *nation* that that Constitution had called into being that continued to grow and develop. The Founders had intentionally created a document that was a framework, not a straitjacket, that would allow the nation to meet new challenges which the men wise enough to draft its inspiring words were wise enough to know they could not possibly foresee. Its broad precepts were the very antithesis of the absolutism that those whom Morris Cohen characterized as having a "fetishism of the Constitution" tried to read into it, hoping to give their political views the imprimatur of absolute right.[24]

That Holmes moored freedom of speech not to an individual human right of self-expression but to the greater interests of society was precisely the reason his 1919 dissent in *Abrams*, with its soaring invocation of the free trade in ideas, survived even the tempests of cold war politics to be cited more than forty times by the Supreme Court in decisions upholding free speech. A full century later, his *Abrams* dissent continues to be invoked with admiration by conservative and liberal jurists alike.[25]

Several of his other free speech dissents proved equally powerful goads to the conscience of later Courts, and equally enduring in their influence. In 1946, citing his *Schwimmer* dissent, the Court overturned its previous ruling, and found in favor of a Seventh Day Adventist who had been denied citizenship for his pacifist beliefs. And the same year, citing Holmes's 1921 dissent in *Milwaukee Social Democratic Publishing*, the Court held that use of the mails is a right, not a privilege, establishing the principle that when the government provides a forum for speech the First Amendment bars any attempt to regulate its content.[26]

Lawyers, scholars, and judges have devoted hundreds of thousands of pages of arguments to disputing the technicalities and legal doctrines of Holmes's free speech jurisprudence, but as the legal scholar Ronald K. L. Collins noted, this is "lawyers' stuff" that misses the monumental consequentiality of what Holmes did. In the shadow of war, in the face of the Red Scare and the vehement disapproval of much of the legal profession and indeed much of the country, Holmes staked his reputation—Boston Brahmin, Civil War hero, preeminent legal scholar, distinguished judge—to defend freedom of speech for communists, pacifists, and foreign-born anarchists. "Free speech in America," Collins concluded, "was never the same after 1919."[27]

Even more important, he built his argument for "freedom for the thought we hate" not only on a legal foundation, but on a philosophical one, which tied his own sturdy skepticism to the democratic experiment itself. As Collins observed, Holmes offered a bargain that still scares zealots and moralists, but which embodies what it means to be a "civilized man," as Holmes would have put it, as well as a citizen in a free land: he proposed giving up the comforts of certainty for the risks of freedom, trading the dogmas of faith for the wisdom to question even our own beliefs, embracing the courage to have more trust in the democratic compromise of ideas than in the triumph of an ideological cause.

Speaking to the fiftieth reunion of his Harvard Class of 1861, Holmes had said, "Life is painting a picture, not doing a sum." More than any other single thing, it was this ability—to see that none of us has all the answers; that perfection will never be found in the law as it is not to be found in life; but that its pursuit is still worth the effort, if only for the sake of giving our lives meaning—which people found so striking about Holmes, as a human being and as a thinker. "His own insistence that we view critically what we love and reverence, and the example of his unfailing courage," Morris Cohen wrote a month after his death, made Holmes both a "titanic" and a "lone" figure.[28]

In another speech at Harvard, which Holmes delivered on "The Profession of the Law" in 1886, he had spoken of the loneliness of original work, the "black gulf of solitude more isolating than that which surrounds the dying man," but whose reward is "the secret isolated joy of the thinker, who knows that, a hundred years after he is dead and forgotten, men who never heard of him will be moving to the measure of his thought."[29] He reaped that reward far more than he ever dared believe, which was the final testimony to the greatness of his skeptical humility.

ABBREVIATIONS

AJH	Amelia Jackson Holmes (mother of OWH)
ASG	Alice Stopford Green
BDA	*Boston Daily Advertiser*
B-F	Urofsky, ed., "Brandeis-Frankfurter Conversations"
CC	Clare, Lady Castletown
CM	Charlotte, Baroness Moncheur
CSRS	Clara Sherwood Rollins Stevens
CW	Holmes, *Collected Works*
EC	Ellen Curtis
EJHC	Edward Jackson Holmes, Collection of OWH Materials
ES	Ethel Scott
FF	Felix Frankfurter
FL	Scott, ed., *Fallen Leaves*
FP	Frederick Pollock
HBHS	Urofsky and Levy, eds., *Half Brother Half Son*
H-E	Peabody, ed., *Holmes-Einstein Letters*
H-F	Mennel and Compston, eds., *Holmes & Frankfurter Correspondence*
HJ	Henry James
HJL	Harold J. Laski
H-L	Howe, ed., *Holmes-Laski Letters*
HLA	Henry L. Abbott
H-P	Howe, ed., *Holmes-Pollock Letters*
H-S	Burton, ed., *Holmes-Sheehan Correspondence*
JA	Josiah Abbott

JBT	James B. Thayer
JRG	Bickel and Schmidt, *Judiciary and Responsible Government*
JSMP	John S. Monagan, Papers
LDB	Louis D. Brandeis
LE	Lewis Einstein
LH	Learned Hand
LLH	Morse, *Life and Letters of Oliver Wendell Holmes*
LJPP	Lewis J. Paper, Papers
MDH	Mark DeWolfe Howe
MDHM	Howe, Research Materials on OWH
NG	Anna "Nina" Gray
NYT	*New York Times*
OH	Oral History
OWH	Oliver Wendell Holmes Jr.
OWHA	Holmes, Papers, Addenda
OWHC	Holmes, Letters to Lady Castletown
OWHP	Holmes, Papers, Palfrey Collection
SJC	Supreme Judicial Court, Massachusetts
TCWJ	Perry, ed., *Thought and Character of William James*
TWF	Howe, ed., *Touched With Fire*
WBLM	W. Barton Leach, Miscellanies
WHT	William Howard Taft
WJ	William James
WP	*Washington Post*

NOTES

The principal archive of Holmes's papers is the group of five collections of Holmes material at the Harvard Law School, all of which have been digitized and are fully accessible on the Web.

Where published editions or typescripts of Holmes's letters have been made, I have cited these more convenient sources rather than the original autograph letters. Mark Howe collected, copied, and prepared typescripts of much of Holmes's correspondence and diaries, and these are found mainly in the Mark DeWolfe Howe Research Materials Relating to Life of Oliver Wendell Holmes Jr. (MDHM) under the name of the individual correspondent. Howe also filed carbon copies of these transcribed letters in a single master chronological file, together with an index; these are in the subseries "Correspondence by OWH, 1864–1934," MDHM, 19-2 to 21-8. (Howe's transcriptions of Holmes's numerous letters to Baroness Moncheur are found only in this general chronological file.) There are occasional mistakes in the dates and contents of the transcriptions, and in these instances I have relied on the original versions, which are mostly in the John G. Palfrey Collection of Papers on Oliver Wendell Holmes Jr. (OWHP) and the Oliver Wendell Holmes Jr. Addenda (OWHA), and can be readily located via the online catalogs of these collections. The two other, smaller collections of Holmes papers at Harvard are the Edward J. Holmes Collection of Oliver Wendell Holmes Jr. Materials (EJHC) and the Letters Written by Oliver Wendell Holmes to Lady Clare Castletown (OWHC). Transcriptions of an additional fifty-four letters from Holmes to Lady Castletown are in a separate group of letters in MDHM. Howe's diary of his year with Holmes, which has also been digitized, is in the Mark DeWolfe Howe Papers at Harvard Law School.

A few other important unpublished Holmes letters and materials that Mark Howe did not collect or copy are scattered among a number of archives: the

Doneraile Papers, National Library of Ireland (a dozen letters from Holmes to Lady Castletown that are not in the Harvard collections); the papers of Justices Felix Frankfurter and Willis Van Devanter at the Library of Congress and John Hessin Clarke at Case Western Reserve University; and the W. Gordon McCabe papers at the University of Virginia. The papers of John S. Monagan, W. Barton Leach, Learned Hand, and Lewis J. Paper at Harvard Law School contain a number of important interviews with and reminiscences by Holmes's secretaries, friends, family, and associates; Columbia University holds oral history interviews of Holmes's secretaries Chauncey Belknap and Harvey Bundy.

Items in manuscript collections are cited in the Notes below by box and folder number: MDHM, 15-2, refers to Howe, Research Materials, box 15, folder 2. Harvard's comprehensive online catalog to archival holdings introduced in 2018 (HOLLIS for Archival Discovery) retains these box and folder numbers in the "Item Identifier" associated with each item-level holding in a collection.

PROLOGUE

1. OWH to CSRS, February 9, 1916, MDHM, 17-39; OWH to NG, February 27, 1913, MDHM, 3-34.
2. Acheson, *Memoir*, 62.
3. OWH to LE, December 20, 1917, *H-E*, 157; Biddle, *Casual Past*, 263; OWH to Kaneko Kentaro, March 12, 1929, Kanda and Gifford, eds., "Kaneko Correspondence," 425.
4. Curtis, Review of *Holmes-Laski*, 267.
5. OWH to NG, March 23, 1921, MDHM, 4-3.
6. Bander, *Holmes Ex Cathedra*, 194.
7. OWH to LE, October 31, 1918, *H-E*, 173; OWH to HJL, November 1, 1926, *H-L*, 2:892.
8. OWH to LE, October 31, 1918, *H-E*, 173.
9. OWH to Patrick Sheehan, September 21, 1908, *H-S*, 25.
10. Remarks to Second Army Corps Association, March 13, 1903, *CW*, 3:537.
11. OWH to LE, August 20, 1911, *H-E*, 63; OWH to ES, August 14, 1914, MDHM, 17-29.
12. OWH to Lucy Clifford, January 21, 1928, MDHM, 14-10.
13. OWH to NG, May 8, 1910, MDHM, 3-32; OWH to LE, October 3, 1920, *H-E*, 193.

14. Hiss, *Laughing Last*, 57; Alger Hiss interview, 18–21, JSMP, 1-8; Monagan, *Grand Panjandrum*, 26.

15. Notes for a Talk on O.W.H., 2, WBLM; Sutherland, "Recollections," 20–21; Hiss, *Laughing Last*, 59; OWH to NG, January 4, 1909, MDHM, 3-31; OWH to EC, January 18, 1926, MDHM, 14-23.

16. Leach, *Recollections*.

17. OWH to NG, September 2, 1895, MDHM, 3-15.

18. Belknap, "Justice Holmes," 9.

19. Derby, "Recollections," 347–48.

20. OWH to Melville W. Fuller, February 9, 1909, MDHM, 14-43.

21. OWH to Fuller, February 10, 1908, MDHM, 14-43.

22. OWH to EC, February 24, 1903, MDHM, 14-21; *CW*, 1:86–87, 124 n. 9.

23. "I should like to decide every case—and write every judgment of the court, but I'm afraid the boys wouldn't see it": OWH to CC, February 11, 1897, MDHM, 13-23.

24. Holmes owned three such notebooks during his lifetime. The last and largest was the "Black Book"; it covered the years 1881–1935, and listed 3,475 books read (Monagan, *Grand Panjandrum*, 105). After Holmes's death, his executor had a facsimile edition privately printed and presented a copy to each of Holmes's secretaries (Hiss, *Recollections*, 32). The original Black Book is now in the Harvard Law School Library; a digital facsimile is accessible on the Web. The two earlier notebooks, covering 1865–66 and 1867–80, list 600 books read; these have been transcribed in Little, "Early Reading of Holmes."

25. OWH to LE, May 29, 1931, *L-E*, 325 (Wodehouse); OWH to ES, May 21, 1923, MDHM, 17-29 (Proust); OWH to ASG, February 6, 1910, MDHM, 15-8 (Dante); OWH to ES, July 16, 1908, MDHM, 17-28 (Camoens).

26. Sutherland, "Recollections," 23; OWH to NG, March 20, 1914, MDHM, 3-35; OWH to LE, June 22, 1914, *H-E*, 97; Hiss, *Laughing Last*, 58.

27. James Rowe interview, LJPP, 1-35; Monagan, *Grand Panjandrum*, 104.

28. OWH to ES, July 30, 1908, MDHM, 17-28; OWH to LE, February 8, 1931, *H-E*, 321.

29. OWH to EC, March 29, 1926, MDHM, 14-23; OWH to LE, June 1, 1925, *H-E*, 242; OWH to NG, July 30, 1930, MDHM, 4-25.

30. Meeting of Holmes Secretaries, Notes of Reminiscences, 4, WBLM; OWH to FF, February 11, 1920, *H-F*, 81–82.

31. Acheson, *Memoir*, 65.

32. OWH to NG, October 18, 1903, MDHM, 3-23; Belknap diary entry,

December 13, 1915, quoted in Messinger, "Holmes and his Clerks," 49; Biddle, *Mr. Justice Holmes*, 112.

33. Hiss, *Laughing Last*, 61; entry for February 21, 1934, Howe, Diary, 26–27.
34. OWH to Patrick Sheehan, December 15, 1912, *H-S*, 56; OWH to NG, December 2, 1910, MDHM, 3-33.
35. Holmes, *Common Law*, 1.
36. Posner, *Essential Holmes*, xi.
37. Holmes, *Common Law*, 1.
38. LH to Arthur Train, May 29, 1941, Hand, Papers, 81-7.
39. Dissenting opinion, Southern Pacific Company v. Jensen (1917).
40. O'Neill v. Northern Colorado Irrigation Company (1916).
41. McAuliffe v. Mayor and Board of Aldermen of New Bedford, 155 Mass. 216 (1892), rejecting an appeal by a police officer fired for violating a rule against political activity.
42. Spade v. Lynn and Boston Railroad Company, 172 Mass. 488 (1899), at 491, dismissing a lawsuit by a woman who claimed emotional distress when a train conductor jostled her while ejecting a drunk passenger.
43. Chadwick v. Covell, 151 Mass. 190 (1890), at 193.
44. Dissenting opinion, Olmstead v. United States (1928).
45. Dissenting opinion, Adkins v. Children's Hospital (1923).
46. Dissenting opinion, United States v. Schwimmer (1929), disagreeing with the government's denial of citizenship to a pacifist.
47. Dissenting opinion, Gitlow v. New York (1925), opposing a conviction for the distribution of communist literature.
48. OWH to HJL, July 2, 1917, *H-L*, 1:91; Speech to the Chicago Bar Association, October 21, 1902, *CW*, 3:533.
49. Schwartz, *History of Supreme Court*, 197.
50. "Walbridge Abner Field," Answer to Resolutions of the Bar, November 25, 1899, *CW*, 3:495; Hale, *Table Talk*, 15, OWHA, 4-8; OWH to LE, July 11, 1925, *H-E*, 244; OWH to NG, November 9, 1906, MDHM, 3-29.
51. Hale, *Table Talk*, 15, OWHA, 4-8.
52. Biddle, *Casual Past*, 263.
53. *CW*, 1:87.
54. Palmer, "Holmes and Hitler," 573; Gregg, "Pragmatism of Holmes," 294. In a similar vein, see McKinnon, "Secret of Holmes."
55. Frank, "Learned Hand," 703–4.
56. Graham, *Washington*, 190–91.
57. OWH to FF, July 15, 1913, *H-F*, 12; OWH to LE, June 1, 1905, *H-E*, 16–17.

58. Alschuler, *Law without Values*, 49, 180.

59. Gilmore, *American Law*, 48–49.

60. Novick, *Honorable Justice*, xvii; White, *Justice Holmes*, 297, 358, 370, 476–77; White, "Holmes as Correspondent," 1761.

61. Graves, *Assault Heroic*, xix–xx.

62. *H-P*, 1:xxxi.

63. Anna K. Codman to MDH, August 11, 1942, MDHM, 14-11.

64. Codman to OWH, March 6, 1931, OWHP, 15-17.

65. Zobel, "What a Medley," 12, quoting note by Nina Gray written on envelope of OWH to NG, June 18, 1901, OWHP, 3-19.

66. Acheson to Michael Janeway, May 24, 1960, McLellan and Acheson, eds., *Among Friends*, 182–83.

67. OWH to FF, December 31, 1915, *H-F*, 42.

68. OWH to HJL, December 15, 1926, *H-L*, 2:905.

69. OWH to NG, July 28, 1915, MDHM, 3-37; OWH to ES, November 7, 1909, MDHM, 17-28; OWH to EC, December 30, 1907, MDHM, 14-22.

70. White, "Holmes as Correspondent," 1761.

71. H. Chapman Rose interview, 12–13, JSMP, 1-14.

72. "Mourns Holmes: Messenger Faithful on Anniversary of Death," *Washington Star*, March 6, 1938, A-12, A-15; "Arthur Thomas, Supreme Court Employe, Dies at 80," *WP*, April 24, 1943, B-7.

73. OWH to FP, August 30, 1929, *H-P*, 2:253.

74. Holmes, "Ideals and Doubts," 3.

75. Gompers v. United States (1914); dissenting opinion, Springer v. Government of the Philippine Islands (1928); Otis v. Parker (1903).

76. Opinions of the Justices to the House of Representatives, 160 Mass. 586 (1894), at 594.

CHAPTER 1: Dr. Holmes's Boston

1. Brooks, *Indian Summer*, 11.

2. *LLH*, 1:204.

3. Brooks, *Indian Summer*, 10.

4. Holmes Sr., "Professor's Story," 93; Holmes Sr., *Autocrat*, 125.

5. Hazard, *Jonny-Cake Papers*, 339; Brooks, *Indian Summer*, 5n, 23–24.

6. Mackay, *Life and Liberty*, 1:67.

7. Mark Twain to Pamela Moffett, November 9, 1869, Twain, *Letters*, 1:168.

8. O'Connor, *Athens of America*, 117.

9. Brooks, *Indian Summer*, 83–84.

10. Holmes Sr., *Professor at Breakfast-Table*, 3–4.

11. O'Connor, *Athens of America*, 114–15; Goodman, "Ethics and Enterprise," 444–46.

12. O'Connor, *Athens of America*, 68–69; Howe, *Holmes of Breakfast-Table*, 64–65.

13. O'Connor, *Athens of America*, 30–33.

14. Puelo, *City So Grand*, 84–85.

15. Adams, *Education*, 47; Hofstadter, *Age of Reform*, 205.

16. O'Connor, *Athens of America*, 10.

17. Ibid., 11.

18. Monagan, *Grand Panjandrum*, 58.

19. Howe, *Unitarian Conscience*, 137; Emerson, *Journals and Notebooks*, 15:244.

20. O'Connor, *Athens of America*, 38–39, 152.

21. Hale, *New England Boyhood*, 18–19.

22. Howe, *Unitarian Conscience*, 23.

23. Adams, *Education*, 33–34.

24. Report to the Ecclesiastic Council of the First Parish of Cambridge . . . on the controversies & difficulties existing between sd. Parish and the Revd. Doct. Holmes, their Pastor, OWHA, 5-6.

25. *LLH*, 1:38–39, 46.

26. Holmes Sr., *Mortal Antipathy*, 26; *LLH*, 1:45.

27. OWH to Morris R. Cohen, February 5, 1919, Cohen, "Correspondence," 15.

28. *LLH*, 1:56.

29. Ibid., 80–81.

30. Ibid., 70.

31. Ibid., 86, 102–3, 108–10.

32. Fitz, "My Dr. Holmes," 543, 546.

33. Holmes Sr., *Puerperal Fever*, 47.

34. Ibid., 56–57.

35. Holmes Sr., *Homeopathy*, iv.

36. Tilton, *Amiable Autocrat*, 208; Hoyt, *Improper Bostonian*, 152–53; Holmes Sr., *Autocrat*, 65. ("You will find that the day you have lectured, something has gone out from you," Dr. Holmes told his successor at Harvard Medical School: *LLH*, 1:180).

37. *LLH*, 1:158–59.

38. Ibid., 159.

39. FF note of conversation with OWH, September 28, 1932, MDHM, 22-26.

40. Fitz, "My Dr. Holmes," 553; *LLH*, 1:177–79.

41. *LLH*, 2:3–10, 280–81.
42. Brooks, *Indian Summer*, 10; *LLH*, 1:206, 246; Howe, *Holmes of Breakfast-Table*, 95.
43. Report of Recitations and Deportments, June 19, 1847, OWHA, 2-1; Charles Eliot to OWH, March 28, 1924, OWHP, 17-15; Edward J. Holmes Jr. to Harlan Fiske Stone, ca. 1944, MDHM, 22-11.
44. Hughes, *Autobiographical Notes*, 176.
45. Excerpts from JBT Memorandum Book "E," 111, MDHM, 15-29; Thayer, *Letters of John Holmes*, 7.
46. Higginson, "Brother's Brother," 175–76, 178; Thayer, *Letters of John Holmes*, 45–46, 237.
47. Thayer, *Letters of John Holmes*, xiii; entry for February 11, 1934, Howe, Diary, 25; excerpts from JBT Memorandum Book "E," 115, MDHM, 15-29; Hughes, *Autobiographical Notes*, 176.
48. Thayer, *Letters of John Holmes*, 290.
49. *LLH*, 2:24.
50. Brooks, *Indian Summer*, 10.
51. *LLH*, 1:247; Holmes Sr., *Autocrat*, 5.
52. *LLH*, 1:211.
53. Emerson, *Topical Notebooks*, 3:30; Brooks, *Indian Summer*, 11.
54. Parrington, *American Thought*, 2:451, 459.
55. Tilton, *Amiable Autocrat*, 344.
56. OWH to CSRS, July 26, 1914, MDHM, 17-39.
57. OWH to FF, June 26, 1928, *H-F*, 231; Recollections of a Holmes Secretary, typescript, 6, WBLM.
58. Howe, *Holmes of Breakfast-Table*, 56; *LLH*, 1:322.
59. OWH to FF, May 21, 1926, *H-F*, 202; Donald Hiss in Louchheim, *New Deal*, 39.
60. OWH to CM, August 29, 1908, MDHM, 19-20.
61. "The Use of Law Schools," oration before the Harvard Law School Association, November 5, 1886, *CW*, 3:474; Notes for a Talk on O.W.H., 2, WBLM.
62. Meeting of Holmes's Secretaries, Notes of Reminiscences, 1, WBLM.
63. WJ to Henry James Sr., March 18, 1873, quoted in Howe, *Shaping Years*, 18; entry for December 13, 1889, Alice James, *Diary*, 69; "Mechanism in Thought and Morals," Address to Phi Beta Kappa Society of Harvard, Holmes Sr., *Pages from Old Volume*, 312.
64. Donald Hiss in Louchheim, *New Deal*, 39; Hiss, *Recollections*, 50; OWH to HJL, March 27, 1923, *H-L*, 1:492.
65. OWH to ES, August 22, 1908, MDHM, 17-28.

66. *LLH*, 1:180.
67. Ibid., 316; Sutherland, "Recollections," 20.
68. Entry for February 22, 1934, Howe, Diary, 28.
69. Leach, *Recollections*.

CHAPTER 2: A New England Boyhood

1. Mackay, *Life and Liberty*, 1:66; Hoyt, *Improper Bostonian*, 164.
2. Address to Tavern Club Dinner, November 14, 1902, *CW*, 3:534; OWH to FP, August 2, 1923, *H-P*, 2:120.
3. Remarks at Dinner of the Alpha Delta Phi Club, September 27, 1912, *CW*, 3:540; OWH to HJL, March 27, 1921, MDHM, 8-7. In the published version of this letter (*H-L*, 1:322–24), Mark Howe omitted the quoted passage about the "extra sheets" of his father's work.
4. Address to Tavern Club Dinner, November 14, 1902, *CW*, 3:534; Remarks at Dinner of the Alpha Delta Phi Club, September 27, 1912, *CW*, 3:540.
5. Address to Tavern Club Dinner, November 14, 1902, *CW*, 3:534–35.
6. OWH to HJL, May 8, 1918, *H-L*, 1:154; anecdotes of Austin Clark, May 1948, MDHM, 22-27.
7. *LLH*, 1:171; Tilton, *Amiable Autocrat*, 161; O'Connor, *Athens of America*, 13–17.
8. Howe, *Shaping Years*, 29–30.
9. Alger Hiss interview, 21, JSMP, 1-8; OWH to Morris R. Cohen, February 5, 1919, Cohen, "Correspondence," 15.
10. *LLH*, 1:197, 200.
11. Howe, *Holmes of Breakfast-Table*, 79–81; *LLH*, 1:200–2.
12. Tilton, *Amiable Autocrat*, 219; note of letter from John T. Morse Jr, to T. S. Perry, September 13, 1918, MDHM, 22-4.
13. OWH to LE, September 10, 1916, *H-E*, 139.
14. T. R. Sullivan to E. S. Dixwell, September 29, 1851, OWHA, 2-2; Howe, *Shaping Years*, 5.
15. Lois Lilley Howe, "The History of Garden Street," 54, MDHM, 23-2; Howe, *Shaping Years*, 5.
16. Thayer, *Letters of John Holmes*, xliii.
17. Howe, *Shaping Years*, 5–7; E. S. Dixwell to OWH, December 10, 1882, OWHP, 17-11.
18. OWH to NG, July 20, 1891, MDHM, 3-14; OWH to LE, April 26, 1918, *H-E*, 164.
19. Adams, *Education*, 53–55.
20. Howe, *Shaping Years*, 36, 45.

21. Felton, *Annual Report, 1859–60*, 39; Howe, *Shaping Years*, 41–42.

22. Entry for January 30, 1934, Howe, Diary, 23.

23. "Books," *Harvard Magazine* 4 (December 1858): 408–11, reprinted in *CW*, 1:139–42.

24. "Notes on Albert Durer," *Harvard Magazine* 7 (October 1860): 41–47, reprinted in *CW*, 1:153–57; "Dr. Huntington," *Harvard Magazine* 7 (October 1860): 64–67.

25. "Editor's Table," *Harvard Magazine* 7 (September 1860): 31–33.

26. Cornelius Felton to Holmes Sr., January 17, 1861, quoted in Howe, *Shaping Years*, 59–60.

27. Menand, *Metaphysical Club*, 25.

28. Howe, *Shaping Years*, 48.

29. Remarks at Dinner of the Alpha Delta Phi Club, September 27, 1912, *CW*, 3:539.

30. Menand, *Metaphysical Club*, 26.

31. Emerson, "The Transcendentalist," *Essays & Lectures*, 203.

32. Chauncey Belknap, Some Words of Justice Holmes, 3, MDHM, 22-26.

33. OWH to Patrick Sheehan, October 27, 1912, *H-S*, 51.

34. OWH to FP, May 20, 1930, *H-P*, 2:264; OWH to HJL, January 13, 1923, *H-L*, 1:474.

35. Howe, *Shaping Years*, 62, 69.

36. Felton, *Annual Report, 1860–61*, 18.

37. Howe, *Unitarian Conscience*, 14; Bowen, *Metaphysical Science*, 31, 47.

38. Howe, *Unitarian Conscience*, 81.

39. Bowen, *Metaphysical Science*, 373.

40. OWH to Morris R. Cohen, February 5, 1919, Cohen, "Correspondence," 14–15; Little, "Early Reading of Holmes," 172; Estate of Justice Holmes: The Library, 109, OWHP, 61-3; Channing, *Works*.

41. Cohen, "Justice Holmes," 208; Howe, *Unitarian Conscience*, 110.

42. OWH to James Bryce, December 31, 1882, MDHM, 13-17; Joseph Stevens Buckminster quoted in Howe, *Unitarian Conscience*, 179; Channing quoted in ibid., 279.

43. OWH to FF, July 15, 1913, *H-F*, 12; Channing quoted in Howe, *Unitarian Conscience*, 279.

44. Bowen, *Critical Essays*, ix–xii.

45. OWH to ES, March 7, 1915, MDHM, 17-29.

46. Holmes, dissenting opinion, Lochner v. New York (1905).

47. Bowen, *Critical Essays*, 181.

48. Holmes, *Common Law*, 1.

49. Bowen, *Documents of Constitution*, v.

50. Gompers v. United States (1914).

51. Bowen, *Documents of Constitution*, iii, v.

52. Hudson County Water Company v. McCarter (1908).

53. Quoted in Howe, *Unitarian Conscience*, 127–28.

54. Holmes, "Natural Law," 42.

55. Bowen, *Critical Essays*, 352.

56. Howe, *Unitarian Conscience*, 276, 289, 294.

57. Ibid., 284; Menand, *Metaphysical Club*, 10, 16.

58. Entry for May 23, 1846, Emerson, *Journals*, 7:197.

59. Puelo, *City So Grand*, 15–16, 19.

60. Ibid., 15, 29.

61. Brooks, *Indian Summer*, 129.

62. Puelo, *City So Grand*, 33; McPherson, *Battle Cry*, 119–20.

63. Amos A. Lawrence to Giles Richard, June 1, 1854, quoted in McPherson, *Battle Cry*, 120.

64. Howe, *Holmes of Breakfast-Table*, 88–90.

65. OWH to Arthur Garfield Hays, April 20, 1928, MDHM, 15-21; OWH to HJL, November 5, 1926, *H-L*, 2:893.

66. Menand, *Metaphysical Club*, 30.

67. R. P. Hallowell to OWH, January 23, 1861, in Howe, *Shaping Years*, 66; Menand, *Metaphysical Club*, 30–31.

68. HLA to JA, August 17, 1863, *FL*, 201; "Memorial Day," address delivered at Keene, N.H., May 30, 1884, *CW*, 3:465.

69. OWH to LE, April 17, 1914, *H-E*, 90.

CHAPTER 3: Harvard's Regiment

1. Miller, "Brahmins Under Fire," 75–76 and n. 1; Fox, *Regimental Losses*, 3; *FL*, 23.

2. Fox, *Regimental Losses*, 164, 471.

3. Miller, *Harvard's Civil War*, 16–17; Speech to the Class of '61, June 28, 1911, *CW*, 3:504.

4. OWH to AJH, May 1, 1861, *TWF*, 3.

5. *FL*, 2; HLA to Mrs. Caroline Livermore Abbott, July 11, 1861, *FL*, 33–34; HLA to JA, May 1861, *FL*, 32.

6. Henry Ropes to John Codman Ropes, January 28, 1862, Ropes, Civil War Letters; Palfrey, *Bartlett*, 3.

7. Henry Lee to OWH, June 10, 1884, OWHP, 19-28. In a letter to his father, Abbott describes Holmes as "6 feet high": HLA to JA, August 17, 1863, *FL*, 201.

8. Cornelius Felton to Holmes Sr., July 20, 1861, quoted in Howe, *Holmes of Breakfast-Table,* 101–2.

9. Howe, *Shaping Years,* 75; Felton to Holmes Sr., June 11, 1861, in Howe, *Holmes of Breakfast-Table,* 101.

10. Holmes Sr. to Felton, July 24, 1861, in Howe, *Holmes of Breakfast-Table,* 102–4.

11. Howe, *Holmes of Breakfast-Table,* 104.

12. Howe, *Shaping Years,* 76.

13. Tilton, *Amiable Autocrat,* 265.

14. Howe, *Shaping Years,* 77; OWH to FF, November 2, 1916, *H-F,* 58.

15. Miller, "Trouble with Brahmins," 39–40.

16. Miller, *Harvard's Civil War,* 10–11.

17. Ferdinand Dreher to John Andrew, December 3, 1862, quoted in Miller, "Trouble with Brahmins," 66.

18. Capt. George Adam Schmitt to Andrew, May 11, 1862, quoted in ibid., 59.

19. O'Connor, *Boston Irish,* 83–89.

20. HLA to Mrs. Caroline Livermore Abbott, May 7, 1863, *FL,* 179; HLA to Elizabeth Livermore, December 21, 1861, *FL,* 93; Palfrey, *Bartlett,* 2.

21. HLA to Mrs. Caroline Livermore Abbott, February 8, 1864, *FL,* 237.

22. Miller, *Harvard's Civil War,* 20–24, 32.

23. Ibid., 32–33.

24. OWH to AJH, September 8, 1861, *TWF,* 4.

25. Miller, *Harvard's Civil War,* 47–49.

26. OWH to AJH, September 11 and 23, 1861, *TWF,* 6–12.

27. Palfrey, *Bartlett,* 11; Bruce, *Twentieth Regiment,* 20.

28. Miller, *Harvard's Civil War,* 55, 68–69.

29. Except as noted, the events of the Battle of Ball's Bluff described here and below are drawn from the excellent account in Miller, *Harvard's Civil War,* 55–80, and from Ballard, *Ball's Bluff.*

30. Bruce, *Twentieth Regiment,* 30.

31. William F. Bartlett to his mother, October 25, 1861, in Palfrey, *Bartlett,* 20; HLA to JA, October 22, 1861, *FL,* 60.

32. HLA to JA, October 22, 1861, *FL,* 62; Palfrey, *Bartlett,* 24.

33. OWH to AJH, October 23, 1861, *TWF,* 13.

34. HLA to JA, October 22, 1861, *FL,* 62; Palfrey, *Bartlett,* 25–26.

35. OWH to EC, February 13, 1921, *MDHM,* 14-22; *TWF,* 24.

36. Holmes's account here and in the following paragraphs is from his diary, *TWF,* 23–33.

37. OWH to AJH, October 23, 1861, *TWF,* 13, 18.

38. Dr. William Hunt to Holmes Sr., November 3, 1861, quoted in Howe, *Shaping Years*, 101.

39. Belknap, "Justice Holmes," 7.

40. Holmes Sr. to Dr. William Hunt, November 12, 1861, in Howe, *Holmes of Breakfast-Table*, 105.

41. White, *Justice Holmes*, 503 n. 16.

42. Holmes Sr. to John Lothrop Motley, November 29, 1861, in *LLH*, 2:158.

43. OWH to FP, January 24, 1918, *H-P*, 1:258; Howe, *Shaping Years*, 112–13.

44. Miller, *Harvard's Civil War*, 97.

45. Ibid., 97, 103–4.

46. HLA to Carry Abbott, August 10, 1862, *FL*, 136; HLA to JA, October 22, 1861, *FL*, 62; HLA to Mrs. Caroline Livermore Abbott, January 8, 1863, *FL*, 159.

47. HLA to JA, September 18, 1863, *FL*, 215, and August 17, 1863, *FL*, 201; HLA to Mrs. Caroline Livermore Abbott, September 6, 1863, *FL*, 212.

48. HLA to JA, September 18, 1863, *FL*, 215.

49. OWH to parents, March [25], 1862, *TWF*, 37.

50. McPherson, *Battle Cry*, 424.

51. Ibid., 425–27.

52. OWH to parents, April 7 and 23, 1862, *TWF*, 38–39, 44; OWH to Holmes Sr., June 13, 1862, *TWF*, 53; Miller, *Harvard's Civil War*, 134–35.

53. OWH to parents, June 2, 1862, *TWF*, 51; Hallowell, *Selected Letters*, 12–13.

54. Entry for January 30, 1934, Howe, *Diary*, 23.

55. "Memorial Day," *CW*, 3:464.

56. OWH to Alfred E. Zimmern, January 22, 1918, MDHM, 18-32.

57. OWH to parents, July 5, 1862, *TWF*, 60; OWH to NG, December 31, 1920, MDHM, 4-3; Belknap, "Justice Holmes," 17.

58. OWH to John C. H. Wu, June 16, 1923, Wu, "Letters," 261–62.

59. According to the D-Day Museum, total U.S. Army casualties in the American airborne landings and beach assaults on D-Day were 6,774; Union casualties at Antietam were 12,400.

60. Ballard, *Ball's Bluff*, 56.

61. For the Twentieth Regiment's action at Antietam, see Miller, *Harvard's Civil War*, 167–76.

62. OWH to FP, June 28, 1930, *H-P*, 2:270.

63. Ibid.; "New England Never Runs," *Harper's Weekly*, November 9, 1861, 706.

64. Hallowell, *Selected Letters*, 16–18.

65. Le Duc, "The Captain," 80.

66. Belknap, "Justice Holmes," 6–7; Findlay, "The Captain," 117–18, 121.

67. Belknap, "Justice Holmes, 7; OWH to parents, September 22, [1862], *TWF*, 67; Findlay, "The Captain," 118.

68. Holmes Sr., "My Hunt," 760.

69. Sergeant, "Holmes," 60; Belknap, "Justice Holmes," 7.

70. Civil War Scrapbook, OWHP. The bloodstained handkerchief is in the OWH Object Collection at Harvard Law School; see also *TWF*, 32 n. 27.

CHAPTER 4: The Wilderness

1. Miller, *Harvard's Civil War*, 93–94.

2. HLA to JA, November 20, 1862, *FL*, 143.

3. Miller, "Brahmins Under Fire," 103–4; Miller, *Harvard's Civil War*, 182, 218.

4. HLA to Elizabeth Livermore, January 10, 1863, *FL*, 161.

5. *H-E*, xvii; OWH to LE, March 8, 1924, *H-E*, 221–22.

6. "Memorial Day," *CW*, 3:465.

7. OWH to parents, November 16, 1862, *TWF*, 69; HLA to OWH, September 5, 1863, *FL*, 211.

8. OWH to Amelia Holmes, November 16, 1862, *TWF*, 70–71; OWH to parents, November 16, 1862, *TWF*, 69.

9. OWH to Amelia Holmes, November 19, 1862, *TWF*, 72.

10. OWH to LE, October 14, 1917, *H-E*, 152.

11. OWH to AJH, December 12, 1862, *TWF*, 74; OWH to LE, August 27, 1917, *H-E*, 146.

12. Miller, *Harvard's Civil War*, 198–99, 206.

13. "Memorial Day," *CW*, 3:465.

14. Miller, "Trouble with Brahmins," 66–67, 71.

15. McPherson, *Battle Cry*, 571–72; Fox, *Regimental Losses*, 164.

16. McPherson, *Battle Cry*, 574; Henry Ropes to John C. Ropes, January 17, 1863, quoted in Howe, *Shaping Years*, 148.

17. HLA to JA, January 19 and 22, 1863, *FL*, 162–64.

18. OWH to HJL, June 1, 1927, *H-L*, 2:948.

19. OWH to Holmes Sr., December 20, 1862, *TWF*, 79–80.

20. Entry for January 30, 1934, Howe, Diary, 22; Remarks to 20th Regimental Association, December 11, 1897, *CW*, 3:519.

21. Howe, *Shaping Years*, 146.

22. OWH to Holmes Sr., March 29, 1863, *TWF*, 86–91.

23. OWH to AJH, May 3, [1863], *TWF*, 92.

24. Acheson, *Memoir*, 62.

25. Entry for January 30, 1934, Howe, Diary, 23; Charles A. Whittier to OWH, May 15, 1863, Civil War Scrapbook, OWHP; OWH to AJH, May 3, 1863, *TWF*, 92. During the First World War, Holmes wrote to an English friend whose son had lost an arm, "I remember when I wished I could compromise by losing my foot": OWH to Lady Askwith, March 3, 1915, MDHM, 13-1.

26. OWH to FP, February 1, 1920, *H-P*, 2:36.

27. Holmes Sr. to Dr. William Hunt, May 25, 1863, *LLH*, 2:25.

28. Sutherland, "Recollections," 23; OWH to HJL, July 19, 1916, *H-L*, 1:6.

29. Holmes Sr. to Dr. Hunt, May 25, 1863, *LLH*, 2:25; Norwood P. Hallowell to OWH, February 7, 1863, Civil War Scrapbook, OWHP; HLA to OWH, May 18, 1863, *FL*, 183.

30. HLA to JA, August 7, 1863, *FL*, 197–98.

31. HLA to JA, July 6, 1863, *FL*, 188.

32. Ibid., 186.

33. Ibid., 184 and n. 2; HLA to OWH, July 28, 1863, *FL*, 194.

34. John C. Ropes to OWH, July 7, 1863, Civil War Scrapbook, OWHP.

35. McPherson, *Battle Cry*, 686–87.

36. Edward P. Hallowell to OWH, August 4, 1863, Civil War Scrapbook, OWHP.

37. HLA to OWH, October 18, 1863, *FL*, 226; HLA to JA, July 27, 1863, *FL*, 192. Abbott's racially offensive comment in his letter to Holmes was omitted from the published version in Scott, *Fallen Leaves*: see Howe, *Shaping Years*, 159.

38. HLA to OWH, September 22, 1863, *FL*, 219.

39. Whittier quoted in OWH to parents, March 18, 1863, *TWF*, 85.

40. Ibid., August 10, 1863.

41. OWH to NG, November 12, 1927, MDHM, 4-19; Donald Hiss in Louchheim, *New Deal*, 34.

42. OWH to CM, April 8, 1912, MDHM, 19-27; OWH to NG, June 5, 1913, MDHM, 3-34.

43. Diary, May 4, 1864, *TWF*, 103.

44. King, Robertson, and Clay, *Overland Campaign*, 111.

45. McPherson, *Battle Cry*, 722; Rhea, *Spotsylvania*, 3–4.

46. Rhea, *Wilderness*, 51–52.

47. Diary, May 4, 1864, *TWF*, 104–5.

48. Diary, May 6 and 7, 1864, *TWF*, 106–7.

49. OWH to Lady Askwith, September 18, 1914, MDHM, 13-1; OWH to CSRS, September 11, 1914, MDHM, 17-39.

50. *FL*, 252–53; Bruce, *Twentieth Regiment*, 353–54; OWH to parents, May 6, 1864, *TWF*, 105.

51. Bruce, *Twentieth Regiment*, 357; Menand, *Metaphysical Club*, 54; "The Soldier's Faith," address on Memorial Day to the Harvard University graduating class, 1895, *CW*, 3:487.

52. King, Robertson, and Clay, *Overland Campaign*, 146.

53. McPherson, *Battle Cry*, 726–27.

54. Diary, May 8, 1864, *TWF*, 108–9.

55. Diary, May 9, 1864, *TWF*, 109–10; OWH to AJH, May 11, 1864, *TWF*, 114. Sedgwick was in fact struck by a shot fired from a Whitworth rifle, a British-manufactured sniper weapon that had a range and accuracy far greater than the standard infantry rifles of the day. It was employed by Confederate sharpshooters throughout the war.

56. "The Soldier's Faith," *CW*, 3:488.

57. Diary, May 12 and 13, 1864, *TWF*, 116–17.

58. OWH to parents, May 16, 1864, *TWF*, 121–23.

59. King, Robertson, and Clay, *Overland Campaign*, 447 (map 73).

60. Diary, May 24 and 29, 1864, *TWF*, 131, 133.

61. Diary, May 29, 1864, *TWF*, 133–34; Sutherland, "Recollections," 22.

62. OWH to parents, May 30, 1864, *TWF*, 136; OWH to AJH, June 7, 1864, *TWF*, 142.

63. OWH to parents, May 30, 1864, *TWF*, 135–36.

64. *TWF*, 137 n. 4.

65. "Memorial Day," *CW*, 3:463; OWH to Lady Pollock, May 13, 1898, *H-P*, 1:86; OWH to FP, December 21, 1886, *H-P*, 1:29; OWH to FF, March 5, 1917, *H-F*, 68.

66. King, Robertson, and Clay, *Overland Campaign*, 310.

67. OWH to AJH, June 7, 1864, *TWF*, 142–43.

68. OWH to parents, June 5, 1864, *TWF*, 140; Diary, June 4, 1864, *TWF*, 139; OWH to Agnes Pomeroy, June 21, 1864, MDHM, 13-8.

69. OWH to parents, June 24, 1864, *TWF*, 148–50.

70. The story that Holmes was the soldier who shouted to Lincoln at Fort Stevens, "Get down, you fool!" has had a long life but is apocryphal. It first appeared in print in 1938 in an article in the *Atlantic Monthly* (" 'Get Down, You Fool!,' " February 1938, 169–73) by the *New Yorker* writer Alexander Woollcott, who said that he had heard it from Harold Laski at a luncheon in New York in 1937.

Laski was well known among his friends for spinning fascinating but totally fabricated anecdotes. The only contemporary account of the incident at Fort Stevens comes from Lincoln's secretary John Hay, who noted in his diary that Lincoln, on returning from the fort that day, had related how "a soldier" had "roughly ordered him to get down or he would have his head knocked off." Although Holmes frequently took visitors to Fort Stevens, and liked to point out where he had seen Lincoln, none of his friends except Laski and Felix Frankfurter ever said they heard Holmes claim he had told the president to get down. Nor do any of Holmes's letters to Laski and others in which he recounts seeing Lincoln at Fort Stevens mention this supposed incident (see for example OWH to HJL, May 27, 1921, *H-L*, 1:339–40; OWH to LE, March 27, 1912, *H-E*, 67). Holmes's secretaries Mark DeWolfe Howe and Arthur Sutherland and his cousin's husband Austin H. Clark were adamant that Holmes never said any such thing on their several visits to the fort with him (entry for October 30, 1933, Howe, Diary, 4–5; Sutherland, "Recollections," 22; anecdotes of Austin Clark, May 1948, MDHM, 22-27).

Like Laski, Frankfurter first recounted the story some years after the justice's death, and probably had his memory unconsciously influenced by Laski or the Woollcott article. The historiography of this incident has been a minor scholarly subspecialty of Civil War historians: see, for example, Hicks, "Lincoln, Wright, Holmes," and Cramer, *Lincoln Under Fire.*

71. Francis A. Walker to OWH, July 23, 1864, Civil War Scrapbook, OWHP.

CHAPTER 5: "Society of Jobbists"

1. "The Soldier's Faith," *CW*, 3:488, 490.
2. "Memorial Day," *CW*, 3:467.
3. Shriver, *What Gusto*, 29; Anecdotes, Marion D. Frankfurter, 5, August 10, 1932, MDHM, 22-26.
4. OWH to Lady Askwith, June 28, 1916, MDHM, 13-1; OWH to HJL, April 8, 1919, *H-L*, 1:194.
5. OWH to HJL, November 22, 1917, *H-L*, 1:112.
6. "I make it a point to get eight hours in bed a night, from 12 to 8 a.m.": OWH to Kaneko Kentaro, April 26, 1931, Kanda and Gifford, "Kaneko Correspondence," 429.
7. OWH to LE, June 27, 1917, *H-E*, 142; Holmes, "Path of the Law," 466.
8. Menand, *Metaphysical Club*, 4; Whitman, *Democratic Vistas*, 11.
9. *TWF*, 57 n. 2.
10. OWH to HJL, November 5, 1926, *H-L*, 2:893.
11. OWH to CC, June 24, 1897, OWHC, 1-3; OWH to Henry Adams, December 31, 1907, MDHM, 12-8.

12. OWH to FP, August 30, 1929, *H-P*, 2:252–53; OWH to HJL, May 12, 1927, *H-L*, 2:942.

13. OWH to Lady Tweeddale, May 6, 1925, *H-E*, 239; OWH to Margaret Bevan, May 11, 1914, and August 19, 1913, OWHA, 1-1.

14. Phillips, *Frankfurter Reminisces*, 79; OWH to John C. H. Wu, June 16, 1923, Wu, "Letters," 261.

15. OWH to LE, January 29, 1914, *H-E*, 88.

16. Howe, *Unitarian Conscience*, 299; Holmes Sr., *Elsie Venner*, 63–64.

17. *H-E*, xvi, xix.

18. Brooks, *Indian Summer*, 184; Emerson, *Journals and Notebooks* 15:64–65.

19. Brooks, *Indian Summer*, 95, 102; Adams, *Education*, 276; O'Connor, *Civil War Boston*, 235.

20. Puelo, *City So Grand*, 70; O'Connor, *Boston Irish*, 60–64, 83–84.

21. O'Connor, *Boston Irish*, 87–88, 93; Fox, *Regimental Losses*, 157; O'Connor, *Civil War Boston*, 237.

22. O'Connor, *Civil War Boston*, 238–39; O'Connor, *Boston Irish*, 223, 233; Hofstadter, *Age of Reform*, 9; Howe, *Unitarian Conscience*, 295–96.

23. Howe, *Unitarian Conscience*, 220–21.

24. Anecdotes, FF, September 28, 1932, MDHM, 22-26; Biddle, *Mr. Justice Holmes*, 35–36.

25. Anecdotes, FF, September 28, 1932, MDHM, 22-26.

26. Howe, *Shaping Years*, 204; Introduction to the General Survey, November 28, 1911, *CW*, 3:440; Address to Brown University Commencement, 1897, *CW*, 3:518.

27. OWH to Henry H. Brownell, May 9, 1865, quoted in Howe, *Shaping Years*, 196; WJ to Henry P. Bowditch, May 22, 1869, Hardwick, *Selected Letters*, 83.

28. OWH to WJ, April 19, 1868, *TCWJ*, 1:509.

29. Menand, *Metaphysical Club*, 59.

30. O'Connor, *Civil War Boston*, 148–49.

31. Howe, *Unitarian Conscience*, 300–1.

32. Holmes Sr. to John Motley, December 22, 1871, *LLH*, 2:190; Brooks, *Indian Summer*, 102–7.

33. OWH to John C. H. Wu, March 26, 1925, Wu, "Letters," 275.

34. "The Use of Law Schools," November 5, 1886, *CW*, 3:475.

35. OWH to Lady Burghclere, September 17, 1898, MDHM, 13-21.

36. OWH to NG, July 17, 1896, MDHM, 3-16; entry for May 11, Diary of Trip to Europe, 1866, MDHM, 28-23; OWH to Lady Pollock, August 11, 1895, *H-P*, 1:59.

37. The initial pages of Holmes's trip diary, OWHP, 57-25, include a long list of people and places to see. The letters of introduction from Sumner and others are in OWHP, 57-24. Unless otherwise noted below, the details of Holmes's trip are from his diary, a typewritten transcript of which is in MDHM, 28-23.
38. Menand, *Metaphysical Club*, 205.
39. Maitland, *Leslie Stephen*, 110–11, 115–16.
40. Nesbitt, "Climbing Justice"; J. Monroe Thorington, American Alpine Club, to MDH, June 9, 1942, MDHM, 28-3.
41. Leslie Stephen to OWH, December 7, 1866, in Maitland, *Leslie Stephen*, 186; Tom Hughes to OWH, December 31, 1866, OWHP, 18-28; memorandum of talk with LH, June 11, 1942, MDHM, 22-7.
42. OWH to CM, January 9, 1915, MDHM, 20-1.
43. OWH to CC, August 9, 1897, MDHM, 13-24.
44. AJH to OWH, July 3, 1866, MDHM, 15-27.
45. Amelia Holmes to OWH, and postscript from AJH, July 16, 1866, MDHM, 15-28.
46. WJ to Garth Wilkinson James, March 21, 1866, quoted in Menand, *Metaphysical Club*, 205.
47. Menand, *Metaphysical Club*, 204.
48. Ibid., 92–94.
49. WJ to Thomas W. Ward, March 27, 1866, James, ed., *Letters of William James*, 1:75–76.
50. WJ to Henry P. Bowditch, January 24, 1869, Hardwick, *Selected Letters*, 78.
51. WJ to OWH, May 15, 1868, ibid., 61–62.
52. WJ to OWH, September 17, 1867, ibid., 34–35.
53. James, *Son and Brother*, 276–79.
54. Menand, *Metaphysical Club*, 73–75; James, *Son and Brother*, 347–48, 398.
55. Menand, *Metaphysical Club*, 205; James, *Son and Brother*, 430.
56. Henry James recounted the actual New Hampshire trip in *Son and Brother*, 425–30. Holmes's 1867 engagement book includes an entry for August 17–26, "off to N. Conway with John Gray" (OWHP, 57-25). A young neighbor girl who accompanied the group of adults on a hike remembered Holmes telling her "the tale of the 'Green-eyed Monster'" which she knew to be the story of his devotion to a beautiful lady of the party and his envy of those he thought more favored." The girl, Olivia Murray, related the incident to Learned Hand eighty years later and also

dated the episode to August 1867 (LH to MDH, November 25, 1947, MDHM, 22-26; Howe, *Shaping Years*, 202–3). Holmes himself encountered her again in Washington in 1903 ("Mrs. Bayard Cutting whom I met as a girl of 10 in the White Mtns. We adored each other then": OWH to EC, February 7, 1903, MDHM, 14-21).

57. HJ to WJ, March 29, 1870, Edel, *Selected Letters*, 77; see also, LeClair, "Henry James and Temple"; Habegger, "William James and Temple"; and Habegger, "James's Rewriting of Temple's Letters."

58. Mary James to Alice James, January 1867, quoted in Strouse, *Alice James*, 99.

59. OWH to NG, August 30, 1914, MDHM, 3-36; James, *Son and Brother*, 428, 479. Holmes told Nina Gray in this 1914 letter that he had "a little package of letters" from Minny Temple, but he apparently destroyed them before his death.

60. HJ to OWH, July 29 [1867?], Howe, "Letters of James to Holmes," 414. Howe dated the letter 1865, then revised that to 1868 (Howe, *Shaping Years*, 306 n. 59), but 1867 seems more likely from other evidence (see n. 56 above).

61. James, *Notebooks*, 239. Sheldon Novick's improbable suggestion that Henry James and Holmes had a homosexual encounter at this time is based on an extraordinarily fanciful reading of the pages in James's notebook in which he recounts this visit to Holmes's mother (Novick, *Young Master*, 470–71 n. 42). Novick's sole evidence is James's use of the words *l'initiation première* at the start of a long preceding passage in which he describes his first success as a writer, and his nostalgic remembrances of the Boston literary world. Novick insists that "the passage seems impossible to misunderstand." But, on the evidence, it would appear that impossibility, like sexual innuendo, is in the eye of the beholder.

62. HJ to WJ, October 16, 1869, Edel, *Selected Letters*, 49; HJ to WJ, April 26, 1869, ibid., 32.

63. OWH to WJ, December 15, 1867, *TCWJ*, 1:505.

64. Anderson, "William James in 1869," 369, 374.

65. Menand, *Metaphysical Club*, 220–21.

66. HJ to Charles Eliot Norton, February 4, 1872, Edel, *Selected Letters*, 92. "The Metaphysical Club" has had a legendary aura that far outstrips the reality of its existence. Henry James provided the only contemporary account of the club, and no one except the philosopher Charles Peirce, writing thirty-five years later, ever said that that was its official name (Menand, *Metaphysical Club*, 201–2).

67. Menand, *Metaphysical Club*, 206–7, 230–31.

68. OWH to FP, August 30, 1929, *H-P*, 2:252; Chauncey Wright quoted in Menand, *Metaphysical Club*, 211.

69. OWH to LE, June 1, 1905, *H-E*, 16–17; OWH to HJL, January 25, 1918, *H-L*, 1:131.

70. OWH to WJ, October 13, 1907, MDHM, 16-18; OWH to WJ, March 24, 1907, *TCWJ*, 2:459.

71. OWH to WJ, May 24, 1896, *TCWJ*, 2:458.

72. OWH to LE, January 6, 1908, *H-E*, 32; OWH to WJ, March 24, 1907, *TCWJ*, 2:460.

73. Entry for July 9, Diary of Trip to Europe, 1866, MDHM, 28-23; Leslie Stephen to OWH, July 4, 1870, Maitland, *Leslie Stephen*, 218.

74. Wu, Review of *Holmes-Laski*, 950.

75. Menand, *Metaphysical Club*, 231.

CHAPTER 6: *The Common Law*

1. OWH to CC, April 30, 1897, MDHM, 13-23; OWH to ES, May 21, 1923, MDHM, 17-29.

2. OWH to CC, October 7, 1896, OWHC, 1-1; OWH to John C. H. Wu, March 3, 1930, Wu, "Letters," 298.

3. OWH to Ralph Waldo Emerson, April 16, 1876, MDHM, 14-32; "The Profession of the Law," address to Harvard undergraduates, February 17, 1886, *CW*, 3:472.

4. OWH to Mrs. Charles S. Hamlin, October 12, 1930, MDHM, 15-16; OWH to HJL, October 18, 1925, *H-L*, 1:793.

5. Howe, *Shaping Years*, 281.

6. OWH to John C. H. Wu, March 3, 1930, Wu, "Letters," 298–99; WJ to Henry P. Bowditch, May 22, 1869, *TCWJ*, 1:297.

7. Diary, 1867, OWHP, 57-25.

8. Entries for March 2 and March 5, ibid.

9. "George Otis Shattuck," Answer to Resolutions of the Bar, May 29, 1897, *CW*, 3:492.

10. Entry for November 24, Diary, 1866, OWHP, 57-25.

11. Holmes, "Memoir of Shattuck," 367.

12. "George Otis Shattuck," *CW*, 3:492–93.

13. Ibid., 494.

14. United States v. Ames (1878).

15. Howe, *Proving Years*, 23; Holmes, "Memoir of Shattuck," 361–62, 365.

16. OWH to Frances Kennedy, March 11, 1872, in Findlay, "The Captain," 121; Little, "Early Reading of Holmes, 184.
17. Howe, *Proving Years*, 6–7.
18. White, *Justice Holmes*, 105, 513 n. 101.
19. Details of their trip here and below are from Fanny's Diary of European Trip, 1874, OWHP, 25-13; many of the passages from her diary are quoted in Howe, *Proving Years*, 97–100.
20. *H-P*, 1:xv.
21. Puelo, *City So Grand*, 88–89, 93–94.
22. Howe, *Proving Years*, 106, 254–55, 255 n. 4.
23. Nancy J. B. Morton to MDH, June 3, 1942, MDHM, 22-28; OWH to HJL, November 5, 1926, *H-L*, 2:893.
24. OWH to John G. Palfrey, February 6, 1905, MDHM, 17-10; OWH to LE, June 7, 1904, *H-E*, 10.
25. Novick, *Honorable Justice*, 433 n. 44.
26. WJ to HJ, November 24, 1872, Hardwick, *Selected Letters*, 93; WJ to Henry P. Bowditch, May 22, 1869, *TCWJ*, 1:297.
27. WJ to HJ, October 2, 1869, *TCWJ*, 1:307; Anderson, "William James in 1869," 378.
28. OWH to Mrs. Charles S. Hamlin, October 12, 1930, MDHM, 15-16.
29. WJ to HJ, July 5, 1876, *TCWJ*, 1:371.
30. Howe, *Proving Years*, 13.
31. Ibid., 11; OWH to JBT, December 10, 1869, quoted in ibid., 12.
32. Ibid., 16.
33. Kent, *Commentaries*, 2:374; Holmes's note on implied warranties is on 2:491 of the twelfth edition, reprinted in *CW*, 2:182–85. See also Howe, *Proving Years*, 21–22.
34. Note on easements, 3:419 of the twelfth edition, reprinted in *CW*, 2:355–57; Holmes, "Theory of Torts," *CW*, 1:326–34.
35. OWH to JBT, July 15, 1872, OWHA, 1-23.
36. *TCWJ*, 1:519.
37. Fiechter, "American Aristocrat," 21–22.
38. Note of conversation with Charles Evans Hughes, November 5, 1942, MDHM, 22-7.
39. JBT to James Kent, December 16 and 17, 1873, OWHA, 1-23.
40. Kent to OWH, December 16, 1873, OWHP, 19-19; Kent to JBT, December 16, 1873, OWHA, 1-23. Holmes had written in the preface, "The notes which have been added to former editions since the author's death have not been retained, with the exception of one by Mr. Justice Kent, the

Chancellor's son, and several by the last and very able editor, Judge Comstock." The two words Kent wanted removed were "very able," which he took as disparaging his father by comparison.

41. OWH to JBT, "Private," n.d., OWHA, 1-23; Kent to OWH, December 20, 1873, OWHP, 19-19.
42. JBT Memorandum Book D, 143–44, MDHM, 15-29.
43. OWH to NG, April 30, 1905, MDHM, 3-27.
44. OWH to CM, January 9, 1915, MDHM, 20-1.
45. OWH to HJL, June 1, 1922, *H-L*, 1:429–30.
46. OWH to James Bryce, August 17, 1879, MDHM, 13-16.
47. Frank, "Learned Hand," 679.
48. Menand, *Metaphysical Club*, 341; Howe, *Proving Years*, 156.
49. OWH to Morris R. Cohen, February 5, 1919, Cohen, "Correspondence," 14; OWH to Lady Pollock, July 2, 1895, *H-P*, 1:58. Holmes mentioned reading the book in a letter to Clara Stevens in 1907 ("I rather think that I last wrote before reading for the first time Darwin's Origin of Species": OWH to CSRS, April 28, 1907, MDHM, 17-38), and the book is on his 1907 reading list (Holmes, *Black Book*, 136).
50. Holmes, *Common Law*, 1–2.
51. Ibid., 1–2, 36.
52. Ibid., 37.
53. Ibid., 24–28.
54. Ibid., 35.
55. Ibid., 153.
56. Ibid., 138–39.
57. Ibid., 38.
58. Ibid., 108.
59. Ibid., 149.
60. Smith, *History of Lowell Institute*, 25–26; "Lowell Institute Lecture," *BDA*, November 24, 1880.
61. "The Common Law," *BDA*, January 1, 1881; OWH to HJL, October 18, 1925, *H-L*, 1:793; OWH to Mrs. Charles S. Hamlin, October 12, 1930, MDHM, 15-16.
62. Howe, *Proving Years*, 249–50.
63. OWH to EC, April 26, 1908, MDHM, 14-22.
64. OWH to HJL, January 25 and February 1, 1919, *H-L*, 1:180, 184.
65. Hughes, *Autobiographical Notes*, 172; OWH to ES, May 27, 1910, MDHM, 17-28.
66. OWH to ES, May 27, 1910, MDHM, 17-28.
67. OWH to Lady Askwith, March 3, 1915, MDHM, 13-1.

CHAPTER 7: Holmes J.

1. Charles Eliot to OWH, November 4, 1881, MDHM, 29-17. His salary as a lecturer is mentioned in OWH to Eliot, January 25, 1870, MDHM, 22-21.
2. Urofsky, *Brandeis*, 49, 78–79.
3. Entry for January 29, 1882, JBT Memorandum Book D, 103–6, MDHM, 15-29; Urofsky, *Brandeis*, 79.
4. Charles Eliot to OWH, February 11, 1882, quoted in Howe, *Proving Years*, 265.
5. Howe, *Proving Years*, 272; Speech to Bar Association of Boston, March 7, 1900, CW, 3:498.
6. The events are related in the entry for December 18, 1882, JBT Memorandum Book D, 140–44, MDHM, 15-29, reprinted in Howe, *Proving Years*, 265–67.
7. OWH to James Bryce, December 31, 1882, MDHM, 13-17.
8. OWH to FF, July 15, 1913, *H-F*, 12.
9. Entries for December 18 and 22, 1882, JBT Memorandum Book D, 140–44, MDHM, 15-29, reprinted in Howe, *Proving Years*, 265–68.
10. Ibid.; OWH to Charles Eliot, October 24, 1881, and Eliot to OWH, November 4, 1881, MDHM, 29-17; E. W. Hooper to William F. Weld Jr., January, 1883, quoted in Howe, *Proving Years*, 269–70.
11. F. W. Parker to OWH, December 17, 1882, MDHM, 29-17.
12. LDB to OWH, December 9, 1882, OWHP, 14-23.
13. OWH to FP, August 27, 1883, *H-P*, 1:22.
14. Holmes, "Law in Science," 452.
15. Oakes Ames to OWH, December 11, 1882, OWHP, 14-2; Wister, *Roosevelt*, 129; OWH to FP, August 27, 1883, *H-P*, 1:22; "William Crowninshield Endicott," Answer to Resolutions of the Bar, November 24, 1900, CW, 3:527.
16. OWH to CC, September 30, 1896, MDHM, 13-23.
17. L. Kinvin Wroth, memorandum, Holmes's Single Justice Sittings, 1–2 and Appendix I:1, MDHM, 24-2; Calendar of Assignments of the Justices of the Supreme Judicial Court of Massachusetts, for the Year Beginning September 1, 1899, ibid.
18. Wroth, memorandum, Holmes's Single Justice Sittings, Appendix II and III, MDHM, 24-2.
19. I am greatly indebted to Hiller B. Zobel, who generously shared with me a literal lifetime's research on Holmes's trial cases. Details of Holmes's trials are mostly to be found in the appeals of his decisions that went to the full court, but even there documentation is often sparse: it was not

usual as today to prepare a complete transcript of a trial, and the appellate record generally consists only of a brief agreed statement of facts and a filing known as a bill of exceptions setting forth the specific legal grounds the losing party is alleging as the basis of its appeal.

In equity cases, where an appellate court has the power to reconsider a case afresh and not merely correct procedural errors that occurred at trial, there was sometimes a more complete "report" of the case prepared by the trial judge that can be found in the case records.

Besides the final appellate decisions published in the *Massachusetts Reports*, which sometimes will directly quote Holmes's findings and orders at trial, the principal primary sources are Holmes's trial reports in the bound volumes of SJC, Records on Appeal, at the Social Law Library, Boston, arranged by case name and session; and the many scattered files of his trial cases found in the dockets of the various county courthouses in Massachusetts, many of which Zobel searched out and copied. Reports of two of Holmes's trials with unusually complete transcripts, *Deshon v. Wood* and *Lamson v. Martin*, are in the Holmes papers, OWHA, 7-9 to 7-13.

Zobel has presented some of his findings in Zobel, "Holmes in Trial Court," and Zobel, "Holmes, Trial Judge." The *Boston Daily Advertiser* published a spare but regular account of court news that mentions occasional cases Holmes heard as a trial justice, with fuller coverage of his more sensational trials.

20. August 4, 1924, B-F, 334–35.
21. Clapp v. Jenkins (Docket # 1171, Suffolk County, Equity, 1883); "Legality of the Standard Time," *BDA*, November 24, 1883; "In Chambers—Holmes, J.," *BDA*, December 5, 1883. Examples of national coverage of the case are "The New Standard Time Legal," *NYT*, December 5, 1883, and "Standing by Standard Time," *Milwaukee Sentinel*, December 5, 1883.
22. Briggs v. Canal Company (Docket # 945, Equity, Suffolk County, 1883), Wroth, memorandum, Holmes's Single Justice Sittings, Appendix II:5, MDHM, 24-2; Dexter v. Campbell, 137 Mass. 198 (1884); Beals v. Case (Docket # 346, Equity, Suffolk County, 1883), Wroth memorandum, Appendix II:8; Russell v. Cole (Docket # 865, Equity, Suffolk County, 1883), Wroth memorandum, Appendix II:6.
23. Jacobs v. Rouse (Docket # 588, Equity, Suffolk County, 1883), Wroth memorandum, Appendix II:2; Boston Standard Cab Association v. Nichols (Docket # 947, Equity, Suffolk County, 1883); "Court Calendar—In Chambers—Holmes, J.," *BDA*, December 12, 1883.

24. *Pittsfield Sun*, September 11, 1883, MDHM, 24-5.
25. OWH to FP, December 15, 1912, *H-P*, 1:204; OWH to LE, January 29, 1914, *H-E*, 88.
26. Drake v. Drake (Docket # 403, Berkshire County, 1887); libellee's answer, Drake v. Drake, MDHM, 24-5; Zobel, "Holmes, Trial Judge," 26.
27. Seaver v. Seaver (Docket # 499, Suffolk County, 1883); "Marital Misery: A High-Toned Boston Couple in the Divorce Court," *St. Louis Globe-Democrat,* June 3, 1882; Zobel, "Holmes in Trial Court," 39.
28. Oliver v. Oliver, 151 Mass. 349 (1890) and SJC, Records on Appeal.
29. Robbins v. Robbins, 140 Mass. 528 (1886) and SJC, Records on Appeal.
30. McCormack, "Law Clerk's Recollections," 713; OWH to EC, December 12, 1919, MDHM, 14-22.
31. Gibson v. Imperial Council of the Order of United Friends, 168 Mass. 391 (1897) and SJC, Records on Appeal; Sargent v. Supreme Lodge of the Knights of Honor, 158 Mass. 557 (1893) and SJC, Records on Appeal.
32. Raymond v. Wagner, 178 Mass. 315 (1901).
33. Jones v. Simpson, 171 Mass. 474 (1898), and SJC, Records on Appeal; White v. Massachusetts Institute of Technology, 171 Mass. 84 (1898), and SJC, Records on Appeal.
34. Transcript, 29, 33, Deshon v. Wood, In Equity, Before Holmes, J., Boston, May 23, 1887, OWHA, 7-9.
35. Ibid., 6–7, 13–18, 39, 43–45.
36. Ibid., 73.
37. Deshon v. Wood, 148 Mass. 132 (1888).
38. Fiske v. Pratt, 157 Mass. 83 (1892), and SJC, Records on Appeal.
39. Dimond, *Superior Court*, 88–89, 92–93.
40. Commonwealth v. Nicholson (Suffolk County, 1884); Commonwealth v. Besse, 143 Mass. 80 (1886); Commonwealth v. Baker (Middlesex County, 1886); Commonwealth v. Allen (Suffolk County, 1885). The trials all received extensive daily coverage in the *BDA*: Nicholson, June 16–19, 1884; Besse, May 19–21, 1886; Baker, December 14–18, 1886; Allen, February 3 and 5, 1885.
41. "The Law," Speech to Suffolk Bar Association, February 5, 1885, CW, 3:469.
42. "William Crowninshield Endicott," Answer to Resolutions of the Bar, November 24, 1900, CW, 3:527.
43. Zobel, "Holmes in Trial Court," 44.
44. Anecdotes, Judge John V. Spalding, January 12, 1946, MDHM, 22-27.
45. OWH to NG, October 2, 1896, MDHM, 3-16; OWH to EC, January 7, 1901, MDHM, 14-21; Acheson, *Memoir*, 58.

46. OWH to CC, March 3, 1898, MDHM, 13-24; OWH to CC, June 3, 1897, MDHM, 13-23.

47. Transcript, 205, Chase v. Hubbard, 153 Mass. 91 (1891), SJC, Records on Appeal; transcript, 104, Deshon v. Wood, 148 Mass. 132 (1888), SJC, Records on Appeal. The transcript of Wood v. Bullard, 151 Mass. 324 (1890), SJC, Records on Appeal, also contains numerous examples of Holmes intervening in testimony to admonish witnesses and counsel; see also Zobel, "Holmes in Trial Court," 38–39.

48. "Judge Lowell: Says He Likes to Try Cases Before Judge Holmes," *BDA*, February 19, 1897.

49. Mason v. Pomeroy, 154 Mass. 481 (1891); Stillman v. Whittemore, 165 Mass. 234 (1896); Amherst College v. Allen, 165 Mass. 178 (1896); Sears v. Mayor and Aldermen of Worcester, 180 Mass. 288 (1902); Record, 5, Gale v. Nickerson, 144 Mass. 415 (1887), SJC, Records on Appeal.

50. I was able to locate 156 appeals of Holmes's trial cases in the *Massachusetts Reports*. In 75 cases his decision was affirmed entirely or substantially by the full court, in 14 he was overruled. In another 67 cases, at the request of one or both parties, he reported the case to the full court without a decision. The cases where he overruled himself on appeal were Wood v. Cutter, 138 Mass. 149 (1884), and Hunting v. Damon, 160 Mass. 441 (1894).

51. O'Connor, *Boston Irish*, 113–15; Rosenbloom, *Economic Maturity*, 24.

52. Puelo, *City So Grand*, 49, 218–23; Rosenbloom, *Economic Maturity*, 25.

53. Rosenbloom, *Economic Maturity*, 5, 8–13.

54. Ibid., 27–28; O'Connor, *Boston Irish*, 151–53.

55. Middlesex Company v. City of Lowell, 149 Mass. 509 (1889).

56. Anchor Electric Company v. Hawkes, 171 Mass. 101 (1898) and SJC, Records on Appeal.

57. Harvey v. Merrill, 150 Mass. 1 (1889), and SJC, Records on Appeal.

58. "Walbridge Abner Field," November 25, 1899, *CW*, 3:496.

59. Crowell v. Cape Cod Ship Canal Company, 168 Mass. 157 (1897), and SJC, Records on Appeal.

60. Towne v. Eisner (1918); Johnson v. United States, 163 Fed. 30 (1st Cir. 1908).

61. Bent v. Emery, 173 Mass. 495 (1899). The question in the case was whether the dredging of mud flats by the city required compensation to the owners.

62. Hubbard v. City of Taunton, 140 Mass. 467 (1886).

CHAPTER 8: Labor, Capital, and Dames

1. OWH to LE, March 31, 1922, *H-E*, 204. Holmes misremembered one detail in recalling these events forty years later, telling Einstein that Fanny

"sent me to Europe" for the summer while she got the house ready; in fact, after their 1882 trip abroad together, Holmes did not travel to Europe again until 1889. Holmes was writing letters from 9 Chestnut Street in March 1884 (see the original letter from OWH to FP, March 9, 1884, OWHP, 10-3) but was still at 10 Beacon Street the previous November (OWH to FP, November 5, 1883, ibid.).

2. OWH to LE, October 28, 1912, H-E, 74–75.
3. OWH to LE, June 1929, H-E, 297; OWH to ES, January 6, 1912, MDHM, 17-28.
4. Katherine P. Loring to MDH, June 4, 1942, MDHM, 22-28; memorandum of talk with Thomas Barbour, January 5, 1946, MDHM, 22-7.
5. Entry for June 16, 1889, Alice James, *Diary*, 35.
6. Thomas G. Corcoran interview, 7–8, JSMP, 1-3; LE to OWH, May 5, 1919, and May 31, 1929, H-E, 186, 296.
7. John E. Lockwood to FF, October 1, 1928, OWHP, 58-27; Katharine Bundy interview, 12, JSMP, 1-1
8. Thomas G. Corcoran to FF, November 4, 1926, OWHP, 58-27.
9. Sutherland, "Recollections," 20–21; Alger Hiss interview, 30, JSMP, 1-8.
10. Graham, *Washington*, 191; Meyer, *Roots*, 171–72.
11. OWH to FP, May 24, 1929, H-P, 2:243; memorandum of talk with FF, August 10, 1964, MDHM, 22-26.
12. OWH to ES, September 24, 1910, MDHM, 17-28.
13. Memorandum of talk with Mrs. E. J. Holmes, October 22, 1954, MDHM, 22-7; Katharine Bundy interview, 13–14, JSMP, 1-1.
14. OWH to HJL, October 30, 1921, H-L, 1:378.
15. OWH to NG, August 7, 1895, MDHM, 3-15. Holmes identifies her only as one of "two little girls—cousins of mine," but Dorothy would have been thirteen at the time, as he mentions.
16. LH to MDH, April 29, 1959, MDHM, 22-26.
17. OWH to LE, August 31, 1928, H-E, 289.
18. Katharine Bundy interview, 14–15, JSMP, 1-1.
19. MDH note of luncheon with Sam Morison and Lewis Einstein, April 5, 1961, MDHM, 22-26; OWH to FP, July 27, 1899, MDHM, 11-8. I am grateful to Dr. Lee Ponsky, professor of urology at Case Western Reserve University, and Dr. Adam S. Kibel, chief of urology at Brigham and Women's Hospital, for their explanations of benign prostatic hyperplasia and their insights into Holmes's condition.
20. Based on a single letter in which Fanny wrote, "You have a wife once a week," Novick concluded, "Holmes and his wife had a vigorous if somewhat routinized sex life, as surviving letters between them clearly

indicate" (Novick, "Holmes's Philosophy," 731). Although Novick stated that Fanny's words "cannot really be misunderstood" (Novick, "Art of Biography," 1232), it is unlikely they were meant in a sexual sense, and they certainly were not an accounting of the couple's "routinized sex life": she was writing from Beverly Farms at the end of the summer when Holmes was attending court in Boston and rejoining her on the weekends, and she was referring to the fact that they were only seeing each other once a week (Fanny Holmes to OWH, n.d., Beverly Farms, OWHP, 18-19; although the letter is undated, it is on Beverly Farms stationery, and she refers to events that place it during the time the court was in session).

21. OWH to Lucy Hale, May 21, 1858, MDHM, 18-35.
22. OWH to EC, January 25, 1903, and February 25, 1904, MDHM, 14-21; OWH to CC, March 12, 1897, MDHM, 13-23.
23. OWH to John T. Morse Jr., June 9, 1887, MDHM, 16-38; Wister, *Roosevelt*, 130. ("I have been in the habit for years of calling at the Grays on Tuesday—to see Mrs. G. and John if he happens to be in": OWH to EC, January 7, 1901, MDHM, 14-21.)
24. Katherine P. Loring to MDH, June 10, 1942, MDHM, 22-28.
25. Phillips, *Frankfurter Reminisces*, 23.
26. OWH to NG, August 29, 1899, MDHM, 3-18; "Charles P. Curtis, Boston Lawyer, 87," *NYT*, April 28, 1948; "American Boat Wins," *NYT*, September 3, 1913; OWH to NG, July 26, 1900, MDHM, 3-19.
27. "What Is Doing in Society," *NYT*, August 3, 1899; "J. S. Stevens Dead on Hunting Trip," *NYT*, March 23, 1935.
28. Memorandums of talks with Charlie Curtis, January 28, 1955, MDHM, 22-7, and Sherwood Rollins, December 8, 1955, MDHM, 28-7.
29. James H. Rowe interview, 4, JSMP, 1-15; Monagan, *Grand Panjandrum*, 93; Biddle, *Casual Past*, 288; Isabella Wigglesworth interview, 14, JSMP, 1-16; Katherine P. Loring to MDH, June 4, 1942, MDHM, 22-28; Katharine Bundy interview, 4, 8, JSMP, 1-1.
30. OWH to LE, August 4, 1923, *H-E*, 216.
31. Howe, *Shaping Years*, 254.
32. OWH to Margaret Bevan, September 7, 1913, and December 26, 1914, OWHA, 1-1.
33. Ibid., September 7, 1913.
34. Rollins, *Threads of Life*, 45–47, 51–53.
35. "Easter Sonnet," CSRS to OWH, OWHP, 22-17.
36. CSRS to OWH, [December 31, 1899], OWHP, 22-17.

37. ES to OWH, September 30, 1896, OWHP, 22-1.
38. Memorandum of talk with Austin Clark, May 1948, MDHM, 22-27. Katherine P. Loring was one who said she had never observed any signs of jealousy in Fanny: Loring to MDH, June 10, 1942, MDHM, 22-28.
39. Fanny Holmes to OWH, n.d., Beverly Farms, OWHP, 18-19 (see also n. 20 above).
40. Memorandums of talks with Mrs. James B. Ayer, October 25, 1955, MDHM, 23-2, and Charlie P. Curtis Jr., January 28, 1955, MDHM, 22-7.
41. Katharine Bundy interview, 4–5, JSMP, 1-1.
42. Hale, *Table Talk*, 11.
43. "The Breakfast Table," *BDA*, May 7, 1888; "In and About Portland: Prominent Bostonians Coming," *Morning Oregonian*, May 25, 1888; "A Beautiful Trip," ibid., May 28, 1888. In his address to the Chicago Bar Association in 1902, Holmes recounted meeting Fuller in Chicago on this 1888 trip: *CW*, 3:532.
44. OWH to Owen Wister, June 8, 1888, MDHM, 18-22; WJ to Henry and Alice James, October 14, 1888, *TCWJ*, 1:409; OWH to CM, January 9, 1915, MDHM, 20-1.
45. Holmes Sr. to Elizabeth Ward, April 13, 1889, *LLH*, 2:264; OWH to Wister, April 14, 1889, MDHM, 19-4; entry for May 30, Diary of European Trip, 1874, OWHP, 25-13; Diary, 1882, OWHP, 57-26.
46. *TCWJ*, 1:411; entry for June 16, 1889, Alice James, *Diary*, 35.
47. Ethel Grenfell to OWH, June 27, 1892, OWHP, 16-22.
48. HJ to OWH, November 13, 1891, Howe, "Letters of James to Holmes," 417.
49. CC to OWH, February 19, 1892, OWHP, 15-3. ("I was staying at Wilton for Easter, & found Lord and Lady Pembroke still full of pleasant recollections & thoughts of a visit from you when you were here in England last": Charles Bowen to OWH April 9, 1891, MDHM, 13-12.)
50. Anna K. Codman to MDH, August 11, 1942, MDHM, 14-11.
51. OWH to NG, August 7, 1891, MDHM, 3-14.
52. Montgomery, "Strikes in Nineteenth-Century," 91–93; Rosenbloom, *Economic Maturity*, 28.
53. Rosenbloom, *Economic Maturity*, 30–31, 33, 36.
54. July 2, 1924, B-F, 328; Post, "Dissent in Taft Court," 1341–42; Holmes, dissenting opinion, Vegelahn v. Guntner, 167 Mass. 92 (1896), at 104.
55. Holmes, dissenting opinion, Commonwealth v. Perry, 155 Mass. 117 (1891), at 123–24.
56. Holmes, "Ideals and Doubts," 3; OWH to HJL, May 24, 1919, *H-L*, 1:207, and August 6, 1917, *H-L*, 1:96; "The Soldier's Faith," *CW*, 3:487.

57. Holmes, "Path of the Law," 467–68; Address to Middlesex Bar Association, December 3, 1902, *CW*, 3:536.

58. OWH to FP, January 20, 1893, *H-P*, 1:44.

59. Opinions of the Justices to the House of Representatives, 155 Mass. 598 (1892), at 607; OWH to NG, May 10, 1892, MDHM, 3-14; OWH to James Bryce, July 17, 1892, MDHM, 13-17.

60. Holmes, dissenting opinion, Attorney General v. Old Colony Railroad Co., 160 Mass. 62 (1893), at 94.

61. Speech at Harvard Law School Association, June 25, 1895, *CW*, 3:492. The one case where Holmes found a Massachusetts statute unconstitutional was Lorden v. Coffey, 178 Mass. 489 (1901).

62. Opinions of the Justices to the House of Representatives, 160 Mass. 586 (1894), at 594. For Holmes's view on powers versus prohibitions, see OWH to JBT, November 2, 1893, MDHM, 18-1.

63. OWH to Owen Wister, April 14, 1889, MDHM, 19-4; Memorial Sketch of Edward Jackson Holmes, EJHC, 2-4.

64. *LLH*, 1:195; Holmes Sr., *Mortal Antipathy*, 23.

65. OWH to Mrs. Charles S. Hamlin, October 12, 1930, MDHM, 15-16; Hale, "Afternoon with Holmes," 108; Dow, *Old Days*, 64.

66. *LLH*, 2:96.

67. OWH to James Bryce, November 5, 1894, MDHM, 13-17.

68. Davis, *History of Judiciary*, 177; Amelia Jackson Sargent will and trust accounts, OWHA, 6-5; statements of rent on Boston properties, July, 1904, OWHP, 55-8; account of sale of 12 Plympton St. and 7 Bow St. properties, Cambridge, September 13, 1901, OWHA, 6-6.

69. Probate appraisal, estate of Epes Sargent Dixwell, March 15, 1900, OWHA, 6-4; Bureau of Labor Statistics, *Consumer Spending*, 6.

70. OWH to CC, June 18, 1897, OWHC, 1-3; Thomas G. Corcoran in Louchheim, *New Deal*, 24.

71. OWH to NG, September 26, 1903, MDHM, 3-23; miscellaneous bills and receipts, 1895, OWHP, 28-1; receipt for house rent, Beverly Farms, A. O. Marshall to Justice Holmes, October 15, 1897, OWHP, 29-9; OWH to HJL, January 1, 1927, *H-L*, 2:911.

CHAPTER 9: Ideals and Doubts

1. Belknap, "Justice Holmes," 15.

2. OWH to FP, January 17, 1891, *H-P*, 1:34–35.

3. OWH to FP, March 22, 1891, *H-P*, 1:35; Tasker v. Stanley, 153 Mass. 148 (1891).

4. Debbins v. Old Colony Railroad Company, 154 Mass. 402 (1891); In re Welsh, 175 Mass. 68 (1900). On the court's institutional norms favoring unanimity, see Tushnet, "Holmes on Supreme Judicial Court," 978, 1002.
5. OWH to CC, May 20, 1897, MDHM, 13-23.
6. "Walbridge Abner Field," November 25, 1899, CW, 3:495.
7. Ibid., 497.
8. Ibid., 496; OWH to NG, August 3, 1893, MDHM, 3-15.
9. Belknap, OH, 12; OWH to CSRS, April 28, 1907, MDHM 17-38.
10. Hamilton v. West End Street Railway Company, 163 Mass. 199 (1895), at 200; American Waltham Watch Company v. United States Watch Company, 173 Mass. 85 (1899), at 87; Weston v. Barnicoat, 175 Mass. 454 (1900), at 458; Nash v. Minnesota Title Insurance and Trust Company, 163 Mass. 574 (1895), at 586; Ryalls v. Mechanics' Mills, 150 Mass. 190 (1889), at 194.
11. Merrill v. Peaslee, 146 Mass. 460 (1888), at 465.
12. OWH to FP, November 2, 1884, H-P, 1:26.
13. Commonwealth v. Pierce, 138 Mass. 165 (1884), at 175, 177–79.
14. Commonwealth v. Kennedy, 170 Mass. 18 (1897), at 20.
15. Nash v. Minnesota Title Insurance and Trust Company, 163 Mass. 574 (1895); Spade v. Lynn and Boston Railroad Company, 172 Mass. 488 (1899); Butler v. New York, New Haven, and Hartford Railroad Company, 177 Mass. 191 (1900).
16. OWH to Lady Pollock, April 11, 1897, H-P, 1:74; Commonwealth v. Sullivan, 146 Mass. 142 (1888).
17. OWH to NG, June 16, 1896, MDHM, 3-15.
18. OWH to Lady Pollock, April 12, 1901, MDHM, 30-9. This letter was omitted from the published Holmes-Pollock correspondence.
19. CC to OWH, Saturday [July] 4, [1896], OWHP, 15-3.
20. Entries for July 11, 15, 22, 27, Diary, 1896, OWHP, 57-26. ("It was in the middle of July that we went to the Exhibition and I noted that you had a quick eye for pictures": OWH to CC, July 6, 1897, MDHM, 13-24.)
21. Monagan, Grand Panjandrum, 71; Castletown, Papers, finding aid, p. 26; Castletown, Ego.
22. Letters from Clare to Bernard Castletown, Castletown, Papers, Ms 35,295(2–5). The arrangements for Castletown's mistress, Mrs. E. Palgrave, are described in Doneraile Papers, Ms 34,187(6).
23. Howe, "Letters of James to Holmes," 419–20; entry for August 16, Diary, 1896, OWHP, 57-26.
24. A brief contemporary description of the house and park during the Castle-

towns' time is in White, "Notes on Buttevant, Doneraile," III:46–49. I am
most grateful to Rosemary Collier, director of national historic properties
in Ireland's Office of Public Works, and to the staff at Doneraile Park for
allowing me to tour the interior of the house, which was under restoration
at the time of my visit in 2017.

25. CC to Bernard Castletown, September 6, 1896, Castletown, Papers, Ms
35,295(4); OWH to CC, January 29, 1897, and September 17, 1896,
MDHM, 13-23.

26. OWH to CC, August 22 and 23, 1896, OWHC, 1-1, and December 4,
1896, MDHM, 13-23; entries for August 23, 24, 27, Diary, 1896, OWHP,
57-26; Nancy J. B. Morton to MDH, June 3, 1942, MDHM, 22-28. A
brief biographical sketch of Gordon McCabe is in Gordon, *McCabe
Memoir.*

27. OWH to CC, September 5, 1896, OWHC, 1-1; December 19, 1896,
MDHM, 13-23.

28. OWH to CC, September 5, 1896, OWHC, 1-1; item for August 29, "Pr
Horses to Boston $12.00," Standley & Larcom, bill to Mrs. O. W. Holmes,
September 2, 1896, OWHP, 28-19. Holmes was listed among the passengers who arrived in New York on August 29 on the *Etruria*: "Arrivals
from Europe," *NYT*, August 30, 1896.

29. OWH to CC, September 17 and 30, November 21, and December 19,
1896, MDHM, 13-23.

30. John S. Monagan, "The Love Letters of Justice Holmes," *Boston Globe
Magazine*, March 24, 1985; Monagan, *Grand Panjandrum*, 71–94.

31. OWH to CC, December 4, 1896, MDHM, 13-23, and, October 7, 1896,
OWHC, 1-1.

32. OWH to CC, May 7, 1897, MDHM, 13-23. La Touche's letters, which
are in private hands, were the remarkable discovery of G. Edward White
and are quoted in White, *Justice Holmes*, 233–34, 236–37.

33. CC to Bernard Castletown, August 30, 1896, Castletown, Papers, Ms
35,295(4).

34. Ibid., September 6, 1896.

35. CC to OWH, n.d., OWHP, 15-3.

36. "In Favor of Strikers," *BDA*, May 29, 1895.

37. Vegelahn v. Guntner, 167 Mass. 92 (1896).

38. Ibid., at 106.

39. Ibid., at 105, 106.

40. Holmes, "Privilege, Malice," 3.

41. Vegelahn v. Guntner, at 107–8.

42. Holmes, "Path of the Law," 467.

43. OWH to HJL, February 19, 1920, *H-L*, 1:243; Holmes, "Path of the Law," 466.

44. OWH to CM, September 1, 1908, MDHM, 19-20; OWH to FP, May 26, 1919, *H-P*, 2:13.

45. Holmes, "Path of the Law," 461.

46. Ibid., 459–61; Holmes, *Common Law*, 110, 214. In his discussion of contracts on p. 317 of *The Common Law*, Holmes introduced the idea of a man with "no scruples" to illustrate that the only real consequence of a contractual condition is the "greater or lesser possibility of having to pay money."

47. Holmes, "Path of the Law," 459.

48. OWH to CC, January 11, 1897, MDHM, 13-23.

49. Horwitz, "Holmes in Legal Thought," 69.

50. Patnoude v. New York, New Haven, and Hartford Railroad Company, 180 Mass. 119 (1901).

51. American Waltham Watch Company v. United States Watch Company, 173 Mass. 85 (1899).

52. Horwitz, "Holmes in Legal Thought," 57.

53. Richard W. Hale to MDH, May 17, 1939, MDHM, 22-18; Holmes, dissenting opinion, Plant v. Woods, 176 Mass. 492 (1900), at 505.

54. OWH to CC, December 8, 1897, MDHM, 13-24; OWH to CC, March 5, 1897, MDHM, 13-23.

55. OWH to CC, June 3, 1897, MDHM, 13-23, and May 28, 1897, OWHC, 1-3; "Heroic Deed and Noble Cause Immortalized in Bronze," *Boston Globe*, June 1, 1897.

56. OWH to NG, July 25, 1897, MDHM, 3-16.

57. OWH to NG, September 2, 1895, MDHM, 3-15.

58. OWH to CC, January 10, 1898, MDHM, 13-24.

59. OWH to CC, March 1898, Doneraile Papers, Ms 34,166(1). I am very much obliged to Ralph Erskine for providing me copies of these letters in the National Library of Ireland from Holmes to Lady Castletown.

60. OWH to CC, April 1, 1898, OWHC, 1-4.

61. OWH to CC, April 15, June 6, 7, and 9, 1898, MDHM, 13-25.

62. OWH to NG, June 20, 1898, MDHM, 3-17; OWH to CC, June 18, 1898, MDHM, 13-25.

63. Entry for July 11, Diary, 1898, OWHP, 57-26; OWH to Lady Burghclere, September 17, 1898, MDHM, 13-21.

64. Entry for August 22, Diary, 1898, OWHP, 57-26.

65. OWH to CC, September 5, 1898, MDHM, 13-25; entries for August 25 and 27, Diary, 1898, OWHP, 57-26; OWH to FP, December 9, 1898, *H-P*, 1:89–90.

66. OWH to CC, September 5 and 8, 1898, MDHM, 13-25.

67. OWH to CC, May 19, 1899, OWHC, 1-5. Her letter is not extant, but Holmes quotes her words in his reply.

68. CC to Bernard Castletown, April 23, 1899, Castletown, Papers, Ms 35,295(5).

69. White, *Justice Holmes*, 243; Bernard Castletown to OWH, June 18, 1899, OWHP, 15-3.

70. Diary, 1901, OWHP, 58-1; OWH to NG, September 15, 1901, MDHM, 3-20.

71. OWH to NG, July 27, 1899, MDHM, 3-17.

72. OWH to EC, December 4, 1901, MDHM, 14-21.

73. Devlin, "Judges in Robes"; Causten Browne to OWH, January 15, 1901, OWHP, 58-15; Alfred Rodman Hussey to MDH, August 8, 1942, MDHM 22-29.

74. OWH to CSRS, July 19, 1902, MDHM, 17-38.

75. George Hoar to Henry Cabot Lodge, July 29, 1902, quoted in Garraty, "Holmes's Appointment," 297.

76. Hoar to Lodge, August 11, 1902, quoted in ibid., 299; Hoar to Lodge, August 7, 1902, MDHM, 22-25.

77. Eben S. Draper to Lodge, March 7, 1902, quoted in Garraty, "Holmes's Appointment," 293; Wagner, "Holmes and Roosevelt," 119–21.

78. Theodore Roosevelt to Lodge, July 10, 1902, Morison, *Letters of Roosevelt*, 3:288.

79. Ibid., 289.

80. OWH to NG, August 17, 1902, MDHM, 3-21.

81. Roosevelt to OWH, August 19, 1902, Morison, *Letters of Roosevelt*, 3:.315.

82. OWH to FP, May 17, 1925, *H-P*, 2:161; Garraty, "Holmes's Appointment," 295 and n. 10; Roosevelt to OWH, August 21, 1902, Morison, *Letters of Roosevelt*, 3:319.

CHAPTER 10: "So Great and So Different"

1. OWH to CSRS, September 8, 1902, MDHM, 17-38; OWH to John Chipman Gray, August 17, 1902, MDHM, 3-8.

2. OWH to CSRS, October 17, 1902, MDHM, 17-38.

3. Editorial, *New York Evening Post*, August 12, 1902, quoted in White, *Justice Holmes*, 306; OWH to FP, September 23, 1902, *H-P*, 1:106.

4. OWH to LE, March 25, 1927, *H-E*, 265.

5. Speech to Bar Association of Boston, March 7, 1900, *CW*, 3:498.
6. OWH to John Chipman Gray, August 17, 1902, MDHM, 3-8.
7. Address to the Chicago Bar Association, October 21, 1902, *CW*, 3:532; Address to Middlesex Bar Association, December 3, 1902, *CW*, 3:537.
8. King, *Fuller*, 287.
9. Address to Middlesex Bar Association, *CW*, 3:536.
10. Acheson, *Memoir*, 41–42.
11. Biddle, *Casual Past*, 271; Acheson, *Memoir*, 41.
12. Derby, "Recollections," 347.
13. Hofstedt, "Court Messengers," 260–61; Lowry, "Justice at Zero."
14. "Uncle Jim Burke," *Washington Bee*, January 5, 1907; information to author from Marshal's Office and Curator's research files, Supreme Court of the United States, January 2017; "Funeral of John Craig," *Washington Bee*, January 11, 1908; Derby, "Recollections," 347. I am very grateful to Matthew Hofstedt, Office of the Curator, U.S. Supreme Court, for providing me information from the Court's archives on Holmes's messengers and the history of the Court messengers.
15. Lowry, "Justice at Zero"; Schwartz, *History of Supreme Court*, 101; Baldwin, "Supreme Court Justices," 156.
16. Schwartz, *History of Supreme Court*, 101.
17. *JRG*, 81–82 and n. 319.
18. OWH to HJL, January 7, 1924, *H-L*, 1:579–80. The lunchbox is now in the OWH Object Collection at Harvard Law School.
19. *JRG*, 81.
20. Entry for November 28, 1933, Howe, Diary, 12–13; *JRG*, 80–81.
21. Acheson, *Memoir*, 56; Baldwin, "Supreme Court Justices," 159.
22. Butler, *Century at Bar*, 65–66.
23. OWH to EC, December 21, 1902, MDHM, 14-21.
24. Ibid., February 7, 1903.
25. John E. Lockwood interview, April 1, 1981, LJPP, 1-26; OWH to NG, March 2, 1903, MDHM, 3-22.
26. Tip-in notes, Otis v. Parker, No. 41, bound volume of opinions, 1902 term, OWHP.
27. Hughes, *Autobiographical Notes*, 173–74; Urofsky, *Brandeis*, 475; McCormack, "Law Clerk's Recollections," 714.
28. OWH to FP, April 4, 1909, *H-P*, 1:154.
29. OWH to CSRS, January 10, 1903, MDHM, 17-38; OWH to Melville W. Fuller, February 5 and 6, 1903, quoted in King, *Fuller*, 291.
30. Derby, "Recollections," 348.

31. Joseph Choate, quoted in Friedman and Israel, eds., *Justices of Supreme Court*, 2:1494.

32. King, *Fuller*, 125.

33. Notes of Reminiscences, 2, WBLM; OWH to ASG, October 14, 1911, MDHM, 15-9; *JRG*, 66–67.

34. "Justice Harlan's Harrangue," *The Nation*, May 30, 1895, 417, quoted in King, *Fuller*, 215–16.

35. OWH to EC, March 3, 1903, MDHM, 14-21; *JRG*, 66.

36. *JRG*, 82 n. 321; OWH to NG, January 4 and 16, 1903, MDHM, 3-21.

37. Acheson, *Memoir*, 65; OWH to FF, March 28, 1922, *H-F*, 138.

38. Schwartz, *History of Supreme Court*, 180–82; People v. Gillson, 109 N.Y. 389 (1888), at 398.

39. Friedman and Israel, *Justices of Supreme Court*, 2:1577, 1603.

40. King, *Fuller*, 313.

41. OWH to EC, November 27, 1904, MDHM, 14-21.

42. OWH to William L. Putnam, July 12, 1910, in "Judge Putnam's Recollections," 529; King, *Fuller*, 134.

43. King, *Fuller*, 291.

44. Bleistein v. Donaldson Lithographing Company (1903).

45. OWH to EC, February 7, 1903, MDHM, 14-21.

46. Belknap, OH, 15; OWH to ASG, January 10, 1911, MDHM, 15-9; OWH to NG, January 13, 1927, MDHM, 4-16; "Dixie Belles Radiant," *WP*, January 22, 1908.

47. OWH to NG, February 8, 1904, MDHM, 3-23; Hale, *Table Talk*, 16.

48. OWH to NG, May 10, 1892, MDHM, 3-14; McCabe in "Presentation of Price Library," 11; OWH to William Gordon McCabe, June 19, 1905, McCabe, Papers, box 2; Donald Hiss in Louchheim, *New Deal*, 40.

49. Acheson, *Memoir*, 49.

50. OWH to EC, January 12, 1903, MDHM, 14-21.

51. OWH to NG, February 15, 1903, MDHM, 3-21; OWH to EC, February 7, 1903, MDHM, 14-21.

52. OWH to EC, January 25, 1903, MDHM, 14-21.

53. OWH to NG, February 8, 1904, MDHM, 3-23; OWH to CSRS, January 10, 1903, MDHM, 17-38.

54. "Justice Holmes Sighed," *WP*, January 31, 1904.

55. Memorandum of talk with Mrs. James B. Ayer, October 25, 1955, MDHM, 23-2; OWH to NG, February 15, 1903, MDHM, 3-21; Mrs. Holmes' Visiting Book, 1905–1909, OWHP, 55-10.

56. OWH to EC, January 12 and February 7, 1903, MDHM, 14-21.

57. Graham, *Washington*, 191; Herbert v. Shanley (1917); OWH to EC, July 31, 1919, MDHM, 14-22.

58. Graham, *Washington*, 191; Meyer, *Roots*, 171. The oft-mentioned story about Fanny and TR comes from Catherine Drinker Bowen's highly fictionalized 1943 biography of Holmes, *Yankee from Olympus*, but there is corroboration of Fanny's mordant observation about Washington wives in a letter Holmes wrote at the time: "My wife has seen tragedies—wives of men whom they had helped to arrive—and when they get here with their clothes they realize that now they are an encumbrance" (OWH to EC, February 7, 1903, MDHM, 14-21).

59. Biddle, *Casual Past*, 289–90.

60. Hale, *Table Talk*, 12.

61. Acheson, *Memoir*, 49, 55; Belknap, OH, 16; Archie Butt to Clara Butt, September 10, 1910, Butt, *Letters*, 2:508. Butt refers to Mrs. Holmes's "treatment of Mrs. Stonewall Jackson at the White House," but does not elaborate. Mrs. Jackson was one of the guests at a dinner at the White House that the Holmeses attended earlier that year ("Supreme Court Justices Dine at White House," *WP*, January 26, 1910).

62. Belknap, OH, 17–18.

63. OWH to NG, December 25, 1903, MDHM, 3-23, and May 8, 1910, MDHM, 3-32; OWH to CSRS, May 10, 1908, MDHM, 17-38.

64. OWH to Anna K. Codman, February 15, 1903, MDHM, 14-11; OWH to EC, January 24, 1904, MDHM, 14-21.

65. OWH to EC, January 12, 1903, MDHM, 14-21.

66. OWH to Anna K. Codman, January 20, 1904, MDHM, 14-11; "Marriage of Miss Brewer to Mr. Wellington Wells," *WP*, February 9, 1904; OWH to NG, February 8, 1904, MDHM, 3-23.

67. OWH to Codman, February 15, 1903, MDHM, 14-11; "New Belgian Minister to Wed Miss Clayton in Mexico," *WP*, November 19, 1901; CM to OWH, August 11, 19[?], OWHP, 20-15; OWH to CM, September 15, 1909, MDHM, 19-22.

68. Liebman, "Lewis Einstein"; *H-E*, xx.

69. *H-E*, v, xx–xxi.

70. OWH to NG, May 3, 1903, MDHM, 3-22.

71. Ibid., April 12, 1903.

72. OWH to EC, April 21 and February 7, 1903, MDHM, 14-21; Appendix I: Opinions of the Court, King, *Fuller*, 339.

73. OWH to NG, May 3, 1903, MDHM, 3-22.

74. OWH to EC, February 8, 1904, MDHM, 14-21.

CHAPTER 11: Due Process

1. OWH to NG, July 11, 1903, MDHM, 3-22; engagement book [1903], OWHP, 58-2; miscellaneous receipts, 1903, OWHP, 13-1. Holmes's engagement book for his 1903 trip to England is listed in the catalog to the OWHP as "c. 1898," however the dates and days of the week he recorded match 1903, as do the details of the trip.

2. OWH to NG, August 14, 1903, MDHM, 3-22, and September 2, 1903, MDHM, 3-23.

3. OWH to Lucy Clifford, January 21, 1928, MDHM, 14-10; OWH to ES, November 28, 1908, MDHM, 17-28. Holmes made similar remarks about the unhumility of Christians in OWH to NG, May 8, 1910, MDHM, 3-32, and OWH to Morris R. Cohen, May 27, 1917, Cohen, "Correspondence," 9.

4. OWH to LE, October 12, 1914, H-E, 101.

5. OWH to LE, August 8, 1925, H-E, 246.

6. OWH to Patrick Sheehan, December 27, 1903, and February 1904, H-S, 11, 12.

7. OWH to Sheehan, January 2, 1904, H-S, 12.

8. Sheehan to OWH, October 6, 1912, H-S, 46, 48.

9. OWH to LE, May 19, 1917, H-E, 141; OWH to EC, February 25, 1904, MDHM, 14-21; OWH to ASG, July 29, 1912, MDHM, 15-9.

10. OWH to NG, April 12, 1903, MDHM, 3-22.

11. Miscellaneous receipts, 1903–1904, OWHP, 31-2, 31-3; OWH to NG, October 18, November 1, and December 25, 1903, MDHM, 3-23.

12. Miscellaneous receipts, 1903–1904, OWHP, 31-4; OWH to NG, October 18, 1903, MDHM, 3-23.

13. OWH to NG, September 26, 1903, MDHM, 3-23.

14. Frankfurter, "Constitutional Opinions," 683.

15. Frank, "Learned Hand," 685; Thayer, *Constitutional Law*, 12–14, 18.

16. Peckham, dissenting opinion, People v. Budd, 117 N.Y. 1 (1899), at 45, 69, 71; Schwartz, *History of Supreme Court*, 181.

17. Urofsky, *Dissent*, 86–87.

18. Slaughter-House Cases (1873).

19. Harlan, dissenting opinion, Civil Rights Cases (1883).

20. In re Jacobs, 98 N.Y. 98 (1885).

21. Schwartz, *History of Supreme Court*, 180.

22. Holden v. Hardy (1898).

23. OWH to HJL, October 23, 1926, H-L, 2:888.

24. Posner, *How Judges Think*, 120.

25. OWH to ASG, December 18, 1914, MDHM, 15-9.

26. Posner, *Law and Literature*, 346–47.
27. Holmes, dissenting opinion, Lochner v. New York (1905).
28. Missouri, Kansas & Texas Railway Company v. May (1904).
29. JBT quoted in Frank, "Learned Hand," 685–86.
30. Louisville & Nashville Railroad Company v. Barber Asphalt Paving Company (1905).
31. Martin v. District of Columbia (1907); OWH to John C. H. Wu, November 4, 1923, Wu, "Letters," 266.
32. Holmes, dissenting opinion, Union Refrigerator Transit Company v. Kentucky (1905).
33. Fiss, *1888–1910*, 143; OWH to ASG, January 10, 1911, MDHM, 15-9. He repeated these views about the Sherman Act many times, for example in OWH to NG, June 28, 1915, MDHM, 3-37.
34. OWH to Franklin Ford, April 6, 1911, Burton, *Progressive Masks*, 84; OWH to LE, October 28, 1912, *H-E*, 74.
35. Fiss, *1888–1910*, 138 n. 94. ("The newspaper story as to the Presdt. and me is pure fiction so far as any communication to me goes": OWH to NG, March 21, 1904, MDHM, 3-24.)
36. OWH to NG, March 21, 1904, MDHM, 3-24; Henry Adams to Elizabeth Cameron, March 20, 1904, Ford, *Letters of Henry Adams*, 429.
37. OWH to John G. Palfrey, April 1, 1904, MDHM, 17-10; OWH to EC, March 18, 1904, MDHM, 14-21.
38. "White House Guests Hear Mrs. Batcheller Sing," *WP*, April 4, 1904; OWH to CM, February 19, 1908, MDHM, 19-19.
39. OWH to FP, February 9, 1921, *H-P*, 2:63–64.
40. Theodore Roosevelt to Henry Cabot Lodge, September 4, 1906, MDHM, 22-23.
41. Walker, "Beef Trust," 499; Swift and Company v. United States (1905).
42. OWH to ASG, February 10, 1905, MDHM, 15-8.
43. Ibid., June 15, 1908; Hudson County Water Company v. McCarter (1908).
44. Georgia v. Tennessee Copper Company (1907).
45. OWH to NG, May 30, 1908, and January 4, 1909, MDHM, 3-31.
46. OWH to ES, December 11, 1908, MDHM, 17-28.
47. OWH to CM, November 18, 1908, MDHM, 19-21; OWH to CSRS, February 1, 1908, MDHM, 17-38.
48. OWH to CM, November 18, 1908, MDHM, 19-21.
49. OWH to NG, July 23, 1904, MDHM, 3-25.
50. Fanny Holmes to OWH, n.d., OWHP, 18-19; entry for June 11, Diary, 1907, OWHP, 58-1.

51. OWH to CM, August 14, 1907, MDHM, 19-18; OWH to NG, September 15, 1907, MDHM, 3-30.
52. OWH to CM, July 8, 1907, MDHM, 19-18.
53. OWH to NG, September 15, 1907, MDHM, 3-30.
54. OWH to CSRS, October 4, 1907, MDHM, 17-38.

CHAPTER 12: 1720 Eye Street

1. OWH to NG, December 25 and November 1, 1903, MDHM, 3-23.
2. Ibid., November 1, 1903.
3. OWH to CC, June 12, 1917, Doneraile Papers, Ms 34,166(1).
4. OWH to EC, February 24, 1903, 14-21; OWH to ES, April 24, 1909, MDHM, 17-28; OWH to NG, November 1, 1903, MDHM, 3-23.
5. Hiss, *Recollections*, 48–49; OWH to LE, May 25, 1918, *H-E*, 166.
6. Derby, "Recollections," 346–47; Sutherland, "Recollections," 20.
7. OWH to NG, December 25, 1903, MDHM, 3-23, and July 23, 1904, MDHM, 3-25.
8. A. J. Sargent will, OWHA, 6-5; OWH to O.W.H. Upham, May 25, 1901, and account of sale of property, 12 Plympton St., Cambridge, September 13, 1901, OWHA, 6-6.
9. OWH to CSRS, March 6, 1908, MDHM, 17-38; "Honor to Justices," *WP*, January 24, 1908; "Social and Personal," *WP*, March 2, 1905; notes of talk with Dorothy Vaughan, May 18, 1948, MDHM, 22-27; Thompson, "Thomas Wayland Vaughan."
10. Inventory of 1720 Eye Street, Estate of OWH, EJHC, 1-13.
11. Ibid.; Sutherland, "Recollections," 21. Fanny listed the household pets in a letter to ES, November 9, 1909, MDHM, 17-28.
12. List of dinner guests during Washington years, OWHP, 55-9.
13. Monagan, *Grand Panjandrum*, 32; Donald Hiss in Louchheim, *New Deal*, 34; Hiss, *Laughing Last*, 59.
14. Canceled checks, Riggs Bank, 1902–1935, OWHP, 35-8 to 45-1; miscellaneous receipts, 1900–1935, OWHP, 30-1 to 35-7.
15. Alger Hiss interview, 19, JSMP, 1-8; James Rowe in Louchheim, *New Deal*, 44.
16. Peppers, "Horace Gray," 19–21.
17. *JRG*, 82–83.
18. OWH to Anna K. Codman, February 15, 1903, MDHM, 14-11.
19. OWH to NG, March 2, 1903, MDHM, 3-22, and November 5, 1905, MDHM, 3-28.
20. Derby, "Recollections," 349; OWH to FF, January 6, 1925, *H-F*, 178.

21. OWH to Arthur Sutherland, May 28 and April 2, 1927, quoted in Sutherland, "Recollections," 19; OWH to CM, October 7, 1909, MDHM, 19-23.
22. Derby, "Recollections," 349; Recollections of a Holmes Secretary, typescript, 4, WBLM.
23. Belknap, "Justice Holmes," 10; Belknap diary entries for November 19 and October 13, 1915, quoted in Messinger, "Holmes and His Law Clerks," 49.
24. Meeting of Holmes Secretaries: Notes of Reminiscences, 1, WBLM.
25. Monagan, *Grand Panjandrum*, 115; Bundy, OH, 62; Notes for a Talk on O.W.H., 2, WBLM; Sutherland, "Recollections," 21; OWH to CM, February 25, 1912, MDHM, 19-26.
26. Notes for a Talk on O.W.H., 2, WBLM; Donald Hiss in Louchheim, *New Deal*, 34.
27. Hiss, *Laughing Last*, 54; Monagan, *Grand Panjandrum*, 116.
28. Biddle, *Mr. Justice Holmes*, 148; Donald Hiss in Louchheim, *New Deal*, 41.
29. Belknap, "Justice Holmes," 3; Belknap, OH, 15–16.
30. OWH to FF, December 19, 1915, *H-F*, 40.
31. Bundy, OH, 62–63; Derby, "Recollections," 352.
32. Alger Hiss to FF, December 13, 1929, Frankfurter, Papers, reel 91; LDB to FF, December 11, 1929, *HBHS*, no. 397.
33. OWH to FF, January 6, 1925, *H-F*, 178; LDB to FF, December 17, 1929, *HBHS*, no. 398.
34. John E. Lockwood to FF, November 5, 1928, OWHP, 58-27; Belknap, "Justice Holmes," 3.
35. Belknap diary entry for November 9, 1915, quoted in Messinger, "Holmes and His Law Clerks," 50; Recollections of a Holmes Secretary, typescript, 4, WBLM; Bundy, OH, 67.
36. Bundy, OH, 66; Biddle, *Casual Past*, 271–72.
37. Biddle, *Casual Past*, 272.
38. Belknap et al., "Remembrances of Holmes," 392.
39. Biddle, *Casual Past*, 281; Hiss, *Recollections*, 49–50.
40. Hiss, *Laughing Last*, 54; Alger Hiss in Louchheim, *New Deal*, 25; John E. Lockwood to FF, May 24, 1929, Frankfurter, Papers, reel 91; H. Chapman Rose to OWH, October 23, 1932, OWHP, 59-1.
41. Messinger, "Holmes and His Law Clerks," 53–54, 63–64 nn. 54–57.
42. Leach, *Recollections*, 4.
43. OWH to CM, December 18, 1910, MDHM, 19-25; OWG to ASG, April 26, 1910, MDHM, 15-8.

44. OWH to William L. Putnam, July 12, 1910, in "Judge Putnam's Recollections," 528–29.

45. OWH to CM, July 14, 1910, MDHM, 19-24; Monagan, *Grand Panjandrum*, 107; OWH to ES, July 11, 1910, MDHM, 17-28.

46. OWH to ASG, September 4, 1910, MDHM, 15-8; OWH to CM, August 31, 1910, MDHM, 19-24.

47. *TCWJ*, 2:250–51; OWH to LE, June 17, 1908, *H-E*, 35, and June 1, 1905, *H-E*, 16.

48. OWH to ES, September 24, 1910, MDHM, 17-28.

49. Ibid.; OWH to ASG, September 4, 1910, MDHM, 15-8, and October 14, 1911, MDHM, 15-9.

50. OWH to ASG, September 4, 1910, MDHM, 15-8; Pringle, *Taft*, 1:533.

51. Pringle, *Taft*, 1:535.

52. OWH to ASG, January 10, 1911, MDHM, 15-9; Pringle, *Taft*, 1:535.

53. OWH to NG, December 15, 1910, MDHM, 3-33.

54. OWH to LE, December 19, 1910, *H-E*, 57–58.

55. The imaginative account of Holmes's 1909 trip to England in Novick, *Honorable Justice*, 293, has Fanny accompanying him. In fact she stayed home. Holmes wrote to a friend on his return to the United States, "I . . . came back in three weeks, not to be away from Mrs. Holmes longer than I could help" (OWH to Kaneko Kentaro, August 2, 1909, Kanda and Gifford, "Kaneko Correspondence," 297).

     What Fanny's 1908 operation was for is unclear from the few letters that refer to it: Fanny Holmes to OWH, May 11, 1908, OWHP, 18-19 ("I suggest that your next visit should be on Thursday instead of Wednesday as my stitches are to come out on Wednesday") and OWH to ES, June 24 and August 22, 1908, MDHM, 17-28 ("Mrs. Holmes is all right again. I was scared but it turned out that there was no need to be"; "Mrs. Holmes is ever so much better, though the pulldown was more lasting than I expected").

56. OWH to Kaneko Kentaro, August 2, 1909, Kanda and Gifford, "Kaneko Correspondence," 296; OWH to NG, September 28, 1909, MDHM, 3-32.

57. OWH to LE, December 19, 1910, *H-E*, 58; OWH to ASG, May 16, 1909, MDHM, 15-8.

58. OWH to CM, December 18, 1910, MDHM, 19-25.

59. Ibid.; Patrick Sheehan to OWH, March 25, 1911, *H-S*, 39.

60. Bernard Castletown to CC, June 3, and July 2, 1912, Doneraile Papers, Ms 34,166(3).

61. OWH to CC, April 14, 1912, Doneraile Papers, Ms 34,166(1).

62. Ibid., April 21, 1912.
63. OWH to ASG, April 5, 1913, MDHM, 15-9; OWH to NG, June 5, 1913, MDHM, 3-34.
64. OWH to NG, October 12, 1913, MDHM, 3-35; OWH to LE, October 2, 1913, *H-E*, 80.
65. OWH to ASG, November 9, 1913, MDHM, 15-9.
66. OWH to ES, June 9, 1912, MDHM, 17-29.
67. Phillips, *Frankfurter Reminisces*, 4–5, 16, 19.
68. Ibid., 35–38; Snyder, *House of Truth*, 8–9.
69. Phillips, *Frankfurter Reminisces*, 17; OWH to HJL, November 25, 1916, and July 30, 1920, *H-L*, 1:37, 272; Lash, *Diaries of Frankfurter*, 30.
70. FF to John Chipman Gray, November 27, 1911, quoted in Snyder, *House of Truth*, 22.
71. OWH to FF, August 14, 1916, *H-F*, 56; OWH to CM, April 9, 1918, MDHM, 20-7; OWH to HJL, May 8, 1918, *H-L*, 1:153.
72. O'Connell and Dart, "House of Truth," 79–81; Snyder, *House of Truth*, 33.
73. Phillips, *Frankfurter Reminisces*, 105; Snyder, *House of Truth*, 61.
74. Phillips, *Frankfurter Reminisces*, 106; Snyder, *House of Truth*, 1–2.
75. O'Connell and Dart, "House of Truth," 79.
76. OWH to FF, March 27, 1917, *H-F*, 70; OWH to John H. Wigmore, November 19, 1915, MDHM, 18-14; OWH to LE, November 24, 1912, *H-E*, 75.
77. OWH to ES, November 12, 1914, MDHM, 17-29; OWH to LE, May 26, 1926, *H-E*, 254; OWH to CM, April 9, 1908, MDHM, 19-19.
78. OWH to LE, February 23, 1919, *H-E*, 183; memorandum of talk with FF, January 2, 1964, MDHM, 22-26.
79. OWH to NG, July 23, 1904, MDHM, 3-25; OWH to CM, September 28, 1919, MDHM, 20-8; OWH to NG, October 12, 1913, MDHM, 3-35; Monagan, *Grand Panjandrum*, 35.
80. Expense account, James Doherty, June 10, 1930, OWHP, 35-2.
81. OWH to ES, July 16, 1908, MDHM, 17-28; OWH to John G. Palfrey, July 17, 1908, MDHM, 17-10; OWH to ES, August 29, 1925, MDHM, 17-30 (the autograph letter, in OWHA, 1-15, includes a hand-drawn map of the arrangement of the property).
82. OWH to NG, June 22, 1918, MDHM, 3-38; OWH to ES, July 13, 1924, MDHM, 17-30, and July 30, 1908, MDHM, 17-28.
83. OWH to ES, September 5, 1915, MDHM, 17-29; OWH to HJL, June 11, 1920, *H-L*, 1:268.
84. OWH to ES, September 24, 1911, MDHM, 17-28 (Dante); OWH to CM,

July 15, 1911, MDHM, 19-25 (Oxford Book); OWH to CSRS, August 4, 1914, MDHM, 17-39 (Descartes); OWH to CM, September 21, 1912, MDHM, 19-27 (Epictetus); OWH to LE, April 28, 1923, *H-E*, 214 (Montaigne); OWH to ES, March 9, 1923, MDHM, 17-29 (Spinoza); OWH to LE, August 19, 1909, *H-E*, 50 (James); OWH to FP, August 2, 1923, *H-P*, 2:120 (Austen).

85. OWH to LE, September 26, 1907, *H-E*, 31 (Tolstoy); OWH to LE, February 5, 1923, *H-E*, 210 (Dickens); OWH to NG, October 18, 1903, MDHM, 3-23 (French novels); OWH to EC, September 3, 1919, MDHM, 14-22 (Buchan).

86. OWH to EC, November 1, 1929, MDHM, 14-23; OWH to CSRS, August 4, 1914, MDHM, 17-39.

87. OWH to CM, October 7, 1909, MDHM, 19-23.

88. OWH to LE, September 20, 1926, *H-E*, 261; OWH to Leslie Scott, October 13, 1907, MDHM, 17-31.

CHAPTER 13: Holmes Dissenting

1. WHT to Horace H. Lurton, May 22, 1909, quoted in Pringle, *Taft*, 1:529–30.

2. Pringle, *Taft*, 2:854.

3. *JRG*, 9.

4. Acheson, *Memoir*, 70; Hughes, *Autobiographical Notes*, 171.

5. *JRG*, 40–43; Friedman and Israel, *Justices of Supreme Court*, 3:1973–74.

6. OWH to FP, February 24, 1923, *H-P*, 2:113; OWH to FF, December 9, 1924, *H-F*, 177.

7. OWH to CM, February 18, 1911, MDHM, 19-25.

8. OWH to ASG, December 18, 1914, MDHM, 15-9; OWH to NG, January 4, 1909, and Christmas 1908, MDHM, 3-31.

9. OWH to FP, February 6, 1926, *H-P*, 2:175; OWH to FF, November 30, 1919, *H-F*, 77; Hughes, *Autobiographical Notes*, 173.

10. OWH to FP, February 6, 1926, *H-P*, 2:175; OWH to NG, May 5, 1928, MDHM, 4-19.

11. Belknap, "Justice Holmes," 5; Friedman and Israel, *Justices of Supreme Court*, 3:1773; Acheson, *Memoir*, 66.

12. *JRG*, 69; Acheson, *Memoir*, 66; OWH to HJL, November 23, 1926, *H-L*, 2:896, and January 4, 1925, *H-L*, 1:693.

13. OWH to ASG, July 5, 1914, MDHM, 15-9; OWH to CM, January 3, 1912, MDHM, 19-26.

14. OWH to FF, October 24, 1920, *H-F*, 95.

15. Tip-in notes, First National Bank of Decatur v. Henry, No. 221, bound volume of opinions, 1907 term, OWHP.
16. OWH to William H. Moody, September 30, 1914, quoted in *JRG*, 234.
17. Ibid.; *JRG*, 232–37.
18. No. 481, bound volume of opinions, 1913 Term, OWHP.
19. McCormack, "Law Clerk's Recollections," 714.
20. Zane, "Legal Heresy," 431, 436 n. 17, 438–41 n. 23.
21. Hughes, *Autobiographical Notes*, 173.
22. OWH to NG, March 18, 1911, MDHM, 3-34.
23. Gompers v. United States (1914).
24. OWH to LE, May 20, 1921, *H-E*, 195; OWH to FP, July 15, 1906, *H-P*, 1:130; Acheson, *Memoir*, 61–62.
25. Acheson, *Memoir*, 62; Standard Oil Company of New Jersey v. United States (1911); OWH to NG, March 18, 1911, MDH, 3-34.
26. OWH to LE, May 20, 1921, *H-E*, 195–96; OWH to ASG, June 7, 1914, MDHM, 15-9.
27. OWH to CSRS, April 16, 1914, MDHM, 17-39.
28. OWG to NG, April 22, 1914, MDHM, 3-35.
29. *JRG*, 946; Post, "Dissent in Taft Court," 1284, 1349 n. 252.
30. ZoBell, "Division of Opinion," 190–94; Urofsky, *Dissent*, 40, 47–49; Henry Billings Brown quoted in ibid., 10.
31. Sunstein, "Unanimity and Disagreement," 773–74, 778–79.
32. King, *Fuller*, 339–41; Post, "Dissent in Taft Court," 1386; Cushman, "Inside Taft Court," 74–76.
33. July 6, 1924, B-F, 330; Holmes, dissenting opinion, Federal Trade Commission v. Beech-Nut Packing Company (1922).
34. July 1 and 3, 1923, B-F, 314, 317.
35. OWH to HJL, November 10, 1923, *H-L*, 1:560; Post, "Dissent in Taft Court," 1350 n. 255.
36. *JRG*, 240; McKenna, dissenting opinion, Marcus Brown Holding Company, Inc. v. Feldman (1921); McKenna, dissenting opinion, Block v. Hirsh (1921); McKenna, dissenting opinion, The Western Maid (1922).
37. *JRG*, 239–41.
38. *JRG*, 238; OWH to FF, June 22, 1920, *H-F*, 94; tip-in notes, Southern Pacific Company v. Jensen, No. 280, bound volume of opinions, 1916 Term, OWHP, quoted in *JRG*, 238–39.
39. OWH to NG, May 5, 1928, MDHM, 4-19; OWH to CM, January 27, 1928, MDHM, 20-26.
40. Hughes quoted in Urofsky, *Dissent*, 12.
41. Freedman, "Habeas Corpus," 1483–84.

42. Ibid., 1484.
43. OWH to CC, November 28, 1914, OWHC, 1-5; "Justice Holmes's Opinion," *NYT*, November 27, 1914.
44. OWH to CM, July 6, 1915, MDHM, 20-2.
45. Holmes, dissenting opinion, Frank v. Mangum (1915).
46. OWH to LE, April 10, 1915, *H-E*, 112.
47. OWH to NG, February 21, 1915, MDHM, 3-37; OWH to John Chipman Gray, February 21, 1915, MDHM, 3-10; OWH to CM, February 28, 1915, MDHM, 20-2.
48. "Police News Notes of a Day," *WP*, June 23, 1915; "Deaths Reported," *WP*, June 25, 1915; OWH to CM, July 6, 1915, MDHM, 20-2.
49. OWH to CM, July 6, 1915, MDHM, 20-2; OWH to ES, July 13, 1915, MDHM, 17-29.
50. Leo Frank to OWH, July 10, 1915, OWHP, 17-26.
51. Memorandum of talk with FF, August 10, 1964, MDHM, 22-26.
52. OWH to CM, July 6, 1915, MDHM, 20-2; May 1, 1910, MDHM, 19-24; February 28, 1915, MDHM, 20-2.
53. Snyder, *House of Truth*, 101–2.
54. OWH to ES, March 10, 1916, MDHM, 17-29; OWH to CM, March 10, 1916, MDHM, 20-4.
55. OWH to ES, March 7, 1915, MDHM, 17-29; Snyder, *House of Truth*, 3; OWH to ES, November 12, 1914, MDHM, 17-29.
56. OWH to HJL, September 7, 1916, *H-L*, 1:17; Editorial Notes, *New Republic*, January 30, 1915, 4; Editorial Notes, *New Republic*, April 24, 1915, 290.
57. "To Justice Holmes," *New Republic*, March 11, 1916, 156.
58. Urofsky, *Brandeis*, 73–74, 154.
59. Ibid., 116–17, 134–35, 281–83, 451.
60. Ibid., 438, 445.
61. OWH to CSRS, May 13, 1916, MDHM, 17-39.
62. Urofksy, *Brandeis*, 459.
63. Ibid., 174, 267.
64. Ibid., 219–20.
65. Peppers, "Brandeis and His Clerks," 73–74.
66. Acheson, *Memoir*, 47; Marquis Childs interview, LJPP, 1-5; Peppers, "Brandeis and His Clerks," 77.
67. HJL to OWH, April 19, 1924, *H-L*, 1:612; LDB to HJL, February 29, 1920, MDHM, 25-18.
68. Urofsky, *Brandeis*, 565–66; Mary Donnellan interview, LJPP, 1-10.

69. OWH to CC, August 27, 1916, Doneraile Papers, Ms 34,166(1).

70. Memorandum of conversation with Austin Clark, May 1948, MDHM, 22-27. Fanny's anti-Semitism was noted by several of their friends. Charlie Curtis's sister-in-law wrote to Holmes after Fanny's death, "Whenever I find myself talking to a Jew whatever kind of passport he may carry I laugh as I remember what dear Mrs. Holmes used to say to you. You said, 'She calls them Keiks and how can I bother with them, but I never notice their noses, it's their conversation I like!!!' It's so true for surely they talk better than any lot of people in the world": Eleanor Roelker Palffy to OWH, March 7, 1931, OWHP, 21-16.

71. OWH to NG, March 5, 1921, MDHM, 4-3.

72. *JRG*, 353.

73. Federal district judge Robert L. Carter, who was a law student at Howard University in 1938 when the school's dean argued a racial discrimination case before the Court, attended the oral argument and witnessed McReynolds's behavior: Robert L. Carter, "The Long Road to Equality," *The Nation*, May 3, 2004. The wife of Erwin Griswold, when he was a young attorney working in the solicitor general's office, was present in Court to see McReynolds's similar treatment of Mabel Walker Willebrandt, who was assistant U.S. attorney general from 1921 to 1929: Harriet Ford Griswold, "Justices of the Supreme Court of the United States I Have Known," *Supreme Court Historical Society Quarterly*, 8:4 (1987): 7–8.

74. Jantzen, "McReynolds and Group Photograph"; *JRG*, 354.

75. Tip-in notes, Evans v. Gore, No. 654, bound volume of opinions, 1919 term, OWHP, quoted in *JRG*, 354.

76. *JRG*, 353; July 3, 1923, B-F, 317.

77. Bunting v. Oregon (1917); Phillips, *Frankfurter Reminisces*, 101–2.

78. OWH to HJL, January 12, 1921, *H-L*, 1:304.

79. OWH to FP, June 14, 1918, *H-P*, 1:267.

80. OWH to Lady Askwith, September 18, 1914, MDHM, 13-1.

81. OWH to CM, August 23, 1914, MDHM, 19-29.

82. Otto von Gierke to OWH, October 1914, OWHP, 17-28; OWH to CSRS, November 12, 1914, MDHM, 17-39.

83. OWH to Margaret Bevan, August 19, 1913, OWHA, 1-1; OWH to CSRS, November 12, 1914, MDHM, 17-39.

84. OWH to FF, March 27, 1917, *H-F*, 70; Sutherland, "Recollections," 22.

85. OWH to CM, April 9, 1918, MDHM, 20-7; OWH to LE, March 10, 1918, *H-E*, 163, and September 2, 1914, *H-E*, 100.

86. OWH to CM, April 9, 1918, MDHM, 20-7.
87. OWH to LE, June 13 and July 11, 1918, *H-E*, 167, 168.

CHAPTER 14: Free Speech

1. Gunther, *Learned Hand*, 137; Snyder, *House of Truth*, 114.
2. Gunther, *Learned Hand*, 7–8, 27.
3. Ibid., 2, 8.
4. Ibid., 8, 79, 156, 159, 504.
5. Masses Publishing Company v. Patten, 244 F. 535 (S.D.N.Y. 1917).
6. LH to Zechariah Chafee Jr., December 3, 1920, in Gunther, "Hand and First Amendment," 768; Masses Publishing Company v. Patten, 246 F. 24 (2d Cir. 1917).
7. Gunther, "Hand and First Amendment," 731–32; LH to OWH, June 22, 1918, in ibid., 756.
8. OWH to Franklin Ford, November 21, 1915, Burton, *Progressive Masks*, 109; OWH to HJL, June 1, 1927, *H-L*, 2:948.
9. LH to OWH, June 22, 1918, in Gunther, "Hand and First Amendment," 755–56.
10. OWH to LH, June 24, 1918, in ibid., 756–57.
11. LH to Charles P. Curtis Jr., January 14, 1954, Hand, Papers, 86-21.
12. Kramnick and Sheerman, *Laski*, 87.
13. Ibid., 66–68.
14. HJL to OWH, October 23, 1927, *H-L*, 2:990; OWH to FP, February 18, 1917, *H-P*, 1:243; HJL to OWH, September 10, 1927, *H-L*, 2:979; HJL to OWH, December 28, 1920, *H-L*, 1:302. The reviews of the Holmes-Laski letters by Abel, Curtis, and West all called attention to Laski's embroidery of the truth.
15. Shils, *Portraits*, 192–93.
16. Curtis, Review of *Holmes-Laski*, 268; entry for January 22, 1931, Webb, Diaries.
17. OWH to HJL, January 15, 1925, *H-L*, 1:702, and October 24, 1928, *H-L*, 2:1105; HJL to OWH, November 13, 1928, *H-L*, 2:1110.
18. Kramnick and Sheerman, *Laski*, 220–21.
19. Woolf, *Downhill*, 229–30.
20. Shils, *Portraits*, 200.
21. OWH to FP, February 18, 1917, *H-P*, 1:243. On Laski's marriage and estrangement from his family, see Kramnick and Sheerman, *Laski*, 46–47, 185–87; HJL to OWH, July 18, 1920, *H-L*, 1:271.
22. OWH to HJL, June 25, 1918, *H-L*, 1:158; June 28, 1918, MDHM, 4-38;

and August 10, 1918, *H-L*, 1:162; HJL to OWH, August 27, 1918, *H-L*, 1:163.

23. Chafee, "Laski and the Law Review," 1399–1400.

24. Kramnick and Sheerman, *Laski*, 91–94, 101–4.

25. HJL to OWH, July 5, 1918, *H-L*, 1:159–60; OWH to HJL, July 7, 1918, *H-L*, 1:160–61.

26. OWH to HJL, June 25 and August 10, 1918, *H-L*, 1:158, 162. On August 19 Holmes wrote Laski, "Don't forget to send me the law book you mentioned containing accounts of the fundamental theories of various who philosophized about the law" (MDHM, 4-38). Holmes's 1918 reading list identifies the book in question: "(F. Gény.) *Science et technique en droit privé positif.* Vol. 2. Article written on Natural Law (August)" (Holmes, *Black Book*, 125).

27. OWH to FP, October 31, 1918, *H-P*, 1:271; HJL to OWH, August 27, 1918, *H-L*, 1:163.

28. Holmes, "Natural Law," 41, 42.

29. Ibid., 40.

30. OWH to LE, September 28, 1918, *H-E*, 171–72; OWH to HJL, September 18, 1918, *H-L*, 1:164–65.

31. OWH to FP, October 31, 1918, *H-P*, 1:270.

32. Healy, *Great Dissent*, 88–91; Debs v. United States (1919).

33. Commonwealth v. Davis, 162 Mass. 510 (1894); McAuliffe v. Mayor and Board of Aldermen of New Bedford, 155 Mass. 216 (1892).

34. Burt v. Advertiser Newspaper Company, 154 Mass. 238 (1891); Cowley v. Pulsifer, 137 Mass. 392 (1884).

35. Commonwealth v. Blanding, 20 Mass. 304 (1825).

36. Ibid., at 313–14, 317.

37. Peck v. Tribune Company (1909).

38. "I am catspawed by Brandeis to do another dissent on burning themes": OWH to HJL, December 3, 1918, *H-L*, 1:176. The only important case Holmes wrote a dissent to that month was *Baltzer*.

39. Tip-in notes, Baltzer v. United States, No. 320, bound volume of opinions, 1918 term, OWHP.

40. Ibid., handwritten returns of the justices. Novick, "Unrevised Holmes," 332, interprets the first two words of White's note to read "Please stall," which not only seems unlikely on its face but makes no semantic or syntactical sense with the words that follow.

41. "Orders New Trial in Espionage Cases," *WP*, December 17, 1918. Healy, *Great Dissent*, 73–75, makes a circumstantial but persuasive argument that Brandeis leaked word of Holmes's planned dissent.

42. OWH to CM, April 4, 1919, MDHM, 20-8.

43. OWH to LH, February 25, 1919, in Gunther, "Hand and First Amendment," 758.

44. Commonwealth v. Kennedy, 170 Mass. 18 (1897); Commonwealth v. Peaslee, 177 Mass. 267 (1901).

45. Schenck v. United States (1919).

46. HJL to OWH, March 18, 1919, *H-L*, 1:191; LH to OWH, [late March], 1919, in Gunther, "Hand and First Amendment," 758–59.

47. Freund, "Debs Case"; OWH to Herbert Croly, enclosure in OWH to HJL, May 13, 1919, *H-L*, 1:202–4.

48. Gunther, "Hand and First Amendment," 745–46; Chafee, "Freedom of Speech."

49. Auerbach, "Chafee," 521–22.

50. Chafee, "Speech in War Time," 944.

51. LH to Zechariah Chafee Jr., January 2, 1921, in Gunther, "Hand and First Amendment," 770.

52. OWH to CM, April 4, 1919, MDHM, 20-8.

53. OWH to FP, April 27, 1919, *H-P*, 2:11; OWH to LE, April 5, 1919, *H-E*, 184.

54. "36 Were Marked as Victims by Bomb Conspirators"; "Sees Bomb Sent in Revenge," *NYT*, May 1, 1919.

55. OWH to LE, May 22, 1919, and March 25, 1927, *H-E*, 186, 265; OWH to FP, June 17, 1919, *H-P*, 2:15.

56. Kramnick and Sheerman, *Laski*, 149; Healy, *Great Dissent*, 241; Snyder, *House of Truth*, 301.

57. OWH to HJL, April 4, 1919, *H-L*, 1:193. Some of Holmes's words were omitted by Mark Howe in the published version of this letter: see the complete typescript in MDHM, 5-1.

58. FF to OWH, May 15, 1920, *H-F*, 89; HJL to OWH, May 11, 1919, *H-L*, 1:201.

59. Kramnick and Sheerman, *Laski*, 128; "The Boston Police Strike," *Harvard Alumni Bulletin*, October 23, 1919, 106.

60. HJL to OWH, May 15, 1919, *H-L*, 1:204; OWH to HJL, May 13 and 18, 1919 (quoting his letter to the Law School Association in support of Pound), *H-L*, 1:202, 204; OWH to A. Lawrence Lowell, June 2, 1919, quoted in *H-L*, 1:211 n. 2; Lowell to OWH, June 10, 1919, quoted in Snyder, *House of Truth*, 286.

61. OWH to HJL, May 18, 1919, *H-L*, 1:204; OWH to NG, September 2, 1919, MDHM, 3-39; OWH to HJL, June 11, 1920, *H-L*, 1:268.

62. Kramnick and Sheerman, *Laski*, 134–35; Healy, *Great Dissent*, 185–87.

63. OWH to HJL, October 26, 1919, *H-L*, 1:217.
64. Dean Acheson heard the story at the time from his Yale and Harvard Law classmate Stanley Morrison, who was Holmes's secretary that year and sat in the adjoining study while the discussion was taking place. In his memoirs (Acheson, *Memoir*, 119), Acheson recalled two of the justices as Pitney and Van Devanter. In a letter to Alexander Bickel, which provided additional details of the meeting, he identified the third as McKenna (Acheson to Bickel, June 2, 1960, Acheson, Papers, 3-34).
65. Menand, *Metaphysical Club*, 430.
66. OWH to Chafee, June 12, 1922, quoted in Healy, *Great Dissent*, 243.
67. Healy, *Great Dissent*, 218–25; Wigmore, "Abrams," 545, 552.
68. Smith, *Chafee*, 51–55; Urofsky, *Brandeis*, 556; Kramnick and Sheerman, *Laski*, 138–40; *Harvard Lampoon*, January 16, 1920.
69. OWH to FF, February 11, 1920, *H-F*, 82; Kramnick and Sheerman, *Laski*, 140–41; LDB to HJL, February 29, 1920, MDHM, 25-18; HJL to OWH, March 28, 1920, *H-L*, 1:255.
70. OWH to HJL, March 31, 1920, *H-L*, 1:256.

CHAPTER 15: Taft's Court

1. OWH to ES, September 24, 1910, MDHM, 17-28; OWH to HJL, May 12, 1927, *H-L*, 2:942.
2. OWH to HJL, January 6, 1923, *H-L*, 1:469.
3. Ibid. ("bullies me"); OWH to HJL, October 9, 1921, *H-L*, 1:374 ("great comfort"); OWH to ASG, January 10, 1911, MDHM, 15-9 ("imbecile statutes"); OWH to HJL, March 4, 1920, *H-L*, 1:249 ("go to Hell").
4. McReynolds, dissenting opinion, Arizona Employers' Liability Cases (1919).
5. Acheson, *Memoir*, 67–68.
6. Holmes, concurring opinion, Arizona Employers' Liability Cases (1919).
7. Old Colony Trust Company statements, 1904–1929, OWHP, 48-1 to 54-6; canceled checks, personal, Riggs National Bank, 1902–1935, OWHP, 35-8 to 45-1; LDB to FF, May 25, 1927, *HBHS*, no. 280; OWH to LE, April 26, 1918, *H-E*, 164.
8. OWH to Lady Askwith, September 17, 1919, MDHM, 13-1. Holmes refers to reading Malthus for the first time in OWH to CSRS, August 23, 1914, MDHM, 17-39. Malthus's *Essay on Population* is on his 1914 reading list (Holmes, *Black Book*, 129).
9. OWH to HJL, August 12, 1923, MDHM, 5-19.
10. Derby, "Recollections," 352; OWH to Morris R. Cohen, November 23,

1919, Cohen, "Correspondence," 18 and n. 34; OWH to FF, March 21, 1928, *H-F*, 225.

11. OWH to LE, May 14, 1916, *H-E*, 128.

12. OWH to ES, March 9, 1925, MDHM, 17-30; OWH to NG, March 5, 1921, MDHM, 4-3.

13. OWH to HJL, March 10, 1921, *H-L*, 1:318; OWH to EC, March 17, 1921, MDHM, 14-22.

14. OWH to LE, February 23, 1919, *H-E*, 182–83.

15. OWH to NG, November 30, 1921, MDHM, 4-5; "Justice Holmes," *New Republic*, February 2, 1921, 294; "Mr. Justice Holmes," *New Republic*, March 9, 1921, 36; OWH to HJL, March 10, 1921, *H-L*, 1:318.

16. Notes of talk with LH, June 11, 1942, MDHM, 22-7; LH to Arthur Train, May 29, 1941, Hand, Papers, 81-7; LH to Charles P. Curtis Jr., February 14, 1954, ibid., 86-21; OWH to ES, March 15, 1921, MDHM, 17-29.

17. OWH to ASG, March 26, 1919, MDHM, 15-9; *JRG*, 478.

18. OWH to ES, February 7, 1912, MDHM, 17-28.

19. Mason, *Taft*, 18–19, 76–77.

20. OWH to FP, July 11, 1921, *H-P*, 2:72; OWH to HJL, May 27, 1921, *H-L*, 1:339; Post, "Dissent in Taft Court," 1276–77.

21. Pringle, *Taft*, 2:997–99.

22. Bundy, OH, 64; OWH to NG, June 28, 1931, MDHM, 4-27.

23. Mason, *Taft*, 198; WHT to Willis Van Devanter, December 26, 1921, quoted in Post, "Dissent in Taft Court," 1311.

24. Lee, *Taft*, 8:xxii. Part of the increased percentage was almost certainly due to the elimination from the docket after 1925 of the large number of uncontroversial cases the Court had easily disposed of unanimously: see Post, "Dissent in Taft Court," 1336–38.

25. Pringle, *Taft*, 2:960; OWH to FP, May 21, 1922, *H-P*, 2:96; OWH to CM, June 2, 1922, MDHM, 20-14; OWH to ES, March 7, 1922, MDHM, 17-29.

26. OWH to CM, June 2, 1922, MDHM, 20-14 (showing appreciation); Post, "Dissent in Taft Court," 1311–12 (modifying opinions); Mason, *Taft*, 205 (past differences with Brandeis); April 17, 1922, *B-F*, 302–3 ("cultivated man").

27. Mason, *Taft*, 195, 216.

28. WHT to Horace Taft, April 17, 1922, MDHM, 17-44.

29. OWH to CM, May 2, 1921, MDHM, 20-12; OWH to FF, April 20, 1921, *H-F*, 110.

30. WHT to Horace Taft, May 7, 1922, quoted in Pringle, *Taft*, 2:967.

31. WHT to Horace Taft, June 8, 1928, quoted in Mason, *Taft*, 259; Urofsky,

Brandeis, 581; WHT to C. P. Taft II, March 7, 1926, quoted in Pringle, *Taft*, 2:969.

32. WHT to LH, March 3, 1923, quoted in Pringle, *Taft*, 2:969.

33. Biddle, *Mr. Justice Holmes*, 145–47; "Justice Holmes at Ninety," *NYT*, March 8, 1931.

34. WHT to LH, March 3, 1923, Pringle, *Taft*, 2:969.

35. WHT to Horace Taft, April 17, 1922, MDHM, 17-44; OWH to NG, December 21, 1921, MDHM, 4-5, and October 12, 1921, MDHM, 4-4; OWH to ES, March 7, 1922, MDHM, 17-29.

36. OWH to CM, June 2, 1922, MDHM, 20-14; OWH to EC, June 23, 1922, MDHM, 14-22 (misdated June 3 in Mark Howe's transcription; see the original in OWHP, 16-7).

37. OWH to John Hessin Clarke, July 1, 1922, Clarke, Papers.

38. Pilcher, "Prostatectomy in Two Stages"; Shackley, "Century of Prostatic Surgery."

39. OWH to EC, July 2, 7, and 12, 1922, MDHM, 14-22. The July 12 letter in particular is very difficult to make out; for the original autograph letter, see OWHP, 16-7.

40. OWH to EC, August 11, 1922, MDHM, 14-22.

41. Anna K. Codman to OWH, July 22, 1922, OWHP, 15-17.

42. OWH to ASG, December 7, 1922, MDHM, 15-7; OWH to EC, August 11, 1922, MDHM, 14-22; OWH to NG, August 25, 1922, MDHM, 4-6.

43. OWH to NG, September 27, 1922, MDHM, 4-6.

44. OWH to NG, November 4, 1922, MDHM, 4-7.

45. Tip-in notes, Jackman v. The Rosenbaum Company, No. 3, bound volume of opinions, 1922 term, OWHP.

46. OWH to NG, November 4, 1922, MDHM, 4-7; OWH to EC, August 11, 1922, MDHM, 14-22.

47. LDB to FF, January 29, 1923, *HBHS*, no. 121.

48. Mason, *Taft*, 170 ("enemies of the Constitution"); WHT to Willis Van Devanter, December 26, 1921, quoted in Urofsky, *Brandeis*, 581 ("break down the prestige"); WHT to Henry L. Stimson, May 18, 1928, quoted in Pringle, *Taft*, 2:969–70 ("two votes . . . not very helpful").

49. Tyson & Brother v. Banton (1927), citing Munn v. Illinois (1876).

50. Weaver v. Palmer Brothers Company (1926); Williams v. Standard Oil Company (1929); Fairmont Creamery Company v. Minnesota (1927); Schlesinger v. Wisconsin (1926); Frost & Frost Trucking Company v. Railroad Commission of California (1926); Louis K. Liggett Company v. Baldridge (1928); Tyson & Brother v. Banton (1927).

51. B-F, 321.

52. John Hessin Clarke to WHT, October 31, 1922, Clarke, Papers; Clarke to Willis Van Devanter, July 28, 1924, Van Devanter, Papers, box 32.
53. Memorandum of talk with FF, January 2, 1964, MDHM, 22-26.
54. Brandeis, dissenting opinion, Jay Burns Baking Company v. Bryan (1924); OWH to FP, May 11, 1924, *H-P*, 2:136–37; HJL to OWH, January 13, 1918, *H-L*, 1:127.
55. OWH to HJL, March 1, 1923, *H-L*, 1:485.
56. OWH to NG, April 21, 1923, MDHM, 4-8.
57. Theodore Roosevelt to Henry Cabot Lodge, September 4, 1906, MDHM, 22-23.
58. OWH to ASG, July 11, 1905, MDHM, 15-8.
59. Taylor, "Disfranchisement in Alabama," 421; Schmidt, "Black Disfranchisement," 847.
60. McCabe v. Atchison, Topeka & Santa Fe Railway Company (1914); Berea College v. Kentucky (1908).
61. Lerner, *Mind and Faith*, 338; *JRG*, 868; Bailey v. Alabama (1911).
62. LH to MDH, April 29, 1959, MDHM, 22-26; Hand gave a slightly different version of the anecdote in *Continuing Legal Education*, 119.
63. Tip-in notes, Buchanan v. Warley, No. 231, bound volume of opinions, 1916 term, OWHP. Holmes's unpublished dissent is also reprinted in the plates following p. 592 of *JRG*.
64. Curriden and Phillips, *Contempt of Court*, 123–36, 154–60, 213–14.
65. King, *Fuller*, 324.
66. United States v. Shipp (1906); OWH to Melville W. Fuller, May 13, 1909, quoted in King, *Fuller*, 327; Curriden and Phillips, *Contempt of Court*, 338.
67. Freedman, "Habeas Corpus," 1502–5.
68. McReynolds's misstatements of the record are discussed in Waterman and Overton, "Aftermath of *Moore*," 121–22.
69. Ibid., 118–19, 123.
70. "Due Process of Law in Arkansas," *New Republic*, March 14, 1923, 55–57; "Legal Lynching and the Constitution," *New Republic*, March 21, 1923, 84–85; Snyder, *House of Truth*, 354.
71. OWH to LE, February 5, 1923, *H-E*, 209.

CHAPTER 16: "My Last Examination"

1. WHT to C. D. Hilles, September 9, 1922; WHT to Charles P. Taft II, May 3, 1925; and WHT to Robert A. Taft, May 17, 1925, quoted in Mason, *Taft*, 161–62.

2. OWH to NG, February 22, 1925, MDHM, 4-13.

3. OWH to LE, January 27, 1925, *H-E*, 231; OWH to HJL, August 16, 1924, and March 5, 1925, *H-L*, 1:646, 719.

4. "Supreme Court," *Time*, March 15, 1926; *New York World*, March 8, 1926, quoted in Snyder, *House of Truth*, 393.

5. OWH to NG, March 14, 1926, MDHM, 4-15.

6. OWH to FF, December 17, 1925, *H-F*, 196; OWH to EC, January 18, 1926, MDHM, 14-23; FF to Elizabeth Shepley Sergeant, June 7, 1926, quoted in Snyder, *House of Truth*, 392.

7. OWH to FF, December 8, 1926, *H-F*, 210; OWH to Sergeant, December 5, 1926, OWHP, 22-7.

8. OWH to Sergeant, December 7, 1926, OWHP, 22-7.

9. Thomas G. Corcoran to FF, December 9, 1926, OWHP, 58-27.

10. Ethel St. Leger to OWH, April 11, 1927, and Bernard Castletown to OWH, April 22, 1927, OWHP, 15-3.

11. OWH to CM, June 18, 1927, MDHM, 20-25; OWH to NG, December 20, 1927, MDHM, 4-19, and April 9, 1927, MDHM, 4-17.

12. OWH to EC, January 5, 1927, MDHM, 14-23.

13. Thomas G. Corcoran to Alger Hiss, February 2, 1931, OWHP, 59-8; John E. Lockwood to FF, November 5, 1928, OWHP, 58-27; OWH to NG, June 26, 1927, MDHM, 4-18.

14. OWH to Lucy Clifford, June 24, 1927, MDHM, 14-10.

15. OWH to LE, June 27, 1917, *H-E*, 142; OWH to Lucy Clifford, April 27, 1927, MDHM, 14-10.

16. Except where noted, the details of the Sacco-Vanzetti case here and below are taken from the excellent and meticulously researched account in Snyder, *House of Truth*, 409–47.

17. OWH to HJL, April 25, 1927, *H-L*, 2:938.

18. OWH to FF, March 18, 1927, *H-F*, 211.

19. OWH to LE, August 14, 1927, *H-E*, 272; OWH to HJL, August 18, 1927, *H-L*, 2:971; Thomas G. Corcoran to FF, September 13, 1927, OWHP, 58-27.

20. Bard v. Chilton, 20 F.2d 906 (6th Cir. 1927); Snyder, *House of Truth*, 455–56, 473–74.

21. OWH to HJL, August 24, 1927, *H-L*, 2:974.

22. OWH to LE, August 14, 1927, *H-E*, 272.

23. Lombardo, *Three Generations*, 74–75, 148–55.

24. WHT to OWH, April 23, 1927, OWHP, 22-25.

25. Tip-in notes, Buck v. Bell, No. 292, bound volume of opinions, 1926 term, OWHP.

26. OWH to HJL, April 29, 1927, *H-L*, 2:939.

27. Dietrich v. Inhabitants of Northampton, 138 Mass. 14 (1884); OWH to ES, September 13, 1910, MDHM, 17-28.

28. Quinn v. Crimmings, 171 Mass. 255 (1898), at 258; Lorenzo v. Wirth, 170 Mass. 596 (1898); Holbrook v. Aldrich, 168 Mass. 15 (1897).

29. OWH to CC, June 18, 1897, OWHC, 1-3.

30. Pokora v. Wabash Railway Company (1934).

31. April 17, 1922, B-F, 303; LDB to FF, November 13, 1927, *HBHS*, No. 297.

32. Urofsky, *Dissent*, 194–96.

33. WHT to Horace Taft, June 12, 1928, MDHM, 17-44 ("nastiest opinion"); WHT to Horace Taft, June 8, 1928, quoted in Mason, *Taft*, 259 ("they are mistaken"); ibid., 161 ("noisy dissenter"); WHT to Robert A. Taft, March 4, 1928, quoted in ibid., 220 ("much of a Constitution"). Taft's majority opinion in *Olmstead* was overturned in 1967 in *Katz v. U.S.*, which held that the Fourth Amendment requires the government under most circumstances to obtain a warrant to intercept private telephone conversations.

34. Sutherland, "Recollections," 25.

35. American Banana Company v. United Fruit Company (1909).

36. The Western Maid (1922).

37. Kawananakoa v. Polyblank (1907).

38. Zane, "German Legal Philosophy," 349 n. 83; Zane, "Legal Heresy," 431, 461.

39. OWH to FP, January 24, 1919, *H-P*, 2:3.

40. Hiss, *Recollections*, 35; LDB to FF, February 29, 1928, *HBHS*, no. 311.

41. LDB note, April 2, 1927, *HBHS*, no. 271 n. 6; McCormack, "Law Clerk's Recollections," 713–14.

42. LDB to FF, April 21, 1929, *HBHS*, no. 363; WHT to Charles P. Taft, May 5, 1929, quoted in White, *Justice Holmes*, 459.

43. OWH to NG, April 26, 1929, MDHM, 4-22; LDB to FF, April 28, 1929, *HBHS*, no. 365.

44. Pringle, *Taft*, 2:970; OWH to ES, October 24, 1923, MDHM, 17-30.

45. OWH to ES, n.d., MDHM, 17-30.

46. LDB to FF, May 11, 1929, *HBHS*, no. 366.

47. OWH to LE, July 11, 1925, *H-E*, 244.

48. United States v. Schwimmer (1929).

49. John E. Lockwood to FF, May 31, 1929, Frankfurter, Papers, reel 91; FF to OWH, May 29, 1929, *H-F*, 240.

50. Rosika Schwimmer to OWH, January 28, 1930, OWHP, 21-38; OWH to Schwimmer, January 30, 1930, MDHM, 17-27.

51. E. B. White, "Talk of the Town," *New Yorker*, June 22, 1929, quoted in Snyder, *House of Truth*, 505.
52. LDB to FF, April 21, 1929, *HBHS*, no. 363; John E. Lockwood to FF, May 24, 1929, Frankfurter, Papers, reel 91.
53. Lockwood to FF, May 31, 1929, Frankfurter, Papers, reel 91; Lockwood in Belknap et al., "Remembrances of Holmes," 394.
54. OWH to CM, October 24, 1929, MDHM, 21-1 ("discreet dames"); Hiss, *Recollections*, 36–37 (reading aloud); OWH to ES, July 30, 1921, MDHM, 17-29 ("Day of Judgment"); OWH to LE, February 10, 1908, *H-E*, 33 ("final examination"); Alger Hiss in Louchheim, *New Deal*, 31 ("little murder").
55. OWH to FF, November 12, 1932, *H-F*, 273; entry for November 10, 1933, Howe, Diary, 9; OWH to HJL, September 9, 1929, *H-L*, 2:1180.
56. WHT to Horace Taft, November 14, 1929, quoted in Pringle, *Taft*, 2:967.
57. LDB to FF, January 9, 1930, *HBHS*, no. 400; January 11, 1930, ibid., no. 401; OWH to NG, January 21 and February 26, 1930, MDHM, 4-24.
58. Hiss to FF, February 27 and March 20, 1930, Frankfurter, Papers, reel 91.
59. OWH to NG, February 26, 1930, MDHM, 4-24.
60. LDB to FF, May 26, 1930, *HBHS*, no. 428; State Tax Commission of Utah v. Aldrich (1942).
61. OWH to ES, December 26, 1929, MDHM, 17-30; OWH to EC, January 23, 1931, MDHM, 14-23.
62. "Death Plucks My Ear," OWHP, 62-3, and audio recording, OWHA, 8-16.
63. 90th Birthday, 1931, OWHP, 59-9.
64. OWH to EC, October 8, 1931, MDHM, 14-23.
65. New Jersey v. New York (1931).
66. Missouri v. Holland (1920).
67. OWH to EC, December 15 and October 27, 1931, MDHM, 14-23; OWH to NG, November 7, 1931, MDHM, 4-28.
68. OWH to NG, Thanksgiving 1931, MDHM, 14-28.
69. Hughes, *Autobiographical Notes*, 299; H. Chapman Rose interview, 12–13, JSMP, 1-14; Monagan, *Grand Panjandrum*, 142; LDB to FF, January 10, 1932, *HBHS*, no. 479.
70. H. Chapman Rose to FF, March 7 and 31, 1932, Frankfurter, Papers, reel 91.
71. OWH to NG, May 2, 1932, MDHM, 4-28; OWH to EC, November 23, 1932, MDHM, 14-25.
72. James Rowe interview, LJPP, 1-35 (dirty jokes); anecdote of Mrs. Ralph Ellis, spring 1933, MDHM, 22-26 (rock in a riverbed); entry for March

6, 1934, Howe, Diary, 29. The milk-price case was Nebbia v. New York (1934). *Tyson* was formally overruled in Gold v. DiCarlo, 235 F. Supp. 817 (S.D.N.Y. 1964), but as the district court noted in its opinion in that case (subsequently affirmed in a brief per curium by the Supreme Court), *Nebbia* had already effectively rejected the "fictional test" of a "business affected with the public interest."

73. Phillips, *Frankfurter Reminisces,* 241–42.

74. The account of FDR's visit here and below is from Donald Hiss in Louchheim, *New Deal,* 36–38.

75. Notes for a Talk on O.W.H., 3, WBLM.

76. "President Sees Holmes Buried at Arlington," *WP,* March 9, 1935; Monagan, *Grand Panjandrum,* 147.

77. Anecdotes, Marion Frankfurter, August 10, 1932, MDHM, 22-26.

78. The parcel with the musket balls was apparently given to Holmes's nephew and subsequently lost, but Holmes's lawyer told Mark Howe of having found it in the safe deposit box after Holmes's death: John S. Flannery to MDH, May 13, 1942, MDHM, 22-29.

EPILOGUE

1. Will of OWH, MDHM, 23-12; Oliver Wendell Holmes Memorial Fund, Senate Document No. 197, May 13, 1940, 76th Cong., 3rd Sess., 5 (copy in MDHM, 23-12). When he retired from the Court, Holmes gave Arthur Thomas his planned legacy at once, and changed his will in a codicil to reflect that fact: check to Arthur A. Thomas, $1,010, June 1, 1932, OWHP, 43-7. The house was eventually sold by the government, and later torn down to make way for an office building.

2. Recommendation to Congress that Bequest of Justice Holmes be Set Aside in a Special Fund, House Document No. 166, April 25, 1935, 74th Cong., 1st Sess. (copy in OWHA, 7-4).

3. John S. Flannery to MDH, May 13, 1942, MDHM, 22-29.

4. Laurence Curtis to Robert M. Benjamin, May 25, 1938, MDHM, 23-12.

5. James H. Rowe Jr. to Robert M. Benjamin, June 6, 1938, MDHM, 23-12.

6. Oliver Wendell Holmes Devise, Senate Report No. 1053, July 21, 1955, 84th Cong., 1st Sess; H.R. 7029, An Act to Establish a Permanent Committee for the Oliver Wendell Holmes Devise, 84th Cong., 1st Sess. (copies in MDHM, 23-11).

7. "Justice Holmes's 1935 Bequest Remains Unfulfilled," *NYT,* May 3, 1983; Katz, "Holmes Devise History."

8. OWH to Lady Tweeddale, April 4, 1931, *H-E,* 323; Speech to Class of

'61, *CW*, 3:504; OWH to John C. H. Wu, September 20, 1923, Wu, "Letters," 264.

9. FF notes, August 10, 1932, MDHM, 22-26.

10. OWH to LE, September 30, 1932, *H-E*, 349; for his requests to destroy letters, see for example OWH to NG, December 27, 1920, MDHM, 4-2; OWH to CC, September 5, 1898, MDHM, 13-25; OWH to CSRS, April 16, 1914, MDHM, 19-29; OWH to FF, July 25, 1921, *H-F*, 119.

11. OWH to HJL, December 9, 1921, MDHM, 5-12. This and the other passages mentioning Holmes's requests that Laski never publish his letters were omitted by Mark Howe from the published volumes of their correspondence, apparently to avoid embarrassing Laski's widow, who was still alive at the time: see Alger Hiss interview, 4–5, JSMP, 1-8.

12. HJL to OWH, December 31, 1921, MDHM, 5-12; *H-L*, 1:v.

13. Alger Hiss interview, 3, JSMP, 1-8; Hiss, *Recollections*, 39–40.

14. FF to OWH, August 4, 1931, *H-F*, 264; OWH to HJL, July 25, 1931, *H-L*, 2:1320.

15. *H-F*, xxxi–xli.

16. Charles P. Curtis Jr. to LH, [early January 1954], Hand, Papers, 86-21.

17. Mencken, "Mr. Justice Holmes."

18. West Coast Hotel Company v. Parrish (1937).

19. United States v. Carolene Products Company (1938).

20. In *Senn* v. *Tile Layers Protective Union* (1937) the Court upheld a Wisconsin statute barring injunctions against peaceful picketing, and in *New Negro Alliance* v. *Sanitary Grocery Company* (1938) similarly held the anti-injunction provisions of a new federal labor law, the 1932 Norris–La Guardia Act, to be constitutional. In *National Labor Relations Board* v. *Jones & Laughlin Steel Corporation* (1937), the Court in a 5–4 decision by Chief Justice Hughes found the act's provisions barring the discharge of workers for union activity valid. And four years later, in a sweeping unanimous opinion by Justice Frankfurter, the Court declared in *Phelps Dodge Corporation* v. *National Labor Relations Board* (1941), "The course of decisions in this Court since *Adair* v. *United States* and *Coppage* v. *Kansas* have completely sapped those cases of their authority."

21. United States v. Darby Lumber Company (1941).

22. Notable examples include *Evans* v. *Gore* (1920), dissenting from the Court's decision that current federal judges were exempt from the income tax on the grounds that the Constitution barred the reduction of the salary of sitting judges, reversed in *Helvering* v. *Gerhardt* (1938); *Long* v. *Rockwood* (1928), dissenting from the Court's decision invalidating a state tax on patent royalties, reversed in *Fox Film Corporation* v. *Doyal*

(1932); *Myers v. United States* (1926) dissenting from the Court's decision striking down a law that prevented the president from removing certain officials without congressional approval, reversed for independent agencies in *Humphrey's Executor v. United States* (1935).

23. Powell v. Alabama (1932).
24. Cohen, "Justice Holmes," 207.
25. Urofksy, *Dissent*, 169–71, lists forty-one Supreme Court free-speech opinions from 1941 to 2011 that have cited Holmes's *Abrams* dissent.
26. Girouard v. United States (1946); Hannegan v. Esquire, Inc. (1946).
27. Collins, *Fundamental Holmes*, 376–77.
28. Speech to Class of '61, *CW*, 3:504; Cohen, "Justice Holmes," 206.
29. "The Profession of the Law," *CW*, 3:472–73.

BIBLIOGRAPHY

Abel, Albert S. Review of *Holmes-Laski Letters*. Edited by Mark DeWolfe Howe. *Louisiana Law Review* 14 (1954): 472–91.

Acheson, Dean. *Morning and Noon: A Memoir*. Boston: Houghton, Mifflin, 1965.

———. Papers. Manuscripts and Archives, Yale University, New Haven, Conn.

Adams, Henry. *The Education of Henry Adams*. 1918. Reprint. New York: Modern Library, 1931.

Alschuler, Albert W. *Law without Values: The Life, Work, and Legacy of Justice Holmes*. Chicago: University of Chicago Press, 2000.

Anderson, James William. " 'The Worst Kind of Melancholy': William James in 1869." *Harvard Library Bulletin* 30 (1982): 369–86.

Auerbach, Jerold S. "The Patrician as Libertarian: Zechariah Chafee, Jr., and Freedom of Speech." *New England Quarterly* 42 (1969): 511–31.

Baldwin, Elbert F. "The Supreme Court Justices." *The Outlook*, January 28, 1911, 156–60.

Ballard, Ted. *Battle of Ball's Bluff*. Staff Ride Guide. Washington, D.C.: Center of Military History, U.S. Army, 2001.

Bander, Edward J., ed. *Justice Holmes Ex Cathedra*. Charlottesville, Va.: Michie, 1966.

Belknap, Chauncey. "Justice Holmes at Work and Play." Typescript filed with Oral History.

———. Oral History. 1975. Center for Oral History Archives, Columbia University, New York, N.Y.

Belknap, Chauncey, et al. "Personal Remembrances of Mr. Justice Holmes by his Former Law Clerks." *University of Florida Law Review* 28 (1976): 392–98.

Bickel, Alexander M., and Benno C. Schmidt Jr. *The Judiciary and Respon-*

sible Government, 1910–21. Vol. 9, *The Oliver Wendell Holmes Devise History of the United States Supreme Court*. New York: Macmillan, 1984. (*JRG*)

Biddle, Francis. *A Casual Past*. Garden City, N.Y.: Doubleday, 1961.

———. *Mr. Justice Holmes*. New York: Scribner's, 1942.

Bowen, Francis. *Critical Essays on a Few Subjects Connected with the History and Present Condition of Speculative Philosophy*. Boston: H. B. Williams, 1842.

———. *The Principles of Metaphysical and Ethical Science Applied to the Evidences of Religion*. Rev. ed. Boston: Brewer and Tileston, 1855.

———. *The Principles of Political Economy*. Boston: Little, Brown, 1856.

———, ed. *Documents of the Constitution of England and America*. Cambridge, Mass.: John Bartlett, 1854.

Brooks, Van Wyck. *New England: Indian Summer, 1865–1915*. New York: Dutton, 1940.

Bruce, George A. *The Twentieth Regiment of Massachusetts Volunteer Infantry, 1861–1865*. Boston: Houghton, Mifflin, 1906.

Bundy, Harvey H. Oral History. 1960. Center for Oral History Archives, Columbia University, New York, N.Y.

Bureau of Labor Statistics. Department of Labor. *100 Years of U.S. Consumer Spending: Data for the Nation, New York City and Boston*. Report 991. Washington, D.C., 2006.

Burton, David H., ed. *Holmes-Sheehan Correspondence: The Letters of Justice Oliver Wendell Holmes and Canon Patrick Augustine Sheehan*. Port Washington, D.E.: Kennikat Press, 1976. (*H-S*)

———. *Progressive Masks: Letters of Oliver Wendell Holmes, Jr., and Franklin Ford*. Newark, D.E.: University of Delaware Press, 1982.

Butler, Charles Henry. *A Century at the Bar of the Supreme Court of the United States*. New York: G. P. Putnam's Sons, 1942.

Butt, Archibald Willingham. *Taft and Roosevelt: The Intimate Letters of Archie Butt, Military Aide*. 2 vols. Garden City, N.Y.: Doubleday, Doran, 1930.

Castletown, Bernard Edward Barnaby FitzPatrick, Lord. *"Ego": Random Records of Sport, Service, and Travel in Many Lands*. London: John Murray, 1923.

———. Papers. National Library of Ireland, Dublin.

Chafee, Zechariah, Jr. "Freedom of Speech." *New Republic*, November 16, 1918, 66–69.

———. "Freedom of Speech in War Time." *Harvard Law Review* 32 (1919): 932–73.

———. "Harold Laski and the Harvard Law Review." *Harvard Law Review* 63 (1950): 1398–1400.

Channing, William E. *The Works of William E. Channing, D.D.* Boston: American Unitarian Association, 1899.

Clarke, John Hessin. Papers. Special Collections Research Center, Case Western Reserve University, Cleveland, Ohio.

Cohen, Felix S., ed. "The Holmes-Cohen Correspondence." *Journal of the History of Ideas* 9 (1948): 3–52.

Cohen, Morris R. "Justice Holmes." *The New Republic*, April 3, 1935, 206–9.

Collins, Ronald K. L., ed. *The Fundamental Holmes: A Free Speech Chronicle and Reader.* Cambridge: Cambridge University Press, 2010.

Continuing Legal Education for Professional Competence and Responsibility. Report on the Arden House Conference, December 16–19, 1958. Philadelphia: American Law Institute, 1959.

Cramer, John Henry. *Lincoln Under Enemy Fire.* Baton Rouge: Louisiana State University Press, 1948.

Curriden, Mark, and Leroy Phillips Jr. *Contempt of Court: The Turn-of-the-Century Lynching that Launched a Hundred Years of Federalism.* New York: Anchor, 2001.

Curtis, Charles P. Review of *Holmes-Laski Letters.* Edited by Mark DeWolfe Howe. *Yale Law Journal* 63 (1953): 266–76.

Cushman, Barry. "Inside the Taft Court: Lessons from the Docket Books." *Supreme Court Review*, 2015, 345–410.

Davis, William T. *History of the Judiciary of Massachusetts.* Boston: Boston Book Co., 1900.

Derby, Augustin. "Recollections of Mr. Justice Holmes." *New York University Law Quarterly Review* 12 (1935): 345–53.

Devlin, Andrea L. "It Is Well That Judges Should Be Clothed in Robes." *Supreme Judicial Court Historical Society Journal* 2 (1996): 123–26.

Dimond, Alan J. *The Superior Court of Massachusetts: Its Origin and Development.* Boston: Little, Brown, 1960.

Doneraile Papers. National Library of Ireland, Dublin.

Dow, Mary Larcom. *Old Days at Beverly Farms.* Beverly, Mass.: North Shore Printing Co., 1921.

Edel, Leon, ed. *Henry James: Selected Letters.* Cambridge: Harvard University Press, 1987.

Emerson, Ralph Waldo. *Essays & Lectures.* New York: Library of America, 1983.

———. *Journals and Miscellaneous Notebooks of Ralph Waldo Emerson.*

Edited by Linda Allardt and David W. Hill. Vol. 15, *1860–1866*. Cambridge: Harvard University Press, 1982.

———. *Journals of Ralph Waldo Emerson*. Edited by Edward Waldo Emerson and Waldo Emerson Forbes. Vol. 7, *1845–1848*. Boston: Houghton Mifflin, 1913.

———. *The Topical Notebooks of Ralph Waldo Emerson*. Vol. 3. Edited by Glen M. Johnson. Columbia: University of Missouri Press, 1994.

Felton, Cornelius Conway. *Annual Report of the President of Harvard College, 1859–60*. Cambridge, Mass.: Welch, Bigelow, 1860.

———. *Annual Report of the President of Harvard College, 1860–61*. Cambridge, Mass.: Welch, Bigelow, 1862.

Fiechter, Frederick C., Jr. "The Preparation of an American Aristocrat." *New England Quarterly* 6 (1933): 3–28.

Findlay, Anna Howell Kennedy. "Where 'The Captain' Was Found." *Maryland Historical Magazine* 33 (1938): 107–26.

Fiss, Owen M. *Troubled Beginnings of the Modern State, 1888–1910*. Vol. 8, *The Oliver Wendell Holmes Devise History of the United States Supreme Court*. New York: Macmillan, 1993.

Fitz, Reginald. "My Dr. Oliver Wendell Holmes." *Bulletin of the New York Academy of Medicine* 19 (1943): 540–54.

Ford, Worthington Chauncey, ed. *Letters of Henry Adams (1892–1918)*. Boston: Houghton Mifflin, 1938.

Fox, William F. *Regimental Losses in the American Civil War, 1861–1865*. Albany, N.Y.: Albany Publishing, 1889.

Frank, Jerome N. "Some Reflections on Judge Learned Hand." *University of Chicago Law Review* 24 (1957): 666–705.

Frankfurter, Felix. "The Constitutional Opinions of Justice Holmes." *Harvard Law Review* 29 (1916): 683–702.

———. Papers. Manuscript Division, Library of Congress, Washington, D.C.

Freedman, Eric M. "Leo Frank Lives: Untangling the Historical Roots of Meaningful Habeas Corpus Review of State Convictions." *Alabama Law Review* 51 (2000): 1467–1540.

Friedman, Leon, and Fred L. Israel, eds. *The Justices of the United States Supreme Court, 1789–1969: Their Lives and Major Opinions*. 4 vols. New York: R. R. Bowker, 1969.

Freund, Ernst. "The Debs Case and Freedom of Speech." *New Republic*, May 3, 1919, 13–15.

Garraty, John A. "Holmes's Appointment to the U.S. Supreme Court." *New England Quarterly* 22 (1949): 291–303.

Gilmore, Grant. *The Ages of American Law*. New Haven: Yale University Press, 1977.

Goodman, Paul. "Ethics and Enterprise: The Values of a Boston Elite, 1800–1860." *American Quarterly* 18 (1966): 437–51.

Gordon, Armistead C. *William Gordon McCabe: A Brief Memoir*. Richmond, Va.: Old Dominion Press, 1920.

Graham, Katharine. *Katharine Graham's Washington*. New York: Knopf, 2002.

Graves, Richard Perceval. *Robert Graves: The Assault Heroic 1895–1926*. London: Weidenfeld & Nicolson, 1986.

Gregg, Paul L. "The Pragmatism of Mr. Justice Holmes." *Georgetown Law Journal* 31 (1943): 262–95.

Gunther, Gerald. *Learned Hand: The Man and the Judge*. 2nd ed. New York: Oxford University Press, 2011.

———. "Learned Hand and the Origins of Modern First Amendment Doctrine: Some Fragments of History." *Stanford Law Review* 27 (1975): 719–73.

Habegger, Alfred. "Henry James's Rewriting of Minny Temple's Letters." *American Literature* 58 (1986): 159–80.

———. "New Light on William James and Minny Temple." *New England Quarterly* 60 (1987): 28–53.

Hale, Edward Everett. "An Afternoon with Oliver Wendell Holmes." *McClure's Magazine*, July 1893, 99–109.

———. *A New England Boyhood and Other Bits of Autobiography*. Boston: Little, Brown, 1900.

Hale, Richard Walden. *Some Table Talk of Mr. Justice Holmes and "The Mrs."* Privately printed, 1935. (Copy in OWHA, 4-8.)

Hallowell, Norwood Penrose. *Selected Letters and Papers of N. P. Hallowell*. Peterborough, N.H.: Richard R. Smith, 1963.

Hand, Learned. Papers. Historical & Special Collections, Harvard Law School, Cambridge, Mass.

Hardwick, Elizabeth, ed. *The Selected Letters of William James*. New York: Farrar, Straus and Cudahy, 1961.

Hazard, Thomas Robinson. *The Jonny-Cake Papers of "Shepherd Tom."* Boston, 1915.

Healy, Thomas. *The Great Dissent*. New York: Picador, 2013.

Hicks, Frederick C. "Lincoln, Wright, and Holmes at Fort Stevens." *Journal of the Illinois State Historical Society* 39 (1946): 323–32.

Higginson, Thomas Wentworth. "His Brother's Brother." *Atlantic Monthly*, August 1899, 175–82.

Hiss, Alger. *Recollections of a Life*. New York: Henry Holt, 1988.

Hiss, Anthony. *Laughing Last*. Boston: Houghton Mifflin, 1977.

Hofstadter, Richard. *The Age of Reform*. New York: Vintage, 1955.

Hofstedt, Matthew. "Afterword: A Brief History of Supreme Court Messengers." *Journal of Supreme Court History* 39 (2014): 259–63.

Holmes, Edward J. Collection of Oliver Wendell Holmes, Jr., Materials. Historical & Special Collections, Harvard Law School, Cambridge, Mass. Digitized collection accessible on the Web. (EJHC)

Holmes, Oliver Wendell, Jr. *The Black Book: A List of Books Read by Justice Holmes*. MS 4075, Harvard Law School Library. Digitized copy accessible on the Web.

———. *The Collected Works of Justice Holmes*. 3 vols. Edited by Sheldon M. Novick. Chicago: University of Chicago Press, 1995. (CW)

———. *The Common Law*. 1881. Reprint. New York: Dover, 1991.

———. "Ideals and Doubts." *Illinois Law Review* 10 (1915): 1–4.

———. "Law in Science and Science in Law." *Harvard Law Review* 12 (1899): 443–63.

———. Letters Written to Lady Clare Castletown. Historical & Special Collections, Harvard Law School, Cambridge, Mass. Digitized collection accessible on the Web. (OWHC)

———. "Memoir of George O. Shattuck, LL.B." *Proceedings of the Massachusetts Historical Society* 14 (1900): 361–68.

———. "Natural Law." *Harvard Law Review* 32 (1918): 40–44.

———. Papers. Addenda. Historical & Special Collections, Harvard Law School, Cambridge, Mass. Digitized collection accessible on the Web. (OWHA)

———. Papers. John G. Palfrey Collection. Historical & Special Collections, Harvard Law School, Cambridge, Mass. Digitized collection accessible on the Web. (OWHP)

———. "The Path of the Law." *Harvard Law Review* 10 (1897): 457–78.

———. "Privilege, Malice, and Intent." *Harvard Law Review* 8 (1894): 1–14.

Holmes, Oliver Wendell, Sr. *The Autocrat of the Breakfast-Table*. 1858. Reprint. Vol. 1, *The Writings of Oliver Wendell Holmes*. Boston: Houghton, Mifflin, 1894.

———. *Elsie Venner*. 1861. Reprint. Vol. 5, *The Writings of Oliver Wendell Holmes*. Boston: Houghton, Mifflin, 1904.

———. *Homeopathy and Its Kindred Delusions*. Boston: Ticknor, 1842.

———. *A Mortal Antipathy*. 1884. Reprint. Vol. 7, *The Writings of Oliver Wendell Holmes*. Boston: Houghton, Mifflin, 1898.

———. "My Hunt after 'The Captain.'" *Atlantic Monthly*, December 1862, 738–64.

————. *Pages from an Old Volume of Life: A Collection of Essays*. Vol. 8, *The Writings of Oliver Wendell Holmes*. Boston: Houghton, Mifflin, 1891.

————. *The Professor at the Breakfast-Table*. 1859. Reprint. Vol. 2, *The Writings of Oliver Wendell Holmes*. Boston: Houghton, Mifflin, 1892.

————. "The Professor's Story." *Atlantic Monthly*, January 1860, 88–99.

————. *Puerperal Fever as a Private Pestilence*. Boston: Ticknor and Fields, 1855.

Horwitz, Morton J. "The Place of Justice Holmes in American Legal Thought." In *The Legacy of Oliver Wendell Holmes, Jr.*, edited by Robert W. Gordon. Edinburgh: Edinburgh University Press, 1992.

Howe, Daniel Walker. *The Unitarian Conscience: Harvard Moral Philosophy, 1805–1861*. Cambridge: Harvard University Press, 1970.

Howe, Mark A. DeWolfe. *Holmes of the Breakfast-Table*. London: Oxford University Press, 1939.

Howe, Mark DeWolfe. Diary. Mark DeWolfe Howe Papers, 29-1. Historical & Special Collections, Harvard Law School, Cambridge, Mass. Digitized copy accessible on the Web.

————. *Justice Holmes: The Proving Years, 1870–1882*. Cambridge, Mass.: Harvard University Press, 1963.

————. *Justice Holmes: The Shaping Years, 1841–1870*. Cambridge, Mass.: Harvard University Press, 1957.

————. Research Materials on Oliver Wendell Holmes, Jr. Historical & Special Collections, Harvard Law School, Cambridge, Mass. Digitized collection accessible on the Web. (MDHM)

————, ed. *Holmes-Laski Letters: The Correspondence of Mr. Justice Holmes and Harold J. Laski, 1916–1935*. 2 vols. Cambridge, Mass.: Harvard University Press, 1953. (H-L)

————. *Holmes-Pollock Letters: The Correspondence of Mr. Justice Holmes and Sir Frederick Pollock, 1874–1932*. 1941. 2nd ed. Cambridge, Mass.: Harvard University press, 1961. (H-P)

————. "The Letters of Henry James to Mr. Justice Holmes." *Yale Review* 38 (1949): 410–33.

————. *Touched With Fire: Civil War Letters and Diary of Oliver Wendell Holmes, Jr.* Cambridge, Mass.: Harvard University Press, 1946. (TWF)

Hoyt, Edwin P. *The Improper Bostonian: Dr. Oliver Wendell Holmes*. New York: Morrow, 1979.

Hughes, Charles Evans. *The Autobiographical Notes of Charles Evans Hughes*. Edited by David J. Danelski and Joseph S. Tulchin. Cambridge, Mass.: Harvard University Press, 1973.

James, Alice. *The Diary of Alice James*. Edited by Leon Edel. New York: Dodd, Mead, 1964.

James, Henry (1843–1916). *The Complete Notebooks of Henry James.* Edited by Leon Edel and Lyall H. Powers. New York: Oxford University Press, 1987.

———. *Notes of a Son and Brother.* London: Macmillan, 1914.

James, Henry (1879–1947), ed. *The Letters of William James.* 2 vols. Boston: Atlantic Monthly Press, 1920.

Jantzen, Franz. "From the Urban Legend Department: McReynolds, Brandeis, and the Myth of the 1924 Group Photograph." *Journal of Supreme Court History* 40 (2015): 325–33.

"Judge Putnam's Recollections of Chief Justice Fuller." *The Green Bag* 22 (1910): 526–29.

Kanda, James, and William A. Gifford, eds. "The Kaneko Correspondence." *Monumenta Nipponica* 37 (1982): 41–76, 223–56, 289–316, 413–36.

Katz, Stanley N. "Official History: The Holmes Devise History of the Supreme Court." *Proceedings of the American Philosophical Society* 141 (1977): 297–304.

Kent, James. *Commentaries on American Law.* 4 vols. New York: Halsted, 1826–30.

King, Curtis S., William Glenn Robertson, and Steven E. Clay. *Staff Ride Handbook for the Overland Campaign, Virginia, 4 May to 15 June 1864: A Study in Operational-Level Command.* Fort Leavenworth, Kans.: Combat Studies Institute Press, 2009.

King, Willard L. *Melville Weston Fuller: Chief Justice of the United States, 1888–1910.* 1950. Reprint. Chicago: University of Chicago Press, 1967.

Kramnick, Isaac, and Barry Sheerman. *Harold Laski: A Life on the Left.* New York: Allen Lane, 1993.

Lash, Joseph P., ed. *From the Diaries of Felix Frankfurter.* New York: W. W. Norton, 1980.

Leach, W. Barton. Miscellanies, Vol. 1. Red Set Collection. Historical & Special Collections, Harvard Law School, Cambridge, Mass. (WBLM)

———. *Recollections of a Holmes Secretary.* 1940. Historical & Special Collections, Harvard Law School, Cambridge, Mass.

LeClair, Robert C. "Henry James and Minny Temple." *American Literature* 21 (1949): 35–48.

Le Duc, Alice Sumner. "The Man Who Rescued 'The Captain.'" *Atlantic Monthly,* August 1947, 80–86.

Lee, Francis Graham, ed. *The Collected Works of William Howard Taft.* Vol. 8, *"Liberty under Law" and Selected Supreme Court Opinions.* Athens: Ohio University Press, 2004.

Lerner, Max, ed. *The Mind and Faith of Justice Holmes: His Speeches, Essays, Letters, and Judicial Opinions.* New York: Modern Library, 1943.

Liebman, George W. "Lewis Einstein." In *Diplomacy Between the Wars: Five Diplomats and the Shaping of the Modern World.* New York: Palgrave Macmillan, 2008.

Little, Eleanor N. "The Early Reading of Justice Oliver Wendell Holmes." *Harvard Library Bulletin* 8 (1954): 163–203.

Lombardo, Paul A. *Three Generations, No Imbeciles: Eugenics, the Supreme Court, and Buck v. Bell.* Baltimore: Johns Hopkins University Press, 2008.

Louchheim, Katie, ed. *The Making of the New Deal: The Insiders Speak.* Cambridge, Mass.: Harvard University Press, 1983.

Lowry, Edward G. "Justice at Zero: The Frigid Austerities which Enrobe the Justices of the United States Supreme Court." *Harper's Weekly*, May 21, 1910.

Mackay, Charles. *Life and Liberty in America; or, Sketches of a Tour in the United States and Canada, in 1857–8.* 2 vols. London: Smith, Elder, 1859.

Maitland, Frederic William. *The Life and Letters of Leslie Stephen.* London: Duckworth, 1906.

Mason, Alpheus Thomas. *William Howard Taft: Chief Justice.* New York: Simon and Schuster, 1964.

McCabe, William Gordon. Papers. Albert and Shirley Small Special Collections Library, University of Virginia, Charlottesville, Va.

McCormack, Alfred. "A Law Clerk's Recollections." *Columbia Law Review* 46 (1946): 710–18.

McKinnon, Harold R. "The Secret of Mr. Justice Holmes: An Analysis." *American Bar Association Journal* 36 (1950): 261–64, 342–46.

McLellan, David S., and David C. Acheson, eds. *Among Friends: Personal Letters of Dean Acheson.* New York: Dodd, Mead, 1980.

McPherson, James M. *Battle Cry of Freedom: The Civil War Era.* New York: Oxford University Press, 1988.

Menand, Louis. *The Metaphysical Club.* New York: Farrar, Straus and Giroux, 2001.

Mencken, H. L. "Mr. Justice Holmes." *American Mercury*, May 1930, 122–24.

Mennel, Robert M., and Christine L. Compston, eds. *Holmes & Frankfurter: Their Correspondence, 1912–1934.* Hanover, N.H.: University Press of New England, 1996. *(H-F)*

Messinger, I. Scott. "The Judge as Mentor: Oliver Wendell Holmes Jr. and His Law Clerks." In Peppers and Ward, eds., *In Chambers.*

Meyer, Agnes E. *Out of These Roots: The Autobiography of an American Woman.* Boston: Little, Brown, 1953.

Miller, Richard F. "Brahmins Under Fire: Peer Courage and the Harvard Regiment." *Historical Journal of Massachusetts* 30 (2002): 75–109.

————. *Harvard's Civil War: A History of the Twentieth Massachusetts Volunteer Infantry*. Hanover, N.H.: University Press of New England, 2005.

————. "The Trouble with Brahmins: Class and Ethnic Tensions in Massachusetts' 'Harvard Regiment.'" *New England Quarterly* 76 (2003): 38–72.

Monagan, John S. *The Grand Panjandrum: The Mellow Years of Justice Holmes*. Lanham. Md.: University Press of America, 1988.

————. Interviews and Reminiscences. Papers. Historical & Special Collections, Harvard Law School, Cambridge, Mass. (JSMP)

Montgomery, David. "Strikes in Nineteenth-Century America." *Social Science History* 4 (1980): 81–104.

Morison, Elting E., ed. *The Letters of Theodore Roosevelt*. Vol. 3, *The Square Deal, 1901–1903*. Cambridge, Mass.: Harvard University Press, 1951.

Morse, John T., Jr. *Life and Letters of Oliver Wendell Holmes*. 2 vols. Boston: Houghton, Mifflin, 1899. (*LLH*)

Nesbitt, John B. "The Climbing Justice: Oliver Wendell Holmes' Season in the Alps." *Summit*, Winter 1993–94, 16–19.

Novick, Sheldon M. *Henry James: The Young Master*. New York: Random House, 1996.

————. *Honorable Justice: The Life of Oliver Wendell Holmes*. Boston: Little, Brown, 1989.

————. "Justice Holmes and the Art of Biography." Review of *The Justice from Beacon Hill*, by Liva Baker. *William & Mary Law Review* 33 (1992): 1219–49.

————. "Justice Holmes's Philosophy." *Washington University Law Review* 70 (1992): 703–53.

————. "The Unrevised Holmes and Freedom of Expression." *Supreme Court Review*, 1991, 303–90.

O'Connell, Jeffrey, and Nancy Dart. "The House of Truth: Home of the Young Frankfurter and Lippmann." *Catholic University Law Review* 35 (1985): 79–95.

O'Connor, Thomas H. *The Athens of America: Boston, 1825–1845*. Amherst: University of Massachusetts Press, 2006.

————. *The Boston Irish: A Political History*. Boston: Northeastern University Press, 1995.

————. *Civil War Boston: Home Front & Battlefield*. Boston: Northeastern University Press, 1997.

Palfrey, Francis Winthrop. *Memoir of William Francis Bartlett*. Boston: Houghton, Osgood, 1878.

Palmer, Ben W. "Hobbes, Holmes and Hitler." *American Bar Association Journal* 31 (1945): 569–73.

Paper, Lewis J. Papers. Historical & Special Collections, Harvard Law School, Cambridge, Mass. (LJPP)

Parrington, Vernon Louis. *Main Currents in American Thought: An Interpretation of American Literature from the Beginnings to 1920*. Vol. 2, *The Romantic Revolution in America*. New York: Harcourt, Brace, 1930.

Peabody, James Bishop, ed. *The Holmes-Einstein Letters: Correspondence of Mr. Justice Holmes and Lewis Einstein, 1903–1935*. New York: St. Martin's, 1964. (*H-E*)

Peppers, Todd C. "Birth of an Institution: Horace Gray and the Lost Law Clerks." In Peppers and Ward, eds., *In Chambers*.

———. "Isaiah and His Young Disciples: Justice Louis Brandeis and His Law Clerks." In Peppers and Ward, eds., *In Chambers*.

Peppers, Todd C., and Artemus Ward, eds. *In Chambers: Stories of Supreme Court Law Clerks and Their Justices*. Charlottesville: University of Virginia Press, 2012.

Perry, Ralph Barton, ed. *The Thought and Character of William James*. 2 vols. Boston: Little, Brown, 1935. (*TCWJ*)

Phillips, Harlan B., ed. *Felix Frankfurter Reminisces*. New York: Reynal, 1960.

Pilcher, Paul Monroe. "Transvesical Prostatectomy in Two Stages." *Annals of Surgery* 59 (1914): 500–4.

Posner, Richard A. *How Judges Think*. Cambridge, Mass.: Harvard University Press, 2008.

———. *Law and Literature*. 3rd ed. Cambridge, Mass.: Harvard University Press, 2009.

———, ed. *The Essential Holmes*. Chicago: University of Chicago Press, 1992.

Post, Robert. "The Supreme Court Opinion as Institutional Practice: Dissent, Legal Scholarship, and Decisionmaking in the Taft Court." *Minnesota Law Review* 85 (2001): 1267–1390.

"Presentation of the Thomas Price Memorial Library." *Bulletins of the University of Virginia* (January 1905).

Pringle, Henry F. *The Life and Times of William Howard Taft*. 2 vols. New York: Farrar and Rinehart, 1939.

Puelo, Stephen. *A City So Grand: The Rise of an American Metropolis, Boston 1850–1900*. Boston: Beacon Press, 2010.

Rhea, Gordon C. *The Battle of the Wilderness, May 5–6, 1864*. Baton Rouge: Louisiana State University Press, 1994.

———. *The Battles for Spotsylvania Court House and the Road to Yellow Tavern, May 7–12, 1864*. Baton Rouge: Louisiana State University Press, 1997.

Rollins, Clara Sherwood. *Threads of Life.* Boston: Lamson, Wolffe, 1897.

Ropes, Henry. Civil War Letters. Boston Public Library, Boston, Mass.

Rosenbloom, Joshua L. *The Challenge of Economic Maturity: New England, 1880–1940.* Historical Paper 113, NBER Working Paper Series on Historical Factors in Long Run Growth. Cambridge, Mass.: National Bureau of Economic Research, 1999.

Schmidt, Benno C., Jr. "Principle and Prejudice: The Supreme Court and Race in the Progressive Era. Part 3: Black Disfranchisement from the KKK to the Grandfather Clause." *Columbia Law Review* 82 (1982): 835–905.

Schwartz, Bernard. *A History of the Supreme Court.* New York: Oxford, 1993.

Scott, Robert Garth, ed. *Fallen Leaves: The Civil War Letters of Major Henry Livermore Abbott.* Kent, Ohio: Kent State University Press, 1991. (FL)

Sergeant, Elizabeth Shepley. "Oliver Wendell Holmes." *The New Republic,* December 8, 1926, 59–64.

Shackley, D. "A Century of Prostatic Surgery." *British Journal of Urology International* 83 (1999): 776–82.

Shils, Edward. *Portraits: A Gallery of Intellectuals.* Chicago: University of Chicago Press, 1997.

Shriver, Harry C. *What Gusto: Stories and Anecdotes about Justice Oliver Wendell Holmes.* Potomac, Md.: Fox Hills Press, 1970.

Smith, Donald L. *Zechariah Chafee, Jr., Defender of Liberty and Law.* Cambridge, Mass.: Harvard University Press, 1986.

Smith, Harriette Knight. *The History of the Lowell Institute.* Boston: Lamson, Wolffe, 1898.

Snyder, Brad. *The House of Truth: A Washington Political Salon and the Foundations of American Liberalism.* New York: Oxford University Press, 2017.

Strouse, Jean. *Alice James: A Biography.* New York: New York Review Books, 2011.

Sunstein, Cass. "Unanimity and Disagreement on the Supreme Court." *Cornell Law Review* 100 (2015): 769–823.

Supreme Judicial Court. Massachusetts. Records on Appeal. Social Law Library, Boston, Mass.

Sutherland, Arthur E. "Sutherland's Recollections of Justice Holmes." Edited by David M. O'Brien. *Supreme Court Historical Society Yearbook,* 1988, 18–25.

Taylor, Joseph H. "Populism and Disfranchisement in Alabama." *Journal of Negro History* 34 (1949): 410–27.

Thayer, James Bradley. *The Origin and Scope of the American Doctrine of Constitutional Law.* Boston: Little, Brown, 1893.

Thayer, William Roscoe, ed. *Letters of John Holmes to James Russell Lowell and Others.* Boston: Houghton, Mifflin, 1917.

Thompson, Thomas G. "Thomas Wayland Vaughan, 1870–1952." Washington, D.C.: National Academy of Sciences, 1958.

Tilton, Eleanor M. *Amiable Autocrat: A Biography of Dr. Oliver Wendell Holmes.* New York: Henry Schuman, 1947.

Tushnet, Mark. "The Logic of Experience: Oliver Wendell Holmes on the Supreme Judicial Court." *Virginia Law Review* 63 (1977): 975–1052.

Twain, Mark. *Mark Twain's Letters.* 2 vols. Edited by Albert Bigelow Paine. New York: Harper, 1917.

Urofsky, Melvin I. *Dissent and the Supreme Court: Its Role in the Court's History and the Nation's Constitutional Dialogue.* New York: Pantheon, 2015.

———. *Louis D. Brandeis: A Life.* New York: Schocken, 2009.

———, ed. "The Brandeis-Frankfurter Conversations." *Supreme Court Review,* 1985, 299–339. (B-F)

Urofsky, Melvin I., and David W. Levy, eds. *"Half Brother, Half Son": The Letters of Louis D. Brandeis to Felix Frankfurter.* Norman: University of Oklahoma Press, 1991. (*HBHS*)

Van Devanter, Willis. Papers. Manuscript Division, Library of Congress, Washington, D.C.

Wagner, Richard H. "A Falling Out: The Relationship Between Oliver Wendell Holmes and Theodore Roosevelt." *Journal of Supreme Court History* 27 (2002): 114–37.

Walker, Francis. "The 'Beef Trust' and the United States Government." *Economic Journal* 16 (1906): 491–514.

Waterman, John S., and Edward E. Overton. "The Aftermath of *Moore v. Dempsey.*" *St. Louis Law Review* 18 (1933): 117–26.

Webb, Beatrice. Diaries. Digital Library, London School of Economics. Web.

West, Rebecca. Review of *Holmes-Laski Letters.* Edited by Mark DeWolfe Howe. *Harvard Law Review* 67 (1953): 361–67.

White, G. Edward. "Holmes as Correspondent." *Vanderbilt Law Review* 43 (1990): 1707–61.

———. *Justice Oliver Wendell Holmes: Law and the Inner Self.* New York: Oxford, 1992.

White, James Grove. "Historical and Topographical Notes, &c., on Buttevant, Doneraile, Mallow, and Places in Their Vicinity." *Journal of the*

Cork Historical and Archaeological Society 2nd ser., 19 (1913): II:257–330, III:1–56.

Whitman, Walt. *Democratic Vistas and Other Papers*. London: Scott, 1888.

Wigmore, John H. "Abrams *v.* U.S.: Freedom of Speech and Freedom of Thuggery in War-time and Peace-time." *Illinois Law Review* 14 (1920): 539–61.

Wister, Owen. *Roosevelt: The Story of a Friendship*. New York: Macmillan, 1930.

Woolf, Leonard. *Downhill All the Way: An Autobiography of the Years 1919 to 1939*. New York: Harcourt Brace Jovanovich, 1967.

Wu, John C. H. Review of *Holmes-Laski Letters*, edited by Mark DeWolfe Howe. *Michigan Law Review* 51 (1953): 948–53.

———, ed. "Some Unpublished Letters of Justice Holmes." *T'ien Hsia Monthly* 1 (1935): 251–302. (Copy in OWHA, 4-7).

Zane, John M. "German Legal Philosophy." *Michigan Law Review* 16 (1918): 287–375.

———. "A Legal Heresy." *Illinois Law Review* 13 (1919): 431–62.

Zobel, Hiller B. "Justice Oliver Wendell Holmes in the Trial Court." *Massachusetts Legal History* 8 (2002): 35–47.

———. "Oliver Wendell Holmes. Jr., Trial Judge." *Boston Bar Journal* 36 (March-April 1992): 25–28.

———. "What a Medley of a Man!" Catalog for Exhibit Honoring the Sesquicentennial of Justice Oliver Wendell Holmes, Jr. Harvard Law School, March 8–June 6, 1991.

ZoBell, Karl M. "Division of Opinion in the Supreme Court: A History of Judicial Disintegration." *Cornell Law Quarterly* 44 (1959): 186–214.

INDEX OF COURT CASES

The full texts of all U.S. Supreme Court decisions are nowadays freely available from many Internet sources and can be readily located through a simple search by case name, so formal citations are not included below.

Full citations to appellate decisions of the Massachusetts Supreme Judicial Court are given in the standard form that refers to their location in the published *Massachusetts Reports*: For example, 148 Mass. 132 is volume 148, page 132 of the *Reports*.

Cases that Holmes heard as a trial justice and that were not subsequently appealed to the full court are cited below by the Massachusetts county or court where they were tried (and, where available, the docket number).

SUBJECT INDEX

Page numbers in *italic* refer to illustrations.